M000191656

霞の如く―源平争乱関連謡曲の研究と翻訳―

Like clouds or mists

Like Clouds or Mists

Studies and Translations of Nō Plays of the Genpei War

edited by

Elizabeth Oyler and Michael Watson

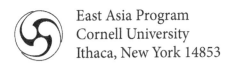

East Asia Program
Cornell University
Ithaca, New York 14853

The Cornell East Asia Series is published by the Cornell University East Asia Program (distinct from Cornell University Press). We publish books on a variety of scholarly topics relating to East Asia as a service to the academic community and the general public. Address submission inquiries to CEAS Editorial Board, East Asia Program, Cornell University, 140 Uris Hall, Ithaca, New York 14853-7601.

Cover Image: Tsukioka Kogyo, Japanese, 1869-1927
Sanemori, from the series "One Hundred No Dramas (Nogaku hyakuban),"
1898–1903. Color woodblock print 37.8 x 25.6 cm (14 7/8 x 10 1/8 in.) (approx.)
Bequest of Henry C. Schwab
1943.833.41
The Art Institute of Chicago
Photography © The Art Institute of Chicago.

Number 159 in the Cornell East Asia Series
Copyright ©2013 Elizabeth Oyler and Michael Geoffrey Watson.
All rights reserved.
ISSN: 1050-2955
ISBN: 978-1-933947-29-7 hardcover
ISBN: 978-1-933947-59-4 paperback
Library of Congress Control Number: 2012955630
Printed in the United States of America

∞ The paper in this book meets the requirements for permanence of ISO 9706:1994.

CAUTION: Except for brief quotations in a review, no part of this book may be reproduced or utilized in any form without permission in writing from the author. Please address all inquiries to Elizabeth Oyler and Michael Watson in care of the East Asia Program, Cornell University, 140 Uris Hall, Ithaca, NY 14853-7601.

In memory of
Karen Brazell,
inspiration to us all

∾ CONTENTS

∼ Foreword

This volume grew out of a workshop held at Washington University in St. Louis in the Spring of 2005 that brought together scholars of two of medieval Japan's most recognizable artistic corpuses: *Heike monogatari* 平家物語 (Tales of the Heike) and the nō drama 能楽. The objectives of the workshop were to focus on the profound connections between the *Heike* and the vast body of nō plays derived from it, and to bring attention to those plays that have so far been absent or understudied in English-language scholarship. After drawing up a list of *Heike*-derived plays that merited the most immediate attention, participants divided themselves into smaller groups to work on individual plays: one group translated the play, while others researched the play's connections to one or more antecedents in the *Heike* and related genres. The result is a series of translations and essays tracing the development of a number of key *Heike* episodes and characters as these are reanimated in a group of nō plays over the course of the fifteenth through seventeenth centuries. Most of the plays translated and discussed in the volume were presented at the workshop, but several others were added because of their close affiliations with these works.

One practical goal of the workshop was to provide English translations of and research about nō plays that could be used in college classrooms. At the same time, we wanted to make the plays meaningful through cultural and historical contextualization for generalists and specialists alike. We started with basic questions: how did writers, performers, and audiences understand individual plays about stories and characters familiar from another work? How were those stories translated into the idiom of nō (and, in many cases, other genres)? A concern that quickly became apparent was the issue of canonicity and the nō: why were some plays embraced by nō schools as they fixed their repertoires, and what place did plays not taken up by these schools hold in cultural traditions in late medieval and early modern Japan?

While exhaustive answers to such questions about actual performance traditions from so distant in the past remain obscure, it is our hope that this volume helps clarify the allusive relationships between the *Heike* and nō, as well as some possible contours marking the borders of the nō canon.

In concentrating on intertextuality, this volume follows the example set by Janet Goff's *Noh Drama and The Tale of Genji* in underlining connections across genres and between works, but in this case the scope is more temporally compressed: the variants of the *Heike* were taking their final forms decades rather than centuries prior to the emergence of nō, and both arts were the objects of patronage by the Ashikaga shoguns. The interplay between them, as well as that between them and other genres telling tales from the *Heike*, was key in a number of developing performance and narrative traditions. Given the sheer number of both variants of the *Heike* and nō plays based on characters from them, we found ourselves in the fortunate situation of confronting more plays and variants than we could possibly address: there are many plays still waiting to be translated and studied. We also discovered, as is so often the case in medieval contexts, that no matter what we did to limit our scope, the webs of interconnectedness between plays and variant texts of the *Heike* constantly suggested relations to others we had not considered, some of which are included here, and some of which we leave for the imaginations of other scholars and translators.

We have organized the volume to follow the order of events presented in the Kakuichi-bon variant of the *Heike*. The basis for the most widely circulating translations of the work, including Helen Craig McCullough's of 1988 and Royall Tyler's of 2012, its rendition of the story of the war is most familiar to both Japanese and foreign audiences. The essays and translations in this volume focus on a series of major events from the *Heike*: Kiyomori's rise (the "Giō" cycle of plays); Yoshinaka's push to the capital; the flight of the Heike and the battle of Ichi-no-tani; and the aftermath of the war. For each event, we include a series of one to three plays preceded by essays about them. In several cases, plays could have been placed differently—*Rō-Giō*, for example, although concerned with the heroine of the "Giō" episode, bears stronger thematic and structural similarities to *Morihisa*—but we have chosen to place them within the more obvious constellation of plays.

Following these is an essay on the thematization of the *Heike* in *Haku Rakuten*, a nō play on a seemingly divergent subject, and a translation of the play. The essay and translation suggest not only how characters and events, but also pervasive ways of thinking about art and culture, were derived from the *Heike*. The book concludes with an essay about transpositions of *Heike* stories into twentieth-century drama, particularly in response to the Japanese experience of the war in the Pacific.

We offer this volume as a step toward a better understanding of a nexus of stories, characters, and arts central to medieval and early modern Japan, and particularly the significant variety of ways plays of the nō theater portray them.

Elizabeth Oyler
Michael G. Watson

1 〜 Introduction

| Elizabeth Oyler

The title of this volume is taken from a formulaic description of battle found throughout the *Heike monogatari* 平家物語 (Tales of the Heike) corpus and elsewhere in Japanese war tales. Warriors fill the field "like clouds or mists" (*unka no gotoku* 雲霞の如く), so dense that they blur into a confused mass that is conveyed through the unexpected metaphor of clouds or mist, something essentially ephemeral. The seemingly paradoxical conjoining of the forceful solidity of battling troops and the ethereality of clouds or mists seems particularly fitting for the hybrid cultural, political, and linguistic space in which both the *Heike* and nō developed. Linguistically, *unka no gotoku* brings together the popular poetic images of clouds (*kumo* くも/雲) and mist (*kasumi* かすみ/霞) in a Sino-Japanese word (*unka* 雲霞) embedded in an expression that relies on both Chinese and Japanese syntax. Such complex expressions became increasingly prevalent in the new kinds of literature and drama emerging during the medieval period, and they represent a salient reflection of the negotiation of the lyrical, phonetic space of *waka* 和歌 poetry and Heian-period (794–1185) *monogatari* 物語 and the sorts of official, historical discourse associated with writing in Chinese characters that are emblematic of the medieval age.

The experimental intermingling of lyrical and historiographical modes in linguistic contexts is mirrored on social registers as well. The warrior class, which had been isolated socially and geographically from authority and cultural production throughout the Heian period, began to encroach on political and cultural spaces that had formerly been occupied only by the central aristocracy. While on the one hand, reverence for established forms and a profound nostalgia for the past remained central to the way the new power-holders thought and wrote about their world, on the other, they were confronted by new realities that shaped the way they framed these impulses and expressed them in literature and drama. Nowhere is this more apparent than in the *Heike monogatari* and the nō drama, two arts deeply involved in articulating the relationship between the new cultural terrain of the present in their reanimations of the past.

No strong consciousness of the warriors as a literary or historical subject occurred before the medieval period. A few early records of warrior exploits had appeared during the late Heian period; it is only with the several conflicts in the 1150s through the 1180s that the warriors become prominent features in literature and historical records. But from the time Minamoto Yoritomo 源頼朝 (1147–1199) won the Genpei War (1180–1185) and created a new branch of government to oversee warrior affairs, warriors and the political office of "shogun" would hold a vital official position, even when its seat was contested or unoccupied, until the 1860s.

Although the *Heike* presents both a new narrative subject and a new mode of expression, even a cursory reading of any *Heike* variant reveals profound debts to traditional modes of writing, particularly to historical writing, and more specifically historical tales (*rekishi monogatari* 歴史物語), a hybrid form that emerged in the eleventh century. *Eiga monogatari* 栄華物語 (Tale of Flowering Fortunes, ca. early twelfth century) and *Ōkagami* 大鏡 (The Great Mirror, ca. 1040–1140) are considered the earliest examples of this genre.[1] Both of these works deviate from earlier histories in their intense focus on the life of Fujiwara Michinaga 藤原道長 (966–1027), the most powerful minister Japan had seen. Earlier histories had been annals concentrating instead on court events, with both the subject and the ordering principle being the succession of sovereigns (*tennō* 天皇). Whereas official histories had been written in Chinese, historical tales were written in the *kana* syllabary, which was, in the Heian period, generally associated with belle-lettristic arts. Historical tales further display experimentation with voice and point of view borrowed from such literary traditions as the "tale" or *monogatari* 物語, of which *Genji monogatari* 源氏物語 (The Tale of Genji, ca. 1008) was the most prominent example.

---

1. William H. McCullough and Helen C. McCullough, trans., *A Tale of Flowering Fortunes: Annals of Japanese Aristocratic Life in the Heian Period*, 2 vols. (Stanford University Press, 1980); Helen C. McCullough, trans., *Ōkagami: Fujiwara Michinaga (966–1027) and His Times* (Princeton University Press, 1980).

The war tales represent yet a further refraction of historical writing, for their subject is the warrior class—and particularly its most memorable representatives—under whose control the realm fell. Even more than historical tales, war tales are eclectic in form and voice. Many variant texts of any given war tale are written in *kanbun* 漢文 ("Chinese writing," a hybrid form of Japanese following Chinese syntax and using exclusively Chinese characters), and all include *kanbun* passages (often quotations of official or religious documents). Yet they simultaneously rely on lyrical *kana* traditions as well: all *Heike* variants include poetry, and often describe scenes of intense personal emotion in conventional lyrical styles, including passages articulated in the alternating 5- and 7-syllable lines associated with *waka*.

The influence of *Heike monogatari* in various artistic spheres was profound. In addition to nō drama, other emerging performance and literary genres relied heavily on the characters and events of the *Heike*—in particular, the *kōwakamai* 幸若舞 ("ballad-drama") and *otogizōshi* 御伽草子 ("companion tales," or short prose narratives), both of which are mentioned in the essays of this volume. As the translations and essays included here suggest, characters appearing only briefly in the *Heike* acquired detailed biographies when they moved into other genres. Such a milieu created an underlying body of narratives about the Genpei period exhibiting productive tensions that strongly affected the way the war is remembered: multiple renditions of any given episode in literary, dramatic, or mixed versions all contributed to the creation of a multifaceted "text" immanent in any individual work or performance. Genpei War heroes were simultaneously men who died on the battlefield in the *Heike* and the ghosts of those men in the nō—a combination of the tangible and the ephemeral; the massed body of soldiers in the heat of the fray and the mists dissipating from a long-ago battlefield.

More often than not, these characters were peripheral to the war or even fictional, but theirs are nevertheless the names that came to be indelibly etched into the cultural memory of the war: the aged warrior Sanemori, the beautiful dancer Giō, the gifted young flautist Atsumori. Creating these characters and giving them meaning within the context of the war is among the great contributions of the medieval narrative and dramatic arts that are the subject of this volume.

TALES OF THE HEIKE

Heike monogatari is among Japan's most enduring and influential works of literature. A chronicle of the Genpei War, it narrates the civil conflict that brought Japan's classical age to a close and ushered in warrior rule. This attenuation of royal authority would place power in the hands of shoguns or their advisors in one form or another until the Meiji Restoration of 1868. Within cultural memory, the war was momentous, a shift in paradigms of governance, social order, and cultural values. Each of these changes is recorded, pondered, and given a variety of explanations in the pages of *Heike monogatari*.

What we refer to as the *Heike monogatari* includes approximately eighty variant texts exhibiting diverse styles, thematic concerns, and even contents. The best known of these today grew out of the oral performance tradition of the *biwa hōshi* 琵琶法師, blind male performers who recited the tale while accompanying themselves on the *biwa*, or Japanese lute. Their art, which has come to be known as *Heike biwa* 平家琵琶 or *Heikyoku* 平曲, was widely practiced during the medieval period, and continued to enjoy warrior patronage through the Tokugawa era (1600–1868). The provenance of the first *biwa hōshi* is not entirely clear—certainly, high-ranking chanters were performing rites for the Genpei War dead from shortly after the conflict's end, and the musical patterning we associate with *shōmyō* 声明, a kind of Buddhist liturgical chant, forms the basis for many of the musical formulae used in *Heike biwa*. In addition, itinerant performers with only loose or no connections to the Buddhist establishment also added narratives about the war to their repertoires.

In both cases, a strong element of ritual attended the development of *Heike* stories. Tales of the war celebrated the acts of the war's victims and served the placatory function of soothing their souls in the afterlife. Custodianship of various duties associated with pacification of the unhappy dead—who might return at any time to cause havoc in the here-and-now—had long been the responsibility of both the Buddhist clergy and outcaste performers like the *biwa hōshi*. From well before the time of the *Heike*, the *biwa* lute played an integral role in such processes—stringed instruments generally were thought to contain the power to communicate between this world and the next—but they also added a dimension of depth and mystery to the stories chanters recited, which simultaneously increased the interest of the reciter's art as an entertainment.

Of these recited texts, the best known today is the Kakuichi-bon 覚一本, or "Kakuichi text," a work purported to capture in written form the oral art of an esteemed performer known as Kakuichi.[2] According to one of its colophons, the Kakuichi-bon was committed to paper in 1371. Organized into twelve base chapters plus one additional chapter (the *Kanjō no maki* 灌頂巻, "Water Consecration Scroll"), it consists of nearly two hundred episodes following a sometimes only roughly chronological order. In the main, it devotes strongest attention to lamenting the deaths of various warriors and their womenfolk, particularly those on the losing side. Thematically, the Kakuichi-bon is strongly colored by a Buddhist world-view that society was in a state of steady decline as generations moved further away from the lifetime of the historical Buddha. This view is captured in the concepts known as *masse* 末世 (the latter age) or *mappō* 末法 (the latter days of the law), referred to often in the *Heike* and other contemporary works. One related thematic frame for the *Heike* is the juxtaposition of Buddhist law (*buppō* 仏法) and royal law (*ōbō* 王法): the tale is about restoration of balance between the two. This concept is elucidated as well in a contemporary treatise known as *Gukanshō* 愚管抄, authored by the Tendai abbot Jien (慈円). The thematic similarities between the *Heike* and *Gukanshō*, as well as other indications of strong ties to the Tendai complex of temples on Mount Hiei (which lies at the northeast corner of Kyoto), have led scholars to posit that Tendai monks, and perhaps even Jien himself, had an editorial hand in this variant.

Many *Heike* variants were never used for recitation. The most annalistic of these read like chronicles, with a higher density of Chinese terminology—some are, in fact, written entirely in *kanbun*, a derivative form of Chinese used in Japan from earliest times, particularly in official discursive contexts. Whereas recitational variants tended to be organized under episodes, many of these nonrecited variants were arranged chronologically under dated entries, if any demarcation was used at all. The oldest *Heike* variant, the Engyō-bon 延慶本, named for the era in which it was written (the Engyō era, 1308–1311), is a nonrecited text. Dating from 1309, it differs from the Kakuichi-bon in style and thematic focus. It is organized chronologically, has a more heterodox worldview, and exhibits a stronger narrative interest on the

---

2. A detailed study of the Kakuichi-bon can be found in Michael G. Watson, "A Narrative Study of the Kakuichi-bon *Heike monogatari*," (Doctoral Thesis, the University of Oxford, 2003).

Genji warriors of the east who won the war.[3]

One of the richest variant texts is known by a discrete title: *Genpei jōsuiki* 源平盛衰記, or "Record of the Rise and Fall of the Minamoto and Taira." A particularly long work, it includes expansions of many of the famous episodes from the *Heike* corpus, as well as additional material and alternative versions of stories. This variant cannot be dated with certainty, it is generally thought to have been composed in the fifteenth century, although some scholars place it earlier. Exhibiting a stronger Confucian bent than most other versions, *Genpei jōsuiki* also is the source for many nō plays and other reworkings of *Heike* tales, including a number of the plays translated here.[4]

A number of other variant texts are mentioned in the essays that follow. The Nagato-bon 長門本 is extant only in seventeenth-century copies but it seems to reflect a somewhat earlier, nonrecited version of the tale. It is named for the region in which it was found: Nagato, the province facing the straits where the final battle of the war was fought, and home to Amidaji 阿弥陀寺, the mortuary temple for the defeated war dead.

The order in which the variants were composed, as well as the directions in which influence circulated among them, are ongoing topics of scholarly debate. As the essays and translations in this volume demonstrate, stories from various texts were clearly known to playwrights and audiences, especially by the late medieval period. The inclusiveness of what it meant to be a "tale of the Heike" points to fundamental characteristics of medieval narrative and drama, broadly speaking: textual integrity was not a concern and the corpus was sufficiently elastic to embrace not only expansions of individual stories but also versions that contradicted each other. The very multiformity of the *Heike* is one of its defining qualities, and one that undoubtedly provided not only actual material but also inspiration to move in creative directions away from it for nō writer-performers as they began to develop their art.

---

3. The Engyō-bon is one important text considered in David T. Bialock, *Eccentric Spaces, Hidden Histories: Narrative, Ritual, and Royal Authority from* The Chronicles of Japan *to* The Tale of the Heike (Stanford University Press, 2007).

4. Bialock, *Eccentric Spaces, Hidden Histories*, 288.

THE NŌ THEATER

The nō theater maintains a cultural status in Japanese performing arts today that far overshadows recitation of the *Heike*. Eloquent introductions to the art, as well as innovative treatments of playwrights, actors, and plays, can be found in a number of English-language works; these are included under separate heading in the general bibliography of this volume. The introductory material in Donald Keene's *Twenty Plays of the Nō Theater* and Karen Brazell's *Traditional Japanese Theater: An Anthology of Plays* provide succinct and particularly helpful introductions for familiarizing those new to nō with its history and performance practices.

The nō theater emerged at the turn of the fifteenth century, in a context in which numerous new and old performing arts were actively vying for popularity. *Sarugaku* 猿楽 evolved from *sangaku* 散楽, which had been transmitted from the continent during the Nara (710–784) period to Japan; it involved a mixture of performing arts—mime, acrobatics, and dance. *Dengaku* 田楽 consisted of ritual performances associated with harvest celebrations. *Ennen* 延年 were songs sung following Buddhist rituals. In addition, such novel arts as *Heike* recitation, *imayō* 今様 singing, and *shirabyōshi* 白拍子 dancing also enjoyed popularity during the period leading up to the creation of the nō.

The earliest performances to be referred to as nō were mounted by *sarugaku* and *dengaku* troupes, which drew from the various popular arts to create dramatic performances framed as plays but showcasing dance and song. Both *dengaku* and *sarugaku* performers in the early Muromachi 室町 period (1333–1573) were organized into troupes, and these were patronized by the major temples and shrines in the capital and surrounding areas. Four troupes of Yamato *sarugaku* performers were clustered around Nara (south of the capital); six others (the Ōmi troupes) were situated near Lake Biwa, to the northeast of the capital. Troupes of *dengaku* performers made their home base in the capital and in Nara. All troupes traveled, performing at a variety of locations, but mostly within the home provinces surrounding Kyoto.

Nō as it is practiced today locates its ancestors in a father and son who were leaders of the Yūzaki 結崎 troupe of Yamato performers: Kan'ami 観阿弥 (1333–1384) and Zeami 世阿弥 (1363?–1443?). The Yūzaki was the youngest of the Yamato troupes, but quickly became the most popular, in part because of Kan'ami's skill as a performer, and in part because of the troupe's experimentation with various forms, such as the integration of the popular dance form of *kusemai*. Kan'ami took his troupe to the capital to perform, and it was in one such performance in 1374 that his troupe caught the eye of the third Ashikaga shogun Yoshimitsu 足利義満 (1358–1408), who, captivated by Zeami's beauty and talent, became an active patron of the troupe.

Yoshimitsu's patronage was foundational for the development of nō, for it was through his tutelage and that of Nijō Yoshimoto 二条良基 (1320–1388), an important poet and advisor to Yoshimitsu, that Zeami became familiar with many of the important literary works and aesthetic concepts that would inform the development of his theories on nō. The elevation of nō from something resembling popular festival entertainment to a serious theatrical form interacting with conventional upper-class canons of taste came about in large part because of these influences. Zeami's works are recognized especially for their focus on character, and most famously the characters of elegant yet suffering women. He wrote extensively about performance, and his treatises provide one of the most important windows on early performance practice.[5] The aesthetic ideals associated with Zeami in the main emphasize the dramatic potential of such poignant characters, although as Tom Hare's contribution to this volume demonstrates, particular theoretical concepts about them are often imbricated with a variety of other ideals and modes of thinking about nō.

Today, Zeami is looked to as the founding father of nō, in part because of the complexity and beauty of many of the plays he wrote or reworked, and in part because he authored numerous treatises, such as *Go on*, discussed in Tom Hare's essay in this volume, about performance. Yet Zeami's style was not the only one affecting the development of the art: the next generation of sarugaku nō playwrights and actors also shaped the repertoire. Zeami's son, Motomasa 元雅 (ca. 1394–1422), and his son-in-law, Zenchiku 禅竹 (1405–1471?), both wrote plays that followed Zeami in creating penetrating portrayals of individual characters, although each approached the task differently; Motomasa's *Shigehira* provides one example of Motomasa's unique style.[6] Other troupes and

---

5. For studies and translations of Zeami's critical oeuvre, see Thomas B. Hare, *Zeami's Style: The Noh Plays of Zeami Motokiyo* (Stanford University Press, 1986); Tom Hare, trans., *Zeami, Performance Notes* (Columbia University Press, 2008); Shelley Fenno Quinn, *Developing Zeami: The Noh Actor's Attunement in Practice* (University of Hawaiʻi Press, 2005); J. Thomas Rimer and Yamazaki Masakazu, trans. *On the Art of the Nō Drama: The Major Treatises of Zeami* (Princeton University Press, 1984).

6. Zenchiku's work is the subject of Paul S. Atkins, *Revealed Identity: The Noh*

other Yūzaki leaders took different approaches to the nō: Nobumitsu 信光 (1435–1516) produced more "theatrical" plays, involving larger casts and more action onstage; the vestiges of all of these playwrights and others can be found in nō plays today.

During the Tokugawa period (1603–1868), the shogunate adopted the nō theater for ceremonial purposes, which effectively ensured that the art would be supported by the government, but also that it would ossify: unlike the emergent theatrical forms of kabuki and bunraku, nō did not begin to incorporate elaborate stage props or alter its general form to accommodate popular taste, but rather took an inward turn, slowing in pace and focusing on an artistry associated with preservation of specific styles of voice and movement. This general trend coincided with the division of nō plays into one of five categories, which became the basis for programs: for a given program, one play from each of the categories was performed in a set order: first a god play (*kamimono* 神物 or *waki* nō 脇能); then a warrior play (*shuramono* 修羅物); then a play featuring a beautiful woman (*kazuramono* 鬘物, literally "wig piece"); then a miscellaneous piece (referred to as *yobanmemono* 四番目物, "fourth category piece"; then a final piece (*kiri* nō 切り能). These desigations are based in part on the character of the protagonist, or *shite*, of the play. In the first, it is a deity, in the second, a warrior, in the third, a beautiful woman; in the fourth, a person or ghost or other being; in the fifth, a demon or monster. In general, nō plays use few actors. One or two *tsure*, or companions, may accompany either the *shite* or the *waki*, the secondary character and often the *shite*'s interlocutor. These share the stage with a chorus and several instrumentalists playing drums and flute. As time passed, the major nō schools thinned their repertoires, as reflected in the 250-piece collection of nō performed today.

Although many of the nō most familiar to Western audiences are *mugen* 夢幻 or "dream" nō, a large body of *genzai* 現在 or "realistic" nō are also among the plays of the official repertoires. The plays that were excluded from these repertoires outnumber those included by a multiple of ten or more, and in the main, they have received significantly less critical attention. Of these, at least a hundred are based on stories from the *Heike*, although some only very tangentially. These are generally referred to as *bangai* 番外 nō, or plays that exist outside (外) the official repertoires (*banshiki* 番式).

Plays of Komparu Zenchiku (Center for Japanese Studies, University of Michigan, 2006).

THE GENPEI WAR

The general subject of all the plays translated in this volume is the Genpei War, a conflict with roots reaching back several generations before the conflict itself. The title of *Heike monogatari* refers to the Taira 平 (or Heike 平家, written with the Chinese characters for "Taira" and "house") clan, a family descended from a son of Sovereign Kanmu 桓武 天皇 (r. 781–806). The prince had been reduced to commoner status as a process of dynastic shedding—in order to lessen competition for the throne, secondary sons were given surnames (the royal family has none) and appointed to mid-level bureaucratic positions.

As recounted in most *Heike* variants and the Kakuichi-bon in particular, the roots of the Genpei War lay with the rise of this branch of the Taira, commonly referred to as the Kanmu Heike. The ancestors of this Taira branch had traditionally held provincial governorships, mostly in the western regions of the realm, where they enriched themselves financially in the lucrative trade with the continent. As a result, in 1131, Taira Tadamori 平忠盛 (1096–1153) was able to ingratiate himself to the Retired Sovereign Toba 鳥羽院 (1103–1156) by providing funds to construct a thirty-three bay hall (Sanjūsangendō 三十三間堂), the Tokujōjuin 得長寿院, in fulfillment of Toba's vow to build a temple. Tadamori was rewarded with courtier privileges at the palace. This placed him in the upper aristocracy; the combination of his wealth and Toba's favor assured him continued success at court throughout his life, and paved the way for his heir, Kiyomori 清盛 (1118–1181), to ascend to even greater heights. In little more than a generation, the Taira had risen from rustic provincials to important members of the central aristocracy in the capital city, Heian-kyō, a social climb of unheard-of speed.

In 1156 and 1159, two disputes between members of the royal house and the regental clan, the Fujiwara 藤原, erupted into armed conflict, and both sides called upon members of two "warrior houses," the Taira and the Minamoto 源 (or Genji 源氏, written with the logographs for "Minamoto" and "clan"), to come to their defense. Like the Taira, the Minamoto had originally descended from the royal family; the main line claimed the Sovereign Seiwa 清和天皇 (850–880) as their ancestor and had proven themselves over the generations as great military men.

In 1156, however, the former clan leader, Tameyoshi 為義 (1096–1156), and his heir, Yoshitomo 義朝 (1123–1160), were divided in their opinions concerning which side to support. Tameyoshi and his

amnesty issued during Tokuko's pregnancy, Shunkan eventually died in exile. Like Giō, his story was taken up again in the nō theater and elsewhere. Thomas Rimer's chapter in this volume addresses, among other things, a modern play about Shunkan, attesting to the enduring interest in the fate of the exile.

Kiyomori's behavior following the Shishi-no-tani affair only inspired further resentment of the Taira fortunes. In 1179, his eldest son Shigemori 重盛 died, an opportunity grasped by Go-Shirakawa to terminate the clan's claims to property rights (and therefore income) Shigemori had held. Kiyomori retaliated by placing Go-Shirakawa under house arrest in the Toba mansion south of the capital. With Go-Shirakawa thus neutralized, Kiyomori was next able to force Takakura's abdication in favor of the infant Antoku.

The first real volleys of what would become known to posterity as the Genpei War came in 1180, when the aging Minamoto Yorimasa 源頼政 (1106–1180) joined forces with Mochihito 以仁 (1151–1180), a disenfranchised royal prince, to challenge Antoku's ascension; this rebellion is the primary subject of the Kakuichi-bon's Chapter Four. Yorimasa was a member of the Seiwa Genji, but of what had become a collateral branch. Having sided with Kiyomori during the Heiji uprising, he had survived that event, but, like Yoshitomo before him, believed he had not been adequately recompensed for his efforts against his kinsman and his demonstrated loyalty to the throne.

The conspirators' plot was discovered early, prompting Yorimasa to flee with Mochihito to Miidera, a temple complex east of the capital. The Miidera monks happily harbored the party and sent requests for support to Enryakuji, the head temple of their own sect (Tendai) and also to Kōfukuji, the head temple of the Hossō sect. Enryakuji, located on Mount Hiei at the northeastern corner of Heian-kyō, did not reply, unwilling to create a rift with Kiyomori. Kōfukuji promised support, but the temple was located in the former capital of Nara, forty kilometers south of Heian-kyō, a distance that proved too great.

Kiyomori began amassing troops for an attack on Miidera. Realizing the impossibility of mounting a defense there, Yorimasa and the prince decided to try to make their way to Nara and the Kōfukuji monks; they were joined by the able-bodied monks of Miidera. Kiyomori's forces met them at the Uji River south of the capital, and a fierce battle ensued. The prince was killed as he tried to escape, and, outnumbered, Yorimasa committed suicide. Kiyomori then ordered his troops to burn Miidera as punishment, an event that brings Chapter Four to a close.

Chapter Five marks an important turning point in the Kakuichi-bon. Yorimasa's revolt had been put down fairly easily, but Kiyomori sensed the tenuousness of his own hold on authority, and soon after the uprising he ordered that the court be moved from Heian-kyō to Fukuhara, a settlement along the inland sea in what is now Kobe. Fukuhara lay within the province of Settsu, over which the Taira had long held power; its physical distance from Heian-kyō, combined with the mountainous terrain to its north and east and the sea to the south, made it a logistically prudent position for a power-holder wary of further military attacks. In the narrative, however, the move to Fukuhara signals the beginning of the end for Kiyomori. Following so many banishments early in the narrative, this removal of the government from its rightful place empties the center of its meaning, disrupting the functioning of the central aristocracy and government officials.

The transfer of the capital was wildly unpopular, and many viewed it as an act of hubris and a break with precedent doomed to have serious karmic consequences. Inauspicious dreams and visions began to haunt the Taira. These were followed soon after by news from the east country that the eldest of Yoshitomo's sons, Yoritomo, had raised troops in Izu, his place of banishment, and was challenging Taira partisans in the area. The Taira in Fukuhara dispatched troops immediately under the command of Taira Koremori 平維盛 (1160–1184), son of Shigemori, and Taira Tadanori 平忠度 (1144–1184), Kiyomori's brother. The Taira met Yoritomo's forces at the Fuji River in Suruga province. Encamped on opposite banks of the river late in the afternoon, the two forces prepared to meet each other the following day. During the night, a flock of birds took wing, startling the already nervous Taira troops, who then retreated in a panic, believing the sound to be a night attack by the seasoned eastern warriors on the opposite bank. They returned to Fukuhara in disgrace. Yoritomo claimed Suruga and Tōtōmi provinces and entrusted them to two retainers. He then retreated to Kamakura, a hamlet in Sagami province that would remain his headquarters throughout the war and beyond, to consolidate his forces.

Chapter Five concludes with the court's return to Heian-kyō from Fukuhara. Essentially an act of capitulation by Kiyomori, it also allowed him to begin an offensive against Genji partisans in Ōmi province, just east of the capital. The Taira were successful in suppressing the opposition. Simultaneously, however, Kiyomori planned an attack on Kōfukuji and Miidera as punishment for their support of Mochihito's rebellion. When they learned of Kiyomori's plans, the monks of Kōfukuji prepared to fight, chasing off and finally decapitating emissaries sent from the capital. Infuriated, Kiyomori sent forces under the command of his son Shigehira and nephew Michimori to punish the Nara monks. After a day battling at Narazaka and Hannyaji, Shigehira's forces were nearing victory. As the sun set, he ordered fires to be lit. This was a fateful decision: his men lit a commoner's house on fire, and the flames, blown by a violent wind, quickly spread to the venerable temples of Nara: Kōfukuji, where many women, children, and elderly monks had fled seeking refuge, and Tōdaiji. The loss of life and damage to sacred properties were enormous, earning Shigehira the enmity of the Nara religious establishment and the censure of all. He came to be considered perhaps the most culpable Taira for this crime, and at the end of the war, he was sent to Nara for execution.

The burning of the Nara temples at the end of Chapter Five parallels the burning of Miidera at the conclusion of Chapter Four and presages the fall of Kiyomori's flowering fortunes. Chapter Six marks a definitive ending of an age: first, Retired Sovereign Takakura and then Kiyomori die in rapid succesion. Takakura's death is attributed to his sorrow over the state of affairs brought about by Kiyomori's ambitions, and three episodes following his death eulogize him. The first celebrates him as a wise and compassionate ruler, and the next two recount love affairs with women of great beauty and sensitivity whom Kiyomori drove from the palace to insure his daughter's success as a consort. The tenor of these episodes is nostalgic and melancholic.

By contrast, Kiyomori's death is dramatic and epic in scale. Consumed by a fever so high that it causes water to evaporate when it touches his skin, Kiyomori died with a curse on his lips: "Build no halls or pagodas after I die; dedicate no pious works. Dispatch the punitive force immediately, decapitate Yoritomo, and hang the head in front of my grave. That will be all the dedication I require."[8] Three eulogistic episodes follow, all of which situate Kiyomori, both in this life and a former one, as a man of unusual talent, destined for greatness. Such episodes serve the important function of placation, and they represent a pattern seen elsewhere in the corpus as well: an important figure dies a death that may leave him with rancor or regret, and a eulogy, ranging from a few lines to the three episodes following the deaths of Kiyomori

---

8. Ichiko Teiji, ed., *Heike monogatari* (jō), NKBZ 29 (Shōgakukan, 1973), 452; Helen C. McCullough, trans., *The Tale of the Heike* (Stanford University Press, 1988), 211.

and parody the royal authority that he challenges; in fright, Go-Shirakawa called upon Yoritomo to punish his cousin. Yoritomo commanded two of his brothers, Yoshitsune 義経 (1159–1189) and Noriyori 範頼 (1156–1193) to attack the capital, and Chapter Eight ends with the ominous comment that:

> Thus the Heike held the western provinces, Yoritomo the eastern provinces, and Yoshinaka the capital. It was just as when the usurper Wang Mang ruled for eighteen years between Former Han and Later Han [in China]. With all the checkpoints closed, those in the provinces could deliver neither official tax goods nor private rents, and people of all degrees in the capital resembled fish in shallow water. Such were the parlous circumstances under which the old year ended and the third year of Juei began.[99]

Minamoto Yoshitsune, the great field general of the Genpei War, becomes a central figure of the narrative in Chapter Nine. The opening episodes describe his men's routing of Yoshinaka from the capital. After a furious final battle, Yoshinaka's troops were reduced to just his most loyal retainers, with whom he reteated to Awazugahara, along Lake Biwa, where he met his end. Yoshitsune then took control of the capital in Yoritomo's name and soon mounted an offensive against the Taira. By attacking their stronghold at Ikuta in a daring descent down the cliffs behind it, he forced them to take to their boats and flee; this is known as the battle of Ichi-no-tani (1184.2.7). During this retreat, one of the most famous episodes from the *Heike* occurs. As he spurred his horse toward the boats, Atsumori 敦盛, a young nephew of Kiyomori, was called back by the Minamoto partisan Kumagai Naozane 熊谷直実 (1141–1208), a seasoned warrior who easily grappled Atsumori—too noble to refuse the challenge—to the ground. Removing Atsumori's helmet, Kumagai was moved by the lad's youth and beauty, which reminded him of his love for his own son, a boy of about the same age. Although wanting to spare Atsumori, he saw his comrades quickly approaching and realized there was no chance for Atsumori to escape. He took the boy's head and then turned his back on the secular world to spend the rest of his life, as the

---

9. Ichiko Teiji, ed., *Heike monogatari* (ge), NKBZ 30 (Shōgakukan, 1973), 174; McCullough, *Tale of the Heike*, 282.

Heike tells it, praying for Atsumori's repose in the afterlife. The tragedy of Atsumori's fate is underlined by the flute Naozane found tucked in the lad's armor: like Tadanori, Atsumori was clearly a man of sensibility and artistic skill, too refined and too young to die in battle.

The "Death of Atsumori" is among the *Heike*'s most popular stories, and it spawned many plays and narratives not only about the event itself but also the fate of the unborn son Atsumori left behind. One version of the boy's life is recounted in the extracanonical nō play *Ikuta Atsumori*, translated in this volume by Lim Beng Choo. Keller Kimbrough's chapter draws connections between the tale recounted in *Ikuta Atsumori* and other narratives, particularly from the Buddhist tradition, that appear to have influenced it. Kimbrough also contributes a translation of *Ko Atsumori emaki*, a Muromachi-period narrative likewise recounting the fate of Atsumori's young son, included for comparison.

Many Taira were killed or captured at Ichi-no-tani, the most important being Shigehira, who had burned the Nara temples. Chapter Ten concerns the aftermath of the battle, and particularly Shigehira's fate. He was taken first to the capital, where Go-Shirakawa attempted to ransom him in exchange for the royal regalia, but the Taira refused this offer. He then was transported to Kamakura, after meeting with his religious mentor, Hōnen Shōnin 法然上人 (1133–1212). In Kamakura, a lovely and sensitive woman named Senju-no-mae 千手前 entertained him; so moved was she by their encounter that, after his execution, she took the tonsure to pray for his soul. Chapter Ten concludes with several episodes narrating the tonsuring and suicide of Shigemori's eldest son, Koremori, who, comprehending the hopelessness of the Taira's position, left the battlefield and went to Mount Kōya, where an old friend administered the precepts and then guided him as he prepared to drown himself, which he did on the twenty-eighth day of the Third Month of 1184. Learning of his death, his beloved wife took the tonsure to pray for his soul.

Meanwhile, there was a lull in the fighting lasting for nearly a year. The Minamoto under Noriyori were unsuccessful in engaging the Taira, and Yoshitsune had been ordered to stay in the capital, in part due to Yoritomo's suspicions about his youngest brother's ambitions. Finally, however, Yoshitsune was permitted to head west to fight the Taira in the First Month of 1185, and his troops defeated the Taira first at Yashima, then at Shido Bay. The fighting at Yashima is the setting for another particularly popular episode from the *Heike*, "Nasu no Yoichi." Challenged to shoot a fan extended on a pole held by a lady on one of the

Taira boats, Yoshitsune called upon the young archer Yoichi to perform the task. Relying on the divine help of Hachiman, Yoichi loosed an arrow, which hit the mark; both Taira and Minamoto forces lauded this act. The Nasu no Yoichi story is the source for the kyōgen play *Nasu*, translated in this volume by Carolyn Morley, whose chapter about the *Heike* in kyōgen also describes a variety of ways in which the *Heike* stories, *Heike* recitation, and *biwa hōshi* are represented in the kyōgen repertoire.

The final battle of the war was fought on the twenty-fourth day of the Third Month of 1185, after Yoshitsune and his men effected a perilous crossing of the straits at Suō, where they joined Noriyori and attacked the Taira in the straits in front of Dan-no-ura. Although the Taira fought heroically, they were outmatched, and as defeat became imminent, many of them committed suicide. The child sovereign Antoku, clutching one of the royal regalia—the sword—was carried into the sea in the arms of his grandmother, Kiyomori's widow. Nearly all the Taira, both men and women, died in this battle, save Tokuko, Antoku's mother, and the Taira commander-in-chief, Kiyomori's eldest living son, Munemori. The prisoners were taken to the capital, and then the important ones were sent on to Kamakura. Tokuko became a nun, and spent the rest of her life performing the heartbreaking task of praying for the souls of her child and most of her kinsmen. Munemori was executed as he traveled back from Kamakura, and Shigehira was sent to Nara to be executed by the monks there.

The ambiguous ending of the war is captured in a number of plays about executions at its conclusion. Paul Atkins translates the haunting *Shigehira*, a play about the sufferings of Shigehira in the afterlife as he endlessly re-lives the burning of Nara. Atkins's accompanying chapter emphasizes the relentlessly pessimistic portrayal of Shigehira's suffering in this particularly bleak play by Motomasa. The play points to one important dynamic motivating the reanimation of such characters beyond the *Heike*: they are at once dead and lingering, distant and near.

Morihisa describes an act of divine intervention that prevents the beheading of this relatively minor character, who appears in the Nagato-bon but not the Kakuichi-bon, and whose story bears strong resemblances to that of *Rō-Giō*. The play is translated by Shelley Quinn, who also contributes a chapter highlighting the play's allusive connections to other works. Naoko Gunji's chapter discusses the performance of *Morihisa* in the context of fund-raising efforts for temple rebuilding following a fire.

Tom Hare's chapter on Zeami's theoretical work *Go on* and the articulation of some of its concepts in "Rokudai no utai" (The Song about

Rokudai) takes up the story of yet another last-minute reprieve, in this case, that of the Taira heir, Rokudai. Hare's discussion of the work as an exemplification of theoretical principles laid out in *Go on* demonstrates the importance of generic structural concerns in recasting this well-known narrative from the *Heike* in the nō corpus. A counterpoint to this excavation of Zeami's theoretical writings is provided by Susan Blakeley Klein's reading of the political dimensions of the play *Haku Rakuten*, which draws on the Genpei War stories and heroes as it describes a confrontation between the Japanese god of poetry and the famous Tang poet Bai Juyi. Her analysis is followed by a translation of the play.

As Thomas Rimer's chapter on modern plays based on the *Heike* (and indebted to the nō as well) suggests, this was as true for the twentieth century as for the fifteenth. *Heike* characters and situations provided points of entry for examining the meanings of war, personal relations, and loss well beyond the scope of medieval Japan. The ongoing generative power of the *Heike* narrative to address changing situations suggests the timelessness of the issues they raise and the emotional responses they evoke. How these were first developed in the nō and how they are connected to related cultural phenomena are the central concerns of the translations and essays in this volume.

Note on Organization, Conventions, and Style

The appendix includes a finding list for *Heike*-related nō plays. For the translation of terms, we follow Royall Tyler's *Japanese Nō Dramas* (Penguin, 1992).

A comprehensive bibliography is provided in the Works Cited. In addition, relatively full citations are included in the footnotes of each piece in the hopes that this will allow readers greater ease in finding reference material. Characters for Japanese names and important terms are also provided at their first appearance in each piece. Standard abbreviations for commonly cited series are used in both the Works Cited and the footnotes. A list of full titles for these series is included at the beginning of the Works Cited.

All titles of literary works are italicized but the names of individual *Heike monogatari* variants are not. Instead, they are identified by the

suffix –bon (-text), for example: Kakuichi-bon or Kakuichi-bon *Heike monogatari*; Engyō-bon or Engyō-bon *Heike monogatari*, etc. We have opted for Engyō-bon instead of Enkyō-bon or Enkei-bon (all written 延慶本) to reflect current scholarly consensus on the correct pronunciation of the era name in which it was written. The *Genpei jōsuiki* is italicized, for although it is considered a *Heike* variant, it has a discrete title. Episodes (*dan* 段) within the *Heike* are placed in quotation marks ("Giō"); where they are identified by number, such as 1.6, the numbers refer to chapter (*maki* 巻) number and episode number, respectively. All such numbering refers to the Kakuichi-bon text ordering, unless otherwise noted. When abbreviated, dates are listed as Western year. lunar month.day (1184.2.7 is the seventh day of the Second Month of 1184). Intercalary months are prefaced by "i": i2 is "the Intercalary Second Month."

As a rule, we have striven for consistency in translation of terminology wherever possible, but individual authors translate some fundamental terms differently—notable examples include "chapter," "book," or "scroll" for *maki* and "episode" or "section" for *dan*. In all cases, we have tried to provide the original Japanese for clarity.

2 ～ Zeami, A Wandering Ghost, and the *Lotus Sutra*: The Story of Giō and Hotoke from *Heike Monogatari* to Nō

| ROBERTA STRIPPOLI

Giō 祇王,[1] the kindhearted female performer loved and abandoned by the ruthless Taira no Kiyomori 平清盛, and her rival and friend Hotoke Gozen 仏御前 occupy a special place in the history of Japanese literature and theater. Their story of love, pain, humiliation, and female solidarity remains unforgotten over many centuries since its first appearance in the *Heike monogatari*. Giō and Hotoke carry a surprisingly heavy weight for fictional characters, and the nineteenth-century temple on the outskirts of Kyoto alleged to have been their retreat is visited every year by thousands of people both for the beautiful red autumn leaves found there and for inspiration derived from their tale.

As her story begins[2] in the *Heike monogatari*, Giō is living in the capital as the concubine of the Taira leader Kiyomori, who lavishes attention on her and provides financial support to her family and friends. One day, a new *shirabyōshi* 白拍子[3] performer, young and ambitious, arrives in town. Her name is Hotoke Gozen 仏御前 (Lady Buddha) and she is determined to sing and dance for the most powerful man in the country in the hopes of obtaining his patronage. Knocking at a famous

---

1. Giō is written in different ways according to the text. The most common variants are: 祇王, 義王, 妓王, and きわう.

2. I am using the text edited and annotated by Tomikura Tokujirō, *Heike monogatari zenchūshaku*, vol. 1 (Kadokawa shoten, 1966), which belongs to the recited (*kataribon*) lineage of the *Tale of the Heike*.

3. The term *shirabyōshi* indicates both the art and the artists, female performers who sang and danced dressed in male clothes. Wakita Haruko, *Josei geinō no genryū: kugutsu, kusemai, shirabyōshi* (Kadokawa shoten, 2001), 132–62.

person's door in search of an audition was a common practice among performers in ancient and medieval Japan.[4] However, Kiyomori refuses to see her; he likes to make his own rules and so he rejects the young woman on the grounds that he already has Giō and there is no place for another *shirabyōshi*, even if her name is "God or Buddha."[5] Giō feels pity for the young artist and manages to convince Kiyomori to allow her to perform. Unfortunately, Giō's act of generosity will lead to her ruin (at least temporarily). Kiyomori shifts his attention to Hotoke and orders Giō out of his residence. Before leaving Kiyomori's mansion, Giō writes a poem on a *fusuma* that sounds like both a testament and a warning to Hotoke:

> Since both are grasses
> in the field, how may either
> be spared by autumn—
> the young shoot blossoming forth
> and the herb fading from view?[6]

Giō's poem may be interpreted as a bitter contestation that, like her own, Hotoke's luck is bound to be short-lived. However, it also shows a first understanding of the Buddhist concept of impermanence. The poem in fact will deeply affect Hotoke later in the story.

Besides losing Kiyomori's affection, Giō can no longer count on his financial patronage; she and her family (her mother and a sister, both also *shirabyōshi* performers) are left to take care of themselves, something to which they are not accustomed. After some time, Kiyomori invites Giō back to perform before Hotoke. Giō initially ignores his summons but eventually is convinced by her mother to pay a visit to this powerful and dangerous man. In what is usually regarded as the most dramatic scene of the story, Giō sings and dances in front of Hotoke, who now occupies what used to be Giō's seat next to Kiyomori. Following a performance that moves everybody except Kiyomori, Giō returns home planning to

---

4. Concerning *suisan* 推参, or the practice of visiting an important person's residence in search of artistic patronage, see Abe Yasurō, "Suisankō," *Gobun* 52 (Osaka daigaku kokugo kokubungakkai 1989), 12–27.

5. Helen Craig McCullough, trans., *The Tale of the Heike* (Stanford University Press, 1988), 31.

6. *Moeizuru mo / karuru mo onaji / nobe no kusa / izure ka aki ni / awadehatsubeki.* Tomikura, *Heike monogatari zenchūshaku*, vol. 1, 126. Translation of the poem by McCullough, *Tale of the Heike*, 33.

commit suicide by throwing herself in a river. Her mother and sister also threaten to commit suicide, but then all resolve to cut their hair, become nuns, and move to a hut in the Saga mountains, near Kyoto, where they can live in peace, meditate on the impermanence of the world, and recite the *nenbutsu* 念仏 to attain rebirth in Amida Buddha's western paradise. One night they hear someone knocking at the hut's door; after an initial moment of terror, they realize that the nocturnal visitor is none other than Hotoke, who shows them her freshly shaven head. Inspired by the poem left by Giō, she has realized the emptiness of her desires and decided to join her former rival. Giō and Hotoke are thus reunited, and Giō's resentment, which would have prevented her spiritual elevation, is now extinguished. In the end, the four women (Giō, her mother, sister, and Hotoke) attain salvation, and their names are even recorded in the Retired Emperor Go-Shirakawa's *kakochō* 過去帳 (memorial register), which supposedly attests to their rebirth in paradise.[7]

The happy ending of Giō's story is even more positive if we take into account that, in at least one version of the *Heike*, the story is placed just a chapter away from Kiyomori's demise.[8] The striking contrast between Giō's voluntary seclusion in pleasant company (and her eventual

---

7. The *kakochō* is a memorial register that was kept in the Chōgōdō 長講 堂 temple, built near the Sixth Avenue by Retired Emperor Go-Shirakawa (1127–1192). The only extant copy, supposedly in Go-Shirakawa's hand, is now considered an Edo-period copy. Tomikura, *Heike monogatari zenchūshaku*, vol. 1, 142.

8. The story stands independent from the main narrative: it is not directly linked to any other event recounted in the *Heike*, nor does Giō's name appear in any other chapter. This means that it could easily be placed almost anywhere in the tale, and thereby serve different agendas. In texts such as the Kakuichi-bon 覚一 本 and Engyō-bon 延慶本, Giō appears near the beginning, just after narratives introducing the fortunate fate of Kiyomori's children. The story reinforces the description of Kiyomori as a ruthless dictator, thus giving additional reasons for his downfall to seem necessary and inevitable. However, in *Genpei jōsuiki* 源 平盛衰記, the Giō episode does not occur until Chapter Seventeen, just after the transfer of the capital to Fukuhara (corresponding to Chapter Five in the Kakuichi-bon). It can be argued that both the Giō episode and the move to Fukuhara are used as examples of the evil deeds Kiyomori commits after he loses his heir Shigemori, known for his wisdom and ability to influence his father's decisions. In the Yashiro-bon 屋代本, the story appears in the usual place in the table of contents, but is actually located in a separate "omitted texts" (*nukigaki* 抜 書) section, placed just at the end of the work (in this case Chapter Twelve) that brings together seven episodes left out of the main text.

salvation) and Kiyomori's painful death may have been evident to the medieval audience, who most likely did not consider Giō a pitiful figure. For centuries after the composition of *Heike monogatari*, the feelings her story generated continued to flow in works from various literary and performance genres, including nō theater, whose repertoire includes a number of plays based on this story.

NOTES ON THE TRANSPOSITION OF STORIES FROM *MONOGATARI* TO NŌ

The plays about Giō and Hotoke are just a few examples of a vast number of nō plays whose plots and protagonists have already appeared in previous literary works such as *Genji monogatari* and *Heike monogatari*. The common practice of basing plays on well-known originals had a number of advantages, recognized at least as early as Zeami's day.

The first is that a character already known to an audience will automatically imbue the play with the atmosphere that usually surrounds his or her story. If the character is a young aristocratic warrior like Atsumori, for example, he will bring a touch of pathos and refinement; if it is a strong figure like Benkei, a sense of vigor. The woman searching for her son in *Sumidagawa* 隅田川 carries with her a feeling of madness and despair typical of such bereft mothers.

In the treatise *Sandō*[9] (The Three Elements in Composing a Play), Zeami discusses the choice of one's source materials, the "seed":

> The seed refers to the choice of a subject based on appropriate traditional sources, the actions of which are both appropriate for theatrical expression and especially effective in terms of the Two Arts of dance and chant. This is, of course, because these Two Arts form the fundamental basis of our whole art. If the subject chosen for the play concerns a character who

---

9. *Sandō* 三道 (also known as *Nōsakusho* 能作書) is a guide to composition written in 1423 by Zeami for his immediate successors. Translated in J. Thomas Rimer and Masakazu Yamazaki, *On the Art of the Nō Drama: The Major Treatises of Zeami* (Princeton University Press, 1984).

cannot be manifested using these Two Arts, then even if the character to be portrayed is a famous person in the past or a person of prodigious gifts, no theatrical effect appropriate to the *nō* is possible. ...

> In terms of women's roles, Lady Ise, Ono no Komachi, Giō and Gijo, Shizuka, and Hyakuman are all famous for their artistic accomplishments in poetry or dance. All of these historical or literary characters, if chosen for the central figure in a nō drama, will of themselves bring an appearance of artistic elegance to the play. ... Thus, creating a character whose very essence is involved in the art of song and dance can be termed choosing the proper seed.[10]

Later in the text, when explaining the "woman's role," Zeami mentions Giō one more time:

> Such characters as Shizuka, Giō, and Gijo represent *shirabyōshi* and so they should chant *waka* poetry, perform extended *issei*, follow the rhythms of the "eight beats," sing using the upper notes of the scale, dance to the rapid rhythm of the drum, and exit while dancing.[11]

Giō brings grace and dignity, along with all the melancholy of her vicissitudes. She is therefore a very appropriate character for an elegant play, a play that recaptures her beauty, artistry, and the drama of abandonment, as it celebrates her qualities. Moreover, she is a *shirabyōshi*, an expert in singing and dancing, the two arts fundamental to nō.

A character like Giō doubles the presence of performance in the play: the singing and dancing of the nō actors on the stage and the two scenes of singing and dancing in her story.[12] The fact that the audience knows and loves the narrative surrounding these two scenes increases its interest for them. Giō, therefore, brings added value to the play.

---

10. Rimer and Yamazaki, *On the Art of the Nō Drama*, 148–49.

11. Ibid., 154.

12. On the role played by performance in the "Giō" episode see Elizabeth Oyler, "Giō: Women and Performance in *Heike monogatari*," *Harvard Journal of Asiatic Studies*, 64:2 (Dec. 2004), 341–66.

Another important advantage that results from drawing from a well-known source is that there is no need to worry about the appropriateness of the topic narrated in the nō play. The playwright does not run the risk of misunderstanding on the part of the audience by drawing inspiration from an obscure and potentially problematic play. A story like Giō's already belongs to the collective imagination; it has been canonized as an important cultural artifact, and there is no fear that the audience may question its legitimacy.

Perhaps the most visible positive consequence of drawing from a well-known source is that the playwright does not need to use precious time and energy to establish the identity of a character.[13] Since nō theater does not make use of extended scripts, it may be a very difficult task to enable the audience to familiarize itself with a new character from just a handful of lines. Regarding the difficulty of introducing new characters and topics, Zeami warns:

> There is also the category of "created nō" in which a new play is prepared without any specific literary source, making use of the affinities between famous places or historical sites, in order to move the audience. Such plays are difficult to compose and require the accomplishments of a highly skilled person of great talent.[14]

What Zeami does not mention is that making an interesting play out of an already celebrated theme presents complications too. The play based on a well-known source needs to capture the essence of the story, yet convey it in a way that an audience already familiar with it finds appealing and still true to the original.

To be appealing, a play needs to be devised to move an audience that knows the finale already. In order to achieve this, variation becomes essential. However, in order for the play to be acceptable, variation must remain compatible with the established conventions of the story on which it draws.

We find innovation often represented by invented elements, like an unexpected extra character or plot twist, which refresh and give new life to an old familiar story, thus enhancing its interest in performance.[15]

---

13. Janet Goff, *Noh Drama and The Tale of Genji: The Art of Allusion in Fifteen Classical Plays* (Princeton University Press, 1991), 3.

14. Rimer and Yamazaki, *On the Art of the Nō Drama*, 149.

15. Variation may also involve elements such as choice of toponym. For

Nō Plays Involving Giō and Hotoke: Old Story, New Twists

There are four known nō plays based on the Giō episode in the *Heike monogatari*. The following analysis addresses the ways the authors drew on this well-known story, how they transformed it, and the consequences of their choices. For this particular task I focus on the texts of the plays, although I will also take into consideration elements related to their actual theatrical performance.

Some of these plays follow the story as narrated in the *Heike monogatari*, others only retain Giō's general identity and introduce different plots and settings. Giō's or Hotoke's name, always mentioned in the title, enables the audience to link the plays to what they already know about the legend from *Heike*-related performances or tales. Other consistently used features that help the audience identify the story correctly are Giō's skill as a *shirabyōshi* performer and her compassionate nature. The presence of Kiyomori is also an important element of the plays. The Taira leader does not necessarily appear as one of the *dramatis personae* but his presence is always hinted at (with the sole exception of *Rō-Giō* 籠祇王) and Giō's association with him constitutes a basic component of her identity.

Novelty is provided variously by the different angles from which the heroines are viewed, by more developed strategies of resistance to male authority, and by new interpretations of the relationship between the two protagonists, as we shall see.

---

example, by referring to the death place of the two Taira warriors Tadanori and Atsumori at Suma (as opposed to Ichi-no-tani), Zeami gives new refined nuances to their story, at the same time changing forever the identity of this famous *utamakura*. Karen W. Brazell, "Subversive Transformations: Atsumori and Tadanori at Suma," in Amy Vladeck Heinrich, ed., *Currents in Japanese Culture* (Columbia University Press, 1997), 35–52.

Giō

Giō, also known in the Kita School as *Futari Giō* 二人妓王, is a *genzai* nō play of the third type, a *kazura mono* 鬘物. The *shite* is Hotoke, the *tsure* is Giō, and the *waki* is Kiyomori's retainer Senō Tarō Kaneyasu 瀬尾太郎兼康, who also appears in Chapters Three and Eight of *Heike monogatari*, where he is described as a valiant and cunning soldier. Since Giō is repeatedly mentioned in Zeami's writings, many scholars of the past have argued that he may be the author, but current scholarship tends to consider the play anonymous.[16]

Giō is a highly elegant play. The nature of its characters, Giō and Hotoke, as well as the numerous references to Chinese and Japanese poetry, create an atmosphere of sophistication and grace that must have appealed greatly to the Muromachi audience. In this play, Hotoke's personality emerges in finer detail than in the *Heike* version of the story. While in most *Heike* texts the narration is exclusively from Giō's point of view, here Hotoke's is central. At the same time the audience has the impression of sitting in the place of Kiyomori, before whom everything happens. The identification of the audience with Kiyomori may be the reason why he does not physically appear in the play.

Giō recaptures the moment of Hotoke's admittance in the residence of the Taira leader. When Hotoke attempted to visit earlier, uninvited, she was rejected by Kiyomori, who had been insulted by her assertiveness. The other antecedent fact, absent from the *Heike* narrative, is that Giō has remained absent from Kiyomori for four or five days in protest, after commenting that she and Hotoke, as entertainers, are alike, and that Hotoke should be given a chance to perform.

Kiyomori finally resolves to let Hotoke into his residence, and the play opens with Senō Tarō summoning Giō, informing her of this decision, and inviting Hotoke to appear with Giō in front of the powerful man.

An important variation should be noticed here. While in the *Heike* Giō and Hotoke meet for the first time at Hotoke's performance, in the nō play they come on stage together, seemingly having spent the last few days in each other's company. This is not the only hint of an already developed

---

16. The text appears in Sanari Kentarō, ed., *Yōkyoku taikan*, vol. 2 (Meiji shoin, 1930), 857–68 (used here and in Susan Matisoff's translation, also in this volume) and in Nogami Toyoichirō, *Kaichū yōkyoku zenshū*, vol. 3 (Chūō kōronsha, 1936 [reprint edition 1971]), 63–72.

friendship between the two: Giō's pleasure when she learns that Kiyomori is letting Hotoke perform seems stronger than that motivated by a general benevolence toward an unfamiliar colleague. Further suggesting their previous acquaintance is the fact that Hotoke immediately invites Giō to join her in the dance before Kiyomori.

This presumed acquaintance is significant. Their familiar story from the *Heike* is about the development of their relationship, and it necessarily traces the many vicissitudes they enounter before they can be together in the Saga hut: Hotoke's memorable performance, Giō's expulsion from Kiyomori's residence, her further humiliation, both women's final resolution to become nuns. In the nō play all these events are done away with, yet the two women have some pre-knowledge of them. In fact, they seem to know much more than they should, given the scarce information provided by the nō script.[17] For example, when Hotoke invites Giō to join her, Giō recites:

> My dancing sleeves are worn
> From constant use,
> Familiar, seen by all,
> Perhaps with no charm remaining.[18]

The impression here is that she is aware she will soon be discarded. It is clear that not only the audience but also Giō and Hotoke themselves know their story as narrated in the *Heike monogatari*. This is another important consequence of drawing from a famous text: the universal knowledge of the source impregnates both the internal and the external discourse of the play. Intertextuality does not involve just the author and the audience of the play, but also deeply affects the characters. It seems as if Giō and Hotoke have read or heard a performance of their own episode

---

17. It could be argued that they overheard this information from the speech delivered by the *ai-kyōgen*, which in the Hōshō school version of the text (reproduced by Sanari on 863) gives away details of their story. The *kyōgen* actor recapitulates Giō's story and says that he thinks she will eventually be discarded. However, I maintain that the *kyōgen* should be considered part of the audience, rather than a character of the play. The *kyōgen* performance should be seen as separated from the nō play proper because it functions as an intermission, and its text is of a different nature than the nō script, codified in a written form centuries later.
18. *Warawa itsumo no mai no sode koto furinureba hitobito mo megarete kyō ya nakaramashi*. Sanari, *Yōkyoku taikan*, vol. 2, 862. Matisoff's translation.

in the *Heike monogatari*, and their behavior is influenced by what they have learned from reading that text or watching that performance.

Later in the play the two women perform together, singing songs in which Kiyomori's beautiful ladies are compared to those of the Han dynasty sovereign Wu Di 武帝. The song about Hotoke states:

> And in the way the human heart
> Can shift, and does so,
> His heart was captivated
> Drawn by every turn of her dancing sleeves.[19]

This describes what is happening in Kiyomori's heart at that very moment. When Senō says that, although enjoying the dance by both women, Kiyomori wants Hotoke to perform solo, Giō reacts by exclaiming:

> No reason for me to be here,
> I shall head for home.[20]

Giō knows her destiny, and her haste to leave well before being dismissed by Kiyomori takes on a new meaning. She is probably not just reacting in anger at being rejected. Knowing from the beginning that Kiyomori will leave her, why would she be upset? More likely, what she is trying to do is to speed up the events, so that her destiny can be fulfilled. She knows that if the story proceeds, she will soon be reciting *nenbutsu* in a hut in the Saga Mountains, free from Kiyomori's authority, and happily reunited with her mother and sister (who do not appear in the nō play) and especially Hotoke.

The ending of the play is dramatic: Giō leaves Kiyomori's residence and the unwilling Hotoke is compelled to continue her dance; yet it clearly hints at future favorable developments.

---

19. *Hitogokoro utsureba kawaru narai yue ka kare ni kokoro kake obi no hikikaete mai no sode.* Sanari, *Yōkyoku taikan*, vol. 2, 866. Matisoff's translation.

20. *Warawa wa kore ni arite mo yoshi nashi. Mazu mazu ieji ni kaeri sōrawan.* Sanari, *Yōkyoku taikan*, vol. 2, 866. Matisoff's translation.

Genzai Giō (Present World Giō)

Genzai Giō 現在祇王 is a very brief *genzai* nō play. Because several Edo-period neologisms appear in the first printed edition of the play (1676) it is believed to have been composed during the Edo period. The playwright is anonymous.[21]

Giō is the *shite*, Kiyomori the *waki*, and an unidentified *gozen*, who appears to be Hotoke, plays the *tomo*. The events take place some time after Giō has been expelled from Kiyomori's residence. Throughout the play Kiyomori and Giō never address each other directly; they seem to communicate exclusively through Hotoke.

Kiyomori introduces himself and announces his intention to make a visit to the Kiyomizu Temple to admire the cherry blossoms. He sends Hotoke to invite the ladies (*minamina* みなみな) to join him in this visit. Giō immediately refuses the invitation:

> Recently I don't know what he is up to,
> but he never calls me.
> Even if I happen to be there, he won't talk to me.
> I won't go [to Kiyomizu]. Thinking about it
> I realize that he has stopped talking to me
> since that Hotoke has arrived.
> He certainly has transferred his affection to her.
> For this reason I won't go.[22]

In the nō play, Kiyomori's summoning of Giō to perform for Hotoke is replaced by a gentle request to accompany the two of them on a flower-viewing excursion. In the *Heike monogatari*, Giō does not have a choice, but here she is able to refuse the invitation, which she does with great decisiveness. Moreover, while in the *Heike* Kiyomori is enraged by Giō's tardiness in answering his messages, here he sounds rather

21. Tanaka Makoto, ed., *Mikan yōkyokushū*, vol. 27 (Koten bungaku, 1976), 14. Text of the play on 79–82.

22. *Sareba kore hodo wa nani to oboshimeshi sōrō yaran. Wagami o mesu koto mo naku. Tamatama mairite mo onkotoba o mo idasarezu sōrō hodo ni. Mairu majiku sōrō. Yoku yoku mono o anzuru ni Hotoke Gozen to yaran no kitaritamaite ato wa wagami ni onkotoba o mo idasarezu sōrō. Sadamete Hotoke ni on'utsuri sōrō to zonjisōrō hodo ni warawa wa waza to mairu majiki to zonji sōrō.* Tanaka, *Mikan yōkyoku shū*, vol. 27, 80–81. All translations from *Genzai Giō* are by the author.

unconcerned by her refusal: "If it is so, she can do as she pleases!"[23] Giō laments her pitiful condition. In the end, after reciting the poem about the young and old grass in the field that will eventually fade (the same one she wrote on the *fusuma* in the *Heike monogatari* version of the story), she decides, tearfully, to leave Kiyomori's residence and return home for good.

Genzai Giō follows the basic plot of the *Heike monogatari*, with the important difference that nothing is left of the solidarity between Giō and Hotoke, not even the fact that Giō interceded for Hotoke at the beginning. The presence of the "grasses in the field" poem is the only element that somehow links the two women.

If the woman-to-woman bond is lost or ignored, Giō's strong character is emphasized. For the first time Giō does not need to employ any special strategy to extract herself from Kiyomori's control. She has no cause to worry about the possible consequences of her refusal, and she is not planning to commit suicide or to become a nun and hide in the Saga mountains: a simple denial is sufficient to free her. Kiyomori, for weakness or lack of interest, immediately gives up his hold over her.

Things do not go as easily for the protagonist of *Yuya* 熊野, a play by Zeami that has many analogies with *Genzai Giō*.[24] This is another play derived from a *Heike monogatari* episode, *Kaidō kudari* (The Journey Down the Eastern Sea Road) in Chapter Ten. In the *Heike monogatari*, events of the life of the former mistress of Taira no Munemori (the second son of Kiyomori) are told in retrospect.[25] The nō play reenacts these events: Munemori does not grant her permission to visit her ill mother because he intends to enjoy her company while flower-viewing at Kiyomizu Temple, the same location Kiyomori intends to visit in *Genzai Giō*. Unlike Giō, Yuya cannot criticize or, even worse, refuse Munemori's order, but she is later released, thanks to a moving poem she composes.

---

23. *Sayō ni sōrawaba sono tōri ni itashi oki sōrae.* Tanaka, *Mikan yōkyoku shū*, vol. 27, 81.

24. Nippon Gakujutsu Shinkōkai, ed., *Japanese Noh Drama*, vol. 2 (Nippon Gakujutsu Shinkōkai, 1959), 35–51.

25. In the Kakuichi version of the *Heike monogatari*, Munemori's mistress is known as Jijū. Yuya is her mother's name. Tomikura, *Heike monogatari zenchūshaku*, vol. 3, 269–70. McCullough, *Tale of the Heike*, 336–37.

HOTOKE NO HARA (BUDDHA FIELD)

Hotoke no hara 仏の原, the only *mugen* nō examined here, is probably the best-known play of the Giō-Hotoke cycle. The author is unknown, but scholars such as Nishino Haruo believe he belonged to Zeami's circle, and can possibly be identified as Komparu Zenchiku.[26]

The *maeshite* is a woman whom the *waki*, a priest on a pilgrimage, meets in a field in Kaga province (now Ishikawa prefecture). The woman is pleased to see the priest and asks him to pray for somebody who coincidentally passed away in that location exactly ten years earlier. The person in question is the dancer Hotoke who, after leaving the hut in the Saga mountains where she had previously retreated with Giō, had returned to her home village in Kaga and died in that very field. After retelling Hotoke's vicissitudes in detail, the woman takes her leave. The priest is impressed by this story, and, following the *ai* interlude, starts intoning a sutra for the soul of the deceased. It is here that the *nochijite*, the ghost of Hotoke, makes her appearance, dances, and then vanishes.

Hotoke no hara casts a sinister shadow over the heroines' destinies. We left them in the *Heike monogatari* safely reunited in prayer in the Saga hut, waiting to be reborn in Amida's paradise. Here, unexpectedly, we run into Hotoke's ghost, still wandering in fields, not reborn, not yet a buddha, asking to be pacified by both the priest, through sutra recitation, and the nō audience, through a therapeutic reenactment of her story.[27]

That Hotoke remains suffering in the afterlife is probably due in large part to the requirements of the genre. *Hotoke no hara* is a *mugen* nō, which inherently requires a ghost. The presence of a wandering Hotoke may, therefore, be partly due to the necessity for a ghost, and not to a bias against her salvation.

This is in fact a play about salvation, a salvation expected not for Hotoke alone, but for all sentient and nonsentient beings, including the

---

26. Nishino Haruo, ed., *Yōkyoku hyakuban*, SNKT 57 (Iwanami shoten, 1998), 429. Text of *Hotoke no hara* on 429–43. The play is also in Sanari Kentarō, ed., *Yōkyoku taikan*, vol. 4 (Meiji shoin 1931), 2787–99 and in Itō Masayoshi, *Yōkyokushū* (ge), SNKS (Shinchōsha, 1988), 227–35. Translated in this volume by David Bialock.

27. *Heike monogatari* recitations, and well as nō performances, could have had the function of pacifying potentially evil spirits (such as those of the warriors who had died violently). Herbert E. Plutschow, *Chaos and Cosmos: Ritual in Early and Medieval Japanese Literature* (Leiden: Brill, 1990), 220–25.

animals and plants that inhabit the field where the play is set.
The field that gives the play its title, *Hotoke no hara* (Buddha Field), is central, and its plants assume great importance. In the *Heike*, we already saw that Giō had written a poem on a *fusuma*, which described the old and young grasses; it later helped Hotoke understand impermanence.
In *Hotoke no hara* the grasses in the field are not just metaphors. Plants, as well as insects, are strongly present, to the point that they may be considered near-characters in the play. They pray, they bow, they finally attain enlightenment if looked at by a buddha (*hotoke*).

> When one Buddha achieving the way
> beholds with clear sight the Dharma world
> grass, trees, and earth
> all achieve Buddhahood.[28]

The passage then states that even the grasses and trees of *Hotoke no hara* will eventually turn into buddhas. According to Japanese Mahayana doctrines, plants and nonsentient objects are endowed with buddha-nature and can be or become buddhas either by their own agency or passively, by being looked at by the nondifferentiating eye of a buddha.[29]
Buddha-nature was the theme of the *imayō* that Giō had sung at her last dramatic performance in front of Kiyomori and Hotoke:

> In days of old, the Buddha
> was but a mortal;
> in the end, we ourselves
> will be buddhas, too.
> How grievous that distinction
> must separate those
> who are alike in sharing
> the Buddha-nature.[30]

---

28. *Ichi butsu jōdō kanken hōkai sōmoku kokudo shikkai jōbutsu.* Bialock's translation. Bialock's base text is Itō, *Yōkyokushū* (ge), 231.

29. Fabio Rambelli, *Vegetal Buddhas: Ideological Effects of Japanese Buddhist Doctrines on the Salvation of Inanimate Beings* (Kyoto: Scuola Italiana di Studi sull'Asia Orientale, 2001).

30. *Hotoke mo mukashi wa bonbu nari. Warera mo tsui ni wa hotoke nari. Izure mo busshō guseru mi o hedatsuru nomi koso kanashikere.* Tomikura, *Heike monogatari zenchūshaku*, vol. 1, 131. McCullough, *Tale of the Heike*, 34.

Rō-Giō (Giō at the Prison)

Rō-Giō 籠祇王, a *bangai* nō, exhibits the greatest plot variation among the plays examined here.[31] During a retreat at Kiyomizu Temple, the *shite*, the famous *shirabyōshi* Giō, hears that her father has been imprisoned and sentenced to death. Not knowing the reason for this punishment, she immediately sets out for Ki province (present-day Wakayama prefecture), hoping to be able to meet him one last time. On her arrival at the prison, the guard (the *waki* role) agrees to let her see her father (the *tsure*) on the condition that she perform a dance afterward. Giō's father is very pleased to see his daughter; he explains that he is being punished because he freed a young prisoner whom he believed was captured by mistake. Giō agrees that setting the innocent free was a compassionate act but laments that nothing can be done to save her father except praying to the Bodhisattva Kannon for mercy. The guard insists that Giō perform the promised dance. Giō is quite reluctant but starts dancing when her father encourages her by reminding her of the days when he was teaching her the secrets of performance:

> How now Giō? Why do you refuse?
> The dance was one that I originally taught you ...[32]

After the dance father and daughter exchange a rosary and a copy of the *Lotus Sutra* and prepare for the father's execution. In the final scene, as he is about to be killed, the executioner's sword miraculously breaks into pieces, and Giō's father is pardoned. The miracle is attributed to the powers of Kannon and the *Lotus Sutra*.[33] The plot's attention to detail and

---

31. The text of the play is in Haga Yaichi and Sasaki Nobutsuna, eds., *Kōchū yōkyoku sōsho*, vol. 3 (Hakubunkan, 1915), 593–98, translated in this volume by Michael Watson, who also presented a paper on it at the conference of the European Association of Japanese Studies in Warsaw in 2003, to which I am indebted.

32. *Ikani Giō, nan to te kotoba shite mōsu zo. Moto yori kono ikkyoku wa chichi wa oshieshi koto nareba* ... Haga and Sasaki, *Kōchū yōkyoku sōsho*, vol. 3, 596. Watson's translation, Chapter Six in this volume.

33. This turn of the events is directly related to Chapter 25 of the *Lotus Sutra* that contains a similar image. The knives belonging to enemies break into pieces and a prisoner is freed. Leon Hurvitz, *Scripture of the Lotus Blossom of the Fine Dharma* (Columbia University Press, 1976), 317. A similar development occurs in the *Heike*-derived nō *Morihisa* (see Chapter 24 by Shelley Fenno Quinn), where Kannon spares the protagonist just when the executioner raises his sword to cut off his head.

the strong emphasis given to the values of justice and filial piety confer on *Rō-Giō* an unmistakable Edo-period flavor.

The most striking transformation here is the substitution of the mother figure, always present in the *Heike monogatari* versions, with a father. Moreover, the cult of Amida Buddha, central in the finale of the Giō story, is replaced with faith in the salvific power of the *Lotus Sutra*. While in the *Heike* the four women pray to Amida for future rebirth in a paradise, here the *Lotus Sutra* brings benefits in this very life, physically preventing the execution of Giō's father.

CONCLUSIONS

When it draws on a preexisting literary work, a nō play necessarily refers to events that took place in the past. It is immaterial if these events were actually historical; what matters is that they manifested themselves in a previous work. It is up to the playwright to decide what to do with these events. In the case of Giō, the authors of the various nō plays had the *shite* recount these events (*Hotoke no hara*), the protagonists reenact them with degrees of variation (*Giō* and *Genzai Giō*), or they did not mention the events at all as in *Rō-Giō*, where the *Heike monogatari* plot is put aside, and Giō is simply a famous dancer who dutifully practices filial piety.

However, the fact that the audience is familiar with these events of the past is taken for granted and constitutes an essential requirement for the "correct" enjoyment of the play. The members of the implied audience know the story of Giō and can interpret the performance according to a body of knowledge they all share.

In our exploration of Giō-related nō plays, we have become aware of an unexpected consequence of the choice of drawing from such a source: not only is the audience familiar with the events narrated in it, but there are instances in which the characters themselves speak and behave as if they were aware of the way their own story ends, even though it has not yet taken place on the stage. This is particularly evident in the case of the play *Giō*, where the protagonists, Giō and Hotoke, reenact a story they already appear to know by heart.

Other differences can be observed with varying relevance. For example the mother figure, who has a central role in all the versions of the *Heike monogatari*, is completely absent in the nō. In *Rō-Giō*, she is even replaced with an absent father, who, in spite of the *shirabyōshi*'s renowned female lineage tradition, "taught her how to dance."

Another important absence is that of the scene usually considered the dramatic climax of the whole Giō story in the *Heike monogatari*: the dance Kiyomori forces her to perform to entertain Hotoke. This part of the story does not find a place in the nō tradition. There are several "requested performances," such as when Giō and Hotoke dance together in *Giō* and when Giō is forced to dance if she wants to see her father one last time in *Rō-Giō*. But the performance in which Kiyomori humiliates Giō by having her sit in a lower place than Hotoke and Giō dramatically sings that "we all possess the Buddha-nature" does not appear anywhere.

How should we interpret these instances of variation, and, more importantly, how do they affect the *Heike monogatari* tradition?

Until modern times, *Heike monogatari* was not perceived as a single text but identified instead with a vast corpus of stories, a multiform tradition.[34] This gave any new teller of the *Heike monogatari* episodes great freedom to manipulate the stories and change any element, giving birth to new texts. Each new text drew meaning from the tradition but at the same time made a contribution to the tradition.

If each *Heike* performance or *Heike* text can be seen as a different but equally authoritative instantiation of the *Heike* tradition, then each *Heike*-related nō play could also be seen as "another performance" of a certain *Heike monogatari* episode. This performance presents an even further variation from the already multiform texts of the *Heike*. It is the *Heike monogatari* tradition that makes each of these performances, each of these nō plays, an authoritative document.[35]

---

34. The Kakuichi-bon, a group of texts connected to the one dictated in 1371 by the blind reciter Kakuichi, started being considered the most autoritative one only a century ago. For an overview of the principal variants of *Heike monogatari* see David Bialock, "The Tale of the Heike," in Steven Carter ed., *Medieval Japanese Writers, Dictionary of Literary Biography* (Detroit: Gale Group, 1999), 73–84. On the canonization of the *Heike* as a work of literature see David Bialock, "Nation and Epic: *The Tale of the Heike* as Modern Classic," in Haruo Shirane and Tomi Suzuki, eds., *Inventing the Classics: Modernity, National Identity, and Japanese Literature* (Stanford University Press, 2000), 151–78.

35. In other words, the concept of equally authoritative performance proposed by John Miles Foley should be applied not just within the same category of nō, but through literary and performance genres, including *Heike* recitation and writing, medieval narratives *otogizōshi*, etc. See John Miles Foley, *Immanent Art: From*

It becomes evident then that a nō play drawing on a well-known source is also making a contribution to the general tradition of the *Heike monogatari*, or, in our case, to the legend of Giō and Hotoke. Versions of the Giō story told in nō plays, but also in *otogizōshi* 御伽草子 (companion booklets), *kōwakamai* 幸若舞 (ballad-drama), and the like, refer to and derive their meaning from a tradition (the tradition of Giō and Hotoke) but at the same time contribute vitally to the construction and transmission through the generations of this very tradition.

Structure to Meaning in Traditional Oral Epic (Indiana University Press, 1991), especially 42–45.

3 ∼ *Giō*

| SUSAN MATISOFF

INTRODUCTION

The text of the nō play *Giō* is based on the longest episode in the *Heike monogatari*. In most versions of the Kakuichi-bon and in the majority of other *Heike* variants in which the episode appears, "Giō" is positioned immediately following "Wagami no eiga" 我身栄華 (or 吾身栄花, Kiyomori's flowering fortunes). Note 8 in Roberta Strippoli's chapter in this volume discusses the position of the episode in other *Heike* variant texts. In *Heike monogatari,* the "Giō" episode serves to cast a dark shadow on the portrayal of Kiyomori. His arbitrary treatment in sending away his formerly beloved dancing girl Giō readily suggests that Kiyomori's behavior merits criticism. In the play *Giō,* in comparison to its source, the prominence of the dancer Hotoke is greatly elaborated, and it is she who performs the *ha no mai* dance at the play's conclusion. Hotoke is the *shite,* by definition the primary role in the play, yet the title reflects the importance of Giō. Both dancers suffer from Kiyomori's arrogant exercise of power, but Giō's psychological experience may be said to be at the core of the play, as it is in the *Heike monogatari* source, while Hotoke is the more physically active character, given two opportunities to dance.[1]

---

1. Another example of a play which has come to be known by the name of the *tsure* rather than the *shite* is *Semimaru* 蝉丸. The suffering of the blind Semimaru is at the core of the plot, but his sister Sakagami, the *tsure,* has the more active role onstage: she dances but he does not. Susan Matisoff, *The Legend of Semimaru, Blind Musician of Japan* (Columbia University Press, 1978; reprinted by Cheng and Tsui, 2006).

In the Kita school tradition the play is entitled *Futari Giō* 二人祇
王, thus reflecting the importance of both dancers, yet retaining the
familiar name of Giō in the title. This is somewhat reminiscent of the
play *Futari Shizuka* 二人静.[2] In *Futari Shizuka* a woman encountered
in living reality is possessed by the ghost of the *shirabyōshi* Shizuka. In
the latter half of the play, the possessed woman and the ghost of Shizuka
are onstage dancing together extensively. But unlike *Futari Shizuka, Giō*
is a contemporary reality play in which all the roles are living beings.
Despite their differences both plays exploit the visual charm of a duet of
dancers, though the position of the paired dance in *Giō* occurs relatively
early in the play while the finale has Hotoke dancing solo. *Futari Shizuka*
has been attributed to Zeami but the authorship of *Giō* has never been
securely established.

Another play to which comparison must be made is *Hotoke no hara*
仏原, translated in this volume by David Bialock. Sanari Kentarō calls
the two pieces "sister plays" (*shimaikyoku* 姉妹曲) and points to the
earlier parts of the Giō episode in *Heike* as the principal source for the
nō *Giō*.[3] *Hotoke no hara* is inspired by material from later in the episode,
and transformed into a dream vision play with the appearance of Hotoke
gozen as a ghost. Sanari points out that both plays, despite their clear
relation to the source episode, are somewhat unusual in that they quote
few lines directly from that source. The inspiration is more conceptual
than textual.

---

2. For a translation and study, see Jacqueline Mueller, "The Two Shizukas:
Zeami's Futari Shizuka," *Monumenta Nipponica* 36:3 (Autumn 1981), 285–98.

3. Sanari Kentarō, ed., *Yōkyoku taikan*, vol. 2 (Meiji shoin, 1931; reprint edition
1965), 857.

Giō | Translated by Susan Matisoff

Third-category *genzai* nō in two acts.
Performed by the Kanze, Hōshō, and Komparu schools.

Time: During the Taira ascendancy, Third Month
Place: Taira no Kiyomori's residence in the capital
Author: uncertain

WAKI	Senō Tarō
MAEZURE / NOCHIZURE	Giō Gozen
MAESHITE / NOCHIJITE	Hotoke Gozen
KYŌGEN	Senō's Retainer

[PART ONE (*maeba*)]

I

To nanoribue *music Senō Tarō enters, followed by his retainer who carries a sword. They stand at the naming pillar* (nanoriza).

SENŌ TARŌ   I am Senō Tarō,[1] one in service to the Lay-Priest Premier.[2] Now Jōkai governs, holding the realm in the palm of his hand. He is at the height of his glory. A dancer called Giō Gozen[3] has held Jōkai's attention for some time now and his affection for her is unparalleled. Day and night he carouses with her at his side. Then there's a woman from Kaga called Hotoke Gozen,[4] another

---

Giō 祇王. The translation is based on the text in Sanari Kentarō, ed., *Yōkyoku taikan*, vol. 2 (Meiji shoin, 1931; reprint edition 1965), 857–68.

1. Senō Tarō Kaneyasu 瀬尾太郎兼康, warrior serving the Heike leader Kiyomori (see note 3). Senō is not mentioned in the "Giō" episode of *Heike monogatari* (Kakuichi-bon 1.6), but he appears elsewhere in the text, doing Kiyomori's bidding (Kakuichi-bon 1.11, 2.4, 2.9, 3.12, 5.14, 7.6).
2. Taira no Kiyomori 平清盛. Jōkai 浄海, his Buddhist name, is one of several epithets by which he was known after undergoing the tonsure.
3. Giō Gozen 祇王御前. The suffix *gozen* shows respect.
4. Hotoke Gozen 仏御前, from the province of Kaga 加賀, north of the capital, corresponding to the southern part of Ishikawa prefecture.

shirabyōshi.[5] She came here, making it known that she wishes to have Jōkai see her. But in commanding response Jōkai stated, "Whatever sort of god or buddha[6] she may be, so long as I have Giō, I've no wish to meet her." But Giō has said to him, "We two are alike, both making our way as entertainers, so it's only right for you to meet her." And after saying that, Giō has absented herself from him for the last four or five days. Now I have been sent to inform her that she is to put in an appearance today. I am to pass this word to Giō Gozen.

Senō advances to the edge of the stage and faces the curtain.

Is anyone there? I have come to report that Giō Gozen and Hotoke Gozen are both to appear by Jōkai's orders.

II

Senō proceeds from bridgeway to main stage and sits at the witness position (wakiza). Giō and Hotoke follow him onstage.

SENŌ   (*addressing Giō*)
   Well, Giō Gozen, why have you been absenting yourself lately?
GIŌ   Even now, the reason I will go is to plead on Hotoke's behalf!
SENŌ   Ah, now that's been settled. He has already stated that Hotoke Gozen is to come to him. (*Turning to Hotoke*) Ah, Hotoke Gozen, you're to appear for him now. Congratulations!

III

HOTOKE   Uneasily, I speak of my own wishes,
   embarrassed at what you may think of me;
   but if I simply keep my silence
   my desires would remain
   like unseen threads,
   "brocade in darkness,"
   as the saying goes.[7]

---

5. *Shirabyōshi* 白拍子. Women dancers distinguished by their masculine-style costuming. The *kyōgen* interlude below gives one version of the history of such performers.

6. Her name, Hotoke 仏, means a buddha.

7. *Tatoete* たとへて "likening," here translated "as the saying goes," suggests that the image of "brocade in darkness" (*yami no nishiki* 闇の錦) is so familiar as

And what would become of me?
She and I are both performers,
decked out in the same finery.
Do I alone have these ill feelings?
CHORUS (*sageuta*) A man of such great reputation,
Does he make distinctions between others?
(*ageuta*)   On the journey crossing from my home
as cold winds blew down from the mountains
as cold winds blew down from the mountains,
clouds lingered round the highest peaks
wrapping the sky in darkness,
nothing to speed me on my gloomy way.
If people of the capital
should inquire of me,
like those high peaks, enveloped,
with thoughts never clearing.[8]
So I am, but with nothing to say,
I merely weep, not to be seen[9]
by those in my home town.

---

to be in general use, rather than a specific reference to its original Chinese source. The phrase *yoru no nishiki* 夜の錦, "brocade by night" appears in *Kokinshū* 古今集 297, by Ki no Tsurayuki 紀貫之. Helen Craig McCullough, *Brocade by Night: "Kokin Wakashū" and the Court Style in Japanese Classical Poetry* (Stanford University Press, 1985), 415. McCullough states that the original source is the *Shi ji* 史記 and cites Burton Watson's translation, *Records of the Grand Historian*, vol. 2 (Columbia University Press, 1961), 55. The passage reads: "'To become rich and famous and then not go back to your old home is like putting on an embroidered coat and going out walking in the night,' he said. 'Who is to know about it?'"

8. This passage draws on a poem by Ono no Sadaki 小野貞樹, *Kokinshū* 937, specifically the syllables underlined in the transcription: 都人いかにと問はば山たかみはれぬ雲居に侘ぶとこたへよ *miyakobito / ika ni to towaba / yama takami / harenu kumoi ni / wabu to kotaeyo*. McCullough's translation is as follows: "If in the city / someone should ask about me / answer that I pine / in distant mountains too high / for the clouds to clear away." *Kumoi* 雲井 "clouds" is here replaced by *omoi* 思ひ "thoughts." *Kokin Wakashū: The First Imperial Anthology of Japanese Poetry*, translated and annotated by Helen Craig McCullough (Stanford University Press, 1985), 206.

9. *Engo* 縁語, "associative words," left untranslated here, link the words *ha* 葉 "leaves," *tsuyu* 露 "dew," and *kakaru* 懸かる "to hang."

IV

SENŌ   Ah, Hotoke Gozen, what fascinating recollections! Now, by his
order you are to appear and dance before him. That is what he has said.

HOTOKE   I go according to his wishes
             We shall sing *waka* in celebration
             and come, Giō Gozen,
             let us dance together,
             side by side.

GIŌ   My dancing sleeves are worn
             from constant use,
             familiar,[10] seen by all,
             perhaps with no charm remaining.

HOTOKE   So you say, and yet,
             donning flowery robes[11]
             and courtiers' caps
             let us dance together,
             sleeve upon sleeve, resplendent.

SENŌ   How enticing, they appear;
             and once in their dancing costumes
             the impression that they make
             will be even deeper.

CHORUS   With a calm expression
             like the shadow of the moon
             lingering at dawn[12]
             worries hidden from others,
             yet my heart knows my shame.
             My uneasy thoughts are shallow
             in the palest light of early morning.

                                      turning toward Senō
             "Let us don our flowery robes,"

---

10. The translation follows an emendation suggested by Sanari to correct a textual flaw.

11. A *kakekotoba* involving *yū* 言ふ "to speak" and *yūgao* 夕顔 "moonflower" is left untranslated here.

12. There is a minimal, partial allusion here to a poem by Mibu no Tadamine 壬生忠岑, *Kokinshū* 625: 晨明のつれなく見えし別より暁許うき物はなし *ariake no / tsurenaku mieshi / wakare yori / akatsuki bakari / uki mono wa nashi*. McCullough's translation is: "The hours before dawn / seem saddest of all to me / since that leave-taking / when I saw in the heavens / the pale moon's indifferent face." McCullough, *Kokin Wakashū*, 140.

so saying, the two set off together,
the two set off together.

Hotoke and Giō exit.

[INTERVAL (*nakairi*)]

SENŌ Is anyone about?

Retainer comes to him.

RETAINER I am here.

SENŌ Hotoke Gozen is coming together with Giō Gozen. Announce that they are to appear before him.

RETAINER Right.

Retainer proceeds to the naming pillar.

RETAINER Now, about that Hotoke Gozen, she's from Kaga and she's sixteen or seventeen years old. Now, to be sure, from ages past, there have been many *shirabyōshi*, but among them all she's a grand beauty. She sings *imayō* with a lovely voice, and she dances with great skill. There can be no woman like her in the capital or countryside. This is how people in the capital city praised her, so Hotoke Gozen thought, "It's only right that I go to Lord Kiyomori since he's the man of the moment. There would be nothing amiss if an entertainer were to show up by her own choice."

She went to his place at Nishi Hachijō, but the Lord-Novice said, "An entertainer of that sort should come when she is summoned. To come without summons is improper. Whether she's a buddha or a god, since I have Giō, I will not see her," and he turned her away. Because of Giō's intervention, Kiyomori summoned her, and when he saw Hotoke Gozen, it appears his affections quickly shifted to her. And Giō, too, is well known as a performer, with looks surpassing others and a particularly nice disposition. The Lord-Novice has loved her deeply, but, seeing how things are now, I think that Giō may surely be discarded.

In general, concerning those we call *shirabyōshi*, back in the time of Retired Emperor Toba[13] there were two women, Shima no Senzai and Waka no Mae. They costumed themselves in exquisite *ōkuchi* and *suikan* along with courtiers' caps. Since they danced wearing swords, their performances were called "male dances." And later they omitted

---

13. Emperor Toba 鳥羽 reigned from 1107–1123 and died in 1156.

the courtiers' caps and danced wearing just the *suikan* and *ōkuchi*, and so, people say, they were called *shirabyōshi*.[14]

Oh, I just meant to tell you about their costumes, not to deliver such a monologue!

He faces the curtain.

Say, Giō, Hotoke, if you're in costume, you should hurry to him! Come! Come!

Senō sits at the villager position (kyōgenza).

[PART TWO (*nochiba*)]

V

Giō enters followed by Hotoke. Both are now costumed as shirabyōshi *and are wearing courtiers' caps.*

GIŌ   How happy I am, my wish now granted!
                The awaited day has come.[15]
                The dancer, appealing as a maidenflower,[16]
HOTOKE   a woman in form yet wearing
                a courtier's tall cap,

---

14. Presumably this has to do with plain, or white-colored costumes, though the explanation is not clear in this regard. This passage closely resembles but is not quite identical to the relevant passage in the "Giō" section of the Kakuichi-bon *Heike monogatari*. Takagi Ichinosuke et al., eds., *Heike monogatari* (jō), NKBT 32 (Iwanami shoten, 1959), 95. The *ōkuchi* 大口, broad-legged trouser-skirt mentioned here but not in the *Heike*, were likely visualized as white. A *suikan* 水干 is a round-necked, loose outer garment covering the upper body. It is a somewhat simplified version of the *karigoromo* 狩衣, originally a hunting robe, that became more generally used. A *tate-eboshi* 立烏帽子 is a tall cap made of lacquered cloth. The *suikan* and *eboshi* together constitute distinctively male dress.

15. There is a pun here on Michinoku no Kefu 陸奥の狭布 "Kefu (village) in Michinoku district." The place name embeds *michi* 満ち "fulfilled" here translated as "granted" and *kefu* 今日 "today."

16. "Maidenflower" translates the name of the flower *ominaeshi* 女郎花 for linguistic felicity rather than botanical accuracy. The source poem here is by Archibishop Henjō 僧正遍照, *Kokinshū* 1016: 秋の野になまめき立てる女郎花あなかしがまし花もひと時 *aki no no ni* / *namamekitateru* / *ominaeshi* / *ana kashigamashi* / *hana mo hitotoki*. Only the underlined syllables are included in the nō. McCullough's translation: "You maidenflowers / marching in coquettish ranks / self-assertively / through the meadows of autumn: / blossoms, too, must soon depart." McCullough, *Kokin Wakashū*, 228–29.

Giō	and a hunting robe,
	patterned in the flowers of the season,
Hotoke	sleeve touching sleeve,
Giō	together, we step to it.
Together	under the beneficence of the lord
	who keeps the realm in order,
	generation upon generation,
Chorus	voices of the common folk
	rise up in song.[17]

Giō and Hotoke dance a chū no mai *in unison.*

Together	The blossoms of spring in Golden Valley
(*kuri*)	suddenly showed signs of decay.[18]
Chorus	The moon of autumn at Gusu pavilion[19]
	became hidden by clouds of oblivion.
Together	The past does not return,
(*sashi*)	leaving us suffused in memories,
	weeping for those long departed,

---

17. This appears to be the text of an *imayō* 今様 here used to flatter Kiyomori. This image of the joyous consent of the governed, originally applied to the mythological Chinese sage-king Yao 堯, had become a commonplace form of praise for a virtuous ruler in Chinese texts familiar in Japan.

18. Golden Valley 金谷 is the place where the Jin 金 dynasty aristocrat Shi Chong 石崇 lived with his beloved singing girl, Lü Zhu 緑珠, until she committed suicide out of loyalty after Shi Chong was arrested and taken to his death at the instigation of a political rival. This may have been known to the nō playwright through commentaries on a poem by Du Mu 杜牧, "The Garden at Golden Valley" 金谷園, in *Du Mu: Plantains in the Rain: Selected Chinese Poems*, translated by R.F. Burton (London: Wellsweep Press, 1990), 30. I am grateful to Robert Ashmore for assistance in tracking down the Chinese allusions in *Giō*.

19. This is a parallel allusion to another Chinese ruler and his dancing-girl mistress. Gusu 姑蘇 pavilion is associated with an ancient story of a doomed romance between Fu Chai, king of Wu 王夫差 (r. 495–473 BCE), and Xi Shi 西施, a legendary beauty. "The vision of the King of Wu's doomed carousing with Xi Shi, heedless of the forces of Yue [越] gathering against him, was a favorite of Tang poets of the eight and ninth centuries." *An Anthology of Chinese Literature, Beginnings to 1911*, edited and translated by Stephen Owen (New York and London: W.W. Norton, 1996), 99. The nō playwright most likely garnered his Chinese literary allusions from such Tang period poems rather than from earlier historical and legendary Chinese sources. Owen includes a translation of one such poem, by Yuan Zhen 元稹 (779–831) entitled, "A Winter 'White Linen Song.'"

	sleeves damp with tears.
CHORUS	How many days must pass
	before they dry?
	and sadly, none can tell,
	when will our last days come?

(*Maikuse*)

CHORUS   In this world of dream and reality
(*kuse*)   we waken today
            from yesterday's illusion,
            yet dream on ever again.
            Though of humble birth
            we set forth upon the path
            of women entertainers, giving pleasure
            at the will of fickle men of passion.
            Our budding blossoms unknown,
            hidden away like logs
            long buried in the earth,[20]
            our splendor concealed.
            Without good social ties
            we are constrained,
            held back from appearing
            like dew-laden pampas grass
            in full plume.
               Now the Taira Prime Minister, Lord Kiyomori,
            leads the martial forces of the realm
            and all must stand in awe of him.
            In his golden, bejeweled mansion
            he has gathered a number of beautiful women.
            The four pavilions of Han Wu Di,[21]
            how could they have surpassed this?
            Giō is known as a woman
            of particular beauty and passion;
            and he came to love her deeply
            from the first time she appeared before him.

---

20. There are two snippets of quotation from the *Kokinshū* preface in this passage.

21. Han Wu Di 漢武帝 (156–187 BCE). Legend had it that this supreme Han dynasty ruler had an eye for beautiful women and aspired to "collect" them even as a child.

	They pledged to be as if
	paired birds with shared wings,
	trees linked by branches intertwined,[22]
	vowed to adhere to one another, it is said,
	through all time, on earth and in heaven.
TOGETHER	And then there is one called Hotoke
CHORUS	another dancer, divinely favored,
	as suits her name, it seems.
	And in the way the human heart
	can shift, and does so,
	his heart was captivated,
	drawn by every turn of her dancing sleeves.
	Enticing and resplendent she appeared,
	soon a cause for Giō to worry
	without a word, yet greatly shamed.

At the end of the dance both assume a semi-kneeling position, with one knee raised.

VII

SENŌ   I say, you both have charmed him with your dancing; but he has directed Giō Gozen to rest while Hotoke Gozen dances solo for him.

GIŌ   No reason for me to be here, I shall head for home.

SENŌ   No, no! Think of his anger if he were told that! Stay here for a while.

(*turning to Hotoke*) Now, Hotoke Gozen, by Jōkai's order, you are to dance a solo for him. This is his directive.

HOTOKE   No, if Giō Gozen is not dancing, I will not dance alone for him.

SENŌ   It is his will. Hurry now, you should dance for him.

HOTOKE   Weighted down by heavy robes of gauze
she resents the weaver's lack of pity,[23]

---

22. An allusion to the closing lines of Bai Juyi's 白居易 "Song of Everlasting Pain" (*Chang hen ge* 長恨歌). For a complete translation see Owen, *Anthology of Chinese Literature*, 442–47. The famous similes of the birds and trees are, respectively, 比翼鳥 (Jp. *hiyoku no tori*) and 連理枝 (Jp. *renri no eda*).

23. This passage draws on the first two lines of a Chinese poem by Sugawara no Michizane 菅原道真, no. 466 in the *Wakan rōeishū* 和漢朗詠集. The title is "The Singing Girl Grows Listless in the Spring" (春娃無気力詩序). A translation

> and at some point I too will bear
> the troubles of her heart, I know.

Hotoke rises and dances as the chorus sings the following lines.

> I know, yet cannot follow my own wishes.
> Hotoke is by her nature a fine dancer
> intoning *waka* and twirling her sleeves,
> again and again she sings.
> Is this the voice of misty spring?
> Are breezes of the season
> scattering the blossoms,
> as her dancing sleeves twirl
> on and on, ever so fascinating!

Ha no mai

HOTOKE
CHORUS

> His feelings may fade,[24]
> his feelings may fade,
> and his affections shift,
> but, Giō Gozen, take it not to heart.
> To Buddha, the source of my name,
> and to the gods I vow,
> I'll speak of no deep bonds to him.
> Together, without deception,
> this she pledged to her.

---

of the full poem: "Her gauze dress becoming a heavy robe / she resents the heartlessness of the woman who wove it! / The pipes and strings play a lengthy tune / she's angry with the musicians for never ending!" *Chinese and Japanese Poems to Sing: The Wakan Rōei Shū,* edited and translated by J. Thomas Rimer and Jonathan Chaves (Columbia University Press, 1997), 142.

24. The expression *hanada no obi* 花田の帯, "a hanada sash" occurs here. *Hanadairo* 花田色 (縹色) is a fugitive pale indigo shade, the easily fading color used metaphorically for fickle human emotion.

4 ⁓ *Hotoke no hara* (Buddha Field)

| David T. Bialock

Introduction

"Hotoke no hara," or "Buddha Field,"[1] belongs to the third category
of nō plays, also known as wig-pieces (*kazuramono*), with authorship
uncertain, though sometimes attributed to Zeami (1363–1443). Although
lacking the classic verbal richness, or "woven brocade" effect, of Zeami's
best known plays, "Buddha Field" is a nearly flawless example of the
dream play (*mugen* nō), with a pared back simplicity of language suited
to its chill wintry mood.

The play is based on the well-known story of the rival *shirabyōshi*
dancers Giō and Hotoke, though the idea of having Hotoke return to
her birth-place in Kaga province appears to be an original touch by
the author, since it is not found in the *Heike monogatari* or the *Genpei
jōsuiki*, the two likely sources for the play's plot. In a departure from other
nō plays based on the *Heike*, the author has made only sparing use of
direct quotation from his source texts, drawing inspiration instead from
scattered verbal hints in several *Heike* variants. The play's location and
associated thematic resonance, for example, may ultimately depend on
a single place-name, Hotoke-ga-hara 仏が原, which occurs only in the
Genpei jōsuiki and Nagatobon *Heike* accounts of the Hakusan protest in
Kaga province. In both versions, the Hakusan monks are said to have
transferred the sacred palanquin to the temple shrine Tsurugi-no-miya

---

1. Classical Japanese does not force a distinction between singular and plural.
In translating the play's title, though "Buddha Fields" makes for more euphonious
English, I have opted for the singular, which seems to work better in conveying
some of the Buddhist doctrinal implications of the play.

金劍宮 at Hotoke-ga-hara.[2] Despite the lack of any connection between this Hotoke-ga-hara and the dancer named Hotoke in the *Heike* tradition, for the play's author Hakusan's location in Kaga province must have been suggestive enough, for the one detail we learn about Hotoke's origins in the *Heike monogatari* is that she was from Kaga province.

The geography of the play's location is further enriched by associations from two poems that occur in the "Giō" episode. The first is composed by Giō, after her dismissal by Kiyomori:

moeizuru mo	Whether newly sprouted
karuru mo onaji	or withering away, both are
nobe no kusa	grasses of the field:
izure ka aki ni	can either avoid the autumn
awadehatsubeki	that awaits us in the end?[3]

The second poem, or *imayō*, is sung by Giō when Kiyomori forces her to return and perform one last time in the presence of Hotoke:

hotoke mo mukashi wa	Even the Buddha of old
bonbu nari	was an ordinary person;
warera mo tsui ni wa	in the end, we too
hotoke nari	will become buddhas;
izure mo busshō	but though everything
gu seru mi o	is one Buddha-nature,
hedatsuru nomi koso	how sad
kanashikere	that distinctions separate![4]

---

2. See Mizuhara Hajime, *Shintei Genpei jōsuiki*, vol. 1 (Shin jinbutsu ōraisha, 1988), 197; and Asahara Yoshiko and Nanami Hiroaki, *Nagatobon Heike monogatari no sōgō kenkyū: kōchū-hen jō*, vol. 1 (Benseisha, 1998), 110–11. In their notes, Mizuhara identifies Hotoke-ga-hara in Book Four of *Genpei jōsuiki* with present day Tsurugi-machi in Ishikawa prefecture, while Asahara and Nanami identify the same place-name in Book Two of the Nagatobon with Ishikawa prefecture's Hara-machi in Komatsu-shi. For a detailed discussion of the place-name Hotoke no hara, see Takahashi Yoshio's study, cited in footnote 7. The equivalent section of the Hakusan incident in the Kakuichi *Heike*, which lacks any reference to Hotoke-ga-hara, occurs in Book One, in the episode "Shunkan no sata Ugawa ikusa" (Kakuichi-bon 1.13, "The Matter of Shunkan and the Battle at Ugawa").

3. Ichiko Teiji, *Heike monogatari* (jo), NKBZ 29 (Shōgakukan, 1973), 54.

4. Ichiko, *Heike monogatari* (jo), 58.

As commentators note, the two poems can be read on several levels: as a literal expression of seasonal decline in the first, a statement of Buddhist nonduality in the second, and in both poems metaphorically of the two dancers, Giō and Hotoke. Taken together, however, their imagery and themes also suggest the medieval Buddhist doctrine on the enlightenment of insentients and sentients, exemplified in the play's "grass, trees, and earth all achieve Buddhahood." Interestingly, the author has avoided direct citation of the poems in the main play,[5] choosing instead to amplify the doctrinal implications of the place-name Buddha Field metaphorically, through a poetic weave of grass and related imagery. The idea that "grass, trees, and earth" could achieve Buddhahood was widespread in medieval literature, partly owing to developments in "original enlightenment" (*hongaku*) doctrine, and it becomes central to the play's meaning through its unifying image of the Buddha Field. This can literally refer to the earthly ground of Hotoke's grass hermitage, and analogically to the enlightened mind-space of the Buddha. At a more theoretical level, the play appears to hesitate among several competing medieval views on the capacity of insentients to achieve enlightenment, with one position implying that insentients are already enlightened and another making their enlightenment dependent on the active contemplation of a buddha.[6] The grassy Buddha Field of the play is both of these spaces at once, and ultimately readers of the play must ask themselves if Hotoke is even in need of the priest's prayers and intercession. The second half of the play,

---

5. The *imayō*, however, is cited by the village resident in the Interlude (omitted in the translation). See "Hotoke no hara," in Sanari Kentarō, *Yōkyoku taikan*, vol. 4 (Meiji shoin, 1931; reprint edition 1965), 2794–96.

6. On the capacity of insentients for enlightenment, Fabio Rambelli writes: "Their theoretical Buddha-nature only allows for an indirect, passive salvation, as for example when a Buddha contemplates his environment with his third eye and sees that everything is non-distinct, non-differentiated from himself. Only in this sense can plants 'become Buddhas.'" Fabio Rambelli, *Vegetal Buddhas: Ideological Effects of Japanese Buddhist Doctrines on the Salvation of Inanimate Beings*, Italian School of East Asian Studies, Occasional Papers 9 (Kyoto: Scuola Italiana di Studi sull'Asia Orientale, 2001), 1–124, esp. 11. For earlier discussions of this problem, see also Donald H. Shively, "Buddhahood for the Nonsentient: A Theme in Nō Plays," *Harvard Journal of Asiatic Studies*, vol. 20, no. 1/2 (June 1957), 135–61; and William R. LaFleur, "Saigyō and the Buddhist Value of Nature," in *Nature in Asian Traditions of Thought: Essays in Environmental Philosophy*, ed. J. Baird Callicott and Roger T. Ames (Albany: SUNY Press, 1989), 183–209. My thanks to Roberta Strippoli for bringing Fabio Rambelli's study to my attention.

climaxing in Hotoke's ecstatic dance, seems to suggest that she is already enlightened, hence the Buddha Field or mind through which sentients and insentients alike achieve enlightenment.

A final word on the location of Hotoke no hara. In the geography of the play, the grassy Buddha Field alternates mysteriously with the snowy alpine heights of Hakusan, a site famous for the practice of mystical mountain religion (*shugendō*), and at times Hakusan's otherworldly chill settles over the play's otherwise autumnal mood. Though the geography may be more poetic than actual, Hotoke no hara, which does not survive as a place-name today, was on the map of the itinerant Buddhist priest Dōkō 道興 (1430–1501), who recorded passing through Hotoke no hara in his travelogue, *Kaikoku zakki* 回国雑記 (*Miscellaneous Record of Travels in the Provinces*, ca. 1486), while on his way to perform austerities on Hakusan's snowy ridges. By the time of Sekioka Yasura's 関岡野州良 (1772–1832) Edo period commentary on Dōkō's travelogue, *Kaikoku zakki hyōchū* 回国雑記標柱, the nō play about the *shirabyōshi* dancers, and the *Genpei jōsuiki*'s and Nagatobon *Heike*'s detailed geography were all part of the established lore of Hotoke no hara.[7] Today, even though the actual place-name has disappeared, the legend of the nō play's marvelous dancer continues to flourish.

---

7. On Hotoke no hara in poetic geography, especially in the travelogue of Dōkō, see Takahashi Yoshio, " 'Hotoke no hara' kō: *Kaikoku zakki no kōtei*," *Gakuen* 481 (January 1980), 76–93. Sekioka Yasura's commentary on Dōkō's reference to *Hotoke no hara* is cited and discussed on p. 86.

Hotoke no hara (Buddha Field)

| TRANSLATED BY DAVID T. BIALOCK

Third-category *mūgen* nō in two acts.
Performed by the Kanze, Komparu, and Kongō schools.
Time: Autumn (Ninth Month)
Place: "Hotoke no hara" in the province of Kaga
Author: Uncertain, sometimes attributed to Zeami

WAKI	Traveling Priest
WAKIZURE	Priest's Companion
MAEJITE	Woman
NOCHIJITE	Hotoke Gozen
AI	A local resident

[PART ONE (*maeba*)]

To shidai music, enter the Traveling Priest and his Companion. They stand at stage-center.

PRIEST AND COMPANION
Everywhere the trees take on a deep autumn red,
Everywhere the trees take on a deep autumn red,
Yet we seek out the deep snows of White Mountain.

Priest faces stage-front.

PRIEST (*nanori*) I am a priest from the capital. Because I haven't performed austerities on White Mountain yet, I departed this autumn with my heart set on reaching the summit of White Mountain.

Priest and Companion face each other.

PRIEST AND COMPANION (*ageuta*)
Along far roads we have come to Koshi,[1]

Hotoke no hara 仏原. This translation is based on Itō Masayoshi, *Yōkyokushū* (ge), SNKS (Shinchōsha, 1988), 228–35. In preparing this translation, I have also consulted the text and notes in Nishino Haruo, ed., *Yōkyoku hyakuban*, SNKT 57 (Iwanami shoten, 1998), 429–33; and on matters of presentation, Royall Tyler, *Japanese Nō Dramas* (London, New York: Penguin Books, 1992). An earlier translation can be found in Shimazaki Chifumi's *The Noh, Volume III: Woman*

> to White Mountain in unknown Koshi,
> to White Mountain in unknown Koshi,
> where even the clouds
> grow bright in the sky
> of Amaterasu the goddess,
> the red of her oak leaves[2]
> a brightly hued pledge
> so high up, peak upon peak
> and already we've arrived;
> our pilgrimage here
> truly cause for thanks;
> our pilgrimage here
> truly cause for thanks.

Priest faces stage-front.

PRIEST (*tsukizerifu*) Traveling swiftly, I've already reached Buddha Field, in the province of Kaga. Since the day grows dark, I think I'll go over to that grass hermitage and spend the night there.

Priest moves to the witness square (wakiza). *Enter Woman as she calls out from the curtain.*

WOMAN (*mondō*) Tell me, reverend Priest, why do you stop at that grass hermitage?

The Priest stands at the witness square and addresses Woman.

PRIEST   How strange! No road or village lies that way, yet a lone woman appears and addresses me. Who might you be?

Woman walks down the bridgeway (hashigakari).

Noh Book 3 (Tokyo: Hinoki Shoten, 1987). Arthur Waley has a brief summary of "Hotoke no hara" in *The Nōh Plays of Japan* (London: Allen and Unwin, 1921).

1. Koshi is an old name for the provinces of the Hokurikudō, corresponding to the modern prefectures of Fukui, Ishikawa, Toyama, and Niigata. "White Mountain" (Shirayama or Hakusan) is a sacred peak on the borders of modern Ishikawa and Gifu prefectures. The place-name appears in the following poem from the *Kokinshū* (8: 391): *Kimi ga yuku / koshi no shirayama / shirane domo / yuki no manimani / ato wa tazunemu.* (Though I don't know / White Mountain of Koshi / where you've gone / I will seek out your tracks / among the drifts of snow.)

2. A passage embellished with several wordplays. The phrase translated "grow bright in the sky" (*amaterasu*) pivots on the name of the sun-goddess (*Amaterasu [ō] kami*), which then extends into the phrases *kami no haha* (mother of the gods) and *hahaso no momiji* (red leaves of the oak).

WOMAN   A woman who lives here in Buddha Field. How timely, and on this of all nights! Your decision to lodge in this grass hermitage is a bit of karma for which I am most grateful. [*She stands at the midpoint of the bridgeway.*] Today happens to be the death anniversary of one in my thoughts. Be kind enough to intone the sutras and perform the Buddhist rites. [*Facing stage-front. In song.*] Hampered as I am by the Five Obstacles and Three Injunctions,[3] it is difficult for me to dispel the clouds of delusion. Please make clear the turbid waters of my heart and guide me along the pure path.

Woman starts walking again.

PRIEST   A request to intone the sutras and perform the Buddhist rites is what any priest would wish. But tell me, who is the deceased I'm to pray for?

WOMAN   Some years ago, there was a dancer from this province called Hotoke Gozen, who went up to the Capital, where her fame as a dancer excelled all others. Afterward, remembering her birth-place, she returned to this province, and it was here that she passed away. This grass hermitage marks her memory, the vestige of one who faded like the dew.

Standing, Priest addresses Woman.

PRIEST (*kakeai*)   How strange! So she whose name was celebrated long ago, Hotoke Gozen, has left behind her name even in death.

Standing, Woman addresses Priest.

WOMAN   In a place named Buddha Field,   (*chanted*)
          her name lingers on in regret for the past.

PRIEST   Doubtless I will pray for the salvation   (*sung*)
          of one whose affinity for Buddhahood is beyond doubt

WOMAN   Assured by her name!
          "When one Buddha achieving the way

PRIEST   beholds with clear sight the Dharma world

WOMAN   grass, trees, and earth

---

3. The Five Obstacles are listed in the *Lotus Sutra*: "Also, a woman's body even then has five obstacles. It cannot become first a Brahma god king, second the god Sakra, third King Mara, fourth a sage-king turning the Wheel, fifth a Buddha-body. How can the body of a woman speedily achieve Buddhahood?" Cited from Leon Hurvitz, *Scripture of the Lotus Blossom of the Fine Dharma* (Columbia University Press, 1976), 201. The Three Injunctions are Confucian and refer to the proper conduct of a woman: as a daughter, obedience to her father; as a wife, obedience to her husband; and as a widow, obedience to her son.

PRIEST AND WOMAN (*facing one another*)
　　　　　　　all achieve Buddhahood."[4]
　　　　　　　Upon hearing this,　　　　　　　*Facing stage-front.*
CHORUS (*ageuta*)

　　　　　　　Even the grass and trees of Buddha Field
　　　　　　　Even the grass and trees of Buddha Field
　　　　　　　Will doubtlessly achieve Buddhahood.
　　　　　　　In gratitude, just now
　　　　　　　even the insects
　　　　　　　noisily crowding the field[5]
　　　　　　　seem to raise their voices in prayer;
　　　　　　　and in the mountain wind and night storm
　　　　　　　whose tranquil sound spreads through the field,
　　　　　　　even the grass and trees grow aware,
　　　　　　　even the grass and trees grow aware.
PRIEST (*mondō*)　　　　　　　　　　　*Addressing the Woman.*
　　　　　　　Now please tell me the story of Hotoke Gozen.
CHORUS　　　　　(*kuri*)
　　　　　　　Long ago, when Taira Kiyomori was Chancellor, there were four
entertainers named Giō, Gijo, Hotoke and Toji, whose brilliance in
the arts of song, music, and dance won them renown in the world.
WOMAN　　　　　(*sashi*)
　　　　　　　At first, Kiyomori kept Giō by his side,
　　　　　　　so enamored was he of her dancing.
CHORUS　　　　　On the sleeves of fair robes
　　　　　　　adorning those voluptuous charms
　　　　　　　a white dew settled
　　　　　　　on her waking and sleeping[6]

---

4. On the implications of this phrase, see my introduction to the play.

5. Lines that echo a poem found in *Kokon chomonjū* 古今著聞集 (Scroll 8):
*Kashigamashi / nomose ni sudaku / mushi no ne yo / ware dani nakade / mono o
koso omoe* (How noisy / the cries of insects / crowding all the field / while I alone
unweeping / brood despondently). Nagazumi Yasuaki and Shimada Isao, eds.,
Kokon chomonjū, NKBT 84 (Iwanami shoten, 1988), 268.

6. A passage embellished by a series of word associations (*engo*) with possible
erotic overtones: jewel (*tama*) in *tamaginu* (jeweled robes, or "fair robes" in the
translation), dew (*tsuyu*) in the expression "white dew" (*shiratsuyu*), and "to fall"
or "settle" (*oki*) of dew, which creates a pivot with *okifushi*, whose primary sense
denotes "rising" and "reclining" as in waking and going to sleep. The play's author
may be drawing hints from the language of the Engyōbon *Heike, Genpei jōsuiki*,

	behind screens never parted
	for her leaving.
	It was just as if she had been a lady-in-attendance at
	the Palace.
WOMAN	And yet she unexpectedly got her chance.
CHORUS	After Kiyomori summoned Hotoke Gozen,
	the object of his affections changed,
	and before she knew it, Giō had been dismissed.
WOMAN	With a dreary wind
	now sighing through her world
	the autumn deepened[7]
CHORUS	and her rain of tears
	never ceased.
(*kuse*)	How true the saying:
	"In this uncertain world
	things never follow
	the heart's desire."
	A flower's glory is brief,
	so why regret, she thought, the scattering
	of my own beauty's flower?
	The tempest blows,
	but the pine stays forever green.
	"To be always sorrowing[8]
	always at a loss
	in this uncertain world,"
	when she pondered these words,
	her own change of fortune

and other variants, which is more explicit about Kiyomori's physical relations with Hotoke and other consorts than the mildly euphemistic language of the Kakuichi *Heike*. See, for example, the comparisons in the commentary on the *Giō* episode in *Engyōbon Heike monogatari zenchūshaku*, vol. 1, ed. Engyōbon chūshaku no kai (Kyūko shoin, 2005), 104.

7. Lines that incorporate two conventional wordplays: *aki* (autumn / weariness) and *fuke* meaning, respectively, "blow" of the wind and "deepen" of the autumn.

8. Possibly an allusion to this poem by Saigyō on the topic of impermanence (*mujō*) in *Shinkokinshū*, 8: 831: *Itsu nageki / itsu omoubeki / koto nareba / nochi no yo shirade / hito no suguran* (To be always lamenting the present / always thinking about the future / because of that / people pass their days / ignorant of the world to come).

	seemed truly a lesson from the Buddha.
WOMAN	So thinking that Amida's Paradise lay that way,
CHORUS	she put her trust in him
	who clears the mind of confusion,
	and in the western mountains
	far from the ills of this uncertain world,
	in the remote depths of Saga
	she resolved to live hidden away
	in the seclusion of a grass hermitage.
	Then unexpectedly, Hotoke Gozen,
	her appearance altered to a nun's, came to visit her.
	"Despite things being what they are,
	although I have renounced the world like this,
	my stubborn heart continues to feel resentful toward you.
	Is it human to have feelings such as yours?
	How true to your name of Hotoke, now!"
	And saying this, Giō joined her hands in prayer
	and shed warm tears of gratitude.
CHORUS	(*rongi*)
	But putting this old tale aside for now,
	tell me, who are you that pray for her?
WOMAN	Who? I can't say, but why ask
	about one whose going was like the dew
	that clings to the needles of Iwashiro's Pine?[9]
CHORUS	If you wish to know
	whither she's gone,
	seek out her tracks in the blank snow[10]
	of this field.

Addressing the Priest.

WOMAN	The grass hermitage would be over here
CHORUS	where she settled her dewlike life
WOMAN	a grass hermitage

---

9. The Iwashiro Pine was celebrated as far back as the *Man'yōshū*. In the present passage, Iwashiro also puns on the verb *iwaji* ("I can't say").

10. The word *shirayuki* (literally "white snow" but here translated "blank snows") contains a pivot on *shira,* suggesting both "I don't know" (*shirazu*) and "white." The lines seem to take up the imagery of snow and tracks alluded to at the beginning of the play.

CHORUS   "Whose owner is Hotoke."[11]
              Having let slip these words,
              her figure flits away,
              and trailing a sleeve through the grass
              she makes a path through the dew,
              and enters the grass hermitage
              enters the grass hermitage.

In the base square (jōza) she faces stage-front, then exits the stage.

[INTERVAL (*ai*): omitted]

[PART TWO (*nochiba*)]

PRIEST AND COMPANION
    (*ageuta*)   The wind in the pine blows
                   chill in these fields,
                   the wind in the pine blows
                   chill in these fields,
                   where on a transient bed of grass
                   we've prayed eternal hours through the night.
                   Thankful to pray
                   for her departed spirit;
                   thankful to pray
                   for her departed spirit.

To issei *music Hotoke Gozen enters and stands at the base square. She faces stage-front.*

HOTOKE (*sashi*)   My thanks to you
                   For intoning the sutra!
                   Already as dawn begins to break
                   the bell of a distant temple faintly tolls
                   and the moon sinks
                   below the rim of that mountain
                   streaked with clouds.
                   Though the storm rages fiercely
                   About your traveler's bed,
                   Do not waken from your dreams.

PRIEST (*kakeai*)   How strange! A dancer's form has appeared

---

11. Hotoke here can refer to Hotoke Gozen and also the Buddha.

	beside my grass pillow in Buddha Field. It must be the spirit of her whom I asked about, Hotoke Gozen.
HOTOKE	*Addressing the Priest.*
	Despite feelings of shame, *(chanted)* relying on the name of one called "Buddha" long ago, in reincarnated form I dance and sing.
PRIEST	With the voice of the Dharma in Paradise *(sung)*
HOTOKE	I perform the rites of Buddha
PRIEST	Here in this field
HOTOKE (*issei*)	at the dance of a Buddha waving her skillful sleeve
CHORUS	even the grass and trees appear to bow.

(dance: jo no mai)

HOTOKE (*waka*)	On my own I will intone the name of Buddha
CHORUS	Each on their own as they return home, who gathered to hear the Dharma who gathered to hear the Dharma.
HOTOKE (*noriji*)	*Facing stage-front.*
	How many worlds will it endure The teaching of the Dharma!
CHORUS	The former Buddha has passed away
HOTOKE	the Buddha to come has yet to appear
CHORUS	the interval of a dream
HOTOKE	is life in this present world!
CHORUS	The bell tolls
HOTOKE	the cock crows
CHORUS	the brief span of a dream-vision in the night. If even the Buddha ceases to be all the more will human beings
HOTOKE (*uta*)	cease to be. Clouds and waters buffeted by the storm
CHORUS	clouds and waters buffeted by the storm, billows reflecting the heaven's expanse,

began from one drop of dew.[12]
Turning out her sleeve
the dancer returns to what?
The instant before a step is taken
is truly the Buddha's dance.
And ending her song
she vanishes away;
ending her song
she vanishes away.

---

12. An idea also recorded in the Chinese Preface to the *Kokinshū*.

5 ⁓ How Giō Saves Her Father's Life: Innovations to the Giō Legend in *Bangai* Nō | Michael Watson

Around two hundred and fifty nō plays are in the current performance repertoire of the Kanze, Hōshō, Komparu, Kongō, and Kita schools.[1] At least thirty of these plays are based on incidents or characters from *Heike monogatari* or related texts. These include eight of the plays translated in this volume (*Giō, Hotoke no hara, Ikuta Atsumori, Kiso, Kiyotsune, Morihisa, Sanemori,* and *Shunzei Tadanori*) together with the plays *Atsumori, Daibutsu kuyō, Ebira, Fujito, Funa Benkei, Ikarikazuki, Kagekiyo, Kanehira, Kogō, Michimori, Nue, Ōhara gokō, Senju, Shichiki ochi, Shōzon, Shunkan, Tadanori, Tomoakira, Tomoe, Tsunemasa, Yashima,* and *Yorimasa*. To this list one could add three variant versions performed by one or more schools (*Genzai Nue, Genzai Tomoe, Genzai Tadanori*) and five plays based on anecdotes in *Heike monogatari* that have little to do with the main Genpei narrative or or characters (*Gendaiyū, Kan'yōkyū, Kenjō, Sagi,* and *Taisanpukun*).

Rō-Giō 籠祇王 ("Giō at the Prison") was once performed by actors of the Kita 喜多 school, but has now fallen out of the active repertoire. In other respects, too, it resembles some of "extracanonical" plays (*bangai yōkyoku* 番外謡曲) on Genpei-periods topics that survive in text alone. More than one hundred of such plays have been identified in the very large corpus of *bangai* nō texts, and more await discovery.[2]

---

1. The total number of plays performed by each school fluctuates as older plays are revived (*fukkyoku* 復曲) and less popular plays are dropped from the repertoire (*haikyoku* 廃曲, "abolished pieces").

2. Further details are given in the Appendix. The surviving corpus of *bangai* plays exceeds three thousand. The largest collection of plays, 2,402 in total, is found in Tanaka Makoto, *Mikan yōkyokushū*, 33 vols. (Koten bunko, 1963–1998).

Some *bangai* nō use characters and incidents from the Genpei War that are not represented in the plays performed today. There are, for instance, plays centering on figures such as Taira no Shigemori, his son Koremori and grandson Rokudai, the courtier Naritsune, and the priest Mongaku, all of whom play important roles in the narrative versions of *Heike monogatari*.[3]

The majority of the extracanonical plays retell episodes directly from a version of the *Heike* narrative, either the recited Kakuichi 覚一 variant or one of the "read" texts such as the Nagato 長門 variant or *Genpei jōsuiki* 源平盛衰記. Examples include plays about the battles of Kurikara, Ichi-no-tani, Yashima, and Dan-no-ura.[4] Some of these plays take the familiar form of a *mugen* 夢幻 ("phantom") nō in which a spirit retells the story of his or her death, following the pattern of canonical plays like *Atsumori* 敦盛 or *Tadanori* 忠度. However, many other *bangai* nō are written as *genzai* 現在 ("present-time") plays, with actions of living characters depicted in chronological time. This is the case with the piece considered here, *Rō-Giō*, the least known of the four plays about the Giō story. Only one female character from *Heike monogatari* is featured in more nō plays than Giō: the woman warrior (*onna musha* 女武者) Tomoe Gozen.[5]

In the nō, there is usually room for more than one dramatization of a particular episode or character. For instance, there are at least two

---

Several hundred *bangai* plays can read in a lightly annotated edition in Haga Yaichi and Sasaki Nobutsuna, eds., *Kōchū yōkyoku sōsho*, 3 vols. (Hakubunkan, 1915; reprint edition, Rinsen shoten, 1987).

3. Plays include *Komatsu kyōkun* 小松教訓, *Koremori* 惟盛 (維盛), *Rokudai* 六代, *Naritsune* 成経, and *Takikomori Mongaku* 瀧籠文覚. Tanaka Makoto, ed., *Mikan yōkyokushū*, vol. 22 (Koten bunko, 1974), 77–83; Haga and Sasaki, *Kōchū yōkyoku sōsho*, vol. 1, 796–802, vol. 3, 608–14, 24–28, vol. 2, 469–71.

4. For *Kurikara otoshi* 倶利伽羅落, see the translation and study in this volume. Six *bangai* plays related to Ichi-no-tani and Dan-no-ura are discussed in Michael Watson, "Spirits of the Drowned: Sea Journeys in *Bangai* Noh from the Genpei War," in Eiji Sekine, ed., *Travel in Japanese Representational Culture: Its Past, Present, and Future*, Proceedings of the Association for Japanese Literary Studies, Vol. 8, Summer 2007, 141–54.

5. Tomoe Gozen 巴御前. The play *Tomoe* 巴 in the current repertoire of all five schools is a *mugen* nō, but the *bangai* plays about her are *genzai* nō dramatizations: *Genzai Tomoe* 現在巴, *Kinukazuki Tomoe* 衣潜巴, *Konjō Tomoe* 今生巴, and *Midai Tomoe* 御台巴 (also known as *Katami Tomoe* 筐巴). Haga and Sasaki, *Kōchū yōkyoku sōsho*, vol. 1, 153–56, 553–56, 806–9; Tanaka, *Mikan yōkyokushū*, vol. 3 (Koten bunko, 1965), 66–72.

plays dealing with the battle of Uji, described in Chapter Four of *Heike monogatari*. One is the well-known *Yorimasa* 頼政, and the other is the extracanonical *Ichirai hōshi* 一来法師. While the former focuses on the defeat and death of Yorimasa, the *bangai nō* retells the earlier part of the story, climaxing in a description of how a handful of warrior-monks defend the bridge at Uji.[6]

The case of *Rō-Giō* is more puzzling. It does not overlap in any obvious way with *Futari Giō* 二人妓王 and *Hotoke no hara* 仏原, the better known plays based on characters in the episode. It seems on first sight to take little from *Heike* but the name of the character Giō, making it one of the most radical adaptations of *Heike* material for the nō stage. There is no mention of Giō's mother and sister, or rival Hotoke. Instead, it deals with Giō and her father—a man who is never mentioned in the matrilineal world of the *shirabyōshi* 白拍子 in *Heike monogatari*.[7]

An early Muromachi play, *Rō-Giō* survives in the tradition of only one of the five nō schools, the Kita school. However, as mentioned earlier, the play has fallen out of the active repertoire. It is omitted from most of the major modern series of nō texts, and for all intents and purposes can be considered a *bangai nō*.[8] The title *Rō-Giō* has two elements, something that is always hard to translate; *Funa Benkei* 船弁慶 or *Sotoba Komachi* 卒塔婆小町 are other examples. "Giō at the Prison" perhaps—certainly not "Giō Imprisoned" as has been suggested.[9] The first element, *rō* (籠), means "prison" or "gaol (jail)," but it is Giō's father who is first a prison guard and then a prisoner himself. The character *rō* originally means a bamboo cage, and it is once used in that sense when Giō's father laments his loneliness in captivity.[10] But otherwise *rō* is used in the play like the more usual character *rō* to mean "gaol" (牢).

Like all plays, this one makes a wide range of allusions: to a Taoist classic, to a famous phrase by the Tang poet Bai Juyi 白居易, to the

---

6. *Ichirai hōshi* is edited in Haga and Sasaki, *Kōchū yōkyoku sōsho*, vol. 1, 686–90.

7. Female performing artists are discussed in detail in Strippoli's chapter in this volume (Chapter 2).

8. Haga and Sasaki, *Kōchū yōkyoku sōsho*, vol. 3, 593–99. The text is also edited in Nonomura Kaizō, ed., *Yōkyoku nihyakugojū-banshū*, revised by Ōtani Tokuzō (Kyoto: Akaoshō bundō, 1978), 277–80.

9. Barbara L. Arnn, "Medieval Fiction and History in the *Heike Monogatari* Story Tradition" (Ph.D. dissertation, University of Indiana, 1984), 143.

10. *Rōchō kumo wo koi* 籠鳥雲を恋ひ (A caged bird yearning for the clouds). Haga and Sasaki, *Kōchū yōkyoku sōsho*, vol. 3, 594.

death poem of Ariwara no Narihira, and to several *waka* from imperial anthologies.[11] More significantly, the play cites copiously from the twenty-fifth chapter of the Lotus Sutra. This famous chapter, the *Fumonbon*, is also sometimes known as *Kanzeonkyō* 観世音経, the Kannon Sutra.[12]

In *Heike monogatari*, Giō looks to Amida Buddha to protect the Saga refuge from hostile male intruders. She places her hope in *Mida no hongan*, Amida's original vow. In the nō play, Giō and her father trust in Kannon's promise, *Kannon no chikai*.[13] The bodhisattva of mercy does not actually appear in the play, but is the prime mover of the plot.

The play opens with the *waki*, who is an unnamed person from Kogawa in Kishū.[14] He reports that an argument with a person in the neighboring village resulted in many people being taken prisoner. A young man was put under the guard of a local person, whom we learn later is Giō's father. He let the young man escape and has now been made a prisoner himself. He is to be strictly guarded and even if someone comes claiming to be a relative, no one is to be allowed to visit him (*taimen wa kataku kinsei* 対面は堅く禁制). His reasons for letting the man escape are unstated, saved for later.

---

11. The phrase *Kyōgen kigo* 狂言綺語, "wild words and specious phrases," by Bai Juyi 白居易 (772–846). *Wakan rōeishū* 和漢朗詠集 588. The final poem in *Ise monogatari* 伊勢物語 was traditionally thought to be written on his deathbed by Ariwara no Narihira 有原業平 (825–880). Further details are given in the notes to the translation that follows.

12. The chapter title *Kanzeon Bosatsu fumonbon* 観世音菩薩普門品 has been translated as "The Gateway to Everywhere of the Bodhisattva He Who Observes the Sounds of the World." Leon Hurvitz, *Scripture of the Lotus Blossom of the Fine Dharma* (Columbia University Press, 1976), 311.

13. *Mida no hongan* 弥陀の本願. The original episode can be found in "Giō" (Kakuichi-bon 1.6). Takagi Ichinosuke, et al., ed., *Heike monogatari* (jō) (Iwanami shoten 1959), 104; Helen Craig McCullough, trans., *The Tale of the Heike* (Stanford University Press, 1988), 36. *Rō-Giō* ends: げに頼みても頼むべきは、是れ観音の誓ひなり "Truly 'trust where you may trust,' this is the Kannon's vow," Haga and Sasaki, *Kōchū yōkyoku sōsho*, 599. The expression *chikai* 誓ひ meaning "promise" or "vow" also occurs in two other passages: Giō's father's trust in Kannon's "vow that / The sea of happiness is immeasurable" 福寿海無量の誓ひのままに and Giō's own wish that her father will be delivered from "all kinds of evil as [Kannon] vowed" 種々諸悪趣の誓ひのままに. Haga and Sasaki, *Kōchū yōkyoku sōsho*, 594, 598.

14. Kogawa 粉川 is in the northeast of modern-day Wakayama 和歌山 prefecture in the Kii 紀伊 peninsula.

The *shite* and *tomo* (companion) then enter; they are Giō and a fellow traveler on their way to Kogawa. In terms of dramatic structure we have a *shidai* passage describing the moment of departure, followed by the *sashi*, where Giō explains who she is and why she is making this journey. A *michiyuki* describing the journey itself follows.

The *Heike* episode begins by describing how Giō loses the patronage of Taira no Kiyomori to another *shirabyōshi*, a newcomer to the capital called Hotoke Gozen. In the Kakuichi version of *Heike*, the two women are termed *asobime* 遊女 and *asobimono* 遊者, the only time these terms appear in this variant.

In the nō, Giō describes herself first as a *yūjo*, another reading of the characters used to write *asobime*. These terms do not translate well. "Dancing girl" or "singing girl" are among the suggestions for *yūjo*—and a *shirabyōshi* both sang and danced—but of course these entertainers were sought after for their physical charms as well as their artistic talents. Conversely in the Kakuichi *Heike*, the word *yūjo* only appears in the compound expression *yūkun yūjo* 遊君遊女, the "courtesans and harlots" summoned to entertain the warriors elsewhere in the narrative.[15]

In the *sashi* section of the nō play, Giō introduces herself as follows:

是は此程都の住む、祇王と申す女にてさむら
ふ。我遊女の道をたしなみ、色香にうつる花鳥
の、声の綾織る旗薄の、いとめづらかに初月の、
雲井にも名を残す身の、花の都の住居かな。[16]

I am a woman called Giō / and live now in the capital, / a performing woman by profession. / There, where flowers spread their hue and scent, / birds sing, and twill is woven by pampas grass, / in the beauty of the new moon / in the cloud-seat, the Palace, / have I made a name for myself, / living in the capital of flowers.

There is no mention of Kiyomori here, or of his residence at Nishihachijō. Instead, Giō is famous at the highest levels, even in the "cloud-seat" (*kumoi*), the Palace. It was true that at this period, Retired

---

15. "Fujigawa" 富士川 (Kakuichi-bon 5.11); "Hikyaku tōrai" 飛脚到来 (6.6); "Daijōe no sata" 大嘗会之沙汰 (10.15 in the Takano MS, 10.15 "Fujito" 藤戸 in the Ryūkoku MS). Translated "courtesans and harlots" in McCullough, *Tale of the Heike*, 190, 208, 357.

16. Haga and Sasaki, *Kōchū yōkyoku sōsho*, vol. 3, 593.

Emperor Go-Shirakawa was himself one of the most active patrons of *imayō* 今様, the form of verse sung by the *shirabyōshi*. But the only link in the *Heike* episode is with the memorial register in the Retired Emperor's temple, a register which still records the names of Giō, her mother, sister, and Hotoke, allegedly in Go-Shirakawa's hand.[17]

Next, Giō explains why she has left the capital. Her "aged father lives in the country" but has become a prisoner "or something" but she cannot imagine what crime (*tsumi* 罪) he has been charged with. Here we have for the first time one of the key motifs of the play, and one that links it to the *Heike* episode of "Giō": a child's concern for her aged parent "in a world where parting is already so close."[18]

When they arrive in the village of Kogawa, Giō tells her companion to search for her father. The *tomo* asks for directions, giving us a second description of Giō:

> いかに此内へ案内申し候。是に渡り候人は、都
> に隠れなき祇王と申す白拍子にて渡り候が、父
> 御に対面の為御下りにて候。よきやうに御申し
> 有つて引き合はされて給はり候へ。

> Tomo: Is there anyone here? This person here is
> the celebrated *shirabyōshi* Giō, and she has come
> to see her father. Please allow her to meet him.[19]

This confirms why she has "left a very special name" in the capital: she is famous as a *shirabyōshi*. The expression *kakurenaki* is used elsewhere in nō for celebrated *shirabyōshi*—in *Futari Shizuka* and *Yamamba*, for example.[20] The *waki* seems to have heard of her, saying that he will make

---

17. A register claiming to be in the hand of Go-Shirakawa survives, and contains the names of the four women, but is a later copy. Ichiko Teiji, ed., *Heike monogatari* (jō), SNBZ 45 (Shōgakukan, 1994), 50, n. 23.

18. *Wakare no chikaki yo no naka ni* 別れの近き世の中に、いかなる罪にか沈み給はん. Haga and Sasaki, *Kōchū yōkyoku sōsho*, vol. 3, 593. Separation through death or another cause may occur at any moment.

19. Haga and Sasaki, *Kōchū yōkyoku sōsho*, vol. 3, 594.

20. Cf. *Futari Shizuka* 二人静, *kakurenaki mai no jōzu nite arishikaba* かくれなき舞の上手にてありしかば ("Then you were well known as a talented dancer"). Nishino Haruo, ed., *Yōkyoku hyakuban*, SNKT 57 (Iwanami shoten, 1998), 401; Chifumi Shimazaki, trans., *The Noh, Volume III: Woman Noh Book 3* (Hinoki Shoten, 1981), 50. In *Yamamba* 山姥, there are two occurences of the phrase *kakurenaki yūjo* かくれなき遊女 ("a dancer renowned far and wide"; "a celebrated dancer").

an exception for her as "the most celebrated and accomplished dancer in the realm" (*tenga ni kakure mo naki mai no jōzu*). He refers to her as "Giō Gozen" 祇王御前 (Lady Giō):

> 【ワキ】 「某に対面と仰せ候人は何くに渡り候ぞ。
> 【シテ】 「恥ずかしながら妾にて候。
> 【ワキ】 「最前も申す如く、総じて囚人の所
> 縁に対面は堅く禁制にて候へども、祇王御前
> の御事は、天下に隠れもなき舞の上手にて候
> 程に、舞を舞うて御見せ候はば、大法を破つ
> て父御に引き合はせ申さうずるにて候。

WAKI: Where is the person who wants to see me?
SHITE: It is me, I am abashed to say [*hazukashina-gara warewa ni te sōrō*].
WAKI: As I said earlier, all relatives of the prisoner [*shu jin no yukari*] are forbidden to see him.
However, as it is you, Lady Giō, the most celebrated and accomplished dancer in the realm, I will break the prohibition and let you meet your father if you perform a dance.[21]

Giō is dismayed: "You say that unless I dance, parent and child will not be allowed to meet."[22] This motif is surely modeled on the *Heike* episode, not merely her reluctance to dance, but how it is connected—again—with her relation to a parent. In *Heike*, Giō is unwilling to perform again before Kiyomori and Hotoke, and only agrees to his demand for the sake of her mother, who fears what Kiyomori may do. In the play, Giō manages to put off the dance for now. The *waki* agrees to let her perform after she has met her father. For the play's structure, apart for anything else, it is essential for the dance to come later. One might also recall the passage in *Hagoromo* where the fisherman demands that the angel dances *before* he gives back the robe.[23]

Nishino, *Yōkyoku hyakuban*, 161, 162; Royall Tyler, trans., *Granny Mountains: A Second Cycle of Nō Plays* (Cornell East Asia Series, 1978), 315, 316.

21. Haga and Sasaki, *Kōchū yōkyoku sōsho*, vol. 3, 594.

22. *Oyako no naka no taimen naru ni, mawaji to iwaba au koto kanawaji* 親子の中の対面なるに、舞はじといはば逢ふ事かなはじ. Haga and Sasaki, *Kōchū yōkyoku sōsho*, vol. 3, 594.

23. Yokomichi Mario and Omote Akira, eds. *Yōkyokushū* (ge) (Iwanami

Giō's father is brought forth. He compares his isolation to a caged bird, to a homing goose that has lost its fellows, a quotation taken directly or indirectly from a tenth-century work in Chinese included in *Honchō monzui* 本朝文粋 ("Literary Essence of Our Court").[24] The same phrases are used in *Heike monogatari* Chapter Ten, in a letter describing how Shigehira must feel as a prisoner of the Genji.[25]

Giō's father ends by praying to Kannon the merciful, asking to be received into Paradise.[26] His quotation is from the *Fumonbon* chapter of the Lotus Sutra, the first of many in the work.[27]

He is amazed to find that Giō has come. She explains. She was on a retreat in the Kiyomizu temple, praying for her father, when she heard that he was charged with some crime (*toga* 咎):

さん候。父御の御祈りの為、此程清水にこもり
て候へば、何事やらん父御前は科を蒙り、籠者
とやらん聞こえ候程に、かちはだしにて是まで
参りて候。扨御科は何事にて候ぞ。

SHITE: When I was on a retreat in Kiyomizu praying for you, I heard that you were charged with some crime

---

shoten, 1963), 328; Royall Tyler, trans., *Japanese Nō Dramas* (London, New York: Penguin Books, 1992), 104.

24. *Rōchō kumo wo koi / kigan wa tomo wo ushinau kokoro, / sore wa hōrui ni koso kike* 籠鳥雲を恋ひ/帰雁は友を失ふ心、それは鳥類にこそ聞け (A caged bird yearning for the clouds, / a migrating goose who has lost his companions— / ask birds what this feeling is like). Haga and Sasaki, *Kōchū yōkyoku sōsho*, vol. 3, 594. The opening is based on the phrase 只籠鳥雲を恋ふるの思あり by Taira no Kanemori 平兼盛. Ōsone Shōsuke et al., eds., *Honchō monzui*, SNKT 27 (Iwanami shoten, 1992), 216.

25. Kakuichi-bon 10.3 "Yashima inzen": *Rōchō kumo wo kouru omoi … kigan tomo wo ushinau kokoro* 籠鳥雲を恋る思ひ、帰雁友を失ふ心 (his thoughts, fretful as a caged bird longing for the clouds [...] his feelings, sad as those of a homing goose lost from its fellows). Takagi Ichinosuke et al., eds., *Heike monogatari* (ge) (Iwanami shoten 1960), 248; McCullough, *Tale of the Heike*, 331.

26. *Zensho ni mukae tori tamae* 善処に迎へ取り給へ (literally, "come to take me to the good place"). Haga and Sasaki, *Kōchū yōkyoku sōsho*, vol. 3, 594.

27. The quotation from sutra is somewhat garbled, with the phrase 福寿海無量 (the sea of happiness is immeasurable) used instead of the standard 福聚海無量. Sakamoto Yukio and Iwamoto Yutaka, eds., *Hokekyō* (Iwanami bunko, 1962), vol. 2, 267; Burton Watson, trans., *The Lotus Sutra* (Columbia University Press, 1993), 306 ("The sea of his accumulated blessings is immeasurable").

and were imprisoned, so I came all the way here on foot. What crime is it, then?[28]

Next, he tells his side of the story.

某番に当たり候時、囚人を見れば未だ若き人な
り。しかも此度の本人にても非ず。痛はしや人
の上だに悲しきに、さこそは親の嘆き給ふらん
と、思はば人を助くるは、すなはち菩薩の行な
れば、たとひ我等は罪に逢ふとも、助けばやと
思ふ一念に、籠を開き夜にまぎれ落とす。

When it was my turn to guard, I saw that one of the prisoners was still young, and had nothing to do with this affair. I felt pity and sorrow for him, and when I imagined how his parents would grieve for him, I thought that helping him would be the act of a Bodhisattva [Bosatsu no gyō], and so I decided to spare him, even if it meant that I would be punished [tatoi warera wa tsumi ni au tomo]. I opened the gaol and let him escape under the cover of darkness.[29]

Oya no nageki 親の嘆き, the grief of his parents, is an example of the Buddhist concept of aibetsuriku 哀別離苦—the suffering of separation from those one loves—one of the great themes of Heike monogatari. One of its final passages recalls the sorrow of separation between husbands and wives and parents and children.[30] We recall how Kumagai hesitates to kill Atsumori because he imagines how the young man's father would grieve (ika bakari ka nageki-tamawanzuran).[31]

Giō's father is to be executed that night, but to have seen her gives him comfort "in this life and the next" (nise anraku 二世安楽).[32]

"If your crime was to help another," Giō replies, "then it is a matter

28. Haga and Sasaki, Kōchū yōkyoku sōsho, vol. 3, 595.

29. Ibid.

30. Kakuichi-bon, Kanjō no maki 灌頂巻, episode 5 "Nyōin shikyo." Ichiko, Heike monogatari (ge), 526; McCullough, Tale of the Heike, 437.

31. いか計かなげき給はんずらん. Kakuichi-bon 9.16 "Atsumori no saigo." Ichiko, Heike monogatari (ge), 233; McCullough, Tale of the Heike, 317.

32. Haga and Sasaki, Kōchū yōkyoku sōsho, vol. 3, 595.

for rejoicing," suggesting that they pray for Kannon for aid, trusting in the power of "the benevolent eye that beholds all sentient beings." Like her father, she quotes from the *Kanzeonkyō*.[33]

In singing nō, among the most rewarding parts to perform are the short exchanges that often precede the first entrance of the chorus, which contribute to the build-up of tension. The *kakeai* in *Atsumori* are a good example.[34] There as in many other plays, the singers are the *shite* and *waki*. In *Rō-Giō* as in plays like *Kiyotsune* 清経 and *Aoi no ue* 葵上, it is the *shite* and *tsure* who exchange shorter and shorter phrases with each other,[35] finishing each other's sentences.

【ツレ】「此一世こそ限りなるを、
【シテ】「此世をだにも添ひ果てもせで

TSURE: The relations between parent and child ...
SHITE: ... are a bond for this life only ...[36]

They end by singing together "... what kind of retribution from a former life is it to die on the point of a sword?"[37] The chorus voices their hope that they can become parent and child in another life, and prays for Kannon in his great pity and compassion to help them in the life to come (後の世 *nochi no yo*). As we shall see, Kannon will come to their aid in *this* life.

---

33. The phrase 慈眼視衆生 *jigen shi shūjō* appears at the end of the verse (*gāthā*) section of the *Fumonbon* chapter of the Lotus Sutra. It is given the *kundoku* reading *jigen wo motte shūjō wo miru* in Oda Tokunō, ed., *Hokekyō kōgi* (Kōyūkazō, 1899), vol. 8, 72. Hurvitz, *Scripture of the Lotus Blossom*, 319 ("His benevolent eye beholding the beings"); Watson, *The Lotus Sutra*, 306 ("he views living beings with compassionate eyes").

34. Yokomichi Mario and Omote Akira, eds., *Yōkyokushū* (jō) (Iwanami shoten, 1960), 236.

35. In *Aoi no ue* 葵上, the section is called *kakeai* 掛ケ合 in Itō Masayoshi, ed. *Yōkyokushū*, vol. 1, SNKS (Shinchōsha, 1983), 20–1. This corresponds to the section called *mondō* 問答 in Yokomichi and Omote, *Yōkyokushū* (jō), 127–8. For *Kiyotsune* 清経, see the *kakeai* section in Yokomichi and Omote, *Yōkyokushū* (jō), 253. In *Rō-Giō*, the *shite* and *tsure* end by singing together. A similar example is found in the *kakeai* of *Kayoi komachi* 通小町. Yokomichi and Omote, *Yōkyokushū* (jō), 78.

36. Haga and Sasaki, *Kōchū yōkyoku sōsho*, vol. 3, 596.

37. *Tsurugi no saki ni kakaran koto, ikanaru zense no mukui zo ya* 剣の先にかからん事の、いかなる前世の報いぞや. Haga and Sasaki, *Kōchū yōkyoku sōsho*, vol. 3, 596.

The *waki* tells Giō to put on her *eboshi* hat and dance. Blinded by tears and unable to dance, she tries to refuse once more. When Giō's father hears of her promise, he asks why she is refusing:

【ツレ】 「尤もの御理にて候。いかに祇王。何と
て辞して申すぞ。<u>もとより此一曲は、父が教へし
事なれば</u>、今日の今は光陰にも、歌舞の菩薩の妙
文なるべし。はやはや謡ひ給ふべし。

> TSURE: It seems very reasonable. How now, Giō? Why do you refuse? *The dance was one that I originally taught you.* So on a day when time passes as quickly as this, it will be like the miraculous words of the Bodhisattva of Dance. You should sing at once.[38]

In *Heike monogatari*, the first *shirabyōshi* dancers were women. Giō and her sister are daughters of a *shirabyōshi* performer. It is a female art, passed down from mother to daughter. Her father's claim to have taught her is startling.

Giō prepares to dance. She knows that if she refuses now, she will be punished. She will do it because it is her father's command (*chichigo no ōse nareba*). In the Kakuichi *Heike*, when summoned by Kiyomori, Giō initially says she is not afraid of punishment, for she fears neither death nor banishment. But her mother cannot face the thought of living her last years in an unfamiliar rustic place.[39] Giō resolves to obey her mother's command.[40]

The text sung during the dance of the *shite* contains more references to "parent and child." They must part like blossoms falling on a dancer's sleeve.[41] "The fragile bond between parent and child is but for one life,

---

38. Haga and Sasaki, *Kōchū yōkyoku sōsho*, vol. 3, 596. Emphasis added.

39. *Narawanu hina no sumai* ならはぬひなの住まひ. "Giō" (Kakuichi-bon, 1.6), Ichiko, *Heike monogatari* (jō), 42, McCullough, *Tale of the Heike*, 34. Note how the same word *hina* (鄙) is used by Giō as she journeys to Kii in the play, n. 13 above.

40. The phrase *oya no mei wo somukaji* 親の命をそむかじ is used both before and after her visit. Ichiko, *Heike monogatari* (jō), 42, 44; McCullough, *Tale of the Heike*, 34, 35.

41. *Hikari no uchito ni asobu naru, kochō no mai no hana no sode, chirigata ni naru oya to ko no, nanika utaite-kanazuran* 光りの内外に遊ぶなる、胡蝶の舞の花の袖、散りがたになる<u>親と子</u>の、何か謡ひて奏づらん. Haga and Sasaki, *Kōchū yōkyoku sōsho*, vol. 3, 597. Emphasis added.

passing in a dream."[42]

The second theme here—and throughout the play—is religious. Giō's dance and song is a ritual act in itself. Her father likens it to the "miraculous words of the Bodhisattva of Dance." This same phrase—歌舞の菩薩 *kabu no Bosatsu*—is repeated by the chorus after her dance.[43]

When Giō sings in *Heike monogatari*, her words carry a Buddhist message that deeply impresses Hotoke Gozen. Giō's performance in the play is a religious act, a path to enlightenment:

> 【地】つらつら無常を観ずるに、飛花葉の
> 風の前、風月延年の遊楽も、狂言綺語の
> 一てん、讃仏乗の因縁まで、津の国の、
> 何はの事か法ならぬ、遊び戯れ数々の
> 【シテ】声仏事を為してこと

CHORUS: If we observe closely the mutability of things, we see how the blossoms and leaves that fly before the wind, even elegant musical concerts and "wild words and specious phrases," can lead to praise of the Buddha. In the land of Tsu, is there anything that is not the Dharma? Play and frolicking of all kind ...

SHITE: ... are [equivalent to] Buddhist chanting.[44]

She begs the *waki* to let her die instead of her father but is told: "Even if you were a man, your life could not take the place of another's. But as you are a woman, it is out of the question."[45]

Her father accepts the fact that he must die, giving her a rosary he received from the holy Hōnen of Kurodani on Mount Hiei (黒谷の法然上人). In return, she presents him with the sutra that she has been reciting for his sake, praying that he will be delivered from evil, and that they might be reunited on the same lotus in Paradise. The chorus sings a prayer to Kannon the merciful.

---

42. 薄き契りは<u>親と子</u>の、一世（ひとよ）に限る夢の内を. Haga and Sasaki, *Kōchū yōkyoku sōsho*, vol. 3, 597. Emphasis added.

43. *Kabu no Bosatsu no myōmon naru beshi* 歌舞の菩薩の妙文なるべし. Haga and Sasaki, *Kōchū yōkyoku sōsho*, vol. 3, 597.

44. Haga and Sasaki, *Kōchū yōkyoku sōsho*, vol. 3, 597. See below for an explanation of the allusion to *Goshūishū* 1197 by a courtesan (*yūjo*) called Miyagi.

45. Haga and Sasaki, *Kōchū yōkyoku sōsho*, vol. 3, 598.

The *waki* impatiently reminds them of the time. Yet when he raises his sword to behead Giō's father, a miracle happens. Light from the sutra blinds his eyes. The sword drops from his hands and shatters.

【ワキ】 (詞) あまりに時刻も移り行けば、か
の老人の首打たんと、太刀振りあぐればこは如
何に。御経の光り眼にふさがり、取り落とした
る太刀を見れば、二つに折れて段々と為る

WAKI: So much time has passed that I raise the sword
to strike off the old man's head when ... what is this?
Light from the sutra blinds my eyes and I drop the
sword. It shatters, breaking into two.[46]

He picks up the sutra and looks at the words that were just read. "There is no doubt," he says. We hear the text itself in the final *kakeai*, this time between the *shite* and *tsure* in unison and the *waki*:

SHITE, TSURE: "If you encounter trouble with the king's law ...
WAKI: ... face punishment, and are about to forfeit your life.
SHITE, TSURE: Think on the power of Kannon.
WAKI: ... and the executioner's sword ...
SHITE, TSURE: ... will be broken to bits!"[47]

The quotation is directly from the *Kanzeonkyō* again, in Chinese word-order and readings. Following this, the chorus repeats the same text, but this time read in Japanese fashion, announcing finally: "Old man, you are saved in time. Go home." Giō's father is pardoned and they

---

46. Haga and Sasaki, *Kōchū yōkyoku sōsho*, vol. 3, 598

47. The text is first read in Sino-Japanese: 或遭王難苦 *Waku zō ō nanku* 臨刑欲寿終 *ringyō yoku jushu* 念彼観音力 *nebi kan'onriki* 刀尋 *tōjin* 段々 壊 *dandan'e*. The chorus summarizes in Japanese: *ōnan no kurushimi ni au tote mo, ni orareru nan no* ("Even if we encounter trouble with the king's law, the sword will shatter into pieces"). Haga and Sasaki, *Kōchū yōkyoku sōsho*, vol. 3, 598. Cf. Sakamoto and Iwamoto, *Hokekyō*, vol. 2, 262; Watson, *The Lotus Sutra*, 304 ("Suppose you encounter trouble with the king's law, / face punishment, about to forfeit your life. / Think on the power of that Perceiver of Sounds / and the executioner's sword will be broken to bits!"); Hurvitz, *Scripture of the Lotus Blossom*, 317 ("Or one might encounter royally ordained woes, / Facing execution and the imminent end of one's life. / By virtue of one's constant mindfulness of Sound-Observer / The knives would thereupon break into pieces").

return together "on the path of joy."[48]

Reference works, when they mention *Rō-Giō* at all, point to the similarity of its central incident with the nō play *Morihisa* 盛久. There too a prisoner escapes death when the executioner's sword shatters— thanks to the intercession of the Kannon. In that case also a pilgrimage to Kiyomizudera is mentioned.[49] Another point in common is that both plays are based in the same kind of realistically featured medieval world. But while the parallels are undeniable, *Rō-Giō* has virtues of its own. On the surface, it seems to have little to do with the story of Giō and Hotoke apart from the fact that Giō is a famous *shirabyōshi*, and reluctant to perform.

As we have seen, one of her reasons for overcoming her reluctance in both cases is her desire to obey and protect an aged parent. In the *Heike* episode, Giō's actions are definitively influenced on two occasions by her mother's words: on deciding whether or not to perform before Kiyomori, and in choosing renunciation of the world rather than suicide after the performance. One of the achievements of *Rō-Giō* is to have explored further the theme of parent-child relations.

Bai Juyi's famous phrase "wild words and fancy phrases" is followed by a reference to a Japanese poem by a *yūjo* called Miyagi, a performing woman like Giō and Hotoke. Miyagi's poem reads as follows:

津の国のなにはのことか法ならぬ遊び戯れまで
とこそ聞け

Tsu no kuni no	In Naniwa in the Land of Tsu
nani wa no koto ka	what is there
nori naranu	that is not the Dharma?
asobi tawamure	even playing and frolicking
made to koso kike.	or so I have heard … [50]

---

48. *Yorokobi no michi ni kaerikeri* 喜びの道に帰りけり. Haga and Sasaki, *Kōchū yōkyoku sōsho*, vol. 3, 598.

49. *Yuya* 熊野 is another play in the current repertory in which Kannon faith 観音信仰 and Kiyomizu play an important role. See Gunji Naoko, Chapter 23, and the Introduction and Translation of the play *Morihisa* 盛久 by Shelley Quinn in Chapters 24–25.

50. *Goshūishū* 後拾遺集 1197. The poet, the *yūjo* Miyagi 遊女宮木, is suggesting that even playing and frolicking with a courtesan like her can lead to the praise of Buddha. Kubota Jun and Hirata Yoshinobu, eds., *Goshūi wakashū*, SNKT 8 (Iwanami shoten, 1994), 389. The text of *Rō-Giō* quotes the words *Tsu no kuni no nani wa no koto ka nori naranu asobi tawamure*. Haga and Sasaki, *Kōchū yōkyoku sōsho*, vol. 3, 597.

A reductive reading would make the whole play an illustration of the verses from the Lotus Sutra, but the religious idea at its heart is this question: "Is there anything that is *not* the Dharma?"—is there anything that cannot lead to enlightenment?

6 ～ *Rō-Giō* (Giō at the Prison)

| MICHAEL WATSON

INTRODUCTION

Rō-Giō 籠祇王 (Giō at the Prison) is a *genzai* play in two acts. It formerly was part of the Kita school repertoire, but it is no longer performed. The playwright is unknown. The *shite* of *Rō-Giō* is Giō, the famous *shirabyōshi* 白拍子 dancer from *Heike monogatari*, but little in the play is derived from the source text. *Rō-Giō* bears close structural and thematic resemblance to *Morihisa*, also translated in this volume: it opens with a *michiyuki* 道行 (travel song), has a dance as its visual center, and turns on a miraculous last-minute reprieve granted by the deity Kannon. The order of the dance and reprieve are reversed from *Morihisa*, creating a somewhat more suspenseful climax.

Rō-Giō opens with Giō, and her attendant traveling from the capital to Kogawa, in Kii province, where Giō's father has been imprisoned. They are met by a man from Kowaka who has been charged with guarding Giō's father. Giō is at first unaware of the nature of her father's crime. The guard agrees to let her meet with her father in exchange for a dance: Giō's fame as a *shirabyōshi* has reached even this remote village.

Giō is united with her father and learns of his crime: while he himself was serving as a jailer, he freed an innocent man, an act Giō praises. The two lament their imminent parting, and the guard intervenes to request that Giō dances. Although weighed by her sorrows, she is prodded into performing by her father. She dances, and then the execution is to take place. Miraculously, however, the sword cannot hit its mark—it has been shattered, we are told, by Kannon's divine intervention to protect the innocent.

83

We can presume that part of the visual pleasure of this play lies largely in Giō's dance; combined with the drama in the last-minute reprieve involving the popular salvific deity Kannon, *Rō-Giō* was most likely quite effective in performance. Moreover, the juxtaposed themes of freedom and captivity, captor and captive, and parent and child suggest a rich complexity of emotional entanglements and their moral consequences that give unusual complexity to this piece.

Rō-Giō (Giō at the Prison)

| TRANSLATED BY MICHAEL WATSON

Fourth-category *genzai* nō in two acts.
Formerly performed by the Kita school.
Time: Third Month, year unknown
Place: Kogawa in Kii province[1]
Author: Unknown

SHITE	Giō
TOMO	Attendant
TSURE	Giō's Father
WAKI	Man from Kogawa[2]

MAN FROM KOGAWA   I am so-and-so from Kogawa in Kishū. Now then, I had an argument with a certain person from the neighboring village. A great number of people were captured and many trophies taken. One of the prisoners who was still young was put under the guard of a local man. Because he let the prisoner escape last night, this guard has himself been made prisoner. I intend now to make sure that

---

Rō-Giō 籠祇王. This translation is based on Haga Yaichi and Sasaki Nobutsuna, eds., *Kōchū yōkyoku sōsho*, vol. 3 (Hakubunkan, 1915; reprint edition, Rinsen shoten, 1987), 593–99. The divisions between prose and sung passages follow a Kita 喜多 school *utaibon* 謡本 libretto kindly provided to me by Richard Emmert. Kita Rokuheita, ed., *Rō-Giō* (Wanya shoten, 1923).

1. The information concerning play category, time, and place follows Kita, *Rō-Giō*, n.p. The province of Kii 紀伊, referred to in the text as Ki 紀, Kishū 紀州 or Ki no kuni 紀の国, is now Wakayama prefecture. Kogawa 粉河 is located in the modern city of Kinokawa 紀の川, and is known for its ancient Tendai temple, *Kogawa-dera* 粉川寺, third in the series of thirty-three Kannon temples visited by pilgrims on the ancient route known as *Saigoku sanjūsansho Kannon junrei* 西国三十三所観音巡礼.

2. In Kita school tradition, Giō wears a young woman's mask (*ko-omote*), a brocaded outer robe (*karaori*) over a kimono (*haku*), and hat (*Shizuka eboshi*). She holds a black fan and has a sutra tucked in her robe. Her father wears a *mizugoromo* cloak and a plain under-kimono (*muchi nōshime*) and carries a crystal rosary (*juzu*). Kita, *Rō-Giō*, n.p.

he is strictly guarded. Is anyone there? Guard the jail strictly. Even if
someone comes claiming to be a relative of the prisoner, all meetings
are strictly forbidden. Be sure to remember this.

GIŌ AND ATTENDANT (*shidai*)
          The morning is fine, with rising clouds as we
          start our journey,
          the morning is fine, with rising clouds as we
          start our journey,
          hurrying on the way to Ki.

GIŌ (*sashi*)   I am a woman called Giō
          and live now in the capital,
          a performing woman by profession.[3]
          There, where flowers spread their hue and scent,
          birds sing, and twill is woven by pampas grass,
          in the beauty of the new moon
          in the cloud-seat, the Palace,
          have I made a name for myself,
          living in the capital of flowers.

GIŌ (*kotoba*)   I have an aged father who lives in the country, but I have
heard that he is a prisoner or something.

    [*sung*]   Even without an aged parent in a world
          where parting is close at hand.
          For what crime could he possibly be charged?[4]
          I am hurrying down to the country to see him once more.

GIŌ AND ATTENDANT
          Spring mists rise as we leave
          the capital in the depths of the moonlit night
          setting off at Yodo ford.[5]
    (*uta*)   The mountain wind scatters flowers,[6]
          as we pass through the dewy reeds of Udono
          travelling on to reach the snows of Kinya,
          to reach the snows of Kinya.

---

3. *Yūjo no michi wo tashinami.* The characters 遊女, read *yūjo* and translated
here as "performing woman," can also be read *asobime.*

4. More literally, "sunk" (*ika naru tsumi ni ka shizumi tamawan*).

5. The *michiyuki* passage describes a journey down the Yodo 淀 river in
Yamashiro province to Udono 宇渡野, and then to Kinya 禁野 and Kitano 交
野 in Kawachi province. All lie within modern Ōsaka prefecture.

6. The libretto indicates that this phrase is to be sung twice. Kita, *Rō-Giō*, 2 *verso.*

In the cherry-hunting fields of Katano,[7]
we are drenched, taking shelter for the night,
even though the rain does not fall.
The moon shines bright over Sumiyoshi and the
    Western Sea,[8]
the waves in the offing visible from afar.
The evening clouds vie with one another
as we arrive in the province of Izumi.
In Shinoda Forest, the *kudzu* leaves
and spring herbs are still in bud,
when we pass through fields and mountains
to the province of Ki,
arriving at the village of Kogawa,
arriving at the village of Kogawa.[9]

Gıō   After hurrying on our way, we have finally arrived in the village of Kogawa. Search this place for the whereabouts of my father.

ATTENDANT As you command. Is there anyone here who can help us?

A local person (ai-kyōgen) *approaches.*

This person here is Giō, a *shirabyōshi* dancer famous in the capital. She has come to see her father. Please allow her to meet him.

[*Giō exchanges words with the local person. He brings her to the man in charge of the prison at Kogawa.*][10]

* * *

---

7. The expressions "snows" and "cherry-hunting" allude to a poem by Fujiwara no Shunzei (*Shinkokinshū* 2: 114) in which the sight of falling cherry blossoms in Kitano at dawn in spring are likened to snow.

8. There is a common wordplay on *sumi* (澄み/住み) in "the moon *shines bright*" and the place-name of Sumiyoshi 住吉. It is now part of Ōsaka prefecture. Western Sea (*nishi no umi*) is a reference to the Setō Inland Sea. The phrase is repeated in Kita performance tradition. Kita, *Rō-Giō*, 2 verso.

9. Giō's journey continues through the province of Izumi 和泉 (southern Ōsaka prefecture) into Ki no kuni 紀の国 (Wakayama prefecture).

10. At this point one would expect to see a short conversation between Giō and an ai-kyōgen actor playing the part of a local person. This is not included in texts of the play.

MAN   Where is the person who wants to see me?
GIŌ   It is me, I am abashed to say.
MAN   As I said earlier, all relatives of the prisoner are
forbidden to see him. However, as it is you, Lady Giō, the most
celebrated and accomplished dancer in the realm, I will break the
prohibition and let you meet your father if you perform a dance.
GIŌ   What, I should perform a dance?
MAN   Exactly.
GIŌ   How sad this makes me. You say that unless I dance,
parent and child will not be allowed to meet. If you would only let
me meet my father, I will show you my dance afterward.
MAN   Agreed. I shall bring you to him first. Then afterward,
you will show me your dance. Is anyone there? Bring this person to
the prisoner.
FATHER   A caged bird yearning for the clouds,
                     a migrating goose who has lost his companions—[11]
                     ask birds what this feeling is like.
                     It is no different for us humans:
                     missing friends left in one's home town,
                     thinking of nothing but karma from an earlier life.
                     Praise be to Kannon the merciful.
                     May he come to receive me into Paradise
                     according to his vow that
                     "The sea of happiness is immeasurable"[12]

---

11. The two images are used in *Heike monogatari*, "Yashima inzen" (Kakuichi-bon 10:3) to describe the feelings of the prisoner Taira no Shigehira 平重衡 after his capture at Ichi-no-tani. The same phrases appear together in the nō play *Higaki* 絵垣 ("Cypress Hedge"). Kajihara Masaaki and Yamashita Hiroaki, eds., *Heike monogatari* (ge) (Iwanami shoten, 1993), 206; Helen Craig McCullough, trans., *The Tale of the Heike* (Stanford University Press, 1988), 331. Koyama Hiroshi and Satō Ken'ichirō, eds., *Yōkyokushū* (jō), SNBZ 58 (Shōgakukan, 1997), 437; Kenneth Yasuda, *Masterworks of the Nō Theatre* (Indiana University Press, 1989), 309. The expression 籠鳥雲を恋ひ *rōchō kumo wo koi* derives ultimately from a work in Chinese by the tenth-century poet Taira no Kanemori 平兼盛 included in Book Six of *Honchō monzui* 本朝文粋. Ōsone Shōsuke et al., eds., *Honchō monzui*, SNKT 27 (Iwanami shoten, 1992), 216.

12. The quoted expression translates 福寿海無量. This is close in meaning and sound to 福聚海無量, a phrase that occurs at the end of the verse (*gāthā*, Jp. 偈 *ge*) section of the twenty-fifth chapter of the Lotus Sutra (*Hokekyō* 法華経). Oda Tokunō, ed., *Hokekyō kōgi* (Kōyūkazō, 1899), vol. 8, 72, where the phrase from the sutra is read *fukujū no umi muryō nari*. Sakamoto Yukio and Iwamoto Yutaka,

GIŌ   How are you, Father? It is I, Giō, come to see you.

[*sung*]   My eyes cloud over and my spirit is troubled
to see you in this state.

FATHER   I am amazed. How have you come here?

GIŌ   When I was on a retreat in Kiyomizu[13] praying for you, I
heard that you were charged with some crime and were imprisoned,
so I came all the way here on foot. What crime is it, then?

FATHER   You are right to wonder. I shall tell you all the details. Listen.

GIŌ   So tell me then.

FATHER   There was fighting in this province, and a great number
of people were killed on this side and the other. Some of those
who were captured alive were put into this prison under the guard
of local men. When it was my turn to guard, I saw that one of the
prisoners was still young, and had nothing to do with this affair. I
felt pity and sorrow for him, and when I imagined how his parents
would grieve for him, I thought that helping him would be the act of
a bodhisattva, and so I decided to spare him, even if it meant that I
would be punished. I opened the gaol and let him escape under the
cover of darkness. Losing a prisoner could not be overlooked and so
I was punished as you see. What's more, I have heard that this night
is to be my last, so I am very happy you have come.

[*sung*]   It would have been lonely
to face death alone,
but to see you here gives me comfort
in this life and the next.
As I speak I shed tears
despite myself.

GIŌ   On the contrary, if your crime was to help another, then
it is a matter of rejoicing. We should pray to Kannon for aid, for the
power of the benevolent eye that beholds all sentient beings.[14]

---

ed., *Hokekyō* (Iwanami bunko, 1962), vol. 2, 267; Leon Hurvitz, trans., *Scripture
of the Lotus Blossom of the Fine Dharma* (Columbia University Press, 1976), 319;
Burton Watson, trans., *The Lotus Sutra* (Columbia University Press, 1993), 306
("The sea of his accumulated blessings is immeasurable").

13. The temple of Kiyomizu 清水 in the capital, an ancient center for the
worship of Kannon Bodhisattva (*Kannon bosatsu* 観音菩薩). See the studies by
Gunji and Quinn in this volume.

14. The phrase "benevolent eye that beholds all sentient beings" translates 慈眼
視衆生, an expression from the Lotus Sutra, and once again from the end of the
twenty-fifth chapter. It is given the *kundoku* reading *jigen wo motte shūjō wo miru*

FATHER	Truly, that is so, but now I do not care for the loss of my life. Enlightenment in the next is my sole wish.
GIŌ	That is true. For your sake it is for the best, I know, yet for myself, the relations between parent and child …
FATHER	are a bond for this life only
GIŌ	and when even in this life one has not spent enough time together,[15]
FATHER	at least in the midst of birth, old age, sickness, and death[16]
GIŌ	without suffering the pain of illness
FATHER	or waiting for death
GIŌ AND FATHER	what kind of retribution from a former life is it to die on the point of a sword?
CHORUS	It cannot be escaped, this retribution in my old age, this retribution in my old age. In another life we may again become parent and child once more. But as for this one, our bond is coming to an end. Thus I beg Kannon in his great pity and compassion to help me in the life to come, to help me in the life to come.
MAN	How now Lady Giō. Take your *eboshi* and put it on quickly.[17] Perform your dance!
GIŌ	Having seen my father in this state, I am blinded by tears and cannot dance. Please forgive me.
MAN	What you say does not make sense. You are trying to deceive us.

---

in Oda, *Hokekyō kōgi*, vol. 8, 72, and translated as "His benevolent eye beholding the beings" in Hurvitz, *Scripture of the Lotus Blossom*, 319.

15. The next four lines alternate between chanted speech and sung styles.

16. Another reference to a passage in the twenty-fifth chapter of the Lotus Sutra. Oda, *Hokekyō kōgi*, vol. 8, 65 (生老病死苦); Hurvitz, *Scripture of the Lotus Blossom*, 318.

17. According to the directions in the Kita school libretto, Giō wears a *Shizuka eboshi* 静烏帽子. This is a tall gold-colored hat, unlike the usual black *eboshi*, and is worn by Yoshitsune's lover Shizuka 静 in plays like *Yoshino Shizuka* or *Funa Benkei*.

FATHER   What are you saying to Giō?

MAN   When this woman came to me first to say that she
wanted to meet you, a prisoner, I broke the rules and let her see you
so that I might able to see the dance I'd heard about. She promised
that after she had seen you she would dance. Now she says that she
will not dance. What do you think of that?

FATHER   It seems very reasonable. How now, Giō? Why do you
refuse? The dance was one that I originally taught you. On a day
when time passes as quickly as this, it will be like the miraculous
words of the Bodhisattva of Dance. You should sing at once.

GIŌ   There is nothing further to say.
                If I do not dance, I will be punished.
                And since Father commands me,
                I shall hold back my tears and calm my heart.

FATHER   Remembering time past,
    [*sung*]   Father weeps as he gives the beat.

GIŌ   Beginning the dance in harmony

FATHER   their sad voices together—

GIŌ   "parent and child, for this life only"[18]—

FATHER   showing regret

GIŌ   from blossoming sleeves,

CHORUS (*shidai*) swirling snow from sleeves,
                raining tears that only increase.[19]

GIŌ   Everything in world is like a dream,

---

18. The relations between parent and child were thought to be for one life
only, whereas husband/wife relations were said to extend over two lives (this life
and the next), and master/retainer relations over three (the past, present, and
future). The expression *oyako wa isse no naka* is used of another daughter/parent
relationship in the nō play *Yuya* 熊野. Koyama and Satō, *Yōkyokushū* (jō), 410;
Royall Tyler, trans., *Granny Mountains: A Second Cycle of Nō Plays* (Cornell East
Asia Series, 1978), 83 ("the lifetime bond that links parent to child"). See also
Hōgen monogatari 保元物語 (Rufubon 流布本 version, section 3.1): *Oyako wa
isse no chigiri to mōsedomo* 親子は一世の契りと申せども ("Though they say
the bond of parent and child is for one life"). Nagazumi Yasuaki and Shimada
Isao, *Hōgen monogatari*, NKBT 31 (Iwanami shoten, 1961), 383; William R.
Wilson, trans., *Hōgen monogatari: Tale of the Disorder in Hōgen* (Tokyo: Sophia
University, 1971), 76. The expression *oyako wa isse* 親子は一世 (*fūfu wa nise,
shujū wa sanze* 夫婦は二世、主従は三世) has become proverbial in Japanese.

19. The Kita school libretto includes the notation *monogi* 物着 at this point,
indicating an onstage costume change for the *shite* performing the part of Giō.
Kita, *Rō-Giō*, 8 *verso*.

CHORUS		nothing now seems real.
	(kuri)	Truly "though I knew this was the way
	[uta]	I would go in the end,
		I did not think it would be
		yesterday or today."[20]
		The white snow of the morning
		melts by the evening.
GIŌ	(sashi)	Lightning flashes, morning dew, flint sparks,[21]
CHORUS		in and out of the light there frolic
		butterflies, and blossoms fall
		from dancer's sleeves as parent and child part.
		Why should we not sing and dance?
	(kuse)	Truly in this world,
		if there is one who remains alone,
		if it is I, she sang,
		whom will I depend on?
		Truly it is only natural, but for myself
		now we must part.
		How long will she remain behind
		in the place her father died?
		The world is a cicada's cast-off shell.
		The fragile bond between parent and child
		is but for one life, passing in a dream—
		a morning-glory that blooms
		in expectation of the evening shadows.
GIŌ		Lasting like the Nagara bridge,[22] but for how long?
CHORUS		When we stop to think
		what a floating world we live in,
		how hateful life seems.
		Truly, as I dwell in this world,
		"unpleasant things increase on my way
		along the rocky paths of Yoshino,"[23]
		and the water that flows touches our feelings.

---

20. A quotation of the poem composed by the tenth-century poet Ariwara no Narihira on his deathbed, according to the account in *Ise monogatari*, section 125.

21. Phrases from the Han dynasty classic *Huainanzi* 淮南子 (Jp. *Enanji*) describing the ephemerality of life.

22. The Nagara 長柄 Bridge in Settsu province, here mentioned in anticipation of the word *nagaraete* ("living on").

23. An allusion to *Kokinshū* 951, an anonymous poem.

I grieve for my father.
If we observe closely the mutability of things,
we see how the blossoms and leaves that fly before the wind,
even elegant musical concerts
and "wild words and specious phrases,"
can lead to praise of the Buddha.[24]
In the land of Tsu,
is there anything that is not the Dharma?[25]
play and frolicking of all kind ...

Giō   are [equivalent to] Buddhist chanting.
Chorus   "Bring light, bring illumination
in the dark gloom of the final road
my father must travel along,
and welcome him into that Land
of Truth and Comfort" she said,
and with the speed of the Bodhisattva of Dance,

---

24. The expression *kyōgen kigyo* 狂言綺語 ("wild words and specious phrases") appears in a prose passage from Bai Juyi 白居易 included in the Buddhist matters (仏事) section of the anthology *Wakan rōeishū* 和漢朗詠集, poem 588. Ōsone Shōsuke and Horiuchi Hideaki, *Wakan rōeishu*, SNKS (Shinchōsha, 1983), 222 (願 以今生世俗文字之業狂言綺語之誤 翻 為当来世世讃仏乗之因転法輪 之縁); J. Thomas Rimer and Jonathan Chaves, *Japanese and Chinese Poems to Sing: The Wakan Rōei Shū* (Columbia University Press, 1997), 588 ("I vow to take the error of the wild words and decadent diction of my worldly literary enterprise in this life and transform it into the karma of praising the Turning of the Wheel of Dharma of Buddha's Vehicle for ages and ages to come"). Portions of this famous passage are quoted twice in *Heike monogatari*, in "Daijin ruizai" (Kakuichi-bon 3.17) and "Atsumori no saigo" (9.16). Kajihara and Yamashita, *Heike monogatari* (jō), 185; (ge), 177. McCullough, *Tale of the Heike*, 124, 317.

25. There is an untranslatable double-meaning in the original, which reads *Tsu no kuni no nani wa no koto ka nori naranu*, with a pun on *nani wa no koto* ("what things," i.e., "all things") and the place-name Naniwa 難波 in Settsu province (*Tsu no kuni*). The phrase is based on a poem by a courtesan known as *yūjo Miyagi* 遊女 宮木 in *Goshūishū* 後拾遺集 1197. 津の国のなにはのことか法ならぬ遊び 戯れまでとこそ聞け *Tsu no kuni no* / *nani wa no koto ka* / *nori naranu* / *asobi tawamure* / *made to koso kike*. "In Naniwa in the province of Tsu, what is there that is not the Dharma. I have heard that even playing and frolicking [can lead to the praise of Buddha]." Kubota Jun and Hirata Yoshinobu, eds., *Goshūi wakashū*, SNBT (Iwanami shoten, 1994), 389. The underlined words are quoted in the nō play. In the original, the mention of Naniwa is apposite, as many prostitutes operated from boats in Naniwa harbor.

	she prayed earnestly.
	The time has now come![26]
	Throwing off her hat and cloak, she cries bitterly.
GIŌ	Ah, how sad this is. Please kill me and spare my father.
MAN	Do not talk nonsense. Even if you were a man, your life

could not take the place of another's. But as you are a woman, it is
out of the question.

FATHER   How now, Giō. Do not lament. Your father must meet
his end. Lamenting serves no purpose.

> I received this rosary
> from the holy Hōnen of Kurodani.[27]
> I give to you.
> Pray for me after I am gone,
> say *nenbutsu* for me.

GIŌ
> This sutra here is one
> that I have been reciting for your sake,
> never letting it leave my person,
> praying that you will be delivered
> from all kinds of evil as [Kannon] vowed,[28]
> that you will attain certain Buddhahood,
> and that I may be reunited with you on the
> same lotus.

CHORUS
> Exchanging rosary and sutra, [he says]
> "Reverence be to Kannon
> in His Great Compassion.
> With the light of mercy in his eye
> may He watch over your last moments."[29]

---

26. *Kore made nari ya ima wa haya*, a phrase that appears also in the plays *Ugetsu* 雨月 and *Nishikido* 錦戸. Nonomura Kaizō, ed., *Yōkyoku nihyakugojū-banshū*, revised by Ōtani Tokuzō (Kyoto: Akaoshō bundō, 1978), vol. 1, 367c, 488a.

27. Hōnen 法然 (1133–1212), founder of the Pure Land (Jōdo 浄土) sect of Buddhism. In *Heike monogatari* (Kakuichi-bon 10.5), Hōnen gives religious counsel to the prisoner Shigehira. Kurodani 黒谷 forms part of the Enryakuji temple complex on Mount Hiei.

28. The expression 種々諸悪趣 ("all kinds of evil") comes again from the twenty-fifth chapter of the Lotus Sutra. Oda, *Hokekyō kōgi*, vol. 8, 65; Hurvitz, *Scripture of the Lotus Blossom*, 318 ("The various evil destinies"); Watson, *Lotus Sutra*, 305 ("In many different kinds of evil circumstances").

29. The phrase 慈悲の眼 *jihi no manako* is probably based on the expression 慈眼視衆生 from the end of the verse section of the Lotus Sutra, Chapter 25.

MAN   So much time has passed that I raise the sword to strike
off the old man's head when ... what is this? Light from the sutra
blinds my eyes and I drop the sword. It shatters, breaking into two.

GIŌ AND FATHER   Father and Giō see this too and—
                 not knowing whether his life had come to an end—
                 are struck dumb.

MAN   What is there to doubt? Taking the text of the sutra that
was just read, he looks at it. There is no question about it—

GIŌ AND FATHER   "If you encounter trouble with the king's law ...

MAN   ... face punishment, and are about to forfeit
                 your life.

GIŌ AND FATHER   Think on the power of that Perceiver of Sounds
                 [Kannon] ...

MAN   ... and the executioner's sword ...

ALL THREE   ... will be broken to bits!"[30]

CHORUS   Truly, how precious is this text.
                 Even if we encounter trouble with the king's law,
                 the sword will shatter into pieces.
                 Doubt not the holy text.
                 Ah how precious the sutra![31]
                 "Now then, old man!
                 You are saved in time.
                 Go home."
                 Her father pardoned, Giō leads him on the
                 joyous way back.
                 Truly "trust where you may trust,"
                 this is the Kannon's vow.

Sakamoto and Iwamoto, *Hokekyō*, 267; Watson, *Lotus Sutra*, 306 ("he views living being with compassionate eyes").

30. Twenty characters of the Lotus Sutra, Chapter 25, are quoted directly, in their Sino-Japanese readings and Chinese word order. Sakamoto and Iwamoto, *Hokekyō*, 263; Hurvitz, *Scripture of the Lotus Blossom*, 317; Watson, *Lotus Sutra*, 304. The following chorus rephrases the opening and closing lines in Japanese.

31. The Kita school libretto indicates a break here in the chorus, suggesting movement on stage. Kita, *Rō-Giō*, 12 *recto*, also introductory notes, n.p. The libretto calls for a repeat of the phrase translated "Now then, old man!" (*kono ue rōjin yo*, more literally "moreover, old man").

7 ∿ The Battle of Tonamiyama in *Bangai* Nō | Elizabeth Oyler

The very existence of the term "*bangai* 番外"—extracanonical—in reference to nō points to the heterogeneity of the works comprising the nō repertoire. What constituted a proper subject for nō and what signified an appropriate exposition of that subject were topics of discussion from as early as Zeami's time,[1] and various aesthetic, social, and political concerns continued to shape the boundaries of the art well into the Tokugawa period, when the current canon of approximately two hundred and fifty pieces was codified.[2] Many more plays lie outside established repertoires than within them, and they were excluded for a wide variety of reasons.

In an effort to elucidate one motivation for the failure of such works to be incorporated into the canon, this chapter considers two lesser-known nō that share superficial characteristics with some of the most famous canonized plays. *Kiso* 木曾, which is performed today only by the Kanze school, and the *bangai* piece *Kurikara otoshi* 倶利伽羅落: they concern the events of the Genpei War and laud central figures from that conflict as described in the variant texts of the *Heike monogatari*. In fact, the particular series of battles they describe, Kiso Yoshinaka's 木曾義仲 victory at Tonamiyama and drive to the capital, is the source for *Sanemori*, the well-known canonical nō describing the tragic battlefield death of the elderly Taira partisan Saitō no Bettō Sanemori

---

1. An extensive and nuanced study of the development of Zeami's own theories of practice and aesthetics for the art over his lifetime in Shelley Fenno Quinn, *Developing Zeami: The Noh Actor's Attunement in Practice* (University of Hawai'i Press, 2005).

2. See Gerry Yokota-Murakami, *The Formation of the Canon of Nō: The Literary Tradition of Divine Authority* (Osaka: Osaka University Press, 1997), 183–202 for a discussion of the political and aesthetic imperatives shaping the canon during the Tokugawa period.

discussed later in this volume. Yet both works exhibit important points of divergence, as well. They describe the battle from the perspective of the victorious Minamoto army, and they lack the coherent focus on one specific character that marks the best of *mugen* nō. This wholly different perspective on the event creates incongruities that are increasingly apparent as appropriate topics for nō, modes of exposition, and aesthetic ideals become more stringently regulated as the art matured.

In the pages that follow, I explore how the narrative of Yoshinaka's victory was reworked in the nō and another performing art that matured alongside it—*kōwakamai* 幸若舞, or "ballad drama." The story of Yoshinaka's victory appears prominently in both, yet ultimately is fully integrated only in the *kōwakamai* repertoire. To what degree did these two arts share material and influence each other? And to what extent does the ultimate near-exclusion from the nō of base narratives like Yoshinaka's victory suggest the vitality of structural and thematic concerns for practitioners and theorists of the nō as they came to define it in relation to other arts?

THE BATTLE OF TONAMIYAMA IN MEDIEVAL PERFORMING ARTS

Kiso Yoshinaka's victory at the battle of Tonamiyama was a vital first step toward Minamoto victory in the Genpei War. By defeating the Taira force sent to subdue him, Yoshinaka reversed the direction of the conflict and began the drive that would lead to the routing of the Taira from the capital. This is a moment in the larger narrative of the war when the border between center and peripheries begins to crumble, as outside forces threaten the centuries-old aristocratic order.

Although the battle at Tonamiyama did not capture the cultural imagination to the degree that later battles in the war would, it nevertheless appears prominently in all major texts of the *Heike monogatari* corpus. It also provides the material for the *kōwakamai* piece *Kiso no ganjo*,[3] as well as the nō *Kiso* and *Kurikara otoshi*.[4]

---

3. Asahara Yoshiko and Kitahara Yasuo, eds., *Mai no hon*, SNKT 59 (Iwanami shoten, 1994), 206–9.

4. Both are translated in this volume. The original text for *Kiso* can be found in

During the Muromachi period, *Heike monogatari* recitation, nō, and *kōwakamai* were patronized by members of the warrior class, and all three are closely affiliated with the interlocking facets of creating and maintaining an official memory of a divisive military conflict: bringing into relief the events central to the narrative of the rise of the shogunate; placating the war's losers; and celebrating its victors. The battle at Tonamiyama represents a somewhat complicated moment within this context—Yoshinaka's drive to the capital was an essential step toward the Minamoto victory, but his later alienation from and death at the hands of his Minamoto kin placed him in an ambiguous position for memorialization, as he had to be celebrated as a victor but ultimately depicted as an enemy to the proper order.[5]

The subject of Yoshinaka's victory at Tonamiyama seems a natural fit for the *kōwakamai*, a genre dedicated to the celebration of warrior culture that feature warriors from the early medieval period as the mainstay of the repertoire.[6] The battle was an early and resounding victory for the Minamoto forces, whose fearlessness and tactical brilliance exemplify the best in warrior behavior. Many *kōwakamai* are overt felicitations, as is the case with *Kiso no ganjo*, which celebrates the sanction of the deity Hachiman, god of war and tutelary deity of the Minamoto clan, for Yoshinaka's military campaign.

The battle of Tonamiyama from the perspective of the victorious Minamoto side is less clearly an appropriate topic for nō. While we find Genpei warriors comprising an important category of nō *shite*, those in canonized *shura* nō are virtually all warriors who have died in battle and are possessed by unquenchable rancor or regret. They are by definition not victors; Sanemori is but one obvious and famous example. This suggests one reason why the nō plays *Kiso* and *Kurikara otoshi* lie at or beyond the peripheries of the canon. The stories they tell do not fit well in the more common modes of presentation of warrior stories in the nō. But as we shall see, the attempt to turn the narrative of the victors so easily

Sanari Kentarō, ed., *Yōkyoku taikan*, vol. 2 (Meiji shoin, 1931), 815–24; *Kurikara otoshi* is included in Haga Yaichi and Sasaki Nobutsuna, eds., *Kōchū yōkyoku sōsho*, vol. 1 (Hakubunkan, 1914), 642–46.

5. See Yamashita Hiroaki, *Ikusa monogatari to Genji shōgun* (Miyai shoten, 2003), 242–58, for a discussion of Yoshinaka's portrayal (and need for placation) in the *Heike* and nō traditions.

6. James Araki, *The Ballad-Drama of Medieval Japan* (University of California Press, 1964) presents a study of the extant repertoire and translations of several pieces.

incorporated into the *kōwakamai* repertoire instead of into nō permits us a glimpse of the connections and artistic negotiations between the nō and other arts patronized by the warrior classes during the formative stages in its development, before the current canon was concretized in the Tokugawa period.

In considering *Kiso* and *Kurikara otoshi*, we must bear in mind that the arts in question came into their own significantly after the events they recount. The earliest attributable date for a *Heike monogatari* variant (the Engyō-bon 延慶本) is 1309. The nō was given shape in the early 1400s. We cannot precisely date the *kōwakamai*, but something resembling its extant repertory seems to have existed by the late fifteenth century. All three were patronized by the warrior class during the Muromachi period, the nō famously by Ashikaga Yoshimitsu 足利義満 (1358–1408). Evidence suggests that *Heike monogatari* was also actively sponsored by Yoshimitsu,[7] and there are records of *kōwakamai* performed at the residences of prominent *daimyō* (大名 great lords) during a slightly later period. The pieces from the *kōwakamai* repertoire very closely resemble the texts from which they were derived (primarily *Heike monogatari* variants and *Soga monogatari* [曽我物語, Tale of the Soga Brothers]) and were strung together by the early Tokugawa era in the *Mai no hon* (舞本, Book of Kōwakamai) to create a longer narrative whose endpoint is the establishment of Yoritomo's Kamakura rule.

Although the significance of warrior patronage cannot be overstated for any of these traditions, we must bear in mind that each art served various roles for its sponsors. *Heike monogatari* and *kōwakamai* are almost exclusively devoted to recording events of the Genpei War and its aftermath. Their characters are members or retainers of the Taira and Minamoto clans, and the wide variety of human experience recorded in them is predicated on the horrors of that war. The connection between these arts and their audiences is clear: *Heike monogatari* and *kōwakamai* celebrated members of the military class and mourned the losses of the war which, by the Muromachi age, had come to be seen as an important watershed in the development of warrior rule. The nō repertoire, by contrast, is much broader, embracing themes and characters from earlier ages and works, as well as those of the Genpei War and the warrior world. The significance for its warrior patrons was more subtle and perhaps more

---

7. See Hyōdō Hiromi, *Heike monogatari no rekishi to geinō* (Yoshikawa kōbunkan, 2000), 76–92, for a discussion about the role of the Ashikaga, and particularly Yoshimitsu, as patrons of recited *Heike*.

important. Nō represented a sort of cultural capital that demonstrated a far-reaching embrace of long traditions and aesthetics. Nevertheless, like *Heike monogatari* and the *kōwakamai*, nō was closely affiliated with memory, and specifically with calling forth a story from the past in order to celebrate and/or assuage the characters involved.

The story of Yoshinaka's confrontation with the Taira forces at Tonamiyama is a vital component in the *Heike monogatari* variants of both the "read text lineage" (*yomihonkei* 読本系) and the "recited text lineage" (*kataribonkei* 語本系).[8] In most texts with clearly delineated episodes (*dan* 段 or *ku* 句), the battle occupies two. The first centers on the writing of Yoshinaka's petition, and the second on the ensuing battle. The first episode generally opens with Yoshinaka's encampment at Hanyū and the laying of his battle plan. It culminates auspiciously: looking around, Yoshinaka spots a shrine gate (*torii* 鳥居) on a nearby mountain. Upon inquiring about its identity, he learns that it marks a sanctuary dedicated to Hachiman, the god of war and tutelary deity of his clan, the Minamoto. He calls his scribe Kakumei to compose a petition (*ganjo* 願書) to the god asking for sanction in the upcoming battle. Kakumei brandishes a brush from his quiver and writes the document, which is itself embedded in the narrative. The petition is presented at the shrine, whereupon doves, symbols of Hachiman, flutter above the gate; Yoshinaka interprets this as a good omen and gives thanks.[9]

In the second episode, the Minamoto effect a night attack on the Taira camp, forcing their erstwhile pursuers into a ravine and decimating their forces. Following this victory, Yoshinaka proceeds triumphantly to the capital and forces the Taira to flee. From this point on, the Taira will be fugitives until their final defeat in the battle at Dan-no-ura almost two years later. The Hyakunijukku-bon variant of *Heike monogatari* combines these two in one *ku* 句 (number 63), "Kiso no ganjo 木曾願書."[10] In all variants, the petition is included as a verbatim quotation (although the

---

8. We find it, for example, in the Engyō-bon 延慶本 (read-text lineage), Hyakunijukku-bon 百二十句本 (recited-text lineage), Nagato-bon 長門本 (read-text lineage), and Kakuichi-bon 覚一本 (recited-text lineage) variants, as well as the *Genpei jōsuiki* 源平盛衰記.

9. For the Kakuichi-bon variant's rendition, see Kajihara Masaaki and Yamashita Hiroaki, eds., *Heike monogatari* (ge), SNKT 45 (Iwanami shoten, 1993), 12–17. An English translation can be found in Helen Craig McCullough, trans., *The Tale of the Heike* (Stanford University Press, 1988), 228–32.

10. Mizuhara Hajime, ed., *Heike monogatari* (chū), SNKS (Shinchōsha, 1980), 186–94.

document does not appear in any historical records),[11] and all underline the importance of its composer, the scribe Kakumei 覚明.

YOSHINAKA'S PETITION

Although we shall see below that Kakumei's petition-writing figures in *Kurikara otoshi* as well, it is indisputably the center of both the *kōwakamai Kiso no ganjō* and the nō *Kiso*, works bearing a striking resemblance to each other and to the general *Heike monogatari* narrative in both exposition of the events and focus on specific characters. Unlike the *Heike monogatari* narratives, however, both the *kōwakamai* and nō culminate before the actual battle: the *kōwakamai* ends with praise for Kakumei's calligraphy, while the nō instead concludes with Kakumei performing a dance.

Both endings represent the kind of auspicious conclusion that became hallmarks of the *kōwakamai* and *shūgen* nō (祝言能, felicitous nō) by the time both arts were clearly codified. Felicitation is defined somewhat differently in each, however. In the *kōwakamai*, warrior prowess and military victory are often celebrated, whereas *shūgen* nō tend to celebrate the auspiciousness of a deity, a ruler, and/or the realm. Nō, in other words, is less specifically interested (at least on a superficial level) with personal or military concerns. Whereas the *kōwakamai* seems not to derive from a specific *Heike monogatari* variant account of the event, the nō *Kiso* suggests that the *Genpei jōsuiki* 源平盛衰記 variant was its closest antecedent. One of the nō's *tsure* is identified as Ikeda no Jirō, who is named elsewhere only in the *Genpei jōsuiki*, and Kakumei's calligraphic prowess is demonstrated by his ability to compose the petition "as if copying an old document" (*kosho wo utsusu ga gotoku nite* 古書をうつすが如くにて), a turn of phrase also found only in the *Genpei jōsuiki*.[12]

Minor differences like these aside, the narrative of Kakumei's composition of the petition is fairly consistent across the *Heike monogatari* variants, and both the *kōwakamai* and the nō adhere to the source narrative: Yoshinaka makes camp, and his troops devise a strategy

---

11. This is true of a number of evidentiary "documents" embedded in *Heike* variants.

12. See Mizuhara Hajime, ed., *Shintei Genpei jōsuiki*, vol. 4 (Shin jinbutsu ōraisha, 1990), 67–70.

to outwit their enemies. Upon learning that the shrine in the distance is devoted to Hachiman, Yoshinaka calls upon Kakumei to compose the petition, which is embedded in document form in the text. The document itself is virtually identical in the nō, *kōwakamai*, and *Heike monogatari* variants. Notably, Kakumei's composition of the petition to Hachiman is the center of both nō and *kōwakamai* pieces, which end with the deity's acceptance of the petition.

Like other *kōwakamai*, *Kiso no ganjo* lauds a warrior hero, or perhaps two—both Yoshinaka's victory and Kakumei's calligraphic prowess are equally privileged. This dual celebration is concretely illustrated by the petition itself. While on one level the petition is proof of Kakumei's skill as a scribe and calligrapher,[13] it also documents Yoshinaka's status as not only a great general but also a member of the illustrious warrior lineage of the Minamoto. In particular, it emphasizes his bloodline through the famous Minamoto ancestor Yoshiie 義家 (1039–1106), narrating a version of Minamoto pedigree we find invoked throughout the war tales by narrators and characters alike to justify the clan's rise to prominence.

The *kōwakamai* then ends with the composition of the petition and the remark that Kakumei's calligraphy was praised by all. In other words, attention in the piece is focused primarily on the composer and the very act of composition. The content of the document itself provides the auspicious context in which the act occurs, but ultimately the composition of the petition, rather than the subsequent battlefield victory, is the cause for celebration. The nō, too, celebrates the composition of the document but takes a slightly different but significant course: only after the chorus informs the audience that Kakumei "concludes the letter" (*ganjo wo kakiowaru* 願書を書きをはる) does the actual scroll appear, as Kakumei sits at the side (*wakishōmen*) and "reads it aloud before his lord" (*takaraka ni yomiagetari* 高らかに読み上げたり). The document remains essential but it is given shape by enacted recitation rather than material presence.

Embedded documents like the *ganjo* here are part and parcel of the *Heike monogatari* from which many *kōwakamai* and nō derive, but they are generally absent from nō, with three notable exceptions: *Kiso, Shōzon* 正尊 (which recounts the reading of a oath [*kishōmon* 起請 文] written by the assassin sent to kill Yoshitsune after the Genpei War),

---

13. Elizabeth Oyler, *Swords, Oaths, and Prophetic Visions: Authoring Warrior Rule in Medieval Japan* (University of Hawai'i Press, 2006), 71–81.

and the well-known *Ataka* 安宅,[14] all of which involve the reading of a document, and which together comprise the nō category of "document-centered pieces" (*yomimono* 読物).[15] Unlike *Kiso*, both other plays use recitation of a document to dramatize a moment of extreme narrative tension: in *Shōzon*, a false oath is coerced; in *Ataka*, the subscription scroll (*kanjinchō* 勧進帳) is improvised by Benkei as proof that his party is not Yoshitsune's (which, of course, it is). It is in fact the *absence* of the actual document that brings drama to that *genzai* nō.[16] In *Kiso*, by contrast, reading the document represents a straightforward dramatization of a felicitous composition. Although *Kiso*'s performance of "reading" points toward a thematization of the performative act that we find utilized in the other *yomimono*, it does so without the vital problematization of "reading" that make both *Shōzon* and *Ataka* suspenseful.[17]

Kiso's significant thematic commonalties with these plays goes beyond the scope of this essay, but one structural element it shares with *Ataka* sheds some light on the border of the nō canon and the nō's relation to *kōwakamai*. Both *Kiso* and *Ataka* conclude with a felicitous "man's dance" (*otokomai* 男舞).[18] As Ivan Grail notes in his introduction to *Kiso* in this volume, a final *otokomai* dance is less common than a "battle dance" (*kirikumi* 切組) for warrior-centered works classed as "fourth-

---

14. Basis for the kabuki *Kanjinchō* 勧進帳 and Akira Kurosawa's film *Tora no o wo fumu otokotachi* 虎の尾を踏む男達 (Those Who Tread on the Tiger's Tail, 1945).

15. For *Shōzon*, see Yokomichi Mario and Omote Akira, eds., *Yōkyokushū* (jō), NKBT 40 (Iwanami shoten, 1960), 204–14. *Ataka* can be found in Sanari Kentarō, *Yōkyoku taikan*, vol. 2 (Meiji shoin, 1930), 77–104, and in the other major collections.

16. *Shōzon* was composed by Kanze Nobutoshi 観世長俊, son of Kanze Kojirō Nobumitsu 観世小次郎信光, who is thought to have written *Ataka*. See Kenneth Yasuda, "The Dramatic Structure of *Ataka*, a Noh Play," *Monumenta Nipponica* 27:4 (Winter 1972), 359. Commentators from Sanari on note the unreliability of this attribution of authorship. See Sanari, *Yōkyoku taikan*, vol. 2, 77. Taken together, the three plays generally suggest the ways in which documents can and cannot provide drama in the nō. For purposes of this study, the fact that *Kiso*'s description of the document represents a straightforward inclusion of a recognized auspicious writing and reciting event is most important.

17. We might also note, however, that many scholars view Kakumei's character as drawn in the *Heike* repertoire as an important prototype for the stalwart monk-retainer Benkei 弁慶, the *shite* of *Ataka*; this particular incarnation certainly supports that theory.

18. This role is fulfilled by a different kind of dance at an earlier moment in *Shōzon*.

category pieces" (*yobanmemono* 四番目物), as *Kiso* is. That *Ataka*—also a *yobanmemono*—successfully integrates the *otokomai* demonstrates the dance's ultimate viability within the codified repertoire, and indeed the power of a *genzai* warrior story, given appropriate contextualization. However, we more commonly see the *otokomai* in the several other *bangai* or near-*bangai* plays that share with *Kiso* corollaries in the *kōwakamai* tradition: *Genpuku Soga* 元服曽我 (The Soga Brothers Come of Age), *Kosode Soga* 小袖曽我 (The Soga Brothers and the *Kosode* Robe), and *Shichiki ochi* 七騎落 (Seven Horsemen Retreat). The dance indicates a general structure sharing a common origin with the *kōwakamai* tradition, one that celebrated warriors specifically and relied heavily on the *Heike* or other war tales not simply for content, but even for verbatim narrative. Notably all are categorized as *yobanmemono*, the rubric best able to absorb pieces that resist thematic and structural classification.

To be sure, categorizing all these works as *yobanmemono* reflects the imperatives of later, Tokugawa-period systems of organizing the repertory—such categories were not considerations for the play's composers. And there are of course compelling, felicitous stories that became extremely successful as nō, of which *Ataka* is but one salient example. But all these *kōwakamai*-like, and perhaps *kōwakamai*-influenced, works share certain elements that made them less appealing as nō as the canon was established. Other considerations certainly also contributed to their lack of success, particularly their high degree of verbatim borrowing from source texts with little or no dramatic innovation. But I would suggest here that their structure, combined with a felicitous focus on the individual accomplishments of military men also contributed to the exclusion or near-exclusion of these plays from the repertoire. None are *mugen* nō 夢幻能, all generally have large casts, all celebrate Genpei-period heroes with felicitous dances. The presence of a play like *Kiso* thus implies the close linkages between the two emerging corpuses of nō and *kōwakamai*, at least in their formative stages. That it is retained in the extant repertoires of only the Kanze school, however, suggests that despite certain thematic and structural resonances, it is lacking in the full range of characteristics expected from the art.

THE WOMAN WARRIOR'S MISSING SWORD:
KURIKARA OTOSHI

The *mugen nō Kurikara otoshi* provides an even more complex example of the give-and-take among the corpuses of *Heike monogatari*, *kōwakamai*, and nō. Its *shite* is the ghost of Aoi 葵, the less prominent of Yoshinaka's two woman warriors. Like *Kiso*, the clearest antecedent for *Kurikara otoshi* is the *Genpei jōsuiki*,[19] the only *Heike monogatari* variant to identify the female compatriot to the more famous woman warrior Tomoe 巴 as Aoi (in other variants, Tomoe's companion is named Yamabuki 山吹). Even in *Genpei jōsuiki*, however, Aoi never actually appears at Tonamiyama; she is first mentioned during Yoshinaka's final battle, when we learn that she had been killed in this earlier confrontation.[20]

Despite these similarities to the source text, the narrative premise of *Kurikara otoshi* is unique to the play: years after the battle, a sword that once belonged to the woman warrior Aoi is unearthed at Tonamiyama, and this triggers the appearance of her ghost to recover it. The vitality of this frame is suggested by the alternative names by which the play's slightly variant texts are identified: *Tachibori* (The Unearthed Sword 太刀掘), *Tachibori Aoi* (Aoi and the Unearthed Sword 太刀掘葵), *Aoi* 葵, and *Aoi Tomoe* (Aoi and Tomoe 葵巴).[21] The play opens with the *waki*, a local person, revealing that he has had a prophetic dream (in the *Tachibori* text, he says simply that it is an auspicious day); this prompts him to plant a field on Tonamiyama.

As the digging begins, a sword is unearthed, and it is seen as a "truly remarkable find" (*makoto ni medetaki onkoto nite sōrō* 誠にめでたき御事にて候). The appearance of the sword triggers the spirit possession of the *maeshite*, a woman identified as Akone no mae. Following an almost comically long *mondō* 問答 (dialogue) sequence, the possessing

---

19. Mizuhara, *Genpei jōsuiki*, vol. 4, 67–70.

20. Other indications of a specific allusive link to the *Genpei jōsuiki* are *Kurikara otoshi*'s descriptions of Kakumei's brandishing of paper and ink to compose the petition, which includes flourishes similar to those found only in the *Genpei jōsuiki* and the nō *Kiso*; we also see the play's mention of lighting torches on the horns of oxen to frighten the enemy.

21. See *Tachibori* ("The Unearthed Sword") in Tanaka Makoto, ed., *Mikan yōkyokushū*, vol. 20 (Koten bunko, 1972), 92–97. Tanaka discusses other names for the play on p. 13.

spirit finally reveals herself to be Aoi, a female general in service to Kiso Yoshinaka during the battle at Tonamiyama. She says that the sword is hers and requests that it be returned. The *waki* agrees to give her the sword in return for an account of the battle fought at Tonamiyama, a plot element reminiscent of the guard's request for Giō to dance in *Rō-Giō*.

Here, the nō takes up the *Genpei jōsuiki* narrative. The *shite* describes the battle in an abbreviated form of the *Genpei jōsuiki*: the Minamoto arrive at Tonamiyama, make camp, and debate strategy. Looking around, they see the gate of a shrine and learn that it is devoted to Hachiman. Interpreting this as an auspicious sign, Yoshinaka has his scribe Kakumei compose a petition, which they then present to the deity; an account of Kakumei's history follows. Night falls, and the Minamoto light torches on the horns of oxen to frighten the enemy, which convinces the Taira to wait until morning to fight. Under cover of darkness, Yoshinaka's men, led by Imai Kanehira 今井兼平, attack the Taira and push them down into Kurikara Valley. The play concludes by borrowing the image of the piled-up bodies of the dead in Kurikara Valley to invoke the piling up of sand to make a stupa as a prayer for the dead.

Kurikara otoshi structurally appears to be what came to be classified as a *mugen* nō of the *shura* category: the *shite* is the ghost of a warrior killed in battle; the piece proceeds through a *mondō* sequence between *waki* and *shite* in which the *shite*'s identity is ultimately revealed; the *shite* recounts the battle scene in which her death occurred; and the piece concludes with prayers for the dead. Within these general parameters, however, a number of fundamental characteristics mark this piece as different from canonical *shura* nō (including the somewhat anomalous *shura* nō *Tomoe*, about the better-known woman warrior).[22]

First, the *waki*'s role seems to end at the *sashi* initiating the *shite*'s description of the battle; he otherwise does not speak. His participation is limited, in other words, to the extended *mondō*, in which he performs the conventional role of drawing forth the *shite*'s true identity. In addition to the abbreviated role for the *waki*, we also find that the *shite*, although continuing to recite lines, falls out of the narrative as a subject when she begins to recount the battle. She is replaced first by Kakumei, the scribe, and then Kanehira, who leads the Genji assault. Kakumei's and Kanehira's actions are described, but there is no close connection between these

---

22. *Tomoe* can be found in Sanari Kentarō, *Yōkyoku taikan*, vol. 5 (Meiji shoin, 1931), 2275–88. It is translated in Chifumi Shimazaki, *Warrior Ghost Plays from the Japanese Noh Theater* (Cornell East Asia Series, 1993), 168–83.

two (or between them and Aoi) that would explain their sharing the position conventionally belonging to the *shite*. And we curiously never actually learn of Aoi's specific fate. Moreover, she appears through a medium: in this respect, the *shite* resembles a *monogurui* 物狂い ("spirit possession"), but, as Tanaka Makoto notes, the characterization is not complete.[23] Finally, the prayers in the *kiri* seem to be directed at the souls of the fallen Taira, rather than the *shite*. And we should also bear in mind that this *shite* in a *shura* piece is a female who died in battle, which makes her a complete anomaly in terms of canonized nō.

In addition to these structural incongruities, the play is explicitly felicitous, which, as we have already established, is unusual for a *shura* nō. It opens with an auspicious dream, and the nearness of a shrine dedicated to Hachiman is seen as a good omen. As in *Kiso*, Kakumei's composition of the petition heralds the god's sanction of the Minamoto side, and Hachiman's support leads to an overwhelming defeat of the Taira. The narrative is told from the perspective of the battle's winners, and is as much a celebration of their victory as a eulogy for the defeated Taira.

It is easy, and, I believe, fair to say that these characteristics contribute to the categorization of *Kurikara otoshi* as *bangai*—it does not adhere to the structure and form from which *mugen* nō derives its almost gravitational power: the frame narrative seems disconnected from the embedded narrative, and the embedded narrative, rather than bringing into relief the specific suffering of an individual, instead is more of a boundless and crowded celebration of a successful battle. In this respect, it looks far more like a *kōwakamai* piece than a *shura* nō, and yet it differs from that repertoire as well: the *shite* is a ghost, and the events do not occur in real time. What are the threads that hold the frame narrative and the embedded narrative together, how are they anchored in each, and why is this combination ultimately problematic in a *mugen* nō?

One clue is the way the document is reconstituted in this version. As in the nō *Kiso*, the act of writing so central to both the *Heike monogatari* original and the *kōwakamai* is displaced: Kakumei composes the petition

---

23. See Tanaka, *Mikan yōkyokushū*, vol. 20, 13. He argues that this is not a real *monogurui*, since it does not fulfill the role completely (the relationship between the spirit and the possessed is unclear throughout the piece and is never addressed beyond the opening of the play). For an English summary of Zeami's theory of *monogurui*, see Quinn, *Developing Zeami*, 45–47. Interestingly for this play in particular, Zeami offers the following advice: "Never cast a female character as the victim of possession by a warring or demonic spirit." Quinn, *Developing Zeami*, 47.

with flourish, but then he recites it (*yomiaguru* 読みあぐる): this is the act given repeated attention in the nō. The document itself, in other words, is overshadowed by its recitation, which again gestures to the thematization of recitation as a kind of performance in the nō.

However, unlike *Kiso*, which not only includes the document verbatim but also makes it the center of the play, *Kurikara otoshi* presents the composition of the document as but one segment of the longer narrative of the battle. The first lines of the document found in all other versions are in fact transposed into the prayer intoned as the petition is dedicated. Certainly, this further emphasizes the vitality of reciting when the episode is translated into nō. But more significantly, it suggests the dismantling of the document in this work: the content is scattered, with vital elements reordered as they are moved to different parts of the piece. We find, for example, the recitation of Minamoto lineage inserted into the long *mondō* leading to the revelation of the *shite*'s identity, rather than in the document itself. The *mondō* consists of a recitation of the names Raikō 頼光 (Yorimitsu), Yoritomo, Yoshitsune, and Yoshinaka: the great Minamoto scions (and here clearly in opposition to the Taira) under whom the most famous warriors of their time fought. This *mondō* in fact is more effective as a *monozukushi* 物尽くし (illustrative list) of Minamoto heroes than as a character revelation. Although it eventually brings us to the *shite*, Aoi, it does so by working its way through the Minamoto lineage rather than eliciting her identity through a description of her individual experience, as we expect from a *shura* nō *mondō*.

The transposition of this element of the original document to the *mondō* section of the play suggests nō form, but more significantly drains the petition of its status as evidentiary document. Yet by maintaining the felicitous theme of an illustrious Minamoto lineage, it demonstrates commonalties with the *kōwakamai*. The inclusion of Yoritomo in the list of Minamoto heroes in the *mondō* is another indication of this strong tie—he is rarely celebrated as a warrior hero except in the *kōwakamai*, where he is consistently included. In *Kurikara otoshi*, these themes are translated into the idiom of nō, but they retain enough of the flavor of heroic battle narrative to render the play idiosyncratic.

The most unusual characteristic of the play, however, is its most provocative: the frame narrative, in which Aoi no mae reclaims her unearthed sword. This seems a clear indication that the author intended to create a *mugen* nō. The narrative of the loss and recuperation of a sword further has vital connections to the broader *Heike monogatari* narrative: the *Heike monogatari* is, among other things, a compensatory narrative addressing the loss of Kusanagi 草薙, the sacred sword carried by the child sovereign Antoku 安徳 when he drowned at Dan-no-ura. In the *Heike monogatari*, the most explicitly compensatory "sword" narrative is the "Swords" episode (Ken 剣; Kakuichi-bon, 11.12), where the loss is explained as a retrieval of the blade by the serpent from whose tail it had originally been taken by Susano-o; the sword has gone back to its former otherworldly owner. In the "Tsurugi no maki" 剣巻 (Chapter on the Swords), a secret piece of the *Heike biwa* performance tradition, the narrative of the loss of Kusanagi is accompanied (and amplified) by a companion narrative in which the recovery of Minamoto family heirloom swords by Yoritomo following the revenge of the Soga brothers restores harmony to the realm.[24] The sword in the frame narrative of *Kurikara otoshi* provides an interesting variation on this story: the lost sword generates a narrative, and the narrative insures restitution of the blade to its proper owner. But the narrative the sword generates is not about its loss; rather, it is about a moment of stunning victory. Why are this sword and this story unearthed here?

One answer lies with the identity of the putative *shite*, Aoi. As mentioned above, alternative names for the play are *Tachibori*, but also *Tachibori Aoi*, *Aoi*, and *Aoi Tomoe*. All of these titles draw attention to the frame narrative rather than the embedded one, and most of them also include Aoi's name in their title. Moreover, Aoi is an anomaly: a woman who died on the battlefield, whose ghost has come after her sword. The case of the more famous Tomoe is instructive here. In most *Heike monogatari* variants and the canonical (if unusual) *shura* play about that woman warrior, she is portrayed first and foremost not as a woman warrior, but rather in the more conventional female roles of lover and, more importantly, shamaness (*miko* 巫) or memorializer.[25] Thematic and

---

24. The "Tsurugi no maki" is not part of most textual *Heike* variants, including those of the "recited-text variant" line. It is included as a *nukigaki* (抜き書き supplemental text) to the Yashiro-bon variant and the *Genpei jōsuiki*, and it comprises one of the three *daihiji* (大秘事 major secret pieces) in the *Heike mabushi* 平家正節, the late eighteenth-century libretto used by sighted performers studying *Heike biwa*. Shida Itaru, "*Heike* Tsurugi no maki," in *Nihon koten bungaku daijiten*, vol. 5 (Iwanami shoten, 1984), 389.

25. Discussed in Tomikura Tokujirō, ed., *Heike monogatari zen chūshaku*, vol. 3, part 1 (Kadokawa shoten, 1967), 60–62. Steven Brown elaborates upon this suggestion of Tomoe's earliest nō characterization in his interpretation of her multiple identities in "From Woman Warrior to Peripatetic Entertainer: The Multiple Histories of Tomoe," *Harvard Journal of Asiatic Studies* 58.1 (1998), 191–

formal concerns of both the *Heike monogatari* and the nō prevent her from fulfilling a role antithetical to this characterization. What does this mean for Aoi, who fell in battle?

Although Aoi is the *shite* of this piece, hers is not the story told in the embedded narrative; she triggers an account of the battle, but it is an account without a clear, sustained subject—the description moves from Yoshinaka to Kakumei to Kanehira. If there is a character with sustained identity, it is perhaps Yoshinaka, who ultimately seems to be the individual celebrated here. In this respect, *Kurikara otoshi* differs markedly from the canonical shura nō *Tomoe* 巴 and *Kanehira* 兼平, both of which are only obliquely about Yoshinaka and truly about their title characters.[26] In *Kurikara otoshi*, by contrast, Aoi is *not* a character in the embedded narrative. But she is, significantly, its teller: note again the absence of the *waki* in the second half of the piece. And the *kiri* seems to present the *shite* taking over the *waki*'s role: it is Aoi who prays for the (Taira) dead. Hers cannot be portrayed as a battle death, and she is instead transformed as the play progresses into a character not unlike Tomoe, or, for that matter, Kenreimon'in in the *Kanjō no maki* (灌頂巻 The Initiates' Chapter); she is a memorializer, someone whose storytelling provides the impetus for the recuperation of a sword and the restoration of order.

But what is Aoi is putting to rest with her narrative? If we examine the role of the sword a bit more, some provocative possibilities emerge. The unearthing of the buried sword begins the play, and the final image of the piece suggests reburial. What is figuratively unearthed is the story of Aoi—a woman killed in battle—a story that cannot be told. Her story is then narratively reinterred here under the weight of Yoshinaka's victory. Interestingly, it is the *shite* herself who enacts this retrieval and reburial: she comes for the sword, tells a story that is not her own, and by doing so deflects attention from herself and her potentially transgressive status. These interpretations raise serious questions about the power of narration, an assumption underlying the memorial arts. What does it mean to begin to tell a story if that story cannot be told? And what does it mean to *not* tell one's story, when given the opportunity to do so?

While structural and aesthetic irregularities undoubtedly contribute to the exclusion of *Kurikara otoshi* from the nō canon, the play's

---

92. See also Yamashita, *Ikusa monogatari to Genji shōgun*, 248–58, and Yamashita Hiroaki, *Biwa hōshi no Heike monogatari to nō* (Kōshobō, 2006), 257–61, for discussion of Tomoe's symbolic placatory roles.

26. Yamashita, *Biwa hōshi no Heike monogatari to nō*, 256–57.

quirky nesting of narratives suggest reasons that exceed the thematic inappropriateness we encountered with *Kiso*. *Kurikara otoshi* not only strikes a felicitous tone where it would more suitable to be nostalgic and mournful; it more importantly suggests the kind of story that was increasingly passed over by the canonization process for the nō, and perhaps also more broadly for arts like both *Heike* recitation and nō whose memorial element was very strong.

Like *Kiso*, *Kurikara otoshi* exemplifies dimensions of memorial narrative that were increasingly being extracted from the nō and left to other narrative and dramatic forms, particularly the *kōwakamai* (and later kabuki and bunraku). *Kurikara otoshi* goes a step further. By dismantling the petition that is the centerpiece of the narrative then deflecting the subject from the putative *shite* and dispersing it among a larger cast of characters, *Kurikara otoshi* draws particular attention to the process of exclusion inherent in canonization. The play opens by purporting to tell the story of the recovery of a woman warrior's sword. However, the impossibility of that task within the structural and thematic confines of the nō results in the fragmentation of not only the evidentiary documentary form that gave some alternative shape to *Kiso* but also to the subject herself. Without a sustained identity, she can have no story, as the reburial at the end of the piece symbolically suggests. Underlined in this play is the dynamic process of defining limits, a theme that subtly mirrors the process of creating a canon: the act of canonization deflects, dismantles, and ultimately excludes not simply the generically inappropriate but also the anomalous and explicitly challenging.

8 ～ *Kiso*

IVAN GRAIL

INTRODUCTION

The text of the nō play *Kiso* 木曾,[1] alternatively titled *Kiso no gansho* 木曾願書 ("Kiso's Petition") or *Hanyū* 埴生 (羽生), is largely based on the *Hiuchi gassen* 火打合戦 ("The Battle at Hiuchi") and *Gansho* ("The Petition") episodes of Book Seven of the Kakuichi-bon 覚一本 and the Rufubon 流布本 *Heike* variants.[2] Episodes dealing with the same subject also appear in the Nagato-bon 長門本 *Heike* variant and the *Genpei jōsuiki* 源平盛衰記 as *Genji ikusa haibun no koto* ("The Genji Divides Its Army") and *Shin Hachiman gansho no koto* ("The Petition to the Divine

---

1. Here translated from *Kiso* 木曾 in Sanari Kentarō, ed., *Yōkyoku taikan*, vol. 2 (Meiji shoin, 1930), 815–24. I have also referred to the texts, notes, and commentaries of *Kiso* in Nogami Toyoichirō, ed., *Kaichū yōkyoku zenshū*, vol. 5 (Chūō kōronsha, 1936), 137–44; Kanze Kiyoyuki and Maruoka Katsura, eds., *Kanze-ryū kaitei utaibon*, vol. 43 [*bangai ni*] (Kanze-ryū kaitei kankōkai, 1925); Ōwada Tateki, ed., *Yōkyoku tsūkai: zōho* (Hakubunkan, 1897), vol. 4, 39–43, Nonomura Kaizō, ed., *Yōkyoku nihyakugojū-banshū* (Kyoto: Akao shōbundō, 1978), 422–23, and Nogami Toyoichirō, *Nō nihyakuyonjū-ban: shudai to kōsei* (Nōgaku shorin, 1976), 239.

2. For the Kakuichi-bon, see Takagi Ichinosuke, et al., eds., *Heike monogatari* (ge), NKBT 33 (Iwanami shoten, 1960), 65–72. For these episodes in the Rufubon (where *Gansho* is titled *Kiso no gansho*), see Utsumi Kōzō, ed., *Heike monogatari hyōshaku* (Meiji shoin, 1939), 374–81.

Hachiman").[3] The inclusion of Ikeda no Jirō Tadayasu[4] as the second *tsure* seems to indicate influence from the *Genpei jōsuiki* narrative. When Minamoto no Yoshinaka (源義仲, 1154–1184) asks about the shrine he sees in the distance, the Kakuichi-bon reads: "Lord Kiso summoned **a local guide** … (*Kiso-dono kuni no annaisha o meshite*)."[5] In the *Genpei jōsuiki*, however, a similar passage is rendered: "Kiso summoned **Ikeda no Jirō Tadayasu, a resident of that province** (*Kiso tōgoku no jūnin Ikeda no Jirō Tadayasu o meshite*)."[6]

As a *genzai nō* play, *Kiso* is included in the plays of the fourth group (*yobanmemono*, to use the Tokugawa-period classification system), which tend to involve human beings whose actions are conveyed through dramatic mimesis in the present.[7] It is a one-act play (*ichidangekinō*) that includes a male dance (*otokomai*) performed in a martial style to a swift rhythm by the unmasked *shite*, Kakumei (覚明, dates uncertain), as its primary dance piece. This feature distinguishes *Kiso* from many other *genzai* plays in the fourth group that instead include a mimed fight scene (*kirikumi*) at the dramatic climax. As an extracanonical (*bangai*) play performed only by the Kanze 観世 and Umewaka 梅若 schools, *Kiso* is distinct from *Heike*-inspired plays in the repertoire of currently performed plays (*genkō kyoku* 現行曲) in that it focuses on felicitations for the certainty of victory in battle.

---

3. See Book Thirteen of the Nagato-bon in Kokusho kankōkai, ed., *Heike monogatari Nagato-bon* (Kokusho kankōkai, 1906), 453–56, and Book Twenty-nine of the *Genpei jōsuiki* in Tsukamoto Tetsuzō, ed., *Genpei jōsuiki*, vol. 2 (Yūhōdō shoten, 1929), 114–19. There is a detailed and very useful breakdown of the *Kiso* text and the *Heike* antecedents corresponding to each passage of the text in Kanze and Maruoka, *Kanze-ryū kaitei utaibon*, vol. 43

4. 池田次郎忠康. Beyond his brief appearance in the *Genpei jōsuiki*, Tadayasu's biography is unclear.

5. Takagi et al., *Heike monogatari* (ge), 69. The expression *kuni no annaisha* also appears in this passage in the Rufubon. See Utsumi, *Heike monogatari hyōshaku*, 378. In the Nagato-bon, Yoshinaka summons "a village elder" (*sato no chō*). See Kokusho kankōkai, *Heike monogatari Nagato-bon*, 455.

6. Tsukamoto, *Genpei jōsuiki*, vol. 2, 116.

7. A certain consciousness that the events are being reenacted, however, seems to slip into the *Kiso* text, where Kakumei's actions are described as follows: "Without a semblance of thought, he presently concludes the letter, *as if copying an old document*" [italics added].

Kiso | Translated by Ivan Grail

Fourth-category *genzai* nō in one act.
Performed by the Kanze school.
Time: Second year of Juei (1183), Fifth Month
Place: Encampment at Hanyū in Etchū[1]
Author: Unknown

SHITE	Kakumei
TSURE	Kiso no Yoshinaka
TSURE	Ikeda no Jirō
TSURE	Five or six of Yoshinaka's troops

Kakumei, Yoshinaka, Ikeda, and Troops enter to issei *rhythm and face each other.*

TOGETHER *(issei)*   Myriad and mighty—
the very gods drew "Deer Slayer"[2]—
whenceforth the way of bow and arrow
has been long-lasting.

Yoshinaka faces the audience.

YOSHINAKA *(nanori)*   I am he who is called Kiso Yoshinaka.

Kakumei, Ikeda, and Troops continue to face each other.

KAKUMEI, IKEDA, AND TROOPS
The Heike take the Hiuchi stronghold
in Echizen by storm.[3]

Kiso 木曾. This translation is based on Sanari Kentarō, ed., *Yōkyoku taikan*, vol. 2 (Meiji shoin, 1931), 815–24. For other texts consulted, see footnote 1 of the introduction to this play.

1. Hanyū 埴生 (羽生) in Etchū 越中, now in the city of Oyabe 小矢部 in Ishikawa prefecture.

2. "Deer Slayer" translates *kago* 鹿児. The bow and arrow (*ame no kagoyumi* 天鹿児弓 and *ame no kagoya* 天鹿児, respectively) that Amaterasu Ōmikami 天照大神 bestowed upon Ame no Wakahiko 天若彦 to govern Japan. For a translation of this story in the *Kojiki* (古事記, 712), see Donald L. Philippi, trans., *Kojiki* (Princeton University Press, 1969), 123.

3.   Hiuchi-ga-jō 燧が城 (火打が城). South of Kaga 加賀 and Etchū 越中 provinces (where the subsequent battles were fought) in the eastern part of present-day Fukui 福井 prefecture.

| | With horsemen a hundred thousand strong,
they push us back to Tonami Mountain.[4] |
| YOSHINAKA | Our forces being but some five thousand strong
we must defend ourselves by strategem. |

KAKUMEI, IKEDA, AND TROOPS

Prepare the white banners, great in number,
and stand them on the Kuro Slope.
There, they will instill doubt
in the hearts of our enemies.
Assemble the troops on the mountain.
Once in the darkness of night, attack from both
front and back, pressing the enemy down
into Kurikara Valley.[5]

Yoshinaka faces everyone else.

TOGETHER (*ageuta*)

Making ready, Yoshinaka,
making ready, Yoshinaka
divides his forces into seven units.
His is the prowess of a powerful warrior.[6]
Leading ten thousand horsemen,
at Hanyū he set up camp,
at Hanyū he set up camp.[7]

IKEDA If I may, my Lord. By your command, we erected a great many
white banners on Kuro Slope. When the Heike forces saw this, they
said: "A massive Genji army is heading this way! If we get closed in, it
will be our doom. This is our most advantageous spot." So they took
up position at a place called Saru-no-baba on Tonami Mountain.

YOSHINAKA   This is precisely what I had hoped. The arrow
exchange shall thus begin tomorrow. Take heed and warn our allies
that we will not engage in battle today. Only when night has fallen

---

4. Tonamiyama, here written 礪並山 (砺並山), now 砺波山. In Etchū 越中 at
the present-day western border of Toyama 富山 prefecture.

5. Kurikara-ga-tani 倶利伽羅が谷, on the border of present-day Toyama and
Ishikawa prefectures. In many *Heike* texts, the name Kurikara is written 倶梨迦羅.

6. *Seibyō* 精兵 ("powerful warrior"). From the four-character term *gōkyū-
seibyō* 強弓精兵 which appears frequently and interchangeably with the above
throughout the *Heike* narrative.

7. In Etchū (present-day Toyama), east of Tonami Mountain and Kurikara
Valley.

will we press our attack hard. Bring this message to all fronts.

IKEDA   As you wish.

YOSHINAKA   Ikeda no Jirō!

IKEDA   Before you, my Lord.

YOSHINAKA   To the north, in the summer thicket on that mountain (*looks toward audience*), I can faintly make out a gem-red enclosure and the beveled beams of a shrine. What is the name of that place? What god is worshipped there?

IKEDA   That is the Hachiman Shrine of Hanyū.[8] This land is its domain.

YOSHINAKA   I have unwittingly set up camp in the domain of Hachiman—what an auspicious sign. Kakumei!

KAKUMEI   Before you, my Lord.

Kakumei bows to Yoshinaka. Ikeda returns to his former position.

YOSHINAKA   I wonder if I should offer a petition to Hachiman, both for future generations and, for the present, as a prayer for victory in this battle …

KAKUMEI   As you command, my Lord, presenting a petition would be most suitable.

YOSHINAKA: In that case, draft me a petition.

KAKUMEI   As you wish.

[sings]   Kakumei receives the order.

Kakumei stands up

CHORUS   From out of his quiver,
            from out of his quiver

Kakumei receives a scroll from the assistant at the base square [jōza]

            he takes a small ink-stone and writing paper.
            He grinds the ink and soaks his brush.
            Without a semblance of thought,
            he presently concludes the letter,
            as if copying an old document,
            and reads it loud before his Lord.

Kakumei sits down at the side (wakishōmen) and unrolls the petition.

KAKUMEI   Let me see:
            "I pay homage and make obeisance[9]
            to the Great Bodhisattva Hachiman,

---

8. The present-day Hachiman Shrine in Isurugi-chō 石動町 in Toyama prefecture.

9. *Kimyō chōrai* 帰命頂礼.

who is the original
ruler of the Imperial court of Japan
and the ancestor of the many generations
of illustrious sovereigns.
To guard the treasured throne[10]
and to give divine favor to the commoners,
it is manifest as the three gold-glimmering forms[11]
and its traces are revealed
in the worldly bodies of the three gods.[12]
For many years now, the man called the Taira Chancellor[13]
has held the four seas in the palm of his hand
and has brought suffering and disorder to the masses.
He is a foe of the Buddhist law
and an enemy of the Imperial law.
In the beginning, my great-grandfather,
the former governor of Michinoku,[14]
devoted his name for the clan's worship of Hachiman.
I, though, am an unworthy descendent.
To try now to achieve this awesome feat,[15]

---

10. *Hōso* 宝祚. The imperial throne.

11. Although *sanjin* 三身 usually refers to the three bodies of the Buddha—the dharma body (*hōshin* 法身), the merit body (*hōjin* 報身), and the response/manifest body (*ōjin* 応、化身), with some variations—several editors have suggested that the expression here could refer to the trinity of Amida, Seishi, and Kannon, since they were also the main objects of worship of Hachiman.

12. *Sansho no kenbi* 三所の権扉. Ōjin tennō 応神天皇, Jingū kōgō 神宮皇后, and Tamayorihime 玉依姫. The three divinities (with Ōjin tennō being the most prominent among them) enshrined as Hachiman, corresponding to the Amida trinity as the worldly incarnations of the god(s).

13. *Heishōkoku* 平相国. Taira no Kiyomori (平清盛, 1118–1181).

14. *Sōsofu saki no Michinoku no kami* 曽祖父前の陸奥の守, Minamoto no Yoshiie (源義家, 1039–1106). He changed his name to Hachiman Tarō in service to the god and thus established Hachiman as the tutelary deity of the Minamoto clan.

15. A decision appears to have been made here to abbreviate the petition for (the sake of) performance. Between the phrases "though unworthy" and "as his descendent" is a much longer passage that appears (with slight variations) in several *Heike* variants and that is here conflated. In the Kakuichi-bon, for instance, the passage continuing from *Yoshinaka iyashiku mo* (rendered here as: "I, though unworthy") reads **Yoshinaka iyashiku mo** *kyūba no ie ni umarete, wazuka ni kikyū no chiri o tsugu*. "**Though humble**, I spring from warrior stock; though inadequate, I pursue my father's calling." Helen Craig McCullough, trans., *The Tale of the Heike*

is like a baby using half a gourd to measure the ocean,
or like a praying mantis
taking an axe to confront a mighty carriage.
However, I will do this solely for the sovereign and
    the state.
I prostrate myself and speak my wishes.
Send down a sign that my words have been heeded.
Secure my victory and make the enemy retreat
in the four directions.
          Second year of Juei, Fifth Month."[16]

Kakumei finishes reading the letter and bows.

CHORUS   Everyone, from Lord Kiso
                through the ranks of his troops,
                praised Kakumei from where they sat,
                saying he was truly accomplished
                in both brush and bow.

YOSHINAKA   Yoshinaka takes out a top arrow[17] and says:

Takes an arrow from the quiver on his back.

CHORUS   Take this with the petition
                and make a dedication at the main hall of the shrine.[18]
                Receiving the arrow, Kakumei holds it up

(Stanford University Press, 1988), 229. The passage continues with an explanation of his military strategies and with more praise for Hachiman, until finally it arrives at the phrase that appears next in the nō text of *Kiso* and is translated here as: "as his descendent" (*kōin to shite*). The line from the Kakuichi-bon reads *Yoshinaka sono* **kōin to shite** *kubi o katamukete toshi hisashi* ("Many years have passed since I first bowed my head before the god **as one of their number**"). McCullough, *Tale of the Heike*, 230. The *Kiso* text and the Kakuichi-bon petition then flow back together, with (*Kiso*), "... to try now to achieve this awesome feat ..." (*kono taikō o okosu koto*). The only difference here is the inclusion of *ima* ("now," which has been included in the translation of the *Kiso* passage) in the Kakuichi-bon. Although this omission slightly garbles the text and makes the translation problematic, the overall meaning of the petition is unchanged.

16. The Kakuichi-bon, Rufubon, and the *Genpei jōsuiki* all record the same date but with the eleventh day included. The Nagato-bon, however, has the date of this petition as the first day of the Sixth Month. See Kokusho kankōkai, *Heike monogatari Nagato-bon*, 456.

17. *Uwazashi* 上差. An extra humming-bulb arrow (*kaburaya* 鏑矢) attached to the side of a full quiver. See Sanari, *Yōkyoku taikan*, vol. 2, 823.

18. *Naijin* 内陣, where the main image of worship of the shrine was kept.

and stands before his Lord.
With solemn dignity,
he takes it to the Hachiman Shrine,
he takes it to the Hachiman Shrine.

Kakumei comes before Yoshinaka, accepts the arrow, fixes it to the letter, and settles down at the stage assistant position (kōkenza) as if praying to Hachiman.

KAKUMEI   If I may, my Lord, the petition and top arrow have been dedicated to the Hachiman Shrine. Now, farmers from this estate have come to wish your army luck in battle. They offer food and wine.

YOSHINAKA   Never has there been anything so auspicious. My army's victory is secured. Well then, they should wish us luck in battle. Kakumei, serve the wine!

KAKUMEI   As you wish.
In the divine winds
blowing through Hachiman Shrine—

While singing, Kakumei opens his fan, pours wine for Yoshinaka, and returns to his former position.

CHORUS   the enemy will scatter—as falling leaves.
YOSHINAKA   Kakumei, dance me a number!
KAKUMEI   As you wish.
CHORUS   The enemy will scatter as falling leaves.

Kakumei opens his fan.

(DANCE: *otokomai*)

CHORUS   In the midst of our drinking revel,
in the midst of our drinking revel,
a wonder appears from Hachiman.

Kakumei looks up, facing the audience.

Wild doves come a-flying wing-to-wing
like the fluttering white banner of our clan!
A sign that the petition has been acknowledged.
Everyone from Lord Kiso

Everyone bows facing the audience

down through the ranks of his troops
together prostrate themselves
as they pray fervently for divine protection.

Now is the time

Kakumei stands and dances

to drive the great forces of the Heike
down into Kurikara Valley and achieve
a decisive victory in this single battle—
all because of the divine powers of Hachiman!

*At the base square (jōza), Kakumei stamps the final beat (tomebyōshi)
and bows to Yoshinaka. Yoshinaka exits the stage followed by the others in
order.*

9 ～ *Kurikara otoshi* (The Fall from Kurikara) | MICHAEL WATSON

INTRODUCTION

In this play, a chance discovery of a sword in the fields near the old battleground causes a woman to be possessed by a spirit of someone who died fighting in that place. The spirit reveals herself to be a woman named Aoi no mae 葵の前, a female general in the Genji army commanded by Kiso no Yoshinaka, who was victorious at the battle of Kurikara.[1]

In the familiar Kakuichi version of *Heike monogatari*, Yoshinaka has just one female general (*onna musha* 女武者), the beautiful Tomoe Gozen 巴御前. Tomoe makes a brief but memorable appearance in Chapter Nine in the episode in which Yoshinaka himself dies.[2] In Genpei jōsuiki 源平盛衰記, a longer version of the narrative for reading, Tomoe is described as leading one thousand riders into battle at Kurikara.[3] The

---

I would like to express my gratitude to William Bodiford and Yamanaka Reiko for their help in understanding the final part of this piece. For further information about narrative and historical background to this play, see Chapters 7 and 8 in this volume.

1. The battle took place on 1183.5.11. Kiso no Yoshinaka 木曾義仲 died in the First Month of the following year.

2. "Kiso no saigo" 木曾最期 (Kakuichi-bon 9.4, "The Death of Kiso"). This episode mentions the name of another of Yoshinaka's female companions, Yamabuki 山吹. Unlike Tomoe, she is not described as female warrior. Ichiko Teiji, ed., *Heike monogatari* (ge), SNKZ 46 (Shōgakukan 1994), 175; Helen Craig McCullough, trans., *The Tale of the Heike* (Stanford University Press, 1988), 291.

3. Mizuhara Hajime, ed., *Shintei Genpei jōsuiki*, vol. 4 (Shin jinbutsu ōraisha, 1990), 65, 72 (巴女一千余騎 *Tomoe-jo issen yoki*).

Nagato version also describes Tomoe fighting at Kurikara[4] but there is no mention of a similar role played by Aoi 葵 at that battle or elsewhere. She appears only in *Genpei jōsuiki*, where we are told:

木曽殿には、葵、巴とて二人の女将軍
あり。葵は去年の春礪並山の合戦に
討れぬ、巴はいまだありと聞く。

Lord Kiso had two female generals, Aoi
and Tomoe. Aoi was killed in the battle of
Tonamiyama, but Tomoe is still alive as I hear.[5]

Nothing more is mentioned in the narrative about Aoi.[6] Other written or oral traditions may have circulated about Aoi, but the versions of the plays seem only to have used information that could be gleaned from the account of the battle in *Heike* versions.

Kiso no Yoshinaka's victory over the Heike army at Mount Tonami is described in all major *Heike* variants.[7] Mount Tonami is the modern *Tonami yama* 砺波山 in Toyama prefecture, close to the western border of Ishikawa prefecture. Although its highest point is just 277 meters above

---

4. Kokusho kankōkai, ed., *Heike monogatari Nagato-bon* (Kokusho kankōkai, 1906), 454.

5. Mizuhara Hajime, ed., *Shintei Genpei jōsuiki*, vol. 4 (Shin jinbutsu ōraisha, 1991), 308. This comes from the episode "Tomoe goes down to the Kantō" (*Tomoe Kantō gekō no koto* 巴関東下向事), which describes Tomoe's parting with Kiso no Yoshinaka just before his death at Awazu, and generally corresponds with Kakuichi-bon section 9.4, "The Death of Kiso," Ichiko, *Heike monogatari* (ge), 175–79.

6. Obviously, Aoi no mae can have no possible connection with the character known by the sobriquet Aoi no ue in *Genji monogatari*. It is perhaps worth noting that she shares a name with another character in *Heike monogatari*, a servant girl in the palace who is loved by Emperor Takakura. Kakuichi-bon 6.3 "Aoi no mae." Ichiko Teiji, ed., *Heike monogatari* (jō), SKBZ 45 (Shōgakukan, 1994), 428–30; McCullough, *Tale of the Heike*, 200–1. This could be the derivation of her name, but it may be more significant that Aoi is a flower name, like Yamabuki ("Japanese rose"), mentioned as Tomoe's female companion in the Kakuichi version.

7. The name Tonami appears in various forms, including 砥浪山 (Kakuichi-bon *Heike monogatari*, 7.4–7.6), 砥波山 (Nagato-bon *Heike monogatari*, Book 13), and 礪並山 (*Genpei jōsuiki*, Book 29). Ichiko, *Heike monogatari* (ge), 27; Kokusho kankōkai, ed., *Heike monogatari Nagato-bon* (Kokusho kankōkai, 1906), 455; Mizuhara, *Shintei Genpei jōsuiki*, vol. 4, 70.

sea level, the sides of the valley are very steep.[8] The Kurikara of the title is a valley lying some five hundred meters to the east of the peak, just over the prefectural border with Ishikawa. Modern maps show the place names Kurikara 倶利伽羅, the "old battle-field" of Saru-ga-baba 猿ヶ馬場, and two "grave mounds" Aoi-zuka 葵塚 and Tomoe-zuka 巴塚. A visit to the area in August 2005 revealed that the "graves" were in fact memorial markers, well posted with signs erected by the local education committee, displaying informative notices. Although the markers do not appear old, the survival of the names Aoi-zuka and Tomoe-zuka suggests that a local tradition has kept alive the memory of the two women warriors who—according to some versions, at least—fought alongside Kiso Yoshinaka.[9]

The main text used for this translation is *Kurikara otoshi* 倶利伽羅落, edited by Haga Yaichi and Sasaki Nobutsuna.[10] Reference has been made to a variant text known as *Tachibori* 太刀堀 ("The Unearthed Sword") edited by Tanaka Makoto.[11] As the texts of *Kurikara otoshi* and *Tachibori* diverge considerably at many points, it is not feasible to note more than a few differences below. Passages from *Tachibori* have been cited in the footnotes either because they are of intrinsic interest or because they help to elucidate obscure passages in *Kurikara otoshi*. Tanaka's critical edition not only gives textual variants from manuscripts and woodblock editions, but also includes musical and structural indications like *kakaru* and *kuse* lacking in Haga and Sasaki's edition. Such terms have been romanized and added where appropriate below. Stage directions are absent from both editions. The opening exchanges between *waki* and *tsure* read very abruptly unless we mentally insert pauses for the changes of location from Hasunuma's residence to Mount Tonami and back again. Triple asterisks have been added at these points.

---

8. The major modern road through the area, National Highway 8, goes under the mountain in a series of tunnels, called, predictably perhaps, "Genpei Tunnel" 源平トンネル.

9. Photographs of the stone memorials with the names of Tomoe and Aoi can be seen on web guide to ancient sites related to nō in the Hokuriku prefectures (*Hokuriku sanken no yōkyoku koseki annai* 北陸三県の謡曲古跡案内, www. tvk.ne.jp/~mugiya/gosei.htm). Accessed January 11, 2011.

10. Haga Yaichi and Sasaki Nobutsuna, eds., *Kōchū yōkyoku sōsho*, vol. 1 (Hakubunkan, 1914), 642–46.

11. Tanaka Makoto, ed., *Mikan yōkyokushū*, vol. 20 (Koten bunko, 1972), 92–97.

Kurikara otoshi (The Fall from Kurikara)

| TRANSLATED BY MICHAEL WATSON

No longer in the performance repertoire.
Time: Some years after the end of the Genpei War
Place: Etchū province, near Mount Tonami
Author: uncertain

WAKI	Hasunuma, a resident of Etchū province
MAEJITE	Lady Akone, later possessed by spirit of Aoi
NOCHIJITE	Spirit of female-warrior Aoi
TSURE	A man in the service of Hasunuma

HASUNUMA   I am Hasunuma Such-and-such from the province of Etchū.[1] I have recently had a prophetic dream[2] and so I am going to have a new field made on Mount Tonami.[3] Today I plan to arrange for this to be done. Is anyone there?

MAN   At your command.[4]

Kurikara otoshi 倶利伽羅落. This translation is based on Haga Yaichi and Sasaki Nobutsuna, eds., *Kōchū yōkyoku sōsho*, vol. 1 (Rinsen shoten, 1986), 642–46. As explained in the preceding essay, reference has been made to a variant text known as *Tachibori* 太刀堀 ("The Unearthed Sword"). Tanaka Makoto, ed., *Mikan yōkyokushū*, vol. 20 (Koten bunko, 1972), 92–97. Both versions are *mūgen* nō. *Bangai* nō are not conventionally assigned to one of the five categories, but in terms of content, this play might be considered a "mad woman" play (fourth category).

1. Hasunuma's personal name is not given. He himself uses the expression Hasunuma no nanigashi 蓮沼の何がし [i.e., 何謀], Hasunuma Such-and-such. A place name in the city of Oyabe 小矢部 in modern Toyama prefecture, formally Etchū 越中 province, Hasunuma is a site of the ruins of a medieval fortress Hasunuma-jō 蓮沼城 and lies about ten kilometers to the west of Mount Tonami.

2. *Kidoku naru yume* 奇特なる夢. There is no mention of this in the play *Tachibori*, where Hasunuma says instead that it is an "auspicious day" (吉日) to clear fields. Tanaka, *Mikan yōkyokushū*, vol. 20, 92.

3. The term *hatake wo hiraku* presumably means clearing previously uncultivated land for agricultural purposes.

4. In the edition of *Tachibori*, the following dialogue is abbreviated. Tanaka,

HASUNUMA Tell everyone to go and make the new field today.

MAN As you command. Everyone will leave early this morning. This is what they will be told.

MAN Listen, now. The master wants all of you to go out and clear the fields.

***

What is this here? A fine sword! How extraordinary. I must bring it at once to show the Master.

***

My Lord! As we were clearing the field, we dug up a sword.

HASUNUMA This is indeed a fine sword. I shall make it one of the treasures of my house.

MAN It is truly a remarkable find.

***

What shall I say?[5] Lady Akone[6] has suddenly gone mad, and says that the sword must be returned. How strange this is! I must report the matter at once. My Lord! People have just told me that Lady Akone who serves here has gone mad and is saying that the sword should be returned.

HASUNUMA It is strange for her to say this. Bring her here to me.[7]

MAN At your command.

[*To others.*] You there! Tell them to bring this Lady Akone here.

Mikan yōkyokushū, vol. 20, 92. The *tsure* appears only later, and in a different role, as a spirit accompanying the *shite*.

5. *Nan to mōsu zo*. Or perhaps, "How shall I put this?"

6. *Akone-no-mae* あこねの前. In the late fifteenth-century play *Niwatori Tatsuta* 鶏龍田, a woman by this name is possessed by the spirit of a rooster stolen by her husband from Tatsuta Shrine. Haga Yaichi and Sasaki Nobutsuna, eds., *Kōchū yōkyoku sōsho*, vol. 3 (Rinsen shoten, 1987), 51–54.

7. In *Tachibori*, the *waki* says that Akone must not be allowed out on the street (*rotō e idete wa kanaumaji* 路頭へ出ては叶まじ) and orders his men to take her into custody (*ori* 檻). Tanaka, *Mikan yōkyokushū*, vol. 20, 93.

AOI[8]	*sashi-koe*	Now when the Heike had taken Hiuchi fortress in Echizen[9] and advanced as far as this mountain, Tonamiyama, why did our warriors[10] not go forth and scatter them?
	kakaru	Our warriors waited in the presence of their leader.[11] What then did Imai no Shirō do?[12]
CHORUS		With six thousand riders he opposed the enemy forces.
AOI		Higuchi no Jirō,[13]
CHORUS		*Ta te ne nu i a u hi to mo e mo* [= Tate Nenoi Aoi Tomoe][14]

---

8. As we learn later, the *shite* has been possessed by the spirit of *Aoi no mae* 葵の前, a female warrior who fought on the side of the Genji army of Kiso no Yoshinaka 木曽義仲, see the introduction above.

9. *Hiuchi ga jō* 燧が城 in Echizen 越前 province. This event is described in *Heike monogatari*, Kakuichi-bon 7.4 "Hiuchi gassen" (The Battle of Hiuchi). The ruins of Hiuchi fortress are located somewhat more than 100 km south of Tonamiyama, in present-day Imajō, Nanjō-gun, Fukui prefecture (福井県南条郡今庄町).

10. *Mikata no tsuwadomo*. More literally, "the allied warriors."

11. The term *onmae* points to their leader, Kiso no Yoshinaka, who is not yet named.

12. Imai no Shirō Kanehira 今井四郎兼平, Kiso's milk-brother (*menotogo* 乳母子) and closest retainer. According to Kakuichi-bon *Heike*, the Genji forces were divided. Kanehira leads a force of 6,000 to a position to the west of Tonamiyama, his brother Kanemitsu leads a force of 7,000 to a position east of the mountain, while Kiso makes camp near Hanyū to the north of the mountain. Kakuichi-bon 7.4 ("Hiuchi gassen"), Ichiko Teiji, ed., *Heike monogatari* (ge), SNKZ 46 (Shōgakukan 1994), 27–28; Helen Craig McCullough, trans., *The Tale of the Heike* (Stanford University Press, 1988), 228.

13. Higuchi no Jirō Kanemitsu 樋口次郎兼光, Kanehira's older brother.

14. たてね縫（ぬ）ひ逢ふ紐巴（ひもともゑ）も. At first sight, this looks as if it should be divided *tatene nui-au himo Tomoe*. This clearly ends in a reference to the famous woman warrior Tomoe, Kiso's mistress, and (according to some traditions) sister to Kanehira and Kanemitsu. However, the context suggests that more of Kiso's warriors are listed here. The opening is surely not to be read *tatene* but *Tate*, a reference to Tate no Rokurō Chikatada 楯の六郎親忠, a close retainer of Kiso's. The expression *nui au himo* appears to mean "a thread sewn together" but this may either be decorative wordplay or a corruption of *Nenui* for Nenoi no Koyata 根井の小弥太／祢の井の小野太 and *Aui mo* for *Aoi mo*, a reference to Aoi 葵. As explained in the introduction to this translation, only *Genpei jōsuiki* mentions the existence of this woman in Kiso's entourage. The name Nenoi completes the list of "the famous Four Heavenly Kings in Lord Kiso's service— Imai, Higuchi, Tate, and Nenoi" 木曽殿の御内に四天王ときこゆる今井、樋口、楯、根井, Kakuichi-bon 9.1 "Ikezuki no sata," Ichiko, *Heike monogatari*

AOI	women warriors—
CHORUS	are such as these to be found elsewhere?
	I do not know—white bows of *mayumi*, [15]
AOI	arrows, lined up together, their battle cries
CHORUS	making a sound like autumn storms.
HASUNUMA	What a strange sight! You there! Are you in someone's
service?[16]	
AOI	I am. I am one who once served a great general.
HASUNUMA	Served a great general, you say.
	Are you then one of Raikō's Four Heavenly Companions? [17]
AOI	I am neither Sadamitsu nor Suetake.[18]
HASUNUMA	Tsuna or Kintoki then?[19]

(ge), 163; McCullough, *Tale of the Heike*, 285. These readings are confirmed by the corresponding passage in *Tachibori*, where the *shite* sings だてねのゐ and the *tsure* continues with あふひも巴も. The Genroku-period edition of five hundred nō texts (*Gohyakubanbon* 五百番本) uses the characters 伊達 for Date (=Tate) and 根の井 for Nenoi. Tanaka, *Mikan yōkyokushū*, vol. 20, 93. The voiced form Date is not surprising. Other names are seen in unvoiced and voiced forms, cf. the name 土肥 Toi/Doi for the famous Minamoto partisan Doi Sanehira.

15. The usual pun on *shira-* "white" and *shira(nu)* "(I) do not know." *Mayumi* (檀) is the name of a tree whose wood was used to make bows, but also contains the word *yumi* "bow," linking this line with the following (*ya nami-tsukurō*, "arrows lined up").

16. In *Tachibori*, the *waki*'s question is less specific: *ika naru mono no tachi-yorite aru zo*. It is the *shite* who announces: "I am one who served a general of old" (*kore wa inishie taishō ni tsukae-mōshishi mono nite*). Tanaka, *Mikan yōkyokushū*, vol. 20, 93.

17. Minamoto no Raikō Yasumasa 源頼光保昌 (936–1021), famous for his victory over the "earth spider" (*tsuchigumo*). Raikō's exploits are described in the "Tsurugi no maki" 剣巻 ("Sword Scroll") of the Yashiro-bon *Heike monogatari* and *Genpei jōsuiki*. Asahara Yoshiko et al., *Yashiro-bon Takano-bon taishō Heike monogatari*, vol. 3 (Shintensha, 1993), 517–23. He features also in the canonical nō plays *Ōeyama* 大江山, *Rashōmon* 羅生門, and *Tsuchigumo* 土蜘蛛. Like Kiso and other figures in Japanese history, Raikō was associated with four warriors, known as *shitennō* 四天王 ("Four Heavenly Kings"). This was originally a Buddhist term for four protective divinities (Jikokuten, Zōjōten, Kōmokuten, and Tamonten) often depicted in sculpture as figures in warrior garb around the four sides of a temple altar or a central sculpture.

18. Usui no Sadamitsu 碓井貞光, Urabe no Suetake 卜部季武. Raikō's retainers.

19. Watanabe Tsuna 渡辺綱, Sakata Kintoki 坂田金時 (公時) Raikō's retainers. They are listed together with the other two *shitennō* in the "Tsurugi no maki" 剣巻. Asahara et al., *Yashiro-bon Takano-bon taishō Heike monogatari*, vol. 3, 518.

AOI (*kakaru*) Not them, either.

HASUNUMA   Then are you a retainer of the Heike?

AOI   My enemies! Do you wish to anger me? I am a retainer of the Genji.

HASUNUMA   Then are you one of Yoritomo's men?

AOI   There are so many warriors. Name the one you mean.

HASUNUMA   Perhaps a retainer of the Lieutenant [Yoshitsune].[20]

AOI   I am not thinking of [21] Suzuki, Kataoka, Mashio, Kanefusa, Benkei or any of the others.[22]

HASUNUMA   So then, one of Kiso's men?

AOI   If so, say who you mean.

HASUNUMA   Imai no Shirō?

AOI (*kakaru*) Not him.

HASUNUMA   Higuchi no Jirō?

AOI   Him neither.

HASUNUMA   Now it's come to me. One of women warriors, Aoi or Tomoe?

---

20. Yoshitsune is referred to by his common appellation *Hōgan* 判官, sometimes translated "Police Lieutenant." By contrast, Yoritomo was referred to by personal name earlier, rather than as his more usual appellation (*saki no) hyōe no suke* (前) 兵衛佐, (the Former) Assistant Guards Commander.

21. *Omoi no yorazu*: more literally, perhaps, "This is unexpected."

22. The list in *Tachibori* begins with Kamei 亀井 rather than Suzuki, but is otherwise identical. Apart from the inclusion of Benkei, the lists are surprising, omitting the names of Yoshitsune's men who are most frequently mentioned in *Heike* variants such as Ise no Saburō Yoshimori, Eda Genzō, Kumai Tarō, and the Satō brothers Tsuginobu and Tadanobu. For a typical list see Kakuichi-bon 9.7 "Mikusa seizoroe." Ichiko, *Heike monogatari* (ge), 196–97; McCullough *Tale of the Heike*, 300–1. (Note that allied warriors are named first, personal retainers last.) The corresponding list in *Genpei jōsuiki* bears more resemblance to the two nō plays: 片岡八郎為春、備前四郎、鈴木三郎重家、亀井六郎重清、武蔵坊弁慶等を始として ("Kataoka Hachirō Tameharu, Bizen Shirō, Suzuki Saburō Shigeie, Kamei Rokurō Shigekiyo, Musashibō Benkei and others." Book 36, "Genji seizoroi no koto," Mizuhara Hajime, ed., *Shintei Genpei jōsuiki*, vol. 5 (Shin jinbutsu ōraisha, 1991), 33. A different Kataoka connected to Yoshitsune is mentioned twice in the Kakuichi variant (Kataoka no Gorō Tsuneharu 片岡五郎経春, Kakuichi-bon 9.7 and 11.11, McCullough, *Tale of the Heike*, 301, 383). This leaves only Mashio 増尾 unexplained. The name is possibly a corruption of Washio (Yoshihisa) 鷲尾 (義久), the name of the hunter's son at Hiyodorigoe who is taken by Yoshitsune into his entourage, serving him loyally until Yoshitsune's death in Ōshū. Ichiko, *Heike monogatari* (ge), 204 (Kakuichi-bon 9.9 "Rōba"); McCullough, *Tale of the Heike*, 305.

AOI   (*kakaru*) I am abashed, for women …
HASUNUMA   … blush, the Aoi flower in bloom … the Aoi flower in
   bloom.[23]
AOI   Though aged in years, I do not hide the name of the two
       flowers. Abashed, I shall depart. Ah, abashed, I shall depart.
HASUNUMA   So, you are Lady Aoi. I shall return the sword to you. If I
   do so, please tell us the story of the ancient battle at this mountain. I
   shall pray for your soul.[24]
AOI   (*sashi*)   My master, Lord Kiso,
           led fifty thousand some riders
           to this mountain, Tonamiyama,
           and made camp in the wood to the north.
CHORUS   A force of one hundred thousand and more Heike riders
           spread out like clouds or mist.
           The Genji were here—
AOI   And the Heike were over there.
           The two opposing camps,
           dragon and tiger in menacing display,
           like lions in combat,[25]
           or Taishaku battling with *aśura*.[26]

───────────

   23. *Iro ni izuru ka aoigusa, aoigusa.* The use of *ka* here is puzzling. Perhaps "Are
you Aoi / the Aoi flower, in full color?" The very similar expression appears in the
play *Genji kuyō* 源氏供養 where the *shite* Murasaki Shikibu identifies herself
by mentioning *murasaki*: 恥かしや　色に出づるか紫の. Itō Masayoshi,
Yōkyokushū (chū), SNKS (Shinchōsha, 1986), 54; Janet Goff, *Noh Drama and The
Tale of Genji: The Art of Allusion in Fifteen Classical Plays* (Princeton University
Press, 1991) 204. ("How ashamed I am. / Is it apparent from the color?"). Here the
waki guesses her identity. In *Tachibori*, the line is sung by the *shite*, a more typical
form of self-revelation. Tanaka, *Mikan yōkyokushū*, vol. 20, 94.
   24. "Lord Kiso had two female generals, Aoi and Tomoe. Aoi was killed in the
battle of Tonamiyama, but Tomoe is still alive as I hear." Mizuhara, *Shintei Genpei
jōsuiki*, vol. 4, 308. Not only is Aoi's death not mentioned in the description of the
battle in book 28, but her name does not appear at any other point in extant texts
of *Genpei jōsuiki*. As mentioned in the introduction, memorials (*tsuka* 塚) for Aoi
and Tomoe can be visited today.
   25. 獅子争の勢 *shishi sō no ikioi.* In *Tachibori*, the base text has ししざ
うのいきほひ *shishi zō no ikioi*, with the Shimomura manuscript using the
characters 獅子象. This gives the meaning "the force of lion(s) and elephant(s)."
   26. The superhuman battles with Titans (Skt. *aśura*, Jp. *ashura* 阿修羅) are
frequently described in *mugen* nō 夢幻能 of the second category, *shuramono* 修
羅物, which depict the sufferings of the spirits of warriors. Another example is

	One of the forces played for time—[27]
CHORUS	Our side. We first made sure to delay
	that the battle might be held on the morn.

The enemy understood this to be true
and both armies made camp for the night.
Meanwhile on our side the question of how
a small force could possible destroy a large one
was the subject of our deliberations when—
looking out from Lord Kiso's camp
toward the east—we could faintly make out
the red sacred fence
and roughly cut roof of a shrine
in the shade of the mountain's dense green foliage—
it was the middle of the Fifth Month of the
second year of Juei.[28]
We learned it was a shrine called Hanyū
dedicated to the Great Bodhisattva Hachiman
the guardian divinity of this clan.[29]
  Lord Kiso was much encouraged, thinking
"This means our army is sure to win!"
Hurrying to the shrine.
to write a petition, he summoned
Kakumei, who obeyed his command,
removing his helmet and tying it to the
    shoulder-cord.
From his armor[30] he brought out a piece of paper,
dipped with ink a brush

---

found in *Shunzei Tadanori*, translated in this volume.

27. *Heike* variants describe how Kiso ensured that only skirmishes were held, leading the Heike to believe that the main combat would occur on the following day. The translation is only a guess and unsatisfactory. The text reads *tsuki hi wo torubeki ikioi ari*, with the variant *ikioitari* in *Tachibori*. Tanaka, *Mikan yōkyokushū*, vol. 20, 95. *Tsukihi* can sometimes refer to the passing of time generally, but strictly speaking it means the passing of days and months.

28. The year 1183. The growth of foliage is at its height in the Fifth Month, during the summer rainy season.

29. Hachiman Daibosatsu 八幡大菩薩 was the guardian divinity of the Genji.

30. More literally, "from the armhole of his armor," like Tadanori when he takes out a scroll of his poetry. "Tadanori miyako ochi" (Kakuichi-bon 7.16). Ichiko, *Heike monogatari* (ge), 76; McCullough, *Tale of the Heike*, 247.

from the writing case in his quiver,
wrote the petition and read it aloud.

(kuse)   This Kakumei was formerly a monk
of the Southern Capital,
trained in the different teachings[31] of the Hossō sect
and learned in matters Japanese and Chinese
He wrote the petition fluently[32] and read it aloud.
Greatly pleased, Lord Kiso ordered
a humming-bulb arrow be presented to the shrine,
and each of the warriors serving him
gave the shrine one top humming-bulb arrow.
"Hail to Great Bodhisattva Hachiman.
We pray to you with heads touching the ground,"[33]
they prayed.

Meanwhile, when night had come,
so that the foe might think
their numbers were great
they brought together a thousand oxen,
lit torches on all their horns,[34]
and drove them so that the light
filled the clouds and sky.
It was the Fifth Month[35]
dark and cloudy
in the pitch-black night
but when stars gathered undimmed[36]

---

31. *Shogaku* 諸学. Some *Tachibori* manuscripts read *shūgaku* 修学, "training."

32. *Mizu wo nagasu gotoku ni*, "as water flows."

33. *Namu kimyō chōhai Hachiman Daibosatsu* 南無帰命頂礼.

34. This incident is described in *Genpei jōsuiki*, Book 29, "Tonamiyama gassen no koto," where the number of oxen is given as "four or five hundred." Mizuhara, *Shintei Genpei jōsuiki*, vol. 4, 72.

35. *Satsuki.* The second mention of this month in the rainy season. *Heike* variants emphasize how dark the night was. "As is typical for the Fifth Month, the moonlight shone hazily in the sky, so that the Genji and Heike could hardly make each other out on the dark and narrow roads under the trees on the summer mountainside" 五月の空の癖なれば、朧に照す月影、夏山の木下暗き細道に、源平互に見え分ず. *Genpei jōsuiki*, Book 29, "Tonamiyama gassen no koto" ("The Matter of the Battle of Tonamiyama"). Mizuhara, *Shintei Genpei jōsuiki*, vol. 4, 71.

36. *Kurakaranu hoshi wo atsumureba.*

the enemy imagined a great force
and dared not attack.
Imai no Shirō with six thousand or more riders

AOI   from the frontal force[37] shouted a battle cry
CHORUS   while fifty thousand riders in the forest behind
raised their voices in the same battle cry.
The enemy warriors fled, taking nothing with them[38]
and plunged straight into Kurikara Valley.
Horses fell on men,
men on horses,
piling up, piling up, on top of one another[39]
as more than seventy thousand riders
plunged into Kurikara,
filled in the valley depths,
making it shallow.

kiri   It is for this that I pray
in truth, for the world hereafter.[40]
Piling up sand to make a stupa,[41]
carefully polishing the golden skin of the Buddha

---

37. *Ōte* 追手, literally "pursuit force." The term is used in *Genpei jōsuiki* where the Kakuichi variant uses *ōte* 大手 (regularly translated as "frontal assault force" by McCullough). The two terms are synonymous.

38. *Toru mono mo toriaezu*, a conventional phrase for such incidents, cf. "Fujigawa" (Kakuichi-bon 5.11) and "Dasaifu ochi" (8.4). Ichiko, *Heike monogatari* (jō), 403; (ge), 118. McCullough, *Tale of the Heike*, 190, 265.

39. The phrase *ochi kasanari* is repeated.

40. It would seem as if Aoi were praying as much for the salvation of the enemy warriors who died at Kurikara as for her own rebirth. However, as Reiko Yamanaka pointed out to me, the *kiri* passage is almost identical to the concluding lines of *Sotoba Komachi* 卒都婆小町. Itō Masayoshi, *Yōkyokushū* (ge), SNKS (Shinchō, 1986), 260.

41. The image of the warriors' bodies piling as they fall (*ochi kasanari*) suggests the image of sand piled up to make a stupa or pagoda (*isago wo tō to kasanete*). This recalls an idea expressed in several sutras, including the Lotus Sutra, Book Two (*Hōbenron*, Expedient Devices): 若曠野中　積土成仏廟　乃至童子戲 聚砂為仏塔. Tamura Yoshihiro and Fujii Kyōkō, *Hokekyō* (Daizō shuppan, 1988), vol. 1, 166. "Or there are those who in open fields, / Heaping up earth, make Buddha-shrines / There are even children who at play / Gather sand to make Buddha-stūpas. / Persons like these / Have all achieved the Buddha Path." Leon Hurvitz, *Scripture of the Lotus Blossom of the Fine Dharma* (Columbia University Press, 1976), 38–39.

presenting flowers of offering[42]
that we might enter the path of awakening,
the path of awakening.

---

42. For translations of the almost identical ending of *Sotoba Komachi* see Royall Tyler, trans., "Komachi on the Gravepost," *Granny Mountains: A Second Cycle of Nō Plays* (Ithaca, NY: Cornell East Asia Series, 1978), 116; Herschel Miller, trans., "Stupa Komachi," in Haruo Shirane, *Traditional Japanese Literature* (Columbia University Press, 2007), 952. The ultimate source may again be the Lotus Sutra, in passages like the following: "If any persons, in stūpas and mausoleums, / To jeweled images and painted images / With flowered and perfumed banners and canopies / And with deferential thoughts make offerings"; "If anyone, even with distracted thought, / And with so much as a single flower, / Makes offering to a painted image, / He shall at length see numberless Buddhas." Hurvitz, *Scripture of the Lotus Blossom*, 40.

10 ᠕ *Sanemori*: Departure from Oral Narrative | Akiko Takeuchi

In *Sando* 三道 (Three Elements in Composing a Play), Zeami instructed that any warrior play based on a character from *The Tale of the Heike* should be faithful to its source. However, as is well known, his own warrior plays often slightly deviate from the *Heike*. In addition, there is a fundamental change that ensues from the adaptation of a story from one theatrical genre (oral storytelling) to another (nō drama): while in oral storytelling, characters' speech and acts are presented through the mediation of a narrator, in nō, narration recedes, and the distinction between narration and characters' speech is often ambiguous. From a narratological perspective, such attenuated narration is the most distinctive trait of nō drama, one which distinguishes it from oral storytelling.

This chapter examines the extent and effect of this peculiar characteristic of narration as it applies in the case of *Sanemori* 実盛, a warrior play by Zeami, which is often said to be more faithful to the *Heike* than any other nō play.[1] I will first outline the differences between oral narration performance (*katari-gei* 語り芸) and nō theater from the viewpoint of narratology as well as theater semiotics.[2] Then, applying this framework, I will examine *Sanemori*, especially its second act. This act, more than three-fourths of which consists of citations taken almost verbatim from the *Heike*, continues to draw the attention of scholars

---

1. For example, see Amano Fumio, "'Heike no monogatari no mama' to iu koto: *Sanemori* wo megutte," *Kokuritsu nōgakudō* 45 (May 1987), 28–29.

2. As space is limited, I have concentrated on presenting a general theoretical framework for making comparisons between nō and oral storytelling in terms of narrative structure, without offering a full argument on the subtlety and complexity of narration in nō.

for its narratological peculiarities, such as a nonchronological order of events and a certain confusion surrounding the role of the *shite* who plays Sanemori's ghost.

For the present argument, the distinction between primary and secondary narrations is especially useful.[3] In the *Heike* chapter "Sanemori" (Kakuichi-bon 7.8), for example, Tezuka Tarō 手塚太郎 reports to Kiso Yoshinaka 木曽義仲 his battlefield clash with Sanemori. Here, the narration that describes the interactions between Kiso and Tezuka is primary; Tezuka's retelling of the clash is secondary narration. In other words, secondary narration is a narration embedded within a primary narration, and one which is not introduced by any other narration. In nō drama, secondary narration is typical for a ghost's retelling of its own past; on the other hand, primary narration depicts incidents as they occur in the dramatic present. As Fujita Takanori points out, primary narration in nō is typically employed at the conclusion of an act, where the disappearance of a protagonist is often described by the chorus as *tote usenikeri* とて失せにけり ("thus saying, s/he disappeared").[4] Primary narration may also appear during the act: sometimes characters' speeches are followed by a tag clause, such as *to iite* といひて ("thus saying"), and their ongoing activities in the dramatic present are verbally described either in the past or present tense.

The theater scholar Anne Ubersfeld has proposed an especially helpful model for analyzing narration in drama.[5] As she argues, in theater there always exists a "twofold situation of communication": one between characters on stage and the other between the stage and the audience. The former may be called "onstage communication" and the latter "theatrical communication." They are inversely proportional to each other: when onstage communication is foregrounded, theatrical communication recedes, and vice versa. Thus, when a given speech clearly functions as onstage communication, such as an imperative, plea, or greeting, its theatrical communication becomes less prominent.

---

3. For a discussion of the levels of narrative, see Gérard Genette, *Narrative Discourse: An Essay in Method,* trans. Jane E. Lewin, ed. Jonathan Culler (Cornell University Press, 1980), 227–34. Genette employs his own terms "diegetic narrative" and "metadiegetic narrative," which correspond closely to primary and secondary narrative.

4. Fujita Takanori, *Nō no korosu* (Hitsuji shobō, 2000), xvi.

5. Anne Ubersfeld, *Reading Theatre,* trans. Frank Collins, ed. Paul Perron and Patrick Debbèche (University of Toronto Press, 1999).

Moreover, this twofold communication model is analogous to the two principal modes of discourse in the novel; that is, speech and narration. In a novel, characters direct their speech, as a function of communication, first and foremost to each other. At the same time, characters' speech is also transmitted to the reader through the narrator. By contrast, narration is solely addressed to the reader. In drama, likewise, characters' speeches are not only addressed to other characters but also to the audience. Primary narration on stage, on the other hand—which is not an indispensable element of drama—is addressed solely to the audience; therefore, it does not function as onstage communication.

Theatrical communication is most restricted in Western "realistic" drama. Such drama aims at creating the illusion of a transparent fourth wall, one through which an audience catches glimpses of the actors on stage. These actors, in turn, perform as if there were no audience, and therefore, no theatrical communication. At the other extreme, oral storytelling is a genre where theatrical communication predominates. Physically and grammatically, the narrator, who is also a reciter, addresses the audience directly. Onstage communication has no physical representation, and characters' speeches and actions are verbally conveyed to the audience only through the voice of the narrator. Furthermore, the narrator often manifests his/her presence by making subjective comments on the narrated incidents. The narrator also manipulates the order of the events in his/her telling through such techniques as flashback and flashforward.

In nō, too, theatrical communication is much more conspicuous than in Western "realistic" drama. This can be clearly seen not only in the use of primary narration, but also at the opening of a play, as characters often introduce themselves directly to the audience, in a *nanori* 名乗リ section, or explain their ongoing voyage from one place to another in a *michiyuki* 道行 section. At the same time, however, compared to oral storytelling, nō theater augments onstage communication at the expense of a mitigated theatrical communication. Many scenes in nō are not only visually but also verbally presented, yet most of these verbal descriptions are secondary narration, that is, a character's telling of the past. In other words, such verbal descriptions form part of the character's own speech, mostly to other characters.

Mugen nō 夢幻能 (dream plays) can then be defined as a dramatic form that enables the playwright to deemphasize primary narration. In this dramatic form, main events are instead delivered by secondary narration, as characters recount the past through a process of onstage communication. In fact, as Fujita Takanori observes, *mugen* nō tends to contain much less primary narration than does *genzai* nō 現在能 (plays set in the present), in which the main actions take place in the dramatic present and are described through primary narration, as in oral storytelling.[6] To put this another way, in the spectrum of narration types available to theatrical genres, Western realistic drama and oral storytelling occupy opposite ends. Nō drama is located somewhere in between, with *mugen* nō rather closer to the drama's end, and *genzai* nō, which involves more primary narration lying toward the oral storytelling's end.

In reality, however, the distinction between primary and secondary narrations in drama is not always clear-cut, due to another essential element of theater: gesture. Gesture is a locus where two disparate settings can converge; when a character speaks of an incident that has occurred offstage, his or her gestures visually reenact this temporally and spatially distant event *on* the stage in the present. For example, in the second act of *mugen* nō, when a ghost relates a past event, accompanied by physical re-presentation, this secondary narration may seem primary, as if the ghost were describing an ongoing act on stage.

The second act of *Sanemori* contains three such instances of secondary narrations that relate past events through the aid of gestures. In the remainder of this chapter, I will examine each of them, paying special attention to the function and nature of these narrations as well as to the twofold communication in them. This study will thus demonstrate how, despite the actors' gestures, Zeami's recurrent emphasis on the ghost's act of speaking to the monk hinders the audience from indulging in an illusionary fusion of the past and the present, and helps keep most of the play within the framework of onstage communication.

First, in the *katari* 語リ section, the ghost of Sanemori narrates to the monk (*waki*) how his severed head was washed with water by Higuchi Jirō 樋口二郎. Although his use of gestures increases as his telling of the story proceeds, little intermingling of past and present actually occurs in this scene, since the one who mimics the movements of the washing of Sanemori's severed head is Sanemori's ghost himself, not Higuchi. Moreover, Sanemori's ghost appears on stage wearing a red brocade robe, highly idiosyncratic attire that seems inappropriate given his white hair and beard, which attest to his great age. The idiosyncrasy of his attire is, in fact, one of the focal points in the play, as it is referred to repeatedly. As a result, it is impossible for the audience

6. Fujita, *Nō no korosu*, xvi.

to forget that the figure who narrates and reenacts Higuchi's washing is Sanemori himself. This visually conspicuous presence of the narrator emphasizes the fact that the scene's narration is a secondary one. It is in fact a narration delivered by a character who belongs to the world of the primary narration, and takes place within onstage communication.

The succeeding *kuse* クセ section takes up another scene from the past. In this episode in the *Heike*, Sanemori, before his final battle, petitions his master Taira Munemori 平宗盛 to wear the red brocade robe, which is permitted only to warriors of the highest rank. Here, Sanemori's ghost wearing the red robe runs ahead of the content of his story. The time gap between the narrating action and the narrated event is thus visually manifested on stage. Once again, a possible fusion of the past and the present is hindered.

Moreover, the description of the past action itself is considerably reduced in this scene. Among ten lines of this *kuse* section in the *Nihon koten bungaku taikei* text, only two are dedicated to the description of the past action: "As for Sanemori's wearing the red brocade robe, it was not that he did so at his own discretion. When he left the capital, he said to Lord Munemori …" (*mata Sanemori ga nishiki no hitatare wo kirukoto watakushi naranu nozomi nari. Sanemori miyako wo ideshi toki munemorikō ni mōsuyō*) and "As he wished, he was granted the red brocade robe" (*to nozomi shikaba akaji no nishiki no hitatare wo kudashi tamawarinu*). The citation of Sanemori's speech to Munemori takes up three and a half lines: from "It is written in the classics that one wears brocade when returning home, loaded with honors" (*kokyō e wa nishiki wo kite kaeru toieru honmon ari*) to "please grant my petition" (*gomen are*). The remaining four and a half lines, that is, the whole second half of the *kuse*, represent a retrospective comment, as the incident itself is compared with the ancient Chinese anecdote of Zhu Maichen 朱買臣.[7]

Although this comment is placed immediately after Sanemori's story, these lines may belong to the narrator; in other words, they may reflect a primary narration addressed to the audience, not the ghost's own comment on himself addressed to the monk. However, the ambiguity of addresser and addressee is soon resolved; the *kuse* section ends with the ghost's declaration of his intention, directly addressed to the other character, the monk: "I will tell you my tale of repentance" (*zange*

---

7. Yokomichi Mario and Omote Akira, eds., *Yōkyokushū* (jō), NKBT 40 (Iwanami shoten, 1960), 272–73. All translations from the play are mine.

monogatari mōsan).[8] This line affirms that the comment as a whole is an onstage communication.

In the final scene of the play, which consists of the *rongi* ロンギ and *chūnoriji* 中ノリ地 sections, Sanemori's ghost reenacts his final battle. As clearly stated at the beginning of the scene—"That agony of the *shura* realm returns here again and again" (*sono mōshū no shura no michi meguri megurite mata koko ni*)[9]—this reenactment is also a form of torture in the *shura* realm, where Sanemori's ghost is suffering in the present; his resentment at having failed in his final battle is the very attachment to the world that prevents him from attaining Buddhahood. In other words, even before Sanemori's gestures cause the secondary narration to mimic a primary one, the scene begins with a fusion of the past and the present. The secondary narration in this scene, due both to its context and physical gestures, thus strongly resembles a primary narration. However, unlike many other plays, this final scene—and the play itself—does not end with short primary narration describing the disappearance of the ghost; rather, the ghost makes a direct plea to the monk, asking for his help in gaining salvation: "please mourn for me" (*ato tomuraite tabitamae*).[10] In other words, after presenting a scene where the secondary narration bears resemblance to a primary narration, the play ends with this strong affirmation of onstage communication.

These three scenes in the second act of *Sanemori* are not presented in chronological order. The episode of the washing of Sanemori's head is presented as the first of the three yet is chronologically the last. The next episode is Sanemori's petition, which is chronologically the first. The battle scene, though at the end of the play, occurs between these two episodes. As is widely known, Zeami's own comments in *Sarugaku dangi* 申楽談義 (Nō Discourses) reveal that he was especially proud of this nonchronological arrangement of events in *Sanemori*, which, as he puts it, creates the effect of *enken* 遠見, or, a "distant view." In narratological terms, this "distant view" can be rephrased as the recognition of the chronological perspective of a given scene; that is, the recognition of the temporal distance that separates the past events from one another, as well as the temporal gap between the narrating and narrated moments. As Genette would argue, such awareness inevitably draws attention to the presence of a narrator—in this case, the ghost of Sanemori—and his

8. Yokomichi and Omote, *Yōkyokushū* (jō), 273.
9. Ibid.
10. Ibid.

narrating act—that is, the fact that these events are told in his "secondary narration."[11] The anachronism in the second act thus strengthens the sense of onstage communication by firmly embedding past events within Sanemori's discourse to the priest.

As Yamanaka Reiko argues, warrior plays around Zeami's time usually depicted battle scenes in the dramatic present, in the form of *genzai* nō.[12] In contrast with this tradition, Zeami chose a *mugen* nō structure for his warrior plays, which, as I have suggested, enabled him to deemphasize primary narration and thus enhance onstage communication, a crucial feature which distinguishes nō "drama" from oral storytelling.[13] In the play *Sanemori*, Zeami pushes this tendency even further. As we have seen, the second act includes various devices to intensify the audience's awareness of onstage communication. Even in the play's first act, which, due to the dramatic actions that fill it, is often described by scholars as close to *genzai* nō in structure,[14] the actions are conveyed mostly by characters' dialogue, not by primary narration. While heavily borrowing from its oral narration source, the play exploits the narration possibilities of the new drama form of nō, one which creates a fictional world on stage beyond the interventions of an ever-present narrator.

---

11. Genette, *Narrative Discourse*, 33–85, 164–69.

12. Yamanaka Reiko, "Ano yo kara furikaette miru ikusa monogatari," in *Gunki monogatari to sono gekika: Heike monogatari kara Taikōki made*, ed. Kokubungaku kenkyū shiryōkan, Kotenkōen shirīzu, vol. 6, (Rinsen shoin, 2000), 128–53.

13. This is especially conspicuous when compared to *Jikken Sanemori* 実検実盛, a nō play by an anonymous author, which relates the scene of Sanemori's head-washing in a *genzai* nō structure. Most of the incidents depicted in *Sanemori* in the secondary narrative are here narrated in the primary.

14. For example, Kōsai Tsutomu, *Nō utai shinkō: Zeami ni terasu* (Hinoki shoten, 1972), 274–82.

11 ～ Sanemori

| MAE J. SMETHURST

INTRODUCTION

In *Heike monogatari*, Chapter Eight, Saitō Bettō Sanemori 斉藤別
当実盛 appears as an old man who wishes to wear a red brocade *hitatare*
直垂 in the battle against the Genji. Munemori 宗盛, the head of the
Heike, grants him permission to wear the *hitatare*, which makes him
look as if he were a general. Sanemori also disguises his age by dyeing
his hair and beard black, and he fights bravely in spite of his age. He is
finally killed by a retainer of Kiso Yoshinaka 木曽義仲, whom he tried
to engage in fighting.

In the nō, Sanemori appears as an old man before the priest Taami
Shōnin 他阿弥上人, who, unlike other priests in *shura* nō, is identified
by name. The *maeshite* identifies himself finally as the spirit of Sanemori,
who asks the priest to pray for him. According to Kōsai Tsutomu,[1] the
play's first half (*maeba*) is like both a *genzai* nō and a *mugen* nō. The nō
reconstructs what was considered a real event: the appearance of the
ghost of Sanemori at Shinowara 篠原, recorded in the Mansai diary for
the year 1414.[2] We learn that the *waki* is talking to the ghost of Sanemori
in the *maeba*, and this is the same ghost dressed in armor with whom he
speaks in the second half (*nochiba*).

The perspective of this nō differs from other *shura* nō. We are watching
a performance of an *odori nenbutsu* 踊り念仏 within the performance
of the *nochiba*. If Zeami wanted his warriors to be connected in some

---

1. Kōsai Tsutomu, "Sakuhin kenkyū: Sanemori," *Kanze* (January 1970), 3–9.
2. *Mansai junkō nikki* 満済准后日記, Ōei 21 (1414).5.21. *Mansai jugō nikki*,
edited by Kyoto Teikoku Daigaku Bunka Daigaku (Rokujō kappan seizōjo, 1918).

way with the arts, as he says in the *Fūshikaden* 風姿花伝, there is an additional layer provided to the dramatization of the *Heike* version in this *shura* nō. Sanemori is connected with a form of the arts that is not poetry or flute-playing, as with *Tadanori* 忠度 and *Atsumori* 敦盛 respectively, but with the real and contemporary performance of the Buddhist *odori nenbutsu*. One might say that the nō is both a *genzai* nō and *mugen* nō throughout, that is, if we think of the ghost of the warrior as a real being contemporaneous to the dramatic time, the being that appeared as a ghost to the people of Shinowara, and the one who is portrayed as the ghost speaking in the nō. The translation of this nō is followed by one of *Genzai Sanemori* 現在実盛, a nō play not included in the current performance repertoire.

Sanemori

| TRANSLATED BY MAE J. SMETHURST

Second-category *mugen* nō in two acts.
Performed by all five schools.
Time: Second year of Juei (1183), Fifth Month
Place: Shinowara in Kaga province
Author: Zeami

WAKI	Priest Taami Shōnin
WAKIZURE	Attending priests
MAESHITE	Old man
NOCHIJITE	The Spirit of Sanemori
AI	Local man

[PART ONE (*maeba*)]

LOCAL MAN   (*nanori*)
    This person lives in the village of Shinowara, in the province of
Kaga.[1] Now, the successor to Yugyō, a person named Taami Shōnin,
who traveled here in accordance with the practice of that itinerant
priest, delivers sermons here every day.[2] But there is something
strange about this: before or after the noontime services he carries
on a monologue. Everyone says that this is strange. Since this person
is regularly near his platform, he has been requested to inquire into
the matter. After noontime I will go and ask him about it. Everyone,
please stand informed of this.

Sanemori 実盛. This translation is based on Yokomichi Mario and Omote
Akira, eds., *Yōkyokushū* (jō), NKBT 40 (Iwanami shoten, 1960), 265–73. This
translation and the footnotes follow closely the translation in my book, *The
Artistry of Aeschylus and Zeami: A Comparative Study of Greek Tragedy and Nō*
(Princeton University Press, 1988).
    1. Now in Kaga City, Ishikawa prefecture, on the Japan Sea.
    2. Ippen Shōnin 一遍上人 (His Reverence Ippen, 1239–1289), founder of the Ji
時 sect. The name Yugyō 遊行 refers to his practice of traveling the country to teach
nenbutsu 念仏 recitation, a custom followed by his successor Taami 他阿弥 Shōnin.

PRIEST TAAMI (*sashi*)

        Although Paradise is a place millions of miles away,
        a long way for one to be reborn,[3]
        although Paradise is a place millions of miles away,
        a long way for one to be reborn,
        here too in one's heart is Amida's country.
        The voices of people, both high and low,
        are heard reciting the *nenbutsu*,

PRIESTS   both day and night in the place of the Law,

PRIEST TAAMI   truly the glory of Amida saves all—

PRIESTS   by virtue of this Vow of His, who is there

PRIEST TAAMI   who would be excluded?

TOGETHER (*ageuta*)

        Just one person even if alone,
        let him pursue Buddha's holy name,
        let him pursue Buddha's holy name,[4]
        when everyone leaves the place of the Law.
        Both hearts that believe and those that do not
        his Vow draws in: will anyone pass through the net? No.
        Both people who believe and those who do not—
        he will help them take passage
        and go to that country aboard the ship of the Law[5]
        that floats along the Way easily, as it is said,
        that floats along the Way easily, as it is said.

While this is sung, Old Man appears quietly and stops at the first pine of the bridgeway (hashigakari). *He is dressed in the costume of an old man, wears an "old-man" mask and carries prayer beads. He turns toward the stage and joins his hands in prayer.*[6]

OLD MAN (*sashi*) The sound of the flutes is heard in the distance above
        a lone cloud,

---

3. The *waki* begins with quotations from Buddhist sutras. Yokomichi and Omote, *Yōkyokushū* (jō), 441, supplementary notes 107 and 105.

4. The beginning of the *ageuta* is borrowed from the words of His Reverence Ippen 一遍 (the Yugyō mentioned by the kyōgen *ai*). Yokomichi and Omote, *Yōkyokushū* (jō), 266, n.13.

5. The "country" is the Pure Land paradise (*gokuraku* 極楽). "Law" (*nori* 法, the Dharma) puns on the word for "embark" (*nori* 乗り).

6. There are more stage directions included in the edition used than I include within this translation.

a holy multitude comes before the setting sun to
give welcome.[7]
Ah, on this holy day as well a purple cloud hovers above.
The sound of the bell and of voices reciting the *nenbutsu* are
heard. It is now time to listen to the sermons,

Faces forward.

But, even if he were not trying to hurry, waves of old age would
make the going difficult, and he cannot approach those in the place of
the Law. Yet, he will listen from outside.

In melody. With one sincere invocation of Buddha's name
the hope of enlightenment that comes from Buddha's
glory shines forth without clouds,
but for one whose vision is impaired by old age
the path is not clear.

*Old Man enters the main stage as he sings, sits down, and joins his hands
in prayer once again.*

Come now, although he is a little late,
The distance from here is not far.
Namu Amidabu.

PRIEST TAAMI (*mondō*)   Well now, old man, indeed you are not
negligent about the daily invocations. Therefore, I think you are
a devout person. Yet other people cannot see your presence. They
all are wondering among themselves whom I meet and what I am
saying. Now,[8] give your name.

Old Man looks at Priest.

OLD MAN   This is an unexpected question you ask. Let me
inform you from the start that I come from far away and am but a
country person. If I had a name worth mentioning, I *would* give my
name. Only, your Reverence's arrival is utterly as if Amida had come
to receive me.

*At this point in the dialogue, Old Man faces forward and sings one line in
a melody that, like a* sashi, *does not follow a beat, but is delivered more
insistently than the words that precede.*

It is fortunate that he has lived long enough
to experience the occasion of these recitations.   (*In speech*)

---

7. These words are based on a poem in Chinese by Jakushō 寂昭, an eleventh-
century monk. See Yokomichi and Omote, *Yōkyokushū* (jō), 267 n. 19.
8. Literally, "today."

> It has the feeling of a blind turtle's discovery
>> of a log floating in the ocean
> or of one eagerly awaiting and seeing the bloom of
>> the *udonge*.[9]
> The happiness of one who has had a rare experience
>> in his old age is exceedingly great.
> Tears of joy on his sleeves are abundant.

Looks down and then up.

> Even as he is, can he be reborn
> in the land of peace and happiness?
> This thought causes incomparable joy.
> On such an occasion, to have to give his name,
> a name that belongs
> to this world of blindness and continual cycles of rebirth,
> is regrettable.

Looks forward.

PRIEST TAAMI   Indeed, what the old man says is exceedingly reasonable; however, you could be saved through repentance of your sins. Just name your name.

Old Man looks at Priest.

OLD MAN   Then I cannot avoid giving my name?

PRIEST TAAMI   That is right. Quickly give your name.

OLD MAN   In that case have the people before you sent away and I will approach you and give my name.

Stands up, goes to the middle of the stage, and sits down.

PRIEST TAAMI   Of course, the appearance of the old man is not seen by the eyes of the other people. And yet, if that is your wish, I shall have the people move away. And you come near and name your name.

Old Man moves to stage center and sits.

OLD MAN   In the past Saitō Bettō Sanemori of Nagai was defeated and killed in the battle here at Shinowara. Word of it has no doubt reached you.

PRIEST TAAMI   He was a Heike samurai, a famous warrior of the bow. But the story of the battle is of no benefit. Just name your name.

---

9. The *udonge* 優曇華 flower was said to bloom but once every three thousand years. According to the Buddhist parable, seeing it bloom is as likely an occurrence as a blind turtle, who surfaces once every one hundred years, discovering in the ocean a floating log with a hole in it and passing his head through that hole.

Old Man faces forward.

OLD MAN   Ah, but it is relevant. It is said that in the water of the pond before you, Sanemori's hair and beard were washed. (*Faces Priest.*) Therefore, it may be that an attachment on his part stays behind. Even today among the people of this area it is said that the form of the ghost is seen.[10]

PRIEST TAAMI   Then is it seen by people even now?

Old Man faces forward.

OLD MAN   A tree not seen among the many other treetops on a
                 mountain
           when in bloom betrays itself as a cherry tree.[11]
           Observe the same thing in the old tree.

PRIEST TAAMI (*fushi*)
           How strange! The story about Sanemori's past
           which I heard, I thought was about another person.
           But how strange, it was about you.   (*In speech*)
           So then, you are the ghost of Sanemori, are you?

Old Man looks at Priest.

OLD MAN   I am the ghost of Sanemori. While the soul is in the other world, part of the spirit remains in this world.[12]

          Faces forward.

PRIEST TAAMI   (*In melody*)
                  In sinful attachment to this transient world
OLD MAN   (*In speech*)
           more than two hundred years have elapsed.
                  (*In melody*)
PRIEST TAAMI But still he cannot be saved, floating on Shinowara's
OLD MAN   pond, in vain, waves wash against the shore at night
PRIEST TAAMI and by day without distinction in the darkness of the soul
OLD MAN   whether in a state of dreams
PRIEST TAAMI or in a state of wakefulness[13]

---

10. The news of the ghost of Sanemori appearing reached the capital a few years before the play was produced and the ghost continued to be seen. By capitalizing on the contemporary event, Zeami creates a nō that is both like a *genzai* nō and *mugen* nō. See Kōsai Tsutomu, "Sakuhin kenkyū: Sanemori," *Kanze* (January 1970), 7.

11. The poem is by Ariwara no Yukihira, *Ise monogatari*, no. 114.

12. "Soul" and "spirit" translate *kon* 魂 and *haku* 魄, respectively.

13. *Utsutsu* 現, reality.

OLD MAN	he is obsessed with this thought.
(ageuta)	At Shinowara
	very much like hoarfrost on the grass
	is the old man.
CHORUS	Like hoarfrost on the grass
	is the old man.
	With him let no one find fault,
	temporarily revealed—
	Sanemori appears.

Old Man looks eagerly at Priest.

> Please, he asks, do not let his name leak out.

Looks down and then forward, stands up.

> Talk about his past will bring shame.

Moves quietly toward the base square (jōza).

> When one thought he was rising
> and leaving his holy presence,
> at the edge of Shinowara's pond,

Moves forward on the stage.

> his shape faded into an apparition and disappeared.
> His shape faded into an apparition and disappeared.

Exits from the stage along the bridgeway.

[INTERVAL (*nakairi*)]

Local Man (ai-kyōgen) comes forward onto the stage.[14]

LOCAL MAN   What? Are you saying that His Reverence was speaking to himself? In that case, I think I will go right to him and make an inquiry.

> *Goes to stage center, turns to Priest, and sits down.*

Today I fear that I am late.

PRIEST TAAMI   Why have you been negligent?

LOCAL MAN   I wanted to come much more quickly, but am late because of many obligations. Now, I want to make an inquiry of Your

---

14. The translation of the *ai* section is based on Sanari Kentarō, *Yōkyoku taikan*, vol. 2 (Meiji shoin, 1931), 1252–1254. The text is from the *Ōkuraryū koshahon* 大蔵流古写本, dating from 1789.

Reverence. Every day at the noon services you carry on a dialogue with yourself, and I hear that everyone at Shinowara is wondering about this. Since they know that I am a person who customarily approaches you, they have asked me to make inquiry. What is this all about?

PRIEST TAAMI How is that? The people at Shinowara are wondering about my carrying on a monologue at the time of the noon-hour invocations?

LOCAL MAN   That's exactly right.

PRIEST TAAMI Pertaining to that subject, I want to pose a question. What I am going to ask is unexpected, but tell me, if you know, about the way in which Saitō Bettō Sanemori of Nagai died long ago at the battle here in Shinowara.

LOCAL MAN   This is an unexpected question you ask. I do not know much about the matter, but will tell you the story as it reached me through hearsay.

PRIEST TAAMI I appreciate your kind consideration.

Local Man turns toward the audience.

LOCAL MAN   Well then, the person called Saitō Bettō Sanemori was from a Northern province, a person who in the middle of his career went to the Minamoto side. It is said that he received the domain of Nagai in Musashi province and gave himself the name Nagai no Saitō Bettō. At the time of the battle at Ishibashiyama he again goes to serve the Taira.

The battle at Shinowara here, it is said, took place well over two hundred years ago. The Taira, wanting to fight Kiso Yoshinaka and further to destroy Yoritomo, send a force of more than 100,000 cavalry to the Northern province. Lord Kiso with 50,000 cavalry went to meet them. They say various encounters took place. Sanemori was an extraordinary old warrior. His hair and beard were white. So wanting to die in battle attired like a young person, he dyed his hair and beard with black ink. His armor plaques were made for him of tanned leather. The protector at his throat was made of the plant *saikachi*. They say that he looked like a first-class young warrior.

However, during the encounter, when the Taira were defeated in the battle and when Sanemori held back and waited for a good rival, one of Lord Kiso's quicker men came forward and cut off his head beneath the ears. In the presence of Lord Kiso it was said, "There is something special about this head." During various discussions, there were some who say that is Sanemori's head and others that it is not. "At any rate," someone said, "have it washed and we shall see."

When he had it washed in the water of the pond here at Shinowara and looked at it, it was the head of no one other than Saitō Bettō. Then moved by Sanemori's example, it is said, everyone, saying that any warrior who carries a bow like him should try to be true to his aspirations, shed tears.

Turns toward Priest.

Anyhow, that's the sort of thing I learned through hearsay. But why was it you asked? I wonder because it is an unusual inquiry.

PRIEST TAAMI   You have related this story in detail, I asked for no other reason than that recently on the occasion of the noon-hour invocations an old man appeared out of nowhere. When I asked him who he was he related the story of a battle of long ago and had scarcely said that he is the ghost of Sanemori when I lost sight of his figure at the edge of the pond!

LOCAL MAN   Oh. Around the time of the noon-hour services you [seem to] carry on a dialogue with yourself because the spirit of Sanemori appears. Therefore, I hope you will pray for the repose of Sanemori.

PRIEST TAAMI   As I too think that way, let me go to the edge of the pond and hold a special *odori nenbutsu* service. Let us pray for his repose. Make an announcement of this to the people of Shinowara.

LOCAL MAN   Leave it to me.

Rises, moves to the right, faces the audience, and makes the announcement.

Everyone, listen. In order to pray for the repose of Sanemori, His Reverence will hold a special *odori nenbutsu* service at the edge of the pond at Shinowara. So all and everyone at Shinowara please attend and stand informed, stand informed.

Returns to Priest and faces him.

PRIEST TAAMI   I appreciate your special attention.

Local Man exits to his seat at stage back right.

[PART TWO (*nochiba*)]

PRIEST TAAMI   Let them pray for that ghost
with a special recitation of prayers.

PRIEST TAAMI AND ATTENDING PRIESTS
     (*machiutai*)   At Shinowara

> at the edge of the pond, over the water of the Law
> at the edge of the pond, over the water of the Law
> deep in invocation,
> in recitation of prayers,
> the clear voices cross.
> Hold a memorial service
> from the first to the last
> watch of night.
> The heart also Westward
> goes with the moon
> light cloudless, clear.
> They ring the bell through the length of the night.

Attending Priests sit down and Priest, facing forward, joins his hands in prayer.

PRIEST TAAMI   *Namuamidabu. Namuamidabu.*

Priest sits down. Sanemori's Spirit (nochijite) *enters and stands by the base pillar* (shitebashira).

SANEMORI'S SPIRIT (*sashi*)

> When one has reached Paradise,   *Faces forward.*
> he has left the world of suffering forever

Looks back toward the bridgeway.

> and the seat of transmigration is far away.
> How great is the joy in his heart!

Faces forward and lowers head.

> That Place is a place from which one does not return.

Raises head.

> Life [there] is without end, Amida Buddha. He is
> filled with hope.

Turns to Priest.

SANEMORI'S SPIRIT (*issei*)

> Every time a person repeats the name of Amida
> Buddha,

CHORUS   then, every time he is saved.

SANEMORI'S SPIRIT

(*noriji*)   As for *namu*—

Stamps with his left foot and moves forward two steps.

CHORUS   that is, to submit one's destiny to Buddha.

SANEMORI'S SPIRIT As for *Amida*—

Stamps with his right foot and moves forward one step.

CHORUS   by virtue
                       of righteous acts

Sanemori's Spirit turns left and flips his sleeve over his arm.

SANEMORI'S SPIRIT   one should without fail be saved.

Brings his sleeve back.

CHORUS   It makes him thankful.

Sanemori's Spirit, with his hands folded in prayer, turns to Priest and then looks forward.

PRIEST TAAMI (*kakeai*) Amazing!
                       On the surface of the pond growing white from
                              the light of dawn,
                       the one faintly floating into view
                       is the old man he just saw,
                       but he is dressed in armor. It is amazing.

Sanemori's Spirit looks at Priest.

SANEMORI'S SPIRIT   A fossil tree
                     that no one knows
                     submerged.
                     From the depths of the heart
                     it is difficult to express
                     the innumerable agonies of the warrior hell.
                     Release him from these.

As the kakeai *continues, Sanemori's Spirit looks forward and then at Priest several times.*

PRIEST TAAMI   So then, your appearance
                     before my eyes and your words
                     are not seen nor heard by the others

SANEMORI'S SPIRIT (*In speech*)
                     only evident to Your Reverence.

PRIEST TAAMI (*In melody*)
                     He sees a form, the traces of snow,

SANEMORI'S SPIRIT   White hair and beard of the old warrior, but

PRIEST TAAMI   brilliant is the appearance

SANEMORI'S SPIRIT   of his outfit, bright

PRIEST TAAMI   in the moon's radiance

SANEMORI'S SPIRIT   in the burning light of the lantern.

CHORUS (*ageuta*)   Not dark

Sanemori's Spirit moves to the right and then to the left.

is the night's mantle
a brocade robe
is the night's mantle
a brocade robe
he wears green armor

Turns to the left and looks at his sword.

and swords with sheaths decorated in gold.

Faces forward and makes the gesture of thrusting with a sword.

But, he asks, under the present conditions,
what kind of treasures are these?

Moves forward and looks intently at Priest.

In the Lake of Treasures, there is a lotus calyx.
This should be the real treasure.

Flips his sleeve over and moves to the left.

Indeed, there is no doubt
the teaching of the Law does not tarnish.

Makes a small turn.

If the golden words you respect,

Turns toward Priest.

why should you not be There?
why should you not be There?

PRIEST TAAMI When he looks at you, you are in the form of one still in the world of transmigration. You should relinquish your attachment and reach the calyx of Amida who destroys all sins.

Priest retires to the front right of the stage.

SANEMORI'S SPIRIT (*kuri*) One invocation of Amida abolishes
innumerable sins.

CHORUS That is, a heart blessed with its own virtue turns [to
Buddha] and aspires [to Paradise].
Do not leave your heart behind in attachment.

SANEMORI'S SPIRIT (*sashi*) The time has arrived; this evening he has received
the teachings difficult to encounter.

CHORUS The tale of shame and repentance—
still he cannot forget the past and recollects how at
Shinowara
he died like dew on the grassy plain.

Sanemori's Spirit looks at Priest.

He will tell his tale.

Looks forward toward the audience.

SANEMORI'S SPIRIT (*katari*) Now then, when the battle of Shinowara was lost, Tezuka no Tarō Mitsumori, a Genji, came before Lord Kiso and said, "Mitsumori, fighting a strange character, has cut off his head. He looks like a leader, but he has not the forces behind him. And again, if you think he is an ordinary warrior, he wears a brocade robe. I insisted that he name his name, but to the end he refused to give it." His accent was that of the Kantō dialect. Lord Kiso said, "Ah, this must be Saitō Bettō Sanemori. If so, his hair and beard should be white, but it is strange that they are black. It may be that Higuchi no Jirō is acquainted with him." When he had Higuchi sent for, on arrival and with but one glance, Higuchi shed tears and said,

Looks down.

"Alas, how piteous! This is indeed Saitō Bettō!

Looks up again.

Sanemori was accustomed to say that,
if at sixty years of age or more one goes to battle,
to compete with young warriors
in order to advance first would be childish.
And again, to be looked down upon by people
as an old warrior would be mortifying.
He would choose to dye his hair and beard
   with black ink
and be killed fighting just like a young man.
That is what he always said.

Looks down.

Indeed he has dyed them.

Looks up.

Have his head washed and look for yourselves."

Opens the fan that he holds.

Scarcely had he spoken when holding the head,

Sanemori's Spirit rises from the stool, then kneels and with both hands on his fan makes the gesture of lifting a head. He moves forward.

CHORUS   he leaves the lord's presence
and faces the pond close-by

Rises and moves forward.

in whose green waters are reflected
the leaves of willow branches hanging above.

Stops, bring the fan to his right hand and looks down.

CHORUS (*ageuta*)   The weather is clearing,
                the wind combs
                the young willows' hair.
                The ice is melted,
                the waves wash
                the old moss's beard.

During the singing of the poem, Sanemori's Spirit extends his left hand forward, kneels, looks at his right side, and with his fan makes the gesture of dipping water two or three times.

                When one looked,

Lowers his fan and looks.

                the black ink flowed away
                and there was the original gray hair.

Returns to the base pillar.

                "Truly any warrior of the bow
                who is concerned about his name
                should be like this.

Faces forward.

                Ah, what a noble warrior!"
                said everyone, shedding tears.

CHORUS (*kuse*)   And then,
                Sanemori's wearing a brocade robe
                was not out of a wish to be selfish.
                Sanemori, when he left the capital,
                said to Lord Munemori,
                "There is a saying in the classics,
                'wearing brocade one returns to his birthplace.'[15]
                Sanemori was from Echizen,
                but in recent years was awarded a domain
                and took residence in Nagai of Musashi.
                Now if he leaves and goes North,
                he will surely be killed in battle.

---

15. See below for an explanation. The expression was much cited in Chinese texts familiar in Japan, such as "The Basic Annals of Xian Yu" 項羽本紀 in Sima Qian's *Shiji* 史記. Burton Watson, trans., *Records of the Grand Historian: Han Dynasty I* (Hong Kong: The Chinese University of Hong Kong and Columbia University Press, 1993), 33.

In his old age, nothing would make him
happier to remember
than being granted this permission [to wear a
    brocade robe]."
Since that was his wish,
Munemori bestowed upon him a red brocade robe.

SANEMORI'S SPIRIT Now, in an old poem as well—[16]
"Maple leaves,

CHORUS while brushing them aside he returns home wearing
    brocade
and the people see him."
That is what a poet wrote.
It is in the spirit of the original saying.
Shubaijin of old let his brocade sleeves
flutter on Mount Kaikei.[17]

Sanemori's Spirit flips his sleeve over his arm.

Now, Sanemori
has brought fame to the four corners of the
    Northern province
and the celebrated warrior's name has lasted through
    generations,
visible to all.
Till dawn
throughout the moonlit night
he will relate his tale of repentance.

CHORUS (*rongi*) Indeed,
with a tale of repentance
purify to the bottom the water in your heart;
leave no impurities behind.

SANEMORI'S SPIRIT That deep-rooted attachment of warrior hell,

Moves forward.

---

16. The poem, not found in the *Heike monogatari*, is an autumn poem found in the *Gosenshū*, no. 404.

17. With the words of the proverb, the Emperor Wu 武帝 persuaded the Chinese scholar, Zhu Maichen 朱売臣 (Jp. Shubaijin), to return home attired in robes of the court, because of the wisdom of this man who had overcome poverty and suffering, and served with honor at Mount Guiji 会稽 (Jp. Kaikei). He then became an official in his homeland. Itō Masayoshi, ed., *Yōkyokushū* (chū), SNKS (Shinchōsha, 1986), 116, n. 7.

moving around and around again to this place
has come. Kiso—

Stamps his foot both before and after expressing the name Kiso.

I intended to grapple with him,
but Tezuka intervened.
Even now that resentment persists.

Mimes a thrust and a parry.

CHORUS   Among Kiso's followers,
who one by one gave their names,
the first to advance was

Sanemori's Spirit appears to be looking for the enemy.

SANEMORI'S SPIRIT Tezuka no Tarō Mitsumori.

CHORUS   A retainer fearing lest his lord be killed

Moves around to the right and goes to the center of the stage.

SANEMORI'S SPIRIT on his horse interceded

Moves to the right.

and to the side of Sanemori

CHORUS   he came. And as he grappled with him,

SANEMORI'S SPIRIT Sanemori said,
"Ah, you want to grapple
with the best warrior in Japan."[18]
Against the front of the saddle he [Sanemori]
pressed him
and cut off and threw away the head.

*During the delivery of these two lines, Sanemori's Spirit thrusts and after a
number of motions mimes the beheading with his fan. He then pretends to
look at an imaginary head held in his hand by its long hair and to drop it
to the ground.*

CHORUS (*chū noriji*)   After that, Tezuka no Tarō
circled around Sanemori on the left,
pulled up the skirt of his armor,
and stabbed him twice with his sword.

*Sanemori's Spirit moves about the stage and looks at his left upper thigh.
He then sits down.*

---

18. Thomas B. Hare, *Zeami's Style: The Noh Plays of Zeami Motokiyo* (Stanford
University Press, 1986), 218, brings out the Kantō dialect here.

	They grappled at close quarters and between the two horses
	fell down with a crash.
SANEMORI'S SPIRIT	Alas, he was an old warrior.
Stands.	
CHORUS	Exhausted from battle,
	an old tree crumpled by the wind,
	whose strength is broken
	beneath Tezuka. As he fell,

Sits down and mimes a fall with his fan.

	retainers came to the spot.
	Finally his head was cut off.
Stands.	
CHORUS	He became one with the earth at Shinowara.
	His form and shadow leave no traces.
	His form and shadow—
	Namuamidabu.
	Please pray in mourning. Please pray.

Sanemori's Spirit flips his right sleeve, takes two steps and folds his fan. Leaves the stage.

12 ⁓ Genzai Sanemori

| MAE J. SMETHURST

INTRODUCTION

Zeami called his nō *Sanemori* a *shura* nō, not a *genzai* nō. The play *Genzai Sanemori* 現在実盛, on the other hand, is a realistic version of the Sanemori story, probably written later than Zeami's nō.[1] In this play, of which my translation follows below, the highly religious dimension of Zeami's version is missing. Another difference is that the play is in dialogic mode up to the *kuse*, when the chorus enters, and the setting shifts from Kyoto to Shinowara.

The dramatic action of the *maeba* takes place in Kyoto, where Sanemori makes preparations to depart for his last battle at Shinowara. The subject matter of this section of the story appears in the narrative mode in the *nochiba* of Zeami's nō. In the *genzai* version, the *shite* is the living Sanemori who comes before the *waki*, Munemori, who grants permission for Sanemori to wear a brocade *hitatare*. As in Zeami's nō, the cowardly behavior at an earlier battle is not mentioned. The *maeba* ends with a celebratory round of sake cup exchanges.

In the *nochiba*, two *tsure*, Yoshinaka and Mitsumori, in battle advance toward Sanemori, who demands to know the latter's name. When the *shite*, Sanemori, dies grappling with a retainer of Yoshinaka, it is the *shite* himself who expresses sadness for his fate. In Zeami's nō it is also the *shite*, but there he is narrating the reaction of Higuchi at three removes from the original.

---

1. Maruoka Katsura, *Kokon yōkyoku kaidai*, revised and augmented by Nishino Haruo (Kokon yōkyoku kaidai kankōkai, 1984), 107.

Genzai Sanemori

| Translated by Mae J. Smethurst

Fourth-category *genzai* nō in two acts.
No longer in the performance repertoire.
Time: Fourth and Sixth Months of Juei 2 (1183)
Place: Kyoto (*maeba*)
            Shinowara (*nochiba*)
Author: Unknown

WAKI	Taira no Munemori
SHITE	Saitō Bettō Sanemori
TSURE	Kiso no Yoshinaka
TSURE	Tezuka no Tarō Mitsumori
TOMO	Attendant to Munemori

MUNEMORI (*nanori*)

    This is Taira no Munemori. Now that I have succeeded
to the position of Minister of State, my responsibility is to administer
to the welfare of the realm. And at this time there are men like Uhyōe
no suke Yoritomo, Kiso no Kanja Yoshinaka, and others.[1] Their
unforeseen rebellion continues. Yoshinaka in particular leads a large
number of men. Accordingly, with the knowledge that he is going up
and attacking along the Hokuriku Road, I have assigned the Komatsu
[Lord of] Third Rank Koremori, and the Echizen [Governor of]
Third Rank Michimori as the generals in charge of fighting the
rebels. Saitō Bettō Sanemori of Musashi said that he should be
allowed to wear a brocade *hitatare* onto the battlefield. He has made
this wish more than once. It will be a memory for him [to live with]
for the rest of his life. I think I must permit him his wish.

    Ah, is someone there?

ATTENDANT   Before you.

Genzai Sanemori 現在実盛. This translation is based on Sasaki Nobutsuna,
ed., *Shin yōkyoku hyakuban* (Rinsen shoten, 1987), 276–80. The text contains no
introduction, stage directions, or commentary.

    1. Yoritomo is referred to as *Uhyōe no suke* 右兵衛佐, Assistant Guards
Commander of the Right, his rank before he was exiled to Izu in 1160.

MUNEMORI   If Sanemori arrives, tell him to come here.
ATTENDANT   Yes, sir.
SANEMORI   (*issei*) (*In melody*)
                    He still remains.
                    His aging body is [like] azaleas
                        growing deep in the mountains recesses—useless.
            Shikashika.[2]
            (*Spoken.*)
MUNEMORI   Sanemori, how are you?
SANEMORI   I stand before you.
MUNEMORI   *You* many times asked about wearing a brocade robe.
    Accordingly permission is granted to do so. Put this on.
SANEMORI   This is an order for which to be thankful. In the past
    Shubaijin wore a brocade robe and waved [its sleeves] at Kaikei
    Mountain. Now Sanemori wants to leave his name in the northern
    country. He must pay back the kindness of his lord. In his old age he
    can remember this. Ah, how fortunate I am!
MUNEMORI   What you say is reasonable. If that *hitatare* is worn to
    meet the enemy, you will not be thought of as a regular samurai.
SANEMORI   And will appear like a general, like his commander. As I
    thought before, if you fight when you are over sixty years of age you
    should dye your hair and beard black.
MUNEMORI   He appears feeling like a young warrior in battle.
SANEMORI   His mind is made up.
CHORUS   An old pine …
                    An old pine fights the flower of a young tree.
                    When he is in the van of battle
                    the mortifying scorn of many people coming face to face
                        with an old warrior is unbearable.
                    So he will dye his hair and beard with black ink.
                    Feeling young he will pass on his name (to posterity).
    (*kuse*)   Now Sanemori was from Echizen.
                    In recent years he received land
                    and lived in Musashi.
                    He was treated kindly in many places.

---

    2. *Shikashika* しかしか ("things like that," "et cetera") appears here in smaller
type in the text to indicate that in stage performance there would be a dialogue
between the *tomo* and *shite*. Sanemori is told that Munemori wanted to see him,
and is brought before him.

	Now he will go to the northern country.
	He intends to die by the sword. He bids farewell.
SANEMORI	In an old song also, the autumn leaves …
CHORUS	Passing through (the autumn leaves), wearing a

Passing through (the autumn leaves), wearing a
    brocade robe,
he goes. Returning home, people admire him.[3]
So it is written in a poem. He returns home
in order to reveal his name.
Sanemori, too, was like him,
receiving this *hitatare*
he offers his name to the northern country.
He will win easily
and not flee with his back to the enemy
Really, he is indeed a warrior.
Really, he is indeed a warrior.
He took the catalpa bow given to him.

SANEMORI	The time has come to say good-bye. He leaves his
	commander.
CHORUS	Sanemori waits for a short time. From Munemori
SANEMORI	in thanks he receives a sake cup. A leave-taking party.
CHORUS	The feelings are incomparably deep.

Sake cups go around many times.
Sake cups go around many times.
"I take my leave," he said—evening waves[4]
    rise then fall
imbued with feelings of actions past.
When will there be another meeting/joining[5]
in this ephemeral, bamboo-like world?
Since this is a strange life,
he had best obey the commander's orders.
On saying these words,
Sanemori sets off for the northern country.

---

3. A reference, as in *Sanemori*, to *Gosenshū* 404 (*momijiba wo / waketsutsu yukeba / nishiki kite / ie ni kaeru to / hito ya miruran*) and the story of Shubaijin (Ch. Zhu Maichen).

4. *Kore made nari to yū nami no / tachiidete on-nagori*, with a pivot on *yū* ("said" / "evening"). The word *nagori* 余波 refers to calm seas when the wind dies down, but also suggests the homonym *nagori* 名残, "memories."

5. The phrase *mata itsu no **yo** ni ai **take** no / fushigi no inochi* … contains a reference to bamboo (*take*) and two words associated with it, both meaning "joints."

Sanemori sets off for the northern country.

[INTERVAL (*nakairi*)]

(The setting changes from Kyoto to Shinowara in Hokuriku.)[6]

TEZUKA AND HIS FOLLOWERS[7] (*issei*)
This is one of Lord Kiso's men, Tezuka no Tarō Mitsumori.
(Spoken)   In the confusion of battle at Ataka Shinowara while Genji and Heike brave samurai fight to gain victory for their side, everywhere there are great martial exploits. I too fight enemies to bring fame to my name. I advance to capture someone.

CHORUS   The place to which he (Sanemori) ran,
the place to which he ran,
wearing a red brocade *hitatare*
green-laced armor,
a horned helmet with a star,
and a gilt-fitted sword,
and mounted on a horse with dappled coat,
he raises his whip and advances.

MITSUMORI (*kakeri*)
Mitsumori sees this.

CHORUS   Mitsumori sees this.
An amazing enemy. A worthy enemy.
Determined not to let him escape,
he speeds his horse closer.
He wants to hear who this person is.
(He says) "Tell me your name, please."

SANEMORI   You ask for a name, but this person does not want to (give his name). You, who are you?

MITSUMORI   A person who lives in Shinano province: Tezuka no Tarō Kanasashi.

CHORUS   Mitsumori names himself and, at the grappling point, pushing and grabbing (at the enemy) Tezuka's retainer comes between them. He fights with his enemy and falls.

SANEMORI   Ah, ha! You are fighting Japan's best. Then as he (Sanemori) is cutting off the head,

---

6. There is no surviving ai-kyōgen text.
7. In the Japanese text the proper names are given rather than the actors' role names, as usual in nō libretti.

MITSUMORI   (another of) Tezuka's retainers went around to the
    bowhand and pulled up his skirt.
SANEMORI   Stabbing twice with his sword.
CHORUS   At close quarters fighting they fall in a heap onto the
                    grass.
SANEMORI   Alas for the old warrior.
CHORUS   Alas for the old warrior.
                Like an old tree crumpling in the wind.
                His strength exhausted,[8]
                he is soon vanquished by the enemy.
                His spirit is fiercely brave.
                His legs are weak like a vehicle with broken wheels.
                As he waves his sleeves his arm is struck by the enemy.
                As he grows weak, weak
                Tezuka's retainer came and fell on top of him.
                Finally his head is taken by the enemy.
                Sanemori's name remains in the world.
                This is the end of Sanemori, the end of Sanemori.

8. *Chikara mo koko ni tsuki yumi no.* The phrase *tsuki yumi* ("zelkova bows")
has not been translated. It is a decorative flourish on the pivot word *tsuki*
("exhausted").

13 ∾ *Shunzei Tadanori*:
Its Background and Related Plays

| Michael Watson

The narrative sources for *Shunzei Tadanori* 俊成忠度 are two episodes in Chapters Seven and Nine of *Heike monogatari*: "Tadanori's Flight from the Capital" and "The Death of Tadanori."[1] In both these episodes, the larger narrative milieu of the crucial stages of the Genpei War they describe and a nexus of nō plays about Tadanori provide important contexts for interpreting the play. "Tadanori's Flight from the Capital" is set in the Seventh Month of 1183, when the capital is under imminent threat by the army of Kiso no Yoshinaka, who has won repeated victories in the Hokuriku campaign. Rather than stand and fight, the Heike decide to abandon the capital and flee to the west. The narrative devotes an episode each to three leading members of the Heike family, describing how each takes leave from a person or persons he loves or reveres. All three episodes have similar titles in the Kakuichi version: "_____ no miyako ochi" ("_____'s Flight from the Capital"). This is paralleled in the ninth chapter, where four episodes are titled "_____ saigo" ("The Death of ___"). The episode depicting Tadanori's leave-taking is the third in the sequence in the seventh chapter, and his death the second in the sequence in the ninth chapter.

The earlier sequence begins with a section about the flight of the Retired Emperor.[2] In the next episode, Taira no Koremori 平維盛 takes

---

1. *Tadanori no miyako ochi* 忠度都落 (Kakuichi-bon 7.16) and *Tadanori saigo* 忠度最期 (9.14). Ichiko Teiji, ed., *Heike monogatari* (ge), SNKZ 46 (Shōgakukan, 1994), 74–77, 226–29; Helen Craig McCullough, *The Tale of the Heike* (Stanford University Press, 1988), 246–47, 313–14.

2. *Shushō miyako ochi* 主上都落 "The Flight of [Retired] Emperor [Go-Shirakawa]" (7.13) has a similar title to sections 7.14, 7.16, 7.17 discussed next,

tearful parting from his wife and two children, whom he leaves behind in the city for their own safety.[3] The last two sections in the sequence focus on Tadanori and Tsunemasa 経正 in a way that seems consciously paralleled. None of the three men will ever return to the city. Tadanori and Tsunemasa will die at Ichi-no-tani just seven months later, and Koremori will be haunted by the memory of the tearful voices of wife, son, and daughter as they begged to accompany him on the flight. He does not take part in the battle of Ichi-no-tani or subsequent fighting, and ultimately takes his own life by drowning.[4]

The three episodes share common themes. Each explores the nature of emotional bonds—between wife and husband/children and father (Koremori), poetry teacher and disciple (Tadanori), religious master and former pupil (Tsunemasa). Those who leave and those who are left behind are bound by memories of a shared past, and by keepsakes left or promises made by the one who leaves, uncertain of what the future holds. "Tadanori's Flight from the Capital" concludes with a passage that jumps forward in time to a period after the war has ended. The function of this prolepsis ("flash-forward") is to remind listeners and readers of what they should know already: that the Heike will be defeated in the war and that Tadanori will die as an enemy of the court. The sequence of episodes that conclude Chapter Seven has a cumulative effect in building up a sense of the finality of the partings and, beyond that, the inevitable fall of Heike. Those who stay in the capital and those who flee realize all too well that theirs will be a parting for all time (kagiri no wakare).[5] The sequence is a powerful illustration of one of the key concepts of Heike monogatari: aibetsu riku 愛別離苦—the suffering of separation from those whom one loves.[6]

Taira no Tadanori 平忠度 (1144–1184) was a younger half-brother to the late head of the family, Kiyomori 清盛 (1118–1181).[7] His father

---

3. *Koremori no miyako ochi* 維盛都落 (7.14, "Koremori's Flight from the Capital").

4. *Koremori no jusui* 維盛入水 (10.12, "The Suicide of Koremori").

5. The phrase comes from the final section of Book Seven, *Fukuhara ochi* 福原落 (7.10, "The Flight from Fukuhara"), where all but the most senior Heike abandon their families as they flee: *kore wa kyō wo saigo, tadaima kagiri no wakare nareba* 是はけふ最後、只今かぎりの別なれば. Ichiko, *Heike monogatari* (ge), 90; "but theirs had been final goodbyes, eternal farewells," trans. McCullough, *Tale of the Heike*, 253.

6. This Buddhist term is specifically referred to twice: Ichiko, *Heike monogatari* (ge), 447, 520; McCullough, *Tale of the Heike*, 404, 435.

7. Tadanori's name is sometimes written 忠教 or 忠則. Texts most often refer

was Taira no Tadamori 忠盛 and his mother a court lady-in-waiting. In a story related early in the first chapter, Tadanori's parents demonstrate their poetic skill and elegance (*fusei* 風情).[8] As their son, Tadanori is from the beginning associated with *waka* poetry and with a refinement found in few of his male relatives, with the principal exceptions of his nephews Tsunemasa and Shigehira. Four of Tadanori's poems feature in the Kakuichi version to Tsunemasa's five and Shigehira's six,[9] but in documented sources outside the bounds of the semifictionalized *Heike monogatari*, Tadanori is the more famous poet, with ten poems in the imperial anthologies, not including the *Senzaishū* poem that is the bone of contention in *Shunzei Tadanori*. His personal anthology also survives.[10]

On his death at Ichi-no-tani, the narrative records how enemy warriors praise him as a model of *bunbu* 文武, highly skilled both in the military arts and in the way of poetry.[11] Although *Heike monogatari* does not dwell on his military achievements, by 1184 Tadanori was a veteran of many campaigns against the Minamoto. In 1179, he took part in the successful attack on Uji, but is not described as playing a notable role in crushing Minamoto no Yorimasa. In later campaigns, Tadanori is mentioned together with his nephews Koremori, Shigehira, Tsunemasa, and Michimori as one of the commanders of the Taira forces. Unlike them, however, he is not held directly responsible for military failures like Fuji River (1180.9), Sunamata (1181.7), or the Hokuriku campaign (1183.4–6). Unlike Shigehira and Michimori, he

---

to him as *Satsuma no kami* 薩摩守, Governor of Satsuma province. See Wada Eiko, "Tadanori," in Ichiko Teiji, ed., *Heike monogatari kenkyū jiten* (Meiji Shoin, 1978), 357.

8. Kakuichi-bon 1.3 "Suzuki" ("The Sea Bass"). Ichiko Teiji, ed., *Heike monogatari (jō)*, SNKZ 45 (Shōgakukan, 1994), 26–27; McCullough, *Tale of the Heike*, 26–27.

9. Tadanori's poems appear in *Heike monogatari*, sections 5.11, 7.16, 8.3, and 9.14, while poems by Tsunemasa appear in 7.3, 7.19, and 8.3, and those by Shigehira 重衡 in 8.2, 10.2, 10.6, and 11.19. It is notable that the Kakuichi version contains no poems by Kiyomori or his heir Shigemori, and only one composed by major characters such as Munemori (11.17), Michimori (9.19), or Koremori (10.1).

10. *Taira no Tadanori ason shū* 平忠度朝臣集, "The Collection of Lord Tadanori." Reizeike Shiguretei Bunko 冷泉家時雨亭文庫, ed., *Chūsei shikashū* 中世私家集, vol. 2 (Asahi Shinbunsha, 1994). *Shinpen kokka taikan*, vol. 3, *Shikashūhen* I, *kashū* (Kadokawa shoten: 1985), 559–61.

11. 武芸にも歌道にも達者にて *bugei ni mo kadō ni mo tassha ni te*. Ichiko, *Heike monogatari* (ge), 229; McCullough, *Tale of the Heike*, 314.

did not participate in the attack on Nara (1180.12) that ends with the death of many innocents and destruction of ancient temples.

Rather than focusing on Tadanori's military activities, the narrative instead shows him in the role of poet. The first extended description of him occurs in the section on "Fuji River" (5.2), just before he sets off with an army sent to attack Yoritomo. Like his father before him, Tadanori is involved with a lady of elegant poetic sensibility, and like his father, he proves himself a worthy match in refinement, first by catching a delicate hint she makes when unable to meet him, and then in the poem he writes in response to hers. Both her hint and his response are explicitly praised for their elegance.[12]

The association of Tadanori with poetic finesse is borne out above all by the episodes with which we are principally concerned, "Tadanori's Flight from the Capital," in which he leaves a scroll of his poems with his poetry master Shunzei, and "The Death of Tadanori," where he is identified by a poem found on his body. In between these episodes, Tadanori is mentioned only twice, in sections 7.19 and 8.3. The latter describes how poems were composed on the night of the full moon in the Ninth Month in Juei 2 (1183), as the exiled Heike think nostalgically of the capital. Tadanori's is quoted first, followed by poems by his elder brother Tsunemori and nephew Tsunemasa. The prominence given to Tadanori's poem is another indication of his stature as a poet within the narrative.

A fuller study of Tadanori would also need to take into account how he is treated in the variant texts of *Heike monogatari*. One relatively short but interesting example must suffice. In the thirty-sixth book of *Genpei jōsuiki* 源平盛衰記 (the Rise and Fall of the Genji and Heike), the episode "Tadanori sees the famous sites" contains a passage not present in the Kakuichi variant relates the events just prior to the battle of Ichi-no-tani.[13] Half a page in length in a modern edition, it consists largely of a string of famous place names in Settsu province, a kind of *tsukushi* (exhaustive list) naming mountains, rivers, inlets, bays, moors, forests, waterfalls, barrier points, bridges, islands, and villages, with several celebrated examples of each. The passage ends by returning to

---

12. The narratorial comments are, respectively, 優にやさしう *yū ni yasashū* ("elegantly") and いとやさしうぞ *ito yasashū zo* ("very elegantly"). Ichiko, *Heike monogatari* (jō), 394, 395; McCullough, *Tale of the Heike*, 185, 186.

13. The full title of the section is 忠度名所名所を見る附難波の浦 賤の夫婦 の事 *Tadanori meisho meisho wo miru (tsuketari) Naniwa no ura shizu no fūfu no koto*. The second part tells the Ashikari 芦刈 story dramatized by Zeami.

Tadanori's feelings of nostalgia: *koko ni utsuri kashiko ni watatte mitamau naka ni mo, Naniwa no ura koso inishie no koto omoiidashitsutsu aware nare* "as he went here and there, crossing over to look in Naniwa Bay he remembered again and again the past—how sad."[14]

In the first key episode serving as a source for the play (Kakuichibon 7.16), Tadanori has apparently already started on his "flight from the capital" (*miyako ochi*) with a small party when he suddenly turns back. The narrator feigns not to know exactly at what point he returns—*izuku yori ya kaeraretariken* "from where was it, then, that he turned back?" As we will see later, other versions of the narrative are less reticent about identifying the place.

Tadanori goes to "the residence in Gojō of Lord Shunzei of the Third Rank," knocks on the gate, and announces his name. There is panic in the capital as the Taira forces flee the city, and the gates of Shunzei's house are firmly closed. His servants are initially fearful of admitting "fugitives" (*ochūdo* 落人), but Shunzei agrees to meet his sometimes pupil, as we later learn Tadanori to be.

Lord Shunzei is the distinguished poetry master, Fujiwara no Shunzei, who was over seventy at this point in time.[15] Tadanori returns for two reasons. First, he wishes to see his master once before he leaves the capital, surely for the last time. Second, he wants to leave something of great personal value with his teacher.

A similar pattern recurs in the following section, "Tsunemasa's Flight from the Capital" (7.17). As a child, Tsunemasa served the abbot (*omuro*) of the Ninnaji, and now "in the midst of the general confusion, he remembered him with longing," so he gallops to the temple gate.[16] Like Tadanori, he is accompanied by a small group of riders. The object of value that Tsunemasa wants to leave behind is a *biwa* or lute. Tsunemasa is already associated in the minds of the audience with the *biwa* by a memorable scene earlier in the seventh chapter (7.4, "Chikubushima"). Like the earlier references to Tadanori and poetry, this prepares listeners or readers for the central object in the scene of farewell. Two nō plays based on this episode are discussed below.

---

14. ここに移りかしこに渡つて見給ふ中にも、難波の浦こそ古への事思ひ出だしつつ哀れなれ. Mizuhara Hajime, ed., *Shintei Genpei jōsuiki*, vol. 5 (Shinjin jinbutsu ōraisha, 1991), 26.

15. Fujiwara no Shunzei 藤原俊成 (1114–1204). His personal name is also read Toshinari.

16. Ichiko, *Heike monogatari* (ge), 77; McCullough, *Tale of the Heike*, 247–48.

In "Tadanori's Flight from the Capital," we do not learn how long
Tadanori has been studying poetry with Shunzei, but it has certainly
been a considerable length of time. As he explains to his teacher, he has
neglected his lessons in the last "two or three years" because of "unrest
in the capital and chaos in the provinces" (*miyako no sawagi, kuniguni
no midare*) and the subsequent problems these have caused his family.
"The fortunes of the family will soon be at an end" (*ichimon no unmei
haya tsuki-sōrainu*), he remarks.[17] Before he leaves the capital, however,
he wishes to leave Shunzei with a scroll of his poems in the hope that
his teacher will think it fit to include even one in the imperial anthology
(*chokusenshū*) that he is editing.

It seems that Tadanori knows that Shunzei has received an imperial
commission to compile an anthology, but realizes that this can only be
completed when the world is again at peace. Shunzei is greatly moved,
and promises to cherish the "keepsake" (*wasuregatami*). Tadanori
rejoices. His wish fulfilled, he has no regrets about dying, whether it be
in the sea or on land. Shunzei watches Tadanori leave, reciting a famous
Sino-Japanese poem of farewell.

The *sashi* section of *Shunzei Tadanori* quotes this poem of farewell:

前途程遠し、思ひをがん山の、夕の雲にはつす

*zento hodo tōshi, omoi wo ganzan
no yūbe no kumo ni hassu.*[18]

I know the way ahead is far. Therefore
I turn my thoughts to the evening
clouds over Goose Mountain.[19]

These are the first two lines of a four-line *rōei* 朗詠, a poem for
singing. The original poem in Chinese was presented by the Japanese
courtier Ōe Asatsuna 大江朝綱 (866–958) to an envoy from Bohai

17. Ichiko, *Heike monogatari* (ge), 75; cf. McCullough, *Tale of the Heike*, 246–
47. Tsunemasa also declares that the fortunes of the Taira are at an end (*ichimon
tsukite* 一門尽きて). Ichiko, *Heike monogatari* (ge), 77.

18. *Omuro Tsunemasa*. Furuya Chishin, *Yōkyoku zenshū* (Kokumin bunko
kankōkai, 1911), vol. 2, 326. For the equivalent passage in the Kakuichi version,
see Ichiko, *Heike monogatari* (ge), 76; McCullough, *Tale of Heike*, 247. *Ganzan* 雁
山 (Ch. Yanshan) is a mountain in China.

19. Translation by Miller and Donnelly from the *sashi* section of *Shunzei
Tadanori*, Chapter 14 in this volume.

(Parhae) 渤海 in northeast Asia.[20] All four lines are quoted in the equivalent passage in Book 32 of *Genpei jōsuiki*, where the narrative has Tadanori deliberately change the third line, singing instead "No date for a later meeting" (後会期無し).[21]

This Sino-Japanese poem also appears in one of the two plays about Tsunemasa, the extracanonical play *Omuro Tsunemasa*.[22] This is a *genzaimono* ("real time" piece), and follows fairly closely the *Heike* narrative of Tsunemasa's leave-taking of the Abbot (7.17), but adding a dance as typical of many nō plays. It is quite possible that the lines are borrowed from the nō play *Shunzei Tadanori*, rather than from the original episode from *Heike monogatari*, or indeed from the ultimate source in the *Wakan roei* collection.

As it turned out, *Senzaiwakashū*, the imperial anthology in question, appeared only two or three years after the final battle of the war, in 1187 or 1188.[23] In a bold but not unique use of prolepsis, the episode ends with an account of what happened to the scroll of poems after peace returned.[24] When Shunzei was editing the anthology, he recalled with sadness how Tadanori looked and spoke on that last occasion.[25] He found

---

20. Ōsone Shōsuke and Horiuchi Hideaki, eds., Wakan rōeishū 和漢朗詠集 (Shinchōsha, 1983), 238 (前途程遠　馳思於雁山之暮雲). *Chinese and Japanese Poems to Sing: The Wakan Roei Shū*, edited and translated by J. Thomas Rimer and Jonathan Chaves (Columbia University Press, 1997), 188 ("The road ahead stretches far for you; / your thoughts race to the evening clouds of Wild Goose Mountain. / A later meeting? the date far off, / we moisten hat strings in tears this morning / at the court of diplomacy"). Poem no. 632 in the section of volume two entitled "Farewell Gatherings" (*senbetsu* 餞別).

21. Mizuhara, *Shintei Genpei jōsuiki*, vol. 4, 154.

22. *Omuro Tsunemasa* 御室経政. Furuya, *Yōkyoku zenshū*, vol. 2, 325–27. Texts of this play appear also under other titles: *Omuro* 御室, *Genzai Tsunemasa* 現在経政, and *Konjō Tsunemasa* 今生経政. See Tanaka Makoto, *Mikan yōkyokushū (zoku)*, vol. 20 (Koten bunko, 1997), "Yōkyoku nayose ichiran," 328, 458, 501.

23. *Senzai [waka] shū* 千載[和歌]集, "Collection [of Japanese Poems] of a Thousand Years." On the two possible dates, Bunji 文治 3 or 4, see Katano Tatsurō and Matsuno Yōichi, eds., *Senzai wakashū*, SNKT 10 (Iwanami shoten, 1993), 434.

24. Other examples of prolepsis in *Heike monogatari* include "Nobutsuna" (4.6) and "Fujito" (10.6). McCullough, *Tale of the Heike*, 142, 356.

25. This reflective comment is a good example of Shuzei as focalizer. Over the course of the episode, focalization shifts from Tadanori to Shunzei. The turning point may come with the expression *koto no tei nani to nō aware nari* 事の体何となう哀れなり, which has been translated as referring specifically to Tadanori, "whose whole bearing conveyed an air of melancholy." Burton Watson, trans., *The*

many poems in the scroll that were worthy of inclusion, but chose just one, entitled "Blossoms at my home" (*Kokyō no hana* 故郷花), that began with *Sazanami ya.*[26] Yet because Tadanori was now an enemy of the court (*chōteki* 朝敵), Shunzei could not identify the poet by name, writing instead *yomibito shirazu*, "Poet Unknown."[27]

Shunzei's caution is understandable. During the course of the war, he seems to have avoided being associated with one side or another. His son, the equally celebrated Teika 定家 recorded a more forthright comment about the conflict. In his diary entry for 1180.9 when the Genji revolt began in earnest, he wrote 世上乱逆追討耳に満つといえども、これを注せず。紅旗征戎わが事にあらず *sejō rangyaku tsuitō mimi ni mitsu to iedomo, kore wo chū sezu; kōki seijō waga koto ni arazu,* "One's ears are filled with news of rebellion and campaigns to crush the rebels, but there is no need to give heed; the red banners [of the Heike] and the expeditions against the barbarian enemy [Genji] have nothing to do with me."[28]

The battle of Ichi-no-tani (1184.2.7) occurred in and around the modern city of Kobe in Hyōgo prefecture. Tadanori was killed in Suma 須磨 on the coast of the Inland Sea. In the final skirmish, Tadanori's right arm was struck off, a fact still remembered in the cities of Kōbe and neighboring Akashi today, both in place names and in a number of separate monuments to his arm and body.[29] Tadanori was the most

---

Tales of the Heike (Columbia University Press, 2006), 76; cf. McCullough, *Tale of the Heike*, 246 ("It was a moving scene").

26. *Senzaishū* 66 (Book One, "Spring Poems, One"). The entire poem is included in the *ageuta* section of the chorus. See the translation by Stephen D. Miller and Patrick S. Donnelly that follows.

27. Ichiko, *Heike monogatari* (ge), 76–77; cf. McCullough, *Tale of the Heike*, 246–47.

28. *Meigetsuki* entry for Jishō 4, 1180.9. Quoted in Sino-Japanese from Hotta Yoshie, *Teika Meigetsuki shishō* (Chikuma bunko, 1996), 42. This famous passage is discussed in Donald Keene, *Travelers of a Hundred Ages* (New York: Henry Holt, 1989), 95–96.

29. There are at least three "arm mounds" (*udezuka* 腕塚), one a simple stone monument in Kōbe-shi Nagata-ku Noda-chō 神戸市長田区野田町, and two in the form of small shrines, one in Kōbe-shi Nagata-ku Komagabayashi 駒ヶ林町 and one in neighboring Akashi-shi Tenmon-chō 明石市天文町, formally called Udezuka-chō 腕塚町. A "body mound" (*dōzuka* 胴塚) in Kōbe-shi Nagata-ku Noda-chō 長田町野田町 is traditionally held to be the place where the rest of his body was buried. The name Udezuka-chō is still used for an area in Nagata-ku. Photographs can be found online in sites such as *Yōseki meguri* 謡蹟めぐり, http://www.harusan1925.net/0321.html. Accessed January 11, 2011.

senior member of the Heike to fall in the battle of Ichi-no-tani, but it also took the lives of many close relatives, including seven nephews and two grandnephews.[30]

"The Death of Tadanori" (Kakuichi-bon 9.14) gives an account of how he dies at the hands of a low-ranking warrior, Okabe no Rokuyata Tadazumi 岡部六弥太忠澄, a Genji warrior from Musashi province.[31] Tadazumi was a member of the Inomata league, the *Inomata-tō* 猪俣党, one of the seven Musashi warrior leagues (*bushidan* 武士団) mentioned in *Heike monogatari*. The play *Shunzei Tadanori* takes place a month after the devastating defeat at Ichi-no-tani, and describes how the same Tadazumi visits Shunzei in order to deliver a poem that he found in the quiver of the man he had killed.

Already by the thirteenth of the Second Month, the heads of the Heike dead were being paraded through the streets of the capital. *Heike monogatari* does not dwell on the Genji's triumphant return to the city, focusing instead on the anxiety of certain of the Heike vanquished, who did not know whether their loved ones were alive or dead.

There is certainly no suggestion in the *Heike* narrative that an insignificant provincial warrior like Tadazumi would have taken it upon himself to visit the house of Fujiwara no Shunzei. Even if he had tried to gain admittance to Shunzei's house, it is hard to imagine that the household would have readily admitted an unknown, low-ranking warrior—judging from the caution shown before they admitted Shunzei's pupil Tadanori eight months before. Unlikely though the situation may be in reality, it works admirably for the purpose of the nō play. Shunzei learns of the fate of his pupil, praises his poetic talent, and reads aloud the poem found on his body. At this point the spirit of Tadanori enters. The rest of the play consists of exchanges between master and dead pupil, interspersed with choral passages.

Their exchange can best be read in the translation itself, but we should note the way it converts the narrative prolepsis into a dialogue.

---

30. According to *Heike monogatari*, at least nine of Tadanori's close male relatives died at Ichi-no-tani: his nephews Kiyofusa 清房, Kiyosada 清定, Tsunemasa (Kakuichi-bon 9.15), Tsunetoshi 経俊, Atsumori 敦盛 (9.16), Michimori 通盛, and Narimori 業盛 (9.18), and his grandnephews Moromori 師盛 (9.18) and Tomoakira 知章 (9.17). In addition, Michimori's wife commits suicide on hearing of her husband's death (9.19). Some deaths are only briefly related in the section "Ochiashi" (9.18 "The Flight"), but others are described in considerable detail.

31. Musashi 武蔵 includes part of modern Tokyo and prefectures to its north.

Tadanori knows already that "Blossoms at my home" has been included in the anthology, but regrets that Shunzei had not identified him by name. This gives Shunzei an opportunity to explain why he was unable to do so. Tadanori is remarkably forgiving, accepting his teacher's assurances that his poetry will make his name "as famous as the stirrups of Musashi."[32]

The chronology is conveniently forgotten here. Only a month has passed since Ichi-no-tani, and the war will not be over for more than another year, so the completion of the anthology is still far off.

The playwright Naitō Tōzaemon 内藤藤左衛門 has created this imaginary encounter by making use of a time-honored practice in Japanese narratives and performed works. This is the technique known by modern scholars as *gojitsutan* 後日譚, a tale that is invented to explain what happened afterward. The play *Ikuta Atsumori* translated in this collection is another example of this, although in that case the initiative seems to have been taken first not in nō but in the genre of short medieval prose tales.

Another example is the canonical nō *Tsunemasa*, which like *Tadanori* takes the form of a phantom play.[33] The *biwa* left by Tsunemasa is placed in front of the Buddhist altar at Ninnaji as part of a service for the deceased. After a priest recounts how he died at Ichi-no-tani, Tsunemasa's spirit appears and describes the sufferings of the *aśura* hell.

Eight surviving nō plays feature Tadanori's spirit as *shite*. Three are canonical plays (*genkō yōkyoku* 現行謡曲), in the current performance repertoire:

32. *Sono na mo sasuga Musashi abumi kakure wa araji ware hito no.* An allusion to *Ise monogatari*, section 13, which begins: *Musashi abumi / sasuga ni kakete;* "just as stirrups from Musashi province hang on their buckles." The *Ise* poem plays on double meanings of *sasuga* (both "stirrup buckle" and "naturally") and *kakete* ("hang" and "depend"), which were *engo* 縁語, words poetically associated with *abumi* (stirrups). See Helen Craig McCullough, *Tales of Ise: Lyrical Episodes from Tenth-Century Japan* (University of Tokyo Press, 1968), 78–79 (translation) and 206–7 (notes). Shunzei here uses the same associated words *sasuga* and *abumi*, while the sound of *kakure* echoes *kakete* in the *Ise* poem.

33. The play is performed by all five schools. The title is written *Tsunemasa* 経正 in the Kanze and Kongō schools, and as *Tsunemasa* 経政 in the Hōshō, Komparu, and Kita. The play has most recently been translated into English in Chifumi Shimazaki, *Battle Noh in Parallel Translations with an Introduction and Running Commentaries* (Tokyo: Hinoki Shoten, 1987), 120–35.

1. *Tadanori* 忠度, by Zeami, a *shuramono* 修羅物
   or warrior play[34]
2. *Shunzei Tadanori* 俊成忠度, the play translated in
   this volume
3. *Genzai Tadanori* 現在忠度 (1), in the repertoire of
   the Kongō school[35]

In *Tadanori*, as in *Shunzei Tadanori*, the *shite* is the ghost of warrior poet himself. On the prompting of the *waki*, a traveling monk in the service of Fujiwara no Shunzei, he gives a much more detailed account of his death at the hands of Tadazumi than we find in *Shunzei Tadanori*. Zeami seems to have been proud of his achievement with *Tadanori*. In *Sarugaku dangi*, he is recorded as saying that the warrior plays *Michimori, Tadanori*, and *Yoshitsune* were "good nō" (*yoki nō*), and that of these *Tadanori* ranked highest.[36]

The remaining plays featuring Tadanori are *bangai yōkyoku* 番外 謡曲 or extracanonical pieces not included in the modern performance repertoire:

4. *Shiga Tadanori* 志賀忠度[37]
5. *Ikuta Tadanori* 生田忠度[38]

---

34. Editions include Koyama Hiroshi and Satō Ken'ichirō, eds., *Yōkyokushū* 1, SNBZ 58 (Shōgakukan, 1997), 147–59. There exist at least five English translations, the most recent being Royall Tyler, *Japanese Nō Dramas* (London, New York: Penguin Books, 1992), 264–76. This has a valuable preface.

35. Tanaka, *Mikan yōkyokushū (zoku)*, vol. 3 (Koten bunko, 1988), 50–55. Two other plays with the same name are mentioned below.

36. *Sarugaku dangi* 申楽談義. Hisamatsu Sen'ichi and Nishio Minoru, eds., *Karonshū, Nōgakuronshū*, NKBT 65 (Iwanami shoten, 1961), 515; Erika de Poorter, *Zeami's Talks on Sarugaku: An Annotated Translation of* Sarugaku dangi *with an Introduction on Zeami Motokiyo* (Leiden: Hotei Publishing, 2002), 108. Yoshitsune is now more commonly known as *Yashima*.

37. Furuya, *Yōkyoku zenshū*, vol. 2, 243–46; Haga Yaichi and Sasaki Nobutsuna, eds., *Kōchū yōkyoku sōsho*, vol. 2 (Rinsen shoten, 1987), 108–12. The work has been traditionally attributed to Zeami 世阿弥 or Zenchiku 禅竹. Tanaka Makoto, *Mikan yōkyokushū (zoku)*, vol. 21 (Koten bunko, 1997), 63.

38. Sasaki Nobutsuna, ed., *Shin yōkyoku hyakuban* (Rinsen shoten, 1987), 16–20. Hida no zenji Mitsumori 飛騨の前司光盛 (*waki*) accompanies Tadanori's son to Ichi-no-tani to pray for his father. There they meet the armored figure of Tadanori's spirit (*shite*) and hear of his death in battle and his suffering in the other world, at eternal war with the *ashura* 阿修羅 (Skt. *aśura*).

6. *Kusakari Tadanori* くさかり忠度[39]
7. *Genzai Tadanori* (2) 現在忠則[40]
8. *Genzai Tadanori* (3) 現在忠度[41]

As noted earlier, "Tadanori's Flight from the Capital" avoids saying exactly where Tadanori turned back to the capital to visit Shunzei. Later versions of *Heike monogatari* in the "read" lineage are less vague: the Nagato version specifies a place name, Yotsuka, while *Genpei jōsuiki* describes him as reaching as far as the lower reaches (*kawajiri*) of the Yodo River.[42] The usual route from the capital to the Inland Sea followed the Yodo River. Intriguingly, however, there seems to be an alternative tradition in extracanonical nō. In two of the plays, Tadanori is said to have turned back at a place called Kitsunegawa 狐河.[43] There is a modern place by this name less than ten kilometers down the Yodo River from the capital, also a plausible place for Tadanori to have turned back.[44]

Of these *bangai* plays, *Shiga Tadanori* 志賀忠度 (or 志賀忠則) most resembles *Shunzei Tadanori*. It too is a *mugen nō*, drawing from

---

39. Tanaka Makoto, *Mikan yōkyokushū*, vol. 27 (Koten bunko, 1976), 39–42. A Ninnaji monk (*waki*) makes a pilgrimage to Suma Beach, where he encounters the "grass-cutter" (*maeshite*) of the title—who resembles Atsumori in Zeami's play of that name. He is revealed as the spirit of Tadanori (*nochijite*).

40. Tanaka Makoto, *Mikan yōkyokushū*, vol. 1 (Koten bunko, 1963), 188–91. The play dramatizes in "real time" the visit to Shunzei (*waki*) by Tadanori (*shite*). The opening borrows other material from *Heike monogatari*, including the passage from Kakuichi-bon 7.13 about how the fleeing Regent reacts when he sees the characters for "spring sun" (Kasuga 春日). Ichiko, *Heike monogatari* (ge), 266; McCullough, *Tale of the Heike*, 243.

41. Tanaka Makoto, *Mikan yōkyokushū*, vol. 17 (Koten bunko, 1971), 171–74. Tadanori (*shite*) turns back to visit Shunzei (*tsure*). This is a Muramachi-period work, extant in many manuscripts.

42. Asahara Yoshiko, ed., *Nagato-bon Heike monogatari no sōgō kenkyū: kōchū-hen ge*, vol. 2 (Benseisha, 1999), 1051. Yotsuka 四つか is identified by the editor as Yotsuka 四塚, southwest of Tōji in the Minami ward of modern Kyoto. This would be a relatively short ride from Shunzei's residence in Gojō. Mizuhara, *Shintei Genpei jōsuiki*, vol. 4, 153 ("Yodo no kawajiri made" 淀の河尻まで).

43. *Kitsunegawa yori hikikaeshi* 狐河より引帰し, in *Ikuta Tadanori*, ed. Sasaki, *Shin yōkyoku hyakuban*, 18. *Kitsunegawa* 狐川, in *Genzai Tadanori* (3), ed. Tanaka, *Mikan yōkyokushū* 17, 171.

44. Yawata Kitsunegawa 八幡狐川, Yawata-shi, Kyoto-fu. There is another Kitsunegawa in modern Kyoto prefecture, but it is in the wrong direction for a journey to Fukuhara on the Inland Sea.

the same two *Heike* episodes. A traveling monk arriving in Shiga by Lake Biwa recalls the poem on the subject of the ancient capital of Shiga by "Poet Unknown" included in the *Senzaishū*.[45] As he wonders who the poet could have been, a villager appears and tells him that the poet was Tadanori, only later to reveal himself as the dead warrior's spirit. The play ends with the spirit describing his death at Ichi-no-tani.

An interesting postscript to the story of Tadanori's meeting with Shunzei can be found in two of the "read" lineage versions of *Heike monogatari*, the early Engyō-bon and the Nagato-bon. These give similar accounts of how another member of the Taira family pauses in his flight to visit his poetry master—none other than Shunzei's son Teika.[46] Teika is moved to tears to be presented with a poem by his pupil, Sama-no-kami Yukimori,[47] and promises to include it in an imperial anthology. He is sorry to hear later that his father did not name Tadanori as the author of the poem included in the *Senzaishū*. When he has an opportunity to select poems for the ninth imperial anthology, the *Shinchokusen wakashū*, Teika chooses the *waka* that Yukimori had given him.[48] More than three reigns had passed since the end of the Genpei War, Teika argued, and therefore there should not be any problem in naming the poet. On first reading, the story seems an invention, simply a variation with a happy ending on the story of how Shunzei was unable to give his pupil credit for his poem. Surprisingly, though, there is evidence that this old account may be true, at least in its broad outlines. In the *Shinchokusen wakashū*, Yukimori's poem is accompanied by a long headnote explaining how he wrote down the poem and left it with Teika in Juei 2 (1183) "at a time when the world at large was not at peace."[49]

---

45. In years 667–672, the capital was at Shiga, in present-day Ōtsu City by Lake Biwa.

46. Kitahara Yasuo and Ogawa Eiichi, eds., *Engyō-bon Heike monogatari: honbun-hen*, vol. 2 (Benseisha, 1990), 89; Asahara, *Nagato-bon Heike monogatari no sōgō kenkyū*, vol. 2, 1053–54.

47. Sama-no-kami Yukimori 左馬頭行盛 (?–1185), son of Kiyomori's second son Motomori. He took his own life at Dan-no-ura, throwing himself into the sea. Ichiko, *Heike monogatari* (ge), 384; McCullough, *Tale of the Heike*, 379.

48. *Shinchokusen wakashū* 新勅撰和歌集, commissioned by Emperor Go-Horikawa in 1232 and completed in 1235. The poem is no. 1193, in Book 17 (*zakka* 2), and credited to Taira no Yukimori.

49. *Ōkata no yo shizuka narazu haberishi koro. Shinpen Kokka taikan*, vol. 1, *Chokusenshūhen, kashū*, 283. The entire headnote is also quoted in Hattori Kōzō, "Yukimori," in Ichiko Teiji, *Heike monogatari kenkyū jiten* (Meiji shoin, 1978), 633c.

14 ～ *Shunzei Tadanori*

| MICHAEL WATSON

INTRODUCTION

Taira no Tadanori 平忠度 (1144–1184) was the most senior member of his family to perish in the battle Ichi-no-tani (1184.2.7). He fought bravely but was outnumbered, dying at the hands of a low-ranking Genji warrior, Okabe no Rokuyata Tadazumi 岡部六弥太忠澄.[1] The play *Shunzei Tadanori* 俊成忠度 is set in the capital one month after the battle. Having discovered the identity of the man he killed from a signed poem in his quiver, Tadazumi decides to bring the poem to Tadanori's poetry master, "Lord Shunzei"—the distinguished Heian man of letters, Fujiwara no Shunzei 藤原俊成 (1114–1204). Tadazumi hands him the strip of paper bearing the poem ("Blossoms at the inn") wrapped around an arrow. When Shunzei reads it aloud, the arrow falls from his hands, in a simple but effective gesture of his shock and grief at the news of his pupil's death. The chorus praises Tadanori for excelling in both the literary and military arts.

As the chorus is singing, Tadanori's ghost slowly enters. The first words he sings are a famous poem of farewell ("I know the way ahead is far"), the very last words Shunzei heard Tadanori sing as he rode off from their final meeting before fleeing the capital with the rest of the

---

1. "The Death of Tadanori" (Kakuichi-bon 9.14 "Tadanori no saigo" 忠度最期). Ichiko Teiji, ed., *Heike monogatari* (ge), NKBZ 46 (Shōgakukan, 1994), 226–29; Helen Craig McCullough, *The Tale of the Heike* (Stanford University Press, 1988), 313–34. For a fuller discussion of this play and related works, see Chapter 13 in this volume.

Heike just seven months before (1183.7).[2] Both knew at the time that he was not likely ever to return. Tadanori has prepared a scroll of more than one hundred of his best poems to present to his poetry teacher in the hope that even one might be included in the imperial poetic anthology that Shunzei had been commissioned to compile. His teacher is moved to receive the scroll, but is ultimately unable to give to Tadanori the literary honors he so desires. When the imperial anthology *Senzaishū* 千載集 is finally completed, two or three years after the hostilities end,[3] Shunzei includes one of Tadanori's poems:

Sazanami ya	Though the capital at Shiga
Shiga no miyako wa	lies in ruin
arenishi wo	the mountain cherries are
mukashi nagara no	as they always were.[4]
yamazakura kana	

Tadanori's status as enemy of the court prevents Shunzei from mentioning Tadanori by name. Instead, he lists the author of the poem as *yomibito shirazu*, "poet unknown."

The play telescopes the chronology for dramatic effect.[5] The grief felt by Shunzei at hearing the news of Tadanori's recent death is followed by his shock at the appearance of the spirit of Tadanori, who knows already of the "Anonymous" poem. Audiences familiar with the original story must have wondered whether Tadanori will react with pride, resentment, or resignation. In fact Tadanori is remarkably forgiving, accepting his

---

2. The immediate source of the poem is an earlier *Heike* episode: "Tadanori's Flight from the Capital" (Kakuichi-bon 7.16 "Tadanori no miyako ochi" 忠度都落). Ichiko, *Heike monogatari* (ge), 76; McCullough, *Tale of the Heike*, 247. Tadanori's leave-taking of Shunzei is the subject of one of the masterpieces of *Heike* illustration, a vividly colored screen painting by Kaihō Yūsetsu 海北友雪 (1598–1677). The screen is in private hands; for a reproduction, see Anzai Tsuyoshi, ed., *Heike monogatari* (Gakken, 1998), 44–45.

3. The date is uncertain, either 1187 or 1188. See footnote 23 in the preceding essay.

4. *Senzaishū* 千載集 66 (Book One, "Spring Poems, One"), quoted in the translation below. The poem is quoted twice in the play, in the *ageuta* section and in the final chorus. The untranslated opening line ("oh gentle waves") functions as a pillow word for Shiga, which lies on the shores of Lake Biwa. Ichiko, *Heike monogatari* (ge), 77; McCullough, *Tale of the Heike*, 247.

5. Commissioned by Retired Emperor Go-Shirakawa in Juei 2 (1183), the anthology was only completed in Bunji 3 (1188).

teacher's assurances that his poetry will make his name "as famous as the stirrups of Musashi."

Evidence for Tadanori's reputation as a poet can be found in the manuscript archives of the Reizei family that preserve his personal poetry collection.[6] Paradoxically, though, the poem that has given him lasting posthumous fame was the one for which he was not given credit at the time. In the climax to this play, Tadanori describes how his spirit is caught up in the violent wars between the *ashura* (titans) and Bonten (Indra).[7] In other second category plays, the troubled spirits of warriors are placated only by the solicitous prayers of the traveling monks who hear their tale. Here, though, the mighty Bonten himself ends the conflict out of admiration for Tadanori's poem on the capital at Shiga.

---

6. See Chapter 13, note 10.

7. Passages describing warring titans occur in other *shura* nō. Examples include *Kiyotsune*, translated in this volume, and *Tomonaga*.

Shunzei Tadanori

| Translated by Stephen D. Miller and
Patrick S. Donnelly

Second-category *mūgen* nō in one act.
Performed by the Kanze, Hōshō, Kongō, and Kita schools.
Time: Third year of Juei (1184), Third Month
Place: The mansion of Fujiwara Shunzei on Gojō Avenue in
        the capital[1]
Author: Naitō Tōzaemon 内藤藤左衛門

WAKI	Okabe no Rokuyata Tadazumi
TSURE	Fujiwara Shunzei
TOMO	Attendant
SHITE	Ghost of Taira no Tadanori

Tadazumi stands at the first pine next to the bridgeway (hashigakari)
carrying an arrow to which is attached a narrow piece of paper.

TADAZUMI   I am your servant, Okabe no Rokuyata Tadazumi, a
resident of Musashi. I killed Satsuma Governor Tadanori with my own
hands at the great battle in the western sea.[2] When I searched his quiver
after he was dead, I found a poem on a narrow strip of paper. I heard
that Tadanori was the student of Lord Shunzei on Gojō Avenue, so I will
take the poem and show it to him.[3]

*So saying, Tadazumi walks onto the main stage and turns in the direction
of Shunzei.*

TADAZUMI   Please tell me the way.

Shunzei Tadanori 俊成忠度. This translation is based on Sanari Kentarō, ed.,
Yōkyoku taikan, vol. 3 (Meiji shoin, 1931), 1437–1448.

1. Taira no Tadanori 平忠度 studied poetry with Fujiwara no Shunzei (also read
Toshinari) 藤原俊成 (1114–1204), whose residence was on Gojō 五条 (Fifth Avenue).

2. The "western sea" (*saikai* 西海) here refers to the Inland Sea between Honshū and
Shikoku. The battle of Ichi-no-tani occurred in and around the modern city of Kōbe.

3. "The Death of Tadanori" (9.14) describes how Tadazumi kills Tadanori,
and discovers his name from a signed poem, but no version of *Heike monogatari*
suggests that Tadazumi later brings the poem to Shunzei.

Attendant stands and appears at the naming pillar (nanoriza).[4]

ATTENDANT	Who is it?
TADAZUMI	Please tell Lord Shunzei that Okabe no Rokuyata Tadazumi is here.
ATTENDANT	I understand.

Attendant appears in front of Shunzei and bows.

	My lord?
SHUNZEI	What is it?
ATTENDANT	Okabe no Rokuyata Tadazumi has come to inquire about something.
SHUNZEI	Please show him here.
ATTENDANT	Yes, sir.

Goes to the nanoriza *and faces Tadazumi.*

	Please come this way.
TADAZUMI	I will.

Goes stage center and sits. Shunzei turns to Tadazumi.

SHUNZEI	Why are you here, Tadazumi?
TADAZUMI	I've come about something in particular. I killed Tadanori with my own hands at the great battle in the western sea. Searching his quiver after he was dead, I found a poem written on a narrow strip of paper. When I heard that Tadanori was knowledgeable about *waka*, I brought this here to show it to you.
SHUNZEI	Please.

Tadazumi pulls an arrow out of his robe, passes it to Shunzei, and returns to his seat. Shunzei takes the arrow.

(*sashi*)	Although it was not as a horseman or archer,
	how touching that he left his name in this world.

Shunzei places the slip of paper in his right hand.

What is the poem's topic? "Blossoms at the inn."[5]

> If I make the shade
> of this tree my inn,
> when night falls

---

4. The *nanoriza* 名乗り座, the "self-naming seat" is another name for the *jōza* 常座, which has been translated throughout this volume as "base square." See plan of the nō stage in Royall Tyler, *Japanese Nō Dramas* (London, New York: Penguin Books, 1992), 21.

5. *Ryoshuku no hana* 旅宿の花.

these blossoms would be
my innkeeper[6]

CHORUS

(*ageuta*)   How sad it is, Tadanori—

Shunzei drops the arrow.

How sad it is, Tadanori.
Fearing the sin of feeling no shame
were he to break his Buddhist vows,[7]
Tadanori walked the path of the five virtues[8]
          with perfection.
By the art of *waka*,
by the sturdy bow and arrow,
he made his name famous.
By excelling on the two paths of words and war,[9]
Tadanori claimed his ship and arrived
at the lotus throne on the far shore.[10]

*On the words "walked the path of the five virtues with perfection," Tadazumi
stands and exits through the side door* (kirido). *Tadanori appears through the
curtain on the words "Fearing the sin of feeling no shame." He arrives at the base
square* (jōza) *as the chorus finish the ageuta.*

TADANORI

(*sashi*)   I know the way ahead is far.
          Therefore I turn my thoughts to the evening
               clouds over Goose Mountain.[11]
          I, who sank beneath the eightfold tides,

---

6. *yuki kurete / ko no shitakage wo / yado to seba / hana ya koyoi no / aruji
naramashi* 行き暮れて木の下蔭を宿とせば花や今宵の主ならまし.

7. *Hakai muzan no tsumi* 破戒無慙の罪.

8. According to Confucian teachings, the five virtues (*itsutsu no michi* 五つの
道, *gotoku* 五徳) are humaneness, righteousness, ritual decorum, wisdom, and
trustworthiness (*jin* 仁, *gi* 偽, *rei* 礼, *chi* 智, and *shin* 信).

9. *Bunbu nidō* 文武二道, the literary and military arts.

10. The far shore (*kano kishi* 彼の岸) is a metaphorical reference to enlightenment.

11. Two lines of a four-line *rōei* 朗詠 (poem for singing), originally in Chinese,
but here read in Japanese: 前途程遠し、思を雁山の夕の雲に馳す *zento hodo
tōshi omoi o ganzan no yūbe no kumo ni hasu*. In *Heike monogatari* (Kakuichi-bon
7.16), it is sung by Tadanori after he bids farewell to Shunzei. Takagi Ichinosuke
et al., *Heike monogatari* (ge), NKBT 33 (Iwanami shoten, 1960), 104; Helen Craig
McCullough, *The Tale of the Heike* (Stanford University Press, 1988), 247. For
further information, see Chapter 13, note 20.

am drawn to spring in the ninefold capital.[12]
I can see myself with you that time we viewed
    the blossoms.
Would I ever want to feel the pain of being
    apart from you?
Not if my life's wish could be fulfilled.

Turning to Shunzei.

Lord Shunzei, Tadanori has come back.

SHUNZEI   This is bizarre! I don't know whether this is dream
                or reality—
            that I can see the Satsuma Governor is so strange.

TADANORI
    Nevertheless, I'm grateful you were kind enough to put a poem
    of mine into the *Senzaishū*.[13] But it bothers me that you attributed it
    to "anonymous."

SHUNZEI
    Understandably so. But restraint prevented me from putting the
    name of the enemy on it. Because your poem is there, your name will
    not be forgotten; please put yourself at ease.

TADANORI   I will. As long as my poem is included ...

SHUNZEI   Your name will be famous as the stirrups of
                Musashi ...[14]

TADANORI   My deep gratitude overflows like the peony ...

SHUNZEI   The poem in this anthology comes from the heart.

TADANORI   On the topic "Blossoms at my home."

CHORUS

    (*ageuta*)   Though the capital at Shiga
                lies in ruin
                the capital at Shiga lies in ruin
                the mountain cherries are
                as they always were.[15]

---

12. "Eightfold" (*yae* 八重) and "ninefold" (*kokonoe* 九重) are ways of expressing
"many" and "great." The "eightfold tides" means the "deep tides" while the "ninefold
capital" refers to its abounding beauty.
13. The *Senzaishū* 千載集 (completed 1188), the seventh of the twenty-one
imperial poetry anthologies, was compiled by Fujiwara no Shunzei, who was the
foremost poet of the time.
14. See Chapter 13, note 32.
15. *Sasanami ya / Shiga no miyako wa / arenishi wo / mukashi nagara no /*

Such a poem will bring you future honor.
In this sad world
brief as lightning,
brief as a butterfly's dream,
brief as a song or dance,
everything obeys the Dharma,
as in Naniwa in the province of Tsu.[16]
Do not doubt that I am Tadanori.

Tadanori moves to center stage and sits.

SHUNZEI

(*sashi*)   Poems are composed according to six genres[17]
in each of the six realms[18] of the Dharma.
CHORUS   Before the age of the gods, song had no fixed form.
TADANORI The brother of Amaterasu Ōmikami,[19]
CHORUS   Susano-o no Mikoto designated song as
thirty-one syllables,[20]
creating an example for all ages to come.

---

yamazakura kana ささ並や志賀の都は荒れにしを昔ながらの山桜かな.
Senzaishū 千載集 66 (Book one, "Spring Poems, One"). In years 667–72, the
capital was at Shiga, in Ōtsu City by Lake Biwa. *Sasanami,* a pillow word for Shiga,
is read *sazanami* in the standard edition of the imperial anthology: Katano Tatsurō
and Matsuno Yōichi, eds., *Senzai wakashū,* SNKT 10 (Iwanami shoten, 1993), 30.

16. Naniwa (present-day Osaka) in Tsu (a province name) is a reference to
a Buddhist poem (*shakkyō-ka* 釈教歌) by the courtesan Miyaki 遊女宮木,
Goshūishū 後拾遺集 1197: 津の国のなにはのことか法ならぬ遊び戯
れまでとこそ聞け *Tsu no kuni no / Naniwa no koto ka / nori naranu / asobi
tawabure / made to koso kike;* "here in Naniwa / in the land of Tsu what is / this
thing called Dharma / I thought it was meant even / for those who gambled
and played." Kubota Jun and Hirata Yoshinobu, eds., *Goshūi wakashū,* SNKT 8
(Iwanami shoten, 1994), 389. *Goshūishū,* the fourth imperial poetry anthology,
was compiled in 1086.

17. The six genres (*rikugi* 六義) refer to a classification created by Ki no
Tsurayuki in the Preface to the *Kokinshū.* The classification is based upon the six
genres in the Chinese *Classic of Songs* (*Shijing* 詩経).

18. The six realms (*rokudō* 六道) refer to the categorization of beings and the
realm in which they live (gods, humans, *ashuras,* animals, hungry ghosts, hell) as
set out in the Buddhist teachings.

19. The Sun Goddess. Her legend is told in the *Kojiki.*

20. The number of syllables found in a *waka* poem.

(*kuse*) When Susano-o no Mikoto planned to live
with the lady, Princess Inada,
he built her a fine home in Izumo.[21]
Seeing the eightfold clouds rising above Izumo,
he composed the poem
    In Izumo
    of the eightfold rising clouds,
    I build an eightfold fence
    to house my wife—
    oh, the eightfold fence[22]
Surely this rare poem composed by a god became an
    example for us.

Tadanori stands and performs.

I gazed across Suma Bay when I lay down to rest.
And I understood the poem "the morning
    mists at Akashi Bay."[23]

TADANORI
CHORUS
After Hitomaro passed out of this world
the art of song, it is said, ceased to exist.
But the writings of Ki no Tsurayuki and Mitsune[24] are
    evergreen,
like needles of pine after they fall.
Like tendrils of vine,
they reach down to us after all this time.
As long as their letters,
like the tracks of birds, last,
    the songs will not die out.

---

21. Present-day Shimane prefecture.
22. This poem can be found in the *Kojiki* 古事記: 八雲立つ出雲八重垣妻篭
み八重垣作るその八重垣を *Yagumo tatsu / Izumo yaegaki / tsuma gomi ni /
yaegaki tsukuru / sono yaegaki wo*. Kurano Kenji and Takeda Yūkichi, eds., *Kojiki
Norito*, NKBT 1 (Iwanami shoten, 1958), 89. For the story, see the translation
by Donald Phillipi, revised in Haruo Shirane, ed., *Traditional Japanese Literature*
(Columbia University Press, 2007), 30–31.
23. The phrase *Akashi no ura no asagiri* comes from a poem by Kakinomoto
no Hitomaro 柿本人丸 (7th–early 8th century). It is included as an anonymous
poem in *Kokinshū* 409: ほのぼのと明石の浦の朝霧に島隠れ行く舟をしぞ
思ふ *honobono to / Akashi no ura no / asagiri ni / shimagakure yuku / fune wo
shi zo omou.*
24. Tsurayuki and Ōshikōchi no Mitsune 凡河内躬恒 are two of the compilers
of the Kokinshū 古今集 (ca. 905), the first imperial poetry anthology.

The songs of Shikishima[25]—
which even the gods accept as offerings—
are like the go-between
who carries tenderness
between man and woman,
husband and wife.

CHORUS   Oh, an evening full of the keen sorrow of parting!

Tadanori assumes a posture of the warrior.

SHUNZEI

It's strange—look at him! His appearance has changed—a ghastly shape—what kind of thing is it?

From the base pillar (shitebashira), *Tadanori looks in the direction of the side* (wakishōmen).

TADANORI

Look there!—The king of the *ashuras*[26] charges up to the Brahmā heaven.[27] Indra[28] confronts him and chases him back to the lower realm.

CHORUS   The enemy's troops scatter,
               the troops scatter
               shouting and screaming.
               On the wave-beaten rocky shore,
               Tadanori, burning with a furious flame,
               draws his sword and slashes.

Tadanori unsheathes his sword and performs.

               His enemy raises their swords as one,
               but after he repels them,
               the enemy vanishes, vanquished.
               Tadanori stood in astonishment
               as a flaming chariot fell from heaven,
               and up from the earth
               a steel blade impaled his foot.
               No longer able to stand or sit—

---

25. Shikishima 敷島 is a poetic name for Japan.

26. *Shura-ō* 修羅王. The *ashuras* (Skt. aśura), one of the six Buddhist realms, are fighting titans who often attack Indra and the gods in his heaven.

27. Bonten 梵天.

28. *Taishaku* 帝釈. Originally one of the Vedic gods of India, Indra later became one of the tutelary gods of Buddhism.

Sitting crosslegged in the middle of the stage, Tadanori casts his sword aside.

> how awful the tortures
> of the king of the *ashuras*
> and his men.

Tadanori faces downward.

TADANORI	And so it was … The poem reads
CHORUS	Though the capital at Shiga

And so it was … The poem reads
Though the capital at Shiga
lies in ruin   *Opens his fan.*
the capital at Shiga lies in ruin   *Stands up.*
the mountain cherries are
as they always were
Because Indra admired the poem,
he lay aside his sword and its torments
and everything turned to darkness.
> Turning away from the lamp,
> together at midnight
> we treasure the moon;
> crushing the flowers underfoot
> we both mourn the spring
> when we were young[29]
With morning light rising fast,
with the rooster's cry,
the figure of Tadanori vanishes.
At daybreak in the mountains
he disappears
among the shadows of the trees,
among the shadows of the trees.

At the base square, he stamps with the final beat (tome-hyōshi).

---

29. *Wakan rōeishū* 27, from a poem by Bai Juyi 白居易 (Po Chü-i). The original Chinese text reads: 背燭共憐深夜月　踏花同惜少年春. Ōsone and Horiuchi, *Wakan rōeishū*, 27; Rimer and Chaves, *Chinese and Japanese Poems to Sing*, 37.

15 ～ Kiyotsune

| CAROLYN MORLEY

INTRODUCTION

Although a minor character in the *Tales of the Heike*, Kiyotsune 清経, a
Taira Middle Captain, is a seductive choice for the protagonist of a nō play.
In the few lines devoted to his suicide in the *Heike*, we learn that he is of
a brooding, sensitive nature, and that he is known for his prowess not on
the battlefield, but on the flute. The antithesis of the robust warriors of the
Minamoto clan, he calls to mind the courtly, overly refined Kashiwagi in
the *Tale of Genji*, a fellow flautist, and a suicide as well. Kiyotsune's death
at his own hand foreshadows the final dark turning in the fortunes of the
Taira. Driven from the capital to Chikuzen with the infant emperor in tow,
they pray at the Usa Hachiman 宇佐八幡 Shrine for deliverance, only
to be devastated by the oracle's dismissal of their prayers. Now, trapped
by the enemy and rejected by the god, Kiyotsune turns to Buddhism to
provide a path of escape from this world through the mercy of Amida.[1]

The nō play *Kiyotsune* by Zeami[2] further complicates the plot by
incorporating a more private story loosely based on such later popular
versions of the *Heike* as the *Genpei jōsuiki*. In that version, Kiyotsune
is said to have given his young wife a lock of his hair when he fled with

---

1. *Heike monogatari*, Kakuichi-bon 8.4 "The Flight from Dazaifu." Ichiko Teiji,
ed., *Heike monogatari* (ge), SNKZ 46 (Shōgakukan, 1994), 116–22. Helen Craig
McCullough, trans., *The Tale of the Heike* (Stanford University Press, 1988), 265–66.

2. The attribution of *Kiyotsune* 清経 to Zeami Motokiyo 世阿弥元清 is based
on the evidence of *Sarugaku dangi* 申楽談義, which includes it in a list of plays
by the playwright. Hisamatsu Sen'ichi and Nishio Minoru, eds., *Karonshū*,
Nōgakuronshū, NKBT 65 (Iwanami shoten, 1961), 520.

his clan from the capital. When she failed to hear from him, and feared she had been forgotten, she sent the lock of hair back to him at Usa.[3] In these versions, his suicide is a response to this rejection. In the nō play, however, the private love story is altered further, and the keepsake of the lock of hair is delivered to Kiyotsune's wife only after his death.

The play opens with Kiyotsune's retainer, Awazu no Saburō, on his way to deliver a lock of Kiyotsune's hair, discovered after his death, to his wife as a keepsake. When she hears that her husband has committed suicide she feels betrayed and refuses the lock of hair. What were their vows of love worth if he could so easily toss his life away? The brooding of Kiyotsune is replaced by the brooding of his wife, the flute that he played before hurling himself into the sea becomes the flute that draws her to him in a dream. Their love provides the means for his return, not so that he can find release, but so that he can bring release to her. After all, Kiyotsune, whose name means, literally, "pure of heart," has already attained release. Compassion, not attachment, has brought him to his wife, an unusual theme for a *shura* nō and one demanding an unconventional format, which Zeami provides.

Most *shura* nō are two-act *mugen* plays in which the *shite* (ghost of the warrior) appears first in disguise and only later in the second act reveals himself, performs a warrior dance, and asks for prayers to be said for his release from *shura* hell. Kiyotsune, on the other hand, is a one-act play in which the ghost of Kiyotsune appears from the first as himself, undisguised. He appears not to the *waki* to ask for prayers for his release, but to the *tsure* (his wife) in order to bring her relief from suffering. His position is clear in his opening lines taken from *Musō Kokushi goroku*, a Zen text, "When the dust of the world clouds the eyes, the Three Realms close in. When the heart is clear, even one's seat is boundless."[4] As Kiyotsune tells her in the final lines of the play, he has been saved from the sufferings of warrior hell by his faith in Buddha whom he called upon before flinging himself into the sea. "Truly, Kiyotsune, pure of heart, has risen to Buddhahood." Nevertheless, her longing for him is so intense that he has responded to her summons. Although he chides her for flinging aside the keepsake of the lock of hair, his tone is one of

---

3. Mizuhara Hajime, ed., *Shintei Genpei jōsuiki*, vol. 4 (Shin jinbutsu ōraisha, 1991), 200–1, in the section titled "The Heike flee to Dazaifu, the poems of the Heiji at Usa Shrine, Kiyotsune drowns himself in the sea."

4. *Musō Kokushi goroku* 夢窓国師語録, cited from Yokomichi Mario and Omote Akira, eds., *Yōkyokushū* (jō) (Iwanami shoten, 1960), 252, headnote 12.

tenderness and pity rather than anger and attachment. Unlike plays in which the theme is the attachment of a man to his lover, Kiyotsune and his wife do not appear together, as a couple, before the *waki* to relate the story of their love and ask for prayers. Kiyotsune is not seeking release; he is bringing release with his story. This theme is underscored when the wife interrupts the recital of his tale to accuse him of giving up hope too easily. The depiction of the events at Usa and, later, the scene of warrior hell are offered not for his own release but in order to aid his wife's understanding of his dilemma as a Taira warrior, which led to his suicide. His death is thus presented to her as inevitable, and not as a rejection of her, laying to rest her worst fears. Zeami thus foregrounds the theme of "love" within the framework of a warrior play, allowing a Buddhist interpretation of the delusions both of love and of warfare to emerge naturally.

Kiyotsune

| TRANSLATED BY CAROLYN MORLEY

Second category *mugen* nō in one act.
Performed by all five schools.
Time: After the death of Taira no Kiyotsune in 1183
Place: Kiyotsune's residence in the capital
Author: Zeami Motokiyo

> TSURE Kiyotsune's wife
> WAKI Awazu no Saburō, Kiyotsune's retainer
> SHITE Kiyotsune, Heike Middle Captain of the Left

Costumes

Kiyotsune's wife wears a *ko omote* 小面 (young woman) mask, and colorful *karaori* 唐織 (Chinese brocade) robe. Awazu no Saburō wears a *kake suō* 掛素袍 (jacket without matching trousers), *shiro oguchi* 白大口 (white, formal divided skirts). Kiyotsune wears a *chūjō* 中将 (young warrior) mask, *nashi uchi eboshi* 梨打烏帽子 (tall court hat, bent at the top, worn over long loose hair), *chōken* 長絹 (silk jacket), and *shiro ōguchi* 白大口 (white, formal divided skirts).

Wife enters without musical accompaniment and sits at the witness square (wakiza). Awazu no Saburō enters to shidai music, dressed for travel in a large woven black hat, and wearing an amulet around his neck. He stops at the base square (jōza) and turns to face the pine on the back wall to sing the shidai. He removes his hat.

SABURŌ (*shidai*)
> Riding the waves along the shore of the eightfold distant seas,
> Riding the waves along the shore of the eightfold distant seas,
> I return to the ninefold capital.

Saburō faces forward.

Kiyotsune 清経. This translation is based on Yokomichi Mario and Omote Akira, eds., *Yōkyokushū* (jō), NKBT 40 (Iwanami shoten, 1960), 249–56. Reference is also made to Koyama Hiroshi et al., eds., *Yōkyokushū* (jō), NKBZ 33 (Shōgakukan, 1973), 198–208; Itō Masayoshi, *Yōkyokushū* (chū), SNKS (Shinchōsha, 1986), 15–26.

(*nanori*)   I am Saburō of Awazu, personal attendant to
Kiyotsune, Middle Captain of the Left. When my lord Kiyotsune was
defeated in the last battle at Tsukushi, he seemed to know that he
would never return home to the capital. Rather than vanish with the
dew by the roadside, at the rough hands of nameless enemy soldiers,
he threw himself into the sea, off the shores of Yanagi-ga-ura, Willow
Bay, in the province of Bungo, and sank with the setting moon into the
night.

Later, when I looked around the ship, I found a lock of his hair.
I have prolonged this useless life of mine to carry his keepsake back
home to the capital.

(*ageuta*)   Long accustomed to a hard country life,
long accustomed to a hard country life,
by chance, in the sad depths of autumn,
I return to the capital,

Puts on his hat again, indicating his journey to the capital.

so different from those springs of long ago.
My traveling cloak already drenched in autumn showers,
my sleeves, soaked through,

Takes a few steps to indicate travel.

secretly, I return in defeat to the capital.
In defeat, to the capital.

(*tsukizerifu*) I have already arrived.

Removes his hat, puts it down at the stage assistant position (kōkenza), and comes forward, facing the Wife, who is seated at the witness square (wakiza).

(*mondō*) Excuse me? Hello? Please relay a message for me.
Saburō of Awazu has come from Tsukushi.

WIFE   What? Saburō of Awazu? There's no need for such formality.
Please come in.

Saburō sits at stage center and bows to the Wife with his hands pressed to the floor.

WIFE   Now, what news do you bring?
SABURŌ   I've come all this way, but how do I begin? I don't know
how to explain.
WIFE   Why, what can this mean? Why do you cry, unable to speak?
SABURŌ   I am ashamed before you.
WIFE   Ashamed? What do you mean? Can my lord have taken
holy vows?
SABURŌ   No, not that.

WIFE   But we had word that he was not injured in the defeat at Tsukushi.

SABURŌ   Yes, it is true that his lordship was not injured. But he must have felt that he could not return to the capital in defeat. Perhaps anything seemed preferable to falling into unknown enemy hands to perish like dew by the roadside. He flung himself into the sea off Willow Bay in Bungo province, to sink like the setting moon in the night.

WIFE   What? You mean he drowned himself at sea?

Shocked, speaking as if to herself.

(*kudoki*)   How could he? Had he been struck down in battle,
              or died on his sickbed,
              then might I have resigned myself to it.
              But for him to die by his own hand ...
              Then, our vows of love were all lies?
              But even if I am bitter, it is of no use.
              Nothing will bring will bring him back.
              And this must be my sorrow.

CHORUS

(*sageuta*)   Nothing lasts in this world.   *Both face front.*
(*ageuta*)   Until now
              I have lived hidden away from prying eyes,
              hidden away from prying eyes,
              weeping always in silence,
              like the soundless wind blowing
              through the pampas grass by my fence.
              But now, why should I care?
              Like the cuckoo on a moonlit night crying until the dawn,[1]
              I'll shed tears openly, not bothering to hide my name,
              I'll shed tears openly, not bothering to hide my name.

---

1. The line is from two poems on the cuckoo. Fujiwara no Sanesada 藤原実定, *Senzaishū* 千載集, no. 161, writes: ほととぎす鳴きつる方をながむればただ有明の月ぞ残れる *Hototogisu / nakitsuru kata o / nagamureba / tada ariake no / tsuki zo nokoreru*; "The cuckoo cries / Yet, when I look up / Only the moon in a dawning sky." Ki no Tsurayuki 紀貫之 in the *Kokinshū* 古今集 160, writes: さみだれの空もとどろにほととぎすなにを憂しとか夜ただ鳴くらん *Samidare no / sora mo todoro ni / hototogisu / nani o ushi toko/ yotada nakuran*; Summer rains / and the sky resounds / Cuckoo, what is your sorrow / that you would cry the night long?

Awazu no Saburō removes the amulet and puts it on his fan to present to Wife.

SABURŌ   (*mondō*)

Please. When I searched the ship, I found this lock of his Lordship's hair, left behind as a keepsake. May the sight of it be a comfort to you.

Awazu no Saburō approaches with the keepsake and gives it to Wife, then returns to center stage and sits. Wife stares at the lock of hair.

WIFE (*kudoki*)   Is this a lock of the Middle Captain's hair?
                      When I look, my eyes grow dim,
                         my heart dies within me.
                      Each time I look at it, my sorrow only deepens.

CHORUS (*uta*)   "Whenever I gaze upon it,
                           this lock of my love's hair only brings me pain.
                         Send it back to Usa, whence it came."[2]
                      All night long I weep and weep for him.
                      Please come to me if only in my dreams.
                      Unable to sleep, I toss on my pillow.
                         "Won't my pillow tell him of my love?
                         Won't my pillow tell him of my love?"[3]

During this chorus, the spirit of Kiyotsune enters along bridgeway and stands at the base square. Meanwhile, Awazu no Saburō quietly exits from the side door.[4]

---

2. *Miru tabi ni / kokoro-zukushi no / kami nareba / usa ni zo kaesu / moto no yashiro ni.* The *waka* plays on the place-name Usa 宇佐 and *usa* 憂さ meaning "melancholy," "sadness." The term *kokoro-zukushi* ("brings me pain") puns on the place-name Tsukushi 築紫 (modern Kyushu). An almost identically worded poem appears in episodes describing Kiyotsune's decision to drown himself in some versions of *Heike monogatari*, including the Engyō 延慶 variant, Book 8, and the *Genpei jōsuiki* 源平盛衰記, Book 33. In these versions, Kiyotsune gives the keepsake to his wife before he leaves the capital, and she returns it to him with this poem when he is at the shrine of Usa in Tsukushi. Mizuhara Hajime, ed., *Shintei Genpei jōsuiki*, vol. 4 (Shin jinbutsu ōraisha, 1991), 201; Kitahara Yasuo and Ogawa Eiichi, eds., *Engyō-bon Heike monogatari: honbun-hen*, vol. 2 (Benseisha, 1990), 137.

3. From a poem of Minamoto no Masamichi 源雅通 in the *Senzaishū*, no. 812: つつめども枕は恋をしりぬらん涙かからぬ夜半しなければ *tsutsumedomo / makura wa koi wo / shirinuran / nameda kakaranu / yowa shi nakereba*; "Though hidden / will not my pillow know of my love? / Since there are no nights / when my tears do not fall?"

4. In the Kanze and Komparu schools a variant performance exists in which Kiyotsune enters to the *netori* melody of the flute as if pulled into his wife's dream.

KIYOTSUNE   *Facing forward, he sings.*

(*sashi*)   "Holy men do not dream,"[5]
                 but who would mistake this for reality?
                 "When the dust of the world clouds the eyes,
                     the Three Realms close in.
                 When the heart is clear,
                     even one's seat seems boundless."[6]
                 For the enlightened, even this world of pain and bitterness
                     is really nothing but a dream, a phantom.
                 Like floating clouds and flowing water,
                     no trace of anyone is ever left behind.[7]
                 Even so, I cannot free myself, and this fickle heart of mine
                     has wandered back into this mortal world.[8]

Steps forward slightly and points to the curtain with fan, then looks back.
Faces front and looks down, then sings softly.

(*shimo no ei*) I dozed off and dreamed of you, my beloved,
                 and so I have come to rely upon my dreams.[9]

Looks up at Wife. Calls out in a clear voice.

(*kakeai*)   My love, from long ago Kiyotsune comes to you.

Wife turns toward Kiyotsune.

WIFE   How strange. Kiyotsune has truly come to my pillow.
                 But my lord drowned—
                 if this is not a dream, how can he appear here?
                 Well, what if it is a dream?
                 I am so grateful to see him. And yet ...
                 And yet, you made a mockery of our vows
                 when you cast yourself from the boat,
                 leaving me only this bitterness.

                                          Struggles not to weep.

---

5. From the *Daie goroku* 大慧語録 by Chikotsu Daie 痴兀大慧 (1229–1312).

6. From *Musō Kokushi goroku* 夢窓国師語録 by Musō Soseki 夢窓疎石 (1275–1351).

7. His attachment begins to disturb his peace of mind.

8. *Enbu no kokyō* 閻浮の故郷, more literally, the homeland of Enbu, the realm of mortals. In Buddhist cosmography, the world in which we live is imagined to form part of a large island known as Enbu 閻浮 (Skt. Jambu).

9. Ono no Komachi 小野小町, *Kokinshū*, no. 553 ("Love Poems II"): うた たねに恋しき人を見てしより夢てふものは頼みそめてき *Utatane ni / koishiki hito wo / miteshi yori / yume chō mono wa / tanomi someteki.*

KIYOTSUNE   If you feel such resentment toward me,
                I, too, have complaints.
         Why should you return my keepsake, meant for your eyes alone.[10]
WIFE   I did not mean to!
                It is only that the grief is more than I can bear.
                  "Whenever I gaze upon it,
                    this lock of my love's hair only brings me pain …"
KIYOTSUNE   Return my grief to Usa, whence it came. To think you
         could return a lock of hair sent with my love … Unless you had
         tired of it, you would have kept my keepsake.
WIFE   You don't understand!
                It may have been meant to comfort me,
                but when I look at it, I go mad, my thoughts a tangle,
                this lock of hair—
KIYOTSUNE   sent especially but to no avail. You return my
         keepsake and this is my resentment.
WIFE   And mine, that you threw away your own life.
KIYOTSUNE   Reproaching each other …
WIFE   and reproached in turn.
KIYOTSUNE   This keepsake has caused such pain.

         Approaches one step toward her.

WIFE   This lock of black hair
CHORUS
(*ageuta*)   is his bitterness to which she adds her own,
                she adds her own.

         Kiyotsune points to Wife with left hand, steps forward to center stage,
         throws back left sleeve and stares at her.

                A resentful trail of tears falls like jewels
                upon the pillowing sleeves this night,
                lined up side by side,
                but, in their anger, each sleeps alone.
                The misery!

         With left sleeve Kiyotsune represses his tears.

                Truly, this keepsake is the cause of my pain.
                "If not for this, I could forget him."[11]

---

10. Chanted speech (*katari*) alternates with melodic singing (*yowagin*) in the
following exchange.

11. Lines based on an anonyous *Kokinshū* poem, no. 746 (Love Poems IV): 形見

Just recalling this poem, my sleeves grow wet with tears,
my sleeves grow wet with tears.

Kiyotsune heads toward the corner pillar (metsukebashira) and then circles left to base square. He performs an open facing movement[12] at the base square seat facing front, and weeping, turns to his Wife.

KIYOTSUNE   (*mondō*)
Please listen to my story of things now past, and
cleanse the anger from your heart.

Goes to stage center in front of the drums and sits on the barrel seat.

(*sashi*)   When we heard that the enemy was already nearing
               the castle at Yamaga in Kyushu,
               we fled, leaving behind our belongings;
               and taking river boats through the night,
               we reached a place called Yanagi, or Willows,
               in the province of Buzen.[13]

CHORUS   The beach was lined with willows, befitting its name,
               and so we settled on this spot
               as a temporary shelter for His Majesty.

KIYOTSUNE   From here His Majesty would make a pilgrimage
               to Hachiman Shrine in Usa.

CHORUS   We had brought offerings intended for the shrine,
               seven horses, and gifts of gold and silver.

WIFE   (*kakeai*)   *Interrupting.*

               When I say this, you may think me
               still mired in my own bitterness,
               and yet, before the reign of His Majesty comes to an end
               or the Heike clan falls, you take your own life.
               Truly, it makes no sense.

こそ今はあたなれこれなくは忘るる時もあらましものを *katami koso / ima wa ata nare / kore naku wa / wasururu toki mo / arashi mono o* (Even this keepsake is now my enemy. If not for this, there would be times I could forget him).

12. The *hiraki* ヒラキ ("opening") is a movement expressing strong emotion. The actor steps back three paces, opening both arms to the side. Nishino Haruo and Hata Hisashi, eds., *Nō kyōgen jiten*, revised ed. (Heibonsha, 1999), 280.

13. Buzen no kuni Yanagi 豊前の国柳 is now part of the city of Kita-Kyūshū in Fukuoka prefecture, overlooking the Kanmon 関門 Straits. Details like "leaving behind our belongings" (*toru mono mo toriaezu*) and "river boats" (*takase bune*) show that the description is based on *Genpei jōsuiki* rather than the Kakuichi version. Mizuhara, *Shintei Genpei jōsuiki*, vol. 4, 199; cf. Ichiko, *Heike monogatari (ge)*, 119.

KIYOTSUNE   Yes, I know. But there was a clear message from the gods
                     that this was a world that we could no longer rely on.
                     Please hear me out.

CHORUS

   (*sashi*)   And so it was, we made our pilgrimage to Hachiman
                       Shrine
                     in Usa where, neglecting nothing,
                     we cried out our prayers before the holy curtains.
                     Then, from within the brocade curtains,
                     a divine voice issued forth, with a sacred message.

KIYOTSUNE   *Solemnly.*

   (*ageuta*)   "Why pray with such passion at Usa
                     where there are no gods to hear your sorrows in
                         this world?"[14]

CHORUS

   (*ei*)   "The hope in our hearts flickered out
                     with the cries of the insects
                     at autumn's end."[15]

     Kiyotsune turns to the right and looks down.

KIYOTSUNE

     Clasps his hands together.

   (*uta*)   Oh gods, buddhas, and the Three Treasures

CHORUS   have you abandoned us?

     Kiyotsune makes a sweeping point with his fan to indicate the Heike clan.

               We cried out, forsaken.
               The whole clan lost heart, its strength gave out.
               They felt hopeless, and with feet dragging,
               they accompanied the sagging imperial carriage.

---

14. 世の中の憂さには神もなきものを何祈るらん心づくしに   *yo no naku no / usa ni wa kami mo / naki mono o / nani inoruran / kokoro-zukushi ni.* A poem quoted from *Heike monogatari*, Kakuichi-bon 8.3 "Odamaki" ("The Reel of Thread"). When the Heike flee to Tsukushi, they pray to the deity of the Usa Shrine for guidance. The oracle gives this ominous warning. Ichiko, *Heike monogatari* (ge), 111; McCullough, *The Tale of the Heike*, 262.

15. さりともと思ふ心も虫の音も弱り果てぬる秋の暮かな *saritomo to / omou kokoro mo / mushi no ne mo / yowari hatenuru / aki no kure kana.* In Kakuichi-bon 8.3, this is the poem written in response to the Usa deity's oracle by Taira no Munemori 平宗盛, leader of the Heike. The poem is included in *Senzaishū* 千載集, no. 333 as a *waka* by Fujiwara no Toshinari (Shunzei) 藤原俊成.

A pitiful sight.

Faces front and stands, then moves forward to front stage center, but abruptly retreats backward to center stage and falls to one knee. Represses his tears with his hand.

(*kuse*)　　　Such was their plight that when they heard
　　　　　　that the enemy were advancing
　　　　　　on Nagato province,
　　　　　　they again boarded a boat

Mimes boarding the boat at stage front.

　　　　　　and pushed off for they knew not where,
　　　　　　their hearts heavy with grief.

Heads toward the corner pillar; looks down.

　　　　　　The things of this world are but a dream.
　　　　　　That is the true reality.

Looks up and makes a large circle to the left, stopping before drums.

　　　　　　In the time of Hōgen, the Heike blossomed
　　　　　　with the flowers of spring.
　　　　　　In the time of Juei, they scattered
　　　　　　with the colored leaves of autumn,
　　　　　　a boat adrift like a single leaf on the waters.[16]

Goes to stage center, makes a sweeping point with his fan, and gazes around to the right. Stamps several times.

　　　　　　The autumn winds blew across Willow Bay,
　　　　　　like enemy forces in the waves of the offing;
　　　　　　white herons flocking in the pines were
　　　　　　like so many Genji flags waving,
　　　　　　causing them to cringe in fear.[17]

Stands before the witness position and looks back toward the pines on the bridgeway. Moves toward base square.

---

16. The Hōgen 保元 (1156–1159) and Juei 寿永 (1182–1184) periods. The same image is used to describe the rise and fall of Heike power and prosperity in the narrative itself. Ichiko, *Heike monogatari* (ge), 72; McCullough, *Tale of the Heike*, 246. In the original, the passage occurs after the Heike abandon the capital in the Seventh Month of Juei 2 (1183). Kiyotsune dies in the Tenth Month, after the Heike are driven from Kyushu. The period ends two months after the devastating defeat at Ichi-no-tani (1184.2.7).

17. The Heike mistake the white color of the herons for the white banners of the Genji.

Kiyotsune, looking deep into his heart,
was convinced of the truth of the oracle engraved in
his mind.

Points with fan as he circles right, goes before drums. Performs an open facing movement and stamps.

"Hachiman takes abode
only in the mind of the righteous."

Faces front again, then raises head and proceeds to center stage. Points to his head with fan.

KIYOTSUNE   How pitiful.

Opens and raises his fan.

CHORUS

If I remain behind, doomed to disappear with the dew,
how long will I suffer, afloat like seaweed pulled by
the waves;
a boat, bobbing in the offing?

He looks down.

And he made up his mind to sink like a gull in the sea.
Was he, without a word to anyone, awaiting his chance?

Circles the stage, decisively, to the right and stops at base square.

Gazing up at the dawning moon, a scene calling for music,
he mounted the prow of the boat.

Removes his fan and using it as a flute, gazes at it and then puts it to his mouth.

Taking his flute from his belt,
in clear, pure tones he played,
and sang and chanted folk songs.

Makes several scattered stamps.

Thinking over what had been, what was yet to be,
over a past to which he could never return, he
exhausted his heart.

Proceeds to the corner pillar; makes a large circle left; goes to before drums.

Some day, he was bound to disappear like the
evanescent waves.
This life is but a journey.

Goes to center stage. Looks tenderly at Wife.

People may think me a fool,
a man with no regrets.
Let them say what they will.

> When I gaze up at the moon,
>   sinking in the western sky,
>   and think of this ephemeral world,
>   I wish that I too might accompany the moon
>   to the Western Paradise.

Turns toward stage front; makes a sweeping point with fan and follows it with his gaze; presses hands together in prayer and then stamps several times.

> With one last cry, "Please come for me,
>   Amida Buddha, Amida Buddha,"

Heads to the corner pillar, and before the witness position, turns toward stage center. Gazing afar with a fan, looks up to the western sky. As if pulled, moves toward base square, then prays, and stamps hard several times. Staring to the west, draws forward.

> he fell with a splash from the boat into the offing
>   and sank to the dregs at the bottom of the sea.

Goes to corner pillar, turns around suddenly and mimes jumping off.

> How sad the end of this suffering body.

With fan raised above head, stares into the depths, then circles left as if pulled by the waves and recedes to the base square where he sits.

WIFE   (*kudoki guri*) Listening to you, my heart grows dark
>   like the lonely heart of the weaver
>   from far-off China, tears sinking into sorrow
>   like falling rain.
>   Ours was a miserable love.

She weeps.

KIYOTSUNE   (*shimo no ei*)

He remains seated.

> Don't say that. The pain of hell is no different
>   from the pain of this world.
>   Sorrow is the same for all, alike.
>   (*naka noriji*) When you fall into warriors' hell …

CHORUS   When you fall into warrior's hell,
>   trees, all around, become the enemy,

Kiyotsune stands and goes forward slightly.

> the rain becomes flying arrows,
>   the earth, sharp swords,
>   the mountains, castles of iron,
>   and the clouds, banners and stricken shields.

*Looks afar. Holds up his fan as a shield in his left hand, then removes
sword with right hand.*

> Our haughty hearts are readied swords.
> Our eyes are blinded by attachment
> to lust, greed, anger, and ignorance—
> enemies of awakening—
> confusing the True Law with delusion.

*Holding his fan as a shield, heads toward the corner pillar and then circles
to the left. From the base square, approaches the witness position.*

> Striking like the waves, retreating with the tide,
> the karma of the seas is revealed in the Western Sea,
> and in the Four Seas.[18]

*Stamps sharply and then heads to before witness position. Waves sword
and retreats to before drums. Kneels on one knee.*

> All that went before, now gone.
> At the end, never failing to chant Amida Buddha's
> name,
> the tenfold prayer, he rides the boat of the Buddha's
> Law—
> without a doubt, as he had prayed.

*Turns to the front and tosses aside sword. Looks at Wife, then stands.
From the corner pillar he circles left to before witness position.*

> Truly, Kiyotsune, pure of heart, has risen to Buddhahood.
> And for this, I give thanks.

*Points fan and goes from the corner pillar to base square. He faces front
and presses his hands together in prayer. He turns toward the witness
position and stamps.*

---

18. Four Seas (*shikai*) refer here to the waters off Shikoku, while the Western Sea
(*saikai*) to the Inland Sea near Kyushu, where Kiyotsune took his own life by drowning.

16 ⌇ Preachers and Playwrights: *Ikuta Atsumori* and the Roots of Nō

| R. KELLER KIMBROUGH

Among the many moving accounts in *Heike monogatari*, none was more famous in the medieval and early-modern periods than that of the young Taira no Atsumori 平敦盛, beheaded on the beach by the Genji warrior Kumagai no Jirō Naozane 熊谷次郎直実 at the battle of Ichi-no-tani 一谷 on the seventh day of the Second Month of Juei 3 (1184). Although the story survives in different forms in different texts of the *Heike*, all manuscripts agree that as the defeated Taira fled to their ships, Kumagai rode his horse upon the shore looking for a Taira noble with whom he might engage. Spotting what appeared to be a general making his way alone through the surf, Kumagai called him back to fight. He pulled the man from his mount and wrested off his helmet, only to discover the teenage Atsumori. Suddenly reminded of his own son, Kumagai thought to let him go. His intentions were thwarted, however, when a group of Genji riders approached, and with little choice he cut off Atsumori's head. Transformed by his experience, Kumagai gave up his life as a warrior and became a Buddhist priest.

In the late-medieval period (mid-fourteenth through sixteenth centuries), the story of Kumagai and Atsumori came to be reproduced in numerous works of fiction, drama, and painting. Tales of Kumagai's spiritual awakening and later life as a priest on Mount Kōya 高野山 were taken up and spread by *Kōya hijiri* 高野聖, the mendicant holy men of Mount Kōya,[1] and Atsumori himself came to be venerated at

---

1. Minobe Shigekatsu, *Chūsei denshō bungaku no shosō* (Osaka: Izumi shoin, 1988), 118–19; Gorai Shigeru, *Zōho Kōya hijiri* (Kadokawa shoten, 1975), 145–46. Gorai points to the *Kōya hijiri's* use of a woodblock-printed prop (the *Uta no e no maki* 歌の会の巻, for which a printing block survives) in preaching about Hōnen, Shinran, and Kumagai.

Suma Temple 須磨寺 (Fukushōji 福祥寺, a Shingon institution now in the city of Kobe), where his flute, which Kumagai is reported to have taken from his corpse, was enshrined from at least the early fifteenth century.[2] By the time the actor and playwright Konmparu Zenpō 金春 禅鳳 (1454–1532?) composed *Ikuta Atsumori* 生田敦盛 in the late fifteenth or early sixteenth century, Atsumori's death had become a popular subject in Buddhist storytelling and nō, having been preceded by the plays *Tsunemori* 経盛 (author unknown; composed in or before the time of Zeami [1363–1443]) and *Atsumori* 敦盛, composed by Zeami prior to 1423.

Although relatively little is known about the personal life of Komparu Zenpō, grandson of the eminent Komparu Zenchiku 金春 禅竹 (b. 1405), Zenpō's authorship of multiple commentaries on the nō reveals his authoritative knowledge of the history and practices of the art. Considering his critical oeuvre, one can only conclude that Zenpō wrote his few plays—around six, it would seem[3]—with an acute awareness of tradition. It is therefore intriguing that while the authors of *Tsunemori* and *Atsumori* chose to emphasize different aspects of the Atsumori account specific to each of the two main textual lines of the *Heike*, Zenpō opted to take an alternative approach, basing his own composition upon an account of Atsumori's posthumous son composed long after *Heike monogatari* proper. Though the immediate oral and/or textual sources of Zenpō's *Ikuta Atsumori* are unknown, the play is related to an early sixteenth-century Tendai Buddhist proselytizing tradition concerning the reunification of fractured families through Buddhist practice and belief. By focusing upon this thematic element, dwelling less upon the death of Atsumori than the meeting of a dead father with his son, Zenpō shaped his composition to evoke the latter tragedies of war—the plight of war orphans haunted by the "ghosts" of their past—setting his own work apart in the larger repertoire of nō.

---

2. Saya Makito, *Heike monogatari kara jōruri e: Atsumori setsuwa no hen'yō* (Keiō Gijuku Daigaku shuppankai, 2002), 39.

3. Omote Akira and Itō Masayoshi attribute Zenpō with the authorship of *Arashiyama* 嵐山, *Ikuta Atsumori*, *Ikkaku Sennin* 一角仙人, *Tōbōsaku* 東方朔, *Hatsuyuki* 初雪, and *Kurokawa* 黒川. Omote Akira and Itō Masayoshi, *Konparu kodensho shūsei* (Wanya shoten, 1969), 66.

TSUNEMORI, ATSUMORI, AND HEIKE MONOGATARI

According to one prominent interpretation of the Atsumori episode in *Heike monogatari*, the story of Atsumori's battlefield demise (*Atsumori no saigō* 敦盛最期, or "The Death of Atsumori" in Helen McCullough's translation of the fourteenth-century Kakuichi-bon 覚一本 variant of *Heike monogatari*)[4] is not about Atsumori at all. Rather, as Mizuhara Hajime has explained, it is one part of a larger episodic account of how Kumagai came to renounce the world and take monastic vows. Mizuhara argues that "The Death of Atsumori" is narratively linked both to "The First and Second Attackers" (*Ichi ni no kake* 一二懸), in which Kumagai's son Kojirō 小次郎 is wounded (and in some texts, apparently killed) as he and Kumagai fight alongside each other at the Taira stronghold at Ichi-no-tani, and, in the Engyō-bon 延慶本 variant and *Genpei jōsuiki* 源平盛衰記, to the account of Kumagai and Kojirō's struggle at the Battle of Uji Bridge, at which Kumagai's heart is said to have first turned to the Way of the Buddha.[5] Following Mizuhara, Saya Makito argues that Atsumori serves as no more than a generic young Taira in *Heike monogatari* whose sole purpose is to be killed so that Kumagai may awaken to the nature of Buddhist Truth. As evidence, Saya points to the seemingly careless and accidental substitution of Taira no Narimori 平業盛 for Atsumori in the corresponding section of *Genpei tōjōroku* 源平闘諍録—an alternate and incomplete text of the *Heike*—which Saya maintains suggests Atsumori's utter unimportance, other than as a stock Taira figure, to the episode that now bears his name.[6]

Unlike most *Heike* texts in the "recited" textual line (*kataribonkei* 語り本系), the Engyō-bon, Nagato-bon 長門本, and other variants in the "readerly" textual line (*yomihonkei* 読み本系) describe how Kumagai

4. Helen Craig McCullough, *The Tale of the Heike* (Stanford University Press, 1988), 315–17.

5. Mizuhara Hajime, *Engyō-bon Heike monogatari ronkō* (Katō chūdōkan, 1979), 357–60.

6. Saya, *Heike monogatari kara jōruri e*, 8–13. The *Genpei tōjōroku* passage is reproduced in Yamashita Hiroaki, ed., *Genpei tōjōroku to kenkyū* (Nagoya: Mikan kokubun shiryō kankōkai, 1963), 203–5. Saya maintains that the Atsumori episode in the Shibu kassenjō-bon 四部合戦状本 text of the *Heike* is an exception: because it intimates the sadness of Atsumori's young lover, the Shibu kassenjō-bon fleshes out Atsumori's character, lending him a depth of his own. Saya, *Heike monogatari kara jōruri e*, 16–18.

wrapped Atsumori's severed head in the boy's *hitatare* 直垂 (a kind of matching shirt and pants worn under armor), and, together with Atsumori's flute or *hichiriki* 篳篥 (a double-reed woodwind instrument employed in traditional court music), sent them to Atsumori's father, Tsunemori.[7] Kumagai is reported to have appended a letter explaining the circumstances of Atsumori's death and Kumagai's own intention to perform services for him in the afterlife, and to have entrusted these to one or two retainers who delivered them to Tsunemori on his ship at Yashima. The Nagato-bon variant in particular emphasizes the depth of Tsunemori's and his wife's grief:

> When the Lord Master of the Office of Palace Repairs [Tsunemori] opened the package he had received, he saw that Kumagai had sent him his son Atsumori's mortal remains. He had been prepared for such notice since the day he set out, but when the time actually came his strength disappeared and he broke down in tears. His wife, the boy's mother, felt as if she were dreaming, and she wept as if to die. How she rued the past, despairing even the day she first saw her husband and he first saw her! Everyone upon the ship, nobles and commoners alike, wet their sleeves with tears. "I had thought that Kumagai was just a barbaric Easterner," Tsunemori said, "but what compassion to have sent these things!"[8]

The Nagato-bon Atsumori account concludes with Tsunemori's formal written reply, remarkable for its staid dignity and the gratitude that it expresses to Kumagai for sending Tsunemori his son's belongings and bodily remains.

The Engyō-bon Atsumori episode also contains Kumagai's letter and Tsunemori's reply, after which it includes an additional, final passage

---

7. The Hiramatsuke-bon 平松家本, Kamakura-bon 鎌倉本, and Hyaku-nijukku-bon 百二十句本 in the recited textual line of the *Heike* do contain the story, but Saya discounts the significance of this by explaining that these works are now understood to be "latter-day composites." Saya, *Heike monogatari kara jōruri e*, 53. The Hyakunijukku-bon Atsumori episode is annotated in Mizuhara Hajime, ed., *Heike monogatari* (ge), SNKS (Shinchōsha, 1981), 109–17.

8. Asahara Yoshiko, ed., *Nagato-bon Heike monogatari no sōgō kenkyū: kōchū-hen ge*, vol. 2 (Benseisha, 1999), 1254.

about Kumagai, returning the story to the character with whom it began and emphasizing the nature of the account as a *hosshin-dan* 発心談 (or *hosshin-tan* 発心譚), or "religious-awakening tale":

> From that time Kumagai's heart turned to the Buddha. He met with Master Hōnen 法然 and took religious vows. His Buddhist name was Rensei 蓮性. He lived in the Renge Valley 蓮花谷 at Mount Kōya, where he prayed for Atsumori in the next life. People say that it was fortunate indeed for [the boy] to have thus brought him to the Way.[9]

Atsumori (or the incident of his death) is identified here as a "Dharma Companion" (*zenchishiki* 善知識, paraphrased in the preceding translation), a term used for human and nonhuman beings and sometimes events that lead one to the path of the Buddha.[10] In the Engyō-bon, which Mizuhara Hajime argues preserves the larger episodic Kumagai account in an earlier and truer form than the Nagato-bon,[11] it is both Kumagai's killing of Atsumori and his later communication with Tsunemori that leads to his renunciation of the present life and his decision to become a priest.

The nō play *Tsunemori* (also known as *Katami okuri* 形見送, "Sending Relics") takes up the story of Kumagai's dispatch of relics to Atsumori's father and employs it as a means through which to evoke the pathos of Tsunemori's and his wife's bereavement and to recount the circumstances of Atsumori's death.[12] Although not currently performed, *Tsunemori* is cited repeatedly in *Sarugaku dangi* 猿楽談義 (Nō Discourses), a compilation of Zeami's reflections on the nō transcribed by his son Motoyoshi 元能, suggesting its prominence in the early repertoire of nō.[13] As a *genzai*

---

9. Kitahara Yasuo and Ogawa Eiichi, eds., *Engyō-bon Heike monogatari: honbun hen*, vol. 2 (Benseisha, 1990), 270. Kumagai was known as "Rensei/Renzei" among members of the Pure Land sect, and "Renjō" among others. Gorai, *Zōho Kōya hijiri*, 144; Minobe, *Chūsei denshō bungaku no shosō*, 123. The full Engyō-bon Atsumori account is translated and discussed in Amy Franks, "Another *Tale of the Heike*: An Examination of the Engyōbon *Heike monogatari*, Ph.D. dissertation (Yale University, 2009).

10. Ichiko Teiji, ed., *Heike monogatari jiten* (Meiji shoin, 1973), 195c.

11. Mizuhara, *Engyō-bon Heike monogatari ronkō*, 361.

12. *Tsunemori* is typeset in Tanaka Makoto, ed., *Mikan yōkyokushū*, vol. 2 (Koten bunko, 1964), 103–9.

13. For textual citations, see Saya, *Heike monogatari kara jōruri e*, 52, and Hisamatsu Sen'ichi and Nishio Minoru, eds., *Karonshū, Nōgakuronshū*, NKBT 65

nō 現在能, a play in which the *shite* portrays a living person (in this case, Kumagai's messenger), *Tsunemori* takes as its central concern the grief of parents who are informed of the loss of their son. Kumagai and Atsumori appear only indirectly, as figures described but never actually seen, and the relics that Tsunemori and his wife receive are referred to in the abstract, without explanation or identification. Tsunemori reads Kumagai's letter for his wife (and the audience) to hear, but it is entirely different from the one in *Heike monogatari*, indicating the liberty that the play's author took with the original *Heike* account. The drama concludes with Tsunemori entrusting Kumagai's messenger with a written response, but the contents of his message are left unspoken. *Tsunemori* thus presents its story in a manner most unlike *Heike monogatari*, which, in its readerly textual line, relies upon the transcribed letters to achieve its emotional effect.

While most *Heike* texts in the recited textual line contain no mention of Kumagai's communication with Tsunemori, they do emphasize the importance of Atsumori's flute, and in this respect their Atsumori accounts starkly contrasts those in the Nagato-bon, Engyō-bon, and other texts in the readerly textual line. The flute, we are told, is a symbol of the refinement and gentility of the Taira nobles, and it is Kumagai's discovery of it that contributes to his decision to become a monk. In the concluding passage of the Atsumori episode in the fourteenth-century Kakuichi-bon text, for example, the *Heike* narrator provides a simple genealogy for the instrument:

> People say that the flute was given to Atsumori's grandfather Tadamori by Emperor Toba because of Tadamori's skill as a flautist. It was then passed on to Tsunemori, who seems to have given it to Atsumori in recognition of his abilities. The flute was called "Saeda" 小枝 [Little Branch]. Music may be a profane pursuit, but in this case it led a warrior to the Buddhist path, which is moving indeed![14]

Like the Engyō-bon, the Kakuichi-bon Atsumori account ends with an allusion to Kumagai's newfound religious devotion. However, the

---

(Iwanami shoten, 1961), 497 and 510.

14. Kajihara Masaaki and Yamashita Hiroaki, eds., *Heike monogatari* (ge), SNKT 45 (Iwanami shoten, 1993), 177. For an alternate translation, see McCullough, *Tale of the Heike*, 317.

Kakuichi-bon and other *Heike* texts in the recited textual line are unique in attributing Kumagai's Buddhist awakening to the power of music—a natural assertion for the *biwa*-playing priests who recited the tale. According to a more substantial and far more creative flute-genealogy in the *otogizōshi Suma-dera fue no iki* 須磨寺笛之遺記 (A History of the Suma Temple Flute), a Suma Temple text composed in the mid-to-late Muromachi period for probable use in preaching, Saeda first belonged to Kūkai 空海 (774–835), the progenitor of the Japanese Shingon 真言 Buddhist sect, who carved it from a bamboo staff that he cut during a metaphysical journey to hear Shakyamuni Buddha preach at Eagle Peak. Kūkai gave the flute to Emperor Saga 嵯峨 (786–842), after which it was enshrined at Tōji 東寺 Temple before being eventually passed down to Atsumori. The *otogizōshi* explains that after Kumagai took the flute from Atsumori's corpse, he showed it to his commander Yoshitsune 義経, who immediately recognized it as one of Kūkai's famous instruments and, with the permission of Retired Emperor Go-Shirakawa, donated it to Suma Temple.[15] According to the Suma Temple record *Tōzan rekidai* 当山歴代 (Historical Ages of Our Institution), Suma Temple was in the possession of Atsumori's flute from well before 1427, when it was stolen and then miraculously returned. A subscription notice (*kanjin-jō* 勧進状) from a Suma Temple fund-raising campaign in 1498 advertises the presence of Atsumori's flute, and a *Tōzan rekidai* entry for 1526 records that Atsumori's flute and portrait were put on public display for ten days that year, attracting awestruck crowds of rich and poor alike.[16]

Zeami famously asserts in his commentary *Sandō* 三道 (The Three Elements in Composing a Play; 1423) that if a play in the martial mode (*guntai no nōsugata* 軍体の能姿) "is to be created around a famous general of the Minamoto or the Taira, one should take special care to

---

15. Gotō Yasuhiro, "*Suma-dera fue no iki* to *Saeda no fue monogatari* wo megutte," *Denshō bungaku kenkyū* 31 (May 1985), 60b–61b and 66a–b; Yokoyama Shigeru and Matsumoto Ryūshin, eds., *Muromachi jidai monogatari taisei*, vol. 5 (Kadokawa shoten, 1977), 291b–4b and 308b–9a. *Suma-dera fue no iki* is also known as *Saeda no fue monogatari* 小枝の笛物語 (The Tale of the Flute "Saeda"). The work was copied or composed by the priest Raikyō 賴慶 sometime before his death in 1610. Gotō argues (55b) that it was written for use in Suma Temple (and broader Kōya Shingon) proselytizing.

16. Saya, *Heike monogatari kara jōruri e*, 39 and 48; Gotō, "*Suma-dera fue no iki*," 47a; Nishiyama Masaru, *Seichi no sōzōryoku: sankei mandara wo yomu* (Kyoto: Hōzōkan, 1998), 74 and 96–97 (note 4).

write the story just as it appears in *Heike monogatari*."[17] True to his word, in constructing his narration of the circumstances of Atsumori's death in his play *Atsumori*, Zeami is remarkably faithful to the Atsumori episode in the recited textual line of *Heike monogatari*.[18] The single most prominent exception occurs in the *ai-kyōgen* 間狂言 interval (which cannot be attributed to Zeami with any reasonable certainty), in which the *ai-kyōgen*—a local villager who happens to speak with an unknown priest, the *waki* Kumagai—explains that Atsumori was killed because he had returned to the shore to retrieve his flute. Although the *ai-kyōgen* deviation from the *Heike* version of events is an apparent violation of Zeami's rule, it is nevertheless consistent with Zeami's earlier pronouncement in his treatise *Fūshikaden* 風姿花伝 (The Transmission of the Flower; ca. 1400) that "if one should take a famous character from the Minamoto or the Taira and bring out the connection between him and poetry and music, then—so long as the play itself is well written—it will be more interesting than anything else."[19] Zeami in fact takes special care to emphasize the importance of music to his drama, remaining loyal to the spirit, if not always the letter, of the *Heike* recited textual line. Insofar as he locates the scene of Atsumori's death at Suma, he may have written his work under the influence of early fifteenth-century Suma Temple proselytizing traditions.[20]

---

17. 源平の名将の人体の本説ならば、殊に殊に平家の物語のまゝに書べし. Hisamatsu and Nishio, eds., *Karonshū, Nōgakuronshū*, 475. Translation slightly modified from Thomas B. Hare, *Zeami's Style: The Noh Plays of Zeami Motokiyo* (Stanford University Press, 1986), 186.

18. *Atsumori* is typeset and annotated (without the *ai-kyōgen* interval) in Koyama Hiroshi et al., eds., *Yōkyokushū* (jō), NKBZ 33 (Shōgakukan, 1973), 223–34, and translated in Royall Tyler, *Japanese Nō Dramas* (London, New York: Penguin Books, 1992), 37–48, and in Arthur Waley, *The Nō Plays of Japan* (New York: Grove Press, 1957), 64–73.

19. Hisamatsu and Nishio, eds., *Karonshū, Nōgakuronshū*, 354. Translation slightly modified from Hare, *Zeami's Style*, 185.

20. Like *Suma-dera fue no iki*, the Suma Temple fund-raising notice of 1498 refers to Atsumori's flute as "Aoba" 青葉, the name that Zeami gave it in *Atsumori*, indicating the possible influence of Zeami's play. The *Tōzan rekidai* entry for 1427, however, refers to Atsumori's flute as "Saeda" 小枝, suggesting that the temple's claim to the instrument was initially unrelated to Zeami's composition. *Suma-dera fue no iki* records that "Saeda" and "Aoba" are two names for the same flute. Gotō, "*Suma-dera fue no iki*," 61b; Yokoyama and Matsumoto, eds., *Muromachi jidai monogatari taisei*, vol. 5, 294a-b.

IKUTA ATSUMORI

Unlike the plays *Tsunemori* and *Atsumori*, Zenpō's *Ikuta Atsumori* is unconcerned with either Kumagai's dispatch of relics or the issue of music. And contrary to Zeami's *Atsumori*, Zenpō locates the site of Atsumori's death at Ikuta, near the eastern gate of the former Taira stronghold at Ichi-no-tani, setting his own composition apart from the geographical context of Suma Temple preaching. The base tale of Zenpō's *Ikuta Atsumori* is most fully recounted in the *otogizōshi Ko Atsumori* 小敦盛 (Little Atsumori), which, in its "old picture scroll" (*ko-emaki* 古絵巻) textual line, dates to the sixteenth century.[21] Like *Ikuta Atsumori*, *Ko Atsumori* tells the tale of Atsumori's son's abandonment by his mother, his adoption by Hōnen, his later reunion with his mother, and his encounter, thanks to his prayers to the Kamo Deity, with his father's ghost at Ikuta 生田. Though all surviving *Ko Atsumori* manuscripts appear to post-date *Ikuta Atsumori*, differences between *Ko Atsumori* in its "old picture scroll" textual line and *Ikuta Atsumori* suggest that rather than the *otogizōshi* having been composed upon the nō play, the two works share an earlier, common source.[22]

The earliest apparent reference to the tale of Atsumori's benighted son is contained in *Shaken nichiroku* 蔗軒日録, the diary of the Zen priest Kikō Daishuku 季弘大叔 (1421–1487). Though suffering from ill health at the time, Daishuku records that in the Third Month of 1485 when he was residing at Kaieji Temple 海会寺 in Sakai 堺, he received

---

21. Matsumoto Ryūshin has classified *Ko Atsumori* manuscripts into two broad textual lines: the "old picture scroll" line, represented by several illustrated *Ko Atsumori* scrolls dating from the late Muromachi period, and the Shibukawa 渋川 (or *Otogi bunko* 御伽文庫 / *Otogizōshi* 御伽草子) line, represented by a number of shorter Edo-period manuscripts. Matsumoto Ryūshin, *Chūsei shōmin bungaku: monogatari sōshi no yukue* (Kyūko shoin, 1989), 86–111. Also see R. Keller Kimbrough, "*Little Atsumori* and *The Tale of the Heike*: Fiction as Commentary, and the Significance of a Name," in Michael F. Marra, ed., *Hermeneutical Strategies: Methods of Interpretation in the Study of Japanese Literature*, Proceedings of the Association for Japanese Literary Studies, vol. 5 (2004), 325–36. The sixteenth-century Keiō University Library *Ko Atsumori emaki* (in the "old picture scroll" textual line) is translated elsewhere this volume.

22. As Matsumoto Ryūshin has observed, however, *Ko Atsumori* texts in the later Shibukawa textual line do show the influence of *Ikuta Atsumori*. Matsumoto, *Chūsei shōmin bungaku*, 98–99.

repeated visits from a blind *Heike* reciter and storyteller by the name of Sōjū 宗住. In a fragmentary notation from the fourth day of that month, Daishuku records that Sōjū performed a piece that he had heard at the residence of a certain "Oda Shikibu" 小田式部—otherwise unknown— about "Master [Atsu]mori's young son" 大夫○盛幼子, "Hōnen Shōnin" 法然上人, and "the novice priest Renjō Hōshi" 小師蓮上法師 (Kumagai Naozane).²³ Minobe Shigekatsu argues that this refers to the story of Little Atsumori (Atsumori's son), and he further suggests that because Daishuku reports that Sōjū finished reciting the ninth volume of *Heike monogatari* on his following visit (on the tenth day of that month), Sōjū likely recited the Little Atsumori account in conjunction with the *Heike* tale of Atsumori's death at the battle of Ichi-no-tani.²⁴

Although the precise origins of the Little Atsumori account are unknown, the tale is similar in many respects to one of several Buddhist tales of lost or abandoned children employed in Tendai preaching from at least the early sixteenth century. As Tokue Gensei and Saya Makito have observed, the two stories are related;²⁵ judging from their contemporaneity, they are cousins in the broader world of medieval Japanese tales. Like the background story recounted by the *waki* in the first part of *Ikuta Atsumori*, the Tendai account concerns a baby boy who is left in the inner tray of a handbox (in *Ikuta Atsumori*, in the lid of a handbox), adopted by a stranger on a visit to Kamo Shrine, and later reunited with his mother. The Tendai *Lotus Sutra* commentaries *Hokekyō jurin shūyōshō* 法華経鷲林拾葉鈔 (Gathered Leaves of the *Lotus Sutra* from a Grove on Eagle Peak; 1512) and *Hokekyō jikidanshō* 法華経直談鈔 (Straight Talk on the *Lotus Sutra*; ca. 1546) contain the story in slightly alternate forms in their chapters on the "Former Affairs of the Bodhisattva Medicine King" chapter (薬王菩薩本事品) of the *Lotus Sutra*.²⁶ As *jikidan* 直談, or "straight talk"-type works, *Jurin shūyōshō* and *Jikidanshō* are two of several fifteenth- and sixteenth-century Tendai commentaries written to explain the *Lotus Sutra* in an unambiguous,

---

23. Cited and discussed in Minobe, *Chūsei denshō bungaku no shosō*, 106–9.

24. Minobe, *Chūsei denshō bungaku no shosō*, 109.

25. Tokue Gensei, *Muromachi geinōshi ronkō* (Miyai shoten, 1984), 170; Saya Makito, "Otogizōshi *Ko Atsumori* no keisei wo megutte," *Mita kokubun* 18 (June 1993), 43–44; Saya, *Heike monogatari kara jōruri e*, 81–82.

26. *Hokekyō jurin shūyōshō*, vol. 4 (Kyoto: Rinsen shoten, 1991), 237–40; *Hokekyō jikidanshō*, vol. 3 (Kyoto: Rinsen shoten, 1979), 358–61. Translations of *Lotus Sutra* chapter titles are from Burton Watson, *The Lotus Sutra* (Columbia University Press, 1993).

straightforward manner, typically by incorporating poems and anecdotes as a means of illustrating and illuminating specific passages and ideas from the *Lotus Sutra*.[27]

Jurin shūyōshō, compiled by the priest Sonshun 尊舜 (1451–1514) at Senmyōji Temple 千妙寺 in Hitachi province 常陸, cites the *Ikuta Atsumori*–related account in its discussion of the following *Lotus Sutra* passage:

> Even if a person were to fill the whole thousand-millionfold world with the seven treasures as an offering to the Buddha and the great bodhisattvas, pratyeka buddhas and arhats, the benefits gained by such a person cannot match those gained by accepting and upholding this *Lotus Sutra*, even just one four-line verse of it![28]

In the course of his explanation, Sonshun draws upon Zhiyi's 智顗 authoritative sixth-century commentary *Fa hua wen ju* 法華文句 (Words and Phrases of the *Lotus Sutra*), after which he quotes from Zhanran's 湛然 *Fa hua wen ju ji* 法華文句記 (Notes on *Words and Phrases of the Lotus Sutra*), an eighth-century commentary on Zhiyi's earlier commentary.[29] Following his own clarification of Zhanran's comments on Zhiyi's explication, Sonshun cites the *Ikuta Atsumori*–related account, presumably as an example of a real-world benefit achieved as a result of accepting and upholding the *Lotus Sutra* (although no such explicit interpretation is provided within the text).

As Sonshun tells the tale, a former intendant of Kamo Shrine once prayed to the Kamo Deity for a child. Later, the intendant took up with one of his female attendants—a woman by the name of Jijū 侍従—and caused her to bear a son. The intendant's wife was enraged, and because she wished to kill the child, the intendant placed him in the inner tray of a handbox and left him near the Kamo River. A man known as the

---

27. For more on these and other Tendai *Lotus Sutra* commentaries, see R. Keller Kimbrough, *Preachers, Poets, Women & the Way: Izumi Shikibu and the Buddhist Literature of Medieval Japan* (University of Michigan Center for Japanese Studies, 2008), Chapter Four.

28. Takakusu Junjirō and Watanabe Kaigyoku, eds., *Taishō shinshū daizōkyō*, vol. 9 (Taishō issaikyō kankōkai, 1924–32), 54a; Watson, *The Lotus Sutra*, 285. Translation by Watson.

29. In Japanese, these works are known as *Hokke mongu* 法華文句 and *Hokke mongu-ki* 法華文句記. For the passages quoted by Sonshun, see Takakusu and Watanabe, eds., *Taishō shinshū daizōkyō*, vol. 34, 143c and 355a.

Tsuchimikado Major Counselor 土御門大納言 had spent the night
in prayer at Kamo Shrine, and as he was returning home at dawn, he
discovered the boy. The man took him home, raised him, and later
sent him to Mount Hiei 比叡 to become a monk. Because the boy was
naturally intelligent, he eventually became a famous priest.

Distraught by the loss of her son, the boy's mother, Jijū, had
immediately taken Buddhist vows. She had wandered the provinces as
a nun, visiting important temples and shrines, constantly seeking news
of her child's next-life rebirth and praying for her own well-being in this
and the future world. After thirty-three years, she had grown lonely for
the capital. She returned to the city, where she heard that a great priest—
her son Sonben Sōjō 尊弁僧正, as-yet unknown to her—was preaching
at Seiryōji Temple 清涼寺. Sonshun explains:

> The nun Jijū visited the temple and listened to the
> sermon. It was wonderful beyond description. After
> it had ended and all the people had left, she stayed
> behind, saying that she had a question for the priest.
> Approaching the holy man and stating that there was
> something on her mind, she asked, "Whose child
> are you, and where do you come from?" "I was an
> abandoned child with neither a father nor a mother,"
> the priest explained, and he told her how he had been
> found. Again, the nun spoke: "Though it will become a
> tale of this Latter Age, please show me the tray in which
> you were left." The man produced the tray. Somehow the
> nun had carried the handbox with her until that time,
> and taking it out now and fitting it with the tray, she saw
> that it was a perfect match. Declaring the priest to be
> her son, she told him her name. Because his true father
> and his adopted father were both still alive, they all met
> together with the priest, which was marvelous indeed![30]

Tales of abandoned sons finding their mothers at or as a result of
visiting Seiryōji Temple are also contained in *Seiryōji Jizō-in engi* 清涼
寺地蔵院縁起 (A History of the Jizō Hall at Seiryōji; composed prior to
1529), Zeami's nō play *Hyakuman* 百万, and the Tokue Gensei manuscript
of the *otogizōshi Kowata kitsune* 木幡狐 (The Kowata Fox; Muromachi

---

30. *Hokekyō jurin shūyōshō*, vol. 4, 239.

period),[31] suggesting that such stories circulated widely in the medieval period. Sonshun's own awareness of this may explain why he quotes Jijū as saying that her story is likely to become "a tale of this Latter Age." Or, Jijū's prophecy may refer specifically to her impending identification of her son by matching the handbox with its inner tray, which, as a narrative device, is one of several variations on a conventional "proof of identity" in late-medieval fiction.[32] In either case, the use of the handbox and its tray in the *Jurin shūyōshō* account is significant to an understanding of *Ikuta Atsumori* insofar as it suggests that the single reference in *Ikuta Atsumori* to a "handbox lid," which is essentially meaningless in the play, constitutes a vestigial trace of Zenpō's source tale.

The *Lotus Sutra* commentary *Jikidanshō* 直談鈔, compiled by the priest Eishin 栄心 at Sugaoji Temple 菅生寺 in Ōmi 近江 province in the years preceding his death in 1546, some thirty years after *Jurin shūyōshō*, reproduces the Sonben/Jijū account in conjunction with an altogether different *Lotus Sutra* passage. According to Ikeyama Issaien, Eishin likely intended *Jikidanshō* as a simplified version of *Jurin shūyōshō* for use in teaching the *Lotus Sutra* to lay audiences at Tendai instructional centers (*dangisho* 談義所) throughout the provinces. To this end, Eishin cut back on difficult or overly abstract explanations and increased the number and prominence of tales in his work.[33] In his "Medicine King" chapter, Eishin includes the *Ikuta Atsumori*–related account in his discussion of the phrase, "like a child finding its mother," in the following *Lotus Sutra* passage:

---

31. The first two examples are cited in Saya, "Otogizōshi *Ko Atsumori* no keisei wo megutte," 44–45, and in Saya, *Heike monogatari kara jōruri e*, 82–85. In a final passage in the two-volume Tokue Gensei *Kowata kitsune nara ehon*, a boy explains to his father that he has heard people say that one can learn the location of a missing parent by visiting the "Sagano Nenbutsu [Hall]," another name for Seiryōji Temple. Yokoyama and Matsumoto, eds., *Muromachi jidai monogatari taisei*, vol. 5, 190a. The *kusemai* from *Hyakuman*, in which the mother dances piningly for her son, is translated in P. G. O'Neill, *Early Nō Drama: Its Background, Character, and Development*, 1300–1450 (Westport, CT: Greenwood Press, 1974), 150–52.

32. In the *otogizōshi Izumi Shikibu*, for example, the poet Izumi Shikibu identifies her long-lost son by fitting his short sword with her matching sheath. In the *otogizōshi Izumi Shikibu*, *Koshikibu*, and *Jippon ōgi*, Izumi Shikibu identifies her child by means of a poem. For a discussion of these works, see Kimbrough, *Preachers, Poets, Women & the Way*, Chapter Three.

33. Ikeyama Issaien, "Kaidai," in *Hokekyō jikidanshō*, vol. 1 (Kyoto: Rinsen shoten, 1979), 6–7 and 12.

> This sutra can bring great benefits to all living beings
> and fulfill their desires, as a clear cool pond can satisfy
> all those who are thirsty. It is like a fire to one who
> is cold, a robe to one who is naked, like a band of
> merchants finding a leader, a child finding its mother,
> someone finding a ship in which to cross the water, a
> sick man finding a doctor, someone in darkness finding
> a lamp, the poor finding riches, the people finding a
> ruler, a traveling merchant finding his way to the sea.[34]

Eishin provides numbered explanations and illustrative accounts for each of these eleven similes.[35] In connection with number five, "like a child finding its mother," Eishin writes that "because all living beings are lost in delusion, they do not know the truth of the various teachings. In this they are like small children abandoned by their mothers, ignorant of direction. But now encountering the *Lotus Sutra* and learning the principle of attaining Buddhahood in this very body, they are like abandoned children who have rediscovered their mothers."[36]

According to Eishin's explanation, we are to understand the Sonben/ Jijū story as a parable about the benefits of discovering the *Lotus Sutra*. The parable is more appropriate to Jijū than it is to Sonben, however, because it is at a Seiryōji Temple sermon—a sermon "wonderful beyond description," probably delivered upon the *Lotus Sutra*—that she happens upon her long-lost son, suggesting the epiphanic importance of her encounter with the *Lotus Sutra*. The parable is all the more effective when one considers that in his capacity as a Tendai priest, Sonben himself has come to represent the sacred scripture. On a more concrete level, Jijū's story is also a tale of the worldly benefits of Buddhism; its lesson—that if one should wish to find a missing relative, one should pray and attend Buddhist sermons—is reinforced by numerous similar accounts in different chapters of the *Lotus Sutra* commentaries.[37]

---

34. Takakusu and Watanabe, eds., *Taishō shinshū daizōkyō*, vol. 9, 54b; Watson, *The Lotus Sutra*, 285. Translation by Watson.

35. *Hokekyō jikidanshō*, vol. 3, 356–63.

36. *Hokekyō jikidanshō*, vol. 3, 358.

37. In one story in the "Benefits of Responding With Joy" chapter (随喜功徳品) of *Jikidanshō*, a brother and sister are said to have been sold into slavery as a result of their stepmother's evil machinations. The sister marries a provincial governor, while the brother becomes a priest. Years later, the two are reunited after the sister goes to hear her brother preach. Eishin concludes by explaining

In *Ikuta Atsumori*, Little Atsumori is indeed reunited with his mother at the site of a Buddhist sermon. Zenpō additionally emphasizes the importance of filial piety in his play (as the ghost of Atsumori explains, it was because of his son's profoundly filial prayer that the Kamo Deity deigned to summon Atsumori from the underworld), and this, too, has its counterpart in medieval Tendai preaching. The *Lotus Sutra* commentary *Jikidan innenshū* 経直因縁集 (Straight Talk on Causes and Conditions), the surviving manuscript of which was transcribed by the priest Shun'yū 舜雄 in 1585, for example, contains in its "Distinctions in Benefits" chapter (分別功徳品) a story of a poor but filial woman from the capital who abandons her son so that she might better support her mother. Her son grows up to be a priest, and he finds her years later when he is lecturing at Tennōji Temple 天王寺. The woman has become old and blind, but her sight is restored in response to his prayers, because, as the narrator explains, "the buddhas recognize filial piety" and reward it in kind.[38]

Eishin's citation of the Sonben story in the context of his explanation of the *Lotus Sutra* simile that a living being finding the *Lotus Sutra* is like an abandoned child finding his mother suggests the possibility of a loose allegorical reading of *Ikuta Atsumori* and the *otogizōshi Ko Atsumori*. In both of these works, the boy's pining for the father he never knew—a sinful,

---

that "due to the merit of hearing lectures on the *Lotus Sutra*, the brother and sister were able to ride in palanquins and carriages in this life and attain rebirth in the Pure Land in the next." *Hokekyō jikidanshō*, vol. 3, 229–32. The story has notable parallels to the tale of Sanshō Dayū 山椒大夫, as Hirota Tetsumichi has observed (*Tendai danjo de Hokekyō wo yomu* [Kanrin shobō, 1997], 222).

38. Hirota Tetsumichi et al., eds., *Nikkō tenkaizō Jikidan innenshū: honkoku to sakuin* (Osaka: Izumi shoin, 1998), 231–32. Saya Makito notes that the *Jikidan innenshū* account is similar to a story in the "Universal Gateway of the Bodhisattva Perceiver of the World's Sounds" chapter (観世音菩薩普門品) of *Jikidanshō*, in which a woman chooses to abandon her three-year-old son in the midst of a famine so that she can feed her father. The son grows up to be an important priest, and he later finds her in the course of a 100-day sermon series. *Hokekyō jikidanshō*, vol. 3, 423–24; Saya, *Heike monogatari kara jōruri e*, 84–85. In their "Encouragements of the Bodhisattva Universal Worthy" chapters (普賢菩薩勧発品), *Jikidanshō* and *Jikidan innenshū* contain an account of a father and two sons in China who are reunited as a result of the sons' filial piety. The younger son's blindness is later cured as a result of their sponsorship of seven days of lectures on the *Lotus Sutra* (during the course of which they collect the joyous tears of all those who come to hear, and apply them to the blind boy's eyes). *Hokekyō jikidanshō*, vol. 3, 538–45; Hirota et al., eds., *Nikkō tenkaizō Jikidan innenshū*, 304–6.

albeit profoundly filial, emotional attachment—is indicative of his deluded state. In *Ikuta Atsumori*, his encounter with his father, whose first words paraphrase the ninth stanza of Su Shi's 蘇軾 Chinese Buddhist verse on the nine stages of bodily decay,[39] similarly suggests an encounter with Buddhist Truth. Finally, the description in *Ko Atsumori* of the boy's later Buddhist devotion (after his meeting with his father, that is) highlights the personal spiritual importance of the event for the boy. Although *Ikuta Atsumori* ends dramatically with Atsumori's anguished return to the world of the dead, the *Ko Atsumori* conclusion suggests that in *Ikuta Atsumori*, too, Little Atsumori will find peace as a result of his supernatural encounter.

When considered in conjunction with *Ko Atsumori*, Zenpō's *Ikuta Atsumori* is peculiar for its elision of most specifically Pure Land Buddhist elements. Other than the unnamed priest's initial statement of allegiance to Hōnen, founder of the Japanese Pure Land sect, *Ikuta Atsumori* contains no identifiable Pure Land references. *Ko Atsumori*, on the other hand, is unequivocally sectarian in tone, from its description of how Kumagai "became a disciple of Hōnen and took up the *nenbutsu* 念仏 with single-minded, unwavering devotion," to its concluding admonition that "we should all chant the *nenbutsu* for the sake of our departed."[40] *Ko Atsumori* describes how Atsumori's widow became a nun and mourned for Atsumori, "chanting the *nenbutsu* day and night" and "recalling their vow to share a lotus-seat in the Pure Land," and it erroneously claims that Little Atsumori grew up to become the eminent Zen'e Shōnin 善恵上人 (Shōkū Shōnin 證空上人; 1177–1247), founder of the Seizan 西山 sect of Pure Land Buddhism.[41]

By examining the Little Atsumori story in its various manifestations, including the *otogizōshi Ko Atsumori* and a puppet play (*ko-jōruri* 古浄瑠璃) of 1645, Muroki Yatarō and Minobe Shigekatsu have identified the influences of several groups of Pure Land preachers, including *Kōya hijiri* 高野聖, nuns of the *Ji* 時 ("Time") sect, and *kanjin* 勧進 (fundraising) priests of Chionji 知恩寺 Temple.[42] Minobe speculates that

---

39. Yokomichi Mario and Omote Akira, eds., *Yōkyokushū*, vol. 2 (Iwanami shoten, 1963), 240, headnote 21.

40. Matsumoto Ryūshin, ed., *Otogizōshi shū*, SNKS (Shinchōsha, 1980), 310–11 and 327 (Keiō University Library text).

41. Matsumoto, *Otogizōshi shū*, 326 and 327. Minobe Shigekatsu argues that Zen'e was confused with Little Atsumori because Zen'e was a disciple of Hōnen and was known to have been acquainted with Kumagai. Minobe, *Chūsei denshō bungaku no shosō*, 122–24.

42. Muroki Yatarō, *Zōtei katarimono (mai, sekkyō, kojōruri) no kenkyū* (Fūkan

the story of Little Atsumori's meeting with his father's ghost derives from an earlier account—now lost—of the meeting of the Chionji intendant Genchi 源智 with his own dead father, Taira no Moromori 平師盛 (1171–84), who, like Atsumori, is reported in *Heike monogatari* to have been killed at the battle of Ichi-no-tani. Minobe suggests that the story was changed to one of Atsumori and his son by the "Kayadō *hijiri*" 刈萱堂聖 (*Kōya hijiri* affiliated with Karukayadō 刈萱堂 Hall on Mount Kōya), who traditionally employed tales of Kumagai in their preaching, and the *Ji-shū* 時宗 nuns of the Mieidō 御影堂 (Shinzenkōji Temple 新善光寺, west of Fifth Avenue Bridge in the capital), who seem to have emphasized the role of Atsumori's widow. There is little trace of the storytelling activities of these particular preacher-entertainers in *Ikuta Atsumori*, however, and whether this is because Zenpō pared them from his play, or because they were absent from his immediate oral and/ or textual source(s), is unknown.

A second and more striking difference between *Ikuta Atsumori* and *Ko Atsumori* is the omission from *Ikuta Atsumori* of the character Kumagai, who, as a disciple of Hōnen, plays a crucial role in the *otogi-zōshi* in raising and caring for Atsumori's son. It cannot be the case that Kumagai was added to the Little Atsumori account after Zenpō's composition of the play, because, as we have seen, Kikō Daishuku refers to him in connection with the story in his diary entry of 1485. What, then, became of Kumagai, and why did Zenpō leave him out? Reading *Ikuta Atsumori* with these questions in mind, it becomes apparent that Kumagai is not missing at all: the *waki*—the priest who introduces himself as a disciple of Hōnen and a companion of Atsumori's son—is Kumagai in all but name. In *Ko Atsumori*, Kumagai serves as a bridge between Atsumori and his son by passing Atsumori's relics on to Little Atsumori in a seemingly symbolic rite of Taira family succession. Similarly, in *Heike* texts in the readerly textual line, Kumagai bridges the gulf between Atsumori and his father Tsunemori by sending Tsunemori his dead son's head. The unnamed priest in *Ikuta Atsumori* also serves as a kind of bridge between Atsumori and his son, for it is he who accompanies the boy on his quest to Ikuta to find his father's remains, and it is he, rather than the boy, who leads them toward the light that reveals Atsumori's ghost.

So why did Zenpō choose to include a Kumagai-figure in his play, yet deny him his name? It is possible that he expected audiences to

shobō, 1981), 347–54; Minobe, *Chūsei denshō bungaku no shosō*, 109–19.

recognize the Pure Land priest's identity on their own. Mizuhara Hajime has argued that in the Engyō-bon and other early texts of the *Heike* (as opposed to *Genpei jōsuiki*, for example), the Kumagai/Atsumori account is narrated from Kumagai's point of view.[43] The priest in *Ikuta Atsumori* similarly narrates the tale of Atsumori's son's encounter with his father's ghost, and audiences may have been expected to recognize the likeness. It seems more probable, however, that Zenpō effaced the priest's identity for an altogether different reason: so as not to distract from the central theme of his composition, namely, the pathos of a war-orphaned child's meeting with his father, and a dead father's meeting with his son. By explicitly including Kumagai within the work, Zenpō would call attention to the relationship between the killer and the killed, thereby returning the tale to its *Heike* origins as a story of one man's (Kumagai's) awakening to Buddhism. As we have seen, it has been argued that in the Atsumori account in *Heike monogatari*, Atsumori serves as no more than a stock Taira figure whose sole purpose is to be killed so that Kumagai may awaken to the nature of Buddhist Truth. It is ironic that in *Ikuta Atsumori*, Kumagai has become the stock figure—an unnamed Buddhist priest, devoid of individual identity—whose only purpose is to narrate events while leading Atsumori's son to his father's ghost, enabling the boy's own allegorical encounter with Buddhist Truth.

CONCLUSION

In composing *Ikuta Atsumori* in the late fifteenth or early sixteenth century, several decades after the plays *Tsunemori* and *Atsumori*, Komparu Zenpō faced the daunting task of writing both in accord with and against tradition. While it may be presumptuous to speak of a Bloomian "anxiety of influence" in the case of Zenpō's formulation of *Ikuta Atsumori*,[44] the fact remains that Zenpō chose to base his composition upon a "new" *Heike* tale, effectively setting his own work apart from that of his forebears. Thomas Hare writes in a discussion of Zeami's nō treatise *Fūshikaden* that "in considering the psychology

---

43. Mizuhara, *Engyō-bon Heike monogatari ronkō*, 360–66.
44. Harold Bloom, *The Anxiety of Influence: A Theory of Poetry* (New York: Oxford University Press, 1973).

of the audience, Zeami concludes that people appreciate the novel; therefore, the actor who can show ordinary things in a new light will succeed."[45] The same can be said of the playwright, both in Zeami's time and beyond. By drawing upon a contemporary storytelling tradition with likely roots in medieval Tendai and/or Pure Land preaching, Zenpō was able to take a new approach to an old theme, incorporating an unnamed Kumagai figure as an echo of the old, and depicting the plight of a posthumous son as a means of newly exploring the physical and psychological consequences of war and reunion.[46]

Considering the performance history of the *Heike* Atsumori episode, Zenpō's departure from tradition may not be as extreme as it seems. Kikō Daishuku indicates in his aforementioned diary entry of 1485 that a blind *Heike* reciter included the Little Atsumori account in his narration of *Heike monogatari*, suggesting that late fifteenth-century *Heike* reciters made little distinction between newer and older *Heike* tales. Furthermore, Mizuhara Hajime proposes that after taking religious vows, Kumagai himself set about telling his story as a means of spreading the Dharma, and that it was his own confessional account of how he killed Atsumori and awoke to the nature of Buddhist truth that came to be incorporated—largely verbatim—in the earliest texts of the *Heike*.[47] Whether or not Mizuhara's assertion is correct, it is certainly true that religious-awakening tales like Kumagai's were employed in early-medieval preaching.[48] With this in mind, it appears probable that the *Heike* Atsumori account (and thus *Tsunemori* and Zeami's *Atsumori*), like *Ikuta Atsumori* and countless other plays, is ultimately rooted in the didactic storytelling traditions of a large and anonymous cast of Kamakura and Muromachi-period preacher-entertainers.

---

45. Hare, *Zeami's Style*, 24.

46. Nishino Haruo and Yamanaka Reiko have suggested a more practical reason for Zenpō's decision to write about Atsumori's son. They say that insofar as many of Zenpō's plays contain a specific role for a child actor, Zenpō may have written them with a particular child in mind—probably his grandson. Personal conversation, March 28, 2005.

47. Mizuhara, *Engyō-bon Heike monogatari ronkō*, 356–81.

48. As one example, Mizuhara cites a passage from the Kamakura-period Pure Land text *Ichigon hōdanshō* 一言芳談抄 (Book of Short Discourses) to the effect that a contemporary priest was employing war tales (*kassen monogatari* 合戦物語) in his preaching. Mizuhara posits that the priest was Kumagai, but there is no way to tell. Mizuhara, *Engyō-bon Heike monogatari ronkō*, 365; Miyasaka Yūshō, ed., *Kana hōgo shū*, NKBT 83 (Iwanami shoten, 1964), 207.

17 ～ *Ikuta Atsumori*

| LIM BENG CHOO

INTRODUCTION

Ikuta Atsumori 生田敦盛 is attributed to Komparu Zenchiku's 金春禅竹 grandson Zenpō 禅鳳 (1454–1532?). Its main source is an episode from Chapter Nine of the *Heike monogatari* (*The Tale of the Heike*).[1] During the battle of Ichi-no-tani 一谷 in the Second Month of 1184, a low-ranking Genji warrior named Kumagai Naozane 熊谷直実 kills Taira no Atsumori 平敦盛 (1169–1184), the youngest son of the Heike general Tsunemori 経盛. Atsumori's premature death foreshadows the ultimate downfall of the once-prosperous and powerful Taira family.[2] The episode is presented not solely as a personal tragedy, but also as an illustration of the uncertainty and transcience of life, as well as of humanity's powerlessness.

The well-known nō play *Atsumori*, attributed to Zeami Motokiyo 世阿弥元清 (1363–1443), reinforces this sentiment. Many years after the battle, the ghost of Atsumori confronts the monk Renshō 蓮生, who turns out to have once been Kumagai Naozane. In his sorrow over their chance encounter on the battlefield, Kumagai has taken religious

---

1. Other Atsumori tales appear in different genres in the later part of the Muromachi period (1392–1573), see for instance, Ichiko Teiji, ed., *Otogizōshi*, NKBT 38 (Iwanami shoten: 1992), 229–40. See also Chapters 16 and 18 by Keller Kimbrough in this volume.

2. The historical Taira Atsumori was killed in the battle at Ichi-no-tani when he was a teenager, as depicted in Zeami's *Atsumori*. For a discussion of some of the possible sources that might have inspired this play, see Sanari Kentarō, ed., *Yōkyoku taikan*, vol. 2 (Meiji shoin, 1931), 263–64.

orders to pray for Atsumori's soul. The play ends with the former enemies reconciled, assured of rebirth on a single lotus leaf. This remarkable denouement highlights the unpredictability of life.[3]

This piece strongly emphasizes philosophical and religious concerns, such as the desire for salvation in a chaotic period. The playwright uses literary techniques to achieve a strong sense of poetic beauty. The aesthetic effect is also strengthened by the regular reference to other classics such as *The Tale of Genji* and poetry anthologies. We identify with the characters through the more abstract emotions evoked by means of poetic imagery and literary allusions and references rather than by individual character's personality traits or heroic actions.

Ikuta Atsumori, produced two generations later, has a very different emphasis. The play opens with a discussion of the mysterious origin of a boy who turns out to be Atsumori's orphan; the child earnestly wishes to meet his father. The separation of parent and child creates keen anticipation on the audience's part: What is the father like? Will he appear? When will he appear?

In the care of the *waki*, Hōnen, the boy visits the Kamo Shrine to pray to see his father. His devotion and sincerity are rewarded with a dream vision, and he is briefly reunited with the ghost of his father at Ikuta, where Atsumori was killed. The play ends with the tearful parting of father and son as the ghost fades away.

In terms of style of presentation, *Ikuta Atsumori* contains a greater number of conversational exchanges than does Zeami's *Atsumori*. There are also fewer poetic allusions and uses of other literary techniques such as *honkadori*.[4] The final battle dance performed by the *shite* Atsumori showcases the skill of the actor playing this role as he struggles with two invisible demonic creatures from hell. It also provides space for the audience to imagine the intensity of the battle.

This is a one-act nō play even though the *shite* character is an apparition no longer living in the present human time. The *waki* character is a monk who is an attendant of the *kokata* (子方 child role), Atsumori's son. Events in the play take place in several different locations, following

---

3. See Karen Brazell, *Traditional Japanese Theatre: An Anthology of Plays* (Columbia University Press, 1997), 126–42 for a translation of the play.

4. Many reasons, of course, can be used to argue for this change, although it is beyond the scope of this introduction to expound on them. A *honkadori* 本歌取り is an allusive variant, a poem written based on expressions in an existing poem.

the child's relentless pursuit of his father.[5]

The first English translation of *Ikuta Atsumori* was published in 1921 by Arthur Waley (1889–1966) under the alternative title of *Ikuta*.[6] Understandably for its time, Waley's rendition is a general appropriation of the play into an English poem. Waley used a style of poetic writing that is familiar to an English-speaking audience, rendering the piece more coherent than the original. This kind of translation presents a "reader-friendly" text to the uninitiated, but compromises certain characteristics of the nō text, such as the practice of repeating the last two lines of certain segments of the play, or the introduction of consecutive image patterns in a manner reminiscent of *renga* 連歌 (linked verse).

5. For a more detailed discussion of Zenpō's work and this play, see Lim Beng Choo, "Performing *Furyū Nō*: The Theatre of Konparu Zenpō," *Asian Theater Journal*, vol. 22, no. 1 (Spring 2005), 33–51.

6. Arthur Waley, *The Nō Plays of Japan* (London: Allen and Unwin, 1921), 74–80.

Ikuta Atsumori

| TRANSLATED BY LIM BENG CHOO

Second category *mūgen* nō in one act.
Performed by the Kanze, Hōshō, Komparu, and Kongō schools.
Time: Autumn, early Kamakura period
Place: I–III:[1] Shrine of the Great Kamo Deity in Yamashiro[2]
            III–VII: The Ikuta Woods in Settsu[3]
Author: Komparu Zenpō (1454–1532?)[4]

KOKATA   Atsumori's child
WAKI   Monk, servant to Hōnen
SHITE   Spirit of Taira no Atsumori

I

*Child stands at front center. Monk stands at the naming pillar (nanoriza)
and faces forward.*

MONK I am a servant of the Holy Priest Hōnen Shōnin of Kurodani.[5]

Ikuta Atsumori 生田敦盛. This translation is based on Sanari Kentarō, ed.,
Yōkyoku taikan, vol. 2 (Meiji shoin, 1931), 263–73. Reference is also made to
Nogami Toyoichirō, ed., *Kaichū Yōkyoku zenshū*, vol. 2 (Chūō kōronsha, 1935),
215–24; Yokomichi Mario and Omote Akira, eds., *Yōkyokushū* (ge), NKBT 41
(Iwanami shoten, 1963), 238–42.

1. The translation is divided into eight sections, following Sanari.
2. Shrine of the Great Kamo Deity (*Kamo no myōjin* 賀茂の明神) in the
province of Yamashiro 山城. There are two ancient Kamo Shrines in what is
now the northern part of Kyoto City. The shrine here is thought to be the Upper
Shrine, *Kamigamo jinja* 上賀茂神社.
3. The Ikuta Woods (*Ikuta no mori* 生田森) is in the province of Settsu 摂津.
A grove by this name is located in the grounds of Ikuta Shrine in the city of Kōbe.
4. Zenpō is identified as the author in *Nihyakujūban utaimokuroku* 二百十番
謡目録 and *Nōhonsakushachūmon* 能本作者注文. The latter lists the name of
the play as *Ikuta* 生田. This is the name by which the play is still known in the
Komparu school.
5. Hōnen Shōnin 法然上人 (1133–1212), the founder of Jōdoshū 浄土宗
(Pure Land) Buddhism. Kurodani 黒谷 is in present-day Kyoto, where Priest
Hōnen was based, and also where the Pure Land sect headquarters were located.

On his way back from a pilgrimage to the Kamo Shrine, his Holiness found a beautiful two-year old boy abandoned underneath the Sagari pine tree.[6] He was left on the lid of a *tebako* box, together with clothing and necessary provisions.[7]

His Holiness had pity on the child and took him back. He raised him with great care, and in no time the child turned ten. This is the child you see before you.

Because the child is saddened by not knowing his parents, His Holiness told the story of the child one day after his sermon. Then out of the crowd came forward a young woman, who claimed that the boy was her child. His Holiness took her aside to ask her for more details, and found out that the boy was the son of Atsumori[8] who was killed at the battle of Ichi-no-tani some years ago.

Having learned of this, the boy was determined to meet his father, so he entered a seven-day secluded prayer session offered to the great Kamo Deity. He requested that the deity grant him a meeting with his father, even if only in a dream.

Today he is completing the prayer session, and I am accompanying him to the Kamo Shrine to offer his final prayers.[9]

They arrive at the shrine. Monk faces forward.

(*tsukizerifu*)   In no time we have arrived at the Kamo Shrine. Do offer your prayers with your heart now.

II

Monk moves toward the right-hand side of Child. Both move to the front of the stage and sit down. Child puts hands together in prayer.

CHILD

(*sashi*)   How grateful I am!
In this awesome shrine ground

---

6. *Sagari matsu* 下り松. Sagari was an old name of an area near the temple of Ichijōji 一乗寺 in Sakyō Ward, Kyoto, in the northeast of the city.

7. *Tebako* 手箱 are small boxes that were used to store daily items.

8. The text refers to Atsumori as *mukan no taiyū Atsumori*, meaning that he was of the fifth court rank, but held no office. His son is described as a "forgotten remembrance," *wasuregatami* 忘れ形見.

9. According to one text, the boy came to say prayers at the shrine for seventeen consecutive days. Nonomura Kaizō, ed., *Yōkyoku sanbyakugojū-banshū* (Nihon meicho zenshū kankōkai, 1928), 140.

surrounded by the sacred vermilion fence
I calmed my heart, cleansed
and clear as the Mitarashi River.[10]
It is here I will ask the deity
to grant my greatest wish.

They end their prayers, lowering their hands.

CHILD AND MONK

(*sageuta*)   Even if it is just in a dream
please grant me
a sight of my dear parent.
(*ageuta*)   Praying with all my might
for my wish to be realized.
Praying with all my might
for my wish to be realized.
I will pray also to the gods at Tadasu—
it would not be right if my prayers were left unanswered.[11]
Please bestow on me what I have asked for.
Please bestow on me what I have asked for.

CHILD

Raises his head as if awakening from a dream. Faces the monk.

(*mondō*) How strange! I had a miraculous dream while I dozed off.

MONK   That is indeed remarkable! What kind of miraculous dream?

CHILD   A heavenly voice spoke to me from behind the main altar
there, [*looks intently toward the front of the stage*] saying that if I really
want to meet my father—even in a dream—I should go to the Ikuta
Woods in the land of Settsu. This is the divine dream I had.

MONK   How very strange! There is no need to return to Kurodani.
I should accompany you to the Ikuta Woods from here. Let us make
haste.

---

10. *Mitarashigawa* 御手洗川, a stream running through the Upper Kamo
Shrine used by worshippers to wash their hands and mouths before proceeding
to the shrine.

11. *Tadasu no kami* 糺の神 refers to the deities of the Lower Kamo Shrine,
known for Tadasu Grove (*Tadasu no mori*). *Tadasu* 糺す also means "to correct,
to make right."

III

Both stand up and face each other.

MONK   (*michiyuki*)
(*ageuta*)   Leaving behind the Kamo Shrine
                 under the mountain shade,
                 leaving behind the Kamo Shrine
                 under the mountain shade,
                 we hurry by Yamazaki
                 and cross the Minase River[12]
                 where the mist is thick and wind strong,
                 piercing our traveling cloaks.
                 Autumn has arrived.
                 Wasn't it just yesterday[13]
                 that we thought we would
                 visit the Ikuta Woods at Settsu?
                 Now at the Ikuta Woods, we have arrived.
                 Now at the Ikuta Woods, we have arrived.[14]

*At "piercing our traveling cloak" Monk moves a few steps forward, then
returns to where he started, indicating that they have arrived. At the end of
the* michiyuki, *Monk faces front.*

---

12. They go down the Yodo River to the Inland Sea. Yamazaki 山崎 lies on the
border between Yamashiro and Settsu. Minasegawa 水無瀬川, a tributary of the
Yodo 淀 River, is often mentioned in poetry. There is a possible allusion here to
a poem by Emperor Go-Toba 後鳥羽 (1180–1239), *Shinkokinshū*, no. 36: 見渡
せば山もと霞むみなせ川夕べは秋と何思ひけん   *mitawaseba / yama moto
kasumu / Minasegawa / yūbe wa aki to / nani omoiken*. The poet admires the sight
of evening in autumn over the misty Minase River.

13. This poem alludes to a poem by Fujiwara no Ietaka 藤原家隆 (1158–1237),
Shinkokinshū, no. 289: 昨日だにとはんとおもひし津の国の生田の森に秋は
きにけり   *kinō dani / towan to omoishi / tsu no kuni no/ ikuta no mori ni / aki
wa kinikeri*; "Wasn't it just yesterday that I thought of visiting the Ikuta Woods at
Settsu? Now autumn has arrived."

14. Ikuta-no-mori lies inside Ikuta Shrine near Sannomiya Station in the center
of modern Kobe. In 1184, it was the site of the eastern entrance to the Heike
stronghold. Takagi Ichinosuke et al., eds., *Heike monogatari* (ge), NKBT 33 (Iwanami
shoten, 1960), 185 *et passim*. The narrative does not mention where Atsumori was
stationed, but Kumagai, the Genji warrior who killed him, was stationed at Ikuta-
no-mori, and was among the first to attack the frontal forces. The Heike stronghold
ultimately fell after it was attacked from the western side at Ichi-no-tani.

MONK (*tsukizerifu*) We have made haste and arrived at the Ikuta Woods at Settsu. The scenic woods and the flowing stream are even better than we heard in the capital. What a beautiful place this is.

> *Looks to his left.*

That field out there, isn't that the field of Ikuta?[15] I think we should go over and take a look.

> *Takes two steps and stops.*

While we were looking around, the sun has suddenly gone down.[16] It looks like there is a dwelling place over there, I see a light. I shall go over and ask for a night's lodging.

> *Both go to the witness square* (wakiza) *and stand. Child sits; Monk follows and sits further down.*

IV

> *A cloth is removed from the large stage prop, a straw-thatched hut, revealing Atsumori sitting on a stool, wearing the "Atsumori" mask.*

ATSUMORI (*sashi*) The five ways are essentially ephemeral.[17]
> Why should one so treasure one's life?
> > "The spirits who guard their tombs flit through
> > the moonlit night,
> > the ghosts who lost their bodies howl in the
> > autumn wind."[18]

---

15. This field (*Ikuta no ono*), like the stream (*Ikutagawa*) and the Ikuta Woods, were all famous poetic sites (*utamakura*).

16. This is an interesting development of the play. A sudden change, usually a fast-forward to the night, seems also to be found in *Yamanba* 山姥. Both plays use this quick time flow as a narrative strategy to introduce the shite.

17. The "Five Ways," *Go-un* 五蘊, refers to the five constituent elements of all existences in Buddhism: 1. matter or form, 2. perception, 3. conception, 4. volition, 5. consciousness. Hisao Inagaki, ed., *A Dictionary of Japanese Buddhist Terms* (Kyoto: Nagata Bunshōdō, 1992 [fourth edition]), 83). Waley has translated the term by breaking it down into the five components it represents: "beauty, perception, knowledge, motion, consciousness." Waley, *Nō Plays of Japan*, 76.

18. These two lines are based closely on the ninth part of 九想詩 "The Nine Faces of Death," traditionally attributed to the Song-period poet Su Shi 蘇軾 (Su Dongpo 蘇東坡, 1036–1101), but possibly an original Japanese work. James H.

	Alas, this dreadful season!
MONK (*kakeai*)	This is very curious.
	Inside this grass hut
	I see a gallant young warrior
	wearing full armor.
	What could this mean, I wonder?
ATSUMORI	*(Raises his face to the monk.)*
	What a foolish man.

All that effort in coming here, was it not just for the sake of meeting me? Shameful as it is to say, this is the spirit of Atsumori of old.

CHILD Tell me, are you my dead father Atsumori? he said.[19]

Despite himself he runs toward him—

While chanting these lines, Child quickly approaches the hut, reaches out to touch Atsumori's left sleeve, then sits down on his right.

CHORUS (*ageuta*) grabbing tightly onto his father's sleeves,
grabbing tightly onto his father's sleeves,

Child holds back his tears. Atsumori turns and looks at him intently.

he cries joyful tears
at the long-awaited reunion[20]

Stanford, "The Nine Faces of Death: 'Su Tung-po's *Kuzōshi*,'" *Eastern Buddhist* 21:2 (1988), 54–77. "The spirits who guard their graves" translates きを守る 幽魂 *ki wo mamoru yūkon*. It has been suggested that *ki* (*ku* in some texts) means "coffin" (棺) or "body" (躯). The glyph used in the Chinese original is 塚 meaning "grave mound." The phrase 塚を守る飛魄 *tsuka wo mamoru hibaku* (flitting spirits who guard grave mounds) appears in *Motomezuka* 求塚, another play centered about the Ikuta area. Yokomichi and Omote, *Yōkyokushū* (*jō*), 72.

19. "He said" translates the interrogative and quotative particles *ka to* that follow direct quotation of the *kokata*'s question. This is followed by narrative description of his actions. Examples are found in other plays. A similar construction with *ka to* occurs at a key point in *Sumidagawa* 隅田川, where the *shite* addresses the spirit of her dead son ("Is that you, my child?") and the *kokata* answers, *Hawa nite mashimasu ka to* ("'Is that you, Mother?' he said."). Yokomichi and Omote, *Yōkyokushū* (ge), 394. In the preceding *kakei* (393), the *shite* describes the mother's own actions in third-person narrative form. See "The Sumida River" in Royall Tyler, *Japanese Nō Dramas* (London, New York: Penguin Books, 1992), 262–63.

20. In the original, the phrase 泣く音に立つる鶯の逢ふ *naku ne ni tatsuru uguisu no ō* ("making a weeping cry, the bush warbler, meeting ...") contains a playful reference to the warbler, which is written with the glyph 鶯 read either *uguisu* or *ō*. This creates a pun on *ō* (逢ふ) meaning "to meet."

forgetting all hardships endured.
How I wish that this transient dream
could become reality.

In the middle of this section Child returns to his seat and sits down, facing forward.

VI

ATSUMORI   (*Raising his face to gaze at the child.*)
(*sashi*)   How pitiful!
                  The beloved child I left behind
                  who should be enjoying a life of splendor,[21]
                  is instead thin and worn.
                  How I grieve to see
                  his inky black sleeves.[22]

Turns from Child to face front, commenting as if to himself.

(*kudoki*)   All this
                  is thanks to your deep filial devotion.
                  Going to the Great Deity of the Kamo Shrine
                  and praying,
                  "Grant me a glimpse of my father
                  if only in a dream!"
                  moved him to take pity on us.
                  The Deity gave a command to the King of Hell
                  who accepted the order
                  and granted me leave for a little while.[23]

Turning to the boy.

                  This meeting of father and child will never happen again.
(*sageuta*)   Under the moon's light as the hour grows late
                  let me tell you tales of the past
                  all night long.

---

21. The term *hanayaka* recalls the brilliant splendor of the Heike before their defeat.
22. Atsumori's child is wearing the black robes of a temple acolyte.
23. Permission to return to the world of mortals (*shaba* 娑婆). The intercession of the Kamo Divinity (*myōjin* 明神) with the King of Hell (*Enma* 閻魔) is found in some versions of the medieval prose tale *Ko Atsumori*. The period of time allowed for the meeting is even shorter, not *shibashi no itoma* as here, but *setsuna no itoma* 刹那の暇, using a Buddhist term for an instant in time. Yokomichi and Omote, *Yōkyokushū* (ge), 242, headnote 3.

Stands up, leaves straw-thatched hut, and starts to dance to the accompaniment of the chorus.

CHORUS (*kuse*)   At the beginning,
when the Heike clan
was basking in extravagant luxury,
we engaged in elegant pursuits,[24]
in all kinds of poetry and music,
seeing off one season
and welcoming another.

Atsumori moves a little closer to the front of the stage.

Why did our fortunes change?

Performs a sashi-mawashi *with fan, looks in the distance, and moves toward the corner pillar* (metsuke-bashira).[25]

Kiso's attack,[26]
completely unexpected:
we were driven to flight
by the enemy,

Moves with short steps, expressing strong emotion.

His Majesty[27]
with all the members of our house,

Staring into the distance.

left the capital of flowers
and started heading west

Stamps several times and goes toward the corner pillar.

to the skies of the Western Sea.
Treading unfamiliar paths,

Turns left at the corner pillar, making a big circle of the stage.

we crossed the mountains

---

24. *Kachō fūgetsu* 花鳥風月, activities like the viewing of flowers and the moon.

25. The "viewing pillar" at the front of the stage, on the left hand side.

26. Kiso no Yoshinaka 木曽義仲 (1154–1184) attacked and occupied the capital in 1183. Kiso is the name of mountainous province where Yoshinaka was brought up. There is an untranslated allusion here to one of its famous sights, *Kiso no kakehashi*, the hanging bridge of Kiso. The word *kake* is used a second time in the meaning of "attack."

27. Emperor Antoku 安徳, just six years old when the Heike fled the capital in the Seventh Month, 1183. His mother Kenreimon'in 建礼門院 was Atsumori's aunt.

and sailed the sea.
For a short while we became
residents of the countryside
far removed from the capital.[28]
When again we finally returned
like the waves on the share
arriving at
the mountain road of Suma,
Ichi-no-tani, and Ikuta Woods

Returns to the center of the stage.

the clan rejoiced,

Gazes forward at the front (shōmensaki).

for the capital is not far from here.

Opens fan.

Just then,

Raises fan.

ATSUMORI   The forces of Noriyori
                 and Yoshitsune[29]

Raises fan.

CHORUS   as vast as clouds or mists,[30]
                 For a time
                 the Heike thought
                 they could put up a fight,
                 but exhausted were their bows

---

28. The expression *amasagaru* 天離がる is a *makurakotoba* (poetic epithet) conventionally modifying *hina* 鄙 (countryside). Literally meaning something like "separated from heaven," it often refers to separation from the capital. After fleeing the capital, the Heike sought refuge in Kyushu. After encountering resistance, they took to their boats again, returning up the Inland Sea to the coastal area of Harima 播磨 and Settsu provinces (modern Hyōgo 兵庫 prefecture).

29. Minamoto Noriyori 源範頼 (1153?–1193), commander-in-chief of the frontal forces attacking Ikuta-no-mori on the east, and his younger brother Minamoto Yoshitsune 源義経 (1159–1189), commander-in-chief of the rear forces that broke the Heike resistance by a surprise attack on Ichi-no-tani to the west.

30. The great size of forces confronting the Heike is expressed through the simile *kumo ya kiri no gotoku nite* 雲や霧ごとくにて, "like clouds or mist." This is a variation of the phrase *unka no gotoku* 雲霞のごとこ (like clouds and fog) that occurs some eleven times in *Heike monogatari* in descriptions of large battle forces, including once in "The Death of Atsumori." Takagi, *Heike monogatari* (ge), 146.

and their luck,
their will to fight had waned.[31]
Dispersed in all directions,
each and every one.

Goes forward to the corner pillar, points fan, makes a large turn to the left, goes to the center-back of stage.

There is a tale of one
who threw herself in the pitiful depths of Ikuta River—

Moves left and right at center-back and prepares for dance.

But alas, what is the use of relating the tale?[32]

VII

ATSUMORI

(*ei*)   I am delighted—
even if this is just a fleeting dream.

Goes forward a little.

This meeting of the parent and child,
our sleeves touching,
(parrot sleeves swinging in dance).[33]

CHORUS   This will linger on in our hearts forever.

(*DANCE: chūnomai*)
Atsumori performs chūnomai *dance. After the dance, he faces front.*

---

31. The phrase *Heike wa un mo **tsuki yumi yatake** gokoro* contains a hidden secondary meaning: "Zelkova bow, arrows of bamboo." The pivot words (*kakekotoba*) are *tsuki* ("run out" 尽き but also "Zelkova wood" 槻) and *yatake* ("valiant" 弥猛 but also "bamboo arrows" 矢竹). The word *yumi* means "bow."

32. An allusion to an ancient legend recorded in the play *Motomezuka* 求塚 (originally called *Otomezuka* 乙女塚 "*The Maiden's Tomb*") where a woman drowns herself in the Ikuta River after neither of the men who love her will give up his suit. The phrase *mi o suteshi* applies also to Atsumori, who loses his life near the same river.

33. *Kakekotoba* (pivot words) yield a second meaning: *ōmu* ("[may] meet" 逢む and "parrot" 鸚鵡) and *furete* ("touching" 触れて and "swinging/shaking" 振れて). The expression *oyako ōmu no sode* appears in the plays *Hyakuman* 百万 and *Minase* 水無瀬. Here "parrot sleeves" refer to the sleeves in dance.

VIII

ATSUMORI   What is that over there? [34]
                Alas, here come the messengers from Hell's Palace
                    "The King of Hell granted you a brief leave," they will say
                "Your late return
                    is enraging the King,"
CHORUS (*chūnori*) And how incredible!
                And how incredible!
                Suddenly dark clouds rise
                and fierce flame blaze up
                amid falling swords.
                Aśura foes
                countless in number,
                reverberate
                as they fill heaven and earth.[35]

    Atsumori looks up and down.

ATSUMORI   Day in day out, the constant warfare
CHORUS   with the *aśura*, my familiar foe.
                He strikes a direct blow
                with his sword.

    Atsumori draws sword and starts dancing.

                Hither and thither
                he runs about,
                sparks flying off his sword
                as he battles on.
                After some time
                the dark clouds
                gradually lift,
                and the *aśura* enemies, too,
                disappear suddenly.
        (*yowagin*) The clear moon shines brightly

---

34. The alternation between chanting (*katari*) and singing (*tsuyogin*) reflects Kongō and Komparu school practice. Yokomichi and Omtoe, *Yōkyokushū* (*ge*), 243. In the Kanze school, only the last phrase is in *tsuyogin* mode.

35. *Shura* 修羅 (Skt. *aśura*) is originally a protective deity in Hinduism. In Japanese Buddhism, however, *shura* are usually fearsome spirits who are constantly engaged in warfare, especially in the realm of the *aśura*, one of the states of existence.

in the serene sky
as dawn breaks.

ATSUMORI (*uta*) How ashamed I am
that my child

Drops the sword and uses a fan.

CHORUS should have witnessed such sufferings.

Faces the Child.

Hurry home, he said,
and pray fervently
for my repose.
In tears he pulls away his sleeves
and bids farewell.

Restrains his tears, moving to the base square (jōza).

His departing visage

Points with his fan, going forward to the viewing pillar and returning to the base pillar (shitebashira).

like the short-lived dew and frost
on the cogon grass[36]
in the morning fields
disappears without a trace,
disappears without a trace.

---

36. 浅茅 *asaji*, with a pivot on 朝 *asa* "morning." Trailing plants such as *asaji*, *mugura*, or *yomogi* had poetic associations with death and decay.

18 ～ Ko Atsumori

R. KELLER KIMBROUGH

INTRODUCTION

On the seventh day of the Second Month of Juei 寿永 3 (1184), the Taira suffered a crushing defeat at the battle of Ichi-no-tani 一谷 in the Genpei War 源平合戦. Among the many casualties was a youth by the name of Atsumori 敦盛, purportedly beheaded on the beach by the Minamoto warrior Kumagai no Jirō Naozane 熊谷次郎直実 (1141–1208) before he could make his escape. His story came to be included in the thirteenth-century *Heike monogatari*, from which it was later singled out for retelling in numerous works of medieval fiction, painting, and drama, including the nō plays *Atsumori* 敦盛, *Tsunemori* 経盛, and *Ikuta Atsumori* 生田敦盛. Atsumori himself came to be celebrated as a kind of medieval cult figure, and his flute, which Kumagai is said to have taken from his corpse, was enshrined at Suma Temple 須磨寺 from at least the early fifteenth century.

Ko Atsumori 小敦盛 (Little Atsumori) dates from the fifteenth or sixteenth century. The most famous of approximately a dozen *otogizōshi* お伽草子 (works of short medieval prose fiction) inspired by specific episodes in *Heike monogatari*, it is distinctively late medieval in content and tone. The story focuses less upon the death of Atsumori than the resulting havoc wrought in the lives of those he left behind; it explores the physical and psychological consequences of war by describing the ways in which three characters—Atsumori's widow, the warrior Kumagai, and a posthumous son (Little Atsumori, from whom the work takes its name)—come to terms with the shared tragedies of their past. Though the war haunts each in a different way, all find solace in the healing powers of truth, fidelity, and Pure Land Buddhism. Even Little

Atsumori, an unwitting victim of a conflict that was over before his birth, finds a way to make peace with a ghost from his past: the father he never knew. Marked by the miraculous revelations, fantastic coincidences, and pungently didactic and emotive narrative style that are so characteristic of the *otogizōshi* genre, his story captures, in microcosm, the struggles of thirteenth-century Japanese society to overcome the crippling wounds of war.

Though scholars have traced *Ko Atsumori's* roots to the oral proselytizing traditions of the wandering holy men of Mount Kōya (*Kōya hijiri* 高野聖) and a variety of Tendai and Pure Land Buddhist preacher-entertainers, the earliest datable reference to the tale is contained in *Shaken nichiroku* 蔗軒日録, the diary of the Zen priest Kikō Daishuku 季弘大叔.[1] In an entry from the fourth day of the Third Month of 1485, Daishuku records that the *Heike* reciter and storyteller Sōjū 宗住 entertained him with a story corresponding to the *Ko Atsumori* account. It may have been around this time, or perhaps somewhat later, that the playwright Komparu Zenpō 金春禅鳳 (b. 1454) adopted the tale of Atsumori's benighted son as the subject of his nō play *Ikuta Atsumori*. Unlike either the Muromachi-period *kōwakamai* 幸若舞 (ballad-drama) *Atsumori* 敦盛 or Zeami's nō play *Atsumori* (composed prior to 1423), both *Ikuta Atsumori* and *Ko Atsumori* identify the site of Atsumori's death as Ikuta 生田 rather than Suma 須磨, suggesting that these works were composed under the influence of some source other than Zeami's *Atsumori* or the Suma Temple cult of Atsumori's flute. The *Ko Atsumori* account of Atsumori's death, which the *otogizōshi* re-creates in its first part, is also clearly based on one or more *Heike* manuscript in the *yomihon* 読み本 (readerly) textual line, rather than the better known Kakuichi manuscript 覚一本 in the *kataribon* 語り本 (recited) line of texts. As a result, it plays down the significance of music in the tale and instead emphasizes the importance of Atsumori's revelation of his name to Kumagai in the moments before his death—a scene that is eerily reenacted at the climax of the story when Atsumori's ghost demands that Little Atsumori, too, tell him his name.[2]

---

1. Minobe Shigekatsu, *Chūsei denshō bungaku no shosō* (Osaka: Izumi shoin, 1988), 106–9. Also see R. Keller Kimbrough, "Preachers and Playwrights: *Ikuta Atsumori* and the Roots of Nō," Chapter 16 in this volume.

2. R. Keller Kimbrough, "*Little Atsumori* and *The Tale of the Heike*: Fiction as Commentary, and the Significance of a Name," in Michael F. Marra, ed., *Hermeneutical Strategies: Methods of Interpretation in the Study of Japanese*

The translation is based upon the sixteenth-century Keiō University Library manuscript in the "old picture scroll" 古絵巻 textual line.[3] The author is unknown.

Literature, Proceedings of the Association for Japanese Literary Studies, vol. 5 (2004), 325–36.
3. Typeset and annotated in Matsumoto Ryūshin, ed., *Otogizōshi shū*, SNKS (Shinchōsha, 1980), 305–27.

Ko Atsumori emaki

| Translated by R. Keller Kimbrough

In the face of their defeat at the battle of Ichi-no-tani, the young Emperor, the Lady of Second Rank, and all the Taira forces dashed to their ships and fled.[1] From among them, Atsumori was somehow left behind.[2] He was riding toward the shore, chasing Lord Munemori's boat, when a warrior by the name of Kumagai no Jirō Naozane appeared.[3] Kumagai wore a dark blue *hitatare*,[4] a suit of armor with shaded green lacing, and a three-plated helmet pulled down low on his head. Sporting a protective cape with a two-bar design, he rode a dark chestnut steed and carried a bow in one hand, an arrow notched at the ready. "Just once I'd like to wrangle with some fine opponent," he was brooding, when he spotted Atsumori, a lone warrior riding out from the direction of Ichi-no-tani.

Atsumori wore a *hitatare* embroidered with ferns and forget-me-nots, a suit of armor with shaded purple lacing, and a helmet of the same design. On his back he bore twenty-five dyed-feather arrows, and in his hand he held a rattan-wrapped lacquer bow. His mount was a gray-dappled roan. The saddle was adorned with a circular crest of eulalia and mistletoe design, and inscribed, in metal, with the character for "wind." His eyes were fixed on a noble's ship in the offing, and he spurred his horse into the sea and pressed it to swim, plunging and bobbing in the surf. Kumagai watched.

Ko Atsumori emaki 小敦盛絵巻. This translation is based on Matsumoto Ryūshin, ed., *Otogizōshi shū*, SNKS (Shinchōsha, 1980), 305–27.

1. The young Emperor was Antoku 安徳 (1178–1185), who later drowned at the battle of Dan-no-ura 壇ノ浦; the Lady of Second Rank 二位殿 (Taira no Tokiko 平時子; d. 1185) was his grandmother, the widow of Taira no Kiyomori 平清盛 (1118–1181), previous head of the Taira clan.

2. Taira no Atsumori 平敦盛 (1169–1184) was the third son of Kiyomori's younger half-brother Tsunemori 経盛 (1124–1185).

3. Lord Munemori 宗盛殿 (Taira no Munemori 平宗盛; 1147–1185) was a son of Kiyomori and Tokiko. Kumagai (or "Kumagae") no Jirō Naozane 熊谷次郎直実 (Taira no Naozane 平直実; 1141–1208) allied himself with Minamoto no Yoritomo 源頼朝 after the battle of Ishibashiyama 石橋山 in the Eighth Month of 1180.

4. A *hitatare* 直垂 (also *yoroi hitatare* 鎧直垂) is a kind of matching shirt and pants worn under armor.

"You there, adrift in the shallows," Kumagai shouted, "you look to be a Commander-in-Chief. It's a disgrace to show your back to an enemy! I am Kumagai no Jirō Naozane, a resident of Musashi province and the fiercest warrior in Japan. Return and fight!" Atsumori was not flurried in the least. Pulling his horse back by the reins, he headed for the shore.

From the moment his horse found its footing, Atsumori brandished his weapon and lumbered to the beach. Kumagai observed his opponent. "Just the sort of adversary I was looking for," he thought, and drawing his great sword, he attacked. Atsumori raised his blade, and after exchanging two or three blows, grappled with Kumagai from atop his steed. They fell to the ground between their horses. Kumagai was a man of prodigious strength, and Atsumori, just a youth. After pinning him down, Kumagai cast away his long sword and drew the short one at his waist. Ripping off Atsumori's helmet, he seized the boy's disheveled hair and wrested back his head. He saw a young fighter, sixteen or seventeen years old, with a lightly powdered face, eyebrows plucked and painted high on his forehead, and blackened teeth.[5] Kumagai was at a loss where to strike. He hesitated before cutting off his head. "Who are you?" he demanded. "Give me your name!"

"You call yourself the fiercest warrior in Japan," Atsumori replied, "but you make a foolish request! What kind of man would give his name when he's held down by a foe? When a warrior gives his name, he gives a trophy to his enemy—a battlefield honor for him to pass on to his heirs. That's what it means to give your name! Now hurry up and take my head, and ask someone else whose it is."

Kumagai spoke: "What you say is true, but this morning, at the Ichi-no-tani fortress gate, my son Kojirō Naoie died at the hand of the Noto Lord.[6] You look to be about his age, and it makes me sorry. I'll pray for you when you're gone, so tell me your name."

"I'd rather not," Atsumori said. "But then, to think there's someone as feeling as you among the Eastern warriors ... and what have I got to hide? I am Atsumori, sixteen years old, holder of fifth court rank with no official post. I am the third son of New Middle Counselor Tomomori. My father is the son of Master of the Office of Palace Repairs Tsunemori, who was himself a younger brother of Chancellor Kiyomori, an eighth

---

5. Atsumori's make-up suggests his gentility and refinement.

6. Taira no Noritsune 平教経 (1160?–1185?) was known as the Noto Lord 能登殿 because he was appointed governor of Noto province when Kiyomori seized power in 1179.

generation descendent of Emperor Kanmu.[7] This was my first battle. Please ... if any of my family survive, give them this flute and *hitatare*." He took from his waist a flute in a rosewood case and handed it to Kumagai. "Now get it over with—hurry up and take my head!"

Kumagai was bewildered, powerless to strike. "Alas!" he thought, "there's nothing so wretched as the life of a warrior. I saw my son Kojirō take a grievous blow by the Ichi-no-tani fortress gate, but we were separated by enemies and allies in the fight, and I lost track of him after that. It was the last time I saw him alive. Noble or humble, all parents love their children—it's an unchanging rule. The Master of Palace Repairs Tsunemori must be waiting anxiously for his son on his ship in the offing. He'll be devastated if he hears he was struck down on the beach. The boy's the same age as Kojirō, and the poor man will suffer like me. If only I could help him to get away ..."

Brushing the dust off the boy's armor, Kumagai set him on his feet. He had him put on his helmet while he himself looked around for a way to escape. He saw a group of thirty riders—what looked to be the Kodama League, flying a banner of a battle-fan design—assembled on the ridge above. To the west, he saw what looked like the Hirayama warriors lined up on their horses, bridles in a row. Others were there, too, countless as the mist. There was nowhere to run. The boy would be unable to make it west to Ogura Valley or Akashi, or east past the harbor at Suma. It was hopeless. Kumagai made up his mind: rather than let him die at someone else's hand, he would kill Atsumori himself, take religious vows, and then conduct rites for him and Kojirō.

Kumagai urged the boy to invoke the name of Amida Buddha for his last ten times. Atsumori turned to the west and recited the *nenbutsu* as he was told.[8] "Do it now, quickly," he said. Kumagai was overwhelmed. He closed his eyes. Then, through his tears, he cut off Atsumori's head.

Stripping off Atsumori's armor, Kumagai found a scroll wedged in a space between the plates. He took it out and saw that it was a collection of a hundred poems. He picked up Atsumori's head, and when he took it to Lord Yoshitsune, he showed him the scroll. Yoshitsune examined the document. "What a pity to have killed a man as refined as this!" he declared, and weeping, he explained: "The poems are in the hand of the

---

7. Atsumori was actually the son of Tsunemori 経盛, not Tomomori 知盛 (1152–1185). Also, Kiyomori was a twelfth generation descendent of Kanmu 桓 武 (737–806), not an eighth.

8. The *nenbutsu* 念仏 is the ritual invocation of Amida Buddha's name.

wife of the governor of Echizen. She composed a hundred of them to while away the hours." Everyone wept when they saw or heard of their commander spilling tears on his armored sleeves.

Kumagai had lost his son, and since taking Atsumori's head, he had come to understand the futile inconstancy of the world. "A man's life is uncertain," he reflected, "it can be gone before the evening sky. The darkness of the long night ahead is all that really matters." The land was at peace, but Kumagai had no worldly ambition. Having set his heart on the Buddha, he ascended Mount Kōya and shaved his head in the manner of a priest. Later, he became a disciple of Hōnen Shōnin and took up the *nenbutsu* with single-minded, unwavering devotion—wonderful indeed![9]

Now there was a lady by the name of Ben no Saishō, daughter of Tōin, the grandson of Lesser Counselor Novice Shinzei, and she was known as one of the most beautiful women in the capital.[10] Atsumori had set his heart on her, and because her feelings had been the same, they had been wed. Atsumori soon had to flee the capital; his grief-stricken appearance at that time was desolate beyond compare. "If I should be killed in the coming battle," he had teased, "you'll probably take up with some Easterner and never think of me again." Though the parting had been bitter, from amid their tears they had said farewell. As remembrances, Atsumori had left with her an Eleven-headed Kannon protective charm and a sword with a rosewood hilt.

From that day forward Atsumori's wife had been mired in sadness. She had worried constantly for her husband's fate, until at last she heard people say that he had been struck down by Kumagai at the battle of Ichino-tani. "Is this a dream?" she cried. "If he had survived, we might have met again … at least that's what I had hoped. But what's to become of me now?" Pulling a robe over her head, she collapsed in a fit of grief. To see her like that was all the more affecting!

Their love had been brief, but as is the way with husbands and wives, the lady was with child. The months passed and she gave birth to a beautiful baby boy. Although she wished to raise him in some deep

---

9. Hōnen 法然 (1133–1212) was the founder of the Pure Land sect of Japanese Buddhism, which advocates the sole practice of the *nenbutsu* to achieve Pure Land rebirth.

10. The Lesser Counselor Novice Shinzei 少納言入道信西 (Fujiwara no Michinori 藤原通憲; 1106–1159) was a scholar and a close attendant of Emperor Go-Shirakawa 後白河天皇. His grandson Tōin 洞院 is unknown, as is Ben no Saishō 弁の宰相.

mountain dwelling or cliffy crag—to keep him as a memento of her husband—the Genji were slaughtering all the Heike children, no matter how young, searching them out even in the womb. Fearing that she, too, would come to grief, she wrapped her baby in a white, lined robe, placed the sword with the rosewood hilt at his side, and left him, in great despair, at a place called Shimomatsu.

At that time, Hōnen had taken Kumagai and his other disciples on a pilgrimage to Kamo Shrine. He heard a baby crying at Shimomatsu, and bringing his palanquin near, he found a beautiful, abandoned little boy. The holy man spoke: "He's surely not a commoner, left wrapped up in a robe like that with a sword at his side. Someone must want him saved. Either that, or he's a gift of the Kamo Deity." The holy man picked him up and took him home, gave him a wet nurse and raised him as his own.

The months and years passed by, and the boy was soon eight. He was more mature than the other children at the temple, and far more intelligent. Once when Kumagai was stroking the boy's hair, Kumagai remarked, "Of all people, this child looks just like that Atsumori I killed at the battle of Ichi-no-tani! It's like he's right here before me," and time and again he wept.

The boy was playing bows-and-arrows with some other children, and he got into an argument over who had won. "You motherless, fatherless orphan," another child railed, "how dare you talk to me like that! It's because the holy man took you in that you act that way." Dejected and chagrined, the boy threw away his bow and arrows and cried.

Though the boy wept for his parents, the other children continued to tease him in this way. He became all the more depressed. Visiting the holy man, he said, "I don't have a mother or father, do I? Oh, how I miss them!" He threw himself to the ground and wailed in sorrow. Hōnen was touched, and he shed tears on the sleeves of his priestly robes. "Poor boy," he said. "You were an abandoned child, without a mother or a father. But I brought you up, so think of me as your mother and father instead." The boy gave it some thought: "The other children sometimes receive visits and letters from their parents and siblings. Why don't I have a mother and father, too?"

Morning and evening he pined. He stopped eating, and he refused to drink water, hot or cold. After seven days, he looked ready to lose his senses, like his life was near an end. Hōnen and the others were alarmed. Summoning his disciples, the holy man spoke: "Look here, everyone. This poor child is dying from longing for his parents. If you've seen or heard anything relating to his family, please say so now." Kumagai raised his voice: "Our poor boy! I do remember one thing. A very pretty lady, about twenty years old, comes to hear your sermons on the six abstinence days every month. She brushes the child's hair when she thinks no one's looking, and then cries her heart out. If there happen to be a lot of people around, she goes home like she doesn't care, but she still acts suspicious."

"Well, then," the holy man said, "we'll hold sermons from today and see who comes!"

Hōnen soon began to preach. Toward the middle of his address, he pressed his sleeve to his face and wept. "Dear audience," he said, "still your hearts and listen. One year when I went to visit Kamo Shrine, I found a baby by Shimomatsu. I've brought him up, and now he's eight. Recently, he's been yearning for his parents. He mourns and cries, he won't eat or drink, and now his life is in danger. Does anyone here know his family? He won't come to any harm, even if he's a Taira. I've raised him myself and I'll make him a priest. I'll go to Rokuhara and beg for a pardon if I have to. But if things go on like this, the poor boy is sure to die!" The holy man broke down in tears. Everyone wept, whether they knew the child or not.

An exceptionally beautiful woman stepped forward from the audience. She wore a trouser-skirt and a twelve-layered robe. Without a word, she set the boy on her knee and began to sob. The poor little child—his handsome features were stretched with sorrow! He looked up at the lady with his sunken, listless eyes, and together they cried. Seeing them there, the holy man stumbled down from his seat; his own tears were moving to behold! All the people wet their sleeves with emotion.

After a while, the lady turned to Hōnen and spoke: "I am Ben no Naishi, a relative of the late Lesser Counselor Nobukiyo.[11] From the time that Atsumori was thirteen and I, fourteen, we shared a fleeting love. Later, in the first year of Genryaku (1184), Atsumori fled the capital. He was sixteen then, and he spoke of many things. Since his son looked just like him, I thought to hide him away as a token of our bond. But then I heard that the Genji were hunting down the Heike heirs—cutting off their heads, even searching them out in the womb. I couldn't stand the thought of suffering such misery again. I didn't know what to do, so

---

11. There is a discrepancy in the text. The lady is earlier identified as "Ben no Saishō" 弁の宰相, not "Ben no Naishi" 弁の内侍. Also, "Nobukiyo" 信 清 is problematic. Matsumoto Ryūshin suggests that it is a Japanese reading of a mistranscription of the Chinese characters for "Shinzei" 信西. Matsumoto, *Otogizōshi shū*, 317, note 7.

although it broke my heart, I decided to abandon my baby. I watched you pick him up and take him to your temple, and then I went home.

"In the eight years since then, I have come to all your sermons on the six abstinence days of every month. I have watched the boy, and I've seen how he's come to look more and more like his father. It makes me long for the old days, and I end up crying. I've suffered so much sometimes, I've been desperate to tell him who I am. But the world being what it is, I've always kept my secret to myself and gone home in tears." The woman poured out her heart. Of all the people there, each and every one was choked with pity. Hearing that this was his mother, the boy was neither happy nor sad—all he could do was cry.

In his free time, Kumagai had been in the habit of taking out Atsumori's silk *hitatare* with the ink design, and the flute in the rosewood case. He would chant the *nenbutsu* and cry. The holy man had seen him and asked what he was always grieving about. Kumagai had replied: "One year during the Heike disturbance, I took the head of Atsumori, the youngest child of the Kadowaki Lord, at Harima Beach in Settsu province.[12] He told me to pass these keepsakes on to his relatives, if any of them survived. But I haven't heard of any family, so I've been carrying them around with me ever since." The holy man had taken a look. "How sad!" he had exclaimed, shedding copious tears.

Hōnen now remembered their conversation. "Where's brother Kumagai?" he asked, and summoned him at once. "You know those relatives of Atsumori's you mentioned," he said, "well, the boy who's been with us all these years—he's his son! And that lady over there is the boy's mother! Those relics of Atsumori's you said you wanted to give his family—you can surrender them now." Kumagai was delighted. Producing the flute and *hitatare*, he explained in detail about Atsumori's final moments. Weeping, he presented the objects to the wife and son. The little boy and his mother passed them back and forth, entranced, and then dissolved into tears—most touching indeed!

After a while, the mother placed her hands on the keepsakes and spoke: "This *hitatare*—I made it for Atsumori when he left the capital. There are ferns on the left sleeve, forget-me-nots on the right, and on the skirt, there is an ink design of two ducks—a male and a female—drifting among the reeds of Naniwa Bay. There is also a poem written here:

---

12. The Kadowaki Lord 門脇殿 (Taira no Norimori 平教盛; 1128–1185) was a younger brother of Kiyomori. Atsumori was a son of Tsunemori, not Norimori.

nagaraete	It wasn't for us
chigirazarikeru	to live on together
mono yue ni	pledging tender vows—
awazu wa kaku wa	yet if we'd never met,
omowazaramashi	we'd never have known such love.

It is his without a doubt. 'So hurtful now, these keepsakes—if not for them, sometimes I might forget.'[13] The way he looked that time ... I wonder if I'll ever escape the memory!" The woman wept. The holy man and Kumagai were similarly overcome.

Kumagai spoke: "So that's why whenever I looked at the child, it was like Atsumori was right in front of me! It makes sense now," and he wept anew. The little boy stared at his father's souvenirs and longed for him all the more. He made a petition to the buddhas, gods, and the Three Holy Jewels: "Please let me see my father—either his bones or his ghost!"[14] Such was his constant prayer.

"It's all because of the Kamo Deity that the holy man took me in and brought me up like this," the boy once thought. "He must be my patron deity. I'll visit him and pray to see my father's ghost." The boy ensconced himself in Kamo Shrine for seven days. He paid obeisance one thousand one hundred thirty-three times a day, prostrating himself in supplication. The deity must have been moved, for on the final, seventh night, he appeared before the boy where he slept. "Among all the children of the world," he said, "there are few who feel deeply for their parents, even when they are alive. How moving, then, that you, who have never seen or known your father, should pray with all your heart for his remains!" The deity recited a poem:

sugisarishi	For love of
sono tarachine no	a parent departed—
koishiku wa	the dew and the frost
Koyano Ikuta-no-	of Ikuta-no-ono
ono no tsuyu shimo	on Koyano Plain.

---

13. The widow quotes a poem, *Kokinshū*, no. 746 (author unknown): かたみ こそ今はあたなれこれなくは忘るるときもあらましものを *katami koso / ima wa ata nare / kore naku wa / wasururu toki mo / aramashi mono wo*.

14. The Three Jewels (*sanbō* 三宝) are the Buddha, the Dharma, and the monastic order.

"What joy!" the boy thought upon receiving the dream-revelation. "My father's bones must lie in Ikuta-no-ono field in Settsu province!" Without a word to his mother or the holy man, he secretly set out. Though ignorant of the way to Settsu, he had heard that it was west. Rustling the dew from the grasses of an unfamiliar road, he wandered forth, pitiful to behold.

Tramping through fields of eulalia, pampas and cogon grass, blind to the way ahead, pillowing his head some nights on frosty bunches of bamboo weed, he eventually came to what he thought was Ichi-no-tani. A thunderstorm was raging, and the boy was endlessly forlorn. All he could hear was the lapping waves, the wind in the pines, seagulls in the offing, and beach plovers exchanging cries. Other than these, he was alone. As he drifted forward, lost, he noticed a glimmering light in the distance. Though it might belong to some goblin, he thought, he was so distressed that he did not care. Stumbling on, he soon observed the hulking frame of an old temple hall.

The boy approached, and in the dim light of a torch, he saw a stranger with painted eyebrows and a lightly powdered face. The man wore a soft pointed hat and paced the veranda in prayer.[15] "Excuse me," the boy called out.

"Who's there?" the man replied. "No one comes around here. Identify yourself!"

The boy wept and explained: "I am from the capital, and I'm searching for my father. I've been walking for the last ten days. But the rain is so heavy and the darkness so dark, I'm at my wits' end. Please give me lodging for the night." "Who is your father?" the man asked.

The boy thought: "The Genji rule the land now, so what will happen if I give him my name? But I'll tell him anyway, and if I lose my life, it will have been for my father, which won't be so bad." He spoke: "My father was a Taira by the name of Atsumori, third son of the Master of Palace Repairs. He was cut down at the battle of Ichi-no-tani. I wanted to find his bones, so I prayed to the Kamo Deity. I had a dream-revelation, and I've come here to search at the Bay of Suma." Without saying a word, the stranger broke down in tears.

After a while the man took the boy by the hand, pulled him up to the veranda and brushed the dew from his rain-soaked clothes. "This way," he said, beckoning him inside. "You must be exhausted, traveling at your young age. Rest here," and he set the child's head upon his knee.

---

15. The stranger's hat was a *nashiuchi eboshi* 梨子打烏帽子, typically worn by a warrior under his helmet.

Though no longer upset or tired, the boy drifted off to sleep. The man spoke, neither in this world nor a dream: "How sad that you should yearn so for a parent you've never seen! It's because of your profound filial devotion that I have come to you now as an apparition. When you were still in your mother's womb, I was struck down by Kumagai here on the Harima shore. It was the spring of my sixteenth year. If you want to serve me in my grave, then study very, very hard, become a man of wisdom and save sentient beings near and far. That will make me happy." He wrote a poem on the boy's sleeve:

koi koite	To the waking world
mare ni au yo mo	I cannot return—
yume nare ya	for love and longing,
utsutsu ni kaeru	a precious meeting this night
mi ni shi araneba	in a dream.

The boy was overjoyed at meeting his father. "Oh, Papa!" he cried, grasping at the man's sleeves, and at that moment, awoke. His mind reeled when he looked around. Where he had seen the temple hall, there was only the wind in the pines; where his father had been, there was only a tangle of eulalia and cogon grass; and where he had pillowed his head on his father's knee, there was only a mossy white thigh bone in a clump of weeds. The boy was overcome. "How cruel!" he cried. "Father, where did you go? Please take me with you! Why did you leave me here alone in the deep grass at the foot of a pine?" He sank into a slough of tears—truly most affecting!

Because the boy could not stay on in this way, he strung his father's bones around his neck and returned to the capital, where he interred each at a different temple or sacred site. Having thus come back to the city, he made his way to Hōnen's temple. The holy man and others had been worried. "We haven't seen our child for some time," they had said, and searched high and low. They were overjoyed now to hear that he had returned. The boy told Hōnen and his mother about all that had happened to him on his trip to Settsu province.

"The child's still so young," people said, "—and to think of the hardships he's endured! His father Atsumori must have been moved by the filial piety in his heart, and appeared to him as a ghost in a dream." Everyone wept at the thought. The months and years passed by and the boy became a blessed priest.

The mother also became a nun at that time. She built a brushwood shack by the Kamo riverbed in the northern part of the capital, and planted morning glories for her fence. Watching her flowers wilt at the touch of the morning dew, she awoke to the fleeting nature of worldly affairs. At dusk, listening to the evening bell at Urin'in Temple, she would gaze at the sun as it set in the west and wonder that Paradise was there. She chanted the *nenbutsu* day and night—so auspicious!—and plucking flowers and burning incense, she prayed for the enlightenment of the many Taira who met their doom at the western sea.[16] In particular she mourned for Atsumori, and recalling their vow to share a lotus-seat in the Pure Land, she prayed for her own rebirth in Paradise.

She composed poems in her spare time:

shiba no to no	My heart
shibashiba isogu	often hastens
kokoro ka na	at my brushwood door
nishi no mukae no	to see the Western Reception
yūgure no sora	in the sunset sky.

kokorozashi	As salvation
fukaki ni ukabu	comes to those most
narai zo to	deeply mourned,
itodo mukashi no	all the more I pray for him
ato wo koso toe	who died so long ago.

Many years passed after the boy became a priest. In the course of his studies he plumbed the deepest truths and came to be known as Zen'e Shōnin of the Western Mountain.[17] It was thanks to his profound sense of filial devotion that his school of Buddhism flourishes in the present day. Those who read this tale should always be dutiful to their parents and teachers. It was a truly wonderful turn of events; we should all chant the *nenbutsu* for the sake of our departed.[18] Amen.

---

16. The Inland Sea, to the west of the capital.

17. Zen'e Shōnin 善慧上人 (Shōkū Shōnin 証空上人; 1177–1247) was a disciple of Hōnen and the founder of the Seizan 西山 (Western Mountain) branch of the Pure Land sect. He was unrelated to Atsumori.

18. According to a *Ko Atsumori* manuscript in the possession of Kōshōji Temple 興生寺, we should all chant the *nenbutsu* for Atsumori's sake. Tokuda Kazuo, "Otogizōshi *Ko Atsumori* no Kōshōji-bon wo megutte," *Gakushūin Joshi Daigaku kiyō* 4 (2002), 50.

19 ~ The *Heike*, the Nō, and Kyōgen Zatō Plays | CAROLYN MORLEY

The treatment of the *Tales of the Heike* (Heike monogatari 平家物語) in the nō and kyōgen theater is revealing of the very different concerns of the two dramatic forms: one with the inner psyche of the character, and the other with the material world. This translates in nō to a focus on the *Heike* as a literary text with universal and spiritual dimensions, and in the kyōgen on the *Heike* as a performance art, recited by specific minstrels at a specific time, in a specific place.

Nō plays of the second category (warrior plays) treat the *Heike* thematically, choosing characters that offer scope for tragic depictions of loss and Buddhist attachment, such as the Taira warriors Tadanori, Atsumori, and Kiyotsune. Kyōgen, on the other hand, developed a group of plays based on *biwa hōshi* 琵琶法師, the blind performers of the *Heike*. These are known as the *zatō* 座頭 (blind man) plays, and to one degree or another they invite the audience into the society and personal relationships of the blind performers. The term *zatō* refers to the lowest rank of the *biwa hōshi* within a *za* (座 guild). In addition to the *zatō* we see mention of other ranks in the *zatō* plays: *sōkengyō* 惣検校 (the highest rank and head of the guild), followed by *kengyō* 検校, *bettō* 別当, and *kōtō* 勾当. The *zatō* plays, together with plays about Buddhist priests, make up a category of plays in the Ōkura 大蔵 kyōgen repertoire[1]

---

1. The earliest Ōkura school text, the *Toraakira-bon* (1642) already lists categories of kyōgen plays by character. Other methods of categorizing the plays were used in Ōkura texts from the Edo period but by late Edo the texts return to categorizing by character-type. The Ōkura school was the first kyōgen school to form in the early Edo period. The Izumi 和泉 and Sagi 鷺 schools followed. Today, only the Ōkura and Izumi schools remain, with many branch families of equal or greater importance. The Sagi school died out at the end of the Edo period with the collapse of government patronage.

designated *shukke zatō* (出家座頭), the priests and the blind men.

In addition to the *zatō* plays, depictions of the *Heike* can also be found in *ai-kyōgen* (間狂言), or interlude plays (and players) within a nō play.[2] As the *ai-kyōgen* for one of the second category *Heike* nō plays, the kyōgen actor normally performs the role of a local who recites the story of the nō play to the *waki*. These recitations are generally quite close to the content of the *Heike* text, although in a vernacular language, and often with picturesque details not found in the original. For example, in the nō play *Yashima* 八島 the *ai* is a salt-maker who happens upon a monk taking shelter in the salt-house. The monk inquires about the battle fought on the beach at Yashima, and the salt maker precedes to tell the story not of Yoshitsune but rather the fight between Kagekiyo 景清 and Mionoya みをの屋, including a graphic and largely fanciful account of them wrestling to the ground.[3] While the *Heike* is treated thematically in the *ai*, the story is reported from the viewpoint of the salt-maker living in the area. The grounding of the story in the salt-maker's words is what makes it kyōgen as opposed to nō.

Although the *ai* role is cited in records as far back as Zeami Motokiyo, *ai-kyōgen* texts were transmitted through the kyōgen actors, and the earliest written texts do not appear until the early seventeenth century. This was the same period in which the kyōgen actors began forming schools and recording their texts in order to receive the patronage of the Tokugawa government along with the nō troupes. A similar formation of *biwa hōshi* had already taken place at least two centuries earlier.[4]

Some of the nō plays also have alternative *ai* (*kae ai* 替間), which are generally more elaborate and active than the usual narrative *ai* (*katari*

---

2. In addition to taking one of two or three roles in a comic skit or *hon-kyōgen* (本狂言) such as the blind man in a *zatō* play, a kyōgen actor also performs as the *ai-kyōgen*. A third role for the kyōgen actor is that of Sanbasō in the ritual performance of *Okina Sanbasō* 翁三番叟 performed annually at the New Year.

3. See Royall Tyler's translation of *Yashima* for a partial translation of the *ai*. Royall Tyler, *Japanese Nō Dramas* (London, New York: Penguin Books, 1992), 338. "They say Kagekiyo went flying, face up, and got a big lump on the back of his neck. Mionoya, now, went flying face down. This was the third moon, mind you, when the flowers fall, and he certainly lost the bloom off the end of his nose." This passage does not appear anywhere in the standard *Heike* text or the nō play. For the *ai* text (Izumi school) see Nonomura Kaizō and Andō Tsunejirō, eds., *Kyōgen shūsei* (Nōgaku shorin, 1974), 746–47.

4. See "*Heike Monogatari* no seiritsu," in Kajihara Masaaki and Yamashita Hiroaki, eds., *Heike monogatari* (jō), SNKT 44 (Iwanami shoten, 1994), 411–45.

ai 語り間) cited above, to the extent that they are sometimes performed independently. In a particularly important *kae ai* for *Yashima* entitled *Nasu* 那須, translated below, the actor takes on four different roles; the complexity of this play is among the greatest in the repertoire. The actor enters as a fisherman and reenacts the "Nasu no Yoichi" episode (Kakuichi-bon 11.4) from the *Heike* during which the Taira taunt the Minamoto from boats off the coast of Yashima. The actor becomes in turn the characters of a fisherman, Yoshitsune, Gotō Sanemoto, and the young archer Yoichi, who is chosen to hit the target on the fan held up by a young Taira woman on a boat out at sea. Because of the complexity of the role, the performance of this *ai* is treated by the Ōkura school as requisite to being recognized as a professional kyōgen actor. Although the play appears in a list of plays as early as the *Tenshō bon* (the first collection of kyōgen plot summaries from 1578) albeit with a slightly different title, *Ogi no mato* 扇の的 (the fan target), the earliest extant version of the text is in the *Kyōgen ki* (狂言記 1660), and it makes its way into Ōkura school texts only in the late Edo period.

While the *ai* roles for the *Heike* nō plays are consistently performed today, the *zatō* plays, which target the blind priests, have all but disappeared from kyōgen performance. Of the more than a dozen *zatō* plays in the repertoire only two are regularly performed today: *Tsukimizatō* 月見座頭 (The Moon-viewing Blind Man) and *Kawakami* 川上 (Kawakami Jizō). These plays share two characteristics that make them palatable for a modern audience: the plays offer a poignant portrayal of the blind man, and neither play hinges on references to the *Heike biwa hōshi*.

The attraction of the first characteristic is self explanatory, the second is important because it points to the fact that the *Heike biwa hōshi* are no longer relevant in contemporary Japan. Much of the original humor of the *zatō* plays centered on the unique society of the *biwa hōshi* who attended annual gatherings, competed with one another for rank within their group, and had a recognized role to play in society. The re-creation of this society on stage provided a buffer to the sometimes brutal and even abusive humor of the plays, making it easier for the audience to identify with the blind musician and his world.

One of the earliest references to a *zatō* play is in the list of plays performed for the subscription performance at Tadasu riverbank in the Fourth Month of 1464.[5] The play listed there was *Chakagizatō* 茶嗅ぎ

---

5. Furukawa Hisashi and Kobayashi Seki, eds., *Kyōgen jiten jikō hen* (Tōkyōdō

座頭 (The Tea-sniffing Blind Priests), in which a *sōkengyō* plays host to the monthly gathering of *kōtō* and *kengyō* to celebrate Benzaiten, the god of music and the arts and the protector of the *biwa hōshi*. In the Sagi Niemon (鷺仁右衛門) text (1724) of the Sagi school,[6] the blind musicians gather at the *sōkengyō*'s home and then entertain one another with a song, followed by chanting of the *Heike* and a dance. The *sōkengyō* then calls on his disciple, Kikuichi, to bring some tea for them to smell. As Kikuichi goes to fetch the tea, a passerby who has been spying on the group dumps some pepper into the cup. When the tea is brought, a fit of sneezing ensues. *Chakagizatō* was one of only seven plays out of 264 that were performed more than six times between 1691 and 1710 for the Ikeda daimyō and the Edo government.[7] Surely the intimate depiction of the *biwa hōshi* at play, in particular at a tea ceremony, was a large part of the attraction.

While the blind-man plays do not universally make specific reference to the role of the *biwa hōshi* as a reciter of the *Heike*, the blind man dresses the same (with variations according to his rank) in all of the plays and performs virtually the same character-type, at least as he appears in the early kyōgen texts onward. The conventions of kyōgen costumes occurred relatively late in the seventeenth century, at the same time as the Ōkura school began systematizing the plays into categories by character-type. The itinerant kyōgen actors of the Muromachi period would not have had the means for the types of costumes that developed later under the patronage of the Tokugawa shogunate.[8]

The *zatō* figure typically is dressed in *kyōgen bakama* 狂言袴 (*hakama* trousers that end at the ankle), a *mizugoromo* 水衣 (gauze jacket), a *sumi tokin* 角頭巾 (a cap with squared corners), and a staff. This costume is very similar to that for the acolyte priests in the *shukke zatō* category. The uniformity of costume was probably an attempt in the Tokugawa period to establish a character-type, the *zatō*, and to associate the low-ranking priests with the low-ranking *biwa hōshi*. In fact, an early

shuppan, 1976), 223.

6. Furukawa and Kobayashi, *Kyōgen jiten jikō hen*, 223. Also found in Izumi school *Kyōgen shūsei*.

7. Kyōgen geinōshi kenkyū kai, ed., *Kyōgen: "okashi" no keifu*, Nihon no koten geinō vol. 4 (Heibonsha, 1970), 42.

8. For more information on kyōgen costume, see Kirihata Ken, "Kyōgen Costumes: The Fascinating World of Dyed Textiles," in Sharon Sadako Takeda and Monica Bethe, eds., *Miracles and Mischief: Noh and Kyōgen Theater in Japan* (Los Angeles: Los Angeles County Museum of Art, 2002), 160–76.

drawing of a *biwa hōshi* in one of the genre scrolls of *Shokunin uta-awase kai* 職人歌合わせ会 (Tradesmen's Poetry Contests) that first appear in the twelfth century shows a blind musician seated with a *biwa* in his lap, dressed in flowing priest's robes. There is no evidence here of the *sumi zukin*, ankle-length *hakama*, or *mizugoromo* that later came to characterize the *zatō* in kyōgen.[9] This suggests that while the character of the *zatō* was based on the *biwa hōshi* figure of the Muromachi period, the costume was created for the stage at a much later date, as would be the case for the other character-types as well. In any case, as far back as the *Tenshō-bon* (1578), two of the six blind-man plays mentioned refer to the recitation of the *Heike*.

By 1642, with the first collection of kyōgen scripts in the Ōkura school by Ōkura Toraakira 大蔵虎明, the *Toraakira-bon* 虎明本, the specific kyōgen *Heike* pattern known as *Ichi-no-tani* 一の谷 (a narrative pattern that takes as its basis a satirical rendition of the battle of Ichi-no-tani from the *Heike*, as explained below) began appearing in the *zatō* plays. This trend continued in the Sagi and Izumi schools, which formed in the early Edo period. While not every *zatō* play contains the so-called *Heike* or *Heikyoku* 平曲 (*Heike* recitation) passage from *Ichi-no-tani*, most refer to some aspect of the life of a *biwa hōshi*, his instrument, the *biwa*, his annual attendance at one of the *biwa hōshi* gatherings, his rank in the *za*, and so forth. In other words, the kyōgen *zatō* is not just any blind priest, but a blind minstrel priest whose trade was the chanting of the *Heike*.

As it turns out, the *biwa hōshi* were a particularly apt target for kyōgen humor. For one thing, both the *biwa hōshi* and the kyōgen actors (originally referred to by Zeami as *okashi hōshi* をかし法師), frequented the same areas in and around Kyoto, performing for local audiences at shrines and temples during the Muromachi period. Moreover, the *biwa hōshi* had achieved a certain reputation by the fifteenth century for their role in embellishing and circulating the *Tales of the Heike*, and were already receiving the protection of the Ashikaga shogunate.[10] In fact,

---

9. Itō Hiroyuki et al., eds., *Nihon no chūsei bungaku* (Shin Nihon shuppansha, 1983), 87.

10. Hyōdō Hiromi, *Heike monogatari no rekishi to geinō* (Yoshikawa kōbunkan, 2000), 1–5. For a more extensive discussion in English of the origins and development of the biwa hōshi and the Tōdō organization, see Susan Matisoff, *The Legend of Semimaru, Blind Musician of Japan* (Columbia University Press, 1978; reprint edition, Cheng and Tsui, 2006), Chapter 1.

the first authoritative, recitative text for the *Heike*, the Kakuichi-bon 覚
一本 (1371), was the work of the *biwa hōshi* Akashi Kengyō Kakuichi
明石検校覚一, whose followers went on to form one of the two main
troupes (*za*) of *Heike biwa hōshi*, the *Ichi-kata za* (一方座). The other
major troupe, the *Yasaka-kata* 八坂方, also from the Kyoto area, is
thought to have preceded the *Ichi-kata*. It is interesting to note that the
only proper name that appears in *zatō* plays is Kikuichi; the *"ichi"* in the
name associates the character with the members of the *Ichi-kata za*, all
of whom had names ending in *"ichi."*[11] The colophon of the manuscript
notes that Kakuichi decided to record his text in order to prevent future
generations from quarreling and dividing over its transmission. The
Kakuichi-bon was subsequently presented to Ashikaga Yoshimitsu two
generations later. This act in itself suggests that the followers of Kakuichi
had organized themselves into a group powerful enough to challenge the
privileged position of the official *biwa hōshi* under imperial protection
in the previous era.[12]

The *biwa hōshi* who recited the *Heike* were known in official records
of the Muromachi and Tokugawa period as *tōdō* 当道 to differentiate
them from their predecessors under imperial patronage. Hyōdō Hiromi
sees the presentation of the Kakuichi-bon as a turning point for the *biwa
hōshi* who in the succeeding generations commanded the recognition of
the shogunate, paying their respects at the New Year and attending and
performing at the inaugurations and memorial services of successive
shoguns in the Tokugawa period. In 1603 when Tokugawa Ieyasu was
inaugurated, the ceremony was attended by the *sōkengyō* (head of the
tōdō) Izu Maruichi (伊豆円一), and is recorded in the Edo-period *Tōdō
daikiroku* (当道大記録 Grand Record of Our Guild) as being in accord
with precedent (先例の通り).[13]

As Hyōdō points out, the Ashikaga's hold on the transmission of
the *Heike* and the *biwa hōshi* weakened considerably after the Ōnin War
in the mid-fifteenth century. Without the protection of the Ashikaga
shogunate, the *biwa hōshi* fell in popular estimation, as well as in terms

---

11. Hyōdō mentions that there is some confusion concerning the character
used to represent "ichi" 一 which is sometimes written *ichi* 市 for city, and may
have originally referred to the eastern area of the capital in which the *Ichi-kata za*
circulated. The *Yasaka-kata* on the other hand were thought to circulate on the
hill (*saka*) from Gion to Kiyomizu where many popular entertainers were based.

12. Hyōdō, *Heike monogatari no rekishi to geinō*, 8–48.

13. Cited in Hyōdō, *Heike monogatari no rekishi to geinō*, 1.

of economic well-being, and the popularity of *Heike* recitation declined with them. From the middle of the fifteenth century until the early seventeenth century, when *Heike* recitation was revived as one of the official ceremonial arts of the Tokugawa shogunate, the *biwa hōshi* were left to fend for themselves among other groups of popular entertainers such as the kyōgen actors, *etoki* 絵解き (picture-tellers), and others. This would suggest that the kyōgen plays' satirical portrayals of the *biwa hōshi* represented something more akin to an attack on fellow performers, still full of their earlier self-importance, in order to take them down a peg or two, than to a cheap shot at the less fortunate. This would be consistent with the humor in other plays in the kyōgen genre. The daimyō 大名 (great lord) in *Imamairi* 今参り is typical. Introducing himself as a great lord, although he has only one field and a servant, he becomes the target of the humor in the play. The difference in the evolution of the *zatō* plays as opposed to those about daimyō or *yamabushi* 山伏 (mountain priests, another character whose relevance is arguably lost on the modern audience), is that even without a familiarity with the mountain priest or daimyō, an audience can tolerate and even enjoy the satiric humor used to deflate the enormous bravado of the characters. When the blind man, on the other hand, ceases to be identified by the audience as a *biwa hōshi*, the humor becomes unacceptable.

The status of the *biwa hōshi* in society and their recognition by the Ashikaga and, later, the Tokugawa governments, had everything to do with their connection to the *Tales of the Heike*. From the first the *Tales of the Heike* appear to have been intended for recital by the *biwa hōshi*, which was not the case for all of the war tales. The earliest source usually cited for the origins of the *Tales of the Heike* is Yoshida Kenkō in his *Tsurezuregusa*. Kenkō tells us that a former nobleman of the Murakami Genji clan and a lay priest (Nakayama Yukinaga 中山行長) recorded the events of the war and then passed them on to a *biwa hōshi* (Shōbutsu 生 仏) for recital. Although there is no way to verify this transmission, scholars assume that the oral tradition is based on some kind of original written text. Since the *biwa hōshi* long had a role in society as lay priests who both celebrated the *kami* of the hearth and land, and prayed for the souls and spirits of the dead, the choice of the *biwa hōshi* was a natural one. Who better to pacify the restless souls of the fallen Heike warriors? Who better to promulgate the myths underlying the legitimacy of the Ashikaga rule? The Ashikaga were, after all, related to the Minamoto (Genji) clan, being a branch of the Seiwa Genji who had established the Kamakura shogunate. Although there is evidence that in the Muromachi period *etoki* were also involved at some point in the recitation of the *Heike*, by the fifteenth century at least, the *biwa hōshi* seem to have had exclusive rights to the performance of the *Heike*.[14] These, then, are the blind men who became the subjects of the *zatō* kyōgen plays.

THE *ICHI-NO-TANI* PATTERN

Of the six *zatō* plays listed in the earliest collection of kyōgen, the *Tenshō-bon* (1578), a collection of short plot summaries, only two make explicit reference to the *biwa hōshi*, although in later editions other references emerge as well. In *Tarashizatō*[15] (no longer extant) a blind man (*zatō*) is looking for a room to spend the night—since the *zatō* were itinerant musicians, this would have been a familiar scene at the time. A woman enters and offers to rent him a room. She leads him to a river and crosses a bridge to the other side. The blind man wades across, and, having gotten wet, removes his robes, and chants the *Heike* as he waits for them to dry. In the meantime, the woman steals his robes and flees. The line from the text is: "He chants the *Heike*, and while he does so, she grabs his clothes and flees" (平家かたる其内いるいとりてにくる). Although there is no way of determining exactly what "Heike" refers to here, it would seem to be the first reference to the *Ichi-no-tani* pattern known as *Heike* in the later kyōgen texts, and only recorded in full in the *Toraakira-bon* in 1642.

The humor of the *Ichi-no-tani* pattern relies on a displacement of emphasis from the serious (the actual text of the *Tales of the Heike*) to the absurd. Musically, the chanting is closer to *shōmyō* 唱名 (Buddhist chant) than to either the nō or the *Heike* styles of chanting. Scholarship suggests that the *Ichi-no-tani* pattern in kyōgen may have been taken from a *hayamonogatari* 早物語, thought to have been short comic pieces recited for practice by novices at *Heike* recitals before the actual chanting of the *Heike* began. Evidence of *hayamonogatari* performed as comic

---

14. Hyōdō, *Heike monogatari no rekishi to geinō*, 13. See also Matisoff, *The Legend of Semimaru*, Chapter 1.

15. Furukawa Hisashi, ed., *Kyōgen kohon nishu: Tenshō kyōgen bon, Torakiyo kyōgen bon* (Wanya, 1968), 22.

relief between *kojōruri* 古浄瑠璃 exists as well. The kyōgen version of *Ichi-no-tani* seems to be based on one of these *hayamonogatari*, but it is altered so that the melody is closer to kyōgen speech style. In kyōgen this musical style is known as *Heike bushi* 平家節 and appears in other plays with an entirely unrelated accompanying verse resulting in further parody.[16] For example, the seaweed seller in *Konbu-uri* 昆布売り (The Seaweed Seller) chants in this manner to hawk his seaweed products, while in *Yobigoe* 呼び声 the master disguises his voice to lure out his servant, Tarō kaja, by chanting his name in kyōgen *Heike bushi*.

In *Donbukattchiri* 井礑 as it appears in the *Sagi Yasunori-bon* 鷺保教本, a *kōtō* and his apprentice Kikuichi are on their way to the mountains for a picnic. As they stroll along, the *kōtō* remarks, "Oh yes. There's something I've been meaning to discuss with you. You haven't progressed much with your *kouta* and *hayamonogatari* practice. Why not let me help you a bit with the *Heike*? (汝にいつぞは言はう言はうと思うていた。そんたもいつがいつまでも、小歌や早物語でも済むまい程に、平家をちと稽古したならばよからう。)[17] The coupling here of the practice of *hayamonogatari* and the *Heike* would seem to confirm the assumption that the *Ichi-no-tani* pattern is related to this genre.

Of the extant *zatō* play texts, six contain the *Ichi-no-tani* pattern in one form or another: *Donbukattchiri*, *Saru zatō* 猿座頭 (The Monkey and the Blind Priest), *Marizatō* 鞠座頭 (The Blind Priest and the Football), *Kiyomizuzatō* 清水座頭 (The Blind Priest at Kiyomizu, also known as *Goze zatō*), *Chakagizatō* 茶嗅ぎ座頭 (The Tea-sniffing Blind Priest), and *Futari zatō* 二人座頭 (The Two Blind Priests). In a seventh, *Kikazuzatō* 聞かず座頭 (The Deaf Blind Priest), the *zatō* uses the chant to ridicule a fellow servant who is deaf, and so is more similar to plays like *Konbu-uri* and *Yobigoe*, cited above, which use only the melody and rhythm of the *Heike bushi* and not the content of the pattern.

The *Ichi-no-tani* pattern begins with the classical opening marker *somo somo* そもそも and diverges from there. The parallel structure and the verbal endings are all recognizable from the *Heike*, however. For the passage to work as a displacement of emphasis from the serious to

16. Kyōgen geinōshi kenkyū kai, ed., *Kyōgen: "okashi" no keifu*, 209–12.

17. Furukawa Hisashi, ed., *Kyōgen shū* (chū), Nihon koten zensho (Asahi Shimbunsha, 1953), 276. *Donbukattchiri* is translated as "Plop! Click!" in Sakanishi Shio, *The Ink Smeared Lady and Other Kyōgen* (Boston: Marshall Jones, 1938; reprint, Rutland, Vt., and Tokyo: Charles E. Tuttle, 1960), 111–17.

the absurd requires that the audience be familiar with the recitation of the *Tales of the Heike* and the role of the *biwa hōshi* as its promulgators. *Donbukattchiri's* version goes as follows:

> そもそも一の谷の合戦敗れしかば、源平互いに
> かかる者はおとがひを切られて逃ぐるもあり、
> また逃ぐる者は踵を切らるるもあり、何が
> 忙はしき時のことなれば、踵を取っておとがひに付け、
> おとがひを取って踵に付けたれば、生えうずことと
> 踵に髭がむくりむくりと生えたるなり。また冬にも
> なれば、切れうずこととおとがひにあかがりが
> ほかりほかりと切れたるなり。

Now then, when they lost the battle of Ichi-no-tani
The Heike grappled with the Genji soldiers.
Some were struck head on and had their chins
whacked off,
And fled.
Others turned tail and their heels were sliced from
behind.
The chaos was such that they grabbed their heels and
Stuck them on their chins,
Scooped up their chins and
Stuck them on their heels.
When they began to grow in place,
Beards started to pop out, pop, pop, pop.
And when they went to shave,
It being winter,
The cracks on their heels suddenly split wide open,
Crackle-crackle-crackle right across their chins.[18]

Although slight variations in the passage appear between the Ōkura, Izumi, and Sagi school texts, in general they follow the *Toraakira-bon*. In the parody of the *Ichi-no-tani* passage in *Kikazuzatō* mentioned above, the *zatō* (Kikuichi) chants:

---

18. Ikeda Hiroshi and Kitahara Yasuo, eds., *Ōkura Toraakira-bon: Kyōgen shū no kenkyū*, vol. 2 (Hyōgensha, 1973), 111 (all translations are the author's unless otherwise noted).

そもそもあのつんぼめは、みみのきこいぬのみならず
おくびょうもの、あほうにてござんなり。

Now then, as for that deaf guy,
Not only do his ears not hear,
He's a cowardly fool as well.[19]

The use of そもそも (Now then …) and the sentence ending ござ
んなり identify it as a *Heike* style pattern like the *Ichi-no-tani* pattern.

Within the context of a play the *Ichi-no-tani* pattern works comically
on several levels. For example, in *Saru zatō*, in which a blind priest and
his wife go cherry-blossom viewing, the humor based on displacement
of emphasis takes a back seat to dramatic irony. The decidedly pompous
blind husband intones the *Ichi-no-tani* passage while his wife is
succumbing to the wiles of a rogue monkey-trainer passing by. Both the
husband and the *Heike* chant are the objects rather than means of satire
here. Oblivious to what is happening around him, he concludes the *Ichi-
no-tani* pattern, "Now that's more like it! A proper tone is essential for
the *Heike*. ..."

Clearly not of the upper ranks of an official guild of *biwa hōshi*, the
blind man's pretensions make him fair game for kyōgen humor. Behind
the husband's back, but in full view of the audience, the monkey-trainer
attempts to seduce the wife. At first, she dismisses his advances but quite
soon, improbably soon in fact, she is seduced into leaving her husband.
In the meantime, her husband is uneasy at his wife's intermittent
absences from his side, and complains to her. Eventually, to ensure her
presence, he ties her to him with a rope, "I won't have it! Where were you?
Forgetting all about your blind husband! I'll fix you." (He pulls out a rope
from his pocket and wraps it around her waist). His wife is angry, "What
are you doing to me? People will laugh!" But the husband responds, "I
don't care if they do. Now I can relax. You're not here to enjoy yourself;
you came to wait on me!" The monkey-trainer makes quick work of this,
untying the wife and fastening the rope to the monkey instead. When
the husband reaches out for his wife, he discovers to his chagrin that she
has transformed into a monkey:

---

19. *Ōkura Toraakira-bon, Kikazuzatō*. Ikeda and Kitahara, *Toraakira-bon*, vol.
2, 430.

"I may be blind but I'm no fool! Now! Pass me the
sake cup! Hey! Hey there! Aren't you going to speak
to me? Are you angry because I scolded you? You're
in the wrong, you know. I didn't mean to say that I
didn't like you. I was just worried that you might get
hurt in the crowd. That's no reason to get so angry
with me. If you're going to behave that way, I'll
just yank you over here beside me. (*He pulls on the
rope and the monkey scratches him.*) Ouch! Ouch!
What long nails! How immodest of you! Draw in
your nails a bit! People will be watching! How can
you scratch your own husband? (*He yanks on the
rope again and the monkey attacks him.*) Oh, how
awful! My wife has turned into a monkey! Where is
everyone? (*He is chased off stage by the monkey.*)[20]

The treatment of the blind husband in this play is similar to that
of the would-be daimyō and bogus priests, two other character-types
frequently the object of humor. In each instance the ridicule is meant to
puncture the character's self-satisfaction and pretensions. At the same
time, there is no denying that the humor in the *zatō* plays is pointed and
cruel. What saves the play is the blind husband's own insistence on his
status as one of the *Heike biwa hōshi* and the pride he takes in it.

The way in which the *Ichi-no-tani* pattern is treated varies
significantly with the play. In *Futari zatō*, for example, instead of the
rogue monkey-trainer tricking the blind husband, we have a *kōtō*
ridiculing his superior, the *kengyō*. A *kōtō* calls on a *kengyō*, hoping to
borrow his *biwa* for a *Heike* gathering at Higashiyama during cherry
blossom time. Unfortunately, the *kengyō* has already sent his assistant,
Kikuichi, on ahead with the *biwa*, so the two decide to go together and
try to catch up with him. The following dialogue ensues:

> SHITE (*kengyō*): Now then, although everyone enjoys
> "blossom viewing," you and I cannot see so we'll enjoy
> "blossom smelling."
>
> ADO (*kōtō*): Wait just a minute! It's called "blossom
> viewing," not "blossom smelling!"

---

20. Izumi school text. Nonomura and Andō, *Kyōgen shūsei*, 189–91.

SHITE: Not at all! Not at all! Don't say that! There's a *waka* (poem) that uses "smelling" with no problem at all.

ADO: How does it go?

SHITE: "*This spring / whether stranger or friend / the sleeves that pass along the road / smell of blossoms.*" When you hear that you realize that it's perfectly all right to say "smelling" the blossoms, don't you think?

ADO: Well, when you put it that way it does seem perfectly all right. But, that can't be a real *waka*, surely! You just made it up to suit the occasion.

SHITE: Hey you! You claim that it's not a *waka*? If that's all you understand of poetry then you'll never make it to *kengyō*. Pay a little more attention to poetry!

As they approach Higashiyama, the sounds of the *Heike* reach them, "We seem to be quite near. You can hear the *Heike* so well, it's as if you could reach out and touch it." They discuss the chanting and the *kōtō* (*ado*) comments, "Whoever it is, he's terrible!" The *kengyō* (*shite*) scolds him and challenges him to chant it himself. Hearing him chant the *Ichi-no-tani* pattern the *kengyō* panics: "Oh no! He's been taking lessons and now he's gotten quite good. I was going to recite *Ichi-no-tani* today too but I can't do it if he's going to. What'll I do? ..." The *kengyō* tries to convince the *kōtō* that his chanting will be an embarrassment and that he really should give it up.

SHITE: Stop! Stop! Look here! You can't recite that way in front of everyone. Give up the *Ichi-no-tani* for today.

ADO: What? Excuse me, sir. Don't say that. You couldn't do as well.

SHITE: Now just a minute you! That's a pretty rude way to talk to a *kengyō*! Your *Heike* can't compare with mine!

ADO: Then let's hear you recite a verse!

SHITE: Listen here! How am I supposed to recite on this mountain path?

ADO: You're right, of course. However, since it's just for my instruction, please allow me to hear a verse.

SHITE: Oh well. If you don't know what it should sound like, you won't realize how bad yours is. I'll recite some for you. Pay attention!

ADO: Thank you, sir.

SHITE: *Now then, having been beaten at the battle of Ichi-no-tani ...*

ADO: Excuse me, sir! That's the part I just recited. Please recite a different part.

SHITE: Now look here! If I don't chant the same part, how will you know what's bad and what's good? You can't chant what you haven't been taught ... so just listen to me.

ADO: Yes, sir.

SHITE: *... the Heike grappled with the Genji soldiers Some were struck head on and had their heels sliced off ...*

ADO: Excuse me, sir! Those "struck head on" couldn't have "their heels sliced off"!

SHITE: Humph. You said that you didn't want me to do the same part of the *Heike*, so I changed it.

ADO: (laughing) Sure you did! Who'd do something like that! I'll put a stop to that *kengyō* mug of yours and send you on your way.[21]

---

21. Izumi school text. Nonomura and Andō, *Kyōgen shūsei*, 579. Although this play is included in the *Kyōgen shūsei*, it is originally from the Ōkura school repertoire.

The play concludes with the *kōtō* facing off with the *kengyō*, shoving him to the ground, and exiting. The *kengyō* is set up for this deflation from the very outset when he waxes eloquent about *waka* and misquotes a famous poem. The audience is fully ready, with the *kōtō*, to see him taken down a peg or two. Moreover, the *Ichi-no-tani* verse works ironically for the audience who can enjoy with the *kōtō* the corrupted version of the pattern offered by the *kengyō*, at the same time as they view the entire interaction from the superior position of their knowledge of the *Heike*. The *Ichi-no-tani* pattern thus provides a wealth of material for humor in the play. The intimate look at the relationship between the *kōtō* and *kengyō*, their feelings of rivalry and friendship, the audience's shared desire (with the *kōtō*) to see the *kengyō* brought low, all help to draw the audience into the world of the *biwa hōshi* and prevent the objectification of the characters.

Myō-on kō 妙音講 AND *Suzumi-no-e* 涼みの会

Like the *Ichi-no-tani* pattern, references within the plays to the *Myō-on kō* and *Suzumi-no-e* serve to mark the *zatō* as part of the world of the *biwa hōshi*. The *Myō-on kō* were monthly gatherings of *biwa hōshi* on the eighteenth of the month to celebrate Benzaiten 弁財天 (also known as Myō-on) by reciting the *Heike*. *Kō* 講 is a Buddhist term for groups that gathered for a reading of the sutras. By the twelfth century however, most of the crafts and trades were organized around a *kō* with a specific protective god (*kami*). As was true of other *kō*, those belonging to the *Myō-on kō* were not just the *biwa hōshi*. In fact the *kō* provided a nexus for the interaction between different groups of craftsmen and entertainers.[22] Since the nō and kyōgen actors also venerated Benzaiten, the *kami* 神 (deity) of the performing arts, presumably the kyōgen actors would have had social interactions with the *biwa hōshi* during the Muromachi period and later.

For the first mention of the *Myō-on kō* in a kyōgen text, we must return again to the *Tenshō-bon* (1578) and the play *Umakarizatō* うまか

---

22. Hyōdō, *Heike Monogatari no rekishi to geinō*, 94–124. For full discussion of the etymology of Myō-on, see Matisoff, *The Legend in Semimaru*.

りざとう.[23] This play is thought to be the basis for the later play *Hakuyō* 伯養, both from the content and from the fact that the *zatō's* name in this version is Hakuyō. Accordingly, a *zatō* enters and says that his name is Hakuyō. He calls on his superior and reports that the *Myō-on kō* is coming up and he intends to go. The superior tells him to go and borrow a horse from the master. When he asks for the horse, however, a *kōtō* shows up and asks for the horse as well. Both of them attempt to lead the horse away. The master tells them to compete for it by singing. They exchange verses ridiculing one another's names. The *kōtō* makes a pun on *haku* (to wear on the foot): "On the road, his footwear broke. Since he can't wear it, let's toss it (him) down the valley." Hakuyō responds with a pun on *kōtō* (dregs of the sake): "Not allowed to enter the banquet hall, the *kōtō* dregs are useless." When the master tries to intervene, Hakuyō tramples on both the master and the *kōtō* before exiting.

In later versions, Hakuyō is sometimes on his way to a *Suzumi-no-e*. The *Suzumi-no-e* was an annual gathering in Kyoto of *biwa hōshi* on the nineteenth of the Sixth Month at *Seiju an* to recite the *Heart Sutra* and the *Heike* and to enjoy the cool of the evening. In the *Toraakira-bon* version of *Hakuyu* the *zatō* enters and announces: "The *Suzumi-no-e* is approaching" (涼みの会も近近になってござる). Both *Chakagizatō* and *Marizatō* mention the *Myō-on kō*. In *Chakagizatō*, the *kōtō* enters and announces, "Today there will be a *Myō-on kō* at the home of the *sōkengyō* so I think I'll go and watch." (今日は座頭共が惣検校の方で妙音講が ござる程に立超え見物いたさうと存ずる.)[24] In *Mari zatō*: "Today I am to be the host for the *Myō-on kō*" (今日は妙音講の当にあたって 御ざる).[25] These references to the *Myō-on kō* or *Suzumi-no-e* would have provided the commoner of the fifteenth and sixteenth centuries with a familiar context within which to view the internal society of the *biwa hōshi*.

Finally, there is an intriguing reference to a memorial service for the Heike clan in an early version of *Futari zatō* in the seventeenth century *Sagi Yasunori* text (1704–1715).[26] The content of the play is completely different from that of the same name in the later Izumi and Ōkura school texts, which, as discussed above, involve the borrowing of a *biwa*.[27] In the

---

23. Furukawa, *Kyōgen kō hon nishu: Tenshō-bon, Torakiyo kyōgen bon*, 19.
24. Nonomura and Andō, *Kyōgen shūsei*, 286–87.
25. Ibid., 473–74.
26. Furukawa and Kobayashi, *Kyōgen jiten jikō hen*, 314.
27. See my translation of a portion of the Izumi school *Futari zatō* play above.

earlier version, a blind priest (盲目の僧) from Yahagi in Mikawa decides to make a pilgrimage to Ise. At Yamada he calls out for a place to stay for the night. Someone appears and offers him a room for rent. The owner then tells him that some time ago a blind priest from Mikawa fell into the river at Monkey Crossing and drowned. The blind priest then begins to chant a Buddhist memorial service for the Heike (*tsuizen no Heike* 追善の平家)—"*Truly the uncertainty of life, like lightning, like the morning dew ...*" (現にや不定電朝露)—when the spirit of the dead priest appears, wearing the old-man mask. The spirit tells his story and then announces that he has achieved Buddhahood through the priest's prayers. In return, he offers to show the priest around the Grand Shrine of Ise. The play ends with a song and dance.

This chant for the memorial service for the Heike appears nowhere else, certainly not in either the *Heike* texts or the nō plays. Presumably the chant was made up by the actors to mimic *Heike*-style recitation by the *biwa hōshi*. Since one of the functions of *Heike* recitation was apparently to release or quiet the souls of the dead Heike clan, the source of the scene seems clear. Although the blind man is not called a *zatō* here, as he is in the revised versions of the play, he functions like one in his act of prayer.

In other respects the play seems remarkably close to the *mugen* nō plays, in which spirits of the dead become manifest in the second scene. There are probably several reasons for this. The kyōgen actors were eager to gain the patronage of the Tokugawa government and the recognition of the nō troupes already receiving this patronage, so a play that paralleled a nō play without parodying it may have seemed appropriate to this purpose. One might also speculate that the play would have been particularly celebratory for the newly established Tokugawa government hoping to lay to rest the souls of their rivals. The fact that the play disappeared quickly from the repertory suggests that it was a little too close to the nō format to accommodate the conventions of the kyōgen stage, the purpose of which was, after all, comic relief. This is the only kyōgen play in which we see the blind priest performing his traditional role of praying for the dead.

CONCLUSION

The role of the *zatō* in the *zatō* kyōgen plays seems quite clearly to be based on the *biwa hōshi* of the Muromachi period. In particular, the period following the Ōnin War was one of fluidity for all of the popular arts. The kyōgen actors, the *etoki*, the *biwa hōshi*, and others presumably would have interacted freely, sharing and borrowing from one another. Glimpses of what those early kyōgen performances would have been like are available in the *Tenshō-bon* (1578), where we see at least six *zatō* plays. A crude and rough humor is characteristic of this text, and the *zatō* plays are no exception. As the kyōgen actors formed schools, recorded texts, and formalized stage and character conventions in the seventeenth century, the character of the *zatō* came to be more strictly identified with the distinguishing attributes of a *biwa hōshi*. These attributes—the *Ichi-no-tani* pattern, the plots centered around the *Myō-on kō* or *Suzumi-no-e*, the emphasis on rank, the use of the biwa as a plot device, the assumption of a spiritual connection between the blind and the afterlife—all contribute to the creation of the rich and mysterious "other" world of the *biwa hōshi*.

Without the common knowledge of the *biwa hōshi* which the audience of the Edo period and earlier would have had, the humor in the plays is very disturbing. However, it is also true that the humor of kyōgen in the sixteenth century, as far as we can guess from the *Tenshō-bon* and the later *Toraakira-bon,* was a rough affair, not only in the *zatō* plays but across the repertoire. Many of the *zatō* plays, for example, end with a sumo match between two blind priests, in which the priests fumble in the air trying to reach one another. Apparently sumo matches between two blind men were a popular form of street corner entertainment in the Kamakura period. According to the *Azuma kagami* 吾妻鏡 they were so prevalent that the government banned them.[28] Since kyōgen routinely lampooned the weak, the vulnerable, and the naïve, the inclusion of such sumo scenes is not surprising.

Much of the cruelty of the humor was transformed during the Tokugawa period through the use of stage conventions, which helped to ensure the depiction of a character-type rather than a particular individual. In this way, the audience could identify with the universal failings and weaknesses revealed by the character-types on stage. This is the secret to the continuing popularity of plays like *Tsukimizatō* and

---

28. Kajihara and Yamashita, *Heike monogatari* (jō), 418.

Kawakami. The blindness in the plays becomes a metaphor for the psychological blindness that affects us all. The *zatō* in *Tsukimizatō* is first befriended, and then tricked by the same passerby on a night of moon viewing. Like us, he is blind to the evil in the man and refuses to recognize that the first man he encountered and the trickster are one and the same person.

In *Kawakami* a blind man regains his sight with the intervention of the bodhisattva only to lose it again. The bodhisattva offers him a bargain, his sight, for his wife. When his wife is told that she must divorce him or he will be blind again, she refuses to do so. His sight quickly fades and with it, his hopes for a different future. What he gains instead is an insight into the workings of karma.

Most of the *zatō* plays have not fared so well, however. Even the winsome humor of *Goze zatō*, which is a love story, has not survived on the modern stage. The plays run the gamut from love stories to tea ceremonies, marital spats, and professional jealousies, and yet their dependence on a familiarity with the *biwa hōshi* and his profession of *Heike* recitation has prevented them from succeeding on stage today. When the world they described was lost, the quirky humor of the *zatō* plays was lost along with it.

20 ～ *Nasu* (Kyōgen)

| CAROLYN MORLEY

INTRODUCTION

Nasu 那須 (*ai-kyōgen* for the nō play *Yashima* 八島)
Source: Jokyō Matsui bon 貞享松井本 (1684–1687)

Nasu 那須 is a *kae ai* for *Yashima* in which the kyōgen actor perform four different roles. The actor enters as a fisherman and reenacts the "Nasu no Yoichi" episode (Kakuichi-bon 11.4) from the *Heike*. Next, he is also Yoshitsune, Gotō Sanemoto, and the young archer Yoichi, who is chosen to hit the target on the fan held up by a young Taira woman on a boat out at sea. The Ōkura school treats mastery of this role as as requisite for recognition as a professional kyōgen actor. The play appears in a list of plays as early as the *Tenshō-bon* (the first collection of kyōgen plot summaries from 1578) with the title, *Ōgi no mato* 扇の的 (The Fan Target), but the earliest extant version of the text is in the *Kyōgen ki* 狂言記 (Kyōgen Record) of 1660. It was included in Ōkura school texts only in the late Edo period.

Nasu (Kyōgen)

| TRANSLATED BY CAROLYN MORLEY

Ai-kyōgen for the nō play *Yashima* 八島

FISHERMAN: Now then, the sun had set on the battle at Yashima, and the decision was made to halt the fighting until the next day.[1] They had just withdrawn, when from the offing an ordinary, small boat rowed out with a lovely girl of seventeen, dressed in a five-layered, light green robe lined in white, and trailing embroidered vermillion trousers. She attached a bright red fan with a sun to the gunwale of the boat, and facing the shore, pointed up at it. The boat quickly pulled up parallel to the nearby shore.

"Come here," she beckoned.

Seeing this, General Yoshitsune summoned Gotō Byōe Sanemoto, "What's the meaning of that?"

Sanemoto listened respectfully, and responded, "My General. It must be a plan to get you to 'take a shot at it.' Then, when the General steps out front with his arrows and approaches the girl, they intend to take careful aim and shoot you. We should do what must be done." And when he said this,

The General commanded, "We must have someone on our side who can shoot."

Sanemoto listened and responded, "As you say sir, on the General's side there are many known for their skill with a bow. Among them the best is Yoichi Munetaka, son of Tarō Suketaka of Nasu in Shimozuke. Although small, he is very skillful. For example, if he's aiming at birds in flight, he'll always hit two out of three without fail."

"Then, bring this Yoichi here," he commanded.

Nasu 那須. Taken from the Jokyō Matsui bon 貞享松井本 (1684–1687). This translation is based on Taguchi Kazuo, ed., *Jōkyō nenkan Ōkura ryū aikyōgen hon nishu (zoku),* Nōgaku shiryō shūsei (Wanya shoten, 1988), 60–63.

1. To compare the Heike episode of "Nasu Yoichi" (Kakuichi-bon 11:4), see Ichiko Teiji, ed., *Heike monogatari (ge),* SKBZ 46 (Shōgakukan, 1994), 356–60; Helen Craig McCullough, trans., *Tale of the Heike* (Stanford University Press, 1988), 366–68.

Yoichi was a lad of barely twenty years. Over his clanging armor, he wore a red court robe, and had removed his helmet and tied it to his breastplate. He came into the presence of the General. The General looked him over. "So this is the Yoichi you mentioned? Hit the target at the center of the fan that young girl has raised, and give those Heike something to look at!"

Yoichi respectfully addressed the General, "I have never done anything like this before. The command should be given to one among us who will not fail you."

The General became furious. In a rage he said, "Those who followed me from Kamakura on this campaign cannot refuse my orders. Those who do not agree to this should withdraw now and return home. We'll settle the score later, in Kamakura!" Yoichi listened, respectfully. Somehow he knew it would be bad form to refuse again. "Although I will probably not succeed, at least I will make an attempt for you." Having said this, he withdrew from the General's presence.

Then, he girded a saddle trimmed in gold with a mistletoe crest on the back of his famous horse, Little Black, and sprang up lightly and with ease. He turned the horse's head and headed him toward the beach. Those around the General exclaimed, "This young fellow will be the one to do it!" And even the General himself looked upon him with confidence. Since he was a bit out of range, he charged into the sea. The horse seemed suddenly to be up to his belly. This was the eighteenth day of the Third Month. And since it was six o'clock in the evening a seasonal north wind blew harshly. The boat was small and the waves, high.

When he saw the boat bobbing up and down, the fan too, unsteady, at that moment, Yoichi closed his eyes. "Amida Buddha, Hachiman, and Daimyōjin of Yūzen in Nasu, please let me strike the center of the fan. If I am to fail in my youth, I will break my bow and kill myself. I will never go home again. If you would have me return home then please let my arrow meet its mark." Then he opened his eyes wide as acorns and when he looked, the wind had quieted down some and the fan appeared easier to hit. Yoichi was slight of build. Yet, his bow was powerful—twelve hands, three fingers in length—and he pulled back and let it fly. Right on target, the arrow whistled through the wind and struck just above the hinge of the fan. Just as his humming-bulb arrow[2]

---

2. A "humming-bulb arrow" (Jp. *kaburaya*, "turnip arrow") made a whizzing sound as it flew because of holes in its large head. This resembled a *kabu* or turnip, hence its Japanese name.

entered the ocean, the fan flew up into the air. It flew up once, twice on the spring breeze, and then suddenly plunged into the sea. The brilliant red fan with the rising sun floated up and down on the foam, looking just like autumn leaves tossing in the waves.

Then the Heike warriors thumped upon the gunwales of their boats, "He's done it! He's done it!" And the Genji warriors rattled their quivers, applauding, "You've done it! Munetaka!"

The General was so pleased that he took that fellow Yoichi to the officer's quarters, and congratulated him, "Have a drink! Drink it dry!"

Well, anyway, that's the way I heard it. I don't know the details. This is just what we've been told of old. Why is it that you ask about it now? It's very odd.

21 ∾ The Nō Play *Shigehira*

| PAUL S. ATKINS

The nō play *Shigehira* 重衡 (or *Kasa sotoba* 笠卒塔婆, among other titles) is a *mugen* (dream) warrior play in which the ghost of the Heike warrior Taira no Shigehira appears to a monk traveling in Nara and asks for release from his sufferings in the afterlife, which are punishments for the destruction of Kōfukuji, Tōdaiji, and other temples in battle. While it appears to have been performed often during the Muromachi period, and there are extant libretti from the late seventeenth century, there is no record of the play having been performed between 1432 and 1983. Its revival sparked a boom in the resurrection of other old nō plays, and *Shigehira* is said to be the most frequently performed of the revived pieces. Such popularity has been attributed to its deft portrayal of the internal state of mind of its protagonist, who is wracked by guilt and rage, but also to the timeliness (and timelessness) of its subject matter— atrocities committed in wartime.[1]

SHIGEHIRA IN HISTORICAL SOURCES AND *THE TALE OF THE HEIKE*

Taira no Shigehira was born in 1156 or 1157, the fifth son of Taira no Kiyomori; his mother was Tokiko. He was awarded Junior Fifth Rank,

The author would like to thank Professors Matsuoka Shinpei and Nishino Haruo for their valuable advice.

1. Matsuoka Shinpei, "Nō 'Shigehira' wo yomu," in Kubota Jun, ed., *Ronshū chūsei no bungaku: sanbun-hen* (Meiji shoin, 1994), 252.

lower grade in 1162 and was subsequently appointed to such posts as Master of the Left Imperial Stables (*sama no kami* 左馬頭), Deputy Director of the Empress's Offices (*chūgū no suke* 中宮助亮), and Chief of the Chamberlains' Office (*kurōdo no tō* 蔵人頭). Eventually he reached the rank of Senior Third and held the post of supernumerary middle captain of the Left Imperial Bodyguards (*sakon'e no gon-chūjō* 左近衛権中将). During the Genpei War, Shigehira distinguished himself as an able commander, defeating such adversaries as Prince Mochihito and Minamoto no Yorimasa (1180.5) and Minamoto no Yukiie (1181.3). He led an expedition to Nara that resulted in the destruction of the Tōdaiji and Kōfukuji temples, and killed thousands, including many noncombatants (1181.12; discussed in detail below). After the Taira's retreat to the west, Shigehira participated in victories over the Genji at Mizushima (1183.i10) and Muroyama (1183.11). This impressive record came to a humiliating end at the battle of Ichi-no-tani (1184.2), where he was captured alive. Upon the urging of Retired Emperor Go-Shirakawa, an offer was made to the Heike to exchange Shigehira for the imperial regalia, which the Taira took with them when they abandoned the capital, but it was rebuffed. Shigehira was transported to Kamakura for an audience with Yoritomo, who acceded to the demands of the monks of Kōfukuji and Tōdaiji and sent Shigehira to Nara for execution. Shigehira's last visits with his wife, with the courtesan Senju, and with Hōnen, the founder of Pure Land Buddhism, are chronicled with great sympathy in *The Tale of the Heike*. He was beheaded at the Kozu River (also called Kizu or Kotsu) on 1185.6.23.

THE ATTACK ON NARA

The Heike attack on Nara is concisely and vividly detailed in *Heike monogatari* 5.14, "The Burning of Nara." In summary, the Taira attacked the Nara temples for their sympathies with the anti-Taira movement, especially their support of Onjōji (Miidera), which harbored Prince Mochihito following his failed uprising. Kōfukuji had pledged to aid Miidera but its forces came too late to avert the death of the prince and the destruction of Miidera. Kōfukuji was the principal target in Nara.[2]

---

2. For further details, see Mikael S. Adolphson, *The Gates of Power: Monks, Courtiers,*

Shigehira, the *Heike* notes, set out for Nara with a total of "more than forty thousand horsemen."[3] The date was 1180.12.28. Seven thousand monks manned fortifications at Hannyaji and Narazaka, strategic sites at the northern edge of Nara, where the town meets the mountains. The monks were roundly defeated, leaving the Taira free to enter Nara itself. By this time it was nightfall, and Shigehira is said to have uttered the fateful words *"hi o idase"*—"Light fires!"—but also connoting something along the lines of "Unleash the flames!"[4] According to *Heike*, a commoner's house was set ablaze, and strong winds caused the flames to spread to temple buildings; the burning of the temples themselves is thus depicted as partly accidental. Aside from the monks who died in battle, the *Heike* records 3,500 dead from fires at Tōdaiji, Kōfukuji, and elsewhere, mainly those too young, old, or weak to fight. Among the material casualties was the famous Great Buddha at Tōdaiji, which melted in the flames.

While powerful temples kept private armies and were notorious for meddling in political matters, the destruction of Kōfukuji and Tōdaiji was shocking. To many it reaffirmed a belief that the world was in the decadent age that Buddhists called *mappō* 末法, in which the teachings of Buddha were abandoned and no one could reach enlightenment. In particular, the aristocrats in the capital, most of whom were of Fujiwara descent, were especially disturbed by the loss of Kōfukuji, the Fujiwara family temple. In a diary entry dated 1180.12.29, Kujō Kanezane noted that "someone came to say that Lord Shigehira had subdued the southern capital [Nara], and was on his way back to the capital. Another said that at Kōfukuji, Tōdaiji, and other [temples] the halls and buildings had been burned to the ground and people had fled to the [Kasuga] Shrine … The Seven Great Temples and others all turned to ashes and dust—is this the end of Buddhism, and of the monarchy? Words fail me. I cannot express this in writing. When I heard the news, it was as if my heart had been torn to shreds."[5] On the same day, Fujiwara no Teika wrote: "Heard the government's forces entered the southern capital and burned the halls, pagodas, and monks' quarters. It is said that both Tōdaiji and

---

and *Warriors in Premodern Japan* (University of Hawai'i Press, 2000), 161–66.

3. Helen Craig McCullough, trans. *The Tale of the Heike* (Stanford University Press, 1988), 194.

4. Kajihara Masaaki and Yamashita Hiroaki, eds., *Heike monogatari* (jō), SNKT 44 (Iwanami shoten, 1991), 318.

5. Ichishima Kenkichi, ed., *Gyokuyō*, vol. 2 (Kokusho kankōkai, 1906), 455–56. See also Takahashi Sadaichi, *Kundoku 'Gyokuyō,'* vol. 4 (Takashina shoten, 1989), 347.

Kōfukuji have already been reduced to smoke. For shame, for shame."[6]
The Tale of the Heike goes to great lengths to demonstrate why the Taira deserved to be removed from power and thereby justify the rule of the incumbent Minamoto. Shigehira's merciless and senseless attack on Nara is a damning example.

THE NŌ PLAY AND ITS INTERPRETATION OF SHIGEHIRA

The nō play *Shigehira* was written sometime in the fifteenth century, long after Tōdaiji and Kōfukuji had been rebuilt. It is mentioned and quoted by Zeami in *Sarugaku dangi* 申楽談儀. Although no definitive evidence exists, current opinion holds that the author was Zeami's son Kanze Motomasa 観世元雅 (d. 1432). Indeed, the relentlessly gloomy tone is consistent with Motomasa's known oeuvre.[7]

In the play, a traveling priest comes to Nara to see its famous temples. He meets an old man on Narazaka who points out the temples that can be seen from the slope (including Tōdaiji and Kōfukuji), then asks the monk to pray for Shigehira. After the interlude, the old man returns in his true form, the ghost of Shigehira. He recounts the moments before his execution at the Kozu River and describes the torments of the *aśura* realm of existence, where he and other ghost warriors do battle every night, unable to quell their own rage.[8] They light their way with torches,

---

6. Tsuji Hikosaburō, ed., *Meigetsuki*, vol. 1 (Zoku gunsho ruijū kanseikai, 1971), 163. See also Meigetsuki kenkyūkai, ed., "'Meigetsuki' (Jishō 4–5-nen) wo yomu)," in *Meigetsuki kenkyū* 5 (November, 2000), 13.

7. The earliest attribution to Motomasa appears to have been by Nishino Haruo. See his essay "Motomasa no nō," in Yokomichi Mario, Nishino Haruo, and Hata Hisashi, eds., *Nō no sakusha to sakuhin* (Iwanami shoten, 1987), 242. A more detailed argument may be found in Matsuoka, "Nō 'Shigehira' wo yomu."

8. *Aśura* (Jp. *ashura* 阿修羅 or *shura* 修羅) is a Sanskrit term that originally referred to a category of ancient Indian gods who waged war against the heavenly Indra gods. In Buddhism it designates one of the six realms of existence (*rokudō* 六道), whose beings are condemned to do incessant battle with one another. Many of the dream nō that concern the Genpei War feature defeated Taira warriors who seek release from the *aśura* realm into which they have been reborn.

which are imagined as the flying fires of Kasuga Meadow (*Kasugano no tobuhi*). Originally signal fires used to warn of the approach of an invasion, the flying fires here are the torches that the warriors carry as they stab each other and hack off one another's limbs night after night. The play ends without resolution, with simply the *shite*'s plea to the *waki* to relieve him of his rage (*shin'i*), which blocks his enlightenment and entry into nirvāṇa.

While the nō play is based on a historical figure, the genre's dramatic conventions dictate that the figure of Shigehira be altered in various ways. First, and most obviously, while Shigehira was only thirty or so at his death, in the play he appears in the guise of an old man. (In this regard it resembles plays such as *Yashima* 屋島, in which the ghost of Minamoto no Yoshitsune, who also died young, assumes the form of an old fisherman.) This choice strips away some of the youthful charm associated with Taira warriors that Zeami favored in writing his own *Heike* plays, and it helps us understand why the first word uttered by the *maejite* in the play is *kurushiki* ("wretched"). Old age is inherently painful and this is part of Shigehira's punishment.

Second, Shigehira has ironically become a resident of the town that he destroyed. In *Heike* as in the historical record, he and his forces spend a single night in Nara before returning to Kyoto the following day. In the play, however, Shigehira has the curious task of acting as a tour guide, telling a monk, of all people, about some of the very temples he once wrecked.

Third, in the *Heike*, Shigehira makes a brief speech before his execution, defending his actions and insists that he was simply following the orders of his father and the emperor (Go-Shirakawa). In the play, Shigehira makes a similar defense, but the reference to Go-Shirakawa is omitted. This may be attributed to a desire to avoid giving offense to the imperial institution—the attempt to shirk responsibility for atrocities committed in war by attributing them to orders from a higher authority is all too familiar to modern audiences, and the elision of the emperor's involvement is especially reminiscent of the postwar situation in Japan. (On the other hand, it is questionable whether Go-Shirakawa had the ability to order or stop the attack on Nara without Kiyomori's assent.) More suggestive is the idea that the focus on Kiyomori, who was both Shigehira's father and lord, is consonant with an intense preoccupation with the bonds between parents and children seen in Motomasa's oeuvre, most especially *Sumidagawa* 隅田川.[9]

---

9. Matsuoka, "Nō 'Shigehira' wo yomu," 267.

Finally, there is Shigehira's experience in the afterlife. This is not addressed in *Heike*, but one is hopeful, as he makes a confession to Hōnen, who symbolically confers upon Shigehira holy orders. Shigehira is a paragon of Buddhist evil—a murderer of monks—and his salvation would paradoxically attest to the efficacy of Buddhist doctrine. Failing that, one would not be surprised to see Shigehira suffering in the realm of hell for his outrageous crimes, but instead he finds himself in the *aśura* realm, like other warriors in dream nō, and he seeks release not from its torments as much as from the rage that keeps him there. In contrast, by the time Shigehira is executed in *Heike*, he seems gripped not by rage but by despair. If anyone needs to be released from the bonds of wrath, it would seem to be the Nara monks themselves. The focus in the play on Shigehira's rage, rather than his crimes, is remarkable but typical of the psychological insight of the great nō playwrights. Rage is both the motivation for Shigehira's sins and his punishment for having committed them.

HISTORY OF THE RECEPTION OF THE PLAY

There is no record of *Shigehira* having been performed between 1432 (which happens to be the year Motomasa died) and 1983, when a performance was organized by Hashi no kai in Tokyo, with Asami Masakuni as *shite*.[10] The reasons for this long hiatus are not known, but one can propose a few hypotheses. First, there is the unremitting gloom of the play, which contrasts with the charismatic melancholy of another play about Shigehira, Zenchiku's *Senju* 千手. We might also bear in mind that Oda Nobunaga ordered the destruction of Enryakuji in 1571, and the play might have hit too close to home while the country was under the control of Nobunaga or his former retainer Hideyoshi.

Since the 1983 performance, *Shigehira* has been performed several times, and is said to be the most successful restorations of a play to the current repertory. In addition, the revival has stimulated research on the

---

10. About the revival, see Matsuoka Shimpei, "Staging Noh," *Acta Asiatica* 73 (1997), 1–15, and "'Shigehira' no fukkyoku," *Geinō* 33:2 (February 1991), 17–19. The 1432 performance is chronicled by Prince Sadafusa (1372–1456) in his diary, *Kanmon nikki* 看聞日記, entry for Eikyō 4.3.14.

play; perhaps its most prolific exponent is Matsuoka Shinpei, who was involved in the original revival (in fact, he wrote a new *ai* interlude for the play, as the old one had been lost).[11]

The best close reading of the play to date is Matsuoka's "Nō 'Shigehira' wo yomu," which provides a thorough examination of the play's themes, motifs, rhetoric, and psychology. Among the many valuable points raised by Matsuoka is his view that Shigehira hallucinates the flying fires of Kasuga, which are actually flashbacks to the burning of Nara by his troops. Matsuoka regards this hallucination as a symptom of Shigehira's mental instability, the signs of a mind disturbed by guilt and the trauma of witnessing unbearable suffering.[12] He also zeroes in on a traditional technique of nō playwrights, the *meisho oshie* (explanation of famous sites); in this case it is Shigehira's description of the temples that he and the monk see as they look out on Nara from Narazaka. Among the various versions of the play, the six temples mentioned appear in three different sequences, but Asukadera always comes last (presumably because it is essential for a wordplay on *asu*, "tomorrow" that leads into the following passage), and Tōdaiji and Saidaiji always come first, in that order. Matsuoka views the erratic progression as a deliberate hint at derangement, especially the jump from Tōdaiji all the way across town to Saidaiji. In Zeami's *meisho oshie*, the progression typically follows topographical order. The willy-nilly flit from one end of town to the next, he argues, is intended by the author to hint at Shigehira's state of mind, and prime the audience for the second act.[13]

But are these truly signs of derangement? With regard to the flying fires, the *waki* too says he sees them, so they cannot be merely the hallucination of the *shite*. And as for the *meisho oshie*, the order of the temples is determined by the *waki*, who is asking the questions; the old man simply replies with information.[14]

---

11. In addition to the works already cited, see "Shigehira," in Matsuoka Shinpei, *Nō: chūsei kara no hibiki* (Kadokawa shoten, 1998), 85–94, and Yamashita Hiroaki, "Nō to Heike no ikusa monogatari: 'Shigehira' wo megutte," *Bungaku* 1:6 (November 2000), 112–24.

12. Matsuoka, "Nō 'Shigehira' wo yomu," 268.

13. Ibid., 260–61.

14. In (1) the version translated, the order of temples is as follows: Tōdaiji, Saidaiji, Hokkeji, Kōfukuji, Futaiji, and Asukadera. The arrangements that appear in other editions are: (2) Tōdaiji, Saidaiji, Hokkeji, Futaiji, Kōfukuji, and Asukadera; and (3) Tōdaiji, Saidaiji, Futaiji, Hokkeji, Kōfukuji, and Asukadera. In my view, the first and last configurations are suspect not necessarily because they

More broadly speaking, I think we must sometimes resist the urge to interpret nō plays by substituting psychological interpretations for supernatural ones. This is not as obvious a point as it seems, because in some of Zeami's plays, the psychological interpretation makes sense. We can often regard the appearance of a ghost in the second half of a *mugen* play as the dream of a monk who has been traveling all day and who nods off as he is reciting a sutra. In some plays the enlightenment of the *shite* is even juxtaposed explicitly against the *waki*'s waking from dream, a natural metaphor but one that leaves the door open for a psychological interpretation of supernatural phenomena. I think that sensibility accounts in part for Zeami's enduring popularity among modern audiences. But we ought to avoid reading the work of other playwrights as if Zeami wrote them, because other playwrights (such as Motomasa and Zenchiku) demonstrate a sincere belief in supernatural phenomena. In Motomasa's case, one thinks of the disagreement between him and Zeami over the staging of *Sumidagawa*. Zeami felt the child should not appear, that we should understand that he was the hallucination of a mother driven to madness by her son's abduction and death. Motomasa put the *kokata* on stage.[15] In doing so he left the other door open, the door that allows us to believe in ghosts as real. However Shigehira's crimes and guilt remind us of our own age, we must continually remind ourselves of the mindset that created such works, one that posited unseen realities that were graspable, but not necessarily created by, the human mind.

---

are out of geographical order, but because some of the phrases used to indicate the position of each of the last four temples relative to the previous one make little sense. For example, in (1), Futaiji is described as "beyond" (*sono sue*) Kōfukuji, which is not the case when viewed from Narazaka. In (3), Hokkeji is described as south of Futaiji, and Kōfukuji beyond Hokkeji; neither reference seems appropriate. Sequence (2), found in the *Higuchi* edition, (*Mikan yōkyokushū zoku* vol. 5, 390–98) appears to be the only version that has internal consistency. See Tanaka Makoto, ed., *Mikan yōkyokyushū zoku*, vol. 5 (Koten bunko, 1989) 390–98. Matsuoka suggests that the author rearranged the order for aural impact ("Nō 'Shigehira' wo yomu," 260), but I wonder whether medieval audiences would have accepted an implausible mapping of Nara in a nō play.

15. See *Sarugaku dangi* in Omote Akira and Katō Shūichi, eds., *Zeami, Zenchiku* (Iwanami shoten, 1974), 270–71.

22 ∾ Shigehira

| Paul S. Atkins

Introduction

There is no definitive information regarding the authorship of *Shigehira*. The most widely accepted theory is that the play was written by Kanze Motomasa (d. 1432), the son and heir of Zeami. It was first advanced by Nishino Haruo, who wrote:

> Set in the shadow of blossoms by the Rainhat Stupa on Nara Hill, *Shigehira* is a dark and depressingly painful play. Shigehira bears not only the torments of the *Aśura* realm, but the karmic guilt of having burned down several temples in Nara on his father's orders. He suffers for the grave sin of having destroyed temples and murdered monks; there is no salvation for him. Insofar as it is a drama of internal emotion, *Shigehira* resembles *Sumidagawa*; like *Morihisa*, *Utaura*, and *Tomonaga* it portrays a character in dire straits with an emphasis on narration, and its diction shares distinctive aspects with *Sumidagawa* and *Tomonaga*. For these reasons is it not highly likely that Motomasa wrote it?[1]

---

1. Nishino Haruo, "Motomasa no nō," in Yokomichi Mario, Nishino Haruo,

Two short passages from *Shigehira* appear in Zeami's collected remarks, *Sarugaku dangi* (Talks on Sarugaku, 1430). This suggests that the play was indeed written by someone in Zeami's circle.[2]

The earliest textual evidence of *Shigehira* is the citation of a few lines in *Sarugaku dangi*, whose postscript is dated 1430. The oldest record of an actual performance is from 1432. There is no record of the play being performed between 1432 and 1983, when it was revived for modern audiences.[3]

Shigehira follows the Kakuichi edition of *The Tale of the Heike* quite closely. The most significant change is the alteration of the name of Shigehira's former attendant. In *Heike*, Tomotoki is generally identified as "Tomotoki, Assistant Deputy Master of the Bureau of Carpentry and of the Imperial Stables of the Right" (*Moku muma no jō Tomotoki*), but in the play he is called "Kondō Tomotoki, Assistant Deputy Commander of the Left Gate Guards" (*Kondō Saemon no jō Tomotoki*). Matsuoka Shinpei suggests that the Tomotoki character is being renamed under the influence of the famous itinerant ascetics of Mount Kōya (*Kōya hijiri*). Tales recounted by the ascetics often included characters who bore the sobriquet "Saemon" (Left Gate Guards).[4]

The play is also known by the title *Kasa Sotoba* (Rainhat Stupa), which refers to a sacred pillar made of stone with a broad top. Two such pillars stand today at a rebuilt Hannyaji, one of the temples destroyed in Shigehira's expedition.

---

and Hata Hisashi, eds., *Nō no sakusha to sakuhin* (Iwanami shoten, 1987), 242.

2. Matsuoka Shinpei, *Nō: chūsei kara no hibiki* (Kadokawa shoten, 1998), 89. For the relevant sections, see Erika de Poorter, *Zeami's Talks on Sarugaku: An Annotated Translation of Sarugaku dangi with an Introduction on Zeami Motokiyo* (Leiden: Hotei Publishing, 2002), 97, 105.

3. Matsuoka Shinpei, "Nō 'Shigehira' wo yomu," in *Chūsei no bungaku: sanbun-hen*, ed. Kubota Jun (Meiji shoin, 1994), 252. The 1432 performance is recorded in the diary *Kanmon nikki* (*Kanmon gyōki*), entry for Eikyō 4.3.14, cited in ibid., 271 n.1.

4. Matsuoka Shinpei, "Nō 'Shigehira' wo yomu," 273, n. 15.

Kasa Sotoba (Shigehira)

| TRANSLATED BY PAUL S. ATKINS

Second-category *mūgen* nō in two acts.
No longer in the performance repertoire, but sometimes revived.

Time: Spring, some time after the Genpei War
Place: Nara Hill in the province of Yamato, near the grave of
       Shigehira
Author: Attributed to Kanze Motomasa

WAKI	A traveling Buddhist monk
MAESHITE	An old man
NOCHIJITE	The ghost of Taira no Shigehira
AI	A villager

[PART ONE (*maeba*)]

Monk enters to shidai *music and stands at base square* (jōza) *facing rear of stage. Alternatively, enters with one or two* wakitsure *(companions), and they line up at the front; in that case, Monk and his companions face each other to sing the* shidai *and* ageuta.[1]

MONK

   (*shidai*)   With spring guiding my heart,
              with spring guiding my heart,
              I will take a journey without grief.

   Faces the audience.

MONK (*nanori*) I am traveling through the provinces and have recently

---

  Shigehira 重衡. Also known as *Kasa Sotoba* 笠卒都婆. This translation is based on Yokomichi Mario and Omote Akira, eds., *Yōkyokushū* (ge) NKBT 41 (Iwanami shoten, 1963), 257–64, with some minor changes. Much of the information contained in these notes is also drawn from this edition. For an overview of the various versions of the play, see Tanaka Makoto, *Mikan yōkyokushū* (*zoku*), vol. 5 (Koten bunko, 1989), 80–82.

  1. The stage directions are from Yokomichi and Omote and are highly conjectural, due to the lack of a modern performance tradition.

been to Kyoto to pray at the shrines and temples in the capital. Now I think I will go make a pilgrimage to the seven temples of the southern capital.[2]

MONK (*ageuta*)   From the capital
I set out again and pass Ide Village,
I set out again and pass Ide Village,
today I see the Mika Plain and the Izumi River,
and the river breeze sends mist
into the spring sky.
In the gentle light of the turning sun,   *Mimes walking.*
is this the southern capital?
Already I have arrived at Nara Hill,
already I have arrived at Nara Hill.[3]

Proceeds to witness square (wakiza) *and sits. Old Man enters to shidai music and stops at base square facing rear of stage. He holds a cane in his right hand.*

OLD MAN

(*shidai*)   Wretched old age is a steep hill,
wretched old age is a steep hill,
but I haven't much farther to go.

Turns to face front.

OLD MAN

(*sashi*)   The blossoms' scarlet has grown old with the
rain's passing,
the willows' green faded
by the wind's deception.[4]

---

2. Nara was capital of Japan from 710–784. The seven temples are Tōdaiji, Kōfukuji, Gangōji, Daianji, Yakushiji, Saidaiji, and Hōryūji.

3. Ide Village is the area around the lower reaches of the Tama River, a tributary of the Kotsu River. The Mika Plain is on the northern bank of the Kotsu, at the base of Mount Mikami. The Izumi River is an old name for the Kotsu River, which runs through the southern part of present-day Kyoto prefecture and is now known as the Kizu River (Kizugawa 木津川). Nara Hill (Narazaka 奈良阪) is a slope at the northern edge of Nara that descends into the city from the mountains that separate Nara from Kyoto prefecture.

4. Following the sixteenth-century commentary *Utaishō* 謡抄, Yokomichi and Omote cite *Paengnyŏn ch'ohae* 百聯抄解 (Jp. *Hyakuren shōkai*) as the source for these lines, which are clearly based on a Chinese poem, but they may have instead been derived from *Danchōshū no nukigaki* 斷腸集之抜書, or even the

Beating its own bones in the cold graveyard,
a demon ghost sobs, resenting the karma of a past life,
while an angel offers flowers in a warm meadow,[5]
rejoicing over and over in the benefits of enlightenment.[6]
These must be merely the fruits of good and bad karma.
Human affairs are like the horse of the old man at the
    fortress;[7]
does anything fail to conform to the Dharma?
Truly, there are no exceptions to the way of the
    world.

OLD MAN

   (ageuta)   Even the song of the aged warbler
grows old, even the song
of the aged warbler grows old.

Its tune sinks into the soul
as it fades away
with the light of the spring sun
I traced slow steps

---

nō play *Sekidera Komachi* 関寺小町, in which they also appear; the plays predate all known texts *of Paengnyŏn ch'ohae*. The Chinese text of the couplet is 花因 雨過紅将老　柳被風欺緑漸低. On *Danchōshū no nukigaki*, see Itō Masayoshi, "Sakuhin kenkyū 'Bashō,'" *Kanze* 46:7 (July 1979), 8–9. On *Paengnyŏn ch'ohae*, see Be Mun-gyŏng, "Yōkyoku to 'Hyakuren shōkai,'" in Kodai chūsei bungaku ronkō kankōkai, ed., *Kodai chūsei bungaku ronkō*, vol. 5 (Shintensha, 2001), 248–68.

5. The edition used has *rin'ya* in *kana* (perhaps to be read 林夜), but here I follow the revised version of the text used for the modern revival, which has *on'ya* 温野. See Tanaka Makoto, *Mikan yōkyokushū (zoku)*, vol. 5, 419. This restores the contrastive parallelism with *kanrin* 寒林 ("graveyard"; literally, "cold forest") and is corroborated by a citation from *Heiji monogatari* 平治物語. See Yokomichi and Omote, *Yōkyokushū (ge)*, 434, n. 67.

6. The original text reads only きしやう; Yokomichi and Omote supply the graphs 帰性 based on their reading of a similar passage from *Yamanba* 山姥. *Yōkyokushū (ge)*, 434, n. 69.

7. The Han collection *Huai nan zi* 淮南子 includes a story (18:7) about a crafty old man who lives near a fortress on the border. One day his horse runs away; while others are dismayed, he remains calm. A few months later it returns, accompanied by a much finer horse. But at this he is concerned. As it turns out, his son breaks his leg riding it. Instead of lamenting, the old man expects good fortune. Indeed, the injury spares the son from being drafted during wartime, saving his life. The tale was well known in medieval Japan as an allegory of the unpredictability of fortune and calamity.

to familiar Nara Hill
and have come to the blossoms' shade,
I have come to the blossoms' shade.

As Old Man finishes singing, Monk rises.

MONK

(*mondō*)   Old man, I have something to ask you.

OLD MAN   What is it?

MONK   I have never been here before, and am dazzled at the sight of the temples.

OLD MAN   Yes, even when I, who am using to seeing them day and night, climb up Nara Hill and look out, I am simply astonished. I can imagine how it would be for someone visiting for the first time. Ask me about the temples you see before you, and I will tell you a little about them.

MONK   First, the massive temple I see toward the east—is that the Hall of the Great Buddha that I have heard of?

OLD MAN   Yes, it is. That is the Great Buddha of Tōdaiji, a vast temple without peer in the three realms.[8]

Monk and Old Man change the direction they are facing with each exchange, as if looking at each temple.

MONK   And the temple I see to the west with the pagoda—which one is that?

OLD MAN   That is the one from Henjō's poem:

"Twining pale
green threads
that string
jewels of white dew—
willows in spring."[9]

(*fushi*)   According to the poem's preface, he wrote this about the willows of the Great Western Temple, that is, Saidaiji.[10]

MONK (*kakeai*)

---

8. The tour begins with one of the temples that Shigehira destroyed. (Kōfukuji is also mentioned later.) Tōdaiji 東大寺 was constructed in 745 by Emperor Shōmu 聖武; its Great Buddha, a massive bronze sculpture of the buddha Vairocana, is well known. It was rebuilt after Shigehira's attack on Nara. The three realms are India, China, and Japan.

9. Variant of *Kokinshū*, no. 27. Archbishop Henjō 遍昭 (816–890) was a poet and Tendai cleric.

10. Saidaiji 西大寺 was erected in 764 by command of Emperor Shōtoku 称徳.

(*fushi*)   How about that temple near the Sao River, where people dry their clothes?[11]

OLD MAN

(*katari*)   That is where they keep a pair of eleven-headed statues made long ago by the monk Ryōkō of China. It is a convent called Hokkeji. [12]

MONK (*fushi*)   And what is the name of the temple I see to the south?

OLD MAN   That is Kōfukuji, which promulgates the Hossō teachings; it is also called Yamashina-dera.[13]

MONK   And what is the temple beyond it called?

OLD MAN   That was founded by Captain Ariwara when he came down from the capital as imperial envoy to the Kasuga Festival—Futaiji, where the chanting of sutras never ends.[14]

MONK   And off there in the distance?

OLD MAN   Although I do not know whether this will be the last day of my life,

CHORUS   *Old man faces front.*

(*ageuta*)   by tomorrow—[15]
at the Asuka Temple the evening bell tolls,

---

11. The Sao River (Saogawa 佐保川) begins at Mount Kasuga and runs west along the northern part of Nara; it was associated in poetry with drying clothes due to its homonym *sao* 竿 (pole).

12. Ryōkō is otherwise unknown. See Yokomichi and Omote, *Yōkyokushū* (ge), 432, n. 58. Hokkeji 法華寺 is said to have been built in 741 on land donated by Empress Kōmyō.

13. Kōfukuji 興福寺 (Yamashina-dera 山階寺) was the Fujiwara 藤原 family temple and maintained its own army and extensive land holdings in the Nara region. It is located adjacent to the Kasuga 春日 Shrine, also affiliated with the Fujiwara.

14. Ariwara no Narihira 在原業平 (825–880) was a courtier, poet, and legendary lover who is conventionally regarded as the protagonist of the *Tales of Ise*. He is said to have donated the land for Futaiji in 847. The Kasuga Festival was held on the first day of the monkey during the Second and Eleventh Months; the Second Month festival was designated as a *rinjisai* 臨時際, or irregular festival, and is indicated in the original but omitted from the translation. A key participant in both events was a middle captain of the imperial bodyguard. See Royall Tyler, *The Miracles of the Kasuga Deity* (Columbia University Press, 1990), 60. Like Shigehira, Narihira held this rank.

15. Pun on place name Asuka 飛鳥 and *asu* 明日 "tomorrow." Asukadera was originally located in the village of Asuka; it was moved to Nara in 718 and renamed Gangōji 元興寺.

at the Asuka Temple the evening bell tolls.
The sound of the demons ringing it fills me with fear.
And now the sound of the famous bell—

Old Man steps forward, listens.

"Is this it?" I think, and the twilight is dreadful.

Looks up.

Yes, even the streets of the Nara capital,

Begins broad left turn to base square.

which has become a thing of the past,
have turned to spring with the flowers in full bloom,
and the eightfold cherry blossoms are lovely,

Faces front, looks.

the eightfold cherry blossoms are lovely.

Villager has entered quietly and is seated at the villager position (kyōgenza).

MONK

(*mondō*)   Well, then, I must leave.

OLD MAN   Before you go, please stand before this marker and pray for the enlightenment of the dead.

MONK   A prayer for enlightenment is a simple matter, but on whose behalf shall it be?

OLD MAN   In your prayer say it is for Shigehira.

MONK   Did Shigehira meet his end at this spot?

OLD MAN   Shigehira was captured alive at Ichi-no-tani and was ordered sent to the Kantō, but due to strong protests from the southern capital, he was beheaded over there at the Kotsu River.[16]

Though he once opened the gates of glory
and was of an illustrious lineage,
having once flourished he then faded,[17]
as you can see before your eyes.

As Old Man finishes singing, he proceeds to the center and sits. At the same time Monk also sits, at the witness square.

CHORUS

(*uta*)   "In the morning, a rouged face

---

16. The river is more commonly known as Kizugawa, but the text has Kozu (Kotsu); at one point there is some wordplay on *kotsu* (bones).

17. *Hito tabi wa sakae hito tabi wa otorouru koto*, a Japanese paraphrase of the phrase 一栄一落 from a Chinese poem by Sugawara no Michizane 菅原道真.

frolics in the streets;
but in the evening, turned to white bones,
it rots in a field."[18]
Vanishing like waves on the Kotsu River,
a pathetic memory.

Old man appears moved.

CHORUS
(rongi)   How painful it is even to hear
the name of Taira no Shigehira.
Now I shall pray for his repose.

OLD MAN   No visitor
stops to pay his respects,
so the shade of the spring grasses shames me,
and this dewlike body flickers.
How sad seem these traces of the dead one!

CHORUS   Yes, a body alive only in appearance—
when will it be unbound? The spring trees

OLD MAN   grow lush, and as for Shigehira's ghost,[19]

CHORUS   his spirit is gone away, but

OLD MAN   the white-haired

CHORUS   hoary old man you see—

Old Man gazes at Monk, stands.

"I am the ghost that has come back," he says
in the light of the evening moon.
That is Mount Mikasa,   *Looks into the distance.*

---

18. Based on *Wakan rōeishū* 和漢朗詠集, no. 793 by Fujiwara no Yoshitaka 藤原義孝. "Morning, you have ruddy cheeks, / the pride of worldly roads! / Evening, you've become white bones / rotting in plains beyond city walls" (朝有紅顔誇世路　暮為白骨朽郊原). Translation from J. Thomas Rimer and Jonathan Chaves, tr., *Japanese and Chinese Poems to Sing: The 'Wakan rōei shū'* (Columbia University Press, 1997), 236. Chinese original quoted from Ōsone Shōsuke and Horiuchi Hideaki, eds., *Wakan rōeishū* (Shinchōsha, 1983), 296.

19. The preceding lines play on Sugata no ike (the name of a famous pond in the Nara region) and the phrase *sugata no ikeru mi*, a body whose appearance lives (but not its soul). *Shigeru* means for a plant or tree to grow lushly, and is partially homonymous with Shigehira's name. *Haru* denotes both the season of spring and the action of clearing or dispelling (the delusive attachments that bar the ghost from entering nirvana).

and this is the rainhat stūpa,[20] *Makes right turn to base square,*
and he hides in the shade of the blossoms, *outstretches arms.*
he hides in the shade of the blossoms.

Exit Old Man.

*Dialogue between the monk and a villager; not extant. Typically, the
monk would ask the villager about what he had seen; the villager would
recount Shigehira's story, tell Monk he had in fact encountered Shigehira's
ghost, urge him to recite a sūtra on his behalf, and exit.*

[PART TWO (*nochiba*)]

MONK

(*ageuta*) On a makeshift pillow, as if dreaming,
            on a makeshift pillow, as if dreaming,
            all through the night as the moon sets
            though I have no ties to him
            I will pray,
            though I have no ties to him
            I will pray for the ghost of Shigehira.

The ghost of Shigehira enters to issei *music, stops at first pine or base
square and faces front.*

SHIGEHIRA

(*sashi*) "Along the streets of Nara,
           now an old village,
           the flowers have not forgotten spring
           and burst into bloom."[21]
           That poem was composed by an emperor.
           Though I am of insignificant station
           and wear a straw raincoat, when spring comes
           it cannot withstand the torments of the Aśura realm—[22]

---

20. Mount Mikasa 三笠山 is located in the eastern part of the city of Nara,
adjoining Kasuga Shrine. A pair of "rainhat stūpas" (so called because of their
shape) is located on the grounds of Hannyaji temple 般若寺. They postdate
Shigehira, but an earlier set may have inspired these lines. The Hyakunijukku-bon
of *Heike* says that Shigehira's head was hung on a nail in front of the rainhat stūpa
at Hannyaji. See Matsuoka Shinpei, "Nō 'Shigehira' o yomu," in Kubota Jun, ed.,
Ronshū chūsei no bungaku: sanbun-hen (Meiji shoin, 1994), 266.

21. Modified text of *Kokinshū*, no. 90, by Emperor Heizei 平城 (774–824; r. 806–809).

22. Complicated wordplay on *mi* (status) and *mino* (rainhat); *haru* (the season

ah, how I miss the mortal world!   *Appears moved.*

SHIGEHIRA

(*issei*)   On Nara Hill, where the oak leaves look
like children's hands,[23] I take in my hands
the catalpa bow.

CHORUS   Among the ranks of the myriad folk,   *Stamps to beat.*

Enters stage proper.

SHIGEHIRA   leave behind your name, brave man,
CHORUS

(*noriji*)   whose heart, once clouded,
shines clear, like the moon
on a night when a voice recites the Dharma,   *Faces Monk.*
a welcome thing indeed.

Places palms together in prayer.

[*A variant has:*

SHIGEHIRA

(*sashi*)   Though I have forgotten as the years pass,
now once again, like a dream from which one is woken,
CHORUS   I will confess the crimes committed
for all the world to see,
and it will link me to
the enlightenment of a Buddha.[24]]

Shigehira sits at center, either on a low stool or kneeling on the stage.

SHIGEHIRA

(*katari*)   Now then, Shigehira was captured alive at Ichi-no-tani,
and he was paraded through Kyoto and Kamakura. Then, due
to strong protests from the southern capital, he was going to be
beheaded at the Kotsu River. At that moment, someone by the name
of Kondō Tomotoki, Deputy Commander of the Left Gate Guards,
pushed his way through crowds of the low and mighty to witness

---

spring, to stretch [a garment]); and *kite* (arrive/wear) makes this passage barely
intelligible. *Minoshirogoromo* refers to a garment worn in place of straw raincoat.

23. Based on a poem from *Kokin waka rokujō* 古今和歌六帖 quoted in
Zeami's play *Hyakuman* 百万; the original is *Man'yōshū*, no. 3836.

24. Yokomichi and Omote's edition is based primarily on a 1686 woodblock
text (*Nihyakuban no gai hyakuban hanpon*); this passage comes from another
version, a copy of the *Yokohon shimogakari utaizoroe* held by the Institute of
Nōgaku Studies at Hōsei University.

Shigehira's last moments. He said, "Shigehira, Tomotoki is here."[25]
Shigehira was glad he had come, as he was an old acquaintance.
When Shigehira said that his last wish was to pray to a statue of
a Buddha, Tomotoki replied, "Easily done." A wooden statue of
a Buddha nearby was borrowed, and placed on the sand in the
riverbed. When Shigehira looked at it, fortunately it was Amida.[26]

(*fushi*)   Then Tomotoki pulled the cord out of the sleeve of the
robe he was wearing. He tied one end to the Buddha's hand and had
the Captain grasp the other. Once Shigehira had surveyed the scene,[27]

CHORUS   he held his hands together, faced the Buddha, and said
with sincerity:

CHORUS

(*kuse*)   "It is said that while Devadatta
               committed the three transgressions,
               the Buddha prophesied
               that even the evil heart
               that destroyed eighty thousand scriptures
               would be known as the Thus Come One Heavenly King.[28]
               Although his sins were truly deep,
               by the karmic link of an encounter
               with the sacred teachings,
               they became instead
               the cause of his attaining the Way.
               Now, Shigehira's transgressions
               were not at all of his own volition;

25. Tomotoki appears in *Heike monogatari* (Kakuichi-bon 10.2 "Dairi nyōbō")
but is otherwise unknown.

26. Amitābha, the buddha of the Western Paradise, especially venerated by
Pure Land Buddhists. Shigehira had been symbolically (but not actually) made a
monk by Hōnen 法然 (1133–1212), founder of the Pure Land school.

27. The text is corrupt. For *yori kumiwatarinureba*, Yokomichi and Omote
propose *nozomitarinureba* ("after [Shigehira] had surveyed the scene").

28. Devadatta (Jp. Daibadatta 提婆達多) was a disciple of the historical
Buddha who later turned against him, committing the Three Transgressions
(disrupting the monastic community, drawing blood from the body of a Buddha,
and killing an *arhan* [Jp. *rakan* 羅漢], a high-ranking Buddhist practitioner).
In the eponymous chapter of the Lotus Sūtra, the Buddha predicted that after
innumerable kalpas had passed, Devadatta too would attain enlightenment, and
would be honored with the title "Heavenly King Thus Come One." Thus Come
One (Jp. *nyorai* 如来, Skt. *tathāgata*) is one of the ten sobriquets of a buddha.

	he was simply following
	the way of the world.
	Of all living beings,
	is there a single one that defies
	its father's command?
	The Buddha can see clearly
	into my heart;
	I wish only to receive the teachings
	and commandments
	of the Three Treasures."[29]
SHIGEHIRA	"With a single prayer,
	Amida Buddha wipes away
CHORUS	infinite sins."

Shigehira stands, moves
When I heard this I thought, *while chorus sings.*
"Before I finish chanting
I will enter the cool path."[30]
Though the light of the setting moon
reached the western sky,
my spirit remained
at the foot of a tree.
Here in the mortal world
to Nara Hill I have returned.
Is the calyx of the blossom
here at the Mikasa grove?[31]
Oh, relieve Shigehira's blind attachment!

(QUASI-DANCE: *kakeri.*)

Shigehira makes a circuit of the stage, expressing his anguished state.

SHIGEHIRA
(*unidentified*)   Ah, how I detest it, coming back from time to time to
wander the mortal world at night. Just when I am about to calm my
heart,   *Standing at base square,*

rage rises in me once more.   *flourishes fan.*

---

29. The Three Treasures are the Buddha, his teachings, and the monastic
community. The corresponding section in *Heike monogatari* has *sanbō no kyōgai*
三宝の境界 (interpreted as "the world of the Three Treasures") but the phrase
makes little sense when rewritten for the play and combined with *uku* ("receive").
See Yokomichi and Omote, *Yōkyokushū* (ge), 433 n. 63.
30. The Western Paradise of the Pure Land.
31. Shigehira wished to be reborn onto the calyx of a lotus blossom in the Pure Land.

SHIGEHIRA
(*kakeai*)   Look at that, traveler.
MONK   Yes, I can see   *Gazes into distance.*
                torches coming from the east.
                What sort of fires are they?
SHIGEHIRA   Those are the famous "flying fires" of the guards of
Kasuga Meadow.[32]
MONK   Yes, I have heard of the flying fires,
                but why are they called that?
SHIGEHIRA   Long ago, war broke out with another country and the
warriors encamped in Kasuga Meadow. The torches and their bonfires
they lit each night moved about such that it looked as if they were
flying, and so this is called the Meadow of Flying Fires. And whenever
we do battle in the Aśura realm, fires are lit in Kasuga Meadow.
                Ah, fend them off!   *Stares toward stage right.*
                At Kasuga
        During the closing lines, Shigehira moves and gestures in accordance with the text.
CHORUS
(*chūnoriji*) are there no guards in the meadow?
                Come out and see. Are there no guards in the meadow?
                Come out and see.[33] Now how much longer
                until tonight's battle in Aśura?
                If dawn breaks, I will be miserable.
                Mount Asama[34] is burning in flames of rage.
                What seemed to be hunters smoking out their prey
SHIGEHIRA   was the light of the flying fires burning the
                Musashi Plain.[35]

---

32. Besides the legend related below, "flying fires" (*tobuhi*, written 飛ぶ火 but also 烽) refers to the smoke signals used by armies in ancient times, especially the border guards of what is now China.

33. Based on the anonymous *Kokinshū*, no. 19: *Kasugano no / tobuhi no nomori / idete miyo / ima ikuka arite / wakana tsumiten* 春日野の飛火の野守いでて見よ今幾日ありてわかなつみてん ("Guardian / of the flying fires / of Kasuga meadow, / come out and look— / How many more days / till I can pick the young herbs?").

34. Mount Asama 浅間 is an active volcano on the border of present-day Nagano and Gunma prefectures. It was a traditional poetic place name associated imagistically with burning passion and linguistically with its homophone *asamashi* (miserable).

35. Alludes to a poem in section 12 of *Ise monogatari*: *Musashino wa / kyō*

CHORUS	What lit the meadow guards' water[36]
SHIGEHIRA	was the flames in my heart,
	reflected in a mirror,
	and what sharpened the blades *Unsheathes sword.*
CHORUS	was the sparks of swords[37]
SHIGEHIRA	stabbing one another,
	hacking off limbs.
CHORUS	The flames have become a shower
	of swords falling on Kasuga Meadow
	like the Grass Cutter,
	the Sword of Gathering Clouds.[38]
	The flying fires seem as numerous as
	the abundant torments
	that shake the mountains and rivers
	of the Aśura realm,

---

wa na yaki so / wakukusa no / tsuma mo komoreri / ware mo komoreri 武蔵野は今日はな焼きそ若草のつまもこもれり我もこもれり ("Do not burn / Musashi meadow today. / Like the young grasses / my husband is hiding inside / and I am hiding inside"). Musashi Plain (*Musashino* 武蔵野) was located in terrain that is now part of Tokyo, Saitama, and Kanagawa prefectures.

36. Refers to a legend about a guard at Kasuga Meadow who was asked by a hunter about a lost hawk. The guard replied that the hawk was at the bottom of his bucket of water (presumably kept to extinguish wildfires in the meadow); when the hunter looked at the water, he saw a reflection of the hawk flying in the sky above. See Zeami's play *Nomori* 野守 (*The Meadow Guard*).

37. The phrase *suwa ittō* is obscure. See Yokomichi and Omote, *Yōkyokushū* (ge), 264, n. 12. *Suwa* is an expression of surprise or warning. *Ittō* suggests a number of sinified compounds beginning with ichi 一 (one). The text gives only the kana いッとう, which many editors (but not Yokomichi and Omote) convert to 一刀 (one sword).

38. The "Sword of Gathering Clouds" (*murakumo no tsurugi* 叢雲の剣) is one of the three imperial regalia (*sanshu no jingi* 三種の神器; the other two are a mirror and a string of jewels). According to myth, the god Susanoo 素戔嗚 slew a huge snake at Kawakami in Izumo province; the sword emerged from the snake's tail. Susanoo then gave it to his sister, the goddess Amaterasu 天照. It was later called the "Grass-Cutting Sword" (*kusanagi no tsurugi* 草薙の剣) and is venerated at Atsuta Shrine in Nagoya. The Taira took the regalia with them when they fled the capital; Emperor Go-Shirakawa offered to return Shigehira to the Taira in exchange for the regalia, but Munemori refused. The sword was lost in 1185 at Dan-no-ura when Kiyomori's widow Tokiko drowned herself with her grandson Emperor Antoku.

Makes turn to corner pillar, then returns to base square.

that shake the mountains and rivers
of the Aśura realm.   *Stretches arms out, then places*
Relieve Shigehira's rage,   *palms together in prayer.*
please relieve his rage!   *Stamps feet.*

23 ～ *Morihisa* and the Cult of Kannon at Kiyomizudera

| Naoko Gunji

Kiyomizudera 清水寺 is a pilgrimage site in Kyoto devoted to the veneration of Kannon. The legendary tales of Kiyomizudera's origins and the miracles associated with its main devotional icon, Jūichimen Senju Kannon 十一面千手観音 (Eleven-headed, Thousand-armed Kannon), were crucial in promoting the cult of the icon, attracting pilgrims to the temple, and soliciting donations from them. These tales were transmitted through various media, including the performing arts. Among the major media to propagate the efficacy of Kiyomizudera's Kannon was the popular nō play *Morihisa* 盛久. It tells how the Kiyomizudera Kannon miraculously saved the life of the warrior Morihisa when he was on the point of execution. Several occasions of performances of this play were recorded in the Muromachi period (1333–1573). Of these, the one in 1478 may have played an important role in promoting the cult of Kannon and pilgrimage to the temple; it was linked closely with the solicitation (*kanjin* 勧進) campaigns that the temple carried out when it needed financial resources for reconstructing its temple complex from the heavy damage due to the Ōnin War (1467–1477). It was in this period that paintings of temple origin tales (*engi* 縁起) and pilgrimage mandara (*sankei mandara* 参詣曼荼羅) were produced to attract the faithful to Kiyomizudera.[1] It seems that the performance of nō plays and

The author wishes to thank Karen Gerhart, Janet Goodwin, Kōhei Kishida, Elizabeth Oyler, Shelly Quinn, Mae Smethurst, and Michael Watson for their helpful comments.

1. The term *sankei mandara* was first used by the modern Japanese art historian Takeda Tsuneo in the exhibition catalogue of the Kyoto National Museum in 1969.

the creation of *engi* paintings and pilgrimage mandara were essential elements in the *kanjin* campaigns, as many temples used them in order to gain immediate economic benefits directly from the public at that time.

Modern scholars have tended to pay little attention to records of historic performances of *Morihisa* because of the fragmentary nature of the evidence; it is true that the programs that list *Morihisa* tell us little about actual performance practice. They do, however, shed a great deal of light on the possible meaning and function of the play when situated within a specific time and space. This chapter focuses on the staging of *Morihisa* in 1478 by positioning it within its original context of solicitation campaigns. I will examine how one specific nō play might have functioned as an integral component of these solicitation campaigns, one aimed to foster the cult of Kannon at Kiyomizudera and to draw pilgrims to the sacred site.

THE MORIHISA STORY

The play *Morihisa* was written by Kanze Motomasa 観世元雅 (1400?-1432), the first son of Zeami Motokiyo 世阿弥元清 (1363-1443).[2] Motomasa had written the script some time before Zeami

---

The term mandara is a Japanese derivation of the Sanskrit term maṇḍala. I prefer to use "mandara" as opposed to "maṇḍala" in this case because the term maṇḍala usually refers to esoteric mandalas such as the Diamond and Womb Mandalas, that is, geometrical configurations of deities or symbols based on Esoteric Buddhist doctrines. In contrast, *sankei mandara* depict the temple or shrine complexes, including their pilgrims, worshipping at the religious site and along the route to the site. The mandara were not hung on the temple walls or altars as devotional and contemplative images but were used on pilgrimage routes as visual aids, mostly for pedagogical and solicitation ends. For the definition of *sankei mandara*, see Shimosaka Mamoru, *Sankei mandara*, Nihon no bijutsu vol. 331 (Shibundō, 1993), 17–20; Elizabeth ten Grotenhuis, *Japanese Mandalas: Representations of Sacred Geography* (University of Hawai'i Press, 1999), 172.

2. *Go on* 五音 (Five Tones), in which Zeami gives his detailed lists of plays in the fifteenth-century repertory, attributes *Morihisa* to Motomasa. In general, the source of the nō *Morihisa* is considered to be the Nagato-bon *Heike monogatari* because the Nagato version is the only text recounting the story of Morihisa that predates the production of the nō script. A comparative reading of the nō play

edited it in 1423.[3] In the play, the protagonist Morihisa, a Taira warrior captured after the Genpei War (1180–1185), is about to be escorted by the Minamoto retainer Tsuchiya 土屋 from Kyoto to Kamakura, where he expects to be executed. The nō play opens with Morihisa begging Tsuchiya for permission to stop at Kiyomizudera in order to pray to the Kannon one last time, explaining that as a devotee of the Kannon of Kiyomizudera he regularly makes pilgrimages there. At the temple, Morihisa expresses farewell to the Kannon and laments his destiny never again to see the cherry blossoms in full bloom in the capital. Guarded by Minamoto warriors, Morihisa travels the Tōkaidō to Kamakura. On arriving, he is informed that his execution will take place either at daybreak or the following evening. At night Morihisa thanks Tsuchiya for escorting him and starts reciting the *Kannon Sutra* 観音経, the twenty-fifth chapter of the *Lotus Sutra*, which he routinely chants. Morihisa quotes one of the verses from the *Kannon Sutra*:

或遭王難苦　臨刑欲寿終　念彼観音力　刀尋段段壊

wakusōōnanku ringyōyokujuju nebikannonriki tōjindandanne[4]

If a person who faces imminent threat of attack should
call upon the name of the Bodhisattva Perceiver of the
World's Sounds, then the swords and staves wielded by
his attackers will instantly shatter into so many pieces
and he will be delivered.[5]

Morihisa and the Nagato-bon *Heike monogatari* by previous scholars demonstrates that both sources tell basically the same story. Some critics, however, claim that the tale of Morihisa in the Nagato version may not necessarily be the only source of the nō script. Rather, the nō *Morihisa* may have been based on several sources, which were formed around the cult of Kannon, orally transmitted, and duly recorded. *Go on* is available in Omote Akira and Katō Shūichi, *Zeami, Zenchiku*, Nihon shisō taikei vol. 24 (Iwanami shoten, 1979), 209. For a comparative reading of the nō script and the Nagato-bon *Heike monogatari*, see Itō Masayoshi, *Yōkyokushū* (ge), SNKS (Shinchōsha, 1988), 494–46; Takemoto Mikio, *Kanami, Zeami jidai no nōgaku* (Meiji shoin, 1999), 512–29.

3. *Ikomasan Hōzanji shozō kichō shiryō denshi gazōshū*, "Zeami jihitsu *Morihisa*," http://mahoroba.lib.nara-wu.ac.jp/y01/htmls/N10/. Accessed January 11, 2011.

4. *Morihisa* in Koyama Hiroshi, Satō Kikuo, and Satō Ken'ichirō, eds., *Yōkyokushū* (ge), NKBZ 34 (Shōgakukan, 1975), 280.

5. Burton Watson, trans., *The Lotus Sutra* (New York: Columbia University Press, 1993), 299 (translation slightly altered).

At dawn Morihisa drops off to sleep and has an oracular dream in which a senior priest appears and explains that he has come from Kiyomizudera, because of Morihisa's piety, to sacrifice himself for Morihisa. When Morihisa is about to be killed, the executioner's sword mysteriously falls into pieces. This scene corresponds to the verse in the *Kannon Sutra* that Morihisa recited. The incident is reported to the shogun, Minamoto no Yoritomo 源頼朝 (1147–1199), who also had the same strange dream. Yoritomo believes that the miraculous event occurred because of Morihisa's faith in the Kiyomizudera Kannon and thus pardons him. Yoritomo invites Morihisa to a banquet, where Morihisa is ordered to perform a dance celebrating longevity, expressing the wish of long life for Yoritomo, the shogunate, and possibly Morihisa himself. The nō play ends with Morihisa leaving the banquet.

The play *Morihisa* emphasizes the miraculous power of the Kiyomizudera Kannon in response to Morihisa's devotions. Since Morihisa is a pious devotee and recites the *Kannon Sutra* even at the very last moment before execution, most believe that Morihisa is saved through his worship of the Kannon at Kiyomizudera.

KIYOMIZUDERA AND ITS MAIN ICON

Kiyomizudera, which literally means "temple of pure water," is located on Mount Otowa 音羽 in the eastern outskirts of Kyoto. The temple was founded in 778 by the priest Enchin 延鎮 (d. 821). Inspired by an oracular dream, he traced a golden-colored stream to its source in the heart of Mount Otowa, where he met a Buddhist recluse by the name of Gyōei Koji 行叡居士 (b.d. unknown). The recluse showed a log of wood to Enchin and told him to carve a statue of Kannon out of it. This icon, Jūichimen Senju Kannon, was later enshrined in a Buddhist hall donated by the Heian military hero Sakanoue no Tamuramaro 坂上田村麻呂 (758–811).[6] This became the Main Hall of Kiyomizudera.

---

6. The Jūichimen Senju Kannon of Kiyomizudera has forty-four arms (usually this type of Kannon has forty-two arms), symbolizing one thousand arms. It is treated as a secret image and kept from public view except in rare occasions. As a substitute for the hidden Kannon, a statue replica of the icon stands before (*maedachi* 前立ち) the closed shrine.

On the altar of this hall, the Kannon was flanked by statues of Shōgun Jizō 勝軍地蔵 on the left and Bishamonten 毘沙門天 on the right, and Kannon's subordinate twenty-eight attendants (*nijūhachibushū* 二十八 部衆), as well as Wind and Thunder gods (*fūjin* 風神 and *raijin* 雷神). It is the miraculous power of this Jūichimen Senju Kannon that saved Morihisa's life.

The original etymology of the name Kannon is "the all-seeing and all-hearing." As this indicates, this deity of Supreme Mercy and Supreme Compassion protects the peace of the world and the welfare of humankind. According to various Buddhist texts such as the *Lotus Sutra* and the *Visualization Sutra*, Kannon makes vows to benefit all sentient beings by protecting them from seven perils (fire, water, wind or rākṣasa, knives or swords, ghosts, shackles, and enemies).[7] Kannon also descends from the Pure Land to attend Amida Buddha, who will escort the faithful to rebirth in paradise. The immense compassion of Jūichimen Senju Kannon is symbolized by its multitude of heads and arms that gave it the name Kannon of Eleven Heads and Thousand Arms. Because faith in Kannon promises worldly benefits in this life and absolution from one's sins after death, Kannon acquired great popularity among all classes of people in Japan.

PILGRIMS AND THE ECONOMIC NECESSITY OF SOLICITATION CAMPAIGNS

Commensurate with the popularity of Kannon itself, temples holding icons of Kannon attracted pilgrims. Kiyomizudera is the sixteenth of the thirty-three sacred temples of Kannon in the Saikoku 西国 (western provinces) pilgrimage. Even before the itinerary of the Saikoku pilgrimage was established in the late Heian period, the Kannon of Kiyomizudera was already worshipped by the elite as one of the seven major Kannon in Kyoto. The Saikoku pilgrimage became increasingly popular among members of all social classes in the Muromachi period.[8]

---

7. Chün-fang Yü, *Kuan-yin* (New York: Columbia University Press, 2001), 117.
8. Hayami Tasuku, *Kannon shinkō* (Hanawa shobō, 1970), 248–317.

Pilgrims not only represented a substantial economic bounty, but also served as vehicles for the mundane and soteriological benefits of worshipping Kannon. The amounts collected by the temple's offering boxes set out in front of various halls reflected the number of pilgrims visiting the temple. These offerings were vitally important for filling the coffers of larger Buddhist institutions like Kiyomizudera, which otherwise relied heavily on income from agricultural estates (*shōen* 荘園) given to them by emperors or high-ranking nobles and warriors. The income from *shōen* estates, however, was limited and therefore not flexible when temples needed extra financial resources. For example, when a fire occurred, temples needed extra money to rebuild damaged buildings. Over the years the *shōen* system weakened in response to changing political and social conditions and collapsed entirely by the late sixteenth century. Moreover, as the imperial court and the elite aristocrats lost their political and economic power, their financial support of temples naturally declined. The collapse of the estate system and the decline in support from the elite necessitated many Buddhist institutions to raise funds from pilgrims for their economic survival. Nonetheless, the Ōnin War, a civil war that ravaged Kyoto, caused a dramatic decline in pilgrims. Because Kiyomizudera was completely destroyed by fire in 1469, the temple desperately needed extra financial resources to restore its buildings.

It was under these circumstances that the solicitation of funds became the primary basis of the temple's income. The most effective way to collect financial resources was to draw pilgrims directly to Kiyomizudera. In order to attract pilgrims, temple officials found two main strategies crucial to success. First, they had to rebuild the temple complex immediately. Second, they had to spread tales of miracles of the Kiyomizudera Kannon. These two strategies were executed through *kanjin* campaigns. The term *kanjin* is an abbreviation of *kan'yū sakushin* 勧誘策進, and its official purpose was to induce lay people to form a spiritual connection (*kechien* 結縁) with a particular Buddhist icon.[9] This religious dimension of *kanjin* was important for both the temple and lay believers; the temple could disseminate Buddhist teachings

---

9. For an example of studies on the solicitation campaigns, see Nakanodō Kazunobu, "Chūseiteki kanjin no tenkai," *Geinōshi kenkyū* 62 (July 1978), 12–35; Janet R. Goodwin, "Building Bridges and Saving Souls: The Fruits of Evangelism in Medieval Japan," *Monumenta Nipponica* 44:2 (Summer 1989), 137–49; Janet R. Goodwin, "Alms for Kasagi Temple," *The Journal of Asian Studies* 46:4 (November 1987), 827–41.

to the public, while the lay people could satisfy their spiritual needs through the practice of *kechien* that would be of special benefit to them in this life and the next. In addition, *kanjin* acquired more pragmatic functions to meet the temple's financial needs. The economic aspect of *kanjin*, soliciting contributions directly from believers, became crucial to the management of religious institutions. During the Muromachi period, especially under the financial strains caused by the Ōnin War, the solicitation of funds served as the central vehicle for the repair and reconstruction of the buildings in the temple complex.

SOLICITATION PERFORMANCES

Faced with a financial crisis, temples had to practice solicitation campaigns effectively, and they chose to employ various forms of media in their campaigns. The performing arts became a major component of the solicitation of funds from the public; by the fifteenth century events frequently took place on the grounds of temples and shrines, on the banks of rivers, and at crossroads of vacant lands in Kyoto.[10] The Muromachi era saw the growing popularity of the performing arts among people at all levels of society.

In order to watch nō performances, the audience was required to make a donation by buying tickets. The price of tickets for nō performances varied with the types of seats. There were two kinds of seats: the general seating area (*shibai* 芝居) and the raised box seat (*zashiki* 座敷). Tickets for the general seating area were purchased normally by commoners at the door on the day of performance, whereas tickets for the box seat were reserved by elite nobles and warriors in advance. Besides purchasing tickets, some audience members donated rice, supplies, or money and in return received *kanjin fuda* 勧進札, "wood or paper strips acknowledging the receipt of their contributions."[11] Although there are

---

10. The earliest documentation of an actual subscription nō is found in an entry of the year 1317 in *Kagenki* 嘉元記. See Hayashiya Tatsusaburō, *Chūsei bunka no kichō* (Tōkyō daigaku shuppankai, 1982), 163–67.

11. Barbara Ruch, "The Other Side of Culture in Medieval Japan," in *The Cambridge History of Japan*, vol. 3, ed. Yamamura Kōzō (New York: Cambridge University Press, 1990), 520.

only a few references to the ticket prices of nō performances during the Muromachi period, Nose Asaji has suggested that the ticket cost of nō plays was similar to that of *kusemai* 曲舞 (a popular song and dance with a lively drum rhythm). In the case of a subscription performance of *kusemai* of 1423, a ticket for the general seating area cost ten *mon* 文, whereas a ticket for a box seat cost between three hundred and five hundred *mon*, about thirty to fifty times as expensive as those for general seats.[12] General seating tickets were more affordably priced for purchase by commoners.

The seating for the nō performances was constructed temporarily in the open air. According to Zeami's *Sarugaku dangi* 申楽談義 (Discourses on the Nō), the stands for solicitation nō were constructed on a lavish scale, measuring sixty-two or sixty-three *ken* 間, approximately 102 meters.[13] In the case of the solicitation performances that took place at the Tadasu riverbank 糺河原 in 1433 and 1464, the stands measured sixty-three *ken*. A sketch of the 1464 performance in the *Tadasu gawara sarugaku zu* 糺河原猿楽図 shows the appearance of the performance space.[14] The stage was surrounded by the stands, which were built in a large circle to accommodate as many spectators as possible. The box seats in the front stand were for the most important spectators, normally the shogun and his party. High-ranking aristocrats, warriors, and monks took their box seats on the other three sides along the perimeter of the stage. Spectators of low-ranking social classes watched from the general seating area on the ground between the stage and the stands. This particular spatial organization enabled the organizer of the *kanjin nō* performance to obtain considerable profits. For this reason, solicitation performances were utilized by many religious institutions as one of the most effective methods in gaining immediate economic benefits from the public.

---

12. Nose Asaji, *Nōgaku genryūkō* (Iwanami shoten, 1938), 1061–62.

13. One *ken,* the width between two pillars, is five *shaku* 尺, approximately 166.5 cm. *Sarugaku dangi* in Omote and Katō, *Zeami, Zenchiku*, 292.

14. See *Ihon Tadasugawara kanjin sarugakuki*, Gunsho ruijū vol. 19 (Yoshikawa kōbunkan, 1984), 814–15. The description that follows relies on Erika de Poorter, *Zeami's Talks on Sarugaku* (Amsterdam: J. C. Gieben, 1986), 24, and P. G. O'Neill, *Early Nō Drama* (London: Lund Humphries, 1958), 79.

Kiyomizudera's Solicitation Campaigns

Before examining how *Morihisa* may have functioned as a means of increasing profits for Kiyomizudera, it is imperative to understand Kiyomizudera's solicitation campaigns, which likely affected the nō performance. Kiyomizudera's solicitation campaigns were headed by Gan'ami 願阿弥 (d. 1486), an itinerant holy man, or *hijiri* 聖, of the Ji sect (*Jishū* 時宗).[15] He had been widely recognized through his other charitable works as a great *kanjin hijiri* in Kyoto even before the Ōnin War. For example, he built a temporary shelter where he provided food to starving people during the great famine of 1461.[16] He also played a leading role in public works projects, such as the construction of the Shijō and Gojō bridges. Gan'ami's *kanjin* campaigns for Kiyomizudera, which had been burnt in 1469 during the Ōnin War, began with the casting of a new bronze bell in 1478 at the crossroads near Seiganji 誓願寺. The names of eighty prominent donors are carved on the surface of the bell. A ceremony was held at the crossroads for the dedication of the bell, and crowded with thousands of people from all levels of society. And four days after the bell was cast, the general public pulled the cart carrying the bell to Kiyomizudera.[17] The ceremony provided an opportunity for Kiyomizudera to raise funds from the public.[18]

As a result of the success of the dedication ceremony of the bell, Gan'ami received an official appointment as the head of the *hongan* 本願, a *kanjin* office, which specialized primarily in the projects of the solicitation as well as the construction and repair of the buildings within Kiyomizudera. Despite the great success of Gan'ami's *kanjin* in 1478,

---

15. The following information regarding Gan'ami's solicitation campaigns for Kiyomizudera is largely from Shimosaka Mamoru, "Hongan to jike," in *Kiyomizuderashi* vol. 1, ed. Kiyomizuderashi hensan iinkai (Kyoto: Hōzōkan, 1995), 267–344.

16. See, for instance, the entry for Kanshō 2.3.26 in *Kyōgaku shiyōshō*, Shiryō sanshū vol. 2 (Zoku Gunsho ruijū kanseikai, 1971), 78–79; the entry for Kanshō 3.2.4 in *Gaun nikkenroku batsuyū*, Dai Nihon kokiroku vol. 13 (Iwanami shoten, 1992), 112.

17. See the entry for Bunmei 10.4.17 in *Haretomi sukune ki* (Meiji shoin, 1971), 35.

18. A few days after the transportation of the bell, *Morihisa* was performed at the same location as the bell had just been cast. I will discuss below the connection between these two events.

however, Kiyomizudera lacked its most important treasure: the sacred main icon, Jūichimen Senju Kannon. The icon had been rescued from the fire that destroyed the Main Hall, and was still housed in a temporary hall. It was urgent to reconstruct the Main Hall so that Jūichimen Senju Kannon, the source of miraculous power, could be enshrined in it.

The *kanjin* mission to rebuild the Main Hall was challenging yet significant. Although the current Main Hall of Kiyomizudera was reconstructed again in the Edo period after the fire of 1629, pictorial and textual evidence demonstrates that the Main Hall in the Muromachi period was similar to the present-day hall that measures thirty-six meters wide by thirty meters deep.[19] A stage connected to the front of the massive Main Hall, where the Kannon is installed, protrudes beyond the edge of the cliff; it is buttressed by wooden beams extending thirteen meters down into the rock below. From this architectural feature, one may easily imagine that the reconstruction project required substantial commitments of time and money.

In order to finance the reconstruction of the Main Hall, Gan'ami and other soliciting monks traveled widely throughout Japan. Their accomplishment is evident in the *kanjinchō* 勧進帳 (subscription document recounting the temple's origin tale [*engi*] and the purpose of *kanjin*) and *hōgachō* 奉加帳 (list of subscribers) that Gan'ami made in 1479. The former document was read in front of potential subscribers to explain the need for raising money. The latter reports approximately 160 subscribers, including Hino Tomiko 日野富子 (1440–1496), who donated one hundred and twenty *kan* 貫 for six wooden pillars.[20] This list also includes many *daimyō* 大名 (great lords) from different regions. Nineteen provinces are mentioned on the list and other documents, ranging from Suruga (present-day Shizuoka) in the east to Satsuma

---

19. For the pictorial evidence, see, for example, *Kiyomizudera engi emaki* and *Kiyomizudera sankei mandara*. *Kiyomizudera engi emaki* is currently preserved at the Tokyo National Museum; reproduced in Komatsu Shigemi, *Kiyomizudera engi, Shinnyodō engi*, Zoku zoku Nihon emaki taisei vol. 5 (Chūō kōronsha, 1994). Two sets of *Kiyomizudera sankei mandara* survive today. One of them is preserved in the Tokyo National Museum; the other is stored in a private collection; reproduced in Shimosaka, *Sankei mandara*, 8–9.

20. *Jōjuin monjo* in Kiyomizuderashi hensan iinkai, ed., *Kiyomizuderashi* vol. 3 (Kyoto: Hōzōkan, 2000), 80–85. One *kan* of copper coins was equivalent to one thousand *mon* of copper coins.

(present-day Kagoshima) in the south.[21] Soliciting monks organized under Gan'ami traveled around the country, targeting elite aristocrats and warriors for donations.[22]

Through the efforts of fund-raising monks, the Main Hall of Kiyomizudera was finally completed in 1484. In a diverse crowd of high and low statuses, Gan'ami arranged a special ceremony for transferring the main icon, the Jūichimen Senju Kannon, to the new hall, an event long awaited by residents of Kyoto. Great numbers surged into the temple complex to witness the rituals and to gain benefits from the Kannon. The rituals of re-enshrining the Kannon were, in fact, reported in many diaries of the elite,[23] including that of Kanroji Chikanaga 甘露寺親長 (1424–1500), who witnessed that monks carried a palanquin in which the Kannon was placed and musicians performed celebratory rituals in front of the newly installed Kannon.[24] For the next ten days Kiyomizudera performed a ceremony of one thousand sutras called *Senbukyō-e* 千部経会, in which either one thousand monks recited a sutra or one monk recited a sutra one thousand times.[25] All of these monumental rites were initiated by Gan'ami.

In the following year, Gan'ami requested permission from Kiyomizudera's head temple Kōfukuji 興福寺 to arrange a public viewing of the Jūichimen Senju Kannon. In general, the display of an icon that is usually hidden (*kaichō* 開帳, opening of a curtain) attracts large numbers of pilgrims and provides special opportunities for them to establish Buddhist karmic bonds with the icon. The direct and

---

21. Among them, the Asakura clan 朝倉氏, the *daimyō* in Echizen (present-day Fukui prefecture), made the largest contribution to Kiyomizudera; for example, Asakura Ujikage 朝倉氏景 (1449–1486) and Asakura Sadakage 朝倉貞景 (1473–1512) each donated one thousand *kan* for fifty wooden pillars. *Jōjuin monjo* in Kiyomizuderashi hensan iinkai, *Kiyomizuderashi* vol. 3, 80–85. Also, for the Shimazu clan of Satsuma, see *Shimazuke monjo* in *Kiyomizuderashi* vol. 3, 85.

22. Shimosaka, "Hongan to jike," 265–344.

23. See the entry for Bunmei 16.6.27 in the following references: *Oyudono no ue no nikki*, Zoku Gunsho ruijū hoi vol. 3 (Zoku Gunsho ruijū kanseikai, 1957), 354; *Inryōken nichiroku*, Zōho zoku shiryō taisei vol. 22 (Kyoto: Rinsen shoten, 1978), 165–66; *Daijōin jisha zōjiki*, Zōho zoku shiryō taisei vol. 33 (Kyoto: Rinsen shoten, 1994), 189.

24. *Chikanaga kyōki*, Zōho zoku shiryō taisei vol. 42 (Kyoto: Rinsen shoten, 1975), 221–22.

25. The *Senbukyō-e* was attended by shogun Ashikaga Yoshihisa. *Shōken nichiroku*, Dai Nihon kokiroku vol. 3 (Iwanami shoten, 1953), 20.

personal contact with the icon is believed to be effective in acquiring spiritual merit that assures happiness in this life and salvation after death. This is why it was a fairly typical strategy in a *kanjin* campaign for a temple to display its hidden icon. Images of Kannon, especially those installed in the temples on the Saikoku pilgrimage route, Kiyomizudera included, are considered so sacred that most of them are kept hidden and are revealed to the public infrequently or, in several cases, not at all. Indeed, throughout its entire history until Gan'ami's time, Kiyomizudera had never shown its Kannon to the public. If such an icon were to be put on display, the temple undoubtedly could expect numerous visitors with cash offerings, and it would have allowed Gan'ami to rebuild many other halls. Nonetheless, his sudden death in 1486 prevented this event, and Kiyomizudera missed a great opportunity for an upsurge in popular devotion.[26] The cancellation of the event indicates how important Gan'ami was as a charismatic leader.

ALTERNATIVE MEDIA FOR SOLICITATION

After the loss of Gan'ami, Kiyomizudera needed to find new ways to attract pilgrims. To this end, the temple produced alternative media, such as illustrated scrolls of the temple's origin tale (*engi*) and pilgrimage *mandara*. The project of producing the *Kiyomizudera engi emaki* 清水寺縁起絵巻 (illustrated handscrolls of Kiyomizudera's origin tales) was initiated by Kanroji Motonaga 甘露寺元長 (1467–1527) in 1517. The lavish production of the scrolls utilized expensive materials and necessitated the collaboration of high-ranking aristocrats, monks, and the finest painters of the day.[27] As is common in such paintings,

---

26. It was not until 1629 that Kiyomizudera first displayed the Jūichimen Senju Kannon, and this display was only for three days. This event followed a fire that broke out in the Kiyomizudera compound in the same year. Because the damage from the fire was so extensive, people started rumors that Kiyomizudera had lost its Kannon. Kiyomizudera needed to display the Kannon not only to deny the rumors but also to collect donations from the public for restoration of its lost buildings. Since that time the *kaichō* of the Jūichimen Senju Kannon takes place every thirty-three years.

27. The most prestigious calligraphers and painters of the time collaborated

the *Kiyomizudera engi emaki* recounts the origin tale of the temple and legendary accounts associated with the miraculous power of its main devotional image, Jūichimen Senju Kannon. For example, the scrolls illustrate how Sakanoue no Tamuramaro, an ardent devotee of the Kiyomizudera Kannon, defeated the northern barbarians under the divine protection of the Kannon. The legendary tale depicted in *Morihisa* is also included in the scrolls. These tales of miraculous events were meant to impress the viewers of the scrolls and solicit donations from them.

Although the functions of painted scrolls of *engi*, founding legends of temples, varied with specific contexts, many of them were used as instruments of solicitation campaigns, in a manner similar to textual *engi*, which were often produced as part of subscription documents. The final inscription on the *Taimadera engi emaki* 当麻寺縁起絵巻 (painted scroll of Taimadera's origin tales) in Ninnaji 仁和寺 in fact explicitly states that it served as a subscription document for restoring the Mandaradō 曼荼羅堂.[28] For another example, when a nun called Sen'amidabutsu 専阿弥陀仏 (b.d. unknown) visited Katsuōji 勝尾寺, she was shown the *Katsuōji engi emaki* 勝尾寺縁起絵巻. Viewing the illustrated scroll of Katsuōji's legendary tales accompanied by a monk's narration of the painting moved the nun so deeply that she decided to donate rice fields to the temple.[29] Also, the courtier Nakamikado Nobutane stated that seeing a set of the painted scrolls of Seiganji's origin tales increased his faith in the main icon Amida Buddha of Seiganji. Given these examples, it is highly likely that the *Kiyomizudera engi emaki* also had a solicitation function and circulated among the elite. The viewers of its elaborate illustrations were probably convinced of the beneficial effects of Kannon and redoubled their devotion to the Kannon.[30] In this way, Kiyomizudera presumably encouraged upper class viewers to make a pilgrimage to the temple and then solicited substantial donations from them.

---

in the production of *Kiyomizudera engi emaki*. The six aristocratic scribes of the scrolls were all prominent figures in the Muromachi cultural realm. They included, for example, Nakamikado Nobutane 中御門宣胤 (1442–1525) and Sanjōnishi Sanetaka 三条西実隆 (1455–1532), who were high-ranking courtiers and masters of calligraphy. The illustrations were rendered by Tosa Mitsunobu 土佐光信 (d. 1522) and his pupils.

28. Komatsu Shigemi, *Taima mandara engi, Chigo kannon engi*, Zoku Nihon no emaki vol. 20 (Chūō kōronsha, 1992), 72–91.

29. Tokuda Kazuo, *Egatari to monogatari* (Heibonsha, 1990), 312–14.

30. See the entry of Bunki 2.4.3 in *Nobutane kyōki*, Zōho shiryō taisei vol. 44 (Kyoto: Rinsen shoten, 1985), 20.

Another important medium in promoting the cult of Kannon was the *Kiyomizudera sankei mandara* 清水寺参詣曼荼羅 (Kiyomizudera pilgrimage mandara), datable to around 1545.[31] Pilgrimage mandara with detailed representations of the temple compound were utilized along pilgrimage routes for preaching, propagation, and solicitation for contribution. Monks and nuns used the mandara as visual aids for guiding pilgrims to the sacred sites, as well as for telling stories associated with the sacred geography. In contrast to illustrated handscrolls, the intended audience here was generally the lower classes. How these mandara were produced remains unclear, but Shimosaka Mamoru has suggested that painting workshops perhaps received the commission of pilgrimage mandara from the *kokuya* 穀屋 (or *hongan*), the office of subscription.[32]

The *Kiyomizudera sankei mandara* depicts pilgrims practicing worship, as well as their entertainments at the height of spring, the most beautiful season of the temple. By showing the pilgrimage routes that the mandara re-creates, a monk or nun invites the viewers to enter from the Gojō bridge at the left lower corner of the painting, and then to travel to numerous locales where they practice worship for benefits. They are guided to the Main Hall, where they can pray to Kannon as well as enjoy the view of cherry blossoms from the stage. In front of many halls, collection boxes are set out, next to which solicitors stretch out wooden collection dippers to the visitors. In this way, the *Kiyomizudera sankei mandara* functioned not only as a map of the sacred site but also as a guide showing where in the temple the pilgrims were expected to donate money. By shifting their perspectives along the passages in the painting accompanied by the monk's or nun's narration, the viewers must have experienced their imaginary pilgrimage to Kiyomizudera.

In addition, the *Kiyomizudera sankei mandara* contains some scenes of the temple's founding legends (*engi*). For example, it depicts the twelfth-century semi-legendary fight between Ushiwakamaru 牛若丸 (Minamoto no Yoshitsune 源義経 in his childhood) and the warrior monk Benkei 弁慶 on the Gojō bridge.[33] In the bottom right corner of the painting are a monk and a hunter who can be identified as the priest Enchin and Sakanoue no Tamuramaro, the founders of Kiyomizudera.

---

31. For a discussion of the use of *sankei mandara*, see Shimosaka, *Sankei mandara*, 17–20; ten Grotenhuis, 172–73.

32. For the detailed analysis of *Kiyomizudera sankei mandara*, see Shimosaka, *Sankei mandara*, 32–48; for a discussion of the painting workshops, see ibid., 66–80.

33. Tokuda Kazuo, "Etoki to monogatari kyōju," *Bungaku* 54 (1986), 191–204.

The same pair of characters appears again, slightly left of the center of the painting.[34] By incorporating legendary tales in the explanation of the sacred map, monks and nuns combined teaching and proselytizing activities into the recitation of the pilgrimage mandara.

MORIHISA AS A SOLICITATION PERFORMANCE

Nō performance functioned in the same way as the pilgrimage mandara and the painted scrolls of Kiyomizudera's origin tales by promoting the cult of Kannon, attracting pilgrims to the temple, and soliciting donations from the viewers. Yet, it had a larger intended audience, both in number and by social classes, than the illustrated scrolls and the pilgrimage mandara. The *Kiyomizudera engi emaki* was probably read by at most three aristocrats at one time; similarly, the *Kiyomizudera sankei mandara* was likely seen by perhaps ten commoners at one time. By contrast, performing arts and their stage settings, in which actual actors created a dramatic scene, reached much broader audiences. As we have seen, the stands constructed for nō dramas could accommodate a large audience with representatives from all levels of society. By omitting unnecessary details, the nō performance captures the essence of the story; at the same time, it conveys the ineffable moods and emotions of the characters to the masses in a straightforward and dramatic manner.

As far as documented in historical records, *Morihisa* was performed on several occasions in the Muromachi period.[35] The earliest documentation of an actual performance of *Morihisa* is found in a program dated to 1478, and it presents an interesting case.[36] Although the program of the play is fragmentary, there are other records from which it is possible to reconstruct the circumstances of that specific

---

34. The pilgrimage mandara utilizes the narrative device of *ijidōzu* 異時同図, in which the same characters are depicted in several different places of the same picture that represent different times.

35. For a list of actual performances of nō plays from the fourteenth to the sixteenth centuries, see Nose, *Nōgaku genryūkō*, 1260–1315.

36. The performance lasted three days, but only the first day of the program survives. Nose, *Nōgaku genryūkō*, 1262.

performance.[37] On the twenty-second day of the Fourth Month of 1478, the Kanze 観世 troupe, one of the most prestigious professional nō troupes, performed *Morihisa* at the crossroads near Seiganji.[38] This event itself was held in part for a solicitation campaign of Seiganji, which had also lost many of its buildings during the Ōnin War.

The *kanjin nō* of 1478 was performed on a grand scale and attended by the ninth Ashikaga shogun Yoshihisa 義尚 (r. 1473–1489), the former shogun Ashikaga Yoshimasa 足利義政 (r. 1449–1473), and his wife Hino Tomiko.[39] *Daijōin jisha zōjiki* 大乗院寺社雑事記, a record kept by the priest Jinson 尋尊 (1430–1508) at the cloister of Kōfukuji, indicates that the stands for the nō of 1478 extended over sixty *ken*, or approximately one hundred meters in length; they looked like the ones built at the Tadasu riverbank in 1433 and 1464, mentioned above.[40] As with the solicitation nō performances at the Tadasu riverbank, the audience for the Seiganji *kanjin nō* consisted of people from all social levels. The box seats were filled with elite warriors, aristocrats, and monks, whereas the general seating areas were occupied by ordinary spectators. Interestingly, this 1478 performance for Seiganji was given at the very site where Kiyomizudera had cast its bronze bell just a week earlier.

The reason *Morihisa* was staged on the same spot where Kiyomizudera's bell had been cast may be simply explained by the fact that the crossroads were one of the common places where performing arts were held. It is, however, important to note that Kiyomizudera also executed its solicitation campaigns around the same time as Seiganji did. Given that the performance of *Morihisa* indeed took place in the midst of *kanjin* campaigns for Kiyomizudera, it was probably not coincidental that the Kanze troupe performed a play that emphasized the miraculous power of the Kiyomizudera Kannon.

---

37. Historical references to this specific event appear in many sources. For example, see *Chikamoto nikki*, Zōho zoku shiryō taisei vol. 11 (Kyoto: Rinsen shoten, 1994), 280; *Chikanaga kyōki*, 12; *Sanetaka kōki* vol. 1 (Zoku Gunsho ruijū kanseikai, 1958), 280; *Daijōin jisha zōjiki*, 411–14; *Haretomi sukune ki* (Meiji shoin, 1971), 36.

38. Seiganji, which is affiliated with the Seizan sect of Pure Land Buddhism, attracted faithful devotees to its main icon, Amida Buddha. Seiganji, due to damage from repeated fires during the Muromachi period, utilized *kanjin* campaigns as a lucrative means of public fundraising.

39. *Haretomi sukune ki*, 36

40. *Daijōin jisha zōjiki*, 414.

As previously mentioned, the prime motivation behind the staging of the *kanjin nō* in 1478 was to solicit funds for Seiganji. The relationship between Seiganji and Kiyomizudera is not specifically documented, yet the solicitation campaigns for both temples were undertaken primarily by itinerant monks and nuns of the Ji sect, to which Gan'ami belonged. Because most of these soliciting monks and nuns did not affiliate with a single institution but rather engaged in various soliciting activities, it is likely that the same monks and nuns worked for these two temples. The monk who initiated and headed Seiganji's solicitation campaigns was called by the title *kanjin hijiri jukkoku shamon* 勧進聖十穀沙門, although his name is unknown.[41] This title referred to an itinerant holy man who did not eat ten kinds of grains such as rice, beans, and sesame. Gan'ami was also sometimes called by this title.[42] As stated earlier, Gan'ami actively contributed to other temples' solicitation campaigns along with Kiyomizudera's. Because of these historical circumstances, it is quite probable that Gan'ami and his colleagues worked for both Seiganji and Kiyomizudera.

Moreover, it seems impossible to isolate the Seiganji performance of *Morihisa* from its connection to Kiyomizudera's solicitation campaign, as these two events took place at exactly the same place and almost the same time. It is also difficult to believe that Gan'ami, a charismatic *kanjin hijiri* who was certainly familiar with various solicitation methods, did not recognize that the performing arts were the most effective way to promote the cult of Kannon, to draw the faithful to the temple and to collect financial resources. In other words, Kiyomizudera may have made the best use of the opportunity, initiated by the Seiganji *kanjin nō*, for its own purposes.

It is important to note that, as mentioned above, collecting money is not the only purpose of *kanjin*; it embodies both economic and religious values. Janet Goodwin argues that *kanjin* was part of Buddhist efforts "to save people's souls," and teaching of Buddhism was a crucial part of *kanjin* practice.[43] It is then plausible that, also in performing *Morihisa* in 1478, Gan'ami intended to convey certain teachings to numerous spectators through the performance of the play. What teachings were they?

---

41. See the entry for Bunmei 9.6.26 in *Nagaoki sukune ki, Shiryō sanshū* vol. 115 (Zoku Gunsho ruijū kanseikai, 1998), 53.

42. See *Gohōkōin ki, Zōho zoku shiryō taisei* vol. 6 (Kyoto: Rinsen shoten, 1994), 19; *Haretomi sukune ki*, 35; *Inryōken nichiroku*, 165.

43. Goodwin, "Building Bridges and Saving Souls," 148.

How did the performance reinforce the Kannon of Kiyomizudera as a source of miraculous power? How did it enhance people's faith in the Kannon? In order to address these questions, the final section of this chapter will be devoted to a brief analysis of the nō text of *Morihisa*.

THE MESSAGE OF *MORIHISA*

Morihisa has been interpreted by modern scholars in various ways, but their interpretations agree in that the primary theme from this play is Kannon's compassion, which can be gained through devotion and pilgrimage. In order to convince the audience of the significance of its theme, the play offers an easily understandable and appealing form. *Morihisa* also addresses one of the most fundamental issues involved in the worship of Kannon, and ultimately resolves it by showing how the protagonist was saved through his faith in the Kannon of Kiyomizudera.

Beginning with Morihisa's last pilgrimage to Kiyomizudera (prior to his departure for Kamakura), the play stresses the importance of pilgrimage to the temple. In this scene he is seated, with his palms pressed together in supplication, in front of the closed cabinet in which the main icon of Kiyomizudera is installed. He asserts:

> All honor and praise to Kannon, whose benevolence and compassion are boundless, whose sacred Vow, like those moxa grasses, will save whomsoever, in just one utterance of his name or one pious thought, believes in him. ... All the more for me, how could my many years of cultivating my precious connection with you be in vain?[44]

The line emphasizes the protection that Kannon provides for worshippers. With the rhetorical question, Morihisa expresses his belief that, because he obtained a karmic link with the Kannon through his faith and pilgrimage to Kiyomizudera, he will be saved. Later, when Morihisa is allowed to recite the *Kannon Sutra* the day before his execution, he holds the sutra scroll and prays:

---

44. Koyama et al., *Yōkyokushū* (ge), 275. Translated by Quinn in this volume.

All thanks and praise for the boundless benevolence
and compassion that is the Bodhisattva's Vow. It is
said that with Kannon's grace even fixed karma may
change. What I ask is that you let your unconditional
benevolence and mercy fall upon me, and lead me
on the path. If he wants for blessings in this life, who
would ask for salvation in the next? If prayers for this
life and the next are in vain, then would it not make the
great saint's Vow a lie?[45]

His bold and straightforward statement repeatedly raises questions
central to the cult of Kannon; the extreme situation that Morihisa is
facing challenges his faith with a doubt as to whether the Kannon's mercy
and compassion are going to save him. This doubt is resolved in the
climactic scene in which the execution sword shatters into pieces and
Morihisa is saved through his devotion to the Kiyomizudera Kannon.
This dramatized scene is designed to prove Kannon's vow to save all
sentient beings under any circumstances.

Other statements made by the characters highlight the primary
message of the play. For example, after the executioner's sword breaks
into pieces, Morihisa, Tsuchiya, and the chorus state the reason why
the protagonist was saved and praise the spiritual power of the Kannon.
Moreover, the old priest who appears in Morihisa's dream asserts
that Kannon's vow is true. All of these passages are carefully inserted
to reinforce the message that a person who undertakes a pilgrimage
and establishes a spiritual tie with the Kiyomizudera Kannon will be
ensured of a reward and will not experience misfortune. Morihisa's
sincere devotion to the Kiyomizudera Kannon is further stressed when
he chants Kannon's name even at the moment of his execution, facing
the direction of the west, where Kiyomizudera is located. The audiences
must have been convinced by what they saw and heard in the play. Such
scenes erased their doubt as to the power of Kannon and deepened
their devotion to the deity. The performance of *Morihisa* must have
encouraged people to spiritually bond with the Kannon of Kiyomizudera
through their pilgrimage in order to obtain this-worldly benefits, as well
as salvation in the next world. The nō performance therefore played a
vital role in the popularization of the Kannon cult. Moreover, the fact
that *Morihisa* was staged in the midst of Kiyomizudera's solicitation

---

45. Koyama et al., *Yōkyokushū* (ge), 279–80. Translated by Quinn in this volume.

campaigns perhaps attests to the significance of the performance of 1478 as an effective medium in conveying its principal message, which was essential to the promotion of the cult of the Kannon and the pilgrimage to the temple.[46]

CONCLUSION

The tales of miracles, which promoted the sacredness of the site and the increase in its pilgrims, were transmitted through various media, including painted scrolls of the temple's origins, pilgrimage mandara, and performing arts. When Kiyomizudera strove to acquire extra financial resources to reconstruct buildings in the aftermath of the Ōnin War, the temple utilized the *Kiyomizudera engi*, *Kiyomizudera sankei mandara*, and nō performances, all of which emphasized the miraculous power of the Kannon of the temple. These art forms, which not only reflected but also enhanced the popularity of Kannon, served as indispensable components in the solicitation campaigns, by helping the temple to fundraise as well as proselytize. The ability of the performing arts to display the miraculous power of Kannon directly and dramatically to large audiences may have played a chief role in attracting pilgrims who wished to obtain worldly benefits in this life and rebirth in paradise. The performance of *Morihisa*, in particular, raises a central issue in the worship of Kannon—the doubt as to whether Kannon really saves the faithful—and resolves it by showing how Morihisa was saved through his faith in the Kannon of Kiyomizudera. It is therefore probable that *Morihisa* played a compelling role in helping the temple promote the cult of the Kiyomizudera Kannon.

---

46. To my knowledge, no records indicate that nō performances took place in the Kiyomizudera compound during the Muromachi period. Yet, even if the play *Morihisa* was performed in a different place, people might have associated it with the stage of Kiyomizudera because this stage has been a landmark of Kyoto for many centuries. In 2000, on the occasion of displaying the hidden Jūichimen Senju Kannon, the nō play *Tamura* 田村, which recounts an origin tale of the temple, was held at Kiyomizudera on the famous stage. Thousands of people crowded Kiyomizudera to witness this special nō ritual. Although this is a recent performance, the combination of the nō play and Kiyomizudera's stage might have been effective in promoting the cult of the Kannon even in the medieval period.

24 ～ Performing Kannon's Grace:
The Nō *Morihisa* | Shelley Fenno Quinn

THE PLAY *MORIHISA* 盛久

In his critical treatise on vocal styles titled *Go on* 五音 (Five tones, undated), Zeami Motokiyo 世阿弥元清 (1363?–1443?) attributes authorship of one passage of *Morihisa* to his son, Kanze Jūrō Motomasa 観世十郎元雅 (?–1432).[1] For this reason, Motomasa is thought to be the author of the play. The passage in question comes near the beginning. It is a *sashi* サシ (recitative) allotted to the *shite* シテ, a hereditary retainer in the defeated Taira 平 clan who goes by the title Shume no Hangan Morihisa 主馬の判官盛久 (Police Lieutenant Morihisa, Head of the Crown Prince's Stables). Morihisa offers it in prayer to the bodhisattva Kanzeon 観世音 (or Kannon 観音) at the Buddhist temple Kiyomizudera

---

1. In *Go on* Zeami enumerates exemplars of five different vocal styles: *shūgen* 祝言 (celebratoriness), *yūgen* 幽玄, *renbo* 恋慕 (passionate love), *aishō* 哀傷 (lamentation), and *rangyoku* 闌曲 (seasoned fluency). Though he does not explicitly label which of his five vocal styles the *Morihisa* passage is supposed to exemplify, it is treated as one of a group of excerpts from nō texts clustered directly after Zeami's discussion of the vocal style having the aesthetic quality of *yūgen* (variously glossed as ineffable "grace," "elegance," "beauty"). He advises that the *yūgen* style should build on the more basic style, *shūgen*, but the melodic line itself should receive less emphasis to allow beauty of mood to come to the fore. It is interesting to note that *yūgen*, a quality that Zeami elsewhere ascribed to certain types of characters (especially those who were "elegant" and female), seems here to be ascribed to the *mode* of exposition—the musical atmosphere—and in reference to the depiction of a warrior. See Omote Akira and Katō Shūichi, eds., *Zeami, Zenchiku* (Iwanami shoten, 1995), 208–9.

清水寺,[2] in the capital of Kyoto 京都. Kiyomizudera was and continues to be an important pilgrimage spot for worshipers of Kannon,[3] and it had been the site of devoted pilgrimages on Morihisa's part for years.

After the Taira defeat in the Genpei 源平 War (1180–1185), the military government (*bakufu* 幕府) founded by the victorious Minamoto 源 clan set out to hunt down the surviving male Taira and execute them. The play opens with Morihisa already held captive after falling into their snare while on one of his daily visits to Kiyomizudera. In the first scene, his jailer and escort, a Minamoto retainer by the name

---

2. Kiyomizudera 清水寺 (Kiyomizu Temple; also pronounced Seisuiji): located in the Higashiyama 東山 hills on the eastern perimeter of the city of Kyoto. The temple was founded in the late eighth century by Enchin shōnin 延鎮上人 (Saint Enchin, d. 821), with the assistance of the celebrated military commander Sakanoue no Tamuramaro 坂上田村麻呂 (758–811). Tamuramaro had been enlightened by Enchin's teachings and erected the main hall to house the sacred statue of Kannon that Enchin had carved. The formal name for the temple dating from that time is Otowa-san Kita Kannonji 音羽山北観音寺. Kiyomizudera is situated on Otowayama 音羽山 (Otowa Hill), where the falls known as Otowa no taki 音羽山ノ滝 (Otowa Falls) are located. The water of this falls is known for its purity, whence the more familiar name for this temple, Kiyomizudera, or "Clearwater Temple." At first the temple belonged to the Shingon 真言 sect, but it joined the Hossō 法相 sect in the late eleventh century upon its affiliation with the Hossō temple Kōfukuji 興福寺 in Nara. In 1965 it gained independent standing as the headquarters and sole member of the Kita Hossō shū 北法相宗 ("Northern Hossō sect"). The principal object of worship at Kiyomizu is the statue carved by Enchin of Jūichimen Senju Kannon 十一面千手観音, "Eleven-headed, thousand-armed Kannon." (For more on this statue and its significance, see Chapter 23 in this volume.) In the play *Morihisa*, this statue, known as Kiyomizu Kannon 清水観音, is depicted as the power that spares Morihisa's life. The temple has always attracted many visitors, especially during the cherry blossom and autumn foliage seasons when the view of the capital from its hillside vantage point is especially splendid. Kiyomizudera is the setting for the nō titled *Tamura* 田村, a warrior play featuring Tamuramaro.

3. Kanzeon Bosatsu 観世音菩薩, the bodhisattva Kanzeon (Skt. Avalokiteśvara, lit. "One who observes the sounds of the world"); a bodhisattva widely revered in Japan from the Nara 奈良 period (710–784) for his boundless benevolence and compassion and for his commitment to offer salvation to all sentient beings. Hereafter referred to by his abbreviated name in Japanese, Kannon. Kannon and Seishi 勢至 (Skt. Mahāsthāmaprāpta), the bodhisattva of wisdom, are the two attendants to the Buddha Amida 阿弥陀 (Skt. Amitābha) who typically appear on either side of him in pictorial and sculptural representations. In East Asia, Kannon is apt to be depicted as female.

of Tsuchiya 土屋 (*waki* ワキ),[4] grants Morihisa permission to pay his respects once more to Kannon at Kiyomizudera before journeying under arrest to the Minamoto headquarters in the town of Kamakura 鎌倉 in the distant Kantō 関東, or eastern region. Well aware that he faces almost certain execution once he arrives, Morihisa's prayer goes:

> All honor and praise to Kannon, whose benevolence
> and compassion are boundless, whose sacred vow
> ... will save whomsoever, in just one utterance of his
> name or one pious thought, believes in him. All the
> more for me, how could my many years of cultivating
> my precious connection with you be in vain?[5] *Casting
> his gaze downward.* Ah, how I shall regret this parting.

From this point, the action of the play moves forward in three steps. Tsuchiya and attendants escort Morihisa to the environs of Kamakura. Little attempt is made in the staging to actually simulate a journey realistically. Rather it is expressed by means of the poetic narrative of a component segment called *michiyuki* 道行 (travel song), which tracks their progress—on both lyrical and geographic planes—from Kyoto to Kamakura. (More will be said about this *michiyuki* section below.) When Morihisa arrives, he continues his prayers to Kannon, with Tsuchiya keeping him company. He dozes off briefly, and when he awakens, he exclaims that while dreaming he has had a prophetic vision, though we learn nothing more at this point about the vision's contents.

---

4. In the Nagato-bon *Heike monogatari* 長門本平家物語, the character of Tsuchiya is identified as Tsuchiya Saburō Moritō 土屋三郎盛遠. In that account, he does not serve as Morihisa's escort to Kamakura but as his would-be executioner once Morihisa gets to Kamakura. In the nō play, Tsuchiya is portrayed as a fellow warrior who empathizes with Morihisa and keeps him company during his prayers. Their camaraderie in the nō serves to bring out a sense of shared warrior ethos. The Nagato-bon lacks any such depiction of the two as kindred spirits. See Kurokawa Mamichi, Hotta Shōzō, and Furuichi Michiyo, eds., *Heike monogatari, Nagato-bon* (Meicho kankōkai, 1906), 736–38.

5. "Cultivating my precious connection with you": gloss of the Buddhist term *chigu kechien* 値遇結縁. To be blessed with a rare encounter with the Buddha or the Buddhist teachings and then to act in such a way as to strengthen the connection. In Morihisa's case, he has long made regular pilgrimages to Kiyomizu. His reasoning is that if one can be saved on the basis of just one pious thought or one invocation of Kannon's name, how much more likely that a person such as he, who has demonstrated his devotion for a long time, will be saved.

The second part of the play stages the attempted execution of Morihisa at Yuigahama 由比ケ浜 beach, just south of Kamakura. The narrative reveals that, as Morihisa waits for the executioner's sword to drop, the opened scroll of the *Kannon Sūtra* (*Kannon-gyō* 観音経) that he is holding emits a light that obstructs the executioner's vision when he raises his sword. He then drops the sword, and it breaks. A stunned Morihisa is immediately summoned into the presence of the Minamoto commander-in-chief, Yoritomo 源頼朝 (1147–1199), and ordered to relate the contents of his dream. We learn subsequently that Yoritomo too had had an unusual dream and had summoned Morihisa to determine whether their dreams were similar.

The ensuing narration of the contents of Morihisa's dream is centered on an important component part existing in many nō plays, called the *kuse* クセ. The chorus steps in to do the narrating for Morihisa, and relates that the night before his intended execution, Morihisa had dreamed that an old man appeared to him to assure him that he would be spared thanks to his steadfast faith in the Kannon of Kiyomizudera. The choral narration continues in the ensuing component, the *rongi* ロンギ (an exchange between chorus and *shite*). The chorus represents Yoritomo's reaction. (Yoritomo is not actually cast as a character in this drama.) We learn that Yoritomo is deeply moved because their dreams have proved identical and has concluded that the bodhisattva has intervened on Morihisa's behalf. Moreover, Yoritomo has pardoned Morihisa. In the third phase of the play Yoritomo serves Morihisa saké and orders him to perform a celebratory dance. Yoritomo is curious to see Morihisa perform, for his reputation as a skilled dancer and singer has preceded him to the Kantō. Morihisa then wastes no time withdrawing from the scene.

SOURCE MATERIALS FOR *MORIHISA*

Motomasa blends source materials from several textual traditions. The tale of Morihisa's deliverance is also recorded in one major variant of the *Heike monogatari* 平家物語 (Tale of the Heike), the Nagato-bon (長門本 Nagato variant). It is found in Chapter Twenty, the final chapter in most recensions of this variant. In the Nagato-bon, Morihisa is introduced as Shume no Hachirōzaemon Morihisa 主馬八郎左衛門盛久 (Hachirōzaemon Morihisa of the Crown Prince's Stables), the youngest son of the Heike retainer Shume no nyūdō Morikuni 主馬入道盛国 (Morikuni, Lay Monk of the Crown Prince's Stables; 1113?–1186). Though his father Morikuni is mentioned in several episodes across *Heike* variants as a trusted elder retainer of the Taira inner circle, Morihisa is thus featured in only one episode in just one major corpus of extant *Heike* variants.[6]

Although the story related in the Nagato-bon is very similar to that in the nō play, there are also marked differences. In the Nagato-bon, it is Yoritomo's wife who dreams of Kannon's intervention on Morihisa's behalf rather than Yoritomo himself. The two versions also conclude differently. After the narration of Morihisa's escape from death, the Nagato-bon ends on a miraculous twist. Morihisa had dedicated a statue of Senju 千手 ("Thousand-armed") Kannon to Kiyomizudera, which is placed to the right of the principal Kannon statue. After Morihisa relates to a priest of Kiyomizudera his escape from death, the priest tells him that, on the twenty-eighth day of the Sixth Month, the very time of Morihisa's escape from execution, the statue he dedicated had suddenly fallen over and an arm had broken. We are left to conclude that Kannon had taken the sword blow on Morihisa's behalf to spare him. It is thought that the Nagato-bon originated at a Buddhist institution, which may shed light on why this version of Morihisa's story concludes on the somewhat

---

6. Morikuni was of Taira lineage. As was the case with Taira no Kiyomori 平清盛 and his immediate relations, who rose to power in Kyoto in the mid-twelfth century, Morikuni was a descendent of Taira no Takamochi 平高望 (late 9th c.). According to one genealogy of the Taira, he is listed as the cousin of Kiyomori's paternal grandfather, Masamori 正盛, and bears the title *Shume no hangan* 主馬判官 Police Lieutenant and Head of the Crown Prince's Stables), the same title as that attributed to Morihisa in the Nagato-bon. See "Heishi keizu" 平氏系図 [Genealogy of the Taira clan] in Kajihara Masaaki and Yamashita Hiroaki, eds., *Heike monogatari* (jō), SNKT 44 (Iwanami shoten, 1991), 393. Morihisa is listed in the same chart as the fourth son of Morikuni, and his title is listed as *Saemon no jō* 左衛門尉, or Lieutenant of the Left Gate Guards. This is also a title ascribed to his father, as in the entry for the nineteenth day of the Tenth Month of 1173 in *Gyokuyō* 玉葉 (Jeweled leaves), the diary of the court aristocrat Kujō no Kanezane 九条兼実 (1149–1207). Cited in Ichiko Teiji, ed., *Heike monogatari kenkyū jiten* (Meiji shoin, 1978), 603. In the Kakuichi-bon 覚一本 version of *Heike monogatari*, Morikuni in his role of trusted elder and retainer is mentioned in sections 2.3, 2.6, 2.7, and 5.12. Another of Morikuni's sons, the Heike retainer and seasoned warrior Etchū no Zenji Moritoshi 越中前司盛俊 is treacherously outwitted and killed at the battle of Ichi-no-tani 一谷 (Kakuichi-bon 9.13). The anecdote about Morihisa's escape from death is not historically documented.

entrepreneurial note that newly carved statues of Kannon might be even more efficacious than old ones.[7]

In his essay on the nō *Morihisa* and its source material, Takemoto Mikio points out that its libretto has no direct quotations of actual lines from the Nagato-bon, nor is there definitive proof that the Nagato-bon manuscripts even predate the composition of the nō play.[8] He also notes that, contrary to the opinion generally held by modern scholars, the Nagato-bon is not the exclusive extant source for the Morihisa anecdote. For instance, the account of the sparing of Morihisa also appears in one of a collection of six short stories (*setsuwa* 説話) titled *"Heike monogatari" hidensho* 平家物語 秘伝書 (Secret writings on *Heike monogatari*), a work dating to sometime between the early and mid Edo 江戸 period (17th to 18th centuries).[9] The manuscript will hereafter be referred to as *Secret Writings*.

Takemoto notes that Morihisa's story in this latter work is at major variance with the Nagato-bon. Most notably, in the account in

---

7. It is thought that the Nagato-bon originated at a former Buddhist temple named Amidadera 阿弥陀寺, located in the proximity of the final battle site of the Genpei War, Dan-no-ura 壇ノ浦. The oldest extant manuscript of Nagato-bon is housed at Akama jingū 赤間神宮 (formerly Amidadera), in Yamaguchi prefecture (4-1, Amidadera-chō 阿弥陀寺町, Shimonoseki-shi 下関市, Yamaguchi-ken 山口県). Though the temple was founded in the ninth century, in the thirteenth century it took on a new identity as the memorial temple for the child emperor who died at Dan-no-ura, Antoku tennō 安徳天皇, and for maternal relatives such as Taira no Tokiko 平時子, his grandmother, and Taira no Tomomori 平知盛, his uncle. The temple underwent restoration in 1289 for that purpose. In 1875, it was converted to its present status as a Shintō 神道 shrine. See Ishida Takuya, ed. *Itō-ke-zō Nagato-bon Heike monogatari* (Kyūko shoin, 1977), "Kaidai," 11–12. This depiction in Nagato-bon of a miraculous connection between a devotional statue and the salvation of a parishioner suggests the dynamics Gunji describes in Chapter 23 in this volume on the cult of Kannon at Kiyomizudera. Specifically, the observation at the end of the Nagato-bon anecdote about new Kannon statues might have been intended as promotion of the cult of the icon for the purpose of attracting pilgrims and soliciting donations analogous to the pattern that Gunji discusses.

8. See Takemoto Mikio, *Kan'ami, Zeami jidai no nōgaku* (Meiji shoin, 1999), 512.

9. See Takemoto, *Kan'ami, Zeami jidai no nōgaku*, 524. This manuscript is in the Bizen Shimabara Matsudaira Bunko 備前島原松平文庫 (library collection of the Matsudaira clan, Shimabara domain, Bizen province). The episode in this collection is titled "Morihisa no koto" 盛久之事 (Concerning Morihisa). This collection is presently housed in the Shimabara Library (Shimabara toshokan 島原図書館), Shimabara 島原 city, Nagasaki 長崎 prefecture, Kyūshū 九州.

Secret Writings, no divine intervention occurs in the execution scene. It is Yoritomo who experiences the prophetic dream, whereupon he immediately dispatches a rider to the beach at Yui to issue a stay of execution to Morihisa. When he subsequently learns that Morihisa has had the same dream, Yoritomo praises him for his piety and pardons him.[10] Takemoto argues plausibly that the fact that there is more than one version of Morihisa's story extant today suggests that, in Morihisa's lifetime, the story was in wider circulation and was more familiar to people than we now might assume.[11] Takemoto's argument for the existence of a body of story material about Morihisa larger than any of its extant variants recalls a dynamic that John Miles Foley delineated concerning oral-connected literature in general. Transmission of traditional story material will involve multiple pathways, making it more useful to think of the story as a network of immanent possibilities that is larger than any one instantiation.[12]

Indeed, Motomasa crafted his own instantiation of Morihisa's story by activating multiple pathways. In addition to his reliance on tale literature such as that introduced above, he drew quite extensively on a performed poem in the *kusemai* style describing Morihisa's journey in captivity from Kyoto to Kamakura. That piece is titled *Tōgoku kudari* 東国下り (Journey to the Eastern Provinces; also titled *Kaidō kudari* 海道下り [Journey east on the sea road]). In *Go on,* Zeami mentions that the lines of this *kusemai* piece were written by the poet Rin'ami 琳阿弥 (dates unknown; also known as Tamarin 玉林), who served the third shogun of the Muromachi bakufu, Ashikaga Yoshimitsu 足利義満 (1358-1408).[13] The original *kusemai* was a rival art of performance

10. Takemoto, *Kan'ami, Zeami jidai no nōgaku,* 526-27. The entirety of the story in *Secret Writings* is quoted herein.

11. Takemoto, Kan'ami, *Zeami jidai no nōgaku,* 528-29.

12. See, for instance, John Miles Foley, "The Impossibility of Canon," in Foley, ed., *Teaching Oral Traditions* (New York: The Modern Language Association of America, 1998), 13-33. It should be mentioned that the pathways for the telling of Morihisa's tale included visual media as well. The *Kiyomizudera engi emaki* 清水寺縁起絵巻 (Illustrated handscrolls of the founding of Kiyomizudera), which was created in the early sixteenth century, introduces Morihisa. See Chapter 23 in this volume.

13. Rin'ami was already a recognized poet of Japanese verse who tried his hand at the *kusemai* format in collaboration with *sarugaku* 猿楽 performers such as Kan'ami 観阿弥. (*Sarugaku,* lit. "monkey music," or *sarugaku no nō* 猿楽の能 were the earlier names for nō.)

that Kan'ami studied and introduced into his own style of *sarugaku*. Subsequently the adapted *kusemai* evolved into the *kuse* section of a nō. In *Go on*, Zeami praises *Tōgoku kudari* as an exemplar of this successful newly adapted style of *kusemai* composition in *sarugaku*.[14]

The portion of *Morihisa* influenced by *Tōgoku kudari* is not the *kuse*, however, but the previously mentioned *michiyuki* 道行 (travel song). Typical of *michiyuki* passages, the lines are larded with references to precedented place names (*utamakura* 歌枕 [poetic loci]) invoked by *waka* 和歌 poets, and with related techniques of double entendre and allusion. Nineteen of the twenty-three *utamakura* mentioned in the *michiyuki* are also mentioned in *Tōgoku kudari*, and in a couple of instances, Motomasa lifts phrases from the *kusemai* piece verbatim (see notes to translation for details). Such references to the *kusemai* composition are lacking in the versions of Morihisa's story in the Nagato-bon or in *Secret Writings*.

Yet the source that was by far the most important inspiration for this nō play traces to another textual lineage, the *Sūtra of the Lotus of the True Law* (*Myō-hō renge kyō* 妙法蓮華経; Skt. *Saddharma-pundarīka-sūtra*). Motomasa draws in particular on Chapter Twenty-five, titled "Kanzeon bosatsu fumonbon" 観世音菩薩普門品 (The Universal Gate of Bodhisattva Kanzeon). In choosing the *Lotus Sūtra* as inspiration for his play, Motomasa was in good company. The influence of that sūtra on East Asian Buddhist cultures has been profound. As stated in *The Princeton Companion to Classical Japanese Literature*: "[It] has been the preeminent scripture in the Mahāyāna of East Asia, both for its doctrinal position and for providing a rich imagery, largely through the parables, both for literature and for the pictorial arts and architecture."[15]

Chapter Twenty-five of the *Lotus* also circulated as its own entity

---

14. *Go on*, Part II: Omote and Katō, *Zeami, Zenchiku*, 223. For the text of *Tōgoku kudari*, see 226–27. For an English translation, see P. G. O'Neill, *Early Nō Drama: Its Background, Character, and Development, 1300–1450* (London: Lund Humphries, 1958), 153–60. Today *kuse* may refer to a sequence of component parts that were adapted from the *kusemai* into *sarugaku*. In its most fully articulated adaptation, it consists of *shidai, kuri, sashi, kuse*, and a reiteration of the *shidai*. Or more commonly, the sequence is abbreviated as *kuri, sashi, kuse*. I have written elsewhere in more detail of the incorporation of the kusemai into sarugaku. See Shelley Fenno Quinn, *Developing Zeami: The Noh Actor's Attunement in Practice* (University of Hawai'i Press, 2005), 115–46.

15. Earl Miner, Hiroko Odagiri, and Robert E. Morrell, *The Princeton Companion to Classical Japanese Literature* (Princeton University Press, 1985), 385.

as of the sixth century and was equally influential as an independent sūtra.[16] Called *Kannon-gyō* 観音経 (*Kannon Sūtra*) in Japanese, it had arrived in Japan by at least the seventh century and has continued to be one of the most familiar and popular of scriptures across all classes of society. Many of the anecdotes in Heian and medieval *setsuwa* collections convey its importance in people's lives and religious practices. For instance, in the eleventh-century tale collection titled *Dainihonkoku hokkekyō genki* 大日本国法華経験記 (Account of miracles from the *Lotus Sūtra*), a Buddhist novice of the Nara temple Tōdaiji 東大寺 describes the twenty-fifth chapter of the *Lotus* as indispensable in the training program that he embarked on at age nine:

> First of all, I read "The Universal Gate of Bodhisattva Kanzeon" out loud. Then in the process of reading it out loud, I became thoroughly versed in all its import, and then gradually started intoning portions of it as I read. When I'd finished that completely, then I studied the other existing Buddhist writings and canonical teachings ...[17]

Nonspecialists too, especially children, routinely learned about Buddhism by first intoning and copying this sūtra.[18]

Kannon-gyō is what Morihisa intones in his prayers to Kannon and what he carries to the execution block. The sūtra underscores the boundless mercy of Kannon and assures the faithful of his sacred vow to intervene in the here and now to ameliorate suffering and offer protection from disaster and human frailty. Reference is also made in the play to another of the sūtra's cardinal teachings, that Kannon is capable of thirty-three incarnations so that he may better minister to human pain and suffering and lead us to enlightenment. The existence since the tenth century of a circuit of thirty-three pilgrimage temples dedicated to Kannon in the western provinces (in which Kiyomizudera now numbers sixteen) reflects the symbolic significance of this number.

---

16. Itō Hiroyuki, Imanari Genshō, and Yamada Shōzen, eds., *Bukkyō bungaku no genten*, Bukkyō Bungaku Kōza, vol. 1 (Benseisha, 1994), 65. The anecdote cited is from Book One, episode sixteen.

17. Book One, episode sixteen. Story collection compiled by the Tendai 天台 priest Chingen 鎮源. Quoted in Itō, Imanari, and Yamada, *Bukkyō bungaku no genten*, 70.

18. Itō, Imanari, and Yamada, *Bukkyō bungaku no genten*, 71.

The portion of the sūtra that is the seed for the action of the play is the precept on the seven tribulations (*shichinan* 七難). The passage adjures that if Kannon's name is invoked just one time in genuine faith, Kannon will hear that voice and deliver that person from suffering, be it from fire, flooding, gale winds, imminent execution, malevolent ghosts, the pillory, or malicious bandits. It is the fourth tribulation, the case of imminent execution by edict of a ruler, that Morihisa endures in this play. The relevant passage in the sūtra states:

> If, again, a man who is about to be murdered calls upon the name of the bodhisattva He Who Observes the Sounds of the World [Kannon], then the knives and staves borne by the other fellow shall be broken in pieces, and the man shall gain deliverance.[19]

This is precisely what happens to Morihisa at the executioner's block, or so we are to believe. When spared execution, Morihisa embodies the miracle promised in this teaching on the seven tribulations. His story becomes a parable affirming the efficacy of Kannon's vow.

THE TEXTUAL AND PERFORMANCE TRADITIONS OF *MORIHISA*

The oldest libretto of *Morihisa*, dated the twelfth day of the Eighth Month of 1423, was copied and edited by Zeami and is one of nine extant holographs known as *Zeami jihitsu nōhon shū* 世阿弥自筆能本集 (Collection of nō libretti in Zeami's hand). The *Morihisa* manuscript is more heavily edited by Zeami than any of the other eight texts in this group. It belongs to Hōzanji 宝山寺 Temple in the Ikoma 生駒 area in Nara prefecture, and is one of five such holographs in their holdings that Zeami had passed down to his son-in-law, Komparu Ujinobu 金春氏信 (known as Zenchiku 禅竹, 1405–1470?).[20] According to Takemoto,

---

19. Leon Hurvitz, trans., *Scripture of the Lotus Blossom of the Fine Dharma* (Columbia University Press, 1976), 25. Original passage found in Sakamoto Yukio and Iwamoto Yutaka, eds., *Hokekyō*, vol. 3 (Iwanami shoten, 1976), 244.

20. A digital reproduction of this manuscript (hereafter referred to as the

the holograph has from thirty to forty revisions in Zeami's hand, though they are principally of an editorial nature and do not alter the dramatic content significantly.[21] My translation of *Morihisa* in this volume is based on this libretto.[22] Takemoto also points out that there is an unusually large number of variations between Zeami's holograph and subsequent libretti of *Morihisa* as a group. He estimates that there are approximately eighty usages shared by the later manuscripts that diverge from the holograph, and that most of the variations occurred relatively early in the performance history—by the beginning of the sixteenth century.[23]

Related to many of these textual variants are established variations in the performance history of this play, which are quite extensive as well. For instance, among the libretti of the Kanze School, there are clear differences in the staging of the play that had taken form by the late Muromachi period. The most conspicuous one comes at the opening of the play. One group of libretti calls for a sequence of component segments that is faithful to the holograph—that is, an opening *mondō* 問答 (segment of prose dialogue) and the *shite*'s prayer scene at Kiyomizudera, followed by the *michiyuki*. A second group of scripts cuts this opening section drastically or entirely, and replaces it with a short speech of self-introduction (*nanori* 名ノリ) by the *waki* to

---

holograph) is available on the internet, making it possible to track Zeami's edits firsthand. See Collection of Digital Images at Ikomasan Hōzanji, http://mahoroba. lib.nara-wu.ac.jp/y01/htmls/N10/index_eng.html. Accessed January 4, 2013.

21. Takemoto, *Kan'ami, Zeami jidai no nōgaku*, 514.

22. I have relied most on the annotated edition of Zeami's holograph in Yokomichi Mario and Omote Akira, eds., *Yōkyokushū* (jō), NKBT 40 (Iwanami shoten, 1960), 413–23. I have also followed the synopsis provided therein of the script for the Kyōgen 狂言 interlude. Yokomichi and Omote base that synopsis on the Teikyō Matsui 丁享松井本 manuscript, owned by the Nogami kinen nōgaku kenkyūjo 野上記念能楽研究所 (The Nogami Memorial Noh Theatre Research Institute of Hōsei 法政 University, Tokyo). I also consulted the annotated edition of Zeami's holograph published in Getsuyōkai, ed., with Omote Akira, general ed., *Zeami jihitsu nōhon shū* (Getsuyōkai, 1997), 33–55. This edition records (in typeset) the original characters that Zeami wrote and specifies Zeami's edits of the original script by Motomasa. Among other manuscripts consulted was the early Edo manuscript named the Kōzan Bunko bon 鴻山文庫本, which appears with annotations in Itō Masayoshi, ed., *Yōkyokushū* (ge), SNKS (Shinchōsha, 1988), 315–25. I have cross-referenced the holograph most thoroughly with this Kōzan Bunko bon.

23. See Takemoto, *Kan'ami, Zeami jidai no nōgaku*, 516.

establish the setting. After the *nanori*, the scene shifts quickly to Kamakura for the attempted execution, Morihisa's audience with Yoritomo, and the final dance. Eliminating the *michiyuki* section deprives the *shite* of an extended passage of poetic narrative adumbrating his state of mind and situates him more immediately in an interaction with Tsuchiya in the prayer scene, followed by the execution scene.

Another type of deviation across libretti of *Morihisa* that is plentiful, though it has less impact on the contours of the action as a whole, is in the components such as the *mondō*, which are in intoned speech, or *kotoba* コトバ・詞. *Morihisa* has more than its share of passages of this type. Small deviations are most apt to occur in *kotoba* passages because they need not be strictly congruent with an instrumental line. Therefore, they can be altered more easily without affecting the synergy of chant and instruments as plotted in the musical score. For more on major differences in staging and lines, see the notes on these points in the translation included in this volume.

Judging from performance records, *Morihisa* does not seem to have been especially popular in the ensuing years. According to one comprehensive performance record compiled from programs dating to the early Edo period, only seven performances of Morihisa were listed between the years 1590 and 1668.[24] Next, taking the performance records compiled by Nose Asaji 能勢朝次 for the period from 1478 to 1599 as my sample, I counted just eighteen performances of the play.[25] Three of those were *kanjin nō* 勧進能 (subscription nō), large open-air performances sanctioned by the authorities for the purpose of fundraising, three were performances at private residences, four took place at Shintō shrines, and eight at Buddhist temples. It was interesting to note that seven of the eight temple performances were held at Nishi Honganji 西本願寺 in Kyoto, the headquarters of the Honganji branch of the Jōdo-Shinshū 浄土真宗 (New Pure Land sect), which "claims salvation by faith in Amitābha [Amida], who is invoked by the prayer formula 'Namu Amida Butsu.'"[26] Surely the popularity that the play seems to have enjoyed in that particular venue is not a coincidence.

---

24. Ennō kiroku chōsa kenkyū gurūpu (1), daihyō, Omote Akira, "Edo shoki nō bangumi nanashu (sono san)," *Nōgaku kenkyū*, Nōgaku kenkyūjo kiyō, no. 24 (1999), 194 (173).

25. Nose Asaji, *Nōgaku genryūkō* (Iwanami shoten, 1938), 1261–97.

26. Nihon Kōtsū Kōsha, *Japan: The New Official Guide* (Tokyo: Japan Travel Bureau, 1975), 665.

Morihisa and Motomasa's Style

A member of the third generation of innovators on the art of Yamato *sarugaku* that we have on record, Motomasa has tended to receive less scholarly attention than his grandfather, Kan'ami, or his father, Zeami. Perhaps this tendency is exacerbated by the fact that Motomasa died in 1432—probably in his early thirties—and left no critical treatises about his craft. Of course we have his plays to go on, and there are his father Zeami's written accounts about him. The image that emerges is of a very gifted playwright who drew on the innovations of his immediate predecessors but also used their precedents to craft works of depth and feeling that are very much his own. *Morihisa* is a good case study in Motomasa's stylistic contributions to the art of playwriting, and it may be useful here to comment very generally on a few of the ways in which the play is indicative of his style, both in relation to what had come before, and in terms of what fresh contributions it made.

First, the play is innovative in terms of how it structures the action, and the *kuse* is a good example of this. Motomasa follows the precedent of his father, Zeami, and his grandfather Kan'ami, by incorporating a *kuse* section into his play. As mentioned above, the *kuse* section is derived from a contemporaneous performing art called the *kusemai*. Not much is known about the original *kusemai* but, judging from extant texts, Zeami's writings, and pictorial representations, the *kusemai* performer sang narrative passages with some dancing and playing of the shoulder drum (*kotsuzumi* 小鼓). Kan'ami is credited with introducing elements from the *kusemai* into *sarugaku*, whereupon they were adapted by Zeami. From Zeami's critical writings, we know that the new *kuse* section made it possible to incorporate extended narrative passages into *sarugaku* texts accompanied with a new type of music that emphasized the beat more than had the traditional *sarugaku* music. So this innovation made it possible to expand the expressive parameters of *sarugaku* by intensifying the narrative voice and diversifying the musical structure.[27]

---

27. The image of a *kusemai* dancer as seen in the illustrated scroll titled *Shichijūichiban shokunin uta-awase* 七十一番職人歌合 (Poetry contest of seventy-one artisans, ca. 1500) is a woman dressed in an upright hat, called an *eboshi* 烏帽子, wide trousers (*hakama* 袴), and a wide-sleeved overrobe, called a *suikan* 水干. The figure is also equipped with a fan in her right hand, and, at her side, a shoulder drum. See Iwasaki Kae et al., eds. *Shichijūichiban shokunin*

One early challenge for *sarugaku* playwrights was how to integrate this new component into their plays. The earliest *kuse* sections, as in many of the plays attributed to Kan'ami, are apt to function in the dramatic action as a "performance within a performance." In Kan'ami's style of *kuse*, the *shite*, typically cast as an entertainer, performs because the plot calls for it, but the contents of the performance do not have a direct relation to the story being dramatized. For instance, in Kan'ami's play *Yoshino Shizuka* 吉野静 (Shizuka in Yoshino), the famed *shirabyōshi* 白拍子 and concubine of the warrior Minamoto no Yoshitsune 源義経 agrees to dance to distract the attention of his pursuers while Yoshitsune flees Mount Yoshino.[28] The tendency in Zeami's plays, on the other hand, was to work the *kuse* into a play as the narrative scaffolding that enables a spirit to cross over from the otherworld to this one in order to retell or reenact his or her story. In such a scenario, the content of the story is important for understanding the *shite*'s character but does not bear directly on the development of

---

utaawase, Shinsen kyōkashū, Kokon ikyokushū, SNKT 61 (Iwanami shoten 1993), 99. Also see 98 and 100 for images of a *shirabyōshi* dancer and a *hōka* performer, respectively. A discussion of the *kusemai* in Zeami's time with a reproduction from the scroll can be found in P. G. O'Neill, *Early Nō Drama*, 42–52. Also recommended is Wakita Haruko, *Josei geinō no genryū: kugutsu, kusemai, shirabyōshi* (Kadokawa shoten, 2001), 131–93.

28. Along with the *shirabyōshi* dancer, a *kusemai* dancer or a *hōka* 放下 (entertainer having the persona of a lay monk) would be likely characters to play the lead in such plays. For instance, see *Hyakuman* 百万 (formerly *Saga no dainenbutsu no onna monogurui* 嵯峨の大念仏の女物狂, Madwoman at the Saga Dainenbutsu), and *Jinen Koji* 自然居士, featuring a *kusemai* performer, a *shirabyōshi* dancer, and a *hōka* performer, respectively. The former version of the madwoman piece *Hyakuman* was performed by Kan'ami and it is likely that he composed it as well. It initially had a *kusemai* with content unrelated to the drama but Zeami later replaced it with a new *kuse* passage that interfaced with the *shite*'s predicament. Along with *Yoshino Shizuka, Jinen Koji*, a fourth-category play, is attributed to Kan'ami. For the texts see Yokomichi and Omote, *Yōkyokushū* (jō), 193–200, 89–95, and 96–105, respectively. Motomasa later reintroduced the same *kusemai* piece that had been in *Saga no dainenbutsu on onna monogurui* originally into his own composition, *Utaura* 歌占, in which its content was only tenuously related to the plot action in a way that hailed back to his grandfather's style. For a comprehensive list of translations in Western languages of nō plays, including all those in the present repertoire, see Michael Watson's database, "Noh Translations," http://www.meijigakuin.ac.jp/~pmjs/biblio/noh-trans.html. Accessed January 4, 2013.

the plot action in the dramatic present. In Zeami's prototypical warrior play, for instance, the *kuse* tends to be situated in the second act. The plot is very simple. The ghost of a fallen warrior appears to relive what has already happened to him, and then disappears.[29]

The *kuse* section of *Morihisa* demonstrates an ingenious melding of these two stylistic tendencies. Motomasa has the *shite* relate the contents of Morihisa's dream from a retrospective stance in a style reminiscent of the Zeami prototype sketched above. The *kuse* thus serves as a vehicle for accommodating the narration of a story that belongs to the subjunctive dimension—that is, the revelation of the miraculous intervention by the bodhisattva. In this regard, Motomasa is employing the *kuse* in a manner similar to his father's preferred pattern—a retelling of information about the *shite*'s identity and story within an irrealis, or supernatural, scenario. At the same time, however, Motomasa introduces the *kuse* section as an element that furthers the plot action in the dramatic present in a way reminiscent of Kan'ami's pattern. That is, the *kuse* also employs the retelling of the dream as a device for furthering the linear dimension, the plot action—in this case, Yoritomo's pardon. Motomasa thus comes up with a hybrid use of the *kuse* that exploits the advantages of the styles introduced by his predecessors. He preserves suspenseful plot action and at the same time exploits the inherent capacity of the narratively organized *kuse* to interject a magical story from the irrealis dimension into the action.

The second point to make about Motomasa's style as reflected in *Morihisa* is closely related to the first. It concerns the kinds of protagonists he tends to choose. Motomasa shows a preference for protagonists that are living in the present, in contrast with his father Zeami's tendency to compose plays that depict spirits returning to this world to retell their stories.[30] At least it can be argued that this preference for characters in living-time scenarios holds for most of those plays that are clearly attested to be by Motomasa, such as the

---

29. For instance, Zeami's warrior plays *Atsumori* 敦盛 and *Sanemori* 実盛. See Smethurst's translation of *Sanemori* in this volume. For the texts in Japanese, see Yokomichi and Omote, *Yōkyokushū* (jō), 233–40, 241–48, and 265–73.

30. Today these two groups of plays are treated as their own classifications, *genzai nō* (living-time nō) and and *mugen nō* 夢幻能 (dream nō), respectively. I would like to make one disclaimer. My observations here involve general stylistic tendencies based on the attested oeuvres of Zeami and Motomasa, but both playwrights are on record as composing plays of either classification.

madness piece *Sumidagawa* 隅田川 (Sumida River), the extremely popular play about a woman from the capital who discovers the grave of her missing child when she travels to the Kantō searching for him; *Utaura* 歌占 (Soothsaying by verse), the story of a shaman who comes back from the dead and is reunited with his son; and the play *Yoroboshi* 弱法師 (Stumbling boy) about a young man who, because he is blind, has been left by his father to wander homeless (though they are ultimately reconciled).[31] All three of these plays feature the motif of parting between parent and child. *Morihisa*, on the other hand, does not treat parting from a loved one, but parting from one's home, from one's past, and (almost) from life itself.

These four plays also suggest a preference for protagonists who are not especially renowned for exploits in literature, legend, or history. This tendency to concentrate on more humble characters seems another departure from his father's recommendation that the playwright choose illustrious and accomplished characters with

---

31. The texts of *Sumidagawa*, *Utaura*, and *Yoroboshi* may be found in Yokomichi and Omote, *Yōkyokushū* (jō), 385–94, 395–403, and 404–12, respectively. One further extant play was attributed to Motomasa by Zeami, *Yoshinoyama* 吉野山 (Mount Yoshino), also titled *Yoshinogoto* 吉野琴 (Yoshino koto), which is a *mugen* piece featuring a *tennyo* 天女 (celestial maiden). It composes a counterexample of the stylistic preference for living-time pieces that I am ascribing to Motomasa. The text of *Yoshinogoto* is available in Haga Yaichi and Sasaki Nobutsuna, eds., *Kōchū Yōkyoku sōsho*, vol. 3 (Hakubunkan, 1915; reprint Rinsen shoten, 1987), 547–50. Zeami also attributes a play no longer extant, titled *Matsugasaki* 松ヶ崎, to Motomasa. There are also four warrior ghost plays that scholars ascribe variously to Motomasa: *Tomonaga* 朝長, *Koremori* 維盛, *Tsunemori* 経盛, and *Shigehira* 重平. It must be said that all these warrior plays of putative authorship adhere to the *mugen* nō classification as well. *Tomonaga* is an important entry in the current canonical repertoire of warrior plays. *Tsunemori* is not in the active repertoire. *Koremori* was also a *bangaikyoku* 番外曲 (play outside of the established repertoire), but has been revived in modern times. This is true for *Shigehira* also. For more on *Shigehira*, see Atkins's translation and analysis in this volume. In *Go on*, Zeami credits Motomasa with the composition of what was probably an independent *kusemai* titled *Kōya no kusemai* 高野節曲舞, eulogizing the great Shingon 真言 sect complex of Kongōbuji 金剛峰寺 (or Kōya-san 高野山). It was later incorporated as the *kuse* section of Zeami's madness play titled *Kōya monogurui* 高野物狂. Omote and Katō, *Zeami, Zenchiku*, 216–17. For information on translations of these plays into Western languages, see Michael Watson, "Noh Translations."

legends that precede them.[32] In practice, Zeami's female characters are apt to have some relation to literary antecedents, and his warrior characters to be important figures in *Heike monogatari* that enjoy the cachet of accomplishment in the courtly arts. In contrast, none of the protagonists of the plays in Motomasa's oeuvre that are mentioned above have substantial connections to courtly culture or reputations for individual accomplishment.

The *shite* of *Morihisa* is of relatively humble standing. The name that he goes by suggests that he has a court affiliation, but only as a palace guard. Though a trusted retainer and a Taira, he is not an illustrious commander or even a member of the immediate family. We are told that he is recognized for his ability to sing and dance, but it seems that Motomasa may have invented that talent out of whole cloth (or taken it from a version of Morihisa's story no longer extant). Perhaps he came up with this talent as justification for the final dance sequence in the play—an obligatory bit of staging at the climax of any *sarugaku* play that is supposed to end auspiciously. In any case, it can be argued that Motomasa knowingly opted to feature a character that had only a bit part in the larger tale of the Taira. Far from banking on the appeal of a famous character to arouse audience interest, Motomasa seems to have intended to arouse audience empathy by expressing simply and plainly the depth of this *shite*'s humility and faith. A certain averseness to dramatic bombast seems firmly rooted here.

Finally, Motomasa's techniques for the invoking of allusion also seem to build on the precedents of his father, but he adds his own distinctive stylistic flavor in this domain as well. In *Morihisa*, Motomasa adheres to Zeami's precepts in *Sandō* that a play should have characters that are familiar and materials that are readily recognizable. After all, what lines stood to be more familiar to the ear of the listener than sacred and well-worn phrases from the *Kannon-gyō*? Motomasa even leaves several of its chanted lines in the original Chinese word order, so confident he seems that they will pose no obstacles to the ears of Japanese audience members.

---

32. In his *Sandō* (The Three Paths), a critical treatise on writing plays, Zeami advises that personages renowned for their abilities in the entertainments of dance and chant make the best protagonists, and that allusions to celebrated poems should be allotted to the *shite* to invoke familiar associations with larger literary themes. For a fully annotated translation of *Sandō*, see Quinn, *Developing Zeami*, 291–302. The passages mentioned here are on 293 and 294, respectively.

So, in principle, Motomasa follows his father's advice. However, his choice of material from a Buddhist sūtra as the seed for his play is very original, as are the resulting tone and upshot of the play.[33] In *Morihisa*, the enactment of the Buddhist parable not only shifts the dramatic focus away from retelling the story of the psyche of a particular individual (outstanding or otherwise) toward a focus on the religious message itself, in a style reminiscent of the morality play. *Morihisa* is about the enormity of Kannon's vow and boundless compassion, which is a mega-message that overarches the specific depiction of any individual history. If there is anything outstanding about Morihisa as an individual among his male Taira cohort, it is the fact that he is still alive. While his unassuming religious piety is singular and exemplary, it represents life choices that are within the reach of everyman. Motomasa has chosen to create a protagonist who is something of an antihero. The character himself sums it up well at the conclusion of his play: "This moment that I am blessed with is not mine or anyone's alone."

Satoi Rokurō has argued that, for Motomasa to have dramatized Morihisa's story so movingly, the playwright must have been himself a believer in Kannon.[34] Perhaps. But one need not be a member of that flock to feel the humility of this character and to sense that his unassuming air reflects a certain preference on the playwright's part for the plain and straight. Perhaps Zeami was addressing such a turn of mind in a passage that he wrote in mourning over Motomasa's death:

> When [Motomasa] was approaching the end of his
> life, he truly achieved understanding and spoke of
> [the importance of] not adding anything unnecessary.
> The mind that knows not to do anything superfluous
> is the one that has a true understanding of nō.[35]

---

33. Buddhist themes were certainly not new to the art of *sarugaku*, but during Kan'ami and Zeami's lifetimes their stream of *sarugaku* had become more secularized in response to shifts in patronage on the part of religious institutions primarily, to that of the Ashikaga *bakufu*. Motomasa's choice to focus on a more overtly religious theme in *Morihisa* perhaps reflects the dwindling of such *bakufu* support.

34. Satoi Rokurō, *Yōkyoku hyakusen, sono shi to dorama*, vol. 2 (Kasama shoin, 1982), 256–57.

35. *Kyakuraika* 却来華 (Flower of Returning, 1433). Omote and Katō, *Zeami, Zenchiku*, 247. The original passage concerns whether Motomasa had mastered the final secrets of the art intellectually, though he did not live long enough to be allowed to actually perform them. The original Japanese is: 最後近く成りし時

分、能々得法して、無用の事をばせぬよし申ける也。無用の事をせぬと
知る心、すなはち能の得法也。*Saigo chikaku narishi jibun, yokuyoku toppō
shite, muyō no koto o ba senu yoshi mōshikeru nari. Muyō no koto no senu to shiru
kokoro, sunawachi nō no toppō nari.* Zeami did not use the term "*nō*" to refer to
the art form. Here *nō* could refer to ability in the art generally, or, as Nearman
chooses to translate the term, "acting." See Mark J. Nearman, trans., "*Kyakuraika*:
Zeami's Final Legacy for the Actor," *Monumenta Nipponica* 35:2 (Summer 1980),
170. I interpret the referent to be Motomasa's overall mastery.

25 ～ *Morihisa*

| SHELLEY FENNO QUINN

INTRODUCTION

Morihisa 盛久 is a *genzai* nō in two parts categorized as a fourth-category, or "miscellaneous" piece. Morihisa appears as a Taira retainer in the Kakuichi-bon *Heike monogatari*, but the story upon which the play is based is only found in the lesser-known Nagato-bon variant. The play was written by Kanze Motomasa 観世元雅 (1400?–1432) and edited by his father Zeami, and it is in the active repertoires of all five nō schools. The *shite* is Morihisa and the *waki* his captor, Tsuchiya. *Tsure* accompanying the *waki* include two palanquin bearers, and—in the modern performance tradition—Morihisa's executioner, as well.

The story enacted in *Morihisa* is a last-minute reprieve, similar in theme and structure to *Rō-Giō* and *Rokudai no utai*, both also translated in this volume. The first part of the play depicts Morihisa's journey in captivity from the capital, Heian-kyō (modern-day Kyoto) to Kamakura, where he will be judged and executed for supporting the losing Taira side in the Genpei War (1180–1185). He is first granted permission to pray to the Kannon at Kiyomizu Temple. At this point begins the lyrical *michiyuki* 道行 (travel song), describing the party's journey along the Tōkaidō 東海道, or Eastern Sea Route, to Kamakura. The *michiyuki* is articulated in the alternating lines of five and seven syllables, the lyrical pattern also associated with *waka* poetry.

Having reached Kamakura, the party rests, and Morihisa dozes off, intoning prayers to Kannon. When he awakens, he reports that he has had a felicitous dream. Tsuchiya hurries the party to the execution ground at Yuigahama. In a dramatic climax, the executioner's sword fails: it breaks in two, we learn, in accordance with Kannon's promise to protect the innocent.

In the interlude, the *ai* marvels at the events; Tsuchiya decides to take Morihisa before the Kamakura Lord, Minamoto no Yoritomo 源頼朝. The second part enacts their interview, in which Morihisa reveals his dream: a promise by Kannon to save him. Having had the same dream and thinking it a divine sign, Yoritomo grants Morihisa a reprieve. Yoritomo asks only that Morihisa, famed for his skill as a dancer, perform once before he leaves. Morihisa obliges, and the play ends with a propitious *otokomai* dance.

Unusual in this play is the opening *mondō* 問答 dialogue between Morihisa and Tsuchiya, a technique emblematic of Motomasa's somewhat unorthodox style. In modern performance, only the Kanze and Komparu schools retain this opening; the others begin with the following *nanori* 名乗 (name-announcing). Also of interest in this piece is the absence of Yoritomo: although a vital character in the play, he is represented only through reported speech.

Morihisa

| TRANSLATED BY SHELLEY FENNO QUINN

TO CHARLES "CHICK" QUINN, IN MEMORIAM

Fourth-category *genzai* nō in two acts.
Performed by all five schools.
Time: Third Month
Place: The Capital
Author: Kanze Motomasa

SHITE	Morihisa (no mask worn)
WAKI	Tsuchiya
WAKITSURE	two palanquin bearers
AI	Tsuchiya's servant

Instrumental section (hayashi 囃子*)*:
flute (*nōkan* 能管), shoulder drum (*kotsuzumi* 小鼓), hip drum
(*ōtsuzumi* 大鼓). There is no stick drum (*taiko* 太鼓) in this play.

[PART ONE (*maeba*)]

After the *hayashi-kata* 囃子方 (instrumentalists) enter down the *hashigakari*
橋懸り (bridgeway) and seat themselves, Morihisa and Tsuchiya enter in
conversation (*mondō* 問答). Morihisa leads, flanked by the two Bearers,
who are holding a palanquin over Morihisa's head, indicating that he is
being transported in their custody. Morihisa carries rosary beads and has a
rolled sūtra scroll tucked into the front of his robe. Tsuchiya follows. In the
modern staging of the play, there is an additional *wakitsure* cast as Morihisa's
executioner, who enters last carrying a sword.

MORIHISA   (*mondō*)
    (*fushi*)   Excuse me, Tsuchiya, sir, but there is something I must
say to you.[1]

Morihisa 盛久. This translation is based on the annotated edition of Zeami's
holograph in Yokomichi Mario and Omote Akira, eds., *Yōkyokushū* (jō), NKBT
40 (Iwanami shoten, 1960), 413–23. For other texts consulted, see Chapter 24,
note 22.

TSUCHIYA   What is it?
MORIHISA

   (katari)   Here in the capital for many years I have been a
believer in Kanzeon[2] of Kiyomizu. Every day without fail I have made
my way there on foot to pray. But if I now go down to the Kantō,[3]
this will be a final parting. So won't you please head this palanquin to
Kiyomizu? I would make my leave with a prayer.[4]

---

   1. The opening of this play has several variants. The one translated here, with
the prose exchange (*mondō* 問答), follows the holograph by Zeami. Of the five
schools of nō performers, the Kanze 観世 and Komparu 金春 schools presently
adhere to this format. However, the Hōshō 宝生, Kita 喜多, and Kongō 金
剛 schools open with a *nanori* 名のり (name announcing) in which the *waki*
introduces himself and the setting to the audience: "I am a retainer of the
Kamakura Shogun, and my name is Tsuchiya. I learned from a trusty informant
that Police Lieutenant Morihisa, Head of the Crown Prince's Stables, was hiding
out at the temple Nariaiji 成相寺 in Tango 丹後 province, and we took him into
custody alive. Now I will accompany him to the Kantō." Yokomichi and Omote,
Yōkyokushū (jō), 414. *Nanori* passages are conventionally used at the opening of
nō plays as of the late Muromachi 室町 period (1336–1573), so inserting one
as an opener may be considered an orthodox touch. When the *nanori* variant is
staged, the *shite* is seated at *jiutaimae* 地謡前 from the opening of the play. The
other characters proceed down the *hashigakari* with the *waki* in the lead. The *waki*
stops at the base square (*jōza* 常座) to face front and deliver the *nanori*. Opening
a play with a *mondō* is very unorthodox, and *Morihisa* is the only play that does
so among the approximately 230 plays in the current repertoire. Yokomichi and
Omote, *Yōkyokushū* (jō), 413. Some other variants of *Morihisa* going back to the
late Muromachi period have more extended *nanori* passages. Itō Masayoshi cites
one example verbatim and notes that, in performance, the longer *nanori* was
likely to replace the opening *mondō* and ensuing *michiyuki* 道行 (travel song)
passages entirely. For details, see Itō, *Yōkyokushū* (ge), 495–96.
   2. Kanzeon Bosatsu 観世音菩薩, the bodhisattva Kanzeon (Skt. Avalokiteśvara,
lit. "One who observes the sounds of the world"); hereafter abbreviated to Kannon.
For more, see Chapter 24 in this volume. Specifically Morihisa directs his prayers
habitually to the statue of Jūichimen Senju Kannon, "Eleven-headed, thousand-
armed Kannon," the central devotional image at Kiyomizudera.
   3. In this context, Kantō refers to the seat of the *bakufu*, established by the
Minamoto clan in the town of Kamakura in eastern Honshū 本州. Formerly
the term was also used to refer broadly to the area of Honshū east of the Ōsaka
Barrier (Ōsaka no seki 逢坂関), which itself marked the boundary between the
capital area and regions to the east. In this period, residents of the capital by and
large considered the Kantō the eastern hinterland.
   4. The *Kōzan bunko bon* 鴻山文庫本 is worded slightly differently, replacing

TSUCHIYA Easily done. [*to the palanquin bearers*] Attention! Head the palanquin in the direction of Higashiyama.[5]

The procession moves onto the main stage and proceeds to the front (shōmensaki). Morihisa steps out of the palanquin and kneels. The Bearers lower the palanquin, and kneel to the rear of Morihisa. Tsuchiya also kneels behind him.

MORIHISA   (*sashi*)   *Faces forward with his hands joined in prayer.*

(*fushi*)   All honor and praise to Kannon, whose benevolence and compassion are boundless,[6] whose sacred vow, like those moxa grasses,[7] will save whomsoever, in just one utterance of his name or one pious thought, believes in him.[8] (*Quietly, he lowers his hands.*) All the more for me, how could my many years of cultivating my precious connection with you be in vain?[9]

---

itoma 暇 in the phrase *itoma no nengan* 暇の念願, lit. "prayerful wish at leave-taking," with *saigo no nengan* 最後の念願, "last prayerful wish." Itō, *Yōkyokushū* (ge), 315.

5. Higashiyama (lit. eastern hills) is the name of a hilly district of Kyoto located to the east of the Kamogawa 鴨川 (Kamo River) along the eastern rim of the city. It is rich in scenic beauty and cultural landmarks, including Kiyomizudera.

6. *Namu ya daiji daihi no Kanzeon* 南無や大慈大悲の観世音. Morihisa is opening his prayer to Kannon with this set eulogy.

7. The single phrase, *sashimogusa* さしも草 suffices to conjure associations with a thirty-one syllable *waka* verse popularly attributed to Kannon: ただ頼めしめぢが原のさしも草われ世の中にあらんかぎりは *Tada tanome / Shimejigahara no/ sashimogusa / ware yo no naka ni / aran kagiri wa* (Just as much as those moxa grasses on Shimeji moor, you may count on me for as long as I am in this world). *Sashimogusa* is mugwort, the ingredient from which moxa is made, and Shimejigahara しめぢが原, the Shimeji moor, was known for mugwort having especially potent medicinal properties. Located in the northern part of present-day Tochigi 栃木 city, at the foot of Ibukiyama 伊吹山, Shimejigahara is also a poetic locus in traditional Japanese poetry. In the poem Kannon vows to followers that placing their faith in him will be just as efficacious as that mugwort. The *waka* puns on *sashimo*, which can also mean "to that extent." This poem (or variants) appear to have circulated widely during the Kamakura period (1185–1336) and the Muromachi period. It is included, for instance, in the collection of poetic criticism titled *Fukoro zōshi* 袋草紙 (Book of Folded Pages; ca. 1156), the tale collection *Shasekishū* 沙石集 (Collection of Sand and Pebbles; 13th c.), and the eighth imperial poetic anthology, the *Shinkokin wakashū* 新古今和歌集 (New Collection of *Waka* Poems Old and New; 1205).

8. Morihisa is alluding to the opening passage of the *Kannon Sūtra* (*Kannongyō* 観音経). See Chapter 24 for more on this sutra.

9. "Cultivating my precious connection with you": gloss of the Buddhist term *chigu kechien* 値遇結縁. To be blessed with a rare encounter with the Buddha or the Buddhist teachings and then to act in such a way as to strengthen the

(Casting his gaze downward.) Ah, how I shall regret this parting.

MORIHISA *(issei)*

> The cherry blossoms of Kiyomizu Temple—

Stands. Bearers again raise the palanquin over his head. Tsuchiya stands.

> will I ever again see them in full bloom?[10]

CHORUS

> For one who won't see spring return, farewell is such sorrow.

MORIHISA

> Otowa Hill too does not make even a sound,

CHORUS

> its inner waterfalls roiling, unheard by men.[11]

Morihisa casts his gaze downward. The entourage stands in a line at front.

CHORUS

(sashi)

> Looking out over the distance, cherry and willow branches interweave,
> and the sky of my old home place is like a brocade,[12]
> When will I ever see it again?[13]

---

connection. In Morihisa's case, he has long made regular pilgrimages to Kiyomizu. His reasoning is that if one can be saved on the basis of just one pious thought or one invocation of Kannon's name, how much more likely that a person such as he, who has demonstrated his devotion for a long time, will be saved.

10. The cherry blossoms of Kiyomizu are a famous emblem of spring in the capital. In the warrior play *Tamura*, for instance, the *shite* makes his entrance saying, "Many a place is famed for cherry-trees, But none can boast such blossoms; Methinks the charity of Kwannon [Kannon] Adds lustre to their hue." Nippon Gakujutsu Shinkōkai, ed. and trans., *The Noh Drama: Ten Plays from the Japanese* (Rutland, Vt., and Tokyo: Charles E. Tuttle, 1955), 25.

11. Otowayama 音羽山 (Otowa Hill), a poetic locus, is located to the rear of Kiyomizudera and is known for its waterfall. Here, *oto* is the simply the first part of the place name and not to be taken literally, but by itself as a word it can refer to sound. The text puns on this morpheme by introducing the idiom *oto ni tateru* 音に立てる, to "raise a cry" or "give voice or expression to," the idea here being that, while Morihisa does not give voice to his sufferings, his inner emotions can be likened to the turbulence of the waterfall. Otowayama is also used as a metonym for Kiyomizudera.

12. All the other manuscripts consulted allot the first two lines of this *sashi* to the *shite*.

13. Allusion to a *waka* by the early Heian poet Sosei 素性 (dates unknown), included in the first imperial anthology, *Kokin wakashū* 古今和歌集 (905), Spring, I, 56, with the headnote: 花ざかりに京をみやりてよめる *Hana zakari ni kyō o miyarite yomeru*; Seeing the capital with the cherry blossoms in full bloom. 見渡せば柳桜をこき交ぜて都ぞ春の錦なりける *Miwataseba /*

<table>
<tr><td></td><td>To think I may not saddens me so
as I resign myself to the eastern road.</td></tr>
<tr><td>MORIHISA</td><td>Born to no good purpose into a warrior clan</td></tr>
<tr><td>CHORUS</td><td>I was someone of wide repute,[14]
so this road I did not expect to travel,
moving eastward beyond the barrier
without a trace, perhaps, crossing Shirakawa River,
whose waves will return but when will I?[15]</td></tr>
</table>

Still standing at front.

CHORUS

(*sageuta*) Who will wait here at "Waiting Hill"?[16]
And [next we pass] Shinomiya-gawara, and Yotsu-no-tsuji,[17]

---

yanagi sakura o / kokimazete / miyako zo haru no / nishiki narikeru; Gazing far afield, / Willow green and cherry pink weave a delicate / brocade of spring so fine / the capital may wear it. Translation in Laurel Rasplica Rodd with Mary Catherine Henkenius, "*Kokinshū*": *A Collection of Poems Ancient and Modern* (Princeton University Press, 1984), 64–65.

14. Presumably a reference to the former prosperity and repute of his clan, the Taira, until their defeat in the Genpei War. Nagato-bon relates that Morihisa's immediate family has served the Taira clan as hereditary retainers for generations. See Kokusho Kankōkai, ed., *Heike monogatari Nagato-bon* (Kokusho kankōkai, 1906), 737.

15. The Shirakawa 白川 River flows from the east through the Kita Shirakawa 北白川 and Okazaki 岡崎 areas, and then joins the Kamo River 鴨川 in the Gion 祇園 area of the city. *Shira* 白 puns on *shirazu* 知らず, or "not know," implying that Morihisa does not know if or when he will return. Librettos of the Komparu, Kongō, and Kita schools replace the suppositional construction *naruran* なるらん with the negative, *narazu* ならず: いつ帰るべきたびなら ず ("not a journey from which I will return").

16. Waiting Hill, a literal gloss for Matsuzaka 松坂, the name of a sloping stretch of road in the area of Hioka 日岡 pass heading east to Yamashiro 山城 province, Uji 宇治 district (now Yamashina ku 山科区 [Yamashina ward] in Kyoto-shi 京都市 [Kyoto city]). *Matsu* puns on the verb *matsu* 待つ, meaning "wait," and the phrase includes a *double entendre*: "this place is where [someone] may await someone," the implication being that no one will await Morihisa's return. The same phrase occurs in the *kusemai* piece *Tōgoku kudari* 東国下り, as well as the *michiyuki* of the play *Semimaru* 蝉丸, usually attributed to Zeami or Motomasa. It is clear that this passage and a number of the passages from the *michiyuki* section of *Morihisa* were inspired by *Tōgoku kudari*.

17. Shinomiya-gawara 四ノ宮河原 and Yotsu-no-tsuji 四つの辻 are a village and a crossroad, respectively, that are also located in the Yamashina area on a

CHORUS

(ageuta)   This is the place
            where people going and returning [meet and] part,
            where people going and returning [meet and] part,
            and where friends and strangers alike
            meet on "Meeting Hill,"[18] nor would the gatekeeper
            ever hold me back as I am now.

The entourage turns to the right and quietly moves to the bridgeway (hashigakari).

            Crossing over the long bridge at Seta[19]
            and reaching "Mirror Mountain," my image looks
                stooped,[20]

---

major artery connecting Kyoto and the Tōkaidō 東海道 (Eastern Sea Road), the main coastal road leading east toward Honshū. Shinomiya-gawara is presently the town of Shinomiya 四宮 in Yamashina ward. Because of its proximity to the pass at Ōsakayama 逢坂山 (Mount Ōsaka), travelers congregated there. The first mora, *shi* 四, in the place name Shinomiya-gawara puns with *shi* 死 denoting death, implying that death is all that awaits Morihisa. The same Chinese character is repeated at the head of Yotsu-no-tsuji in a bit of wordplay. The two lines in which these place names occur come from the *kusemai* piece *Tōgoku kudari*.

18. "Meeting Hill," a literal gloss for the place name Ōsaka 逢坂. *Ōsaka no seki* was a barrier gate at Ōsakayama, east of the capital, north of Otowayama 音羽山 (Mount Otowa), and south of *Biwa ko* 琵琶 (Lake Biwa) in Ōmi 近江 province. The barrier itself fell out of use after the eighth century but the place name remained an important poetic locus (*utamakura*). The libretto quotes the first four lines of the *waka* attributed to the legendary Heian poet Semimaru 蝉丸, which is included in the miscellaneous grouping of poems in the anthology *Gosen waka shū* 後撰和歌集 (compiled 951), 1089. The final line of the poem is: "Ōsaka no seki." In this context the transience of existence, as embodied in travel, and in Morihisa's plight is adumbrated.

19. Seta-no-nagahashi 勢多の長橋 ("Seta long bridge," also known as Seta-no-karahashi 勢多の唐橋) is a celebrated *utamakura* in Ōmi province, present-day Ōtsu 大津 city, Shiga 滋賀 prefecture. The bridge crosses the Seta River, which is fed by Lake Biwa. It was an important link for travelers on the Tōkaidō.

20. Kagamiyama 鏡山 ("Mirror Mountain") is an *utamakura* in present-day Shiga prefecture, on the border between Yasu 野洲 and Gamō 蒲生 districts, west of Lake Biwa. It had a well-trafficked post town at its base. This is an allusion to a miscellaneous poem in the *Kokin waka shū* 899: 鏡山いざ立ち寄りて見てゆかん年へぬる身は老いやしぬると *Kagamiyama / iza tachi yorite / mite yukan / toshi henuru mi wa / oi ya shinuru to* (well now I'll go to / Mirror Mountain gaze upon / it and then travel / on for I wonder if I've / aged in all these

> though I'm not that on in years,
> old my wasted body seems passing through the Oiso
> woods[21]

They pass the first pine.

> to end at Mino, Owari.[22]

They turn to face the curtain at the far end of the bridgeway.

CHORUS

(*sageuta*)   From the Atsuta shoreline,[23] our path hidden
by the waves at evening tide,
we take the winding way through fields

At the third pine, they turn back toward the stage.

> to reach Narumi inlet,
> then to Eight Bridges[24] and the Takashi hills,[25]

---

years I've lived). Translation in Rodd, "*Kokinshū*," 308.

21. "Oiso woods" (Oiso-no-mori 老蘇の森): *utamakura* located in the northern part of Gamō district, Shiga prefecture. *Oi* 老 puns on "old age."

22. The author has run together the names of two provinces, Mino 美濃 and Owari 尾張 to create a pun with *mi no owari* 身のをはり, or "end of one's being," i.e., death. Mino province corresponds to the southern part of present-day Gifu 岐阜 prefecture, and Owari to the western part of Aichi 愛知 prefecture.

23. Atsuta shoreline (Atsuta no ura 熱田の浦) is an area of shore in the southeast section of the present city of Nagoya 名古屋. Atsuta was very famous as the site of an important shrine, Atsuta jingū 熱田神宮. Narumi inlet (Narumigata 鳴海潟) was then a portion of shoreline adjoining Atsuta no ura just to the south. In the medieval period, Narumigata was still an inlet on Ise wan 伊勢湾 (Bay of Ise), though it is landlocked now. Both are *utamakura* of Owari province (Aichi prefecture) and are now within the Nagoya city limits. Morihisa and entourage found the coastline of Atsuta under water due to the evening tide, so they took a roundabout route through a field and emerged at Narumigata.

24. Eight Bridges, or Yatsuhashi 八橋, is an *utamakura* of Mikawa 三河 province (Aichi prefecture), the name of a spot "where the waters of a stream branched into eight channels, each with its own bridge." Translation from *Tales of Ise* in Helen Craig McCullough, *Classical Japanese Prose: An Anthology* (Stanford University Press, 1990), 42. In the ninth episode of *Ise monogatari* 伊勢物語, the putative hero, Ariwara no Narihira 在原業平, stops at Yatsuhashi to admire the *kakitsubata* 杜若 (irises) and compose a poem with reference to them before continuing his own journey to the East. Reference to this place thus conjures up images of Narihira's journey east away from his home in the capital.

25. Takashi hills (Takashiyama 高師山; also read Takashi-no-yama) is an *utamakura* with two possible referents. It is the name of a hill in Mikawa province,

They stop at the first pine and face front.

                then to Eight Bridges and the Takashi hills.

CHORUS

(*rongi*)   From Shiomi slope to [the post town] Hashimoto,[26]

They remain standing at the first pine.

                Where we cross the long bridge at Hamana Lake,[27]

MORIHISA   Traveling robes—

                Did I ever think I'd come this way and see,

                Did I ever think I'd come this way and see,

                Myself alive yet—can it be?

                Sayo no Nakayama.[28]

Atsumi gun 渥美郡 (Atsumi district) (present-day Toyohashi 豊橋 city, Aichi prefecture). It is also the name used to refer to a hilly area stretching from Hamana gun 浜名郡 (Hamana district) in Mikawa province (Aichi prefecture) along the coast to the western edge of Hamana ko 浜名湖 (Lake Hamana) in Tōtōmi 遠江 province (now western Shizuoka 静岡 prefecture). As an *utamakura*, it is associated with both provinces. Yokomichi and Omote, *Yōkyokushū* (jō), 416, n. 43. Itō notes that the earliest extant example of its use seems to be in the Heian *waka* anthology titled *Kokin waka rokujō* 古今和歌六帖 (compiled by 987) and that it became established in medieval times as an *utamakura* of Tōtōmi province. Itō, *Yōkyokushū* (ge), 316, n. 10. Sanari also places it in Tōtōmi. Sanari Kentarō, *Yōkyoku taikan* vol. 5 (Meiji shoin, 1931), 3098, n. 1. The NKBZ edition, on the other hand, suggests the province of Mikawa, identifying the location as a hillock in Takashi chō 高師 (Takashi ward), Toyohashi city, Aichi prefecture. Koyama et al., *Yōkyōkushū* (ge), 277, n. 21.

    26. Shiomi Hill (Shiomizaka 潮見坂) is the name of a stretch of sloping road located in the Shirasuka 白須賀 area in the town of Kosai 湖西, on the western edge of Hamana ko. Hashimoto 橋本 was formerly a post-town on the Tōkaidō located on the seaward side of Hamana ko. The town has been renamed Arai 新居.

    27. Hamana Lake is an *utamakura* of Tōtōmi province. It was famed for its Hamana Bridge (Hamana no hashi 浜名の橋), also an *utamakura*. The bridge, which was approximately seventeen meters long, stretched across the Hamana River, flowing from the lake into the ocean to the south. It was lost in the earthquake of the Eighth Month of 1498; the quake also inundated permanently the strip of land that the river had traversed.

    28. An allusion to a poem on the travel theme, *Shinkokinshū*, no. 987, in which the *utamakura* Saya no Nakayama 小夜の中山 is mentioned: 東の方へまかりけるに、よみ侍りける西行法師 (Composed when departing for the East (Priest Saigyō). 年たけてまた超ゆべしと思ひきや命なりけりさやの中山 *toshi takete / mata koyubeshi to / omoiki ya / inochi narikeri / Saya no Nakayama*

Gazes off into the distance.

CHORUS   The Ōi River's many shifting pools and shallows,
              its waves left behind, we strike out over Mount Utsu,[29]
MORIHISA   and coming to Kiyomi inlet,[30]
CHORUS   we set out along Miho inlet and Tago bay[31]
              and see the gleaming snow

Morihisa gives sweeping gaze to the right.

              on Mount Fuji's peak, and Mount Hakone.[32]

(Did I ever think to scale these heights again in old age? Alive is what I am, Saya no Nakayama!). Translation by Charles J. Quinn, Jr. The *utamakura* Sayo (or Saya) no Nakayama refers to a stretch of sloping road in Tōtōmi province (southern Shizuoka prefecture) connecting the town of Kakegawa 掛川 with the village of Kanaya 金谷 in Harihara gun 蓁原郡 (Harihara district). Because it is a winding road surrounded by deep valleys, it has been recognized since Heian times as an especially dangerous spot on the Tōkaidō. It is a much invoked *utamakura*.

29. Ōigawa 大井川 (Ōi River) flows at the border between Tōtōmi and Suruga 駿河 provinces (central part of Shizuoka prefecture) and lets out into Suruga bay. As an *utamakura*, it is noted for its rough waters. Utsunoyama (Mount Utsu) corresponds to *Utsunoya tōge* 宇津ノ谷峠 (Utsunoya pass) in Suruga province (Shizuoka Prefecture). It enjoys canonical stature as an *utamakura* in *Ise monogatari*. The "Ōi" (Ohowi) in Ōigawa puns with *ohoi* 多い, meaning "many." *Utsu* in Mount Utsu (*Utsunoyama* 宇津の山) puns with *utsu* 打つ, "strike."

30. Kiyomigata 清見潟 (Kiyomi inlet) is an *utamakura* of Suruga province. It is a stretch of shoreline celebrated for its natural beauty, located in present-day Okitsu-chō 興津町 (Okitsu ward) in Shimizu-shi 清水市 (Shimizu city), Shizuoka prefecture.

31. Allusion to a poem by Yamabe no Akahito 山部赤人, *Man'yōshū* 万葉集, Book 3, no. 318: 田子の浦ゆ打出て見れば真白にそ富士の高嶺に雪は降りにける *tago no ura / yu uchidete mireba / mashiro ni so / Fuji no takane ni / yuki wa furinikeru*; "When from Tago shore / We rowed far out and turned to look, / Pure white it was, / The towering cone of Fuji / Gleaming under fallen snow!" Edwin A. Cranston, *A Waka Anthology, vol. 1, The Gem-Glistening Cup* (Stanford University Press, 1993), 300. Miho inlet 三保, now in Shizuoka, is famous for its pines (Matsubara). Tago no ura 田子の浦 (Tago bay) is a stretch of coast from the Okitsu shore up through Kanbara 蒲原 and Fuji 富士 cities. It is scenic with a view of Mount Fuji to the north.

32. Fujisan 富士山 (Mount Fuji) is located on the border between Kai 甲斐 and Suruga provinces (Shizuoka and Yamanashi 山梨 prefectures). Fujisan occupies a sacred place as *utamakura* and as an icon of Japan, one of the "three renowned mountains." Hakoneyama 箱根山 (Mount Hakone) is an *utamakura* of Sagami 相模 province (located on the border of Shizuoka and Kanagawa 神

Faces front and gazes slightly upward and outward.

As the starlit night at length starts to dawn,

The entourage moves down the bridgeway to the main stage and stops before the chorus.

already we have reached Kamakura,[33]
already we have reached Kamakura.

Morihisa seats himself on a stool (shōgi 床几) in front of the chorus. The palanquin bearers remove the palanquin from over Morihisa and withdraw, kneeling behind the hayashi. Tsuchiya kneels at the stage assistant position (kōken-za), as does the executioner when his part is included. The following recitative is expressed with deep feeling; Morihisa remains seated throughout.

Morihisa

(*sashi*)   The true course exists in the void, though dust obstruct it,[34]

奈川 prefectures). It belongs to the same volcanic mountain range as Fujisan.

33. Kamakura 鎌倉 was the locale that Yoritomo chose as the seat of his military government and it remained so until the *bakufu* crumbled in 1333. Kamakura is located on the northwestern shore of the Miura 三浦 peninsula.

34. *Muchū ni michi atte jinai o hedatsu* 無中に路あって塵埃を隔つ: a reference to a Zen 禅 precept propounded by the Sōtō school (Sōtō-shū 曹洞宗) patriarch Dongshan Liangjie 洞山良价 (807–869). The same line appears in the Case 43 of *Fo guo Yuanwu chan shi Bi yan lu* 仏果圜悟禅師碧巌録; (Blue cliff record of the Zen master Engo; Jp. *Bukka Engo zenji Hekigan roku*), only the predicate differs: *izu* 出づ (leave, emerge from, be removed from) rather than *hedatsu* 隔つ (part from, interpose, set apart). One modern commentary for this passage of *Hekigan roku* glosses this phrase as, "When the true nature of things comes into relief, then from within the void, a passageway that transcends this material world opens." Iriya Yoshitaka et al., eds. *Hekigan roku* (Iwanami shoten, 1994), vol. 2, 125. Yokomichi and Omote note that the verb *hedatsu* is preferred in Sōtō Zen texts, and the identical phrase appears in an edition of Dongshan Liangjie's teachings compiled in Japan as *Tōzan Gohon zenji goroku* 洞山悟本禅師語録 in 1738 by the Japanese priest Genkei 玄契 (ca. 1716–1738). Whereas the predicate *izu* suggests that the Zen acolyte who experiences the true nature of things—non-dual emptiness or the void—thereby removing himself from worldly attachment, or "dust." By contrast, *hedatsu* may be interpreted to mean that the "dust"—worldly attachment—gets in the way of following the truth path in the void. However, the meaning of *hedatsu* may also be interpreted as "parting from," as in the acolyte parting from the "dust" once he is on the true path in the void. Yokomichi and Omote hold that *hedatsu* must have the former meaning since this passage does not seem to depict Morihisa as

truly I knew not where I went,
over mountains, across waters,
to arrive down in the Kantō.
A hundred years of privilege, a dream in the dust,[35]
the briefest glint, like a grain of gold in the sand.[36]

---

having achieved enlightenment. Yokomichi and Omote, *Yōkyokushū* (jō), 457, appendix entry #224. Itō corroborates this reading of *hedatsu* as "obstructing," glossing the entire phrase as: "the path to enlightenment exists in the absolute sphere of nothingness [void], in which [the duality of] being and non-being has been transcended, but the dust [defilement] of human passions obstructs that path." Itō, *Yōkyokushū* (ge), 317, n. 16. Both editions point out that this phrase occurs in the aforementioned Buddhist texts in reference to the third of a system of Dongshan's Five Ranks (Dongshan wu wei 洞山五位) proscribed for training the Zen acolyte in the non-dual relations between universality and particularity (*wu wei pian zheng* 五位偏正): the level in which "enlightenment emerges from universality," that is, the level in which the boundaries of self are dissolved in the absolute realm of the void, enlightenment emerging at that instant. Also see Chang Chung-Yuan, *Original Teachings of Ch'an Buddhism: Selected from The Transmission of the Lamp* (New York: Pantheon Books, 1969), 48. The Kōzan Bunko *bon* manuscript attributes the character for dream (*mu* 夢) rather than for void (*mu* 無) in the phrase *muchū* (in the void/in a dream), such that the phrase conflates dream and reality: "the true course exists in a dream," which Sanari preserves in his modern gloss of this phrase from the play: "Even in this world like a dream there is a path called the Buddha's path, and if one enters upon it, one can remove oneself from all worldly defilement." Sanari, *Yōkyoku taikan*, vol. 5, 3098. Furthermore, an extended commentary on *utai* 謡 texts of the late sixteenth century titled *Utaishō* 謡抄 (Commentaries on nō librettos) gives the following interpretation of the same phrase: "since the destination exists in dream, this is not a path that has dust [defilement]." See Geinōshi kenkyūkai, ed. *Nō* (San'ichi Shobō, 1978), 548.

35. The playwright continues the conceit of "dust," a metaphor here for attachment and desire in this world. One hundred years of prosperity are like a dream in this world of attachment and desire. A tacit reference perhaps to the erstwhile prosperity of Morihisa's clan prior to their defeat in the Genpei War.

36. One instant may be pivotal in attaining enlightenment. The slightest instant can be as rare and precious as one speck of grain of gold filtered out of innumerable grains of sand. According to Itō, this line is found in Book Three of a Southern Song Buddhist commentary titled *Xutang he shang yu lu* 虚堂和尚語録 (Jp. *Kidō oshō goroku*, Quotations from the sayings of Priest Xutang; pub. 1269). Itō, *Yōkyokushū* (ge), 317, n. 19. This writing circulated widely among affiliates of the Rinzai 臨済 branch of the Zen 禅 sect in medieval Japan. See *Zenseki deetaa beesu: Zenseki no bu: goroku: Kidōroku* (IRIZ) (Database of Zen

Truth to tell, estranged from the capital by
　　intervening clouds,
from friends too, with whom I had vowed
　　"a thousand years,"[37]
in this changing world, alas, I am alone,
truly my fate shrouded in the clouds and mist
of these Kamakura hills.

He remains seated.

MORIHISA

(*unnamed passage*)

Humiliation such as this is too much to endure. Oh, let them kill
me right away.

Tsuchiya moves quietly to base square (jōza).[38]

TSUCHIYA

(*mondō*)　　Excuse me, I have something to tell you.

Standing at base square, Tsuchiya turns toward Morihisa.

MORIHISA　　What might it be?

*He moves from stool to a kneeling position. While speaking, Tsuchiya
moves toward him a bit and kneels facing him.*

TSUCHIYA　　A messenger has just arrived with word that, because

---

writings: Zen writings section: records of quotations; *Kidōroku*) http://iriz.
hanazono.ac.jp/data/zenseki_208.html. Accessed January 11, 2011.

37. Clouds now come between Morihisa and his home in the capital, and he is
separated from the people to whom he had vowed lasting friendship. This image
seems to parallel the previous one, in which dust/defilement is interposed between
Morihisa and the path he seeks to enlightenment. Itō speculates that Morihisa may
refer here to Taira warriors of repute such as Etchū Jirōbyōe Moritsugu 越中次郎
兵衛盛次, Morihisa's nephew, and Akushichibyōe Kagekiyo 悪七兵衛景清 (Taira
no Kagekiyo 平景清), based on the fact that they are referred to in Nagato-bon. Itō,
Yōkyokushū (ge), 317. They are mentioned together with Morihisa as Taira warriors
who are still at large. Kokusho Kankōkai, *Heike monogatari Nagato-bon*, 736.

38. In the other librettos consulted, after hearing this line, Tsuchiya moves to
the base square and, facing front, says: [unnamed passage] *Ara itawashiya zōrō
Morihisa no hitorigoto o ōse sōrō zo ya*, "Oh, how painful! Morihisa is talking to
himself." Then Tsuchiya turns to Morihisa and announces himself. Morihisa asks
him to approach. There are other small differences in the ensuing prose exchange
between the holograph and the subsequent group of variant librettos. For an
example, see Itō, *Yōkyokushū* (ge), 317–18.

you are a prisoner of consequence, you should be put to death without delay.

MORIHISA I am very glad to hear this. I was just saying so. Humiliation such as this is too much to bear, so I was just expressing my desire to be killed right away, and that very wish has been fulfilled! Now then, I suppose it will be directly?

TSUCHIYA No, I've been informed that it will be at daybreak or tomorrow evening.

MORIHISA   *Quietly in intoned prose.*

I see. Now then, they say that personal discretion plays a part in official matters. There are no words to thank you for your kindness during this time. If alive, why wouldn't I repay my debt to you? But if I am put to death shortly, if then too I might rely on you for even one recitation of the *nenbutsu* for my repose, (*Recitative*) then it would be as if your kindness extended to two worlds,[39] and my gratitude would truly go beyond words. (*Intoned prose*) Every morning and every evening I recite the *Kannon Sūtra*. Especially, with this night being my last, I would like to do so.[40]

Morihisa removes the sūtra scroll from the front of his robe and holds it in his left hand.

MORIHISA

(*unnamed passage*)

All thanks and praise for the boundless benevolence and compassion that is the Bodhisattva's Vow.[41] It is said that with Kannon's grace even fixed karma may change.[42]

---

39. Two worlds (*nise* 二世): this life and the afterlife.

40. The other librettos consulted add an additional line here that further accentuates the shared esprit of *shite* and *waki*. Itō reads, *Nakanaka no koto on-kokoro shizuka ni ondokuju sōrae. Tsuchiya mo kore nite chōmon mōshi-sōrō beshi* なかなかのことおん心静かにおん読誦候へ。土屋もこれにて聴聞申し候ふべし "Of course, recite [the sūtra] with a quiet mind. I too will be here to listen." Itō, *Yōkyokushū* (ge), 318.

41. The Bodhisattva refers here to Kannon. "Boundless benevolence and compassion" is the set phrase and epithet used in prayers to Kannon.

42. Kannon's compassion is so powerful that it can even override something as predetermined as karma. According to the NKBT editors, this statement is taken from a Chinese collection of commentaries on the *Lotus Sutra* titled *Fa hua wen ju ji* 法華文句記 (Jp. *Hokke monguki*), and a similar phrase also appears in book eight of the historical tale *Masukagami* 増鏡 (Greater mirror, 1368–1375).

(Sashi)   What I ask is that you let your unconditional
                  benevolence and mercy
             fall upon me, and lead me on the path.[43]
             If he wants for blessings in this life,
             who would ask for salvation in the next?[44]
             If prayers for this life and the next are in vain,
             then would it not make the great saint's Vow[45] a lie?

He unrolls the scroll and holds it in both hands to read the following.

             You might incur a king's wrath and punishment,
             but even if facing the execution block,
             only pray to Kannon, and the [executioner's] sword
             will instantly break to pieces.[46]

He raises the opened scroll in reverence.

TSUCHIYA

  (mondō)   Hearing this passage confirms that indeed there is hope
  for your life.

MORIHISA   An engaging hearing you give me! According to

Yokomichi and Omote, *Yōkyokushū* (ge), 418. *Fa hua wen ju ji* is based on
commentaries by the Chinese Tiantai patriarch Zhiyi 智顗 and was compiled by
the Tiantai monk Zhanran 湛然 (Jp. Tannen; 711–82).

43. "Unconditional benevolence and mercy" 無縁の慈悲: unconditional
because the bodhisattva's benevolence and mercy embrace all sentient beings
without discriminating between those who have a previously cultivated karmic
connection and those who have not. Morihisa refers in the abstract to the path
to enlightenment, but in this context, he is probably referring to the Pure Land.

44. Worshipers of Kannon believe that blessings received in this world such as
health, longevity, prosperity, etc., should not be cultivated as ends in themselves, but
that as one progresses in one's quest for liberation from the root causes of suffering
on the wheel of birth and death, such worldly benefits will occur quite naturally. See
Hayami Tasuku, *Kannon shinkō jiten* (Ebisu Kōshō Shuppan, 2000), 24.

45. Kannon's vow.

46. This is a verbatim quotation of the passage from the *Kannon-gyō* in which
Kannon vows to deliver from tribulation all those who call on him in prayer: "One
might encounter royally ordained woes, / Facing execution and the imminent
end of one's life. / by virtue of one's constant mindfulness of Sound-Observer
[Kannon] / The knives could thereupon break into pieces." Leon Hurvitz, trans.,
Scripture of the Lotus Blossom of the Fine Dharma (Columbia University Press,
1976), 317. Morihisa's recitation of this phrase preserves the original Chinese
syntax of the lines, but he intones each character in a Japanese *onyomi* 音読
pronunciation (as is typical for a Japanese speaker chanting a sūtra in Chinese).

this passage, even if one must incur a king's punishment, the
[executioner's] sword will break into pieces,[47]

TSUCHIYA   Or take the passage about enemies in battle who will
                all be put to flight,
                their flying arrows failing to find their mark.[48]

MORIHISA   Truly they offer hope, and yet, it's not that

He looks at the scroll. Recitative.

                By no means do I recite this sūtra for the purpose of
                staying alive.

*Tsuchiya moves forward to the middle of the stage, seats himself, and looks
at the scroll's contents.*

MORIHISA AND TSUCHIYA   *Reading from the sūtra scroll.*

                (*unnamed passage*)
                All the various evil realms: hell, the realm of hungry
        spirits, that of beasts—the sufferings of birth, old age, illness, death—
        bit by bit he will extinguish them all.[49]

MORIHISA AND TSUCHIYA (*sageuta*)

                If it is as this passage says,   *Both gaze at the scroll's contents.*

CHORUS   Then even the evil realms—
                The three evil paths, can be avoided.[50]

Morihisa again raises scroll in reverence.

                I am thankful and do not regret the end of this life,

---

47. Morihisa paraphrases the original Chinese scripture in Japanese here,
making its content more readily understandable to a Japanese listener.

48. The passage in question is quoted from *Kannon-gyō*: "When disputes go
through civil offices, / When they terrify military camps, / By virtue of constant
mindfulness of Sound-Observer [Kannon] / The multitude of enemies shall all
withdraw and scatter." Hurvitz, *Scripture of the Lotus Blossom of the Fine Dharma*,
318. For the original text, see Sakamoto and Iwamoto, eds., *Hokekyō*, vol. 3, 266.
The ensuing reference in the play to arrows missing their mark seems to be the
playwright's embellishment.

49. Also quoted from *Kannon-gyō*. Hurvitz's English translation reads: "The
various evil destinies / Those of hell, ghosts, and beasts, / As well as the pains of
birth, old age, sickness, and death, / All little by little are extinguished." Hurvitz,
Scripture of the Lotus Blossom of the Fine Dharma, 25. For the original text, see
Sakamoto and Iwamoto, *Hoke-kyō*, vol. 3, 264.

50. Three evil paths (*san akudō*): The three evil transmigratory paths
determined by karma: path of hell (*jigoku* 地獄), path of starving beings (*gakidō*
餓鬼道), path of beasts (*chikushōdō* 畜生道).

Quickly lowers scroll and looks upward.

But nothing grieves me more than thoughts of the next.

Lowers his gaze.

CHORUS

(*ageuta*)   In the past, on Eagle Peak,

Morihisa rolls up scroll and holds in left hand. Tsuchiya turns to the front.

in the past, on Eagle Peak,
the Buddha known as the Lotus, [51]
and now the Master residing in the West, [52]
and Kannon too, who appears in this world on our
    behalf—

Still seated, Morihisa appears to drift off to sleep.

the divine blessing of these three worlds is the same. [53]
So how could one such as I, close to execution,
fail to be included in the Vow?
Morihisa's path after death
is surely not dark. There is hope!

The ai, Tsuchiya's servant, emerges from behind the curtain, silently traverses the bridgeway, and seats himself at the villager position (kyōgenza).

(*unnamed passage*)

How mysterious!

Morihisa awakens from dream and raises head.

While in a short slumber, I received a clear visitation. How

---

51. Ryōzen 霊山 (short for Ryōjusen 霊鷲山; Skt. Grdhrakūta) is also translated as Vulture Peak. The spot where the historical Buddha Śākyamuni first preached the contents of the *Lotus Sūtra*. Here he is referred to as the "Lotus."

52. "The West" (*saihō* 西方) is an abbreviation for *Saihō gokuraku* 西方極楽, the Buddhist paradise in the western direction. A reference to the Pure Land, where the Buddha ("Master") Amida resides.

53. The three figures are essentially the same but are manifested as Śākyamuni in the world of the past, Amida in the future Pure Land paradise, and Kannon in the present, who remains among sentient beings to lead us to enlightenment. A *gāthā* attributed to the Chinese monk Huisi (Jp. Eshi) 慧思 (515–577). According to Itō, this phrase and variants occur in a number of writings, including the Heian period collection *Kōyō shū* 孝養集 (Tales of filial piety). Itō, *Yōkyokushū* (ge), 320, n. 1. The collection is attributed to the Shingon 真言 ecclesiast Kōgyō daishi 興教大師 (1095–1143).

humbled and grateful I am!

He lowers his gaze.[54]

TSUCHIYA AND PALANQUIN BEARERS[55]

(*kakeai*)   With that, the cock was crowing the dawn

Tsuchiya stands up.

The hour has arrived.

Addressed to Morihisa.

The order is to depart immediately.[56]

MORIHISA   I have been waiting, ready for this moment,

Chanted with resolve. Looks at his left hand.

So in my left hand, I have my sūtra scroll, its text inscribed in gold leaf,

Recitative.

and in my right hand, [fragile as my life],

Looks at right hand.

a string of rosary beads.[57]

Raising his head.

Since now this is my end,
and this the path of my departure from this world,

Recitative.

I set out with faltering footsteps.

Stands.
The two palaquin bears lower the palanquin over Morihisa. Recitative.

---

54. While dozing, Morihisa had a vision. He makes brief reference to that fact here as he awakens. More is said about the content of the vision later in the *kuse* section of the play.

55. All of the lines in this *kakeai* section that the holograph allots to Tsuchiya and the palanquin bearers in unison are allotted solely to the *waki* in the other variants consulted.

56. For the beach of Yui (Yui no migiwa 由比の汀, now Yui-ga-hama 由比ヶ浜) on the coast of Sagami province, Kamakura district, or what is today the southern shoreline in the city of Kamakura. This is the execution site where Morihisa is to be beheaded.

57. *Migi ni wa omoi no tama no o no / inochi wa ima o kagiri nareba* 右には念ひの玉の緒の、命は今を限りなれば: *tama* 玉 or "bead" is a pivot (*kakekotoba* 掛詞) embracing both the meanings *omoi no tama* 念ひの玉, "prayer beads" and *tama no o no inochi* 玉の緒の命 "[my] life [fragile] as a string of beads."

TSUCHIYA AND PALANQUIN BEARERS

> Flanked by warriors in front and behind,
> here too the cock's crow signifies parting.[58]

MORIHISA

Recitative.

> With the temple bell tolling at daybreak,
> Moved from jail cell to palanquin,

TSUCHIYA AND PALAQUIN BEARERS

Recitative.

> and hurried off to the beach at Yui.

Morihisa and entourage circle right from front to base square.

Chorus

(*shidai*)　At dawn, emerging from the path of dreams,[59]
At dawn, emerging from the path of dreams
[just a brief] respite on my way to the next world?[60]

*Morihisa turns to face front. Tsuchiya crosses to witness square
and stands. The Bearers withdraw the palanquin and exit by side
door* (kirido). [*When casting includes a* wakitsure *as executioner,
he remains standing at* jiutaimae (*before chorus*).]

TSUCHIYA　　　　　　　　*Still standing.*

(*kakeai*)　Having now arrived on the water's edge at Yui,
the spot is fixed, the fur cushion laid out.

Pointing at corner pillar (metsuke-bashira), *he addresses Morihisa.*

> "Now seat yourself quickly."

Morihisa moves deliberately to metsuke-bashira *and seats himself cross-legged.*

---

58. *Kore mo wakare no tori no koe* これも別れの鳥の声: the cock's crow is
a poetic image associated with the parting of lovers before break of day. Here as
well it is used to signify parting, but of a different order.

59. *Yumeji o izu* 夢路を出づ ("emerge from the path of dreams"): Morihisa
wakes up from the domain of slumber and dream and the brief respite that it affords.
Another possible interpretation is that he awakens from the dream world, i.e., illusion.

60. *Nochi no yo no tabine naruran* 後の世の旅寝なるらん ("[just a brief] respite
on the way to the next world?"): later textual variants replace *tabine* 旅寝 (a shelter
on one's travels) with *kadode* 門出 (departure [as on a trip]). Whereas Motomasa's
choice of *tabine* suggests his dream provides a brief respite from the road to death,
the revised *kadode* reframes his dream as the initial step on that road. Motomasa's
original line effectively foreshadows the dénouement, in which Morihisa's dream
itself proves the key to his delivery from execution. According to Itō, *kadode* became
the normal usage as of the late Muromachi period. Itō, *Yōkyokushū* (ge), 321, n. 13.

MORIHISA   Morihisa promptly took his seat,
            thought about Kiyomizu being in that direction,

He opens sūtra scroll, and holds it open before him with both hands as he reads.

            and turning to the West, intoned
            Kannon's name as he waited.

Tsuchiya unsheathes sword and moves behind him.

TSUCHIYA   Taking hold of his sword,[61] and circling behind him,
            while he was intoning the *nenbutsu*,
            he raised the sword—

Raises sword.

            but what is this—
            the light reflected by the sūtra blocked his vision.

Drops sword on stage in front of Morihisa.

            When the dropped sword was inspected,

Gazes down at sword.

            it had broken in two and lay in pieces.
            What could this possibly mean?

Surprised.

MORIHISA   Morihisa, not expecting this,

Lowers arms holding unrolled sūtra. Looking dazed, he stares straight ahead.

            was simply astonished.

---

61. "Taking up his sword" (*tachi tori* 太刀取り). It is also possible to gloss *tachitori* as the noun "executioner," so the following two interpretations of the clause are possible: "While taking up his sword and circling behind" (*Tachi tori ushiro e meguri tsutsu*) or "While the executioner (*tachitori*) circled behind" (*Tachi tori uchiro e meguri tsutsu*). Because of the ambiguity, it is not clear whether in the earliest staging the *waki* was acting as executioner (*tachitori*) here or whether there was a separate character, an additional *wakitsure* cast in that role. Subsequently, casting the executioner as a separate character became the established staging. My translation follows the casting as delineated in the NKBT edition, i.e., with no *wakitsure* in the executioner's role. Yokomichi and Omote, *Yōkyokushū* (jō), 420, n. 1. Note that it is possible to read this specific passage as the would-be executioner narrating his own actions from a first-person perspective. However, the *shite* recounts his actions in the passages before and after this one from the third-person remove of a narrator, and for the sake of narrative coherence, I have done the same for the executioner's lines here.

TSUCHIYA

Turning toward him.

But wait—what doubt can there be?

The passage from the holy sūtra we just recited:

MORIHISA

Recitative.

"Even when facing execution,

TSUCHIYA   only pray to Kannon

MORIHISA   and the [executioner's] sword will instantly break to pieces."

CHORUS

(*uta*)   Without a cloud of doubt, as in the scripture,

Still holding the open sūtra in both hands, Morihisa raises it up in reverence.

The sword has broken to pieces.

Morihisa directs gaze at the sword.

The Age of Decline[62] is not upon us after all.

How precious this holy sūtra.

With both hands, Morihisa raises sūtra upward before his face in gesture of reverence.

Presently [His Lordship] heard of this

Rolls up sūtra scroll and places in left hand. Morihisa and Tsuchiya turn to face each other.

and ordered [Morihisa] to appear before him quickly, sending envoy after envoy,

Still seated, Morihisa bows to Tsuchiya.

so Morihisa did what he was told

Morihisa stands and withdraws to kōken-za. Tsuchiya moves to witness square and kneels.

and paid a visit to the Kamakura Lord.

And paid a visit to the Kamakura Lord.

(*shaberi, mondō*)

---

62. The Age of Decline (*masse* 末世): reference to the period of the decline of the Buddhist Law (*mappō* 末法), widely believed to have begun in 1052 and expected to continue for 10,000 years. During this period, historical Buddha's teachings remain, but there is no practice of them or evidence of enlightenment resulting from them.

[INTERVAL (*nakairi*)]

Throughout this kyōgen 狂言 *interlude, Morihisa is removed from the action and remains quietly at the* kōken-za. *Stage attendants remove his Buddhist stole* (kesa 袈裟), *and he is dressed as a warrior with an overrobe added to his unlined robe* (hitatare 直垂), *a ceremonial hat* (eboshi 烏帽子), *and a dirk.*

The kyōgen *actor* (ai アイ), *Tsuchiya's Servant, approaches from stage assistant position to base square and stands facing the audience to deliver his lines. He points out that a truly singular event has occurred. The executioner is very experienced, and it is unlikely that it was a mistake on his part. Morihisa is a devout believer in Kannon, and this must have been Kannon's doing.*

Next Servant moves to center stage, faces Tsuchiya, and seats himself. He asks Tsuchiya if he does not agree that the events that have just occurred are the result of divine intervention. Tsuchiya concurs. Tsuchiya orders the ai *to relay the message to Morihisa to put on a* hitatare *and* eboshi, *and appear before Yoritomo.*

The ai *stands and returns to base square, once more facing the audience. He exclaims that Morihisa is indeed a lucky fellow to have his life spared and be called before the shogun. Next he turns toward Morihisa, who waits at the stage assistant position, kneels, relays the Tsuchiya's message, and retreats to be seated at the villager position.*

Morihisa moves forward to stand at base square. Tsuchiya remains kneeling at witness square.

[PART TWO (*nochiba*)]

TSUCHIYA (*mondō*)
　　　　　Now then, Morihisa, His Lordship has something to say to you.

Morihisa promptly falls down on both knees, turns toward front, places both hands on the floor in front of him, and bows deeply.[63]

　　　　　At daybreak [His Lordship] received a telling vision in a dream, and certainly there are grounds for believing you have received one as well. You are ordered to confirm whether you had such a dream.

Still kneeling deferentially, hands on floor, Morihisa turns toward Tsuchiya to respond.

---

63. Morihisa's bow is performed facing downstage center (*shōmensaki*) where we are to imagine that Yoritomo is seated.

MORIHISA   Now that things have come to this, what point is there
to secrecy? I did receive a visitation.

He lowers his gaze.

TSUCHIYA   In that case, Morihisa, explain in detail the nature of
your vision before His Lordship, for he will hear you out.

MORIHISA   *Maintaining the same posture.*
      Yes, sir.

*He stands and moves to before drums (daishōmae) and then to center
(shōchū), where he kneels facing front.*

CHORUS
   (*kuri*)   Amida's oath not to take up Buddhahood till all his
                        forty-eight vows were filled,[64]
                        is not just now beginning.
                        The light of his great compassion, boundless and timeless,
                        where would there be a place it does not reach?

Morihisa continues kneeling at center.

MORIHISA
   (*sashi*)   This being so, placing my faith in his merciful light,
CHORUS   through day and night, dawn and dusk,
                              without fail,
                        I have recited that holy scripture,[65]
                        and especially at such a time as this,
                        knowing how close I am to execution,
                        I do not lapse for even an instant.
MORIHISA   From last evening till before dawn this morning,
CHORUS   as I remained seated thus quietly.

Morihisa remains in a kneeling position.

---

64. In the *Muryōju-kyō* 無量寿経 (*Sūtra of the Buddha of Infinite Life*, Skt.
Sukhāvatī-vyū-ha sūtra) Amida, when still a bodhisattva, made forty-eight vows
for the salvation of all sentient beings, and when he fulfilled them, he entered
nirvana. The sūtra teaches that those with genuine faith in Amida may be reborn
in his paradise, *Gokuraku jōdo* 極楽浄土 (the Pure Land, Skt. *Sukhāvatī*).

65. The *Kannon sūtra* (*Kannon-gyō*). The sūtra teaches that if one invokes
Kannon's name just one time in genuine faith, Kannon will hear that voice and
deliver one from suffering.

CHORUS

(*kuse*) When light still had not dawned at the six windows[66]
suddenly one patch of sky
was ethereally bright,[67]
and of all things, an old priest
who looked to be past eighty,
wearing a *kasāya* stole,[68] clove-yellow in hue,
fingering his rosary beads of crystal,
and leaning on a cane, its handle in the shape of a dove,
said in an exquisite voice,
"I have come here all the way from Kiyomizu
in Higashiyama in the capital
on your behalf.[69]
How could Kannon's original Vow
of boundless benevolence and compassion ever be in
vain?
Calling out my name but once,
when done with genuine faith in me,
will deliver you from a king's punishment.[70]

MORIHISA All the more for you, [Morihisa], for many years and
months,[71]

---

66. *Rokusō* 六窓 ("six windows"): a Buddhist term referring to the six sense organs (eyes, ears, nose, tongue, body, and mind), the sources of earthly desire. In this context, the term can be interpreted as both referring to a state between slumber and the full coming to one's senses, and to the time of day prior to the arrival of dawn.

67. "Ethereally bright," translating *kyomei nari* 虚明なり, meaning unclear. I have followed Itō's interpretation: brightness arising from a miraculous cause rather than from a natural one. Itō, *Yōkyokushū* (ge), 323, n. 10.

68. A surplice or stole (Jp. *kesa* 袈裟, Skt. *kasāya*) making up an important part of a Buddhist monk's habit. It is a long overrobe draped from the left shoulder to under the right arm.

69. Here it is becoming clear that Kannon of Kiyomizu has appeared to Morihisa in his dream.

70. A paraphrase of the passage from the *Kannon-gyō*. Note that the passage is repeated as a refrain throughout the play,

71. It is clear from the pronoun for "you" in the original Japanese, *nanji* 汝, that a superior is addressing an inferior here, i.e., these are Kannon's words addressed to Morihisa, although it is the *shite* who is allotted the line. This line is the *ageha*, a short melodic passage interjected into the choral chant by the *shite* at a point two-thirds of the way through the *kuse*.

CHORUS   your painstaking earnestness has stood out,
                  your awakening exceeds that of others,
                  you may put your mind at rest.
                  I will sacrifice myself
                  to spare your life," [the old priest] said,
                  whereupon the dream ended.
                  Morihisa thought what an awesome thing is this,
                  and his heart's rejoicing knew no bounds.
CHORUS
    (*rongi*)   Yoritomo listened to this.

Morihisa places both hands on the floor in front of him and bows to (the imaginary) Yoritomo as Yoritomo addresses him.

                  "The dream I experienced at daybreak
                  was just the same," [Yoritomo] said,
                  moved to no end by the clear sign of divine sympathy.[72]
MORIHISA
    Still bowing.

                  At this point Morihisa
                  felt as if awoken from a dream.
                  Unable to hold back his tears,

He performs a pattern to express the suppression of his tears, and stands.

                  he made to take his leave.[73]

Turns his back to the audience and proceeds to base square.

CHORUS   "Morihisa, wait a moment,"

Morihisa halts at base square.

                  raising his curtain, [Yoritomo] called.
MORIHISA   Having no recourse—[Morihisa went back][74]

---

72. Starting here and continuing throughout this *rongi*, the chorus steps in to narrate the words and thoughts of Yoritomo, who is not physically represented on stage. Though it is common for the chorus in nō to narrate thoughts and words of a character on stage, especially those of the *shite*, it is rather unusual to mouth the dialogue of a character who does not appear on stage.

73. Note that Morihisa is referring to himself by name and relating his own actions as a narrator might throughout this *rongi*. This is not in itself unusual in nō dramaturgy, but it is unusual to have the *shite* thus collaborate with the chorus to narrate a conversation with someone (Yoritomo) who is not physically represented on stage.

74. One possible reading here is that when Yoritomo calls on him to come back,

He turns back to center, seats himself, and bows. While the chorus chants the
following, Tsuchiya serves the saké from the imaginary Yoritomo to Morihisa.

CHORUS   "A toast to Morihisa's life, [may it be] a thousand autumns

Tsuchiya employs his open fan as a scoop to ladle the saké. He moves with
it to Morihisa's side, and tips the fan in his direction to suggest that he is
pouring it for him.

and ten thousand springs," [His Lordship] said,
and bestowed on him a cup of saké.

Morihisa extends his fan with both hands in front of him to suggest that
it is the vessel in which he is receiving the saké, and then tips his open fan
toward his mouth to indicate that he is drinking sake from it.

MORIHISA
   (*issei*)   Chrysanthemum wine—the seed of a thousand years,
                or so I have heard.[75]

Morihisa is resigned to the possibility of once again being condemned to death.
Nishino Haruo, *Yōkyoku hyakuban*, SNKT 57 (Iwanami shoten, 1998), 427, n. 14.
   75. *Tane wa haru zo to kiku no sake* 種は春ぞと菊の酒. This phrase puns
and pivots on *kiku*, which may refer either to the chrysanthemum (*kiku* 菊) or to
the action of hearing something (*kiku* 聞く), as in hearing some kind of news:
"Chrysanthemum wine, the seeds of spring, or so I have heard." All the other
manuscripts consulted have *chiyo* 千代 (thousand years/long time) instead of
haru 春 (spring): 種は千代ぞときくの酒 (*Tane wa chiyo zo to kiku no sake*),
and I have translated that variant. The idea is that chrysanthemum has life-giving
properties that will endure a thousand years. It is a phrase that Morihisa utters
as he receives saké from Yoritomo. Chrysanthemum saké thus has an auspicious
image. Made by steeping saké in chrysanthemum blossoms, it was served at
court, for instance, to toast to longevity on the occasion of the chrysanthemum
festival on the ninth day of the Ninth Month. In this instance, it is probably used
metaphorically as an image of long-life. In effect, Morihisa is acknowledging
the saké he has received, alluding to its salubrious properties, and returning
Yoritomo's wishes for a long life. The link between chrysanthemum-related elixir
and longevity traces to the Chinese legend of the Daoist immortal Peng Tan 彭祖
(Jp. Hō Tan). Peng Tan's legend creates an added link between chrysanthemum
dew and the *Kannon-gyō*, which may be the reason that the playwright chooses to
allude to this legend here. He had been a favored attendant to the founder of the
Zhou 周 dynasty of China, Emperor Mu 穆王 (Jp. Bokuō), but had committed
an indiscretion and was banished to the wilderness. Emperor Mu taught him two
lines from the *Kannon Sūtra* to protect him there. Hou Tan would copy the lines
on chrysanthemum leaves, and the dew from those leaves, mixed with nearby
stream water, formed an elixir that allowed him to live seven hundred years. In
Japan, Hō Tan was also known as *Kikujidō* ("Chrysanthemum boy"), which is

Morihisa closes fan. Tsuchiya returns to witness square and is seated.

CHORUS   Ah, petals falling on these sleeves![76]

TSUCHIYA

(*mondō*)   Now then, Morihisa, His Lordship has something to say to you.

Morihisa remains seated at center.

Word has reached His Lordship that you have served the Taira house for generations, that you are a warrior of great prowess, and what is more, you are a skilled dancer. Talk of Shume no Morihisa's performance on the occasion of Lord Shigemori's mushroom gathering party last year in Kitayama has reached us as far away as here in the Kantō.[77] Especially at such a happy moment as this, [His Lordship] wishes you to perform, even if just one piece.

---

also the title of a fourth-category nō play (also known as *Makurajidō* 枕慈童) about his auspicious story. Allusion to the elixir here of course underscores the efficacy of the *Kannon Sūtra*, the basis for the Morihisa parable. Librettos of the Komparu, Kongō, and Kita schools substitute the phrase *kiku no mizu* 菊の水 (chrysanthemum dew) for *kiku no sake*.

76. Itō offers the plausible interpretation that this line is a continuation of the preceding one, and Morihisa's joy makes it seem to him as if the blossoms produced by the chrysanthemum seeds are falling auspiciously on his sleeves. Itō, *Yōkyokushū* (ge), 324, n. 3. Perhaps the falling petals are emblematic of the munificence that Yoritomo has shown Morihisa. They are also an image frequently employed to adumbrate the beauty of a dancer's sleeves, and we are approaching the concluding section with the *otokomai* 男舞 dance.

77. Tsuchiya, the *waki*, again relays Yoritomo's thoughts as if Yoritomo is present. Morihisa is referred to as Shume (or Shime) 主馬, lit. "Stablemaster" but here this functions simply as a name (*sei* 姓). Yokomichi and Omote, *Yōkyokushū* (jō), 422, n. 19. Taira no Shigemori 平重盛 (1138–1179) was the eldest son of Taira no Kiyomori 平清盛 (1118–1181), the head of the clan during its political ascendancy in Kyoto in the twelfth century. Though capable by all accounts, Shigemori's premature death precluded him from becoming the next head of the clan. He is referred to here by the metonymic sobriquet Komatsu-dono 小松殿, taken from the location of his Kyoto mansion. Kitayama 北山, lit. northern mountains, is the name of the hilly wooded area on the northern perimeter of Kyoto. Shigemori's hosting of a party there to gather wild mushrooms is not historically attested. The term used to refer to Morihisa's dance is *ranbu* 乱舞, dance performed to entertain at social gatherings that was an alternative to the dances of the formal court repertoire of *bugaku* 舞楽. It seems to refer often to extemporaneous dance matched to the chanting of the then popular verse form *imayō* 今様。

MORIHISA

Seated, he bows during the following.

(unnamed passage)

How thankful I am! How thankful I am!
What is difficult to attain is opportunity,
what is difficult to turn away from is an order from on high.[78]
This moment that I am blessed with
is not mine or anyone's alone.[79]

(kakaru)   A time of peace when all hearts are in concert,
not only throughout this realm
but people elsewhere too,
this Land of the Rising Sun,
also home to the place named "China Plain."[80]

(DANCE: *Otokomai*)

Morihisa dances to the instruments.

CHORUS

(uta)   The banquet's springtime revelry at its height,

At base square (jōza), *Morihisa stamps.*

The cloudless sun's rays balmy,

At side (wakishōmen), *he executes a* sashimawashi *pattern with his fan.*

---

78. The Japanese for this adage is: 得難きは時なり。去り難きは貴命なり
Egataki wa toki nari. Sarigataki wa kimei nari. According to Itō, the same adage
with slight variations appears in the early Han dynasty collection of philosophical
writings titled *Huainanzi* 淮南子 (Jp. *Enanji*). Itō, *Yōkyokushū* (ge), 325, n. 9.
Zeami employs a similar parallelism in his play *Saigyō-zakura* 西行桜 (Saigyō
and the cherry tree): "What is difficult to attain is opportunity; what is difficult to
encounter is a good friend." Yokomichi and Omote, *Yōkyokushū* (jō), 294.

79. 世もて私あるべからず *yo motte watakushi aru bekarazu.* The phrase
in the holograph can be interpreted either as, (1) X is a definite fact that no
individual can dispute; or (2) X cannot be attributed to one individual alone.
Subsequent manuscripts adhere to a less ambiguous variant, as quoted below
from the early Edo Kōzan Bunko 鴻山文庫 text: *yo mote tameshi aru bekarazu*
世もて例あるべからず, or "[Other] examples [such as this] must not exist." Itō,
Yōkyokushū (ge), 324.

80. "China Plain" is a gloss of Morokoshigahara 唐土が原, an *utamakura* and
the name of a plain located in Sagami province (Kanagawa prefecture). Morokoshi
is another name for China in early Japanese, so here the term connotes that
Chinese people too are in sympathy with or adhere to the splendid state of affairs
brought us by Yoritomo and the Kamakura *bakufu*.

celebrating His Lordship a thousand autumns,
Tsurugaoka's pine needles[81]

Sweeps gaze outward. Moves to center stage.

never depleted,
the laurel vine [growing ever longer].[82]

Seats himself facing front.

MORIHISA   Much too awed to linger,[83]

Bows deeply. Stands and moves to base square.

CHORUS   much too awed to linger,
Morihisa makes his excuses
And takes his leave,

Facing front, Morihisa executes the yūken ユウケン *pattern.*

while in his heart rejoicing,[84]

Stamps twice.

while in his heart rejoicing.

---

81. Tsurugaoka 鶴岡: a reference to the Kamakura shrine Tsurugaoka Hachimangū 鶴岡八幡宮. The shrine is dedicated to Ōjin, his mother Empress Jingū, and the goddess called Himenokami 比売神. Together these three constitute Hachimanjin 八幡神. Introduced to its present site by Yoritomo in 1180, the shrine was held in special reverence by his clan. In the play the shrine is also a metonym for the Kamakura *bakufu*. The two first mora in the place name Tsurugaoka pun auspiciously with *tsuru* 鶴, or crane, a cultural icon of longevity.

82. Laurel vine: *masaki no kazura* まさきのかづら, an evergreen shrub. Immortalized as a metaphor for the longevity of the *Kokin wakashū* collection in Ki no Tsurayuki's 紀貫之 canonical preface to that work, the *Kanajo* 仮名序 (*Kana* Preface): *Matsu no ha no chiriusezu shite, masaki no kazura, nagaku tsutawari* 松の葉の散り失せずして、まさきの葛長く伝はり (The needles of the pine do not all fall; the laurel vine trails long). Ozawa Masao, ed., *Kokin wakashū*, NKBZ 7 (Shōgakukan, 1971), 62.

83. *Nagai wa osore ari* 長居は恐れあり, glossed here as "much too awed to linger." *Nagai* literally means "staying in one place for a long time." It forms a pivot with the preceding phrase, with *naga* read as the complement of the phrase *masaki no kazura*, i.e., laurel vine [is] "long" and the subject of the ensuing phrase, i.e., a "long stay" is intimidating.

84. Zeami's holograph is the only extant libretto to conclude with *kokoro no uchi zo ureshiki* 心のうちぞ嬉しき, translated here as "while in his heart rejoicing." The other manuscripts have: *kokoro no uchi zo yuyushiki* 心のうちぞゆゆしき, which may be glossed variously: "His inner heart was awe-inspiring/admirable," or "His judgment [of the situation] was awe-inspiring/admirable."

26 ～ Genre and the *Heike* Plays in Zeami's *Go on* | TOM HARE

The problem of genre is endemic to nō and its predecessor, *sarugaku* 猿楽, and is a self-conscious concern of playwrights in the tradition from the days of Zeami to the present (if not, in fact, from the days of Kannami [also Romanized as "Kan'ami"]).

In the *gobandate* (五番だて Five Categories), one finds hints of a universal cosmology, similar in certain ways to the *rokudō* (六道 Six Paths) or *jūdō* (十道 Ten Paths) of Buddhism, with gods, *shura*, the human, animal and demonic worlds finding places among *waki* nō, *shura* nō, wig plays, etc., but a brief examination of the last two categories (of miscellaneous plays and *kiri* nō) quickly disabuses one of the notion that this comparison can be carried out with any comprehensiveness or consistency.

So also, in Zeami's own typologies of performance, one finds suggestions of broad cosmological inclusiveness. Curiously enough, though, the earliest version, that in *Fūshikaden* (風姿花伝, "Transmitting the Flower Through Effects and Attitudes"), is actually more comprehensive than later typologies, such as the *Santai* 三体 or *Go on* (五音, "Five Classes of Singing" [also translated in this volume as "Five Tones"]). Figure One shows the way some of these typologies are configured. From the *Ongyoku kuden* of 1419 (音曲口伝, "Oral Instructions on Singing") through the *Nikyoku santai ningyōzu* of 1421 (二曲三体人形図, "Figure Drawings of the Two Arts and the Three Modes") and *Go on* of around 1430, one reaches tentatively toward a consistency based on the recurrence of *shūgen* (祝言) and *bōoku* (ばうをく or ぼうをく¹),

---

1. *Bōoku* is written in kana in most of Zeami's works, but in one text, the graphs 亡臆 "a devastated heart," appear. Scholars have also suggested 望憶, "longing thoughts," and 亡憶, "devastated thoughts." Some versions of the original text write 茅屋 alongside the original kana. This means "sedge-thatched hut" and is presumably a metaphor for the life of lonely poverty that gives birth to the

and the conceptual similarity of other categories, even if the terminology varies from text to text (*yūgen* 幽玄 seems to relate to *yūkyoku* 幽曲, *koi* 恋 to *renbo* 恋慕, and *shukkai* or *jukkai* 述懐 to *aishō* 哀傷).[2] But serious obstacles to understanding remain, and it seems likely that we will learn more from mining inconsistencies for the insights they may afford us, than from forcing the repertory into an incomplete or logically unsustainable typology.

FIGURE 1. PERFORMANCE TYPOLOGIES IN ZEAMI'S PERFORMANCE NOTES

A. 祝言   ばうをく*

B. 祝言   幽玄   恋   述懐   ばうをく

C. 祝言   幽曲   恋慕   哀傷   闌曲

D.   女 老人 直面 物狂 法師 修羅 神鬼 唐事

E. 児姿遊舞 老体(老舞) 女体(女舞) 軍体 砕動風鬼 力動風鬼 天女

A. 音曲口伝 Oral Instructions on Singing Sixth, Month, 1419
B. 三道   *The Three Ways*, Second Month, 1423
C. 五音曲條々 *Articles on the Five Classes of Singing*
   (also 五音 *Five Classes of Singing*) not dated, thought to be before 1430
D. 風姿花伝 (物學條々 1400) *Transmiting the Flower Through Effects and Forms*
E. 二曲三体人形図 *Figure Drawings of the Two Arts and Three Modes*, Seventh Month, 1421

*亡臆? 望憶? 亡憶? 亡国[之音]？

---

emotion in question. All the same, none of these graphs really makes very good sense, and it has been suggested that Zeami may have meant 亡国之音 *bōkoku no on*, "the music of a land about to fall," but did not say what he meant because the phrase was itself bad luck. See Thomas B. Hare, *Zeami's Style: The Noh Plays of Zeami Motokiyo* (Stanford University Press, 1986) 265–66, n. 30.

2. These terms are not amenable to translation in a fully reliable way, but heuristically we might render them as follows: *shūgen* is "congratulatory" or "auspicious" singing, *yūkyoku* entails melodic beauty and sensitivity added to the basic character of *shūgen*. *Koi* is romantic love, and *renbo*, "love and longing." *Jukkai* or *shukkai* expresses regret at the passing of time or at one's failure to be properly recognized and rewarded. *Aishō* means the emotional state resulting from pain, grief and injury.

One reason for the problem is the sheer number of typologies in Zeami's *Performance Notes*.[3] In addition to those already mentioned, there are also *ō no koe* わうの声 and *shu no koe* 主の声, two forms of vocalization in singing; 六義 *rikugi* "Six Principles"; 五調子 "Five Musical Modes"; 五位 "Five Ranks"; 九位 "Nine Ranks"; and so on. Another perhaps more interesting reason is Zeami's attempt to mix different perspectives on performance within individual typologies. Thus, *shūgen* is a largely ideologically motivated category, whereas *aishō* and *yūkyoku* are primarily thematically and aesthetically motivated.[4]

More importantly, the ideological and thematic matrices for the creation of nō plays are increasingly at odds with Zeami's concern for virtuosity in the *Performance Notes*, and in the end, virtuosity is a more important priority.[5] How such a virtuosity would be expressed is only apparent in performance, and this is not available to us today, but we might find, even in the texts cited in *Go on*, some ways in which the problems of virtuosity and genre are mutually implicated.

For our present purposes, I will look specifically at a piece from *Go on* relating to *Heike monogatari* and discuss how it is treated in the martial tale and how it is transformed for the nō stage. Among the possible choices are *Morihisa* 盛久, *Sobu* 蘇武 (i.e., *Sotoba nagashi* 卒塔婆流), *Nue* 鵺, *Tadanori* 忠度, *Sanemori* 実盛, *Kaidō kudari* 海道下り, *Saigoku kudari* 西国下り, and *Rokudai no utai* 六代の歌. Of these, *Morihisa* and *Sanemori* are discussed elsewhere in this volume. *Tadanori* is already well known, and Zeami's citation from it in *Go on* is a mere fragment from the entrance of the *shite* of the last act. *Kaidō kudari* and *Saigoku kudari* are long and heavily dependent on the conventions of the catalogue song, and not as successful as the last piece mentioned above, *Rokudai no utai*, which will serve best for our discussion here.

---

3. This is the translation I will use to refer to Zeami's *Nōgakuron* 能楽論.

4. *Shūgen*, for instance, introduces an ideological element which, even in the exemplary play, *Takasago*, does not hold up entirely to scrutiny if one takes the definition of *shūgen* strictly. (See the discussion in Hare, *Zeami's Style*, 77–78.) Even the overarching aesthetic of *yūgen*, although not necessarily alien to *shūgen*, is in the end indifferent to it, and often tends toward a combination of beauty and sadness, rather than beauty and felicity or auspiciousness.

5. *Yūgen* may carry some of the weight of virtuosity, except that in making it indispensable in (good and productive) *sarugaku* performance, Zeami in a certain sense lowers the standard. That leaves the primary typological category for "virtuosity" that of *rangyoku*.

Zeami himself says of the piece, "I was asked by an august person to take certain source materials and render them into *jo-ha-kyū* form, and offer them up; this is the resulting song."[6] His explicit acknowledgment of its significance gives us good reason to investigate it further.

The story of the young samurai Rokudai in the various narrative traditions of *Heike monogatari* is situated in a highly significant place, near the end of the twelfth chapter. It might be seen as a culmination of the events narrated in *Heike*, in that it focuses on the ruthless extirpation of the last generations of Heike sons and plays out the theme of conflict and revenge, seemingly to exhaust the threat to Genji power. It might even have comprised the end of the *monogatari* itself, were not the entire enterprise capped by the final chapter of the tale, *Kanjō no maki* 灌頂巻 ("Initiates' Chapter" or "Water Consecration Scroll"), a book which brings to conclusion a subjective view of the events of the Genpei War from a remarkable and dissonant perspective, emphasizing the tragedy and futility of the struggle.

The Rokudai story is well suited to its role in the tale as a whole. It carries with it the pathos and suspense we associate with earlier celebrated stories in the work, but sits, all the same, apart from those events. By the time Rokudai becomes a problem for the Genji, the war is over. His presence is important only as part of a mop-up operation carried out with something like the bloodthirsty cruelty of a slaughter of innocents.

The account begins ominously, with suspense and foreboding and a tone of venality and wickedness:

平家の子孫といはん人尋ね出したらん輩においては、所望は請ふによるべし[7]

Rewards await the asking for such parties as succeed in searching out people said to be descendents of the Heike.

---

6. Omote Akira and Katō Shūichi, eds., *Zeami, Zenchiku*, Nihon shisō taikei vol. 24 (Iwanami shoten, 1979), 230.

7. I have used the text in Takagi Ichinosuke et al., eds., *Heike monogatari* (ge) NKBT 33 (Iwanami shoten, 1960), 393, also making reference to the online version of the text at http://etext.lib.virginia.edu/japanese/heike/heike.html. The online text reproduces a version of *Heike monogatari* edited by Yamada Yoshio and printed in 1933 by Hōbunkan. All translations are my own unless otherwise stated.

There follows a pathetic story of the helter-skelter search for anyone who can be tainted with the Heike name. Even poor children who happen to have light skin are betrayed by self-professed nursemaids and babysitters, and torn away from the arms of their parents to be drowned, buried, crushed, or stabbed.

With this hideous background, the story of Rokudai begins: he is the child of Koremori, an important Heike scion, and great grandson of the evil Heike strongman, Kiyomori himself. As such, he would be a prize catch for the Genji, and his mother and her attendants have taken care to seclude the child. The Genji have nearly called their searches to an end, when one of them, peeping through the gaps in a fence, happens to catch sight of a charming young prince who has just run outside to apprehend a little white puppy. The scene must seem deeply ironic to readers who are familiar with the *Tale of Genji*, for it is in very similar circumstances that little Murasaki is first spied by Genji's party. So as well is Princess Onna San-no-miya first glimpsed by Kashiwagi in the same work.

In Murasaki's case, it was her custody and eventually her virginity that were at stake, and with Onna San-no-miya, the fateful peeping led to its own form of tragedy, but here the stakes are still higher. Rokudai is not only a true lineal descendent of the Heike, but he is also somewhat more grown-up than many of the slaughtered innocents in the lead-up to his story, so capturing him means coming to a decision about how he then is to be killed. When he is eventually led away, the women in the household (notably his mother and his wet nurse) raise a wail, and his trusty companions, Saitōgo and Saitōroku (who appear in alternating roles, depending on the version of *Heike*), follow in his trail.

Much of the interest is here, in depictions of the mother and wet nurse in their anguish about what to do, and the earnest impotence of Saitōgo and Saitōroku, but as the story moves on, there is further opportunity for pathos in an exchange of letters between the captive Rokudai and his mother. Suspense builds to the climax, a last-second rescue through the intercession of the near super-hero, the priest Mongaku. This is the climactic moment:

> 既に今はの時に成しかば、若君御ぐしの肩にか
> ゝりたりけるを、よにうつくしき御手をもて前
> へ打越し給ひたりければ、守護の武士ども見ま
> ゐらせて「あないとほし。いまだ御心のましま
> すよ。」とて皆袖をぞぬらしける。其後西にむ
> かひ手を合て静に念佛唱つゝ頸をのべてぞ待給

ふ。狩野工藤三親俊切手にえらばれ、太刀を引
側めて左の方より御後に立廻り、既に切り奉ら
んとしけるが、目も暮れ心も消果て、何くに太
刀を打つくべしとも覺えず、前後不覺に成りし
かば、「仕つとも覺候はず、他人に仰附られ候
へ。」とて、太刀を捨て退にけり。「さらば、
あれ切れ、これ切れ。」とて、切手を選ぶ處
に、墨染の衣著て月毛なる馬に乘たる僧一人、
鞭をあげてぞ馳　「あないとほし、あの松原の
中に、世にうつくしき若君を、北條殿の斬らせ
たまふぞや。」とて、者どもひしと走り集りけ
れば、此僧「あな心う」とて、手をあがいてま
ねきけるが、猶おぼつかなさに、きたる笠をぬ
ぎ、指上てぞ招ける。北條「仔細あり。」とて
待處に此僧走ついて、急ぎ馬より飛おり、暫く
息を休めて、「若君許されさせ給ひて候。鎌倉
殿の御教書是に候。」とて取出して奉る。

Since it seemed that his last moment had arrived, the
young prince took hold of his hair where it hung down
over his shoulders and, with his ever-so-lovely hand,
pulled it up out of the way. Thereupon the samurai in
the employ of the deputy [Hōjō Tokimasa] all looked
at him, "Oh, how sad! See how he keeps his noble
composure even now," and they wept into their sleeves
at the sight. The prince then turned to the west, put
his palms together and chanted the Holy Name of
Amida as he stretched forth his neck. Kano no Kudōzō
Chikatoshi had been selected as executioner; he held
his sword up close and walked up behind Rokudai from
the left, but even as he was about to cut him down, his
vision grew dark and he felt dizzy; he couldn't imagine
where to strike and went faint: "I'm afraid I cannot
carry out the deed. I beg you, call upon someone else
to do it," said he, and tossed his sword off to the side.

"If that's it, then you do it, no, you," said the deputy,
and as he was deciding who should finish the job, a
priest in a black cassock rode toward them on a cream-
tinted dapple grey horse, his whip high in the air, at a

full gallop. "Oh, how sad! There on that field of pines, can Hōjō really mean to have ever so lovely a young prince put to death!" and with that, the priest headed straight for where the crowd pressed together: "Oh, what a miserable business this is!" waving his arms wildly in the air to get their attention, then fearing this wasn't enough, he took off his straw hat and held it high so that he might get their attention. Lord Hōjō said, "Wait a minute," and once the priest had run up to where they stood and dismounted, he let him catch his breath. The priest took out a letter and handed it over, "'The young prince has got a reprieve. Here is a letter from His Lordship in Kamakura."[8]

The story is minutely observed, and the element of suspense is skillfully deployed by setting out a perilous situation for a character who is already sympathetically situated within the narrative. The exchange of dialogue between his unwilling executioners, remarks about his courage and beauty, a minute-by-minute account of the events that seem to portend imminent execution—everything is carefully articulated to produce the maximum audience engagement and a powerful sense of relief when Rokudai is reprieved. The events proceed chronologically and are ordered in a linear and easily comprehended fashion. The narrative is straightforward, clear and written in a style that suggests an eyewitness account, although some of the formulaic elements of *Heike monogatari* are also evident.[9] The arrival of Mongaku exemplifies the best in a last-minute reprieve.

If the story seems to suggest a Hollywood Western, perhaps that merits our admiration for its fulfillment of the basic features of suspense narrative. It is easy to imagine the story being turned into a playscript with only the smallest changes, and that is what one might be led to expect by Zeami's injunctions about being true to source materials. However, Zeami handles it quite differently.

---

8. In this case I have used the Hōbunkan text mentioned above: Yamada, *Heike monogatari*, 1933. It seems a bit more vivid than the NKBT text, but those who prefer the latter may refer to Helen McCullough's translation in *The Tale of the Heike* (Stanford University Press, 1988), 414.

9. In, for instance, the repetition of the phrases *ana itoshi* and *yo ni utsukushi* in the passage.

In Zeami's treatment, formalist concerns are evident from the beginning. He prefaces the piece with this note, as mentioned before, "I was asked by an august person to take certain source materials and render them into *jo-ha-kyū* form, and offer them up. This is the resulting song."

Zeami's situation of the story in the configuration of *jo-ha-kyū* tempts us to try dividing his text into the requisite parts, but however that division might be constructed in its particulars, we cannot help but notice certain structural elements in the text, as a schematized rehearsal of it reveals. (The full translation of this passage as it appears in *Go on* follows this chapter.)

First we find a rather generic statement about impermanence, in Buddhist Sino-Japanese, then a *nanori*, or self-introduction, which raises more questions than it answers. For our purposes here, let us call the person delivering these lines the "waki."

The *mise-en-scène* at Hasedera which follows is lovely, comparable to many of the *ageuta* of the first *dan* in well-known plays, but as soon as it is over, we find, in an abrupt change of pace, these lines:

爰にあはれなる事の候、御堂の西の脇に
局しつらひて、女性の籠りて候 ... 10

Something deeply affecting has happened here: A
room has been partitioned off, back to the west side of
the temple hall, and a lady has taken refuge there.

I would suggest this is the real *ha*, not the point Zeami identifies (between the *shidai* and the *nanori*, earlier) but then, maybe this should be considered the *ha* of the *ha*).

What follows is a masterful description of a troubling scene, with, in Zeami's own version, much more attention to the nature of hearsay in the situation, than in the version that has been incorporated into the repertory of the Kita and Kanze schools, in which the signals of hearsay are played down.[11] The version in *Go on* reads as follows:

---

10. This is the version from *Go on* printed in Omote and Katō, eds., *Zeami Zenchiku*, 230. For ease of understanding, I have followed Omote in supplying *kanji* for some words originally written exclusively in *kana*.

11. The piece is extant (in addition to Zeami's version in *Go on*) in various woodblock editions, starting with one by Kōetsu. The present-day Kanze text is printed with helpful annotations and a modern Japanese translation in Sanari

あさましき御事をこそ聞きてさぶらへ、只今集
まり上りたる旅人、駿河の国千本の松原とかや
にて、平家の棟梁六代御前、只今斬られさせ給
とて、人の集まるを見て候と申を聞きてさぶら
ふとて、なみだにむせび臥し転びたり

"I've heard terrible news. Travelers on their way back to
the capital have come together here just now, and they
say they saw a crowd assembled, talking about how His
Lordship, the Heike chief Rokudai has just been slain
at a place called the Pine Grove of Senbon, or some
such, in the province of Suruga. I heard the travelers
talking about this," she says and collapses in tears.

After this there are general observations about grief, in the form of
references to Confucius and Bo Juyi, and then a broad statement about
how Confucian morality is an inadequate resort in times of tragedy. A
statement of sympathy for the grieving women follows this.

In the remainder of the piece, statements of stark pessimism give
way to denial on the part of the mother, and eventually to a rehearsal
of the religious precautions she took to prevent the very events she has
heard reported. In the end, she makes a fervent call upon the bodhisattva
Kannon, which is apparently answered in the arrival of Saitōgo and
Saitōroku, who report Rokudai's miraculous reprieve.

Kentarō, *Yōkyoku taikan* vol. 7 (Meiji shoin, 1974 [1931]), 72–77. See also Sanari's
discussion of the woodblock editions, 3–7. The passage in question reads: 唯今
あさましき事をこそ聞きて候 ［さふら］へ。集まり上りたる旅人、駿
河の国の千本の松原にて、平家の棟梁六代御前の斬られさせ給ふを。
見て候と申す者の候 ［さふら　ふ］と申しもあへず伏しまろびたり
("I've just heard terrible news. [There are] travelers on their way back to the
capital who have come together here, and there's someone who says he saw how
His Lordship, the Heike chief Rokudai has just now been slain at a place called
the Pine Grove of Senbon, in the province of Suruga." But before she can even
finish saying this, she collapses in tears.) In this version, the phrase 集まり上り
たる旅人 is left hanging, and the attendant reports that there is an eyewitness to
the execution. In Zeami's version, the attendant does not mention an eyewitness,
but says that she saw people assembled talking about the execution. The Sanari
text uses the standard auxiliary verb *safurafu* (Modern Japanese: *sōrō*) whereas
Zeami uses the voiced *saburafu* (a specifically feminine form of the auxiliary) for
the attendant whereas the more general reported speech of the crowd is not so
marked (in Zeami's text it is written with the *kanji* 候 alone).

Zeami's text can be read as the account of an outright miracle. He says,

するがの千本にてすでに、斬られさせ給ひ
しを、上人其時に、駒を早めて走り下り、
喜びの御教書にて、助からせ給ふと…

"At Senbon in the province of Suruga,
after Rokudai had been cut down,
a holy man—at that very time—
raced his pony over, dismounted,
and saved his life
with felicitous orders from on high.[12]

This is a fascinating departure from the *Heike* text that has yet to be persuasively accounted for in this little-studied piece, but it is only part of the sophisticated epistemological context in which Zeami reads the story. Note that he nests the narrative within gossip and messengers' reports, and reflects that discursive nesting in a nesting of subjectivities. We are given, at different removes, the perspectives of the mother, the serving woman, Saitōgo and Saitōroku, the assembled crowd and the figure we have been calling the *waki*. Zeami's reworking of the material moves the point of view away from the chronicling of Genji murders, which occupies the last part of Chapter Twelve of the *Heike* (almost as if it were a list), to situate the point of view in a bystander, a wandering priest, very much the "waki" of a conventional nō play, but here the conventionality ends, for a wonderfully suspenseful and touching account of an apparent tragedy and the last-minute reprieve, all in reports from a vantage point removed not only from the principal, Rokudai, but also from his mother.

Technically speaking, the entire song is very well disposed, and this particular passage is a tour-de-force. It shows many of the characteristics of the narrative centerpiece of a classic play, that is, of a *kuri-sashi-kuse* sequence, even though the Kanze school classes it as *jō, kudoki, kusemai*.[13] Notice, among other things, how the rescue comes just with the *ageha* of

---

12. Sanari's text is substantially the same, but he inexplicably translates the crucial passage into modern Japanese as 駿河の千本で将に斬られようと遊ばしたところへ … i.e., "… At Senbon in the province of Suruga, as Rokudai was just about to be cut down …"

13. Kanze Sakon, ed., *Kanzeryū yōkyoku zoku hyakubanshū* (Hinoki shoten, 1973), 1280–82.

the *kuse*, a high point in the narrative, where, in a full nō, the chanting would change from the unison eight voices of the chorus to a solo part for the *shite*.

The construction of a subject in this play is technically very different from that in the *Heike* narrative. The *Heike* narrator assumes, on the one hand, a more knowledgeable perspective on the events, whereas the inaccuracy of the narrative of hearsay in *Rokudai no utai* allows for the depiction of a subject, the "waki," as it were, who is at the same time its voice—all the more so on the occasion of performance, where this piece is not performed as a play, but as a virtuosic recital piece, a *rangyoku* 乱曲.[14]

More intriguing still: it is this "waki" who is the ethical center of the piece; it is his subjectivity from which all the other subjects in the play are seen, and his subjectivity itself is thematized by Zeami in such intriguing lines as:

夢も現も隔てなく、向去却来の境界に至る

("there is no separation between dream and substance
and I arrive in the realm of facing about and doubling
back.")

This is an explicitly Zen expression.[15] The term apparently originated in the aspirations of a bodhisattva, who, having come to full enlightenment, nonetheless remains in the phenomenal world to save other sentient beings. In Zeami's *Performance Notes*, the term refers to the complete virtuoso who, having mastered all the technique and transcendence of the art, resorts to unorthodox and normally uninteresting performance techniques, imbuing them with a fresh interest and excitement. Here, in reference to a character in a song, it is not entirely clear what Zeami intends, although it seems to focus our attention on the subjectivity of the "waki" as the best informed point of view in the piece. The "waki" might be said to have come to a deep level of realization, even before the events of the piece begin, only to discover

---

14. In the Kanze school, this is designated as one of the *Sankyoku* 三曲, three special virtuoso pieces.

15. There are examples of it in *Kōchi zenji kōroku* 宏智禅師広録 ("The Wide-Ranging Sayings of Zen Master Hongzhi") and elsewhere, and it is crucially an element in the title of Zeami's late text from the performance notes, *Kyakuraika* 却来花, "The Flower in … Yet Doubling Back." Hongzhi (1091–1157) was a Zen monk of the Song dynasty.

another level of complexity in his reality, attested in the grief, near tragedy, and miraculous reprieve of the events recounted. Perhaps this is a further epiphany for an already deeply perceptive, fully aware Zen adept?

It is fitting that this piece, so individually and self-consciously constructed by Zeami in a late text, should thematize an element of Zeami's theory of performance, elsewhere articulated only in technical and rather abstruse ways. One only wishes the piece found its way onto the nō stage in a more fully articulated and accessible way. As a recital piece it is very rarely performed and little known.

The comparison of narrative sources with their dramatic transformation on the Japanese stage provides one of the surest testimonies of the vitality of tradition in the literary and performance arts of Japan. We see tradition in this particular case from an unusual and transgressive perspective, a fact that may, indeed, give us some reason to reconsider what "tradition" itself means in the seemingly so heavily canonized and weighty world of nō drama.

27 ⟶ *Rokudai no utai* (The Song about *Rokudai*)

| TOM HARE

INTRODUCTION

Rokudai no utai 六代の歌 today appears only in Zeami's *Go on* 五音 (Five Classes of Singing). *Rokudai no utai* dramatizes the *Heike monogatari* account of the execution of Rokudai, Kiyomori's great-grandson and last significant male heir.[1] It roughly follows the account in the final chapter of *Heike monogatari* of Rokudai's capture and reprieve. The *Heike* describes the boy's tense youth, as the new shogun, Minamoto no Yoritomo 源頼朝, vascillates about the need to have him executed. Once Rokudai reaches adulthood and takes the tonsure, things seem less uneasy, but while in his thirties, he is executed on the orders of the shogunate. *Rokudai no utai* is a dramatic recasting of his story. We find him as a youth and experience the happy ending of a last-minute reprieve obtained by Mongaku 文覚, the priest famous in the *Heike* tradition as a *deus ex machina*.

The fragment of the play found in Go on is set in Hatsuse, where Rokudai's mother is in retreat; we learn that she has been there praying fervently for her son's safety after he has been apprehended. The priest (who seems to fulfill the role of *waki*) recounts the woman's suffering; her prayer to Kannon, and news that her son has been spared bring the reader to the happy conclusion of the play.

---

1. Rokudai is the only son of Koremori, the eldest son of Shigemori, who was Kiyomori's heir.

Because Zeami's discussion of *Rokudai no utai* in *Go on* is the only extant form of the piece, little can be noted about its performance. However, it resembles both *Rō-Giō* and *Morihisa*, also translated in this volume in its theme and, to a degree, its structure: all involve *michiyuki* 道行 (poetic travel sequences) and a last-minute-reprieve. Like *Rō-Giō*, the affection between child and parent (here, Rokudai and his mother) heightens the dramatic tension in the play.

Numerous later plays that are no longer in the active performance repertoire about Rokudai and Mongaku survive in the corpus of *bangai yōkyoku*.

Rokudai no utai
(The Song about Rokudai)[1]
| Translated by Tom Hare

(I was asked by an august person to take certain source materials and render them into *jo-ha-kyū* form, and offer them up; this is the resulting song.)[2]

> If in nightfall at a traveler's lodging,
> the transience of this world is plain to see,
> then in the vanishing of dewdrops on the wind,
> we find the likeness of all things' mutability.

(In this case, from the *jo* here, we have the tone of *rangyoku*.)[3]

> I am a humble priest with no fixed residence, wandering the provinces wherever my affinities may take me, and in a world where famous sites and ancient ruins present themselves, I can either pay heed or pass them by; there is no separation between dream and substance, and I arrive in the realm of facing about and doubling back.[4]

Rokudai no utai 六代の歌. From Zeami's *Go on* 五音, *"Five Sorts of Singing,"* Tom Hare, *Zeami: Performance Notes* (Columbia University Press, 2008), 406–13. This translation is based on Omote Akira and Katō Shūichi, eds., *Zeami, Zenchiku*, Nihon shisō taikei vol. 24 (Iwanami shoten, 1979), 230–32. I have also referred to the annotated text in Sanari Kentarō, *Yōkyoku taikan*, vol. 7 (Meiji shoin, 1974), 72–77. For further details, see Chapter 26 in this volume.

1. Hatsuse (or Hase) Rokudai 泊瀬六代 was the son of Koremori 維盛 and great grandson of the Heike dictator, Kiyomori 清盛. As such he was the focus of deep suspicion on the part of the Genji, even as just a child. In the account of his life given in the last chapters of *Tales of Heike*, Book 12, he is hunted out of seclusion with his mother and sisters at about age twelve, and captured. The priest Mongaku 文覚 manages to procure a pardon for him from Yoritomo 頼朝 just as he is about to be executed, and he takes the tonsure, to survive until about thirty when suspicions about him arise again and he is finally executed, the last of Kiyomori's direct line.

2. Smaller print in parentheses is used for Zeami's interlinear comments.

3. This is a note written in next to the line "then in the vanishing …" in one manuscript.

4. 向去却来. This unusual word also appears in *Articles on the Five Sorts of*

(*tadakotoba*)

Here in the land of Yamato, where the miraculous
power of the Savior Kanzeon is particularly strong, I will go into
retreat for a time and admire the landscape around this mountain
temple:

(*sageuta*)   Mountain peaks stand tall,
valleys all around,
Houses vanish seamlessly into the clouds,
the vespers bell resounds through rain.

(*jō*)   Dusk has begun to fall
at that bend in the river, clouds rise in waves,
at that bend in the river, clouds rise in waves,
and bring the sea to mind; Potalaka[5] must be just like this:
Secluded Hatsuse Temple, how rich in blessings!
It's true, after all, as they say,
"with snow fallen on Hatsuse Mountain,
a fishing skiff shoves off from the shoals ..."[6]
the view is justly famous, here at the Kaku River,[7]
the view is justly famous, here at the Kaku River.

(*tadakotoba*)

Something deeply affecting has happened here: a room has
been partitioned off, back to the west side of the temple hall,
and a lady has taken refuge there. There seems to be some grave
apprehension pressing upon her; although the reason isn't clear,
it's plain from her appearance, and in the words she cannot keep
entirely secret, that there is some cause of grief that keeps her
weeping and wailing on and on.

Singing; apparently it is an extension of the Buddhist term *kyakurai* 却来, a kind of
recursion on the part of an enlightened being back into the world of phenomena in
order to save other sentient beings. In Zen, *kyakurai* takes on additional meanings,
involving the dialectic unenlightened/enlightened.

5. Potalaka 補陀落 (Jp. Fudaraku) is a paradise over which Kannon (Skt.
Avalokiteśvara) presides. Many medieval Japanese assumed it could be reached
across the sea from the southern tip of the Kii peninsula in central Honshu.

6. *Man'yōshū*, no. 2347: *Amawobune Hatuse no yama ni furu yuki no kenagaku
kohishi kimi ga ne zo suru*, "How long I have languished in longing for you, long as
the snow falling on Mount Hatsuse, where the fisher boats draw up; now I can hear
you coming."

7. The name, perhaps, of a stretch of the Hatsuse River, but also for a pun on
kaku, "thus."

(*sashi*)
From time to time a person who appears to be her serving maid
comes out of the room and circles the four sides of the temple
hall. She seems to be performing the Thousand Paces,[8] but before
she can finish all the steps, she hurries back into the room, and
says, "I've heard terrible news. Travelers on their way back to the
capital have come together here just now, and they say they saw
a crowd assembled, talking about how His Lordship, the Heike
chief Rokudai, has just been slain at a place called the Pine Grove
of Senbon, or some such, in the province of Suruga. I heard the
travelers talking about this," she says and collapses in tears. The
lady, for her part, had reassured herself that no matter what, this
would never happen, but now she raises her voice in an unstinting
wail and falls to the floor weeping. So now, the rest of us all realize
that the lady must be the mother of Rokudai.

(From this point, *Aishyau* [*aishō*].)

(*jō*)	As we've been told,
(*shioru*)	Confucius felt a fire kindled in his heart
	when he had to part from his child Liyu,
(*shioru*)	and Bo Juyi conceived a hatred for medicine,
	left at the bedside when his child died before him.
(*ge*)	The framer, on the one hand,
	of "Benevolence, Integrity, Propriety, Wisdom and
	Trust,"
	a founding Master, on the other,
	of the Way in writing;
	If men like these were so stricken by grief,
	how much more then, someone in these latter days,
	and a woman at that: in her mind
	the grief at parting from someone so beloved
	could only be expected,
	but this sadness passed all reasonable bounds,
	and moved the hearts of the bystanders too,
	to soak their sleeves in tears.
	After a while, the mother,
	wiping away her tears said,

---

8. A devotional practice performed in the hope that one's wishes will be
fulfilled by supernatural intercession.

"All the same, my child put his trust in the succor of a
  holy saint—
how could that have been in vain!
What's more, if he were really slain, then Saitōgo and
  Saitōroku[9]
should come running with the news;
and if we caught wind of it from strangers first, then
  how is it
that they haven't at least come along in the strangers'
  wake to confirm the story?"
Before she could even finish speaking, her words, like
  leaves,
were moistened with a dew of tears; however would
  her heart forget the slightest part of this?
how would she live on in the world
with this beloved boy of hers,
the seed of his line, already gone!

(*kusemai*)

"Strike the bell at Hatsuse,
and the sound will strike deep in my thoughts:
the world makes its sense in the impermanence
of each and every action, and the little time given over
to a mother for her child is but the trifle of a vision or
  a dream;
this, I thought I understood long ago, but now,
faced in earnest with this deprivation,

(*nobe*)   all my erstwhile resolution is vanished in an instant,
I am cast into darkness,
my heart is seared unbearably with longing,
I can think only that my being
is on the verge of disappearance.
But even so, even as I hear
my child is lost to me

---

9. Sons of the warrior Saitō Sanemori 斎藤実盛. When Koremori left his wife
and children in the capital in the summer of 1183, he assigned these young men
to protect his son Rokudai. See *Heike monogatari,* "Koremori's Flight from the
Capital" (Kakuichi-bon 7.14). For Sanemori, subject of the nō *Sanemori* and
Genzai Sanemori, see the chapter by Akiko Takeuchi and translations by Mae
Smethurst in this volume.

I cling to the hope,
the precious sanctuary of belief—

(*nobe*)   All praise to Kanzeon, Great in Compassion!—
I put my faith in her originary vow, that's all I desire,

(*nobe*)   Rouse thy faith in

(*kakeiri*) [10]   Kannon's might,
'which sunders to pieces the slayer's blade …'[11]
Pray be true to that vow!
shatter the enemy's sword, and save my child!"

(*jō*)   At just that moment
a man appeared and announced
that Saitōgo had arrived;
the mother called out,
what's happened, what's happened?
and his answer filled her with joy.

(*yoru*)   "At Senbon in the province of Suruga,
after Rokudai had been cut down,
a holy man—at that very time—
raced his pony over, dismounted,
and saved his life
with felicitous orders from on high,"
said he, whereupon
the mother—her heart must have been overwhelmed—
was unable even to discern her own happiness,
and sat in a stupor of amazement.
"What a blessing," said she,
and put her hands together in prayer, her sleeves
were moistened with unconscious tears,
she must have felt her robes would never dry.

---

10. Omote notes the use of the same term in *Jinen Koji* 自然居士, *Utaura* 歌占 and *Yukiyama* 雪山, but suggests that in contrast with its usage in those pieces, here it is not an indication of a rhythmic pattern, but is to be understood with the direction "nobe."

11. *Lotus Sūtra*, VIII. 25, "The Universal Gateway": "If … a man who is about to be murdered calls upon the name of the bodhisattva He Who Observes the Sounds of the World, then the knives and staves borne by the other fellow shall be broken in pieces, and the man shall gain deliverance." Leon Hurvitz, trans., *Scripture of the Lotus Blossom of the Fine Dharma* (Columbia University Press, 1976), 312. Hurvitz's "He Who Observes the Sounds of the World" is a translation of the name of the Bodhisattva Kan(ze)on 観世音, or Avalokiteśvara.

28 ∿ Nō as Political Allegory: The Case of *Haku Rakuten*

| Susan Blakeley Klein

INTRODUCTION

In the nō play *Haku Rakuten*, the Sumiyoshi Daimyōjin (guardian deity of *waka* poetry) confronts the Tang dynasty poet Bo Juyi 白居易 (772–846) (known as Haku Rakuten 白楽天 in Japan) who has been sent as an envoy by an unnamed Chinese emperor.[1] After besting Haku Rakuten in a poetry contest, the Sumiyoshi deity leads a host of deities and dragon gods in summoning up a "divine wind" (*kamikaze* 神風) to blow the poet back to China. Gerry Yokota-Murakami has noted that the deity as depicted in this play "might be considered the symbol par

I would like to express my gratitude to LeRon Harrison, whose excellent translation of *Haku Rakuten* for a graduate seminar first got me interested in the play, and to research assistant Junko Matsuura, for her tireless persistence in uncovering related materials. Many thanks to Araki Hiroshi 荒木浩, who translated this chapter for publication: Susan Blakeley Klein, "Seijiteki gui toshite no nō: *Haku Rakuten* wo megutte," *Osaka Daigaku Daigakuin Bungaku Kenkyūka Kiyō*, vol. 50 (March 2009), 29–68. Thanks are due also to Junko Hizume, who proofread the Japanese version, and to Ken Robinson and Anne Walthall, who read the chapter in draft form and offered invaluable suggestions for improvement.

1. The Sumiyoshi Daimyōjin 住吉大明神 is actually not singular, but plural—as will be discussed below, the deity is a complex of at least three male deities and a female deity. However, as the figure appearing in the nō play *Haku Rakuten* is an old man, I will provisionally use the masculine singular here to discuss the deity. Haku Rakuten is the Japanese reading of Bo Juyi's 白居易 family name (白, Ch. Bai or Bo) and his "capping" or "courtesy" name" (楽天, Ch. Letian).

excellence of *bunbu ryōdō* 文武両道, the dual way of brush and sword, the samurai ideal."[2] In *Heike monogatari* and *Genpei jōsuiki*, the focus of this volume, the Sumiyoshi deity is also depicted as a deified warrior-poet, and it is clear that elements of the deity's representation in *Haku Rakuten* are based on these war tales. And yet, for the most part, Sumiyoshi's role as one of the "gods of war" (*gunjin* or *ikusagami* 軍神)[3] has been entirely overshadowed by his persona as the guardian deity of poetry. Although most modern nō scholars have recognized that the *kamikaze* in the second half of *Haku Rakuten* resonates with the *kamikaze* of the Mongol invasions, the sea battle in the second half of *Haku Rakuten* is nevertheless read as a purely aesthetic exercise, ignoring any hints of martial posturing in the text.

There are a number of reasons why the image of Sumiyoshi as a martial deity has tended to be neutralized in modern scholarship. First, although in the medieval period Sumiyoshi was frequently identified as one of the "gods of war," scholarship on the Sumiyoshi Daimyōjin has focused almost entirely on how the deity came to be considered the preeminent guardian of *waka* poetry.[4] Unlike the Hachiman deity, a much more famous god of war strongly identified with warrior culture in general and Minamoto no Yoritomo in particular, the Sumiyoshi deity is closely associated with the imperial family and court culture. Little historical spade-work has been done to unearth the military involvement of the Sumiyoshi Shrine (and the Tsumori clan of *kannushi* 神主, or "chief priest") in the unstable political landscape of medieval Japan. One focus of this chapter will therefore be an attempt to remedy that scholarly lacuna.

---

2. Gerry Yokota-Murakami, *The Formation of the Canon of Nō: The Literary Tradition of Divine Authority* (Osaka University Press, 1997), 156.

3. As Thomas Conlan notes, the "gods of war," which included both Buddhist deities and kami, were never authoritatively identified. See the discussion in Thomas Conlan, *State of War: The Violent Order of Fourteenth-Century Japan* (Center for Japanese Studies, University of Michigan, 2003), 173.

4. Among numerous articles, see Katagiri Yōichi, "Wakakami toshite no Sumiyoshi no kami," *Suminoe*, no. 175 (1985), 18–25; Miwa Masatane, "*Chikuen shō* karon no seisei to hatten: kajin toshite no Sumiyoshi myōjin wo megutte" *Nagoya Daigaku kokugo kokubungaku* 13 (November 1963), 25–40; and Hosaka Miyako, "Tsumori-ke no kajingun (2): Sumiyoshi myōjin no shimei," *Gakuen*, no. 433 (1974), 43–80 (reprinted in *Tsumori-ke no kajingun* [Musashino shoin, 1984], 30–61). In English, see Susan Blakeley Klein, *Allegories of Desire: Esoteric Literary Commentaries of Medieval Japan* (Harvard University Press, 2002), 190–98.

A second reason may be ideological. The play can be read as a straightforward rejection of Chinese poetry in favor of *waka*, and one can easily imagine it being used to lend propagandistic support of Japan's war effort in the first part of the twentieth century. Since the play is generally acknowledged to be well written and extremely interesting to perform, it may not be surprising that in the post-war period scholars and actors have tended to downplay its martial elements.[5] Instead, most scholars have taken a more moderate position: *Haku Rakuten* allows for the important role of Chinese poetry as an influential source in the development of Japanese literature, while nevertheless asserting the superiority of native verse. In this reading, the play becomes a contest on the level of "anything you can do, I can do better," and any uncomfortable political resonances are suppressed.[6]

A third reason involves issues of historicism and the nature of political allegory itself. For a text to be identified as political allegory, one must be able to place it within a specific historical context. A poem, for example, that is written for a specific political purpose (say, petitioning for reinstatement to office), but cloaks that purpose in metaphorical language, may be impossible to identify as political allegory if all hints of the original circumstances in which the poem was written are removed. In the case of nō plays, we often have only the vaguest idea of when a play was written and by whom, much less for what purpose. Even if a play had been written explicitly as a political allegory of contemporary events, over time, as the original context in which the play was composed fades from memory, it would be increasingly difficult to read the play as allegorical.

----

5. Although I have not been able to find any concrete evidence to support the idea that *Haku Rakuten* was deployed ideologically to support the war effort, the fact that in a recent *zadankai* (round table discussion) on the play, the nō actors and critics go out of their way to downplay the play's more jingoistic aspects seems significant. See Asami Shinkō, Hirose Shintarō, and Kiyoda Hiroshi, "*Haku Rakuten* o megutte," *Kanze* (February 1984), 41–46.

6. Takemoto Mikio, for example, argues that the play is an extended meditation on the practice of *kudai waka*, or *waka* written on the topic of Chinese couplets, and although I do not have the space to discuss that idea here, the use of a series of alternating and complementary Chinese and Japanese verses to structure the first half of the play gives credence to that interpretation. The first half of the play certainly evinces a much more ambivalent attitude toward China and Chinese poetry than the second. See Takemoto Mikio, "Sakuhin kenkyū: *Haku Rakuten*," *Kanze* (February 1984), 4–12.

Nevertheless, it is hard to believe that nō plays are as purely aesthetic and disconnected from politics as scholars tend to assume today. We know, for example, that in the fourteenth and fifteenth centuries patronage of the Kanze troupe came almost entirely from the Ashikaga shogunate, and it seems unlikely that nō plays directed toward warrior patrons would have been completely apolitical. And we know that in the late sixteenth century Toyotomi Hideyoshi commissioned a group of ten nō plays celebrating his military exploits.[7] However, in the Edo period, plays with such obvious political content were excluded from the canon. Edo period kabuki and bunraku puppet theater were also outlawed from directly representing contemporary events on stage, yet they found ways to circumvent this obstacle in order to meet the desires of their audience. Nō, on the other hand, became, essentially, a depoliticized theater (albeit a theater that had important symbolic effects in supporting the Tokugawa ideology).[8] Modern critical methodologies, which have treated nō as a purely aestheticized object of study, have also played a role in the neutralization of political content. It is not surprising, then, that even if a play such as *Haku Rakuten* was written explicitly as a political allegory, its political content became relatively easy to ignore.

Although I have raised a multitude of issues, in this chapter I will restrict myself to examining three interrelated questions that should help us think about *Haku Rakuten* as political allegory (as well as link to the overall theme of this book). First, how does Sumiyoshi's deified poet-**warrior** image as exemplified in *Haku Rakuten* develop historically? And how is this image related to the representation of the deity in *Heike monogatari* and *Genpei jōsuiki*? Second, given that the Sumiyoshi deity actually plays a relatively minor role in medieval war tales (particularly compared to such deities as the Kumano Gongen or Hachiman) and that Sumiyoshi also appears to play a comparatively small role in the historical record of the Mongol invasions, why might the author *of Haku Rakuten* have chosen the Sumiyoshi deity for its central role? Third, Kume Kunitake and Takano Tatsuyuki (and more recently Amano Fumio) have argued that *Haku Rakuten* is actually a composite allegorization of two events that roiled the capital in the summer of 1419. All three scholars

---

7. See Steven Brown's chapter on the Hideyoshi plays in *Theatricalities of Power: The Cultural Politics of Noh* (Stanford University Press, 2001), 119–28.

8. Eric Rath's recent book *The Ethos of Noh: Actors and Their Art* (Harvard University Press, 2003) addresses the issue of Edo period nō as ideology; see also Thomas Looser, *Visioning Eternity: Aesthetics, Politics, and History in the Early Modern Noh Theater* (Cornell East Asia Series, 2008).

posit the possibility that the play may have been commissioned by the shogun Ashikaga Yoshimochi. Is their case viable? If so, how might the image of Sumiyoshi in the play relate to the position of the Sumiyoshi Shrine vis-à-vis the warrior elite of the shogunate? Before we turn to those questions, however, let us begin with a brief overview of the play itself.

SYNOPSIS OF THE PLAY

The Tang dynasty poet Haku Rakuten has been sent by the Emperor of China to ascertain how clever the Japanese people are. He arrives at Matsura Bay in Kyushu, but before he can land, the Sumiyoshi deity appears in the guise of a humble old fisherman (*okina*). As a test, Rakuten composes a "Chinese" poem:

青苔衣を帯びて	A green moss robe worn
巌の肩に懸かり	draped over the cliff's rocky shoulders,
白雲帯に似て	white clouds like a sash
山の腰を囲る	enwrap the mountain's waist.[9]

Rakuten does not expect the old man to understand it, but the old fisherman not only interprets the poem correctly, he provides a response poem in Japanese:

OLD FISHERMAN: The phrase "green moss" refers to the green moss that drapes the shoulders of the cliff and looks like a robe. The white clouds look like a sash enwrapping the mid-section of the mountains. How amusing, how amusing. In Japanese *uta* the same sentiment would go this way:

苔衣	The robe of moss
着たる巌は	worn by the cliff
さもなくて	has no sash, so
衣着ぬ山の	perhaps it could use
帯をするかな	the robeless mountain's *obi*?[10]

---

9. *Seitaikoromo o obite | iwao no kata ni kakari | hakuun obi ni nite | yama no koshi o meguru.* Itō, *Yōkyokushū*, (ge), 82.

10. *Kokegoromo | kitaru iwao wa | samo nakute | koromo kinu yama no | obi o*

Although the old fisherman implies that his *waka* is simply a translation of the Chinese couplet, in fact it is a sly critique of Rakuten's rather pedestrian use of parallel and antithetical imagery. The deity then goes on to explain the miraculous efficacy of *waka* poetry, and when Haku Rakuten expresses surprise that in Japan even someone as lowly as a fisherman is capable of composing poetry, the deity cites the famous line from the Kana Preface to the *Kokinshū* that "all living beings, without exception, compose poetry" (*iki toshi ikeru mono izure ka uta o yomazarikeri*). He also cites an anecdote in support of that claim from *Kokinwakashū jo kikigaki* (Lecture notes on the *Kokinshū* preface), a thirteenth-century commentary popularly understood to be an oracular revelation from the Sumiyoshi deity manifesting as a venerable old man. In the anecdote, when the sounds of a warbler's chirping song are copied down, they form a Chinese couplet that is then easily translated into a *waka*.[11] The deity notes that if even birds in Japan can compose poetry (implicitly both in Chinese and Japanese), why not an old fisherman?

After hearing this, Haku Rakuten recognizes that the Japanese are much more sophisticated than he had expected, and he decides to return to China without even setting foot on land. Before he has a chance to do so, however, the Sumiyoshi deity reappears leading a host of native deities and announces:

> The Sumiyoshi deity's
> power is such
> that you cannot subdue Japan!
> Quickly return
> as the mounting waves
> turn back, Rakuten.

Dancing across the waves, the deity stirs up a storm and sends Haku Rakuten swiftly home:

> Sumiyoshi has appeared
> Sumiyoshi has appeared
> as have Ise, Iwashimizu, Kamo, Kasuga,

---

suru kana. Itō, *Yōkyokushū*, (ge), 82.

11. *Kokinwakashū jo kikigaki: sanryū shō,* in Katagiri Yōichi, ed., *Chūsei Kokinshū chūshakusho kaidai,* vol. 2 (Kyoto: Akao Shōbundō, 1973), 225–28 (hereafter *Kokinwakashū jo kikigaki*).

Kashima, Mishima, Suwa, Atsuta,
and the Dragon King Shakara's
third daughter
the deity of Itsukushima at Aki.
Floating across the waves
dancing to the Sea Green Melody,
as the eight Dragon Kings
play musical accompaniment,
soaring over the waves,
heavenly robes in playful dance,
sleeves stirring a wind, a divine wind
blowing the Chinese boat back
from here to China.
Truly wondrous
these deities and our sovereign
truly wondrous
this age of deities and our sovereign
how auspicious our untroubled land,
how auspicious our untroubled land![12]

This is a metaphorical sea battle, in which no blood is spilt, but it is striking that the Sumiyoshi deity leads all the other deities, including Amaterasu Ōmikami, in the dance. In order to understand the deity's representation here as warrior-poet-god, we need to examine the deity's historical development, including its origin off the coast of Kyushu; career as guardian deity of sea-farers, with power over wind and waves; appearance in human form as an *okina* (venerable old man); role as protector of the imperial lineage and the nation as a whole; and its manifestation as the guardian deity of poetry.

THE EARLY CAREER OF A DEITY

The Sumiyoshi deity actually has a multiple identity: at the very least it is made up of the three masculine deities Sokutsutsuno-o no mikoto, Nakatsutsuno-o no mikoto, and Uwatsutsuno-o no mikoto, and a fourth

---

12. Itō Masayoshi, ed., *Yōkyokushū* (ge), SNKS (Shinchōsha, 1988), 87.

female deity, the deified Regent Jingū. The three masculine deities were born along with eleven others, including Amaterasu, when Izanagi used seawater to purify himself after returning from Yomi, the land of the dead. This lustration was supposed to have occurred in an inlet on the northern coast of Kyushu: the *Kojiki* and *Nihon shoki* state the lustration occurred at the plain of Awaki[ga]hara 檍原 by the river-mouth of Tachibana in Himuka (日向, now read Hyūga) in Tsukushi.[13] The place name Awakigahara allows for a pun on *awa* 泡 (foam), and Sumiyoshi occasionally appears in poetry in conjunction with the phrase "foam of the white waves" (*shiranami no awa* 白波の泡). But in medieval poetry and the nō, the reading of Sumiyoshi's birthplace is often changed to Aokigahara 青きが原, thereby enabling an association with the "blue-green (sea) plain."

It is likely that the original shrine of Sumiyoshi was in Kyushu. There are two subordinate shrines still extant in that area, one in Fukuoka prefecture (formerly Chikuzen province) and one in Yamaguchi prefecture (formerly Nagato province). Thus, although the main shrine is now near Osaka, it is not surprising that the deity would appear off the coast of Kyushu. In the second half of the play, when the Sumiyoshi deity appears in its true form to expel the foreigners, its origin at Aokigahara is mentioned explicitly:

On the western sea
emerging from the blue-green waves
at Aokigahara ...[14]
the Sumiyoshi deity
appears before you.[15]

As Yokota-Murakami has noted, the deity's origin in a lustration purification ritual provides a subtext of ridding impurities that resonates with the idea of expelling foreigners.[16]

---

13. 日向の小戸の橘の檍原 *Himuka no odo no Tachibana no Awakihara*. Itō Masayoshi paraphrases the pertinent section from the *Nihon shoki* in *Yōkyokushū* (chū), SNKS (Shinchōsha, 1986), 289, fn. 17; the full text is also quoted in Nishimoto Yutaka, *Sumiyoshi Taisha* (Gakuseisha, 1977), 28–29; in English, see Donald L. Philippi, trans., *Kojiki* (University of Tokyo Press, 1968), 68–70.

14. Note that this identical line is used in the nō plays *Takasago*, *Ugetsu*, and *Iwafune* to identify the Sumiyoshi deity's manifestation.

15. Itō, *Yōkyokushū* (ge), 86–87.

16. Yokota-Murakami, *The Formation of the Canon of Nō*, 16.

The next "historical" appearance of Sumiyoshi occurs in connection with Regent Jingū's mythical conquest of the Three Kingdoms in the Korean peninsula. According to the *Nihon shoki* and *Kojiki*, the deity's tripartite masculine form (along with Amaterasu) possessed Jingū and then her minister Takeshi-uchi no Sukune, encouraging her to attack "a land to the west" where "gold and silver, as well as all sorts of eye-dazzling precious treasures, abound."[17] This oracle occurred while Jingū and her husband Emperor Chūai were in Kyushu at the head of an army attempting to subdue the Kumaso. The "raging" forms (*aragami* or *kōjin* 荒神) of the Sumiyoshi and Suwa deities were understood as having accompanied Jingū and protected her during her military expedition. Sometime after the successful conclusion of the invasion, the main Sumiyoshi Shrine was established in Settsu province (south of modern-day Osaka) and Jingū was enshrined in the fourth shrine there. This association with Jingū was probably central to the belief that the Sumiyoshi deity was a protector of the imperial lineage, an idea that appears frequently in Heian-period *waka* poetry.[18] The connection between the imperial court and the shrine was cemented when Emperor Shirakawa (r. 1072–1086) included Sumiyoshi Shrine in the central seven of twenty-two shrines receiving official court recognition, and the shrine subsequently became a major stopping place on the pilgrimage route to Kumano.

The Sumiyoshi deity is also generally identified as the Sea-brine Deity (Shiotsuchi no kami), or Old Man of the Sea (Shiotsutsu no oji), who appears in the *Nihon shoki* and *Kojiki* stories about the "Luck of the Sea, Luck of the Mountain," as well as in the "Akashi" and "Suma" chapters in *Genji monogatari*. In the guise of a supernatural old man, he is understood as a deity with control over the waves, wind, and sea creatures. He can, on the one hand, unleash storms and, on the other hand, guarantee safe passage for sailors and others who go down to the sea in ships. Any vessel venturing across the sea to China or Korea stopped first at the Sumiyoshi Shrine in Settsu province to request the deity's protection, and stopped on its way back to thank the deity for its

---

17. Philippi, trans., *Kojiki*, 257.
18. The typical format for Heian-period poems invoking the Sumiyoshi deity is to refer to the ancient age of a pine tree in the shrine enclosure, understood as an embodiment of the deity, and to express the wish that the emperor (*kimi*) live to a similarly ancient age. For several examples, see Hosaka, "Tsumori-ke no kajingun (2)," 72–74.

safe return. This aspect of the deity's powers explains both Sumiyoshi's initial appearance as an old fisherman and his ability in the second half of the play to call up the divine wind (*kamikaze*) that sends Haku Rakuten swiftly back to China.

Because of the deity's associations with Regent Jingū's expedition and as the guardian deity of sea navigation, the Sumiyoshi Shrine became closely affiliated with travel and trade between Japan and both Korea and China. When the Japanese government's envoys were sent to China and Korea, they paid homage at the shrine, coming and going, and the shrine appears to have received a percentage of the profits in goods from successful voyages. These profits were thought to have become the basis for the famous Sumiyoshi "treasure market" (*takara no ichi*), held each year in the Ninth Month.

But how did Sumiyoshi develop as a guardian deity of the path of *waka* poetry? Even in the earliest historical period the deity appears to have been particularly responsive to petitions in the form of poems: two *chōka* in the *Man'yōshū* (1020 and 4245) can be read as petitions by wives asking the deity to protect their husbands during sea voyages. A third poem (4243), a short envoy, is presented as an oracular revelation from the deity itself promising a safe and swift journey. In *dan* (段, episode) 117 of the tenth-century *Ise monogatari* the deity appears in response to a poem presented by an anonymous emperor commenting on the age of the "princess pine" (*himematsu*) on the shore of Sumiyoshi. The deity offers a poem in turn that assures the emperor of its continuing protection.

The thirty-ninth *kannushi* of the shrine, Tsumori Kunimoto 津守国基 (1023–1102), was the first of a long line of excellent poets in the Tsumori family, each of whom furthered the connection between the Sumiyoshi deity and *waka* poetry. Starting in the late eleventh century, individual poets began dedicating hundred-poem sequences to the deity, and by the early twelfth century Sumiyoshi had been firmly established as the deity to whom poets directed prayers for excellence in composition. From 1128 onward poetry contests began to be held regularly at the shrine. The strong connection between Sumiyoshi and poetry was further encouraged in the late thirteenth century by the development of poetic commentaries on the *Kokinshū* and *Ise monogatari* attributed to oracular revelations by the Sumiyoshi deity appearing as a venerable old man.[19]

---

19. In *Allegories of Desire* (110–13) I argue that the forty-eighth *kannushi* Tsumori Kunisuke 国助 (1242–1299) may have had a hand in the development of secret commentaries like *Kokin wakashū jo kikigaki* that presented themselves

These commentaries, although initially secret, had been disseminated into popular culture by the time *Haku Rakuten* was written. As noted above, the commentary *Kokinwakashū jo kikigaki* in particular forms the textual source (*honsetsu* 本説) of the first half of the play. The identity of Sumiyoshi as the guardian deity of Japanese poetry is obviously necessary for the poem contest that forms the centerpiece of the first half.[20]

These, then, are the main features of the Sumiyoshi deity in the period leading up to the Genpei War. Although there was an initial association of Sumiyoshi's "raging" aspect with Regent Jingū's attack on Korea, for the most part during the Heian period the deity's military identity subsided and its identity as the guardian of sailors and of the imperial lineage predominated, along with a growing emphasis on the deity's connection to the composition of *waka* poetry. Given the dictum in the *Kokinshū* Kana Preface that poetry's primary purpose is to pacify and harmonize, it makes sense that the Sumiyoshi's deity's powers with regard to poetry would be seen as primarily benign in a period that was relatively free of war, both internal and external. But over the course of the twelfth century, as the political landscape became increasingly unstable, it was only natural that Sumiyoshi's martial side would come to the fore again.

Thomas Conlan notes in his analysis of sacred war that religion "cannot be conceived as a refuge from the 'baser' endeavors of politics and war, nor can religious institutions be portrayed as bastions of peaceful sentiment that somehow remained impervious to the vicissitudes of the political order."[21] In a time of war, when kami and buddhas were thought to mingle on the battlefield with men, and having deities on your side was seen as vital to victory, shrines and temples were increasingly drawn into taking sides, if for no other reason than that there were real rewards

---

as oracular revelations of the Sumiyoshi deity. As the fortunes of the court declined, other private sources of revenue needed to be developed, and popular faith in the deity as a protector of poets may have been seen as one source.

20. Ironically, the popular image of Sumiyoshi as a white-haired old man (*okina*) which features so prominently in the nō play is actually modeled on an image of Bo Juyi as an old man with a brush in one hand and paper in the other. Ōgushi Sumio has argued that the images of both the poet Kakinomoto no Hitomaro and Sumiyoshi as *okina* are based on a famous Chinese landscape screen depicting an "old age celebration" that Bo Juyi held to celebrate his sixtieth year. Ōgushi Sumio, "Hitomaro zō no seiritsu to Tōji Sansui Byobu," *Bijutsu kenkyū*, no. 164 (1952), 85–110. In English, see Klein, *Allegories of Desire*, 87–88.

21. Conlan, *State of War*, 166.

for having performed prayers and rituals on behalf of the winners. In this context, and given the Sumiyoshi deity's martial origins, it is not surprising that it came to be viewed as one of the gods of war. The actual developmental process, however, is difficult to ascertain, because the composition of texts such as *Heike monogatari* and *Genpei jōsuiki*, which represent Sumiyoshi as a fully idealized and deified warrior-poet, postdate the Genpei War by two hundred years and are not reliable historical accounts. We know, however, that just prior to the Genpei War, in Retired Emperor Go-Shirakawa's collection of *imayō*, *Ryōjin hishō* 梁塵秘抄 (Songs to make the dust dance on the beams, ca. 1169), the Sumiyoshi deity was included in a *monozukushi* list of the "warfare gods west of the barrier" (*seki yori nishi naru ikusagami*).[22] And *Azuma kagami* depicts two incidents involving priests from Sumiyoshi shrines that provide corroborating evidence of the deity's "remilitarization" in response to civil war.

The first incident occurred as Minamoto no Yoritomo was preparing to attack the Izu Deputy Governor Kanetaka, the initial move in what was to become the Genpei War. In 1179 the Heike had exiled Saeki Masasuke 佐伯昌助, a priest of the Sumiyoshi Shrine in Chikuzen province, to Izu province. On 1180.4.27, Masasuke's younger brother, Masanaga of Sumiyoshi 住吉昌長,[23] attended Yoritomo. He was accompanied by Nagae Yoritaka 永江頼隆, a former retainer of Hatano Yoshitsune 波多野義常 and a descendent of a priest of the Ise Shrine. *Azuma kagami* notes, "As these two have indicated their desire to serve the Minamoto cause, and as they are greatly experienced in matters of Shinto ritual, His Lordship has accepted their offer of service that they might conduct secret prayers on his behalf."[24]

---

22. *Ryōjin hishō* (no. 249) in Kawaguchi Hisao and Shida Nobuyoshi, eds., *Wakan rōeishū, Ryōjin hishō*, NKBT 73 (Iwanami shoten, 1965), 388; in English see Gladys E. Nakahara, *A Translation of Ryōjinhishō, A Compendium of Japanese Folk Songs (Imayō) from the Heian Period (794–1185)* (Edwin Mellen Press, 2003), 194. The barrier was Ōsaka Barrier, located in modern-day Ōtsu City, Shiga prefecture.

23. It is not clear whether this designation means that Masanaga actually was a priest at the Sumiyoshi Shrine in Settsu province. It seems more likely that he, like his brother, came from Chikuzen.

24. Jishō 4 (1180) 7/23, *Azuma kagami* (translation mine) in *Azuma Kagami* (vol. 1), edited by Kuroita Katsumi, Shintei zōho Kokushi taikei no. 22 (Yoshikawa kōbunkan, 1932; reprint 1991), 31 (hereafter *Azuma kagami*). Martin Collcutt translates this section in "Religion in the Life of Minamoto Yoritomo," in P. F.

Masanaga subsequently performed a divination ritual to determine a propitious day and hour for the attack on Kanetaka, choosing the seventeenth day of the Eighth Month between 3 a.m. and 5 a.m. When rain and the nonappearance of critical support threatened to interfere with this plan, Masanaga performed a ritual to exorcise the spirits of disaster and calamity. Yoritomo was so concerned that the ritual be successful that he himself participated, handing a mirror to Masanaga at one point in the proceedings. Yoritaka, for his part, performed one thousand purification prayers (*oharae* 御祓え).[25] And on the night before the attack, we are told that Masanaga was assigned to conduct prayers for the safety of the troops.[26]

This account suggests that a ritualist from one of the Sumiyoshi shrines was crucial to the planning and execution of Yoritomo's initial attack. As numerous other entries in *Azuma kagami* attest, Yoritomo felt it was a matter of vital urgency to make sure the native deities were on his side. In particular, *Azuma kagami*, *Heike monogatari*, and *Genpei jōsuiki* provide plentiful evidence of Yoritomo's strong faith in the Hachiman deity, which he considered a tutelary deity of his clan.[27] One of the main identities of Hachiman is Emperor Ōjin, the son of Regent Jingū, who as we have seen was strongly connected to the founding of the Sumiyoshi shrines. Given their relationship, it is probably not surprising that there was often a Sumiyoshi sub-shrine within Hachiman shrine complexes, and that the Sumiyoshi deity plays an important role in the *Hōjō-e* 放生会 (release of life ceremony) central to the Hachiman cult.[28] These multiple connections may have contributed to Sumiyoshi being considered a god of war along with Hachiman, and helps explain why Yoritomo would have been so pleased to welcome a ritualist from a subsidiary shrine.

Kornicki and I. J. McMullen, eds., *Religion in Japan: Arrows to Heaven and Earth* (Cambridge University Press, 1996), 95–98.

25. Jishō 4 (1180) 8/16, *Azuma kagami* vol. 1, 33.

26. Jishō 4 (1180) 8/17, *Azuma kagami* vol. 1, 34.

27. Collcutt provides numerous examples in "Religion in the life of Minamoto Yoritomo."

28. As it happens, the *Hōjō-e* is performed on the eighteenth day of the Eighth Month, and Yoritomo's initial plan would have meant that the ritual, understood as a pacification for war dead, would take place the day after the attack. For a description of the role of the Sumiyoshi deity in a current version of the *Hōjō-e*, see Jane Marie Law, "Violence, Ritual Reenactment, and Ideology: The *Hōjō-e* (Rite for the Release of Sentient Beings) of the Usa Hachiman Shrine in Japan," *History of Religions* 33:4 (May 1994), 353–54.

After these initial entries in *Azuma kagami*, there is no mention of the Sumiyoshi deity or the main shrine until nearly the end of the war, when we find an entry for 1185.2.19. Minamoto no Yoshitsune had just won a decisive battle at Yashima. At this point Tsumori Nagamori, the governor of Settsu province and the forty-fourth *kannushi* of the main Sumiyoshi Shrine

> arrived at the capital and, permitted an audience with the retired emperor Go-Shirakawa, declared: "On the sixteenth, while the annual *kagura* dance was being performed at the shrine, a humming-bulb arrow appeared from the Third Hall (*sanshinden*) and proceeded west." As His Lordship [Yoritomo] has recently offered prayers for the pacification [of the Heike], is this not a miraculous revelation?[29]

The Japanese here is ambiguous, but it is possible that Yoritomo had recently offered prayers specifically to Sumiyoshi, perhaps even at the shrine, and the arrow was understood as an oracle indicating the deity's affirmative reply to those prayers. Nagamori was one of Go-Shirakawa's elite Northern Quarter Guards, and although there is no earlier mention of the main Sumiyoshi Shrine, it is likely that at the time Go-Shirakawa aligned himself with Yoritomo and the Genji, the shrine did as well. There is some evidence to support this assumption from an Edo period text, the *Hachimangu honki*, which states that in the aftermath of the Genpei War Yoritomo rewarded the shrine for its efforts on his behalf: "In old days [the Sumiyoshi Shrine] possessed land in many places and there were a large number of shrine attendants [社人]. Gifts of land from Yoritomo and other shoguns, and from the Lord of the province are recorded. Now [Genroku era] they have 360 *koku* of Shinryō 神領 [shrine property]."[30]

The omen was considered an important enough event for it to have been included in *Heike monogatari*, where the same story appears with added commentary:

> The Sumiyoshi Chief Priest Nagamori went to the

---

29. Bunji 1 (1185) 2/19, *Azuma kagami* vol. 1, 139.
30. Richard Ponsonby-Fane, *Suminoe no Ohokami* (Nagai shuppan insatsu kabushikikaisha, 1935), 34. One *koku* is approximately equivalent to 45 gallons.

Retired Emperor's palace after Yoshitsune's departure from the capital [for Yashima]. "During the Hour of the Ox on the sixteenth, there was the sound of the humming-bulb arrow flying westward from the Third Hall of our shrine," he reported through Treasure Minister Yasutsune. Greatly pleased, the former sovereign [Go-Shirakawa] gave him a sword and other treasures for the god.

When Empress Jingū attacked Silla long ago, the deity of the Ise Shrine assigned two rough spirits (*aramitama*) to accompany her. The spirits stood in the prow and stern of her ship, and she vanquished Silla with ease. After her return to Japan, one spirit stayed in Sumiyoshi district in Settsu province. He is the one known as Sumiyoshi Daimyōjin. The other spirit selected Suwa district in Shinano province as his abode. He is the one known as Suwa Daimyōjin.[31]

The equivalent section in *Genpei jōsuiki* differs in some details:

On the night of the sixteenth day of the Second Month of Genryaku 2 [1185], at the Hour of the Rat [midnight], officials and others on duty heard the sound of a humming-bulb arrow coming from the Third Hall of Sumiyoshi Shrine, proceeding to the west. The *kannushi* Nagamori sent the ritualist (*gonhōri*) Aritō with a report for the emperor. The destruction of the enemy [at Yashima] was because of the deity's protection of the military. When the emperor heard this news, he summoned Nagamori and Aritō to present a sword and other treasures for the deity.

Here, the victory at Yashima is understood as due specifically to the protection of the Sumiyoshi deity. After a digression to discuss the participation of the Sumiyoshi deity in Jingū's invasion, *Genpei jōsuiki* continues:

---

31. Takagi Ichinosuke et al., eds., *Heike monogatari* (ge), NKBT 33 (Iwanami shoten, 1960), 376; Helen Craig McCullough, trans. *The Tale of the Heike* (Stanford University Press, 1988), 372.

As for the two raging deities [Sumiyoshi and Suwa]:
one was established in Settsu province in Sumiyoshi.
This is now Sumiyoshi Myōjin. He controls the waves
on the wide ocean and confers safe passage over the
water, and facing the window of the imperial palace,
protects the imperial body. From the age of the gods,
the shrine style has been *chigi no katasogi* (千木の方
削[32]); the deity is the life-force of the green of the pine
(松の緑生ひかはり); in form he appears as a white-
haired old man (皎皎たる考翁). "How many reigns
have passed?"[33]

In these passages from the three war tales, we can see the Sumiyoshi
deity's identity as a god of war being buttressed by a description of the
deity's involvement in Jingū's invasion. Sumiyoshi's "raging" or "rough"
aspect (荒みたま or 荒みさき) is able to control the ocean wind and
waves and guarantee safe passage. He is also identified as the creative
life force of the pine tree (made famous by the nō play *Takasago*), and
his dominant manifestation is as a white-haired old man. Sumiyoshi is
shown specifically here as defending the imperial line descended from
Regent Jingū, a point subtly reinforced by an allusion to the poem ("How
many reigns have passed?") from *dan* 117 of *Ise monogatari*, in which the
deity manifested to assure an emperor of its continuing protection. It is
natural, then, for the deity to play a notable role in expelling any invasion
from foreign countries, even if they come in the form of poets.

Although the Sumiyoshi deity had become, once again, a god of war,
as depicted in *Heike monogatari* the deity apparently still responded best
to petitions composed in the form of *waka*. The idea that native deities
both communicate in *waka* poetry and respond best to petitions written
in the form of *waka* makes its first appearance in *Heike monogatari*

---

32. 千木 (*chigi*, literally "thousand trees") is an ornamental architectural
style common to some of the oldest shrines in Japan (including Ise, Izumo and
Sumiyoshi). At each end of the shrine's ridgepole the tips of two crossbeams
intersect above the roof line. *Katasogi* is a distinctive way of cutting the ends of
the crossbeams which was used at Sumiyoshi Shrine; it is mentioned in a famous
Shinkokinshū poem (no. 1855) attributed to the Sumiyoshi deity, who it is said to
have appeared in the form of an old man to complain about the dilapidated state
of the shrine. See footnote 34 below.

33. *Genpei jōsuiki* in Mizuhara Hajime, ed., *Shintei Genpei jōsuiki*, vol. 6 (Shin
jinbutsu ōraisha, 1991), 22 (hereafter *Genpei jōsuiki*).

when Taira no Yasuyori, who had been exiled along with Lesser Captain Naritsune and Bishop Shunkan to Kikai-ga-shima, carves one thousand stupas (*sotoba*) from sticks of driftwood in order to petition the deities to obtain his pardon. On each stupa he writes the character *A* in Sanskrit, the era, month, day, his own name and his priestly name, and adds two poems. Yasuyori initially got the idea for the poem stupas from a dream in which two leaves of a *nagi* tree that grows in the Kumano area appear in the offing; when he and Naritsune pick them up, they find they bear the words of a poem, apparently gnawed by insects. The poem promises that because their prayers have been so fervent, they will assuredly return to the capital. Yasuyori casts the stupas into the sea with a prayer to various gods, including Kumano and Itsukushima, that the stupas reach the capital. One of the wooden stupas reaches the Itsukushima Shrine in Aki, where a good friend of Yasuyori is staying. He finds it in the tide, and takes it back to the capital, where it helps gain Yasuyori's pardon from Taira no Kiyomori.

Two issues raised here are also central to *Haku Rakuten*. The first is that in Japan, even creatures such as birds and insects are capable of composing poetry. In *Haku Rakuten* this ability is understood to prove the superiority of the Japanese generally: Bo Juyi decides to return to China directly after hearing the anecdote from *Kokinwakashū jo kikigaki* in which a bird composes a *waka* poem. The second issue is the miraculous efficacy of *waka* poetry, particularly as a means for communication with the gods. This second point is elaborated in a brief interpolation in *Heike monogatari* and a much longer one in *Genpei jōsuiki*:

> Kakinomoto no Hitomaro's thoughts followed a small boat "going island hid"; Yamanobe no Akahito watched cranes among the reeds; the Sumiyoshi god thought of his shrine's crossbeams;[34] the Miwa god pointed to the cedar at his gate. Ever since the divine Susano-o originated the thirty-one-syllable Japanese poem long ago, the gods and buddhas themselves have expressed their multifarious emotions in verse.[35]

34. In the poem (*Shinkokinshū* 1855) the deity complains about the cold, intimating that the chill is due to frost falling through the shrine's crumbling crossbeams. It is usually interpreted as a request for funds to rebuild the shrine, directed at an emperor.

35. McCullough, *Tale of the Heike*, 93–94 (translation modified).

Genpei jōsuiki continues:

> *Waka* is a means to transform the ruler of the country, a source for filling the heart/mind with peaceful thoughts ... Sumiyoshi and Tamatsushima are not the only guardian deities of this path [of poetry]; at Ise, Iwashimizu, Kamo and Kasuga (among others) countless oracular revelations and messages in dreams have been given in the form of poems.[36]

Genpei jōsuiki here specifically raises an issue central to *Haku Rakuten*: Sumiyoshi as the guardian deity of *waka* poetry was likely to be particularly susceptible to petitions addressed in the form of poems, but other deities are susceptible as well, and it does not seem coincidental that the deities listed in *Genpei jōsuiki*, except for Tamatsushima, are identical to those in *Haku Rakuten* and listed in the same order. At any rate, it is notable that in the Regent Jingū's invasion, the Sumiyoshi and Suwa deities were directed by Amaterasu to guide her ship; in the nō, Sumiyoshi takes the lead in coordinating the attack. The play was certainly written by someone who was a proponent of the Sumiyoshi Shrine.

Although as we have seen, the Sumiyoshi deity's image was reformulated as a warrior-poet in response to the growing instability of the country, it seems likely that the depiction of Sumiyoshi deity in *Haku Rakuten* as the preeminent martial defender of Japan against foreign countries is actually a product not of the Genpei War, but the Mongol invasions of 1274 and 1281. Kaizu Ichirō argues that the ideology of *shinkoku shisō*, Japan as the "land of the kami," developed specifically in

---

36. *Genpei jōsuiki*, vol. 1, chapter 7, 337–38. The rest of the passage from *Genpei jōsuiki* goes on to align the power of poetry with Buddhist dharani (magical spells), and paints a picture of Sumiyoshi as a syncretic deity encouraging the dual path of *waka* and Buddhist enlightenment. The other major allusive subtext, *Kokinwakashū jo kikigaki* (224), also implicitly aligns the efficacy of *waka* with the power of Buddhist sutras. Interestingly, in *Haku Rakuten* this correlation is eliminated, along with almost any Buddhist references. Since it is fairly certain that the play was revised, probably by Kanze Nobumitsu, it is possible that at that point, or perhaps in the Edo period, any Buddhist elements were removed to make it more "orthodox," that is, more appropriate for use as a *shūgen* (auspicious or celebratory) play. See Takemoto Mikio's summary of the case for Nobumitsu's revision in "Sakuhin kenkyū: *Haku Rakuten*," 4–9.

response to the threat of foreign invasion.[37] Kaizu presents a number of examples in which warriors involved in the battles claimed to have seen deities in the form of supernaturally strong generals or as terrifying dragons rising out of the sea to unleash their full fury on the Mongol fleet and includes a couple of anecdotes in which the Sumiyoshi deity figures.[38] We know that during the Mongol invasions, Sumiyoshi Shrine was the site of prayers and rituals for the defense of the nation, [39] and

---

37. Note that this concept was understood rather differently in the medieval period than in the modern. Whereas in the twentieth century the kami were represented as uniquely invincible defenders of the nation, medieval depictions of kami involved in the Mongol invasions represented Chinese deities as powerful rivals. This was because after the invasions, like warriors who wished to be rewarded, shrines presented descriptions of their deity's participation in battle. These descriptions used a similar narrative structure to those used by warriors: the deity faces a series of initial setbacks because of the power of the enemy deities, but strengthened by the power of the shrine's ritual prayers the deity is ultimately able to defeat them. See Kaizu Ichirō, *Kamikaze to akutō no seiki: Nanbokuchō jidai o yominaosu* (Kōdansha, 1995), 40–44; for a typical warrior narrative see Thomas Conlan, *In Little Need of Divine Intervention: Takezaki Suenaga's Scrolls of the Mongol Invasions of Japan* (Cornell East Asia Series, 2001).

38. Kaizu, *Kamikaze to akutō no seiki*, 40–44; the Sumiyoshi deity is mentioned on 43. Kaizu also (49) describes a document issued by Mount Koya asking for recompense for defense efforts made by the Jishu kami of Amano Shrine. According to the document various kami met for a strategy session on the fifth day of the Fourth Month (which according to a captured Mongol was the day after the Mongol fleet set out) and in this session the Amano deity was selected to lead the battle. According to a second oracle, on the thirtieth day of the Seventh Month the Sumiyoshi Shrine deity and Hachiman Daibōsatsu fought under the command of the Amano Shrine deity. The veracity of the oracle is verified by the argument that it was vouchsafed to a *miko* of the Hirota Shrine (supposedly independent of Mount Koya's influence). Although here the Sumiyoshi Shrine deity follows the lead of the Amano Shrine deity, the basic narrative is similar to the second half of *Haku Rakuten*. These examples, in which shrines apparently cooperated in their efforts to get rewards from the court and shogunate, appear to have been quite common, and such narratives may have served as a model in the creation of the play.

39. In the Second Month of 1268 (Bun'ei 5) the Kamakura shogunate received an official letter from the Mongols, who were hoping to browbeat the Japanese into becoming a tributary state voluntarily. On the fifteenth a meeting was held in the office of the retired emperor, and on the twenty-second, an order for prayers for the defense of the nation against foreign countries was sent to the twenty-two shrines, including Sumiyoshi. Aida Jirō, *Mōko shūrai no kenkyū: zōhoban*

there is some evidence that at least the subsidiary shrine in Chikuzen was rewarded by the Kamakura shogunate for its role.[40]

To sum up, in *Haku Rakuten* we can see displayed all of the powers attributed to the Sumiyoshi deity in *Heike monogatari* and *Genpei jōsuiki*, as well as during the Mongol invasions. Obviously, he is the defender of *waka* poetry; he appears as a humble old fisherman (the Old Man of the Sea) who is nevertheless able to control the winds and through his dance upon the ocean along with the other deities, blow Haku Rakuten back to China. In his role as protector deity of the path of *waka* poetry, Sumiyoshi is the ideal poet, capable of winning the poetry contest; in his role as protector deity of the nation, Sumiyoshi is the ideal warrior, capable of defeating the Chinese militarily.

(Yoshikawa kōbunkan, 1982), 56. According to Kaizu Ichirō (*Kamikaze to akutō no seiki*, 45), in 1277 the shogunate drew up a ritual calendar that assigned each of the great shrine complexes a specific month when it would be responsible for rituals of national protection. Sumiyoshi Shrine was assigned the Ninth Month (probably because its main festival occurred on the thirteenth of that month). Kaizu compares this structured year-round system of prayers to the preparations in Hakata, where warriors were assigned specific months when they were responsible for taking on the roles of national defense guard (*ikkoku keigo banyaku*) and building the defense wall (*ishitsukijaku*). Kaizu provides more documentary evidence of the participation of Sumiyoshi and its subsidiary shrines on pages 96 and 106-7. In addition, we know that Eison 叡尊 (1201–1290), a high-ranking priest of the Kai Ritsu Shingon sect who was central to the defensive ritual effort by *kenmitsu* Buddhist institutions, performed public prayers for the defense of the nation at the Sumiyoshi Shrine in 1268 and 1275. Shinshū Ōsaka-shi shi hensan iinkai, ed., *Shinshū Ōsaka-shi* vol. 2, chapter 2, section 4, part 3 (Osaka City, 1988) 245–47 (the author wishes to thank Nodaka Hiroyuki 野高宏之 of the Editorial Office of Osaka City History in the Osaka Municipal Central Library for providing a photocopy of the section on the history of the Sumiyoshi Shrine during the Mongol invasions).

40. According to a petition for payment of a promised reward written by Fujiwara Kunikado 藤原国門, an official of the Buyū 武雄 Shrine of Bizen province, after the first Mongol invasion in 1274 six shrines were initially chosen to receive rewards of land, based on the efficacy of the shrine's prayers, and the Sumiyoshi Shrine in Chikuzen province was one of them. Aida Jirō, *Mōko shūrai no kenkyū: zōhoban* (Yoshikawa kōbunkan, 1982), 85.

HAKU RAKUTEN AS POLITICAL ALLEGORY

The scholarly lack of interest in the Sumiyoshi deity's martial aspect is surprising, if for no other reason than the obvious resonances between the plot of *Haku Rakuten* and the Mongol invasions of 1274 and 1281. The setting is just off the coast of Kyushu, near where the two invasions occurred. Prior to the invasions, in the late 1260s, Khubilai Khan (1215–1294) sent emissaries to Japan to see whether Japan would become a tributary state voluntarily; in the play the poet Haku Rakuten has been sent to test the "sagacity" of the Japanese, although here the test is of how sophisticated the Japanese are at their leisure activities (*motte asobi*). The *kamikaze* aroused by the dance of Sumiyoshi and the other deities at the end of the play certainly resonates with the typhoons popularly believed to have destroyed the Mongol fleet. Nō scholars have generally written off these resonances as purely metaphorical. But if we assume, as most scholars do, that the play was written either by Zeami or someone contemporaneous to him in the early fifteenth century, why would the Mongol invasions suddenly be a focus of attention, albeit an apparently light-hearted focus? Would the play's confrontational attitude toward China make more sense if understood in the context of the Ashikaga shogunate's relations with Ming China and Chosŏn Korea?

In fact, as early as 1916 the historian Kume Kunitake (1839–1931) argued that *Haku Rakuten* was not simply a light-hearted poetic contest but should be understood as an explicit political allegory. In the early postwar period, the theater scholar Takano Tatsuyuki made a similar argument, apparently without knowledge of Kume's earlier essay.[41] Both scholars pointed to a military crisis in Ōei 26 (1419) as forming a possible historical subtext to the play. The crisis erupted when, in the Sixth Month of 1419, the government of Chosŏn sent a fleet of warships to attack pirate (*wakō*) bases on the island of Tsushima. This "invasion" (subsequently known in Japan as *Ōei no gaikō* 応永の外寇) was supposedly defeated by an army of deities who called up a *kamikaze*. The same summer, an

---

41. Kume Kunitake, "Yōkyoku Haku Rakuten wa kessaku nari–yūdai naru taigai shisō to Ōei no gaikō," *Nōgaku*, vol. 14 (January 1916), 18–30, and Takano Tatsuyuki, *Nihon engekishi*, vol. 1 (Tōkyōdō, 1947), 327–31. See also the synopsis of both arguments in Amano Fumio, "*Haku Rakuten* to Ōei no gaikō: Kume Kunitake to Takano Tatsuyuki no shosetsu o kenshō suru," *Zeami: chūsei no geijutsu to bunka*, 1:1 (February 2002), 128–46.

envoy from the Ming Emperor arrived in the port of Hyōgo, attempting to renew diplomatic relations between Ming China and Japan.

Both Kume and Takano believed that *Haku Rakuten* was written specifically for Yoshimochi in celebration of the successful defeat of the Korean "invasion" as well as the shogun's rejection of the Ming envoy, who was forced to return to China empty-handed without ever stepping foot on shore in Hyōgo. Kume actually went so far as to assign historical figures to the main roles: in the first half the *waki* is supposed to be the Ming envoy Roen 呂淵 and the *shite* is the Zen priest Gen'yō 元容 sent by Yoshimochi to meet him. In the second half, Kume argues that the *nochijite* is the Kyushu *tandai* (deputy) Shibukawa Yoshitoshi 渋川 義俊, who was believed at the time to have participated in the defense of Tsushima.[42] This possible political subtext, which explains both the evident xenophobia and the strikingly martial character of the deity, has been given little credence by literary scholars until very recently, when Amano Fumio wrote an article on *Haku Rakuten* that outlined Kume and Takano's arguments and suggested further historical evidence that might support their position.[43] To evaluate their arguments we need to review the historical incidents themselves.

I will start with the second event first, because the cessation of diplomatic relations was a contributing factor to the attack on Tsushima. The shogun Yoshimochi had discontinued the extremely lucrative trade agreement between China and Japan in 1411, claiming that his father Yoshimitsu, on his deathbed, had expressed regret that he had offended the native deities by receiving envoys from a foreign country and vowed never to do so again.[44] According to Tanaka Takeo, the Ming emperor

---

42. Kume, "Yōkyoku *Haku Rakuten* wa kessaku nari," 26–27. Note that there appears to be some confusion about who the *tandai* was at the time, both in contemporaneous diaries and modern scholars' accounts. Shibukawa Mitsuyori 渋川満頼 (1372–1446) replaced Imagawa Ryōshun as *tandai* in 1395; Mitsuyori stepped down sometime in 1419 and his son Yoshitoshi (1400–1434) took his place.

43. Amano, "*Haku Rakuten* to Ōei no gaikō." Both Itō Masayoshi (*Yōkyokushū*, [ge], 456) and Nishino Haruo (*Yōkyoku hyakuban*, 540) mention the possibility of the Ōei invasion as subtext for *Haku Rakuten*, but neither pursue the idea further.

44. Yoshimochi initially accepted the envoy sent in late 1408 by the Ming Emperor to perform special obsequies for Yoshimitsu and appoint Yoshimochi as the new King of Japan; he sent the envoy and his entourage back four months later in Japanese ships. In 1410 a Japanese mission arrived at the Chinese court to express thanks for the Ming Emperor's gifts and his confirmation of Yoshimochi

Chengzu actually contemplated sending troops to attack Japan because of this, but the Chinese ultimately chose instead to persist in their attempts to get Yoshimochi to reopen relations.[45] In 1417 Emperor Chengzu sent a message that rebuked Yoshimochi, but left the way open for a renewal of good relations. When there was no response from the shogun, Chengzu sent another rescript, harsher in tone. Chengzu took pains to warn the Japanese that the Chinese armed forces were not like the Mongol invaders, who had been good at riding and shooting but not at seamanship. One can imagine how Yoshimochi would have received this not very veiled threat, which seemed to be a replay of the threatening letter sent by the Mongols before the invasion of 1274.[46]

The Ming Emperor's envoy Roen had arrived in the summer of 1418, hoping to restore friendly relations, but Yoshimochi was adamant in rejecting the emperor's overtures. Now, in the summer of 1419, Roen returned to the port of Hyōgo just a few weeks after the attack on Tsushima. He could not have chosen a worse possible moment, and it is clear that the coincidence was seen as anything but coincidental by the highly suspicious shogun, shogunate and court. Yoshimochi responded to Roen through an intermediary, the Zen priest Gen'yō, explaining his refusal to reopen relations on the grounds that in the past the country

---

as the successor of Yoshimitsu. But by 1411 Yoshimochi had evidently changed his mind, since in that year he refused to receive an envoy from China who carried a friendly letter and a gift of money. It is not clear why Yoshimochi discontinued a trade that was so lucrative. Both George Sansom and Pierre Souyri argue that Yoshimochi was acting out of resentment toward his father, who had always favored his younger brother Yoshitsugu, combined with the influence of his senior counselor Shiba Yoshimasa 斯波義将 (1350–1410) who had been skeptical of Yoshimitsu's policies. Given how lucrative the trade was (Yoshimitsu financed the construction of the extravagant Kitayama villa with the profits) it is a puzzling decision on Yoshimochi's part. George Sansom, *A History of Japan: 1334–1615* (Stanford University Press, 1961), 173–75; Pierre François Souyri, *The World Turned Upside Down*, trans. Käthe Roth (Columbia University Press, 2001), 146.

45. Tanaka Takeo, "Japan's Relations with Overseas Countries," in John Whitney Hall and Toyoda Takeshi, eds., *Japan in the Muromachi Age* (University of California Press, 1977), 168.

46. See the comment quoted below from a contemporary diary, *Mansai jugō nikki*, which compares this note with the threatening note sent prior to the Bun'ei invasion of 1274. Ōei 26 (1419) 7/23, *Mansai jugō nikki* vol. 1, edited by Kyoto Teikoku Daigaku Bunka Daigaku (Rokujō kappan seizōjo, 1918), 334–35 (hereafter as *Mansai jugō nikki*).

had never been subordinate to foreign countries, and the previous lord, Yoshimitsu, became ill because he broke this prohibition when he accepted the title of "King of Japan" (日本国王) in order to pursue trade with China.[47]

One might note that Yoshimochi's ostensible explanation for why he ended diplomatic relations—that the native deities were offended by Japan's subordinate position—resonates nicely with the overall attitude depicted in *Haku Rakuten*. It is ironic, however, that throughout most of its career the Sumiyoshi deity was actually strongly associated with foreign trade. In fact, it is likely that Yoshimitsu's earlier effort at foreign relations with Ming China was the historical subtext for the nō play *Iwafune* 岩船 (The Indestructible Warship), which is set in the famous Sumiyoshi treasure market and celebrates the profits to be made from foreign trade supported by a strong military empowered by the gods.

At about the same time that the Chinese were sending threatening notes, the Chosŏn government was becoming fed-up with marauding Japanese pirates who were staging almost continuous raids on the coastal granaries of the Korean peninsula and China. After the reunification of the Northern and Southern Courts in 1392, Yoshimitsu had gotten enough control of Kyushu to make some headway in the suppression of the *wakō* (pirates), for which he received a letter of gratitude from the Chinese in 1407. However, his son Yoshimochi's lack of interest in trade also extended to an unwillingness to spend scarce resources to suppress pirates, and there was a resurgence of pirate activity, some of which originated out of the island of Tsushima, located about equidistant from Japan and Korea.

This tense situation was exacerbated in 1418 when the provincial governor (*shugo* 守護) of Tsushima, Sō Sadashige 宗貞茂, died, leaving behind only a young son, Sadamori 貞盛.[48] Sadashige had maintained

---

47. "[Before his death, my father, Yoshimitsu] received from a fortune teller the following prognostication: 'Since antiquity our country has never declared itself a vassal of a foreign country, but you departed from the stance taken by preceding enlightened sovereigns. You accepted the [Chinese] calendar and the seal [with the title "King of Japan"] and did not refuse them. This is the reason for your illness.'" Ishii Masatoshi, ed. *Zenrin kokuhōki*, in Tanaka Takeo, ed., *Zenrin kokuhōki Shintei zoku zenrin kokuhōki* (Shūeisha, 1995), 140. English translation from Charlotte von Verschuer, "Ashikaga Yoshimitsu's Foreign Policy 1398 to 1408 AD.: A Translation from Zenrin Kokuhōki, the Cambridge Manuscript," *Monumenta Nipponica* 62:3 (Autumn 2007), 265. See also Amano, "*Haku Rakuten* to Ōei no gaikō," 135.

48. The following description of the invasion is based on Nakamura Eikō,

friendly relations with the Chosŏn government, and was working with that government to establish safe passage for trading ships. Because Sadamori was too young to lead the family, he was taken in hand by Sōda Saemontarō 早田左衛門太郎. The Sōda family were related to the Sō family, but since they had been heavily involved in piracy along the Korean coast, the Chosŏn government received with dismay the news that they were now in charge on Tsushima island. Its worst fears appeared to be confirmed in 1419 when a large fleet of pirate ships from Tsushima that had banded together for an attack on Ming China ransacked granaries along the coast of Chosŏn as well.[49] When the new ruler, Sejong (r. 1418–1450) and his advisors met to figure out an appropriate response, it was suggested that the government take advantage of the pirates' absence to attack their home base and then lie in wait for their return. Sejong ordered a full-scale attack on Tsushima, and sent a threatening message to Sadamori on the twenty-ninth day of the Fifth Month suggesting that Sadamori act in accordance with his father's longstanding friendship with Chosŏn. According to Korean records, 227 ships carrying 17,285 men and rations for sixty-five days set sail on the nineteenth day of the Sixth Month and anchored the next day in shallow water off the shore of Tsushima. They sent a second letter to Sadamori, but received no reply so they set about destroying ships and burning houses, as well as creating a defensive barrier to prove their willingness to stay. On the twenty-sixth the Koreans invaded the center of the island. Lured into a trap by the Japanese, they retreated after suffering major losses. In the meantime, a typhoon off the coast of China had sunk most of the pirate fleet. Sadamori (or his advisors) sent a report on the battle to the shogunate, including the fact that there had been a typhoon, and requested permission to

---

"Ōei no gaikō," in Kokushi Daijiten Henshū Iinkai, ed., *Kokushi daijiten* vol. 2 (Yoshikawa kōbunkan, 1980), 444–45. For brief discussions in English of the situation on Tsushima in and around the time of the invasion, see Kenneth R. Robinson, "From Raiders to Traders: Border Security and Border Control in Early Chosŏn, 1392–1450," *Korean Studies* 16 (1992), 105–6, and "The Tsushima Governor and Regulation of Japanese Access to Chosŏn in the Fifteenth and Sixteenth Centuries," *Korean Studies* 20 (1996), 31–32. Robinson's articles clarify the role of Tsushima in developing diplomatic and trade relations between Chosŏn and Japan during this period.

49. Nakamura Eikō ("Ōei no Gaikō," 444) argues that the attack was an act of desperation caused by a famine on Tsushima, and that the pirates first requested food from the Chosŏn government, only attacking when their request was turned down.

negotiate. When the Koreans learned that the typhoon had sunk the pirates, they negotiated a friendly truce and sailed back to Chosŏn. Apparently both the Koreans and the Japanese chose to view the military action as a victory for their side.[50]

It seems obvious to us today that this invasion was on a very different order from the Mongol invasions of a hundred and fifty years before. It was limited in scope, focused only on dealing with the *wakō* pirates, and mounted by the Chosŏn government with no official participation by China (although Chinese mercenaries may have been involved). It had no connection to the arrival of the Ming envoy Roen. In historical retrospect, the Tsushima invasion was a mere blip on the screen in an age of much more serious civil unrest.[51] However, in the capital at the time the coincidental timing of the two events appears to have created widespread panic, largely conditioned by the government's previous experience of the Mongol invasions and the shogun Yoshimochi's paranoia about the Chinese.[52]

Evidence of how the court and shogunate reacted to the simultaneous appearance of the Ming envoy and the attack on Tsushima comes primarily from two diaries: *Mansai jugō nikki* 満済准后日記 and *Kanmon gyoki* 看聞御紀. The first is by Mansai 満済 (or Manzai, 1378–1435), an adopted son of Yoshimitsu and the head priest of Godaiji temple. Mansai

---

50. For example, in a recent historical survey, one of the major accomplishments attributed to King Sejong is that he "defeated the Wakō pirates on Tsushima Island." See Patricia Ebrey, Anne Walthall, and James Palais, eds., *Pre-Modern East Asia: To 1800* (Houghton Mifflin, 2006), 297.

51. One indication of modern historians' lack of interest is the range of dates given in various accounts (for example, both Takano and Sansom have the invasion occurring in the Seventh Month rather than the Sixth). The lack of agreement about dates is probably another symptom of the confusion generated by unsubstantiated rumors at the time. On the other hand, Nakamura Eikō has focused attention on the invasion as a turning point in Japanese and Korean relations.

52. Note that a previous invasion of Tsushima by Koryŏ forces in 1389, in which more than three hundred pirate ships and innumerable coastal dwellings were destroyed, does not seem to have occasioned anything like as much concern. This may have been because the shogun at the time, Yoshimitsu, was actively pursuing diplomatic and trade relations with Ming China and therefore was not likely to have been under the misapprehension that they or the Mongols were invading. For a detailed account of the 1389 attack, see Benjamin Harrison Hazard, "Japanese Marauding in Medieval Korea: The Wakō Impact on Late Koryŏ" (Ph.D. Dissertation, University of California, Berkeley, 1967), 269–70.

was a trusted counselor to three shoguns, Yoshimitsu, Yoshimochi, and Yoshinori, advising them on issues of both domestic and foreign politics. His diary is considered an extremely reliable source for understanding the internal workings of the shogunate during his lifetime, and as a high-ranking prelate he refers often to matters involving religious rituals. *Kanmon gyoki* was written by Gosukō-in Fushiminomiya Sadafusa Shinnō 後崇光院伏見宮貞成親王 (1372–1456), the father of Emperor Go-Hanazono 後花園 (r. 1429–1464). Sadafusa's diary is considered less reliable in the sense that it often relies on hearsay and rumor, but it presents a clear picture of the heightened state of anxiety in the capital during the summer of 1419. It is also useful in this context because of Sadafusa's strong interest in the supernatural.

It is apparent from entries in these diaries that the arrival of the Ming envoy not long after reports of the attack on Tsushima was considered extremely ominous; in fact, it seems likely that it was the coincidental timing of the two events that encouraged the widely disseminated rumor that the Chinese (or Mongols) had made plans to stage a large-scale invasion. For example, although Mansai earlier mentions ritual prayers mounted in response to a "foreign invasion" it is not until the Chinese envoy arrives that he appears to become worried:

> One Chinese ship (*tōsen* 唐船) arrived at Hyōgo Bay, and on the nineteenth of this month the Chinese envoy presented a letter at the Fukugenji Temple in Hyōgo. ...

> As in the Bun'ei period [the first Mongol invasion of 1274], we did not pause to consider yes or no, but simply rejected it. The Mongols attacked Tsushima, with great numbers of dead on both sides. There is a rumor that there was a dispatch letter, but while I was at Ryūkyoji, there was no one to investigate the truth, so I am simply presenting the rumors.[53]

The language here is ambiguous, but Mansai appears to be collapsing the Bun'ei invasion of 1274, when the Mongols attacked Tsushima and inflicted great damage and numerous casualties, with the current invasion by Chosŏn. This mistaken belief was encouraged by reports

---

53. Ōei 26 (1419) 7/23, *Mansai jugō nikki*, 334–35.

from warrior officials in Kyushu, at least as reported in the diaries. For example, Mansai records that on the seventh day of the Eighth Month, while he was in attendance on Yoshimochi, a dispatch from the "Kyushu shōni" (deputy assistant governor of Dazaifu)[54] arrived:

> In the dispatch it said that an advanced guard of more than five hundred Mongol ships approached Tsushima. Shōni Daisōemon 少貳代宗右衛門 and more than seven hundred followers engaged in battle again and again. On the twenty-sixth day of the Sixth Month, they fought all day. The foreigners were defeated and it is said that more than half of them died or were captured. It is said that we captured two of their commanders alive and forced them to confess. Among those five hundred ships there were mainly Korean soldiers. [One of the confessions claimed that] about twenty thousand Chinese warships (唐船) had been ordered to attack Japan on the sixth day of the Sixth Month, but a great wind (大風) arose, the Chinese warships were forced to retreat, and more than half of them were sunk. This is what the dispatch said. The two captured generals confessed that they were Korean. According to the letter, during the battle, various supernatural events occurred.[55]

Mansai was present when the dispatch was read, and so this record of the dispatch's contents is probably fairly reliable. We know that the coerced confession by the two commanders—that twenty thousand Chinese warships had been planning to attack Japan on the sixth day of the Sixth Month but had been sunk by a typhoon—was false, and it may have been made up by the Kyushu officials to exaggerate the importance of

---

54. Members of the Shōni 少弐 clan were the hereditary *Dazai no shōni* 大宰少弐 (also written 少弐 or 少貳) so in the diary entries it is not always clear if the family or the title is meant. Here the title is written 九州少貳, and so it seems likely to be the position. Although Shōni Mitsusada 少弐満貞 (?–1433) is not named specifically, he was the *Dazai no shōni* at the time.

55. Ōei 26 (1419) 8/7, *Mansai jugō nikki* vol. 1, 336–37. It appears as though the dispatch by Shōni Mitsusada discounts any effort by the *tandai* Shibukawa Yoshitoshi, possibly because there was great animosity between the Shōni and the Shibukawa at the time.

their supposed defense of Tsushima. The dispatch also notes that various supernatural events occurred during the battle on the twenty-sixth, but unfortunately the manuscript is missing a number of characters so it is hard to tell what those events might have been.

In an entry from *Kanmon gyoki* dated the eleventh day of the Eighth Month, Sadafusa reports a similar rumor:

> The Chinese (唐人) invaded on the twenty-sixth day of the Sixth Month at Tsushima Bay. The Shōni, Ōtomo, and Kikuchi engaged in battle. The foreign troops were defeated, and our side suffered minimal losses. It is said that we captured two of their generals alive. A great wind blew and many Chinese ships (唐船) were destroyed and sunk. It is said that there were approximately twenty-five thousand Chinese ships. Two commanders were captured and taken to Hyōgo. Six days ago a dispatch arrived. Everyone in the country was overjoyed. The Muromachi lord [Ashikaga Yoshimochi] was extremely pleased. Both courtiers and samurai celebrated with music and dance … Everyone from ministers on down participated in the celebration. It is a source of wonder that although this is called a "degenerate age" the hearts of the kami were reached.[56]

This entry may be based on the same dispatch recorded in *Mansai jūgo nikki*, but with greater exaggeration: the Chinese ships now number 25,000, and rather than being part of an earlier proposed invasion now constitute the invasion of Tsushima itself.

Subsequently, on the thirteenth day of the Eighth Month, Sadafusa records a dispatch he says is from the Kyushu *tandai* (deputy) Shibukawa Mochinori 渋川持範:[57]

---

56. Ōei 26 (1419) 8/11, *Kanmon gyoki* 看聞御記, in Hanawa Hokiichi 塙保己一, ed., *Zoku gunsho ruijū: hoi*, supplementary vol. 2, part 1 (Zoku Gunsho Ruijū Kanseikai, 1985), 196 (hereafter *Kanmon gyoki*).

57. According to *Kanmon gyoki* the signature on the letter is Shibukawa "Mochinori" but at the time the Kyushu *tandai* was either Shibukawa Mitsuyori 満頼 or Yoshitoshi 渋川義俊. The historian Tanaka Yoshinari (1860–1919) argued that this mistake in itself points to the letter being a fabrication, but it is also possible that it was simply a mistake on the part of Sadafusa. Tanaka also

About the foreign invasion. Six days ago, a dispatch came from the *tandai*, which I am recording here for posterity.

On the twentieth day of the Sixth Month, a mixed group of Mongols and Koreans, in approximately five hundred warships, reached Tsushima. They attempted to invade the island. Our leading Shōni was granted permission to fight. Shortly thereafter, ships arrived in the bays and ports and battle was waged day and night. We do not know how many soldiers of the enemy and on our side died. Things quickly got difficult. All of the armies of the nine provinces participated. On the twenty-sixth day of the same month, it became a life and death struggle. We [know we] killed about 3,700 of the enemy soldiers. We are not sure how many more were killed. There were about 1,300 enemy ships afloat. Pressure was put on the invaders day and night. In skirmish after skirmish enemy ships were boarded and sunk. During the battle a number of supernatural events involving kami occurred. There was a series of marvelous occurrences. The enemy boats were shaken by wind and rain. Lightning struck. Hail fell. It was so cold that the [enemy soldiers] could not grasp their weapons. We do not know how many drowned. During this time, strange things happened. This is a difficult time of year for a battle. We do not know where they came from, but four great ships appeared, hung with marvelous military banners. One of the commanders was said to be a woman. Her power was immeasurable. She boarded the Mongol boats and forced three hundred soldiers into the sea. Besides the followers of the general of the Mongols, there were twenty-

notes that although the letter claims participation by clans located in Kyushu, there is no evidence in family records supporting this. In fact, given their lack of correspondence with the account in Korean records, both reports were probably retroactive fabrications meant to take credit for a military defense that, as in 1389, was mounted mostly by those on Tsushima. Tanaka Yoshinari, *Ashikaga jidai shi* (Meiji shoin, 1923; reprint Kōdansha, 1979), 115–16.

eight criminals (*toga no mono* 咎のもの). Some were immediately put to death by the sword. Seven were left alive by orders from above. On the twenty-seventh about halfway through the night, most of the foreign fleet withdrew. There were rumors that Mongols were killed, but it is not certain. On the second day of the Seventh Month the rest of the enemy ships withdrew. This matter was quickly resolved by the power of the deities. The fortune (*onun* 御運) of our leader[58] is very auspicious. Details have been summarized from the dispatch.

Fifteenth day of the Seventh Month, Tandai Mochinori 探題持範

Although they say this is a degenerate age, [this victory is due to] the power of the deities. Their protection of our country is unrivaled (吾国擁護顕然也). This dispatch tells the true story.[59]

It is clear from this entry that although in reality the typhoon had little connection to Tsushima islanders' successful resistance against the invading forces, it was already being treated as a *kamikaze,* a divine wind sent by the native deities to defend Japan as they had done a hundred and fifty years previously. In addition, the entry describes the participation of deities in the actual sea battle, appearing out of nowhere on four mysterious boats commanded by a female commander. If *Haku Rakuten* was, in fact, written with the Ōei invasion in mind, the *kamikaze* in the second half of the play would have originated from widely disseminated rumors such as this.

The court and shogunate's belief in the participation of the native deities in the defense of the country was furthered by a series of omens and strange events that *Kanmon gyoki* and *Mansai jugō nikki* record occurring from the fourteenth day of the Sixth Month onward. For example, at Izumo Shrine, in the middle of the night on the fourteenth, the voices of ten- to twenty-thousand people were heard yelling; when dawn broke and they looked inside the shrine there was blood on the

---

58. 上様 *uesama*: shogun or emperor.
59. Ōei 26 (1419) 8/13, *Kanmon gyoki* part 1, 197–98.

sacred sword, and the shrine was filled with blood.[60] While Yoshimochi was in attendance at Hachiman Iwashimizu Shrine, the eastern *torii* gate collapsed for no apparent reason.[61] On Mount Kamo, dozens of trees suddenly all withered at once.[62] On a windy and rainy night (the sixteenth) in the Seventh Month an enormous light appeared over the sea and flew toward Atsuta Shrine, knocking down houses along the street leading up to the shrine. A young girl became possessed and explained that this phenomenon was due to the deities at Ise and Hachiman.[63] All of these events were, of course, understood as supernatural warnings by the native deities that Japan was in danger from a foreign invasion. In response, the shogun Yoshimochi is recorded as having repeatedly ordered various shrines and temples to perform ritual prayers for the defense of the nation.

The diaries also provide anecdotal evidence that the deities themselves participated in repelling the foreigners. Besides the story given above of a supernaturally powerful female commander, there is a story about a mounted female commander appearing from Hirota Shrine to lead an army (the shrine attendant who witnessed this was said to have become insane),[64] and a statue of the Kitano Tenjin is reported to have suddenly pointed to the west and flown off, leaving the shrine door open.[65]

A few of the deities mentioned in the second half of *Haku Rakuten* make their appearance in these contemporary diary accounts, and yet Sumiyoshi is conspicuously absent. Why, then, does Sumiyoshi take the lead in the nō play? On some level, the choice of Sumiyoshi may seem overdetermined; no other deity combined all of the required characteristics. In particular, the deity's identity as the guardian deity of *waka* is vital for the poetry contest with Haku Rakuten in the first half of the play, and *Kokinwakashū jo kikigaki*, which forms the backbone of the deity's argument for the superiority of *waka* poetry (and therefore Japan), was supposed to have been an oracular revelation from the deity itself. But as noted earlier, it is striking that the deity takes the lead militarily,

---

60. Ōei 26 (1419) 6/25, *Kanmon gyoki* part 1, 190–91; Ōei 26 (1419) 6/26, *Mansai jugō nikki* vol. 1, 331.

61. Ōei 26 (1419) 6/25, *Kanmon gyoki* part 1, 191; Ōei 26 (1419) 6/24, *Mansai jugō nikki* vol. 1, 331.

62. Ōei 26 (1419) 6/26, *Mansai jugō nikki* vol. 1, 331.

63. Ōei 26 (1419) 7/19, *Mansai jugō nikki* vol. 1, 334.

64. Ōei 26 (1419) 6/25, *Kanmon gyoki* part 1, 191.

65. Ōei 26 (1419) 6/29, *Kanmon gyoki* part 1, 190–91.

even commanding Amaterasu, particularly when we see no mention of the deity in either of the diaries. Both Kume and Amano suggest that the Sumiyoshi deity was chosen simply because the deity was thought to have originated off the coast of Kyushu, and so was geographically appropriate, but this seems a weak explanation.[66] If we assume that the play was written specifically to showcase the deity for Ashikaga Yoshimochi, it might also be useful to look at the history of the relationship between the shrine and the Kamakura and Ashikaga shogunates.

THE HISTORY OF THE SUMIYOSHI SHRINE AND THE SHOGUNATE

As we have seen, Sumiyoshi was one of the gods of war who supported the winning side during the Genpei War. We have some evidence that Yoritomo rewarded the shrine for its support, but it appears that in subsequent years the shrine continued to be strongly associated with the court and the emperor. A hundred years later, in the period after the Mongol invasions, the Kamakura shogunate set to work improving its relations with shrines, to reward them for their role in defending the nation. According to Andrew Goble, from 1313 onward a shrine restoration program was created that

> sought to reward shrines for their part in the defense effort by enhancing their ability to collect provincial levies and donating lands for their support. By thus building up the position of shrines, the *bakufu* also hoped to provide an extra level of institutional control over provincial warriors, drawing them into formal obligations to religious institutions. In a more theoretical vein, the *bakufu* had provided concrete evidence (repelling the Mongols) to support its long-standing claim to be the defender of the nation; and it was now possible to claim further that it partook of the divine protection afforded by the gods.[67]

---

66. Amano citing Kume, "*Haku Rakuten* to Ōei no gaikō," 145.
67. Andrew Goble, *Kenmu: Go-Daigo's Revolution* (Harvard University Press, 1996), 92.

We know that the Sumiyoshi shrines appealed to the shogunate for recompense after the Mongol invasions and were likely to have benefited from the shrine restoration program.

Despite its appeal to the shogunate, however, it is clear that in the fourteenth century the Sumiyoshi Shrine continued to be closely connected with the court over and against the shogunate. Goble has detailed how Emperor Go-Daigo used a variety of esoteric rituals, some of them Tachikawa-influenced, to try to overthrow the Kamakura shogunate. Go-Daigo also extended his efforts to shrines near the capital with ties to the imperial family. Goble lists the Ise, Gion, and Usa Hachiman shrines as having benefited from Go-Daigo's largesse.[68] But there is evidence that Sumiyoshi Shrine did as well. According to Richard Ponsonby-Fane, in 1321 (Genkō 1) Emperor Go-Daigo sent a secret rescript to the head shrine administrator Tsumori Kuninatsu (津守国夏) "soliciting the aid of Suminoe no Ohokami for the overthrow of Hōjō Takatoki."[69] In 1333, perhaps as a reward for his successful overthrow of the Hōjō, Go-Daigo awarded to the shrine the proceeds of a tax on ships coming into the port of Sakai; soon after the shrine was awarded the rights as steward (jitō) and proprietor (ryōke) of Sakai's northern estate (kita no shō).[70] Go-Daigo visited the shrine in the Second Month of 1337, after he had been overthrown by Ashikaga Takauji. In 1352, Go-Daigo's son Go-Murakami, in exile in Yoshino, visited the shrine. After the visit Kuninatsu was promoted to Upper Third Rank, an "almost unprecedented honor," and numerous other official positions were awarded to the Tsumori family during the next fifteen years.[71] Go-

---

68. Goble, *Kenmu*, 92–93.

69. Ponsonby-Fane, *Suminoe no Ohokami*, 29. See also Asao Naohiro, *Osaka to Sakai* (Iwanami shoten, 1984), 158.

70. Sakai was divided into northern and southern estates; the northern estate (closer to Sumiyoshi Shrine) was in Settsu province and the southern estate was in Izumi province. Asao Naohiro (*Osaka to Sakai*, 150–59) presents documentary evidence that the Tsumori family was given control of the northern estate of Sakai as a reward for the Sumiyoshi Shrine's support of the Southern Court; they may also have gotten control of the southern estate during this period. In English, see V. Dixon Morris, "Sakai: From Shōen to Port City," in Hall and Toyoda, *Japan in the Muromachi Age*, 148, and Ponsonby-Fane, *Suminoe no Ohokami*, 10, 33.

71. Ponsonby-Fane, *Suminoe no Ohokami*, 36. A chart of official positions is provided in Hosaka Miyako, "Tsumori-ke no kajingun [1]: Tsumori ichimon to kakei," *Gakuen* 421 (1975), 42–53; and Hosaka, *Tsumori-ke no kajingun*, 20–28. The evidence for this promotion comes from the *kotobagaki* of a poem written

Murakami returned to the shrine in 1360 and lived there until his death in 1368; during this period the base of operations for the Southern Court was a temporary palace (*angū*) within the shrine (legend has it that Go-Murakami took over the Tsumori family's personal residence).

From this evidence it seems clear that the Sumiyoshi Shrine threw its lot in with Go-Daigo and the Southern Court. However, with Go-Murakami's death it must have rapidly become obvious to those in charge at the Sumiyoshi Shrine that they had chosen to back the wrong horse. Three pieces of evidence indicate that the shrine suffered setbacks from 1368 until 1392, when Ashikaga Yoshimitsu finally managed to reunify the Southern and Northern courts. First, virtually no official positions were awarded to the Tsumori family during this period.[72] Second, in 1373 the tax revenues from shipping in Izumi Sakai were transferred to the Hachiman shrine attached to Tōdaiji in Nara; in 1376 the edict was expanded to include a tax on ships at Settsu Sakai.[73] Third, according to a letter recorded in *Aguchi jinja monjo* 開口神社文書, by 1381 the Sakai northern estate was no longer under the control of Sumiyoshi Shrine.[74] The loss of income for the shrine must have been considerable, and one can only assume the Tsumori family would have been making active attempts to win back the shogunate's favor. One means they might have used to get to Yoshimitsu and his coterie of artists and aesthetes (*dōbōshū* 同朋衆) was the image of Sumiyoshi as both patron deity of poetry and defender of the country.

I think I have found one clue that they succeeded in Imagawa Ryōshun's poetic travel diary, *Michiyukiburi*, widely disseminated in the capital not long after it was written in 1371. Imagawa Ryōshun 今川了俊 (1326–1419) was himself a nearly perfect embodiment of the dual ideals of poet and warrior, and *Michiyukiburi* combines elements of both a travel diary and war tale. In 1371 Ryōshun was appointed by Yoshimitsu to the

---

during the emperor's visit.

72. As noted above, whereas prior to Go-Murakami's death in 1368 the Tsumori family was showered with court positions, including several governorships, between 1368 and 1392 they only received one position. From 1392 onward, the Tsumori family apparently regained favor: eighteen official positions were assigned to the Tsumori by Emperor Go-Komatsu between 1392 and 1412, and six official positions were assigned by Shōkō (r. 1414–1428). See Hosaka, *Tsumori-ke no kajingun*, 20–28.

73. Morris, "Sakai: From Shōen to Port City," 148.

74. Asao, *Osaka to Sakai*, 157.

position of Kyushu *tandai* and commissioned to destroy the Southern Court at its bastion in Kyushu. *Michiyukiburi* describes Ryōshun's nine-month journey to Kyushu, at the head of a very large army (although because Ryōshun attempts to make *Michiyukiburi* as much like a poetic travel diary as possible, the army is almost never mentioned). Along the way Ryōshun is particularly drawn to sites made famous by the Genpei War, and throughout the work, the narrative is almost literally haunted by the Heike. For example, toward the end of the diary, Ryōshun has arrived at the bay of Dan-no-ura. Dan-no-ura was supposedly named for a platform (*dan* 壇) that Regent Jingū built along the bay (*ura* 浦) to offer prayers for success in her invasion of the Three Kingdoms. But Dan-no-ura is also, of course, famous as the scene of the last battle of the Genpei War, where the Heike met their final defeat. Ryōshun seems to particularly identify with the child emperor Antoku, who drowned at Dan-no-ura; he dreams of him and offers prayers at a shrine devoted to his memory.[75] In the same area there is also a subsidiary Sumiyoshi Shrine.

At this point in *Michiyukiburi* Ryōshun is waiting impatiently for the tailwinds he needs to cross over to Matsura in Kyushu. There are allied troops waiting for him at Matsura, and Ryōshun worries that they will disband if his warships are unable to cross in a timely manner. He therefore prays first to the deified Regent Jingū at Anatotoyora Shrine, offering three poems, and then offers four poems to the Sumiyoshi Myōjin at the Nagato Shrine, "taking the number from four shrines [at the main shrine in Settsu province]."[76] The poems are as follows:

> *Ukigumo no / oikaze machite /*
> *ama no hara / kamiyo ni terase / hi no hikari mimu*

> I wait for tailwinds
> to chase the floating clouds
> so I may see the sunlight that shone
> upon heaven's plain
> in the age of the gods.

---

75. Imagawa Ryōshun, *Michiyukiburi*, in Nagasaki Ken et al., eds. *Chūsei nikki kikō shū* (Shōgakukan, 1994), 416–17, 422–23. In English, see James Barrett Heusch, "Wayfaring: Imagawa Ryōshun and His *Michiyukiburi*" (M.A. Thesis, University of California, Berkeley, 2002), 122–23, 128–29.

76. Imagawa, *Michiyukiburi*, 417; Heusch, "Wayfaring," 123.

Sue no yo no / mabori mo shirushi /
chihayaburu / kami no naka ni mo / hisa ni henureba

Their protection
is apparent
even in these latter days[77]
since of all the magnificent deities
they have been venerated the longest.

Yawaregeru / hikari morasu na /
shiranami no / awaki no hara o / ideshi tsukigake

Do not spare us any
of your gentle light,
oh moon that emerged
from the froth of white waves at
Awakinohara.

Kamigaki no / matsu no oika wa /
wa ga kuni no / yamato kotoba no / tane ya narikemu

The ancient pines
within the sacred enclosure—
were they not the seeds for
the poetry of
our land of Yamato?[78]

In the first poem, Ryōshun points specifically to the Sumiyoshi deity's power to raise a wind. The second praises the protection of the deity, even in this degenerate age. The third poem compares Sumiyoshi's birth, during Izanagi's lustration in the foam of white waves at Awakinohara, to the emergence of the rising moon. And through the phrase, "do not spare us any of your gentle light," Ryōshun points to the medieval concept of *wakōdōjin* (和光同塵 gentled light, same dust), that buddhas and bodhisattvas temper their radiance and become kami, mingling with

---

77. Sue no yo 末の世: the "latter days" of *mappō* (the decline of the dharma).
78. Imagawa, *Michiyukiburi*, 417–18; translations (modified) from Heusch, "Wayfaring," 124.

the dust of this world for our salvation. The last poem is particularly significant, since it specifically links Sumiyoshi's embodiment in a pine tree to the origin or seed (*tane*) of Japanese poetry (*Yamato kotoba*).

Sumiyoshi makes one more appearance in Ryōshun's diary. Ryōshun composes another poem on the thirteenth day of the Eleventh Month, upon recalling a story about a monk named Sōkyū[79] who in the Ninth Month of that same year had wanted to cross from Takasaki castle, but found the wind unfavorable:

> That night in his boat he had a dream. An old man of about eighty with white hair and sidelocks, wearing an *eboshi* court cap and immaculate white robes, appeared. He spread his left sleeve and said, "Set out upon this." As he waved the sleeve a tailwind blew and Sōkyū crossed over to here. In his dream-state he thought, "It is the great god of Sumiyoshi!" When he awoke it was already daybreak and the wind had picked up, so he put out and arrived in a place called Kudamatsu in Suō within a day.[80]

Here Sumiyoshi appears in his most common medieval guise, as a venerable old man with the power to control the wind and waves. Subsequently a favorable wind began to blow and Ryōshun was able to reach Matsura in time. A second miracle occurred at Matsura as well: the troops waiting there were about to disband when they saw in the distance a flotilla of about forty ships. Thinking that this was Ryōshun's fleet arriving at last, they stayed for another day. However, the mysterious ships simply kept on sailing. Ryōshun proclaims, "Without a doubt [these events] are the result of actions by the deities. They say poems always move the deities; my humble poems were accepted by them as an offering."[81] Ryōshun went on to successfully defeat the last vestiges of the Southern Court, although it took twenty more years to unify the succession.

Imagawa Ryōshun's *Michiyukiburi* appears to have been fairly widely

---

79. According to Heusch ("Wayfaring," 126, fn. 337), Sōkyū 宗久 (dates unknown) was a contemporary of Ryōshun's and was used by him as a messenger on occasion.

80. Imagawa, *Michiyukiburi*, 418–19; translation from Heusch, "Wayfaring," 125–26.

81. Imagawa, *Michiyukiburi*, 420; Heusch, "Wayfaring," 128.

disseminated soon after it was written, and it is possible that it had an influence on the writing of *Haku Rakuten*. Elements that reappear in the play include the deity's appearance in a dream as a venerable old man; the waving of sleeves to produce a wind; and mysterious ships appearing off the coast of Kyushu. The fact that the warrior-poet Ryōshun relies primarily on the Sumiyoshi deity at a key moment in his successful attack on the forces of the Southern Court, only a few years after the death of Go-Murakami at the Sumiyoshi Shrine in Settsu province, may indicate an abrupt shift in the shrine's political allegiance. At the very least it indicates the shrine's support of the shogunate in whatever position it decided to take with regard to the problem of the Northern and Southern courts.

As noted above, Kume Kunitake argued that the *waki* and *shite* roles in *Haku Rakuten* are allegorical portrayals of historical figures involved in the 1419 incidents. Most nō scholars today are unwilling to go this far.[82] But I think it is noteworthy that Imagawa Ryōshun, a model warrior-poet who evidently revered the Sumiyoshi deity and whose travel diary's representation of the deity has close parallels to the representation in *Haku Rakuten*, died in 1420.[83] The play may very well have served not only as a celebration of the defeat of the Chosŏn navy at Tsushima and the repulsion of the Ming envoy from Hyōgo Bay, but also as a memorial celebration of Ryōshun, who spent more than twenty years of his life in Kyushu working for the shogunate's interests. Of course, there would have been a certain amount of irony to such a memorial, given Ryōshun's role in making it possible for Yoshimitsu to establish diplomatic relations with Ming China.[84]

---

82. See Amano's discussion, *"Haku Rakuten to Ōei no gaikō,"* 145.

83. According to Araki Hisashi, the scholarly consensus is that Ryōshun died in the Eighth Month of 1420 at the age of ninety-six. Araki Hisashi, *Imagawa Ryōshun no kenkyū* (Kasama shoin, 1977), 551.

84. Yoshimitsu was moved to finally defeat the Southern Court precisely because he wanted to initiate a lucrative trade agreement with Ming China, and it was clear that the Chinese would not sit down to the table until Yoshimitsu could (1) prove to them he was the legitimate ruler of Japan (they had been dealing with Prince Kaneyoshi [懐良親王] of the Southern Court) and (2) he could show that some real effort was being made to control the *wakō* pirates off the coast of Kyushu. To achieve both aims, Yoshimitsu needed control of Kyushu. Once Ryōshun managed to pacify Kyushu and Yoshimitsu successfully reunited the Southern and Northern courts, Yoshimitsu was able to initiate his first successful mission to China, headed by Soami 其阿弥, a member of his *dōbōshū*,

Leaving aside *Haku Rakuten* as a possible memorial to Imagawa Ryōshun, the argument that the play was written as a political allegory would certainly be aided by evidence that the Sumiyoshi Shrine had made some kind of claim for the deity being one of the kami that defended Tsushima with a *kamikaze*. So far, scholars have not uncovered evidence in diaries or other historical records to prove this. There is, however, one last piece of pertinent evidence that has not previously been discussed: a secret commentary written in first person as though it were an oracular revelation of the Sumiyoshi deity. According to the colophon, it was composed in 1420:

> From the time Izanagi and Izanami first created the land, as long as Amaterasu Ōmikami has governed the world, I have dwelt in the shade of the pine at Sumiyoshi, where thousands of hearts have attached a myriad of word-leaves to events and called them poems. Therefore I especially praise and enjoy this path [of poetry] and resolve to protect, to every bay and every border, those who love *waka* and strive to pursue the path of aesthetic pleasure (好色).[85] I do this because *waka* pacifies evil hearts and moderates the violent. The kami on my left is the Ikkyo deity.[86] The deity reprimands those who do not appreciate sentiment (情) and passion (色) and who criticize the significance of poetry. The kami on my right is the Tsurugiyama deity.[87] This deity appears with eight swords to govern the country without chaos and to eliminate threats from other countries. Because I govern the land and protect the world; because I promote the path of poetry, which makes people sensitive to sentiment by keeping the five lines of poetry from being disordered; and because I appear provisionally to save people and

as chief envoy. See the discussion in Kawazoe Shōji, "Japan and East Asia," in Kozo Yamamura, ed., *Cambridge History of Japan: Volume 3 Medieval Japan* (Cambridge University Press, 1990), 423–38.

85. 和歌を好み、好色を道とせむ物. *Kōshoku* (好色) here means both eroticism and aesthetic sentiment or appreciation.

86. 一挙, also possibly pronounced Ikko. It is unclear who this deity might be.

87. 剣山, most probably the Tsurugi Hachiman deity.

promote moral sentiment, I am known as the founder of the path of *waka*, and I have recommended this path of poetry to the emperors of successive reigns. I now appear to you as an otherworldly old man (幽翁) of eighty years, dressed in a red robe. You are not to reveal this image to others.[88]

Here we have a document that might well have been composed specifically in response to the Ōei invasion. Although it is much more strongly Buddhist in temper than the play, it portrays Sumiyoshi as both guardian deity of *waka* poetry and martial defender of the country. The dating provides us with a firm basis to argue that the Sumiyoshi Shrine might have claimed responsibility for helping to defeat the invaders.

Interestingly, the last signature on the commentary colophon is by Kanpaku Takatsukasa Masamichi 鷹司政通. Masamichi, who was *kanpaku* from 1823 to1842, and who died not long after the Meiji Restoration in 1868, is known for having at first been antagonistic toward the "invasion" by Mathew Perry's black ships, but later to have advocated the imperial restoration. Perhaps he saw new relevance in Sumiyoshi's declaration of his willingness to defend Japan "to every bay and border."

CONCLUSION

Arguing for *Haku Rakuten* as political allegory, Kume Kunitake makes the following point:

In the theater arts, the historical context in which a work was produced is always related to its content. Sometimes the work describes an actual incident, sometimes it creates a new trend. Sometimes it faces censorship. Sometimes it goes against the trends of the time. In any case, the historical background cannot

---

88. その形を人にかたどる事勿れ: literally, you are not to draw this image for other people. *Katadoru* may be a mistake for *kataru* (to tell), or it may mean that the image is not to be reproduced. *Akone no ura kuden*, in Sasaki Nobutsuna, ed., *Nihon kagaku taikei* vol. 4 (Kazama shobō, 1973), 398.

be ignored. If we separate theatrical arts from their time, we simply cannot evaluate them. Authors are of their time. Sometimes later readers cannot understand the meaning of a work. Or even if they understand it, they may not think it has any value. This is because trends and customs change. An extreme example would be utensils that we no longer know how to use. If something is too closely tied to its time, it will not endure for long.[89]

Kume's plea for the importance of historicism in nō scholarship, made almost ninety years ago, is finally beginning to be taken to heart by contemporary nō scholars. If we do not pay attention to the historical context in which nō plays were written, and in particular to the patronage networks that supported the nō troupes, we may be missing the whole point of the play, at least as understood by audiences at the time.

The three canonical plays in which the Sumiyoshi deity plays a leading role, *Takasago*, *Iwafune*, and *Haku Rakuten*, emphasize different aspects of the deity's identity. *Takasago*, by far the best known of the three, shares with *Haku Rakuten* the representation of Sumiyoshi as guardian deity of poetry and celebration of the peacefulness and prosperity of the current (shogunal) reign, but also represents the deity as fertile life-force, symbolized by the long-lived, evergreen pine tree. Amano Fumio has argued that *Takasago*, like *Haku Rakuten*, was written for the Shogun Yoshimochi, and that it has a hidden political background that would have given it an allegorical subtext for its contemporary audience.[90] The much less well-known play *Iwafune*, on the other hand, seems almost diametrically opposed to *Haku Rakuten*: *Iwafune* stresses the deity's role in foreign trade with China, while in *Haku Rakuten* the Sumiyoshi deity appears to reject all things Chinese. How are we to understand such different representations? If we follow Kume's suggestion, and attempt to place the plays back into their original historical context we can see that *Iwafune* would have been strongly connected to pursuits that Yoshimitsu

---

89. Takatsukasa Masamichi (1789–1868) became *kanpaku* in 1823, and in 1842 he became *dajōdaijin*. After Perry's arrival he originally sided with the shogunate, but later switched to supporting the imperial cause. The shogunate was angered by this betrayal and forced his resignation in 1848. He took the tonsure in 1868 and died not long afterward.

90. As quoted in Amano Fumio, "*Haku Rakuten* to Ōei no gaikō," 130–31.

valued highly: art (in this case poetry), commerce (lucrative trade with China) and the welfare (wealth) of the country. *Haku Rakuten* and *Takasago*, on the other hand, eschew foreign relations and commerce, concentrating instead on the unchanging stability of a Japan defended by the Sumiyoshi deity, who is both virile warrior and poetic master. This viewpoint would have suited Yoshimochi, who although a strong patron of the arts was vehemently antagonistic toward foreign relations. We can see how each play, in its own way, may have helped refurbish the image of the Sumiyoshi Shrine and reestablish connections with the Ashikaga shogunate after the shrine's disastrous alliance with Go-Daigo and the Southern Court.

Although the Ōei invasion and the arrival of the Ming envoy caused ripples of anxiety throughout the capital, by the time the play was performed it is likely that Yoshimochi already understood the threat had not been nearly as serious as it appeared originally.[91] It might for that very reason have been thought an appropriate focus of such a light-hearted allegory. And in later years, as the historical incidents of the summer of 1419 were overshadowed by much more serious political events, the political subtext was simply forgotten. A subsequent revision of the play (probably by Kanze Nobumitsu[92]), which transformed *Haku Rakuten* into a two-act play with a humorous *ai-kyōgen* interlude, would have furthered this process of erasure. And in the Edo period, precisely because the political subtext had been neutralized, the play was allowed to enter the canon, although a lingering taint of "unorthodoxy" has caused some

---

91. Amano Fumio "*Takasago* no shudai to seiritsu no haikei: Ōei nijūkyū nen no Aso Daigūji zasshō no jōraku to Yoshimochi no chisei o megutte," *Engekigaku Ronsō*, vol. 7 (December 31, 2004), 14–51. Amano argues that the unusual identification of the *waki* in *Takasago* with a historical person, "Tomonari, the head of the shrine of Asonomiya in Higo," is related to a lawsuit brought by two feuding members of the Aso family that was probably settled by the shogunate sometime in Ōei 30. With this political event in the background, the setting of *Takasago* in the Engi era and the reference to "kimi" (the Engi Emperor), would have been understood by the audience at the time to be allegorical references to the present Ōei era and the shogun Yoshimochi. Amano also provides firm evidence for Yoshimochi's depth of interest in *waka* poetry, which is a main focus of interest in both *Takasago* and *Haku Rakuten*.

92. In the eleventh month of 1419 Yoshimochi asked for and received a more detailed account of the invasion of Tsushima from Sō Sadamori and his advisors. He would also have received a copy of the negotiated treaty, which should have allayed his fears that the attack was coordinated with the Chinese.

scholars to doubt the traditional attribution to Zeami.[93] Having restored
Haku Rakuten's historical subtext, one question now facing us is, how
many other plays that we have blithely assumed were purely aesthetic are
actually political allegories of this kind?

---

93. As noted above, Takemoto Mikio argues that Kanze Nobumitsu revised
the play, based on a comparison with Nobumitsu's similar revision of the play
Ukon. Takemoto, "Sakuhin Kenkyū: *Haku Rakuten*," 7.

29 ⮑ *Haku Rakuten*

| Susan Blakeley Klein

Introduction

Haku Rakuten is a *kami* (or *waki*) nō, a felicitous piece of the first category that would open a traditional program of nō. It is comprised of two acts separated by an interval; both the play and the interval are translated here. The *shite* is the Sumiyoshi Daimyōjin, a deity known for its patronage of poets and seafarers, two themes interwoven in this dramatic celebration of the superiority of Japanese poetry over its Chinese counterpart. The deity appears first in the guise of an old fisherman and is accompanied by one *tsure*. The *waki* is the famous Tang-period poet Bai (or Bo) Juyi 白居易 (772–846), known popularly in Japanese as Haku Rakuten 白楽天, who has crossed the ocean to test the poetic acumen of the Japanese. Two *tsure* accompany him. The *ai* is a subsidiary deity of the Sumiyoshi Shrine.

In the first part of the play, Haku Rakuten arrives off the coast at Matsuragata in the province of Hizen (Kyushu), at the western edge of the realm. After an exchange of poetry, in which the Sumiyoshi deity demonstrates the superiority and miraculous efficacy of waka poetry, Haku Rakuten realizes that the Japanese are cleverer than expected, and he decides to return home without setting foot on land. The Sumiyoshi deity promises to come back and perform a dance to entertain the poet, but after the interlude, in which the *ai* recapitulates the encounter in narrative form, the deity returns in his true form accompanied by a number of other deities (none of whom are represented on stage). Together they dance up a divine wind (*kamikaze*) that blows Haku Rakuten back to China, celebrating the fact that "in this age of the deity and sovereign, our country is immovable" (*kami to kimi ga yo no ugokanu*

443

kuni). The structure of the play is conventional for *kami* nō: the first part culminates in a *kuse* dance and the second in a *shin-no-jo-no-mai* dance. The adversarial relationship between *shite* and *waki*, and the *waki*'s retreat following their confrontation, however, are unusual for *kami* nō.

Although as discussed in the accompanying chapter in this volume, the image of the Sumiyoshi deity as an ideal warrior-poet is linked to the development of that image in *Heike monogatari*, there is no confirmed source (*honzetsu*) for the plot of the play.[1] There is a source, however, for the Sumiyoshi deity's culminating argument for the superiority of Japanese poetry, in which he quotes the famous line from the Kana Preface to the *Kokinshū* that "all living beings, without exception, compose poetry" (*iki toshi ikeru mono izure ka uta o yomazarikeri*) and supports that claim with an anecdote about a young acolyte transformed into a bird who chirps a Chinese poem (easily translated into Japanese). The anecdote appears to have been taken directly from *Kokinwakashū jo kikigaki* (Lecture notes on the *Kokinshū* preface), a thirteenth-century commentary popularly understood to be an oracular revelation from the Sumiyoshi deity himself.[2] The implicit message, that if even a bird can compose poetry in Japan, then how much more so the Japanese people, appears crucial to convincing Haku Rakuten to return home.

The original source of the two poems exchanged by Bo Juyi and Sumiyoshi is thought to be a Chinese couplet and waka response in section four of the *setsuwa* collection *Gōdanshō* 江談抄 (The Ōe Conversations). *Gōdanshō* was compiled by Fujiwara Sanekane (藤原 実兼 1085–1112) from conversations with Ōe no Masafusa (大江匡 房 1041–1111), an accomplished scholar of Chinese poetry. Section four of *Gōdanshō* is mainly made up of commentaries and anecdotes related to Chinese poetry, focusing particularly on poets featured in the *Wakan roeishū*. The Chinese couplet is attributed to Miyako no Arinaka,[3]

---

1. According to Itō Masayoshi, the Naikaku Bunkozō *Kingyoku yōshū* 金玉 要集 records a similar poetic exchange at Myōshū Bay (明州の津) in China between Haku Rakuten and the Sumiyoshi deity manifesting as an old man. Itō takes this to indicate at least some version of the story existed in *setsuwa* form prior to the play. Itō Masayoshi, *Yōkyokushū* (ge), SNKS (Shinchōsha, 1988), 453 and Itō Masayoshi, *Yōkyoku zakki* (Tokyo: Izumi shoin, 1989), 200–1.

2. *Kokinwakashū jo kikigaki: sanryū shō* in Katagiri Yōichi, ed., *Chūsei Kokinshū chūshakusho kaidai*, vol. 2 (Kyoto: Akao Shōbundō, 1973), 225–28.

3. Arinaka (dates unknown) was the son of Miyako no Yoshika (都良香 834–879) who had fourteen Chinese couplets included in the *Wakan rōeishū* 和

a minor poet of Chinese verse:

白雲似帯囲山腰
青苔如衣負巌背
　　在中詩

A contemporary *yomikudashi* translation:

白雲は帯に似て／山の腰を囲り
青苔は衣の如く／巌の背に負はる⁴

hakuun wa obi ni nite / yama no koshi o meguri
seitai wa koromo no gotoku / iwaho no se ni oharu

White clouds—encircling like a sash / the waist of the mountain;
green moss—draping like a robe / the shoulders of the cliff.

Akinaka's verse is paired with a waka response by an anonymous lady-in-waiting (*nyōbō* 女房:):

苔衣／着たる巌は／まびろけて
衣着ぬ山の／帯するはなぞ⁵

kokegoromo / kitaru iwaho wa / mabirokete
kinukinu yama no / obi suru wa nazo

The green moss robe
worn by the cliff
is loosely draped [i.e., it wears no sash to close it];
why then does the robeless mountain
wear an *obi*?

Akinaka's poem is a straightforward example of the Chinese style of

---

漢朗詠集. Arinaka had two couplets included, numbers 325 and 407. Kawaguchi
Hisao, ed. *Wakan Rōeishū* (Kōdansha gakujutsu bunko, 1982), 249 and 304.

4. *Genbun* version section 4, number 7, in Gotō Akio, Ikegami Jun'ichi, Yamane
Taisuke, eds., *Gōdanshō, Chūgaishō, Fukego*, SNKBT 32 (Iwanami shoten, 1997),
508. The *yomikudashi* version was produced by Yamane Taisuke, with headnotes
by Gotō Akio, 108.

5. The *genbun* version is in hiragana; the kanji here are from the *yomikudashi* version.

parallel and antithetical imagery (A is like B, A2 is like B2). Here, green moss hanging on a cliff is compared to a robe hung loosely over the shoulders and white clouds encircling the mid-section of a mountain are compared to an *obi* sash around the waist. The lady-in-waiting's witty rejoinder makes fun of Akinaka's rather pedestrian effort by pointing out the obvious disconnect between the two images—why does the cliff wear a moss-robe but no sash, the mountain wear a cloud-sash but no robe? In so doing she shows off her own more considerable talents: although, according to the normative gender assumptions of the day, as a woman she is not supposed to even understand Chinese, she is able to extemporaneously offer a humorous critique in the form of a waka poem.

By assigning Akinaka's poem to Bo Juyi and the lady-in-waiting's poem to Sumiyoshi, one could easily make the argument that the Sumiyoshi deity, disguised as an old man, is playing a role parallel to that of the lady-in-waiting in the original context. At first Bo Juyi expects nothing of such a humble figure, but when he realizes that even so lowly a person as a fisherman in Japan is capable of not only appreciating Chinese poetry, but critiquing it, he figures that his test of the sagacity of the Japanese is over and it is time to return home. The subversion of gender hierarchy (female cleverly trumps male) in the original context becomes the subversion of political hierarchy (Japan cleverly trumps China) in the play.[6]

With regard to authorship, most scholars agree that the play was written during Zeami's lifetime (c.1363–c.1443). The first recorded performance was in 1464 (Kyūkawara kanjin sarugaku 糺河原勧進猿楽), on a program with *Takasago* and *U no Ha*, but given how few plays were recorded from the fifteenth century, that date is simply used as the outer limit for the play's composition. Takemoto Mikio takes the position that the play is not by Zeami, because it does not conform to Zeami's typical structure for a *waki nō* and there is little evidence of Zeami's

---

6. The version of the poem presented in the *Haku Rakuten* is slightly different than the *Gōdanshō* version, and reverses the order of the original poem:

青苔衣を帯びて/巌の肩に懸かり *seitai koromo o obite / iwaho no kata ni kakari /*
白雲帯に似て/山の腰を囲る *hakuun obi ni nite / yama no koshi o meguru*

"A green moss robe worn / draped over the cliff's rocky shoulders;
white clouds like a sash / enwrap the mountain's waist."

One possible reason for the reversal is that it allows the Sumiyoshi deity to claim that his Japanese poem is only a "translation" of the Chinese poem, when actually, as noted above, it is a sly critique.

trademark richness of rhetorical imagery.[7] However, both Itō Masayoshi and Amano Fumio believe that it is likely to have been written by Zeami for several reasons. First, in *Kintōsho* 金島書, an essay written by Zeami in 1436 while he was in exile on the island of Sado, Zeami quotes a very similar version of the poem, in the same reversed order as the play, and attributes it to Bo Juyi.[8] Second, the idea that "all living beings, without exception, compose poetry" appears in both Zeami's *Rikugi* and as a central theme of the play *Takasago*, and so we know that Zeami also had access to some form of *Kokinwakashū jo kikigaki*. Itō Masayoshi takes this as strong circumstantial evidence of Zeami's authorship; he believes that although the play is somewhat different in character from the usual Zeami *waki* nō, it is possible that he was intentionally creating a new form, a more lighthearted variant of *iwaigoto* or celebratory nō.[9] Amano Fumio makes a similar argument: "First of all, *Haku Rakuten* was probably written after 1419, which strongly supports the idea that Zeami wrote it, and it provides a perfect example of how the shogun was the patron of nō (and Zeami) during its peak of development."[10] Amano admits the counter evidence that Zeami does not mention *Haku Rakuten* as one of the "model new plays" in *Sandō*,[11] but he suggests that perhaps because the play was so clearly based on a recent incident (the 1419 invasion of Tsushima island), it was not considered appropriate as a model. And he admits that the play could have been composed by another of Yoshimichi's favorites, Zōami, who is just as likely as Zeami to have had access to appropriate materials to construct the play.

All scholars appear to agree with Yokomichi Mario's assessment that the play was originally written as a *monogi* one-act play with a costume-change on stage; based on similarities to *Ukon*, a play firmly attributed to Zeami that was revised by Kanze Nobumitsu, Takemoto and Itō believe it was revised by Nobumitsu as a two-act play and thus helped form the basis for Nobumitsu's new style of *furyū nō teki waki nō*.

7. Takemoto Mikio, "Sakuhin kenkyū *Haku Rakuten*," *Kanze* (February 1984), 4–12.

8. Omote Akira and Katō Shūichi, eds., *Zeami, Zenchiku,* Nihon shisō taikei 24 (Iwanami shoten, 1974), 250. In English, see Susan Matisoff, trans., *"Kintōsho:* Zeami's Song of Exile," *Monumenta Nipponica* 32:4 (winter 1977), 445–46.

9. Itō, *Yōkyokushū* (ge), 453–56.

10. Amano Fumio, "*Haku Rakuten* to Ōei no gaikō: Kume Kunitake to Takano Tatsuyuki no shosetsu o kenshō suru," *Zeami: chūsei no geijutsu to bunka* 1:1 (February 2002), 128.

11. Amano, "*Haku Rakuten* to Ōei no gaikō," 146.

Haku Rakuten

| Translated by Susan Blakeley Klein

First-category nō in two acts.
Performed by the Kanze, Komparu, Kongō, and Kita schools.
Time: Early Heian period, season not specified
Place: Matsuragata in the province of Hizen
Author: Unknown

WAKI	Haku Rakuten[1]
WAKIZURE	Chinese Companions
MAESHITE	Old Fisherman
TSURE	Fishermen Companions
AI	A lesser deity who serves Sumiyoshi
NOCHIJITE	Sumiyoshi Deity

[PART ONE (*maeba*)]

Haku Rakuten and two companions enter to okitsuzumi *music. Haku Rakuten stands at center stage and faces forward; his companions wait on the bridge.*

HAKU RAKUTEN (*nanori*) You have before you a courtier of the Prince of Tang China, known as Haku Rakuten. To the east there lies a country called "Nippon."[2] I will swiftly cross to that land, entrusted

---

Haku Rakuten 白楽天. This translation is based on Itō Masayoshi, ed., *Yōkyokushū* (ge), SNKS (Shinchōsha, 1988), 78–87. Itō based his text on the early Edo period *utaibon* published by Hon'ami Kōetsu 本阿弥光悦 (1558–1637), using other texts to fill in lacunae and obscurities. I have also consulted various other edited versions, including those in Nishino Haruo, ed., *Yōkyoku hyakuban*, SNKT 57 (Iwanami shoten, 1999), 540–45; and Yokomichi Mario and Omote Akira, eds. *Yōkyokushū* (ge), NKBT 41 (Iwanami shoten, 1963), 305–8.

1. Haku Rakuten (Ch. Bai Letian) is how the Japanese refer to the Tang dynasty poet Bai (Bo) Juyi 白居易 (772–846). Letian is his "capping" or "courtesy" name (Ch. *zi* 字).

2. Haku Rakuten refers to Japan as *Nippon*, whereas the Sumiyoshi deity uses *Nihon*. In order to preserve the distinction, I will leave *Nippon* untranslated, while translating *Nihon*.

with the task of testing the sagacity of the Japanese. Even now I embark upon the seaways.

The Companions move to the main stage.

HAKU RAKUTEN AND COMPANIONS   *Facing each other.*

(*shidai*)   Our boat rows out toward the rising sun,[3]
our boat rows out toward the rising sun,
and the country we will visit.

(*ageuta*)   Across the Eastern Sea
the boat travels far along wave-filled paths,
the boat travels far along wave-filled paths.
In the wake, setting sun lingering;
in the cloud-trailing heavens,
a moon emerging from beyond

Rakuten mimes traveling.

mountains, already come into view—
before we know it
we have arrived in the land of Nippon,
we have arrived in the land of Nippon.

Rakuten ends up at the witness square (wakiza); *his companions stand in front of the chorus.*

HAKU RAKUTEN (*tsukizerifu*)
Crossing the sea lanes, in no time at all, here is the land of Nippon. Let us drop anchor here and stay awhile; I want to gaze upon this Nippon.

Old Fisherman carrying a fishing pole and two Companions enter to shin no issei *music, appropriate for the appearance of a disguised deity. Companions stand at the first pine, the Old Fisherman stands at the third pine.*

FISHERMAN AND COMPANIONS   *Facing each other.*

(*issei*)   Dawn dimly breaks over Tsukushi's sea
of unknown fires;[4]
the moon alone lingers on.[5]

---

3. 日の本 *hi no moto*: "the place from which the sun rises"; a term used by the Chinese for Japan, which lay to their east.

4. しらぬひの (不知火の) *shiranu hi no*: a *makura kotoba* for Tsukushi (modern Kyushu); it refers to mysterious lights that were said to glimmer in the sea off the coast.

5. The *shimogakari* version includes the following two lines assigned to the

Companions move to center stage; Old Fisherman takes the fishing pole off his shoulder and holding it in his right hand, moves to base square (jōza).

FISHERMAN   *Facing front.*

(*sashi*)   The great waves toss and toss, their turquoise blue soaking the sky.[6]

FISHERMAN AND COMPANIONS   *Facing each other.*

When Han Rei left the land of Etsu
poling his small boat
across the misty waves of the five lakes,[7]
it must have looked like this—
how lovely this sea view is!

(*sageuta*)   From Matsura Bay
to the west, we see no hills, only the dawn[8]

---

tsure: 松風よりの浦の秋ひと葉や舟を見せつらん *matsukaze yori no ura no aki / hitoha ya fune o misetsuran* (a pine breeze on the autumn bay / a single leaf appears like a boat). The line is based on a legend that a Chinese courtier saw a willow leaf floating in the water and made a boat out of it. It may also be based on *Gyokuyō wakashū* 玉葉和歌集, no. 715 (Book 5, Autumn): 月残る磯部の松を吹き分けて入る方見する秋の浦風 *tsuki nokoru / isobe no matsu o / fukiwakete / irukata misuru / aki no urakaze* (the moon lingers in a pine on the rocky shore, whose waving [branches] reveal the direction of autumn's bay breezes). Since this line is the only indication that the play takes place in autumn, it may have been removed to make the play seasonless. Itō, *Yōkyokushū* (ge), 80, fn. 4.

6. Here the fisherman describes the scene before him in the style of Chinese verse, setting up the comparison with Fan Li 范蠡 (Jp. Han Rei), a minister to the King of Yue 越 (Jp. Etsu) who lived in the fifth century BCE. Having served the king brilliantly, Fan Li rowed away from the court at Yue to become a recluse. Yue was a kingdom in the Warring States Era (770–403 BCE). The entire section hints at the imminent arrival of Haku Rakuten.

7. This imagery is based on *Wakan rōeishū* 和漢朗詠集 couplets 406 and 505, both of which describe Fan Li rowing away from Yue in the mist. The first couplet is on the theme, "Seeing clouds, you can tell the presence of sages." Here the mist might be understood as an auspicious sign for the sage Haku Rakuten.

8. 松浦潟西に山なきありあけの月の入る *Matsuragata nishi ni yama **naki** ariake no tsuki no iru*: the phrase contains an untranslatable pun on absence (*naki*) and presence (*ari*). Haku Rakuten set out when the moon was rising from behind mountains to the east; now the fishermen reverse the imagery, telling us the moon is setting to the west in the "mountainless" sea. The implication is that Haku Rakuten has accomplished the journey to Japan in the space of a single night, a point that is reiterated more clearly below. Since it is not actually possible

(*ageuta*)	moon setting and
	clouds drifting like boats in the offing[9]
	clouds drifting like boats in the offing
	anchored together in the early morning
	sea—is China in that direction?

*Old Fisherman stays at center stage; Companions exchange fishing poles for fans and move to the corner pillar (*metsukebashira*).*

> The voyage along sea lanes is not far,
> a single night's sailing, they say,
> he's arrived already, his journey a memory,
> like the dawn moon,[10]
> already a memory, like the dawn moon.

HAKU RAKUTEN   *Facing front.*

(*mondō*)   I've crossed over the high waves of 10,000 *li*[11] and arrived in the land of Nippon. I see a small boat floating nearby and there appears to be an old fisherman in it. Could he be a man of Nippon?

OLD FISHERMAN That is so, I am an old fisherman of Japan. And you are Haku Rakuten of the Tang court, am I right?

HAKU RAKUTEN

(*kakeai*)   This is strange—although this is the first time
I have crossed to this land,
you already recognize me as Haku Rakuten.

---

to sail from China to Japan in such a short space of time, this may be meant to imbue Haku Rakuten's journey with a certain miraculous quality; or it may more generally imply that movement (of both people and ideas) between China and Japan was relatively effortless.

9. The Hon'ami Kōetsu text has 雲も浮かむや沖つ波 *kumo mo ukamu ya okitsu nami* (clouds drifting like waves in the offing). Most other *utaibon* have 雲も浮かむや沖津船 *kumo mo ukamu ya okitsu fune* (clouds drifting like boats in the offing), and I have chosen to use that here because it makes more sense with the following line, 互にかかる朝まだき海 *tagai ni kakaru asa madaki umi* (anchored together in the early morning sea). One possible reading of these lines is that the fishermen see another boat (Haku Rakuten's) anchored, like theirs, in the offing.

10. つきも程なき名残かな *tsuki mo hodo naki nagori kana*: the expression *tsuki* pivots to mean both "arrival" (着き) and "moon" (月). Someone (the implication being Haku Rakuten) has arrived in no time at all, like the moon, which in no time at all has set and become a memory.

11. A *li* is a measure of distance equal to about a third of a mile.

How can this be?

FISHERMAN'S COMPANIONS

> Although your honor comes from China,
> your name and reputation precede you here in Japan
> and cannot be hidden.

HAKU RAKUTEN

> Even if my name is known,
> I still would not expect you
> to recognize me in person!

OLD FISHERMAN

> The rumor that Haku Rakuten has come
> to measure the sagacity of the Japanese
> has spread throughout the land of the rising sun[12]
> and so when, to the east, in the offing
> a boat appeared, every person thought
> "He's come at last to Tsukushi."[13]

Companions move to front of the chorus.

CHORUS

(*ageuta*)

> "It's here, it's here," the long-awaited boat
> in Matsura Bay[14]
> "It's here, it's here," the long-awaited boat
> in Matsura Bay's
> offing, we can plainly see

Fisherman looks off to the right.

> the Chinese vessel of the Chinese man—
> Haku Rakuten—   *Facing Rakuten.*
> how could we mistake him?
> But how irksome, this noisy chattering[15]
> of the Chinese man! Since his language
> is unintelligible,

---

12. 聞こえは普き日の本 *kikoe wa amaneki hi no moto*: the term *amaneki*, which means "universally" or "widely," is often used in conjunction with the universally enlightening light of buddhas and bodhisattvas; here it pivots to mean "the rumor has spread widely in Japan, the source of the sun that shines universally."

13. 心づくし *kokoro zukushi* contains multiple pivots on *tsukushi*: "to realize" (心付く), "to wonder about someone" (心尽くし), and the place-name Tsukushi (筑紫).

14. まつらぶね *matsurabune* contains a *kakekotoba* pivot on *matsu*: "to wait" (待つ) and "Matsura boat" (松浦船).

15. 言さやぐ *koto sayagu*: unintelligible chatter; a *makura kotoba* for *kara* (Chinese).

why waste our precious time? Let us cast our fishing lines.[16]

Old Fisherman mimes fishing by moving to the side (wakishōmen) *where he drops his fishing line off the edge of the stage.*

Why waste our precious time? Let us cast our fishing lines.

HAKU RAKUTEN (*mondō*)　I have something to ask of you. Please draw your boat a little closer. In Nippon, with what do you divert yourselves these days?

Old Fisherman lets the pole drop and taking up his fan, moves to center stage.

OLD FISHERMAN　And what diversions does your honor have in China?

HAKU RAKUTEN　At the Tang court we divert ourselves with composing *shi* verses.

OLD FISHERMAN　In Japan we console our hearts by composing *uta*.

HAKU RAKUTEN　What is this "uta"?

OLD FISHERMAN　The marvelous sutras of India were the basis of the *shi* of China; Chinese verses are the basis of the *uta* of my country. Because *uta* have been gentled by their movement through the three countries, they are called Yamato *uta*, "greatly gentled songs."[17] You must surely know this, and are merely testing an old man's knowledge.

HAKU RAKUTEN　No, I had no such intention. Come, I will compose a poem on the scene before us. Listen to it:

> A green moss robe worn
> draped over the cliff's rocky shoulders,
> white clouds like a sash
> enwrap the mountain's waist.[18]

16. 釣り竿のいとま惜しや *tsurizao no itoma oshi ya* contains a *kakekotoba* pivot: *ito* "[fishing] line" (糸) and *itoma* "spare time" (暇).

17. A much abbreviated version of an explanation given in the thirteenth-century commentary *Kokinwakashū jo kikigaki* 古今和歌集序聞書 (Lecture notes on the *Kokinshū* preface). The *ateji* for Yamato 大和 can also be read 大きに和らぐ (greatly gentled or harmonized). An even more abbreviated version appears in the nō treatise *Rikugi* ("Six principles"), which Zeami gave to Zenchiku. Both passages are quoted in Itō, *Yōkyokushū* (ge), 82, fn. 3. See also Katagiri Yōichi, ed., *Chūsei Kokinshū chūshakusho kaidai*, vol. 2 (Kyoto: Akao shōbundō, 1973), 224.

18. The original source of the two poems exchanged by Rakuten and the Sumiyoshi deity is thought to be a Chinese couplet and a *waka* response in section four of the *setsuwa* collection *Gōdanshō* 江談抄 (The Ōe Conversations).

Do you understand it, old fisherman?

OLD FISHERMAN The phrase "green moss" refers to the green moss
that drapes the shoulders of the cliff and looks like a robe. The white
clouds look like a sash enwrapping the mid-section of the mountains.
How amusing, how amusing. In Japanese *uta* the same sentiment
would go this way:

> The robe of moss
> worn by the cliff
> has no sash, so
> perhaps it could use
> the robeless mountain's *obi*?

HAKU RAKUTEN
　　(*kakeai*)　　How strange, though he is a lowly old fisherman,
he composes a linking poem with such sentiment.
What kind of person could he really be?

OLD FISHERMAN I am an ordinary, nameless man and yet the
composing of *uta* is not limited to human beings. "Each and every
living creature composes *uta*."[19]

HAKU RAKUTEN So among those creatures that live and breathe,
among even the birds and beasts

OLD FISHERMAN evidence of their composing poetry

HAKU RAKUTEN in our gentle country[20]

The Chinese couplet is attributed to Miyako no Arinaka 都在中, a Heian period
poet of Chinese verse; the response poem is by an unnamed lady-in-waiting.
The Chinese poem in its original form reads: 白雲似帯囲山腰, 青苔如衣負
巌肩 (note that the lines are reversed in the nō play). In *Kintōsho* 金島書, an
essay written while Zeami was in exile, Zeami quotes a very similar version of the
poem, in the same order as the play, and attributes it to Bo Juyi. Itō takes this as
possible evidence of Zeami's authorship; it also might indicate that the attribution
to Bo Juyi precedes the composition of the play. Itō, *Yōkyokushū* (ge), 453–54;
Zeami, *Kintōsho* in *Zeami, Zenchiku*, edited by Omote Akira and Katō Shūichi,
Nihon shisō taikei 24 (Iwanami shoten, 1974), 250.

19.　生きとし生けるものごとに、歌を詠まぬはなきものを: based on a
line from the *Kokinshū* kana preface. 花に鳴く鶯、水に住む蛙の声を聞けば、
生きとし生けるもの、いづれか歌をよまざりける *hana ni naku uguisu, mizu
ni sumu kawazu no koe wo kikeba, iki toshi ikeru mono, izure ka uta wo yomazarikeru*
(Hearing the song of the warbler in the flowers, the voice of the frog living in the
water, each and every living being, is there any that does not compose song?).

20. The term 和国 (Jp. *wakoku*) was first used by the Chinese for Japan;
originally the characters were 倭国. The character for the term 倭 was changed

OLD FISHERMAN	is frequently found.
CHORUS	
(*ageuta*)	I know naught of China, but here in Japan
	the warbler singing among the blossoms,
	even the frog dwelling in the pond,
	compose *uta*.
	Why then shouldn't an old man
	compose Yamato *uta*[21]
	like everyone else?

Sits and slips off mizugoromo robe.

(*kuse*)	As for the story about the warbler
	composing a poem,
	was it in the reign of Empress Kōken, I wonder?[22]
	At the usual time in spring,[23]
	a person dwelling in the Takama Temple
	in Yamato province
	listened to a warbler who came to sing
	in the plum blossoms at the temple eaves;
	it sang "*sho yō mai chō rai*

---

to 和 by order of Empress Genmei (r. 707–715) when the palace was moved to Nara in Yamato 大和 province. Both 和国 *wakoku* and 大和国 *Yamato no kuni* share the character 和 (gentle, harmonious), which emphasizes the connection of Japan with the pacifying power of 和歌 (*waka*) poetry.

21. For "Yamato uta" the *shimogakari* version has 腰折れ歌 (*koshiore uta*, literally, "broken hipped *uta*"), a poem whose link between upper and lower *ku* is weak, and is therefore considered mediocre. The implication is that an old man can at least write bad poetry.

22. Empress Kōken reigned 749–58. The following story is based on *Kokinwakashū jo kikigaki*: A priest had a greatly beloved disciple who died and left him grief stricken. However, as the years passed he forgot all about him. Then one spring, he heard a warbler (*uguisu*) singing in the plum blossoms by the temple eaves. When he copied down the song, he found the sounds formed characters that could be read as a poem. He realized from the poem that his disciple had been reincarnated as a warbler. The passage is quoted by Itō, *Yōkyokushū* (ge), 83, fn. 17; for the original, see Katagiri, *Chūsei Kokinshū chūshakusho kaidai*, vol. 2, 225.

23. 式年の春の頃 *shikinen no haru no koro*: Itō takes *shikinen* to mean "each year as usual"; Yokomichi Mario points out a similar usage in Zeami's *Nikyoku santai ningyō zu*. Itō, *Yōkyokushū* (ge), 83, fn. 19. Yokomichi and Omote, *Yōkyokushū* (ge), 436, fn. 85.

fu sō gen pon sei."[24]
Copied out in characters,
he realized the song
formed a thirty one-syllable poem:

OLD FISHERMAN   Although I come
                    each morning
CHORUS   in early spring,
                    I return to my nest
                    without meeting you.[25]
Beginning with the warbler's song,
the examples of birds and beasts,
like humans, composing *uta*
are as countless as pebbles
on the rough seashore.[26]
Each and every living creature
composes *uta*.

CHORUS
   (*rongi*)   Truly, this custom of our gentle country,
                    truly, this custom of our gentle country,
                    which even a humble fisherman understands,
                    is cause for thankfulness.
OLD FISHERMAN   And of the diversions of our gentle country—
                    composing poetry and melodies for dancing—
                    I will show you a wide assortment.

---

24. The "Chinese" poem is identical to the one given in *Kokinwakashū jo kikigaki*: 初陽毎朝来 不相還本栖. Katagiri, *Chūsei Kokinshū chūshakusho kaidai*, vol. 2, 225.

25. The waka "translation" is also identical to the poem given in *Kokinwakashū jo kikigaki*: 初春の朝ごとには来たれども会はでぞ還る本の栖に *hatsu haru no / ashita goto ni wa / kitaredomo / awade zo kaeru / moto no sumika ni.* Katagiri, *Chūsei Kokinshū chūshakusho kaidai*, vol. 2, 225.

26. 例は多くありそうみの浜の真砂の数々に *tameshi wa ōku* **Ariso** *umi no hama no masago no kazukazu ni* contains a *kakekotoba* pivot on *ari*: "the examples are many" (多くあり) and "Ariso Sea" (荒磯海). Ariso Sea is an *uta makura* whose original meaning was "rough sea"; by the time of the *Kokinshū* it was being linked in love poems with "grains of sand on the beach" to indicate "countless" (as in, "How do I love thee? Let me count the ways …"). But in the *Man'yōshū* the phrase *ariso* was used in conjunction with the ancient Chinese kingdom of Yue ("the rough sea waves at Etsu Bay" 越の海のありその浪も) and so here may be hinting again at a connection to China. For Etsu (Ch. Yue) see footnote 6.

CHORUS	The amusement called Bugaku
	who shall perform it?
OLD FISHERMAN	Is there no one else? Then gaze
	as I alone will dance.
CHORUS	For drums, the crashing waves,
	for flute, the cries of the dragon,
	for dancer, this ancient, furrowed man, *Stands.*
	atop the furrowed waves[27]
	floating on the blue-green sea
	dancing to the Sea Green Melody.

Moves to base square position.
Facing the audience.

OLD FISHERMAN

(*ei*)   This Land of Reed Plains[28]

CHORUS   will not be troubled

for ten thousand reigns.

Old Fisherman moves to the bridge and then exits to raijō *music;*
Companions follow.

[INTERVAL (*nakairi*)]

A subsidiary deity of Sumiyoshi Shrine enters and stands at base square.

SUBSIDIARY DEITY   (*nanori / shaberi*)

I am a deity of the local shrine, who serves the Sumiyoshi deity. The deity has heard that a Chinese man named Haku Rakuten, intending to measure the sagacity of the Japanese, has crossed over to our land and has arrived at this bay. The deity regards his entering into Japan as a matter of utmost importance so he took the guise of a lowly fisherman and rowed out in a small boat. When he drew near to Haku Rakuten's boat, Rakuten turned toward the deity and asked, "Are you a man of Japan?" To which the deity replied, "That is so, I am an old fisherman of Japan." When Rakuten asked, "In Japan with what do you divert yourselves these days?", the deity replied, "In Japan, we ordinarily console our hearts by composing *uta*. In China

---

27. 老いの波 *oi no nami*: "furrowed waves," a poetic term for the wrinkles that come with old age.

28. 葦原の国 *Ashiwara no kuni*: another term for Japan, frequently used in the *Nihon shoki* and *Kojiki*.

what do you do?" To which Rakuten replied, "At the Tang Court, we write *shi* verses to console ourselves." Rakuten added, "It's not likely that a lowly old man will comprehend it, but I will compose a verse in Chinese for you: '

> A green moss robe worn
> draped over the cliff's rocky shoulders,
> white clouds like a sash
> enwrap the mountain's waist.

Do you understand, old man?" The deity replied, "This sentiment is also used in Japanese *uta*. I will use this verse's sentiment as the basis for a linking *uta*." He composed:

> The robe of moss
> worn by the cliff
> has no sash, so
> perhaps it could use
> the robeless mountain's *obi*?

Haku Rakuten hearing this, said, "A poor fisherman having this much poetic sentiment is truly strange." To which the deity replied, "It is a custom in our gentle land for not only men but even fowl and beasts to compose *uta*. The Sanskrit sutras became the basis for Chinese poetry, and our court took Chinese poetry to create *uta*. Because they greatly harmonize the poetry of all three countries, they are called Yamato *uta*, "greatly harmonizing *uta*." The warbler flew to the plum blossom branches and sang out a Chinese poem:

> *sho yō mai chō rai,*
> *fu sō gen pon sei*

When composed as a Japanese poem, it runs:

> *hatsu haru no*   Although I come
> *ashita goto ni wa*   each morning
> *kitaredomo*   in early spring,
> *awade zo kaeru*   I return to my nest
> *bi o suru kana*   without meeting you.

The *uta* composed by a frog:[29]

---

29. From *Kokinwakashū jo kikigaki*: "The governor of Iki, Ki no Yoshisada (壱岐守紀良貞) went to Sumiyoshi beach in order to inquire about 'forgetting grass' (*wasuregusa*), and there met a beautiful woman. When he promised to meet her again, the woman said, 'Should you think of me with affection, come to this beach.' When he went back to look for her, the woman was no longer

> *Sumiyoshi no*   As I'll never forget
> *ura no mirume mo*   our meeting and the seaweed by
> *wasureneba*   Sumiyoshi bay
> *kari ni mo hito ni* how could I ever forget the man
> *towarenuru kana*   who inquired after me?

The *uta* written in cow's drool:[30]

> *kusa mo ki mo*   Upon hearing that
> *hotoke ni naru to*   even plants and trees
> *kiku toki wa*   become bodhisattvas
> *kokoro aru mi wa*   this being with feelings
> *tanomoshiki kana*   is now at ease.

In this way the deity related various examples of poems. Rakuten was greatly shocked and thought, "This is not what I expected Japan's wisdom to measure up to. It is best if we quickly return home." That being the case, in accordance with the Sumiyoshi deity's oracular request to lighten Haku Rakuten's mood, we lesser deities have come forth first to comfort him for having traveled so far for naught. As we know he wishes that he could compose an *uta*, we offer this one:

> *Sumiyoshi no*   In a corner of
> *sumi ni suzume no*   the Sumiyoshi shrine
> *su o kakete*   a sparrow makes its nest;
> *sa koso suzume ga*   by so doing he's sure
> *sumiyokaru ran*   to live a good life.

The subsidiary deity performs a celebratory three-part dance (sandan no mai) and then exits.

---

there. A frog came up onto the beach, and hopped by him. When he looked down at the tracks, they were in the form of characters (*moji*). When he read them aloud, they formed a poem: 住吉の浜のみるめも忘ねば仮にも人に又 とはれぬる *Sumiyoshi no / hama no mirume mo / wasureneba / kari ni mo hito ni / mata towarenuru* (Just as I'll never forget our meeting and the seaweed on Sumiyoshi beach, I'll never forget the man who inquired again). Looking at the poem, the man realized the woman had become a frog, and he returned home." The poem includes a common *kakekotoba* pivot on *mirume* meaning "meeting" and "seaweed"; *tohi* (*towarenuru*) means both "inquire about someone" and "to mourn for someone." This passage is quoted in Itō, *Yōkyokushū* (ge), 86, fn. 1. See also Katagiri, *Chūsei Kokinshū chūshakusho kaidai*, vol. 2, 225–26.

   30. Neither this poem nor the next is found in *Kokinwakashū jo kikigaki* and were probably written specifically for the *ai-kyōgen* interlude. The "cow drool" poem lightly spoofs the idea of *sōmoku jōbutsu*, that insentient trees and grasses can also attain enlightenment.

[PART TWO (*nochiba*)]

The Sumiyoshi Deity, appearing now as a splendidly dressed, venerable old man, enters to deha *entrance music (appropriate for supernatural characters) and stands at the first pine on the bridge facing the audience.*

SUMIYOSHI DEITY

   (*issei*)   Blue-green sea waves mount
                like mountains,

CHORUS   drumming to the Sea Green Melody.

Sumiyoshi Deity enters onto the stage and standing at the base square and performs the slow-tempo shin no jo no mai *dance. From "on the western sea" the Sumiyoshi Deity dances and mimes actions.*

SUMIYOSHI DEITY   *Raising his fan.*

   (*waka*)   On the western sea,
                emerging from blue-green waves
                at Aokigahara[31]

CHORUS   appearing before you
                the Sumiyoshi deity,
                Sumiyoshi deity,
                Sumiyoshi

SUMIYOSHI DEITY

                appears before you.

                    Making a small circuit of the stage.

   (*uta*)   Sumiyoshi,
CHORUS   the Sumiyoshi deity's

                    Deity makes a series of stamps.

                power is such

---

31. The use of *Aokigahara* may be based on a poem by Urabe Kanenao (卜部兼直) in the *kami* section of *Shoku Kokinshū* 続古今集 (completed 1265): *nishi no umi ya / Aoki no ura no / shioji yori / awareideshi / Sumiyoshi no kami* (Sumiyoshi deity, who has come forth from the sea lanes of Aoki Bay in the Western Sea). In his annotation to the play *Takasago*, Itō paraphrases a section from the *Nihon shoki* that describes the birth of the three deities of Sumiyoshi: when Izanagi returns from the land of the dead and reaches "Himuka no odo no tachibana no Awaki[ga]hara (日向の小戸の橘の檍原) he purifies himself and the three deities are born." Itō Masayoshi, *Yōkyokushū* (chū), SNKS (Shinchōsha, 1986), 289, fn. 17. In *Nihon shoki*, Awaki[ga]hara is identified as in Tsukushi (that is, in modern Kyushu). See also Nishimoto Yutaka, *Sumiyoshi Taisha* (Gakuseisha, 1977), 28–29. Note that the identical line is used in *Takasago*, *Ugetsu*, and *Iwafune*.

                                    Turns to face Rakuten at base square.
           that you cannot subdue Japan!
           Quickly return
                                         A sweeping point to indicate the waves.
           as the mounting waves
           turn back, Rakuten.
                                         Points directly at Rakuten and stamps.
CHORUS
     (*nakanoriji*)   Sumiyoshi has appeared
                                              Faces forward, two stamps.
                   Sumiyoshi has appeared
                   as have Ise, Iwashimizu, Kamo, Kasuga,
                           Moves to corner and makes a circuit of the stage.
                   Kashima, Mishima, Suwa, Atsuta,
                   and the Dragon King Shakara's
                   third daughter
                   the deity of Itsukushima at Aki.[32]
                   Floating across the waves
                                              Another sweeping point.
                   dancing to the Sea Green Melody,
                                              Facing the audience.
                   as the eight Dragon Kings
                                     Several stamps with overhand point.
                   play musical accompaniment,[33]
                   soaring over the waves,
           Spins and flips left sleeve while Rakuten and companions exit stage.
                   heavenly robes in playful dance,   *Unflips sleeve.*
                   sleeves stirring a wind, a divine wind
           Uses fan to send wind after exiting Rakuten.
                   blowing the Chinese boat back

---

32. Although the chorus lists eight deities and the eight dragon kings, only the Sumiyoshi deity actually appears on stage.

33. 八りんの曲 *hachirin no kyoku*: according to *Utaishō*, the term *hachirin* is obscure, but seems to mean either eight kinds of musical instruments or eight kinds of music. See Itō, *Yōkyokushū* (ge), 87, fn. 10.

Flips left sleeve.

from here to China.

Looks into distance after Rakuten, and makes a series of stamps.

Truly wondrous   *Unflips sleeve.*
these deities and our sovereign

At center stage, flips sleeves and keeps both arms raised while circling to back.

truly wondrous   *Spins at base square.*
this age of deities and our sovereign
how auspicious our untroubled land,   *Unflips sleeves.*
how auspicious our untroubled land![34]

The deity flips left sleeve and performs final stamps.

---

34. The earliest manuscripts of Haku Rakuten have 動かぬ国ぞめでたき *ugokanu kuni zo medetaki* (How auspicious our untroubled land), but at some point the line was changed to 動かぬ国ぞ久しき *ugokanu kuni zo hisashiki* (long may our land be untroubled). All schools now use the latter.

30 ∾ EPILOGUE

The Tale of the Heike in the Theater of the Twentieth Century: Three Examples

| J. THOMAS RIMER

The Tale of the Heike seems to serve as one quintessential source book for nō and other forms of medieval theater, as the preceding chapters in this volume have shown. In addition, *Heike* has continued to show a robust life ever since, providing inspiration and topics for kabuki and other forms of popular theater down to the twentieth century, where its characters and subjects have resurfaced again in animé, manga, and television dramas. Each succeeding age, of course, adapts borrowed material to suit its own concerns, and so *Heike*, its larger themes, and its characters, come out a bit differently on each historical occasion. As a kind of footnote to the present volume, I thought that it might be of interest to examine some newer variations on those venerable themes.

Here I would like to indicate some uses to which the *Heike* has been put in the modern theater, usually called *shingeki* 新劇, that form of spoken Japanese drama based on the imported examples of Shakespeare, Ibsen, and Chekhov, which eventually became the major form for serious dramatists during the last hundred years or so. Perhaps it is not so surprising, given the adaptability of the *Heike* narrative to the nō, for example, that such material might be used again in still other forms of theater. In the case of the modern theater, however, the uses to which the classic text has been put reveal other fresh possibilities not explored to any great extent in the nō plays discussed in this volume. The resiliency and resonance of the *Heike* is in fact exceptional.

One of the first tasks facing a dramatist of any period is the need to seek within the complex corpus of *Heike* incidents, characters, and themes, the material most suited to a dramatic presentation. In the case of the three plays examined here, all highly respected in their time, their respective authors, as indeed did the authors of the nō plays in the Muromachi period and beyond, chose to follow the path of what we might call "name recognition"—they chose to focus on characters and incidents associated with those characters which were already well-known to Japanese audiences. It is not surprising, then, that among the multiple foci found in these three disparate dramas, the characters of Taira no Kiyomori, the Retired Emperor Go-Shirakawa, and the two celebrated Minamoto brothers, Yoritomo and Yoshitsune, take pride of place. In this regard, it might be said that these modern dramatists are, in their own way, following the precepts of Zeami himself who suggests in his *Sandō* (三道 The Three Elements in Composing a Play) and elsewhere that, by making use of characters and material from other sources, the audience gains much of its pleasure from the recognition of this material, and the variations played upon it, as the play proceeds. That strategy is employed in all three of these plays. Art is made of life observed, of course, but it is also made of art: prior precedent can inform and broaden the intuition of the author.

The three playwrights whose works I discuss below chose different elements within the *Heike* narrative on which to focus their attention. The three plays are presented in historical order.

The first is *Shunkan*, written by Kurata Hyakuzō (1891–1943), celebrated in his time as an important and highly acclaimed writer on religion and related cultural matters. He developed a deep interest in philosophy through his encounter with the work of Nishida Kitarō (1870–1945), the greatest figure during the first half of the twentieth century. Some of these high-minded concerns are obvious from his celebrated closet drama concerning Shinran, *Shukke to sono deshi* (出家とその弟子 The Priest and His Disciples), which he wrote in 1917, then revised in its final form in 1921. Originally meant to be read, not staged, the drama remains perhaps his most famous work and was translated into English in 1922 by Glen W. Shaw. Some of the same ideas were developed in his book-length series of essays, *Ai to ninshiki to no shuppatsu* (愛と認識との出発 The Origins of Love and Understanding), written in 1922. This account of Kurata's continued search for personal authenticity within the confusions of modern culture remained popular through the 1950s, going through edition after edition.

His *Heike* play *Shunkan* went through a number of stages. The final version is in three acts. The first act was written in 1919 but the play was not completely finished until 1923. The play was staged the same year at the Meijiza in Tokyo and starred one of the leading actors of the day, Ichikawa Sadanji (1880–1940), as Shunkan. The last stage revival for which I find a record was in 1953.

As a theatrical character, the priest Shunkan has a long pedigree, with celebrated dramatic versions of his life and death in nō, bunraku, and kabuki; indeed, the melodramatic vision of Shunkan, abandoned on his island and left alone to die, has been beloved of writers, visual artists, and audiences alike for many centuries. However, in his version, Kurata has decided to reduce the significance of his exterior narrative through the adoption of a consistently interior view of Shunkan's character. Outer plot devices remain the same and are mostly taken from Chapter Three of *Heike*, with one significant exception, noted below, but the dramatic focus gives pride of place to the priest's self-scrutiny of his own interior motives. Because of this dramatic structure, many of the incidents that push the original narrative forward must now be presented as flashbacks, producing an inordinate number of speeches that begin "I remember … ," "Did you know that … ?" and similar framing devices.

The assumption on which the dramatic tension is constructed, and one with which Kurata knew his audience was familiar, is the undying hatred that Shunkan feels for the despotic Kiyomori; and indeed, it was of course Shunkan's participation in a plot to remove Kiyomori that placed him in exile in the first place.[1]

In Act One, Kiyomori (who never appears on stage) is quickly defined as the arch-villain of the drama. Early in the opening scene, Shunkan, himself of course a Buddhist priest, berates his fellow-exile Yasuyori for his dependence on religious ritual as a means of salvation.

> SHUNKAN: No more thrusting your god on me, if you please, I am sick of it. I tell you plainly that I do not believe in your god, who was so outrageously unjust as to abandon us in this strait, abandoning us in favor of the monstrous Kiyomori.

> YASUYORI: That is blaspheming against the Preserver—

---

1. The cycle of episodes about Shunkan and his co-conspirators appears as a primary narrative thread running from Chapters One through Three of *Heike*, beginning with "Shishi-no-tani" ("The Plot at Shishi-no-tani"), and concluding with "Sōzu shikyo" ("The Death of Shunkan"). See Hiroshi Kitagawa and Bruce Tsuchida, trans., *The Tale of the Heike*, vol. 1 (University of Tokyo Press, 1975), 50–191.

SHUNKAN: The case before us is disgustingly analogous to that of a silly dog kept by a cruel master. Trusting in what cannot be trusted in, the whining creature creeps up to him, wagging his tail obsequiously, and with eyes appealing for pity.

YASUYORI: [*weakly*] And you liken me unto the dog?

SHUNKAN: The master, who has found a new dog of his own choice, is mercilessly determined to get rid of the old, his sole interest now centering in the contrivance of a method best suited to his fancy in dispatching the animal—

YASUYORI: Don't Shunkan, don't! Don't, by Buddha's Divine Compassion!

SHUNKAN: [*in a defiant tone*] Perhaps it is high time we should bid a long farewell to God, that we may transfer our devotion to the Evil One.[2]

Shunkan, who portrays himself as a hero fighting tyranny, rejects the "justice" of his oppressor.

SHUNKAN: "Come what may, I have done right before God and man." It is this idea that has hitherto supported me through all my afflictions. But now I have come to waver in it. I am more disposed to think that I have been dragged into the irresistible current of circumstances. I feel I have been engulfed in the monstrous vortex of—not others' ambition, but rather of human malevolence which has never been stilled from time out of mind. Had we not risen in arms, some other men would assuredly have done so. Ours was simply the lot so chosen, and nothing more or less than that. In short, we were taken possession of by malignant spirits hovering about the three stages of existence. ... It seems to me that human wickedness is so deep-rooted that it is capable of overwhelming with utmost ease the feeble attempt at resistance by two or three. ... And I am but a baffled swimmer struggling in that fearful eddy. My own desires are completely subjugated by those of the spiritual horde, the horror of which is that the latter come to assume the aspect of my

---

2. Kurata Hyakuzō, *Shunkan: A Play*, trans. by Kan'ichi Andō (Kenkyūsha, 1925), 29–30.

own inclinations. Ah, then there is a nightmare I had not long ago, nay, I should say a vision, for I saw it in broad daylight. It was a horrible spectacle of countless ghosts fighting in mid-air. I could hear distinctly in the air the clashing of blades. ... [3]

By the end of Act One, sensing the depths of his loneliness, Shunkan probes deeper still into his feelings.

SHUNKAN: I hate to be hated, and love to be loved. Still, in spite of myself, my unruly tongue makes me say what I should not, while perverse thoughts steal into my mind. Methinks a capricious demon has taken up its abode within me. I am entirely at the mercy of my woeful temper. Mine is an abandoned soul bound to eternal solitude. And then my rude personality is such as can hardly reconcile itself to harmonious intercourse. I curse myself! I hate myself! And I pity myself! [4]

At an earlier point, Shunkan cries out that his soul is a snake. "And this snake of a soul of mine keeps raising its head in restless watch for some safe refuge, which is denied it. Is it that I am a lost mortal, doomed to hell?" [5]

In Act Two, the ship approaches bringing tidings from the capital. The three exiles, Naritsune, Yasuyori, and Shunkan, pledge that, whatever happens, they will live or die together and that they will support each other in whatever trials may follow. Shunkan, however, remains apprehensive concerning their loyalty.

When the ship arrives, Motoyasu, the official sent to bring the other exiles back, seems, unlike the villain-like treatment given him in the kabuki version of the story, a man of some compassion. But he can do nothing.

SHUNKAN: I appeal to the man in you. Do take me back with you.

MOTOYASU: I have no personal grudge against you, sir. On the contrary, I am filled with the deepest sympathy for you in your present predicament. I am even willing to comply with your request, provided no blame fall on my head.

---

3. Kurata, *Shunkan*, 39–40.
4. Kurata, *Shunkan*, 54.
5. Kurata, *Shunkan*, 45.

SHUNKAN: If by your procurement I could regain my home, you should be repaid tenfold for your service; you may count on it, sir.

MOTOYASU: [*reflects*] Somehow my heart misgives me that I shall be called to account for this. ... Well, sir, I am not so sure of the point at issue as you are. At least, I am not so certain of it as I am of the safety of the wisdom which would dictate to me the carrying out literally what is ordered in the letter of pardon and nothing else.[6]

Inevitably, by the end of the act, both the other exiles have made a decision, personally painful for both of them, to return without their partner. The best they can do is to offer to intercede with Kiyomori on Shunkan's behalf. He is, as he feared, to be abandoned.

Act Three, which recounts Shunkan's death, is perhaps the most eloquent section of the play, and shows one significant deviation from the narrative as presented in the original *Heike* texts.

The act opens with a powerful soliloquy by Shunkan, now lying on a bed of seaweed in his clumsily built hut. A portion of his rantings will suggest the somber tone of this long scene.

SHUNKAN: Wherefore can I not shuffle off this mortal coil? Have I not been fasting for more than twenty days? And yet I cannot starve myself to death. It seems life refuses to let go its grim hold on me. Is it so ordained for me to drag out my miserable destiny forever? As the snake will tenaciously keep on living, be it ever so famished, so my senses persistently cling to me when all the vitality has gone from my limbs. Is it Fate's design that I should entirely commend myself to her tender mercies? Let me die! Oh, let me die! Mayhap I am no more, my resentment alone still living. I am resentment itself. I am a spiteful ghost, still living ... [7]

As in the original *Heike* narrative, Shunkan's faithful servant Ariō now appears and is shocked to see the changes in his master.

In the final scene of the play, Shunkan, in a state of ghastly exhaustion, hurls out his bitterness at the universe.

---

6. Kurata, *Shunkan*, 77–78.
7. Kurata, *Shunkan*, 126–27.

SHUNKAN: I absolutely withdraw [my belief in Justice] in the name of the Devil. I hate this world, this remorseless world which has wrought nothing but bitterness and wrong my whole life through. And I never forget it. This is a perverse world, where vice triumphs over virtue—a world worse than nothing. Such a world should be given over to the proper charge of the devil. Come then, Devil! Now I address thee in the most friendly spirit I have ever felt toward thee. Now I know how and why the vindictive ghosts are brought forth in the three worlds. What else will the departed spirit of such a one as myself, predestined to wretchedness, become but a vindictive ghost?[8]

Kurata's major change in the *Heike* narrative comes in the final episode that concludes the play. In the original, after Shunkan's death:

"Ariō held the lifeless body, looked up to heaven, then cast himself down on the ground and wept futile tears. ... Ariō allowed Shunkan to lie undisturbed. He tore down the hut. Around the body, he piled up dry pine branches and put reeds upon them. Then he lighted the pyre. The smoke billowed up, heavy with brine. When the cremation was finished, he gathered up the whitened bones. Then he placed them in a container, hung this around his neck, and secured passage on a merchant vessel bound for Kyushu. Upon reaching home, Ariō went to Shunkan's daughter and told her everything from beginning to end."[9]

Kurata, however, contrives a much more overtly theatrical ending.

ARIŌ: [*addressing the corpse*] Listen my master! Your humble servant will follow you anywhere, everywhere you go. [*carries the corpse on his back*] O merciful Buddha, I renounce this world. I am anxious to rid myself of this horrid world, the sooner the happier. I will go off with my master. I am an ignorant creature, and I implore thy forgiveness if the step I am taking is not right. And,

---

8. Kurata, *Shunkan*, 138.
9. Kitagawa and Tsuchida, *The Tale of the Heike*, vol. 1, 191.

oh, bless the after life of my hapless master I pray thee,
and redeem his soul from damnation for eternal bliss.
[*selecting a spot of death*] Now, then I command my
soul into thy merciful hands, O Buddha! [*hurls himself
headlong from the cliff into the sea, with* SHUNKAN'S *body
on his back*].[10]

Kurata's flair for a strong stage image is certainly best realized in this
scene, even though in order to create this particular example of dramatic
intensity, he was forced to give up the final touching encounter between
Ariō and Shunkan's daughter. Ariō's own death, as reconceived by Kurata,
is indeed a peculiar one by *Heike* standards, and suggests, it seems to me,
the playwright's debt to the strategies of Western drama, or melodrama,
if you will, with which he was very well acquainted. I will discuss this
aspect of his work later in this chapter.

The second play I would like to introduce is one by an important
contemporary dramatist, Yamazaki Masakazu [born 1934], entitled *Yabō
to natsugusa* 野望と夏草, which might be translated as *Intrigue and
Summer Grasses*, written in 1970 and staged at that time by the Kumo
Troupe. Even given the disparity in the attitudes and writing skills of these
two playwrights, *Intrigue* is definitely a postwar play. A variety of characters
are now brought forward. We see not only Kiyomori, but members of the
royal family, including Go-Shirakawa and the deposed Emperor Sutoku.
That very fact that an emperor could now become a character in a drama
shows a freedom of expression unlikely in prewar times.

Yamazaki has brilliantly analyzed the complex narrative line
concerning Go-Shirakawa and Kiyomori that runs through much of
the original *Heike*, pulling out occasional suggestions that allow him to
create believable and complex characters. For example, there are a few
hints in the *Heike* that Kiyomori may well have been the illegitimate
son of a nobleman, even an emperor.[11] A small Buddhist stupa, brought
from a holy site in China, apparently stands as proof, and in Yamazaki's
play, this potent prop appears at several key moments. Kiyomori's wife
and daughter, as well as a number of court figures, are powerfully and
evocatively sketched.

Like the play by Kinoshita Junji described below, *Intrigue* deals

---

10. Kurata, *Shunkan*, 140–41.
11. See the section "Gion nyōgo" ("Lady Gion") in *Heike monogatari*
(Kakuichi-bon 6.10). Kitagawa and Tsuchida, *The Tale of the Heike*, vol. 1, 377–9.

with the shift in power from the nobility to the warrior class, one of the dominant themes of the original *Heike* narrative, and there is at least a suggestion that the play echoes as well shifts in prewar and postwar Japanese society. The play is basically constructed as a kind of duel between the two major forces in this contest for power, Kiyomori and Go-Shirakawa.

Reading the text suggests to me that, even on the stage, as is the case with so many modern and contemporary dramas, the result would constitute a drama of talking heads, since most of the action, from the beginnings of the intrigues to the final fall of the Taira clan, takes place off stage. But the talk itself is brilliant. The spoken dialogue is colloquial, yet manages to sound classical, even poetic 'or heroic at times. In that sense alone, the play can be judged a tour de force of linguistic skill on the part of Yamazaki.

The play is in three acts, set respectively in the summer of 1156 (just after the Hōgen Revolt), in the winter of 1159 (just before the Heiji Revolt), and in the Sixth Month of 1176. The events portrayed in Act One are drawn from the early chapters of the *Heike*, as the duel between these two powerful figures begins. In the early scenes, Kiyomori insists, with evident sincerity, that he only wants to serve the imperial family. He is apparently content to know his place. Thus he is baffled by the attitudes of Go-Shirakawa, who, now planning to abdicate, does not want to be forced into taking any particular stance that will fix too firmly any future responsibilities. Indeed, it is precisely this kind of role imposed from outside that he wishes to give up. The disparate character of these two powerful men is well captured in a sequence in which Go-Shirakawa, with considerable irony, sets out to test Kiyomori's skills as a possible courtier, which would certainly include a devotion to the arts. For the blunt Kiyomori, Go-Shirakawa remains a wily adversary. The subject of the discussion is *fūryū* 風流, an aesthetic term difficult to define in English, but which is most commonly rendered into English as "elegant" or "refined."

> GO-SHIRAKAWA: Well then, do you know what *fūryū* is? After all, your mother was a woman of quality, so she surely had some training in the ways of the arts and elegance. So then, Kiyomori, let me ask you: if you were to think of a poem about fireflies, what might that poem be? Let us say that you saw fireflies glittering in the tall grass, what would this sight make you, with your deep artistic inclinations, think of? Please tell me.

KIYOMORI: I am just a simple warrior and I know nothing about those *imayō* songs that you collect. Still, I can say I would probably remember the chapter on fireflies in *The Tale of Genji*. I remember a lovely poem about fireflies by Tamakazura.

GO-SHIRAKAWA: "Rather, the firefly, who burns with an inner flame and utters no cry, is the one whose devotion passes all that words can say."[12] Well, that's just the kind of answer I would always expect you to give. As for me, I think of something a little different. [*He comes close and spits out his words.*] If I look at those summer grasses and see something glittering there, Kiyomori, they are the eyes of a dead man.

KIYOMORI: [*drawing back*] What are you saying?

GO-SHIRAKAWA: Those are the eyes of a dead man, killed on the battlefield, one who hates you and who has been violently done to death. Someone you have driven to his grave. One who from sheer will power stares at you continuously, with no eyelids to cover over those eyes of his.

KIYOMORI: My Lord, this is a children's game you are playing with me.

GO-SHIRAKAWA: No, no. I am not saying this to frighten you. It is such a beautiful image, don't you think? A body, buried in the back of a summer garden, those eyes burning in a body no longer capable of thought. And, if you can really find this beautiful, then you will have begun to know what true *fūryū* is.

KIYOMORI: Are you saying that human hate can be beautiful? And that to respond to that is beautiful?[13]

Act Two intensifies the protracted duel between the two. By the end of the act, Kiyomori and Go-Shirakawa are altogether at loggerheads.

---

12. Go-Shirakawa quotes Tamakazura's poem in the *Hotaru* chapter ("The Fireflies"). The translation is Royall Tyler's, *The Tale of Genji* (New York: Viking Penguin, 2001), vol. 1, 457.

13. Yamazaki Masakazu, *Yabō to natsugusa* (Kawada shobō, 1970), 20–21. Translations are by the author.

Act Three opens seventeen years later. Kiyomori's daughter, who is in fact in some ways afraid of her father, has allowed herself to be married to the young emperor, Takakura. By marrying into the imperial family, she hopes, among other things, to placate him through having a child, who will be born later as the child emperor Antoku. However powerful Kiyomori may be, the Emperor should remain, at least in theory, still high above him. Awa no Naishi gives Kenreimon'in some advice, then thinks of her own situation and reflects how her father was executed after the Heiji uprising in 1159.[14]

AWA NO NAISHI: If I, like you, the Empress, could bring happiness to the His Majesty, the Emperor ... if the Emperor would grant the same favor to me, then if I had a son ... perhaps then my father's wrath might somehow be placated.

KENREIMON'IN: You, give birth to a child of the Emperor? Why should this be?

AWA NO NAISHI: [*laughing forlornly*] For a woman like myself, that kind of happiness is surely beyond me. Still, I am at an age when it might be possible ... If I could receive such a favor, then my father's blood would flow in the veins of the imperial family forever. It is for this reason ...

KENREIMON'IN: But why? Why something like this, for your father? ...

AWA NO NAISHI: Perhaps this is all just an inference on my part, so far as I can determine. Yet if there is one thing certain in this world, is it not the bloodlines of the Emperors? This line will carry on forever. Longer than any reputation as a great hero that one might earn. Yes, just think of those who have given commands to the whole country since the beginning of time, and how good it would be for a father to be the grandfather of such a one.[15]

---

14. Awa no Naishi, the daughter of the scholar Shinzei and at this early stage in the events a confidante of Kiyomori's wife, Tokiko, will become at the end of the play an important companion to Kenreimon'in herself, when at the conclusion of the war the Empress is exiled to the temple of Jakkōin in the mountains north of Kyoto.

15. Yamazaki, *Yabō to natsugusa*, 87–88.

Later in Act Three, Kiyomori and Go-Shirakawa have an intense debate, in which Kiyomori finally reveals his true feelings of hatred for his rival.

> KIYOMORI: What you say is not true. I fought by myself. And I won by myself.

> GO-SHIRAKAWA: If that is the case, then why do you reproach me now? Well, perhaps I suppose you found that I incited conspirators against you. Yet, even supposing that this were true, there is no reason why you should have been afraid of anything I tried to do to you. Let me continue. After all, it is my conviction that the one fated to win will win. The one who has the strength to win, and who is possessed of the good luck needed to win, will go from victory to victory without help from anyone. And if you have the confidence of your lineage and the will of Heaven, and if you truly possess confidence in yourself, then you surely have no reason to fear poor Go-Shirakawa, who does not even possess one soldier.

> KIYOMORI: It is not that I am afraid of you. I hate you.[16]

In the end, Go-Shirakawa warns Kiyomori that he can no longer go back to being a simple samurai. Kiyomori's long-sought change in status, ironically, has now in fact sealed his fate. Powerful recriminations are now leveled by Go-Shirakawa at Kiyomori concerning the burning of the temples at Nara, the incident that takes place early in the *Heike* narrative.[17]

> KIYOMORI: If I go to Hell for this ...

> GO-SHIRAKAWA: Then I will fall into Hell as well. But, at this moment, you have been able to peer into the depth of my soul. And if you saw Hell there, then you are indeed the illegitimate son of the Emperor Shirakawa, with his fierce, bottomless heart. This is proof of your lineage, more than any stupa I can give you.

---

16. Yamazaki, *Yabō to natsugusa*, 95–96.

17. See section "Nara enshō" ("The Burning of Nara") in *Heike monogatari* (Kakuichi-bon 5.14). Kitagawa and Tsuchida, *The Tale of the Heike*, vol. 1, 340–44.

KIYOMORI: [*groaning*] You … you are the very devil himself.

GO-SHIRAKAWA: It would be wise to remember this. When the support you can give is gone, then you will no longer be able to protect the peace and prosperity of the Heike clan. [GO-SHIRAKAWA *holds out the stupa; after a moment of tension,* KIYOMORI *tries to grab it; his wife screams and falls in a faint. The stage grows dark; one can only see the silhouette of the two men facing each other.*][18]

Paralleling the structure of the original *Heike* narrative, Yamazaki includes an Epilogue, in which the various characters in the drama reflect on the frightening events that have taken place. The conversation between Kiyomori's daughter Kenreimon'in and Awa no Naishi, is particularly poignant.

AWA NO NAISHI: If you must speak of the deepest crimes, then I am the one who is guilty. Without discrimination, my heart urged me on, and there must have been many times when I riled up the feelings of your father. Even when he sought peace and would have given up his efforts, it was I who encouraged him, spurred him on.

KENREIMON'IN: There is no difference between us. You see, I too am filled with regrets. It is I who gave birth to a royal child, and there was no reason why my father should have fought those above his station. I did not see the suppleness that lay behind his strength, with all those traitors lurking around him.

PRIEST [a *biwa hōshi*]: These words show that you have a kind heart. Please do not feel any anxiety. For those who have fallen, we must sense some feeling of consolation.

KENREIMON'IN: No, it is we who must pray for salvation. Everything has sunk away, nothing is left, yet why it is that those of us who remain must go on living, year after year?[19]

The play ends with just such a series of images, recriminations, revelations, and regrets.

---

18. Yamazaki, *Yabō to natsugusa*, 115.
19. Ibid., 119.

Reading the play today, there seems to be, in addition to the psychological deepening of the original *Heike* narrative, another layer of meaning of a more contemporary sort, for there are certainly some parallels, although not specifically articulated by Yamazaki, between Go-Shirakawa and Emperor Hirohito. It seems clear, in scene after scene, that Go-Shirakawa does not want to know precisely what is going on in the country; he merely tries to balance the contending forces through indirection. In some ways, the play seems to be using the *Heike's* historical framework to look back on World War II, just as the final scene in the original looks back on the sorry results of the struggle between the Taira and the Minamoto.

The third play that deals with the *Heike* remains, in terms of multiple productions at least, the most successful of the three. *Shigosen no matsuri* 子午線の祭り (Requiem on the Great Meridian), by Kinoshita Junji 木下順二 (1914–2006), one of the greatest of modern playwrights, was first produced at the National Theatre in 1978 and has been revived half a dozen times, despite the complex and expensive nature of the staging required.

The play deals with the incidents that take place in the final books of the *Heike*, when the Taira suffer a stunning defeat at the battle of Dan-no-Ura in 1185. As in the other two plays, all of the characters presented are historical personages except for Kagemi, an important female role. Here, she is portrayed as the mistress of Taira no Tomomori.

Not surprisingly, the dramatic thrust of the play is built on the tensions of the two sides; in this, Yoshitsune represents the Minamoto, Tomomori the Taira. But again, as in *Shunkan*, major figures in the drama, and the power and force they represent, lurk behind the events portrayed on stage. In the Kinoshita play, the two are, not surprisingly, Go-Shirakawa and Yoritomo.

Unlike Yamazaki, Kinoshita does show battle scenes on stage, where a chorus is employed to chant portions of the actual *Heike* text. The play is long and complicated, difficult to sum up briefly in any adequate fashion. Suffice it to say that Kinoshita's lifelong sympathies for the common folk and their problems may suggest why, earlier in his career, he was dubbed the "Arthur Miller of Japan." In the context of these battles, Kinoshita seems to pose this question: where, in this tangle of egos and lusts for power, do the common people receive justice? When society undergoes such huge shifts, what meaning, if any, can be taken from them? These questions too have strong contemporary resonances. In setting up the contrasts he seeks, Kinoshita creates an effective dialogue in a kind of contemporary language, while many of the chorus passages use language closer to that of the original *Heike.*

Kagemi, the now-dead mistress of Tomomori, appears to him just before the final battle, and in the course of a poetic exchange, redolent of resignation and regret, she makes an ambiguous, somewhat mystical statement that comes close to explaining both the title and, for Kinoshita, the significance of his play.

> KAGEMI: Look around you, my lord. Let your eyes rest on anything that has no feeling. Why do you think that when we insubstantial, transient creatures gaze up at the flickering stars, our thoughts deepen as they do? Isn't it because of the lack of feeling in the circling of those skies? Don't we gain solace and strength? Doesn't it help us to understand the import of the lives we lead? [TOMOMORI *is on the verge of breaking down;* KAGEMI *embraces him gently and clings to him.*] Great events in the world of men are utterly unfeeling too. Fix your eyes on the absence of feeling my lord, fix them there firmly and gaze deeply into it. … [*She fades gradually, until she disappears.*]

> TOMOMORI: [*to* KAGEMI, *as though she were still there, even though she is now gone*] Yes, Kagemi, I understand. … Fix my eyes firmly on it … on that absence of feeling … gaze into it, you say? … That's the only time we fleeting human beings can commune with things eternal, the only time that thoughts can pass from one to the other. That's right, Kagemi, isn't it? [*He recovers himself. Calling offstage in a loud voice.*] Launch a boat and summon Kagekiyo here![20]

Before the final battle, the main tension sustaining this long and complex drama is the attempt by warriors on both sides to grasp the obscure purposes of the figures above them who manipulate them for reasons they cannot always identify.

Early in the play, for example, Tomomori tries to understand, just as did Kiyomori in the Yamazaki play, the shifting mentality and maneuverings of Go-Shirakawa. One of his comrades, Noritsune, says that in fact there seems no apparent purpose in Go-Shirakawa's actions. Tomomori does not agree.

---

20. Kinoshita Junji, *Requiem on the Great Meridian and Selected Essays,* trans. Brian Powell and Jason Daniel (Nan'undo Publishing, 2000), 205–6.

TOMOMORI: On the contrary, everything you say seems to point to his having a very clear purpose. What he wants is to have the Heike and the Genji weighted equal in the scales. And the boy Emperor in position above them there. Then he can rule the country himself from behind the emperor, with everything neatly balanced. Hence the glut of edicts—he's desperate to achieve this. So Go-Shirakawa's thinking is in line with our own hopes and plans and must also be in line with Yoritomo's too. It's not long since Yoritomo was suggesting to Go-Shirakawa that the Heike and the Genji should take turns at having responsibility for the court and ruling the land. And it was only the year before last that he was at the great shrine of Ise petitioning the gods that the peace of the nation and prosperity among the people would follow from punishing the unjust and rewarding the loyal, Heike and Genji alike.

TOKITADA: What are you saying we should do, then?

TOMOMORI: We should ask him to put forward another peace plan.[21]

For his part, Yoshitsune has trouble understanding the motivations of his older brother Yoritomo, particularly in terms of any alliance with Go-Shirakawa. Yoshitsune wants to remain loyal to the throne. He cannot fathom his brother's true attitudes. The result puts him in a double bind worthy of a classical *jōruri* text of Chikamatsu.

BENKEI: Do you remember last summer? You were given a government post by Go-Shirakawa, without Yoritomo being consulted. Then in the autumn you accepted a court promotion from him. And straight afterward you were allowed to attend the imperial court. None of this was at all pleasing to your brother, and that's the reason the commission to defeat the Heike came to your brother Noriyori first, then took a very long time to come to you.

YOSHITSUNE: I know, I know—you told me that before. But in the end Yoritomo did commission me to defeat them, didn't he?

---

21. Kinoshita, *Requiem on the Great Meridian*, 94–95.

BENKEI: Noriyori wasn't getting any results though. …
You were simply your brother's last resort.

YOSHITSUNE: Nonsense! I have won a tremendous victory
here at Yashima.

BENKEI: That's got nothing to do with this.

YOSHITSUNE: [*pause*] So then Benkei … what am I to do?

BENKEI: My lord … I'm afraid I cannot answer that.

YOSHITSUNE: What am I to do? What am I going to do? I
try to please my brother Yoritomo and it doesn't work. I
try to fit in with Go-Shirakawa's wants and that's no good
either. So what on earth am I meant to do?[22]

Finally, all questions seem swept away in the final battle, which
occupies much of Act Four. Effectively written, and for an enormous
cast, the result on stage must be quite spectacular. The use of the chorus
in particular gives the spectator a sense of aesthetic distance from the
turmoil on stage, as though the audience were indeed in the position
of those unfeeling stars, looking down, as though through the wrong
end of a telescope, at these tiny figures with their insignificant yet
gripping concerns. The play certainly reflects Kinoshita's commitment
to common citizens, and the sufferings they must undergo; and here too
his play, like Yamazaki's, by suggesting historical parallels, casts light on
the imperfect way in which Japan has been ruled in modern times. For
all of its historical concerns, *Meridian* is a play of our own time as well.

I have chosen to discuss these three plays, each eloquent in its
treatment of the material taken from the *Heike*, because they are each
typical of the concerns of their respective periods. Kurata's *Shunkan*, for
example, shows the author's desire to create a play of noble proportions,
worthy of Western examples he admired, and with a Faustian theme.
In some ways the play is larger than life, yet for all its melodrama, the
dramatist strives relentlessly for a sense of interiority and roundness
of character quite unlike kabuki's portrayal of Shunkan, for example.
Yamazaki, for his part, attempts to create characters able to speak with

---

22. Kinoshita, *Requiem on the Great Meridian*, 148–49.

eloquence and suggest through their attitudes deep human passions and the clash of relationships. Kinoshita seeks to find a way to show the collapse of something truly noble, but with striking contemporary overtones.

But I have chosen still another reason for juxtaposing these three plays together. For it is important to note that all three of these dramatists have used theatrical strategies based on what they have learned from the dramatist that each of them most admired—William Shakespeare.

From the time that Shakespeare's work was introduced into Japan in the late nineteenth century, he was regarded not only as a supremely gifted playwright, but, in the words of the eminent modern director Senda Koreya 千田是也 (1904–94), "a modern dramatist" as well. Shakespeare's use of heroic themes may have resembled certain aspects of traditional Japanese theater, kabuki in particular, but his remarkable ability to enter into the minds and emotions of his characters, then render these feelings into powerfully effective stage language, allowed his works to serve as a models, along with those of Ibsen and Chekhov, for a truly modern Japanese theater in which the importance of the spoken language is paramount. The first translation of the entire corpus of Shakespeare's work was undertaken by the great writer, dramatist, and scholar of the early twentieth century, Tsubouchi Shōyō 坪内逍遥 (1859–1935). As those translations in turn became removed from shifting contemporary speech, newer versions began to appear and continue to do so. Shakespeare, in various versions, can be found in every bookstore and on stage after stage in Tokyo and elsewhere. Perhaps it is not so surprising that all three of these playwrights continued to feel the centrality of Shakespeare in the creation of their own work. Here are some observations on each.

Kurata attended Tokyo's prestigious First Higher School in Tokyo, where the Headmaster, the celebrated Nitobe Inazō 新渡戸稲造 (1862–1935) upholding his brand of "Christian cosmopolitanism," had an enormous effect on the mental and spiritual lives of his young students. At this time, doubtless the most celebrated incident in the school's history took place when a student, Fujimura Masao, committed suicide by jumping from the Kegon waterfall at Nikko. Before his leap, he wrote his own epitaph:

> Ensconced in the vastness of space and time,
> I, with my meager body, have tried to fathom the

enormity of this universe.
But what authority can be attributed to Horatio's
philosophy?
There is, after all, only one word for truth:
"incomprehensible."
My agony over this question has brought me, at last,
to a decision to die.
And yet now, standing at the precipice,
There is no anxiety in my heart.
For the first time, I realize that great sorrow is
at one with great happiness.[23]

As Donald Roden points out in his analysis of the incident, by questioning Horatio's philosophy, Fujimura "was empathizing with Hamlet's own reaction to his friend's self-assuredness. ... Hamlet was posing existential questions for which Horatio's down-to-earth philosophy had no answers."[24] I mention the incident here because it shows that, for the young intelligentsia of the time, of which Kurata was very much a part, Shakespeare had been fully absorbed into their mental world; the reference would have been understood and sympathized with by all. And in some ways, Kurata's whole career, including the Faustian and Shakespearian ambitions revealed in his dramas, show him trying to work out his own sympathetic responses to the matters of life and death proposed by Hamlet's questions.

Readers might have noted that, in fact, the English used in his translation of Kurata's text by Andō Kan'ichi has a certain Shakespearian ring to it. The original Japanese text of the play, long out of print, is hard to come by, but when I was able to examine a copy, I was at first rather surprised to find that the original is in a highly colloquial kind of stage language, quite different in tonality from the translated version. On reflection, though, perhaps this is not so surprising. Kurata wanted his audiences to experience a truly modern drama; Andō wanted to underscore to Western readers the debt that Kurata owed to classical European literature.

---

23. This translation is taken from Donald Roden's excellent study of the Higher School and its place in Meiji education, *Schooldays in Imperial Japan: A Study In the Culture of a Student Elite* (University of California Press, 1980), which contains a thorough account of this incident and its importance. See 164.

24. Roden, *Schooldays*, 169–70.

Yamazaki Masakazu, born several decades later, came from a more cosmopolitan background, since as a child he lived in Manchuria, where his father was employed. At the end of the war, Yamazaki recounts his own first powerful encounter with Shakespeare.

> My father was ill, on the verge of death. I sat at his
> pillow and read to him the works of Shakespeare in the
> Tsubouchi Shōyō translation. Manchuria had fallen. It
> was the period when both Nationalist and Communist
> troops were occupying the country. The streets were
> full of those dead from cold or starvation. Even in our
> own home only the stove in my father's sick room could
> be kept burning. Under such circumstances, this book
> of Shakespeare remained the only item of literature on
> our bookshelves. With the sound of cannons booming
> in the distance, I watched my father's face, from which
> consciousness seemed slowly to be fading, even as I
> read to him. *Coriolanus, Henry IV, The Tempest*. ... I
> certainly didn't understand every word I read there.
> Yet my reading those plays aloud seemed somehow a
> suitable way to attack the miseries of reality through
> the strength that Shakespeare's strong imagination
> gave to me.[25]

Yamazaki has commented as well that such circumstances led him to attempt to create a theater in which "a man's fate could be thrust directly onto the stage of history."[26] And indeed, read from a Shakespearian point of view, the portrayal in *Intrigue* of Kiyomori and his wife does owe something of its effective energy to Yamazaki's nuanced understanding of the dynamics between Macbeth and Lady Macbeth. Certainly, he could assume that, at least for his generation, those resonances would be understood and appreciated.

Kinoshita Junji, for his part, remains best known as a playwright, but his lifelong interest in Shakespeare produced a number of important essays on that subject. He was particularly interested in Shakespeare's use of language as a means to reveal psychological subtlety, and in

---

25. Yamazaki Masakazu, *Mask and Sword: Two Plays for a Modern Japanese Theatre* (Columbia University Press, 1980), 184–85.
26. Yamazaki, *Mask and Sword*, 184.

his writings, he often compared the differences in the strategies of Shakespearian stage language with those used in kabuki. These, for him, reveal gaps and leaps in logic which the actor's art is obliged to fill. In one sense, Kinoshita's own lifelong quest was to create a viable Japanese stage language without those gaps, one which can both make use of the classical language, binding it to present relevance, and create dialogue in which the psychological logic of contemporary speech can be heightened and refined. Throughout, Shakespeare has remained his chief model.[27]

In conclusion, let me return to my original point that art is essentially made of art. In the case of these three plays, it can be said that the "art" to be recognized is that engendered by the example of the *Heike* itself. Modern audiences can quickly recognize these historical personages and know something of the thrust of their characters. But a second source, and almost as important a one, is the example provided by Shakespearian drama. Shakespeare has long since been absorbed into Japanese literary, and indeed general culture, providing fresh and challenging contours for audiences, performers, and dramatists alike. The *Tale of the Heike* has again entered a rich period in the theater.

---

27. For a sample of his observations on Shakespeare, see the essays accompanying *Requiem on the Great Meridian* in the same volume.

⌁ APPENDIX
Nō Plays of the Genpei War,
A Finding List | Michael Watson

The purpose of this appendix is to provide suggestions and hints for those wishing to explore further the vast reception history of nō plays of the Genpei War, both for the inherent interest of adaptations, prequels and sequels, and for the light that these new versions may reflect on to the earlier narratives.

In the following two sections, information is provided about a large number of premodern and early modern nō plays of the Genpei War. Part A below gives an overview of plays that are based on episodes of the Kakuichi-bon *Heike monogatari*, with the plays listed in the order of those episodes. Part B contains a considerably larger number of plays in alphabetical order by title. Further details are available online on a webpage containing additional entries, short plot descriptions for many plays, and bibliographical information omitted here for reasons of space.[1]

Defining "Genpei War–related" plays in a fairly narrow way, one could arrive at a sum of some thirty-two plays in the current repertoire, or thirty-five including close variants.[2] This represents well over ten percent

---

1. See Michael Watson, "Genpei Tales and the Nō" (Premodern Japanese Studies Website 2012), <www.meijigakuin.ac.jp/~pmjs/biblio/genpei-noh.html>. Corrections and suggestions are welcome.

2. Of these Genpei plays, fourteen fall in the second traditional category (*Atsumori, Ebira, Ikuta Atsumori, Kanehira, Kiyotsune, Michimori, Sanemori, Shunzei Tadanori, Tadanori, Tomoakira, Tomoe, Tsunemasa, Yashima, Yorimasa*); five in the third category (*Giō, Hotoke no hara, Ōhara gokō, Senju, Yuya*); twelve in the fourth category (*Daibutsu kuyō, [Genzai Tadanori], Fujito, [Genzai Tomoe], Kagekiyo, Kiso, Kogō, Morihisa, Rō-Giō, Shōzon, Shichiki ochi, Shunkan*); and four in the fifth category (*Funa Benkei, [Genzai nue], Ikarikazuki, Nue*). Titles

of plays performed today, more than from any other single source. By including plays that are no longer performed (*bangai yōkyoku* 番外謡曲) as well as those that dramatize digressions like *Kan'yōkyū*, *Sagi*, or *Taisanbukun*, a recent authoritative Japanese reference work on *Heike monogatari* lists more than eighty plays "related to *Heike monogatari*."[3] Although this is much larger number than many might expect, it still excludes plays of great Genpei interest like *Ikuta Atsumori*, *Settai*, and *Funa Benkei*, presumably for having only a tangential connection with the Kakuichi version of *Heike monogatari*. Rather than restricting our lists of plays to Muromachi-period works on the *Heike* alone, we have adopted much broader criteria. *Ikuta Atsumori* is included together with many other plays that imagine "what happened next" to characters that appear in *Heike monogatari* or closely related works. *Settai* and *Funa Benkei* are also included, even though strictly speaking they belong not to what we might call the "*Heike* cycle" proper, but instead to the "Yoshitsune cycle," a large group of plays concerning Minamoto no Yoshitsune and his followers.[4] A reading of the play *Settai*, for example, can enhance our appreciation for the episode of Tsuginobu's death in the battle of Yashima.[5] No one interested in the *Heike* cycle would want to ignore *Funa Benkei*, a play that vividly dramatizes an incident in the

placed in square brackets are Kongō school variants. With the publication of the present collection, the only play of the core group of thirty-two not available in English translation is *Shōzon*. For bibliography and further information, see Paul Atkins, "The Index" (Japanese Performing Arts Resource Center, 1998–1999) <www.glopac.org/Jparc/eni/eni.html> and Michael Watson, "List of noh plays in alphabetical order of the Japanese titles" (Premodern Japanese Studies Website, 2012) <www.meijigakuin.ac.jp/~pmjs/biblio/noh-trans.html>.

3. Takemoto Miko, "*Heike monogatari* kanren enmoku ichiran," in Ōtsu Yūichi, et al., eds., *Heike monogatari daijiten* (Tōkyō shoseki, 2010), 617–19.

4. The terms "*Heike* cycle" and "Yoshitsune cycle" refer to what some Japanese scholars call, respectively, *Heike monogatari mono* 平家物語物, nō plays related to *Heike* variants, and *Yoshitsune mono* 義経物 or *Hōgan mono* 判官物. The latter are usually based on *Gikeiki* 義経記 or on works in the genre of *kōwakamai* 幸若舞 ("ballad drama"). For an overview of Yoshitsune legends in nō and *kōwakamai*, see Helen Craig McCullough, *Yoshitsune: A Fifteenth-Century Chronicle* (Tokyo University Press/Stanford University Press 1966), 54–61.

5. Kakuichi-bon 11.3 "Tsuginobu saigo." Kajiwara Masaaki and Yamashita Hiroaki, eds., *Heike monogatari* (ge), SNKT 45 (Iwanami shoten, 1993), 271–73; Helen Craig McCullough, trans., *The Tale of the Heike* (Stanford University Press, 1988), 365–66.

flight of Yoshitsune from Daimotsu Bay hinted at by a brief reference to the violent winds caused by the the angry spirits of the Heike.[6] The list of eighty *Heike*-related plays in the *Heike monogatari daijiten* omits many of the Tokugawa-period plays that feature characters and incidents from the Genpei period. The fact that the majority of extant manuscripts and printed editions date from this period testifies to a continued interest both in reading and performing older plays and in producing original new plays. This Appendix includes examples of Genpei plays composed from the fifteenth to nineteenth centuries, excluding only *shinsaku nō* composed from the Meiji period to the present. The online version includes more comprehensive set of examples from all periods.

In the interests of completeness, we have followed the lead of Japanese scholars in including plays based of any kind of narrative material in *Heike* texts. Zeami's *Taisanbukun*, for example, is based on an anecdote about Kiyomori's son-in-law, the "Cherry-Blossom Counselor." *Kan'yōkyū* dramatizes a famous incident in Chinese history, while plays like *Sagi* ("Heron") or *Akoya no matsu* re-enact older Japanese stories that appear in *Heike* texts.[7]

If we include the large number of relevant *bangai yōkyoku*, there are examples of nō for each of the twelve numbered books—more literally "scrolls," *maki*—of the Kakuichi-bon *Heike monogatari*, as well as the final "Initiate's Chapter" (*Kanjō no maki*). To all appearances it would seem that playwrights or their patrons looked for subjects that had not been dramatized before, filling in the gaps in the narrative, as for example with the plays about the death, capture, or escape of relatively minor characters like Moromori, Nobutsura, or Kumagai's son Naoie. We should also note the development of prominent clusters of plays about a single figure, as with the plays about Mongaku (Book Five), Tomoe (Book Nine), Yokobue (Book Ten), and Rokudai (Book Twelve). The cluster of "Battle of Uji Bridge" plays (Book Four) and "Moon Viewing" plays (Book Five) illustrate a similar phenomenon: multiple plays about a single event, but with variations of perspective depending on which character is foregrounded. The fewest number of nō are to be found for Books One and Six, with five plays each, and Book Eight, with just three. Dozens of plays deal with the great battles of the war, which fall

---

6. Kakuichi-bon 12.5 "Hōgan no miyako ochi." Kajiwara and Yamashita, *Heike monogatari* (ge), 354 (*Heike no onryō no yue to zo oboekeru*); McCullough, *The Tale of the Heike*, 408.

7. Further details about the sources of these plays are given in Part B, below.

in Books Seven, Nine, and Eleven. However, it is important to note that the demand for plays went well beyond a desire for representation of the vanquished Heike or victorious Genji. Of the numerous plays written about the Kikaigashima exiles of Books Two and Three, only one is now staged, the popular *Shunkan*.

All *Heike* texts refer to a greater or lesser extent to important earlier clashes between Genji and Heike warriors in 1156 and 1159, yet relatively few plays are based on the main accounts of the revolts, *Hōgen monogatari* and *Heiji monogatari*. Entries for all known examples have been included below.[8]

Section B provides more information about individual plays, their form and content, possible sources, major text editions, and summary of translations. For further bibliographical details, see the online resources cited above.[9]

---

8. See the entries in Section B for *Akugenda, Higekiri, Kamata, Taki mōde, Tametomo, Tomonaga, Yoshitomo, Yōka, Yuki Yuritomo,* and *Zaimoku Yukihira.* Only *Tomonaga* is in the current repertoire, while *Tametomo* is the only play directly about the Hōgen revolt known to me. For complete English translations of the narrative accounts, see Royall Tyler, *Before Heike and After:* Hōgen, Heiji, Jōkyūki (CreateSpace Independent Publishing Platform, 2012).

9. See footnote 2 above. As new translations appear, bibliographical references will be added to the online database.

PART A
PLAYS LISTED IN THE ORDER OF EPISODES IN THE KAKUICHI-BON *HEIKE MONOGATARI*

The list below orders plays according to the sections (*shōdan* 章段) of the Kakuichi-bon *Heike* that are their direct or indirect source. When the play is related in only a very indirect way with the Kakuichi version, its title is given in parentheses. One example is *Rō-Giō*, where the only link is with the figure of Giō herself. Another is *Shichiki ochi*, where the source is *Genpei jōsuiki* rather than the Kakuichi-bon, in which the incident is not mentioned. Section titles are given in romanization, Japanese, and English according to the edition by Kajiwara Masaaki and Yamashita Hiroaki and the translation by Helen Craig McCullough.[10] Plays marked with a double asterisk (**) are *genkō yōkyoku* 現行謡曲, that is to say, plays in the modern performance repertoire of at least one of the five schools, Kanze, Hōshō, Komparu, Kongō, or Kita.[11] A single asterisk indicates other plays thought to date from the Muromachi period. When different plays are known under the same title, they are distinguished by number.[12] See Part B for editions and other details.

1.5 **Wagami no eiga** 吾身栄花 Kiyomori's Flowering Fortunes
> **Taisanpukun 泰山府君

1.6 **Giō** 祇王 (Giō)
> **Giō 祇王, *Futari Giō* 二人祇王
> **Hotoke hara 仏原
> **(*Rō Giō* 籠祇王) (formerly in the repertoire of the Kita school)

---

10. Kajihara Masaaki and Yamashita Hiroaki, eds., *Heike monogatari*, SNKT 44–45 (Iwanami shoten, 1991–1993). McCullough, *Tale of the Heike*. Readers should also consult the most recent translation of the Kakuichi-bon: Royall Tyler, *The Tale of the Heike* (New York: Viking, 2012).

11. For details concerning current performance repertoire, we have followed Nishino Haruo and Hata Hisashi, ed., *Nō kyōgen jiten* (Heibonsha, 1987; revised and expanded 1999).

12. Such titles are numbered according to the entries in Tanaka Makoto, "Yōkyoku nayose ichiran," *Mikan yōkyōshū (zoku)* (Koten bunko, 1987–1998), vol. 20, 209–542, vol. 21, 59–481, vol. 22, 11–167.

1.15 **Mikoshiburi** 御輿振 Petitioning with Sacred Palanquins
➤ *Mikoshiburi* 御輿振

2.6 **Kyōkunjō** 教訓状 The Admonition
➤ *Daifu* 内府, *Shigemori* 重盛, *Komatsu kyōkun* 小松教訓[13]

2.8 **Dainagon ruzai** 大納言流罪 The Exile of the Major Counselor
➤ *Naritsune* 成経 (→2.10)

2.9 **Akoya no matsu** 阿古屋之松 The Pine of Akoya
➤ *Akoya no matsu* 阿古屋松

2.10 **Dainagon no shikyo** 大納言死去 The Death of the Major Counselor
➤ *(Akoya no matsu* 阿古屋松)

2.15 **Yasuyori notto** 康頼祝言 Yasuyori's Prayer
➤ *Iōgashima* 硫黄島

2.16 **Sotoba nagashi** 卒都姿流 Stupas Cast Afloat
➤ *Sotoba nagashi* 卒塔婆流, *Sobu* 蘇武, *Yasuyori* 康頼 (1)
➤ *Waka no uranami* 和哥の浦なみ
➤ *Yasuyori* 康頼

3.2 **Ashizuri** 足摺 The Foot-Drumming
➤ *Shima no wakare* 嶋の別れ
➤ **Shunkan* 俊寛, *Kikaigashima* 鬼界島

3.6 **Raigō** 頼豪 Raigō
➤ *Raigō* 頼豪

3.7 **Shōshō miyako gaeri** 少将都帰
➤ *Naritsune* 成経 (→2.8, 2.9, 2.10)

3.8 **Ariō** 有王 Ariō
➤ *Kikaigashima* 鬼界島, *Iōjima* 硫黄嶋
➤ *Fumi Sōzu* 文僧都

3.14 **Kane watashi** 金渡 The Transmission of Gold
➤ *Iōzan* 育王山 (Mount Yuwang)

3.15 **Hōin mondō** 法印問答 An Exchange of Views with the Dharma Seal)

---

13. A small portion of this play survives as a performance "piece" (*rangyoku* 乱曲) in the Kanze school. Kanze Sakon, *Kanzeryū zoku hyakubanshū* (Hinoki shoten: 1990), 1239–40. See the discussion in Tom Hare, "Genre and the *Heike* plays in Zeami's *Go on*," Chapter 26 in this volume.

➤ *Hōin mondō* 法印問答

4.1 Itsukushima gokō 厳島御幸 The Imperial Journey to Itsukushima
➤ *Itsukushima mōde* 厳島詣 (also →2.6)[14]

4. 5 Nobutsura 信連 Nobutsura
➤ **Chōbyōe no jō* 長兵衛尉, *Chōbyōe* 長兵衛, *Nobutsura* 信連
➤ *Nobutsura kassen* 信貫合戦

4.6 Kiō 競 Kiō
➤ *Fukui Takiguchi* 福井滝口
➤ **Nakatsuna* 仲綱 (→4.12)
➤ *Genzai Yorimasa* 現在頼政 (→4.12)

4.11 Hashi gassen 橋合戦 The Battle at the Bridge
➤ **Ichirai hōshi* 一来法師 (1), *Jōmyōbō* 浄妙坊
➤ *Ichirai hōshi* 一来法師 (2)
➤ *Magakigashima* 籬が島

4.12 Miya no gosaigo 宮御最期 The Death of the Prince
➤ (*Koga no watari* 古河の渡)
➤ *Tatsuzaki* 竜崎
➤ ***Yorimasa* 頼政

4.15 Nue 鵺 The Thrush Monsters
➤ ***Nue* 鵺
➤ ***Genzai nue* 現在鵺 (Kongō school)

5. 1 Miyako utsuri 都遷 The Transfer of the Capital
➤ *Amida no mine* 阿弥陀の嶺, *Shōgun no tsuka* 将軍の塚

5.2 Tsukimi 月見 Moon-Viewing
➤ **Kojijū* 小侍従
➤ *Matsu yoi kojijū* 松宵小侍従
➤ *Tsukimi* 月見
➤ *Tsukimi ryūjin* 月見竜神

5.4 Haya uma 早馬 The Fast Courier
➤ ***(Shichiki ochi* 七騎落)

5.5 Chōteki zoroe 朝敵揃 An Array of Court Enemies
➤ ***Sagi* 鷺

---

14. In this case and elsewhere, the play draws on material from more than one *Heike* section.

5.6 **Kan'yōkyū** 咸陽宮 The Xianyang Palace
  ➤ **Kan'yōkyū* 咸陽宮
  ➤ *Keika* (1) 荊軻 (Jing Ke)
  ➤ *Keika* (2) 荊軻 (Jing Ke)

5.7 **Mongaku no aragyō** 文覚荒行 Mongaku's Austerities
  ➤ (*Kesa gozen* 袈裟御前)
  ➤ *Taki Mongaku* 滝文学
  ➤ *Takikomori Mongaku* 滝籠文覚, *Mongaku Takigomori* 文覚滝籠

5.8 **Kanjinchō** 勧進帳 The Subscription List
  ➤ *Kanjin Mongaku* 勧進文学 (1) (→4.9)
  ➤ *Kanjin Mongaku* 勧進文学 (2) (→4.9)

5.9 **Mongaku nagasare** 文覚被流 Mongaku's Exile
  ➤ *Mongaku nagashi* 文学流

5.10 **Fukuhara inzen** 福原院宣 The Retired Emperor's Fukuhara Edict
  ➤ *Ningyō* 人形, *Ningyō Mongaku* 文覚人形

6.2 **Kōyō** 紅葉 Autumn Leaves
  ➤ *Momiji* 紅葉

6.4 **Kogō** 小督 Kogō
  ➤ **Kogō* 小督

6.6 **Hikyaku tōrai** 飛脚到来 The Arrival of the Couriers
  ➤ *Saijaku* 西寂

6.8 **Tsukishima** 築島 The Man-Made Island
  ➤ *Matsuō dōji* 松王どうじ
  ➤ *Tsukishima* 築島

6.10 **Gion nyōgo** 祇園女御 The Gion Consort
  ➤ *Gion* 祇園, *Gion zata* 祇園沙汰

7.1 **Shimizu no kanja** 清水冠者 Shimizu no Kanja
  ➤ *Shimizu no kanja* 清水冠者

7.3 **Chikubushima mōde** 竹生島詣 The Visit to Chikubushima[15]

---

15. In the play *Chikubushima* (all five schools), the Dragon God and Benzaiten appear to the imperial messenger visiting the island's shrine. There is no direct connection with an earlier *Heike* episode, which gives an account of Tsunemasa's visit to the island and his vision of a white dragon (*byakuryū*), but both works

> *Chikubushima Tsunemasa* 竹生島経正

7.5 Ganjō 願書 The Petition
> **Kiso 木曾
> *Kiso ganjo* 木曾願書
> *Kakumei* 覚明

7.6 Kurikara otoshi 倶梨迦羅落 The Descent into Kurikara
> *Kurikara otoshi 倶利伽羅落, *Tachibori* 太刀堀, *Aoi* 葵, *Aoi Tomoe* 葵巴

7.8 Sanemori 実盛 Sanemori
> **Sanemori 実盛
> *Genzai Sanemori* 現在実盛
> *Jikken Sanemori* 実験実盛

7.9 Genbō 玄肪 Genbō
> *(*Yōka* 楊賀)

7.16 Tadanori no miyako ochi 忠度都落 Tadanori's Flight from the Capital
> **Genzai Tadanori (1) 現成忠度 (Kongō school)
> *Genzai Tadanori* (2) 現在忠則
> *Shiga Tadanori 志賀忠度 (志賀忠則) (→9.14)
> **Shunzei Tadanori 俊成忠度 (→9.14)

7.17 Tsunemasa no miyako ochi 経正都落 Tsunemasa's Flight from the Capital
> *Genzai Tsunemasa 現在経正, *Omuro Tsunemasa* 御室経正
> **Tsunemasa 経政 (経正)

7.18 Seizan no sata 青山之沙汰 Concerning Seizan
> **Kenjō 絃上, *Genjō* 玄象

8.3 Odamaki 緒環 The Reel of Thread
> *Odamaki 小手巻

8.4 Dasaifu ochi 太宰府落 The Flight from the Dazaifu
> **Kiyotsune 清経

8.7 Mizushima gassen 水島合戦 The Battle at Mizushima

---

draw on similar legends about the sacred island. For an introduction and translation of the play, see Royall Tyler, *Japanese Nō Dramas* (London: Penguin Books, 1992), 58–67.

- ➢ (*Kiyofusa* 清房)
- ➢ *(*Mizushima Tarō* 水島太郎)

9.1 Ikezuki no sata 生ずきの沙汰 The Matter of Ikezuki
- ➢ *Sasaki* 佐々木, *Surusumi Ikezuki* 磨墨生食, *Umakoi* 馬乞

9.4 Kiso no saigo 木曽最期 The Death of Kiso
- ➢ **Kanehira* 兼平
- ➢ **Tomoe* 巴
- ➢ **Genzai Tomoe* 現在巴 (Kongō school)
- ➢ *Katami Tomoe* 筐巴
- ➢ *Kinukazuki Tomoe* 衣潜巴
- ➢ *Konjō Tomoe* 今生巴
- ➢ *Midai Tomoe* 御台
- ➢ *Muan Shōnin* 無庵上人
- ➢ (*Shibabune* 柴舟)
- ➢ (*Yoshiakira* 義明)

9.9 Rōba 老馬 The Old Horse
- ➢ **Michimori* 通盛

9.10 Ichi ni no kake 一二之懸 First and Second Attackers
- ➢ *Naoie* 直家

9.11 Nido no kake 二度之懸 The Double Charge
- ➢ **(*Ebira* 箙)
- ➢ *Kawara Tarō* 河原太郎
- ➢ *(*Kajiwara zaron* 梶原座論, *Zashikiron* 座敷論)
- ➢ *Nido no kake* (1) 二度掛, *Ichi-no-tani senjin* 一谷先陣.

9.12 Saka otoshi 坂落 The Assault from the Cliff
- ➢ *Rōba* 老馬
- ➢ *Nido no kake* (2) 二度掛.

9.14 Tadanori saigo 忠度最期 The Death of Tadanori
- ➢ **Tadanori* 忠度
- ➢ *Ikuta Tadanori* 生田忠度
- ➢ *Kusakari Tadanori* 草苅忠度
- ➢ **Shunzei Tadanori* 俊成忠度 (→7.16)

9.16 Atsumori no saigo 敦盛最期 The Death of Atsumori
- ➢ **Atsumori* 敦盛
- ➢ **Ikuta Atsumori* 生田敦盛, *Ikuta*生田
- ➢ *Genzai Atsumori* 現在敦盛

> *Ichiya Atsumori / Hitoyo Atsumori* 一夜敦盛
> **Katami Atsumori* 筐敦盛
> **Kōya Atsumori* 高野敦盛, *Renshō* 蓮生
> *Kumagai* 熊がひ
> (*Suma goto* 須磨琴)
> *Suma no fue* 須磨の笛
> *Suzume no mori* 雀森
> (*Tsunemori* 経盛)

9.17 Tomoakira saigo 知章最期 The Death of Tomoakira
> ***Tomoakira* 知章

9.18 Ochiashi 落足 The Flight
> ***Michimori* 通盛
> *Hirosawa hime* 広沢姫
> *Moromori* 師盛
> *Saka otoshi* 坂落[16]

9.19 Kozaishō minage 小宰相身投 Kozaishō's Suicide
> *Matsuo no ura* 松尾浦

10.6 Kaidō kudari 海道下 The Journey Down the Eastern Sea Road
> *Kaidō kudari* 海道下[17]

10.7 Senju no mae 千手前 Senju-no-Mae
> ***Senju* 千手, *Senju Shigehira* 千手重衡
> **Shijū Shigehira* 侍従重衡

10.8 Yokobue 横笛 Yokobue
> **Yokobue* 横笛 (1), *Takiguchi* 滝口
> *Yokobue* 横笛 (2), *Yūrei Yokobue* 幽霊横笛

10.9 Kōya no maki 高野巻 The Book of Kōya
> *Kōya no maki* 高野乃巻

10.12 Koremori no jusui 維盛入水 The Suicide of Koremori
> **Koremori* 惟盛 (維盛) (→12.9)

10.14 Fujito 藤戸 Fujito
> ***Fujito* 藤戸

---

16. See entry in Part B below regarding the placement of this play.

17. Rather than a play as such, this is a performance "piece" (*rangyoku* 乱曲) like *Rokudai no uta*. See again Hare, "Genre and the Heike plays in Zeami's *Go on*."

11.1 Sakaro 逆櫓 Reversed Oars
- ➤ *Zaron* 座論 (2)

11.2 Katsuura Ōzakagoe 勝浦大坂越 Katsuura Beach and Ōzakagoe Pass
- ➤ *(Sakurama* 桜間)

11.3 Tsuginobu saigo 嗣信最期 The Death of Tsuginobu
- ➤ *Kikuō* 菊王
- ➤ **Settai* 接待
- ➤ *Yashimadera* 八島寺, *Tsuginobu* 次信 (継信) (1)
- ➤ *Tsuginobu* 次信 (2).

11.4 Nasu no Yoichi 那須与一 Nasu no Yoichi
- ➤ *Nasu* 那須, *Nasu Yoichi* 那須与一 (1), *Horo* 母衣
- ➤ *Nasu no Yoichi* 那須与市 (2), *Ennen Nasu no Yoichi* 延年那須与一

11. 5 Yumi nagashi 弓流 The Dropped Bow
- ➤ **Yashima* 八島
- ➤ **Kagekiyo* 景清
- ➤ *Kumade Hōgan* 熊手判官

11.8 Tōya 遠矢 Distant Arrows
- ➤ *Tōya* 遠矢

11.9 Sentei minage 先帝身投 The Drowning of the Former Emperor
- ➤ *Nii no ama* 二位尼
- ➤ *Sentei* 先帝, *Noritsune* (1) 教経

11.10 Noto dono saigo 能登殿最期 The Death of Noritsune
- ➤ *Shin'ichi* 真都, *Noritsune* (2) 教経
- ➤ **Ikari kazuki* 碇潜
- ➤ (*Tsukushi no urakaze* つくしの浦風)

11.12 Ken 剣 Swords[18]
- ➤ **Gendaiyū* 源大夫
- ➤ **Kusanagi* 草薙
- ➤ *Yatsurugi* 八剣
- ➤ *Higekiri* 髭切
- ➤ **Rashōmon* 羅生門

---

18. Many plays included in this section draw on a much longer account of swords, the "Tsurugi no maki" 剣の巻 ("The Sword chapter") found in the Yashiro and Rufubon variants of *Heike monogatari* and *Genpei jōsuiki*.

11.19 Shigehira no kirare 重衡被斬 The Execution of Shigehira
➤ **Kasa sotoba* 笠卒塔婆, *Shigehira* 重衡, *Shigehira sakura* 重衡桜
➤ **Tatara Shigehira* 鑪重衡

12. 5 Hōgan no miyako ochi 判官都落 Hōgan's Flight from the Capital
➤ ***Shōzon* 正尊
➤ ***(Funa Benkei* 船)
➤ **(Noriyori* 範頼)
➤ **(Yukiie* 行家)
➤ *(Ashiya Benkei* 蘆屋弁慶)

12.7 Rokudai 六代 Rokudai
➤ *Iori Rokudai* 庵六代
➤ **Rokudai* 六代, *Rokudai Mongaku* 六代文学, *Muchi Mongaku* 鞭文学 (→12.8)

12.8 Hase Rokudai 泊瀬六代 Hase Rokudai
➤ **Mongaku* 文覚, *Mongaku Rokudai* 文覚六代
➤ **Saitō Go* 斎藤五, *Saitō Go Rokudai* 斎藤五六代
➤ *Hase Rokudai* 長谷六代 (1)
➤ *Rokudai no uta* 六代の歌, *Hase Rokudai* 長谷六代 (2)

12.9 Rokudai kirare 六代被斬 The Execution of Rokudai
➤ **(Takamura* 篁)
➤ **Tomotada* 知忠

Kanjō no maki 灌頂巻 **Ōhara gokō** 大原御幸 The Imperial Journey to Ōhara
➤ ***Ohara gokō* 大原御幸

Part B

Plays listed in alphabetical order, with bibliography and notes on selected plays

In the entries below double asterisks (**) are used for plays in the repertoire and single asterisks for plays of Muromachi period in origin. The remaining plays date from the early modern (*kinsei*) period. [19] The name of a school is listed in parentheses in cases when the play has now fallen out of that school's repertoire. Plays in the repertoire have been formally divided into the five categories: "first" ("god plays"; *wakinō*), "second" ("warrior plays"; *shuramono*), "third" ("woman" or "wig plays"; *kazura mono*), "fourth" (miscellaneous; *yobanme mono*), and "fifth" ("concluding plays"; *kirinō*).[20] Text editions are referred to by the abbreviations listed below in order of publication, with volume numbers only cited.[21] English translations are referred to by author date only. For full bibliographical information concerning Japanese editions and translations into English and other Western languages, see the online resources cited in footnote 2 above.

Kokumin [国民][22] Furuya Chishin, ed. Yōkyoku zenshū. 2 vols. Kokumin bunko kankōkai, 1911.[23]

Shinhyaku [新百]. Sasaki Nobutsuna, ed. *Shin'yōkyoku hyakuban.* Hakubunkan, 1912, reprint edition, Kyoto: Rinsen shoten, 1987.

---

19. A convenient guide to dating can be found in Takemoto Mikio, "Nōsakuhin zenran" 能作品全覧 in Takemoto Mikio and Hashimoto Asao, eds., *Nō kyōgen hikkei* (Gakutōsha, 1995), 53–120. For a detailed index to a much larger number of nō plays, see Tanaka, "Yōkyoku nayose ichiran."
20. For *bangai yōkyoku*, the indications are tentative, following Maruoka Katsura, *Kokin yōkyoku keidai*, revised and enlarged edition by Nishino Haruo (Kokin yōkyoku kedai kankōkai, 1984).
21. For page references, see the corresponding entry in Watson, "Genpei Tales and the Nō."
22. The Japanese terms in square brackets are abbreviations widely used in nō scholarship. See, for example, Takemoto and Hashimoto, *Nō kyōgen hikkei*, 55.
23. Reference is only made to the second volume, which prints a large number of *bangai yōkyoku* from two Edo collections, the three-hundred play collection of Jōkyō 3 (1686) and the four-hundred play collection of Genroku 2 (1689).

KYS [叢書] Haga Yaichi and Sakaki Nobutsuna, eds. *Kōchū Yōkyoku.* 3 vols. Hakubunkan, 1913–1915; reprint edition, Rinsen shoten, 1987.

Meichō 【名著】 Nonomura Kaizō 野々村戒三, ed. *Yōkyoku sanbyakugojūshū* 謡 曲三百五十番集. Nihon meicho zenshū kankōkai, 1928. [This edition is the base text for the UTAHI collection of online texts. See Watson, "Genpei Tales and the Nō" for links.]

Zensho [全書] Nogami Toyoichirō and Tanaka Makoto, eds. *Yōkyoku shū*, 3 vols. Nihon koten zensho. Asahi Shinbusha, 1949–1957.

Taikan [大観] Sanari Kentarō, ed. *Yōkyoku taikan.* 6 vols. Meiji shoin, 1930–1931.

Bangai [番外] = Tanaka Makoto, *Bangai yōkyoku (Kakuen-bon).* Koten bunko, vol. 33. Koten bunko, 1950.

Zokugai [続外] Tanaka Makoto, *Bangai yōkyoku zoku (Kakuen-bon).* Koten bunko, vol. 57, Koten bunko, 1952.

NKBT 40, NKBT 41 [大系] = Yokomichi Mario and Omote Akira, eds. *Yōkyōkushū.* 2 vols. NKBT 40–41. Iwanami shoten, 1960, 1963.

MYS [未刊] Tanaka Makoto, ed. *Mikan yōkyōshū.* 31 vols. Koten bunko, 1963–1980.

MYSZ [続外] Tanaka Makoto, ed. *Mikan yōkyōshū zoku.* 22 vols. Koten bunko, 1987–1998.

NKBZ 33, NKBZ 34 [全集]. Koyama Hiroshi, Satō Kikuo, Satō Ken'ichirō, eds. *Yōkyokushū.* 2 vols. NKBZ 33–34. Shōgakukan, 1973–1975.

SNKS [集成] Itō Masayoshi, ed. *Yōkyōkushū.* 3 vols. SNKS. Shinchōsha, 1983–1988.

SNKZ 58, SNKZ 59 [新編全集]. Koyama Hiroshi and Satō Ken'ichirō, ed. and trans. *Yōkyōkushū (jō).* SNBZ 58–59. Shōgakukan, 1997–1998.

SNKT 57 [新大系] Nishino Haruo, ed. *Yōkyoku hyakuban.* SNKT. Iwanami shoten, 1998.

*Adachi Shizuka 安達静. *Bangai yōkyoku.* (Third category.) Yoshitsune cycle. →*Gikeiki; kōwakamai Shizuka.* Text: MYS 21.

*Aiju 愛寿; **Aiju Tadanobu** 愛寿忠信. *Bangai yōkyoku.* (Fourth category.) Yoshitsune cycle. Text: KYS 1; MYS 19.

**Akogi 阿漕. All five schools. Fourth category. →*Genpei jōsuiki,* Book 8 ("Sanuki no in no koto"). Text: SNKS (jō).

*Akoya no matsu 阿古屋松. *Bangai yōkyoku.* (Fourth category.) Author: Zeami, possibly a revision of an earlier work. →*Kojidan* 古事談, book 2 (episode relating to Sanetaka); *Genpei jōsuiki,* Book 7; Kakuichi-bon 2.9. Text: NKBT 40; MYS 8 (*Akoya*) and MYS 1, MYS 19 (*Akoya no matsu*). A version of one passage survives as a performance piece (*rangyoku*) in the Kanze school. Revival performed in 2012.

*Akugenta 悪源太. *Bangai yōkyoku.* (Fourth category.) →*Heiji monogatari,* Book 2 (Gakushūin-bon, SNKT 43) or Book 3 (Kotohira-bon, NKBT 31). Text: KYS 1; Kokumin 2:72–77.

Amida no mine 阿弥陀の嶺. *Bangai yōkyoku.* (Fifth category.) Also known as *Shōgun no tsuka* 将軍塚. →Nagato-bon 9; *Genpei jōsuiki,* Book 16; cf. Kakuichi 5.1 "Miyako utsuri." Text: Bangai.

Ashiya Benkei 蘆屋弁慶. *Bangai yōkyoku.* Yoshitsune cycle. →cf. *Gikeiki,* Book 4; Kakuichi 12.5 "Hōgan no miyako ochi." Text: KYS 1.

**Ataka 安宅. All five schools. Fourth category. Possibly by Kanze Kojirō Nobumitsu 信光 (1424–1516). Yoshitsune cycle. →*Kōwakamai* works *Togashi* and *Oisagashi.* Text: NKBT 41; SNKS (jō); NKBZ 34; SNKZ 59; SNKT 59. Translation: NGS (III) 1960; Yasuda 1989; Chambers in Shirane 2007.

**Atsumori 敦盛. All five schools. Second category. Attributed to Zeami. →Kakuichi-bon 9.16 "Atsumori no saigo." Text: NKBT 40; SNBT 58; SNKS (jō). Translation: Waley 1921; Shimazaki 1987; Yasuda 1989; Tyler 1992; Bethe and Emmert 1995; Brazell 1998; Wilson 2006.

Chikubushima Tsunemasa 竹生島経正. *Bangai yōkyoku.* (Fourth category.) →*Genpei jōsuiki,* Book 28. Kakuichi-bon 7.3 "Chikubushima." Text: MYS 20.

*Chōbyōe no jō 長兵衛尉. *Bangai yōkyoku.* (Fourth category.) →Kakuichi-bon 4.5 "Nobutsura." Text: KYS 2; Kokumin 2:169–71;

MYSZ 9 (two variants).

**Daibutsu kuyō 大仏供養 ("The Dedication Rite for the Great Buddha"). All five schools. Known as *Nara mōde* 奈良詣 ("Pilgrimage to Nara") in the Komparu school. Fourth category. Akushichibyōe Kagekiyo (*shite*) fails in his attempt to assassinate Yoritomo (*tsure*) in Nara. A post-Genpei war incident related to a *kōwakamai* piece. Text: KYS 2; Taikan 3.

*Daifu 内府 ("The Palace Minister"). *Bangai yōkyoku.* (Fourth category.) →Kakuichi-bon 2.6 "Kyōkunjō." Text: KYS 2; MYS 22 (*Komatsu kyōkun*); MYSZ 5 (*Shigemori*); MYSZ 9.

**Ebira 箙 ("The Quiver"); *Ebira no ume* 箙の梅. All five schools. Second category. →Nagato-bon 16. Text: KYS 1; Taikan 1. Translation: Wilson 1969.

**Eboshi ori 烏帽子折. Kanze, Hōshō, Kongō, Kita schools. Fourth category play by Miyamasu. Yoshitsune cycle. Text: NKBT 41. Translation: Waley 1921; Shimazaki 1998.

*Ennen Nasu Yoichi 延年那須与一. *Bangai yōkyoku.* See *Nasu no Yoichi.*

**Fue no maki 笛の巻. Kanze school. Fourth category. Yoshitsune cycle. Related to *Hashi Benkei.*→*Gikeiki*, Book 3. Text: Taikan 4.

**Fujito 藤戸. All five schools. Fourth category. In the battle of Fujito (1184.11.26), →Kakuichi-bon 10.14. Text: NKBT 41; NKBZ 34; SNKS (*ge*); SNKZ 59; SNBT 57. Translations include: Wilson 1974; Tyler in Bethe and Emmert 1992.

Fukui Takiguchi 福井滝口. *Bangai yōkyoku.* (Fourth category.) →Kakuichi-bon 4.6 "Kiō." Text: Shinhyaku.

Fumi sōzu 文僧都. *Bangai yōkyoku.* Also known as *Ariō* 有王.→Kakuichi-bon 3.8 "Ariō"; 3.9 "Sōzu shikyo." Text: MYS 7.

**Funa Benkei 舟弁慶 (船弁慶). All five schools. Fifth-category nō by Kanze Nobumitsu (1424–1516). Yoshitsune cycle. →*Gikeiki*, Book 4; cf. Kakuichi-bon 12.5 "Hōgan no miyako ochi." Text: NKBT 41; NKBZ 33; SNKZ 58; SNBT 57. Translation: Sansom 1911; NGS (I) 1955; Yasuda 1989; Tyler 1992 ("Benkei aboard Ship").

**Futari Shizuka 二人静 ("The Two Shizukas"). Kanze, (Hōshō), Komparu, Kongō, Kita schools. *Mugen* nō by Zeami. Third category. Yoshitsune cycle. →*Gikeiki*, Book 5. Text: NKBT 41; SNKZ 58; SNKZ 58;

SNKT 57. Translation: Suzuki 1932; Mueller 1981.

**Gendaiyū 源太夫. Komparu school. First category. Also known as *Atsuta* 熱田. Source: "Tsurugi no maki." Text: KYS 1; Taikan 2.

**Genjō 玄象. All five schools. Known as Kenjō 絃上 in the Kanze school. Fifth category. Text: KYS 1; Taikan 2. Translation: Fenollosa/ Pound (1916), as "Genjo."

Genzai Atsumori 現在敦盛. *Bangai yōkyoku*. (Fourth category.) Encounter between Kumagai Naozane (*shite*) and Atsumori (*tsure*). →Kakuichi-bon 9.16 "Atsumori." Text: MYS 1.

Genzai ebira 現在箙. *Bangai yōkyoku*. (Fourth category.) Also known as *Kagesue* 景季 or *Ume Genta* 梅源太. Text: Shinhyaku.

Genzai Giō 現在祇王. *Bangai yōkyoku*. (Fourth category.) Kiyomori (*waki*) demands that Giō (*shite*) returns to dance before him. Text: MYS 27.

**Genzai nue 現在鵺. Kongō school. (Fifth category.) →Kakuichi-bon 4.15 "Nue" 鵺. Text: KYS 1; Kokumin 2.

Genzai Sanemori 現在実盛. *Bangai yōkyoku*. (Fourth category.) →Kakuichi-bon 7.8 "Sanemori." Text: KYS 1. Translated in this volume.

**Genzai Tadanori 現在忠度. Kongō school. Fourth category. →Kakuichi-bon 7.16 "Tadanori no miyako ochi." Text: MYSZ 3. There are two *bangai yōkyoku* variants: MYS 1; MYS 17.

Genzai Tomoe 現在巴. *Bangai yōkyoku*. (Fourth category.) Formerly performed by the Kongō school. →Kakuichi-bon 9.4 "Kiso no saigo." Text: KYS 1.

*Genzai Tsunemasa 現在経正. See *Omuro Tsunemasa*. →Kakuichi-bon 7.17 "Tsunemasa no miyako ochi." Text: KYS 3.

Genzai Yorimasa 現在頼政. *Bangai yōkyoku*. (Fourth category.) →Kakuichi-bon 4.6 "Kiō"; 4.12 "Miya no gosaigo.". Text: MYS 5.

**Giō 祇王. Kanze, Hōshō, Kongō, (Kita) schools. Third category. Known as *Futari Giō* in the Kita school. →Kakuichi-bon 1.6. Text: Taikan. Translated in this volume.

*Gion 祇園; *Gion zata* 祇園沙汰. *Bangai yōkyoku*. →Kakuichi-bon 6.10 "Gion nyōgo." Text: MYS 4.

Hase Rokudai 長谷六代 (1). *Bangai yōkyoku.* →Kakuichi-bon 12.7 "Rokudai"; 12.8 "Hase Rokudai." Text: MYSZ 11.

**Hashi Benkei 橋弁慶. All five schools. Fourth category. →*Gikeiki*, Book 3. Text: KYS 3; Taikan 4.

**Hashi Benkei no mae* 橋弁慶前. Yoshitsune cycle. (Fourth category.) Text: MYS 2.

Hayauchi Mongaku はやうち文学. *Bangai yōkyoku.* (Fourth category.) →Kakuichi-bon 12.8 "Hase Rokudai." Text: MYS 29.

Higekiri 髭切. *Bangai yōkyoku.* (Fourth category.) →Kakuichi-bon 11:12 "Ken"; "Book of Swords." Text: MYS 23; MYSZ 11 (variant).

Hirosawa hime 広沢姫. *Bangai yōkyoku.* Text: MYS 30. ⇒The character has not been traced, but her suicide may be modeled on Kozaishō's. Kakuichi-bon 9.19 "Kozaishō minage."

Hōin mondō 法印問答. *Bangai yōkyoku.* Kakuichi-bon 3.15. Text: MYS 20.

Horo 母衣. *Bangai yōkyoku.* Also known *Nasu* 那須, *Horo Nasu* 母衣那 須. Text: Zokugai. →Kakuichi-bon 11.4 "Nasu no Yoichi."

Hotoke no hara 仏原. Kanze, Kongō schools. →Kakuichi-bon 1.6 "Giō." Text: SNKS (*ge*); SNKT 57. Translated in this volume.

**Ichirai hōshi (Ichirai hosshi)* 一来法師 (1). *Bangai yōkyoku.* (Fourth category.) →Kakuichi-bon 4.11 "Hashi gassen"; *Genpei jōsuiki*, Book 15. Text: Kokumin 2; KYS 1.

Ichirai hōshi 一来法師 (2). *Bangai yōkyoku.* →Kakuichi-bon 4.6 "Kiō," 4.11 "Hashi gassen." Text: MYSZ 1.

Ichiya Atsumori / Hitoyo Atsumori 一夜敦盛. *Bangai yōkyoku.* →9.16 "Atsumori no saigo." Text: MYS 25.

Ichiya Kagekiyo / Hitoyo Kagekigo 一夜景清. *Bangai yōkyoku.* (Fourth category.) Text: MYS 25.

**Ikari kazuki 碇潜. Kanze, Kongō schools. Also known as *Hayatomo* 早友. Fifth-category play possibly by Komparu Zenpō 金春禅鳳 (b. 1454). → Kakuichi-bon 11.9, 11.10, 11.11. Text: KYS 1, Taikan 1. Translation: Gabriel in Brazell 1988 ("The Anchor Draping").

*Ikedori Morihisa 生捕盛久. *Bangai yōkyoku.* Fifth category. Text: Bangai.

**Ikuta Atsumori 生田敦盛. All schools. Called *Ikuta* 生田 in the Komparu school. Second category. Attributed to Zenpū. → *Ko Atsumori no emaki.* Text: Taikan 1; NKBT 41. Translation: Fenollosa/Pound 1916; Waley 1921. Translated in this volume.

Ikuta Tadanori 生田忠度. *Bangai yōkyoku.* (Second category.) →9.14 "Tadanori saigo." Text: Shinhyaku.

Iōgashima 硫黄島 (1) ("Sulphur Island"). *Bangai yōkyoku.* (Fourth category.) →Kakuichi-bon 2.15 "Yasuyori notto," 3.2 "Ashizuri." Text: MYS 25.

Iori Rokudai 庵六代. *Bangai yōkyoku.* Hōjō no Shirō Tokimasa captures Rokudai. The parting of Rokudai and his mother. →Kakuichi-bon 12.7 "Rokudai." Text: Bangai; MYS 21.

*Iōzan 育王山. *Bangai yōkyoku.* First category play. →Kakuichi-bon 3.14 "Kane watashi." Text: MYS 1, 21 (variant).

Ishiyama Yoshihira 石山義平. *Bangai yōkyoku.* (Second category.) →*Heiji monogatari.* Text: Shinhyaku.

Itsukushima mōde 厳島詣. *Bangai yōkyoku.* (Fourth category.) The pilgrimage of Emperor Takakura to the shrine. →Kakuichi-bon 4.1 "Itsukushima gokō." Text: MYS 8.

Jijū Shigehira 侍従重衡. *Bangai yōkyoku.* →Kakuichi-bon 10.6 "Kaidō kudari." Text: KYS 2.

Jikken Sanemori 実検実盛. *Bangai yōkyoku.* →Kakuichi-bon 7.8 "Sanemori." Text: KYS 2; Kokumin 1.

Kaidō kudari 海道下. A performance "piece" (*rangyoku* 乱曲). →Kakuichi-bon 10.6 "Kaidō kudari."

**Kagekiyo 景清. All five schools. Fourth category. →Kakuichi-bon 11.5 "Yumi nagashi." Text: NKBT 41; NKBZ 34; SNKS (*jō*); SNBZ 59; SNKT 57. Translation: Stopes/Sakurai 1913; Fenollosa/Pound 1916; Waley 1921; NGS (II) 1959; Shimazaki 1998; Emmerich 2002.

*Kajiwara zaron 梶原座論. *Bangai yōkyoku.* (Fourth category.) →Kakuichi-bon 9.11 "Nido no kake." Text: KYS 1:446. Kokumin 2:23–26; KYS 2.

Kakumei 覚明. *Bangai yōkyoku.* (Fourth category.) →Kakuichi-bon 7.5

"Ganjō." Text: MYS 26.

*__Kamata__ 鎌田 (1). *Bangai yōkyoku.* (Second category.) →*Heiji monogatari,* Kotobira-bon version (NKBT 31); *kōwakamai* piece *Kamata.* Text: Shinhyaku.

*__Kamata__ 鎌田 (2). *Bangai yōkyoku.* (Fourth category.) →*Heiji monogatari.* Text: MYS 4.

*__Kamei__ 亀井. *Bangai yōkyoku.* (Second category). Yoshitsune cycle. Text: MYS 4.

**__Kanawa__ 鉄輪. All five schools. Fourth-category play. →"Tsurugi no maki." Text: NKBT 41; SNKS (*jō*). Translation: Kato in Keene 1970 ("The Iron Crown"); Shimazaki 1998 ("The Iron Tripod").

**__Kanehira__ 兼平. All five schools. Second category. →Kakuichi-bon 9.4 "Kiso no saigo." Text: SNKS (*jō*) 329–. Translation: Jones 1963; Shimazaki 1993; Richard 2004.

__Kanjin Mongaku__ 勧進文学 (1). *Bangai yōkyoku.* (Fifth category.) →Kakuichi-bon 5.8 "Kanjinchō," 5.9 "Mongaku nagasare." Text: MYS 9.

__Kanjin Mongaku__ 勧進文学 (2). *Bangai yōkyoku.* (Fifth category.) →Kakuichi-bon 5.8 "Kanjinchō," 5.9 "Mongaku nagasare." Text: MYS 4.

**__Kan'yōkyū__ (often read *Kannyōkyū*) 咸陽宮. Kanze, Hōshō, Kongō, Kita schools. Fourth category. →Kakuichi-bon 5.6. Text: KYS 1; Taikan 2.

*__Kasa Sotoba__ 笠卒塔婆. *Bangai yōkyoku.* See entry for *Shigehira* 重衡 (1).

*__Katami Atsumori__ 筐敦盛 (形見敦盛). *Bangai yōkyoku.* (Fourth category.) →*Genpei jōsuiki,* Book 38 ("Kumagai Atsumori no kubi wo okuru"). Text: KYS 1.

__Katami Tomoe__ 筐巴. *Bangai yōkyoku.* (Second category.). →Kakuichi-bon 9.4 "Kiso no saigo." Text: MYS 16.

*__Katari Suzuki__ 語鈴木. *Bangai yōkyoku.* (Fourth category.) Yoshitsune cycle. Text: KYS 1.

__Kawara Tarō__ 河原太郎. *Bangai yōkyoku.* (Second category.) →Kakuichi-bon 9.11 "Nido no kake." Text: MYS 29.

__Keika__ 荊軻 (1). *Bangai yōkyoku.* (Fourth category.) →Kakuichi-bon 5.6 "Kan'yōkyū." Text: MYS 10.

__Keika__ 荊軻 (2). *Bangai yōkyoku.* (Fourth category.) →Kakuichi-bon 5.6

"Kan'yōkyū." Text: Bangai.

Kenjō 絃上. *Bangai yōkyoku.* All five schools. Known as *Genjō* 玄象 in the Kanze school. Kakuichi-bon 7.18 "Seizan no sata". Text: KYS 1. Translation: Fenollosa/Pound 1916.

Kesa gozen 袈裟御前. *Bangai yōkyoku.* (Fourth category.) →*Genpei jōsuiki,* Book 18, cf. Kakuichi-bon 5.7 "Mongaku no aragyō." Text: MYS 27.

Kikaigashima 鬼界島. *Bangai yōkyoku.* →Kakuichi-bon 3.8 "Ariō." Text: MYS 4; MYS 18 (variant, also known as *Iōshima* 硫黄島).

Kikuō 菊王. *Bangai yōkyoku.* (Second category.) →Kakuichi-bon 11.3 "Tsuginobu saigo." Text: MYS 9.

Kinukazuki Tomoe 衣潜巴. *Bangai yōkyoku.* (Second category.) →Kakuichi-bon 9.4 "Kiso no saigo." Text: KYS 1.

Kiso 木曾. Kanze school. Also known as *Kiso ganjo* 木曾願書. →Kakuichi-bon 7.5 "Ganjo." Text: KYS 1; Taikan 2. Translated in this volume.

Kiso ganjo 木曾願書. *Bangai yōkyoku.* (Fourth category). →Kakuichi-bon 7.5 "Ganjo." Text: Hyōshaku 7.

Kiyofusa 清房. *Bangai yōkyoku.* (Second category.) Source unknown, but cf. Kakuichi-bon 8.7 "Muroyama." Text: MYSZ 3.

Kiyoshige 清重. *Bangai yōkyoku.* (Fourth category.) Yoshitsune cycle. →*Kiyoshige,* a *kōwakamai* concerning Suruga Jirō Kiyoshige and Kajiwara Kagetoki. Text: MYS 19.

Kiyotsune 清経. All five schools. Second category. Author: Zeami. →Kakuichi-bon 8.4 "Dazaifu ochi." Text: NKBT 40; NKBZ 33; SNKS (*chū*); SNKZ 58; SNKT 57. Translation: NGS (I) 1955; Shimazaki 1987. Translated in this volume.

Koga no watari 古河の渡. *Bangai yōkyoku.* (Fourth category.) The ferryman may be the spirit of Minamoto no Yorimasa. Text: MYS 10.

Kogō 小督. All five schools. Fourth category. →Kakuichi-bon 6.4. Text: KYS 1; Taikan 2. Translation: Watson 1998; Shimazaki 1998.

Kojijū 小侍従. *Bangai yōkyoku.* →Kakuichi-bon 5.2 "Tsukimi." Text: Bangai.

Konjō Tomoe 今生巴. *Bangai yōkyoku.* *Genzaimono.* (Fourth category.)

→*Genpei jōsuiki*, Book 35; cf. Kakuichi-bon 9.4 "Kiso no saigo." Text: KYS 1; Kokumin 2:54–57.

*Koremori 維盛 (惟盛). *Bangai yōkyoku.* (Second category.) Attributed to Motomasa. →Kakuichi-bon 10.12 "Koremori no jusui"; 12.9 "Rokudai no kirare." Text: Kokumin 2; MYSZ 7 (two variants).

*Kōya Atsumori 高野敦盛, *Renshō* 蓮生. *Bangai yōkyoku.* (Second category.) Text: KYS 1; MYSZ 4.

*Kumade Hōgan 熊手判官. *Bangai yōkyoku.* (Second category.) →Kakuichi-bon 11.3 "Tsukinobu saigo," 11.5 "Yumi nagashi." Text: KYS 1; MYSZ 3 (three variants).

Kumagai 熊がひ. *Bangai yōkyoku.* (Fourth category.) → Kakuichi-bon 9.16 "Atsumori." Text: MYSZ 3.

Kurama 鞍馬; **Kurama Genji** 鞍馬源氏. *Bangai yōkyoku.* (Fifth category.) Yoshitsune cycle. →*Gikeiki*, Book 1. Text: MYS 1.

Kurama hōgan 鞍馬判官. *Bangai yōkyoku.* (Fourth category.) Yoshitsune cycle. →*Gikeiki*, Book 1. Text: MYS 9.

**Kurama tengu 鞍馬天狗. All five schools. Fifth group. Attributed to Miyamasu. →*Gikeiki*, Book 1. Text: NKBT 41; NKBZ 35; SNKZ 59.

*Kurikara otoshi 倶利伽羅落. *Bangai yōkyoku.* (Fourth category.) →Kakuichi-bon 7.6; *Genpei jōsuiki*, Book 29. Text: KYS 1; MYS 20 (variant titled *Tachibori* 太刀堀, "The Unearthed Sword"). Also known as *Aoi* 葵 or *Aoi Tomoe* 葵巴. Translated in this volume.

Kusakari Tadanori 草苅忠度. *Bangai yōkyoku.* (Second category). →Kakuichi-bon 9.14 "Tadanori saigo." Text: MYS 28.

**Kusanagi 草薙. Hōshō school. (Fourth category.) → Kakuichi-bon 11.12 (*Ken*) and *Tsurugi no maki* ("Book of the Swords"). Text: KYS 1; Taikan.

Magakigashima 籬が島. *Bangai yōkyoku.* →Kakuichi-bon 4.11 "Hashi gassen"; 4.12 "Miya no gosaigo." Text: MYS 30.

Matsu yoi Kojijū 松宵小侍従. *Bangai yōkyoku.* (Third category.) →Kakuichi-bon 5.2 "Tsukimi." Text: MYSZ 13.

Matsuō dōji 松王どうじ. *Bangai yōkyoku.* The spirit of the drowned "human pillar" Matsuō appears to Kiyomori's retainer Nanba Tsunetō. →Kakuichi-bon 6.8 "Tsukishima." Text: MYS 30.

Matsuo no ura 松尾浦. *Bangai yōkyoku.* →Kakuichi-bon 9.19 "Kozaishō."
Text: MYS 30.

Michimori 通盛. All five schools. →Kakuichi-bon, Book 9. Text: NKBT
40; SNKS (*ge*); SNKT 57. Translation: Wilson 1969; Shimazaki 1993.

Midai Tomoe 御台巴. *Bangai yōkyoku.* (Fourth category.) →Kakuichi-
bon 9.4 "Kiso no saigo." Text: MYS 3.

Mikoshiburi 御輿振. *Bangai yōkyoku.* (Fourth category.) →Kakuichi-
bon 1.15. Text: MYS 3.

Mizushima Tarō 水島太郎. *Bangai yōkyoku.* (Second category.) Source
unclear, cf. Kakuichi-bon, Book 8. Text: MYS 30.

Momiji 紅葉. *Bangai yōkyoku.* →Kakuichi-bon 6.2 "Kōyō" 紅葉. Text: KYS 3.

Mongaku (Rokudai) 文覚 [文学] (六代). *Bangai yōkyoku.* →Kakuichi-
bon 12.8 "Hase Rokudai." Text: KYS 3 (Rokudai); MYA 25 (Mongaku,
variant). Also an alternative name for several plays about the monk
Mongaku.

Mongaku nagashi 文学流 (1). *Bangai yōkyoku.* →Kakuichi-bon 5.9
"Mongaku nagasare." Text: MYS 31.

Morihisa 盛久. All five schools. →Nagato-bon 20. Text: NKBT 40;
NKBZ 34; SNKS (*ge*); SNKZ 59; SNKT 57. Translated in this volume.

Moromori 師盛. *Bangai yōkyoku.* →Kakuichi-bon 9.18 "Ochiashi." Text:
MYS 14.

Muan Shōnin 無庵上人. *Bangai yōkyoku.* →Kakuichi-bon 9.4 "Kiso no
saigo." Text: MYS 3.

Nakatsuna 仲綱. *Bangai yōkyoku.* (Fourth category.) →Kakuichi-bon 4.6
"Kiō"; 4.12 "Miya no gosaigo." Text: MYS 12.

Naoie 直家. *Bangai yōkyoku.* (Second category.) →Kakuichi-bon 9.10
"Ichi ni no kake." Text: MYS 29.

Naritsune 成経. *Bangai yōkyoku.* (Second category.) → Kakuichi-bon 3.7
"Shōshō miyako gaeri"; 2.8 "Dainagon ruzai"; 2.9 "Akoya no matsu";
2.10 "Dainagon no shikyo"; also *Genpei jōsuiki*, Books 16–17. Text:
KYS 3.

Nasu 那須, *Horo* 母衣, *Nasu Yoichi* 那須与一 (1). *Bangai yōkyoku.* (Fourth category.) →Kakuichi-bon 11.4 "Nasu no Yoichi." Text: Zokugai.

Nasu no Yoichi (2) 那須与市 (那須与一), also titled *Ennen Nasu no Yoichi* 延年那須与一. *Bangai yōkyoku.* (Fourth category.) →Kakuichi-bon 11.4. Text: MYS 2.

*Nido no kake (1) 二度掛. *Bangai yōkyoku.* (Fourth category.) →Kakuichi-bon 9.9 "Roba"; 9.11 "Nido no kake." Text: KYS 3.

Nido no kake (2) 二度のかけ. *Bangai yōkyoku.* (Fourth category.) →Kakuichi-bon 9.11. Text: MYS 29.

Nii no ama 二位尼 ("the Nun of Second Rank"), also titled *Nii dono* 二位殿. *Bangai yōkyoku.* (Second category.) →Kakuichi-bon 11.9 "Sentei minage." Text: MYS 13.

Ningyō 人形. *Bangai yōkyoku.* Possibly based on a *kōwakamai* titled *Mongaku.* Cf. also Kakuichi-bon 5.10 "Fukuhara inzen." Text: MYS 2, MYS 13 (variant), MYS 23.

*Nobutsura 信連. See *Chōbyōe no jō.*

Nobutsura kassen 信貫合戦. *Bangai yōkyoku.* (Fourth category.) →Kakuichi-bon 4.5 "Nobutsura." Text: MYS 29.

Noguchi hōgan 野口判官. *Bangai yōkyoku.* (Second category.) Yoshitsune cycle. →*Gikeiki*, Book 8. Text: KYS 3; MYSZ 10 (variant).

*Noriyori 範頼. *Bangai yōkyoku.* →*Dainihonshi*, cf. Kakuichi-bon 12.5 "Hōgan no miyako ochi." Text: KYS 3; MYS 16; MYS 18; MYSZ 10 (two variants).

Noritsune 教経. *Bangai yōkyoku.* (Second category.) Text: MYSZ 10. ⇒*Noritsune* is also an alternative name for two other plays, *Sentei* and *Shin'ichi.*

**Nue 鵺. All five schools. Fourth category. →Kakuichi-bon 4.15 "Nue" 鵼. Text: NKBT 40; NKBZ 34; SNKS (*ge*); SNKZ 59. Translation: Tyler 1978 (as "Nightbird"); Yasuda 1989.

Numa sagashi 沼捜. *Bangai yōkyoku.* (Fifth category.) Yoshitsune cycle. Text: Shinhyaku; MYS 23 (a shorter variant).

*Odamaki 小手巻. *Bangai yōkyoku.* →Kakuichi-bon 8.3 "Odamaki" 緒環. Text: KYS 3.

**Ohara gokō 大原御幸. All five schools. Third category. Known as

Ohara gokō 小原御幸 in the Kita school. (In both cases O- is read short.) →Kakuichi-bon *Kanjō-no-maki* 3 "Ōhara gokō." Text: SNKZ 58; NKBZ 33; SNKZ 58. Translation: Hochstedler in Keene 1970.

Ohara iri 大原入. *Bangai yōkyoku.* (Third category.) →Kakuichi-bon K.2 "Ōhara iri." Text: MYS 4.

Oikuma Suzuki 追熊鈴木. *Bangai yōkyoku.* Yoshitsune cycle. Text: KYS 1:327f.

*****Okazaki** 岡崎. *Bangai yōkyoku.* Yoshitsune cycle. Text: KYS 3:557–59 (*Yoshimizu* 吉水).

Okkake Suzuki (1) 追駆鈴木. *Bangai yōkyoku.* (Fourth category.) Yoshitsune cycle. Text: KYS 1 (*Oikuma Suzuki*).

Okkake Suzuki (2) 追駆鈴木. *Bangai yōkyoku.* (Fourth category.) Yoshitsune cycle. Text: MYS 21. For another treatment of this episode, see *Katari Suzuki.*

Omuro Tsunemasa 御室経正. *Bangai yōkyoku.* (Fourth category.) →Kakuichi-bon 7.17 "Tsunemasa no miyako ochi." Text: KYS 3 (supplementary section, pp. 1–6). Also known as *Genzai Tsunemasa* 御室経正.

Raigō 頼豪. *Bangai yōkyoku.* (Fourth category.) →One of "read" variants (Engyō-bon, Book 3; Nagato-bon, Book 6; *Genpei jōsuiki*, Book 10), cf. Kakuichi-bon 3.6. Text: MYS 15.

*****Rashōmon** 羅生門. Kanze, Hōshō, Kongō, Kita schools. Attributed to Nobumitsu. Based on "Book of the Swords" in Yashiro-bon *Heike monogatari.* Text: NKBT 41.

*****Rō Giō** 籠祇王. Kita school, but no longer in active repertoire. Fourth category. Kakuichi-bon 1.6 "Giō." Text: MYS 24. Translated in this volume.

Rō Kagekiyo 籠景清. *Bangai yōkyoku.* (Fourth category). Text: MYS 3.

Rōba 老馬. *Bangai yōkyoku.* (Fourth category). →Kakuichi-bon 9.12 "Saka otoshi." Text: MYS 31.

*****Rokudai** 六代. *Bangai yōkyoku.* →Kakuichi-bon 12.7 "Rokudai." Text: KYS 3 (*Rokudai*); MYS 24 (*Rokudai Mongaku* 六代文学); MYSZ 19 (*Muchi Mongaku* 鞭文学).

*****Rokudai no uta** 六代の歌. *Utai* included in Zeami's *Go on.* Also referred to as *Utaimono Hase rokudai* 謡物長谷六代 and *Hase Rokudai* [*Hatsuse Rokudai*] 長谷六代. →Kakuichi-bon 12.7 "*Rokudai.*" 12.8 "*Hase Rokudai.*" Text: Taikan 7. Translated in this volume.

**Sagi 鷺. All five schools. Fourth category. →Kakuichi-bon 5.5 "Chōteki zoroe." Text: KYS 2; Taikan 2.

*Saijaku 西寂. *Bangai yōkyoku.* (Fourth category.) →Kakuichi-bon 6.6 "Hikyaku tōrai." Text: KYS 2; Kokumin 2.

*Saitō Go 斎藤五. *Bangai yōkyoku.* (Fourth category.) →Kakuichi-bon 12.7 "Rokudai." Text: Kokumin 2:530–39 (*Saitō Go Rokudai*); KYS 2 (*Saitō Go Rokudai*); MYSZ 5 (*Saitō Go,* two variants).

Saka otoshi 坂落 (1). *Bangai yōkyoku.* (Fourth category.) Text: MYS 10.

Saka otoshi 坂落 (2). *Bangai yōkyoku.* (Fourth category.) Text: MYS 25.

*Sakurama 桜間. *Bangai yōkyoku.* (Fourth category). →*Genpei jōsuiki,* Book 42 (Battle of Katsura), cf. Kakuichi-bon 11.1 "Katsuura Ōzakagoe." Text: KYS 2.

*Sanada 真田. *Bangai yōkyoku.* (Fourth category.) Also called *Ishihashiyama* →*Genpei jōsuiki* 20. Text: KYS.

**Sanemori 実盛. All five schools. Second category. Author: Zeami. →Kakuichi-bon 7.8. Text: NKBT 40; SNKS (*chū*); SNKZ 58; SNKT 57. Translation: NGS (I) 1955; Smethurst 1989. Translated in this volume.

*Sasaki 佐々木. *Bangai yōkyoku.* →*Genpei jōsuiki* 23, cf. Kakuichi-bon 9.1 "Ikezuki no sata." Text: KYS 2; Kokumin 2.

*Sekihara Yoichi 関原与市 (与一). *Bangai yōkyoku.* (Fourth category.) Yoshitsune cycle. →*kōwakamai, Kurama ide* (*Azuma kudari*). Text: KYS 2; Taikan 3.

**Senju 千手 All five schools. Third category. Also known as *Senju Shigehira* 千手重衡. →Kakuichi-bon 10.7 "Senju-no-mae." Text: SNKS (*chū*); SNKT 57.

*Sentei 先帝. *Bangai yōkyoku.* (Second category.) →Kakuichi-bon 11.9 "Sentei minage." Text: MYS 2; MYSZ 7 (variant *Noritsune* 教経 [1]).

**Settai 接待. Kanze, Hōshō, Hongō, Kita schools. Fourth category. →*Gikeiki,* Book 8. Possibly related to a *kōwakamai* titled *Yashima* *no ikusa.* Text: KYS 2; Taikan 3; Zensho. Translation: NGS (II) 1959 ("Hospitality").

Shibabune 柴舟. *Bangai yōkyoku.* (Second category.) Cf. Kakuichi-bon 9.4 "Kiso no saigo," but this does not describe the death of Yoshinaka's retainer Nenoi at Awazu. Text: MYS 28.

**Shichiki ochi 七騎落. All five schools. Fourth category. →*Shibu gassenjō-bon Heike monogatari*; *Genpei jōsuiki*, Book 22. Text: KYS 2; Taikan 3. Translation: Smethurst 1998 ("Seven Warriors in Flight").

*Shiga Tadanori 志賀忠度 (志賀忠則). *Bangai yōkyoku.* (Second category.) →Kakuichi-bon 7.16 "Tadamori no miyako ochi"; 9.14 "Tadamori saigo." Text: Kokumin 2; KYS 2; MYSZ 5 (two variants), MYSZ 21.

*Shigehira 重衡 (1) *Bangai yōkyoku.* (Second category.) Also known as *Kasa sotoba* 笠卒都婆 or *Shigehira sakura* 重衡桜. Sometimes attributed to Zeami. →Kakuichi-bon 11.19 "Shigehira no kirare." Text: KYS 1; Kokumin 2:202–6; NKBT 41, MYSZ 5 (five variants). Translated in this volume.

**Shigehira 重衡 (2). *Bangai yōkyoku.* (Third category.) See entry for Senju 千手.

*Shigemori 重盛. See entry for *Daifu.*

*Shijū Shigehira 侍従重衡. *Bangai yōkyoku.* (Third category.) →Kakuichi-bon 10.7 "Senju no mae." Text: KYS 2.

Shikoku ochi 四国落. *Bangai yōkyoku.* (Fourth category.) Yoshitsune cycle. Text: MYS 27.

Shima no wakare 嶋の別れ. *Bangai yōkyoku.* (Fourth category.) →Kakuichi-bon 3.2 "Ashizuri." Text: MYS 28.

Shimizu kanja 清水冠者. *Bangai yōkyoku.* (Fourth category.) →Kakuichi-bon 7.1 "Shimizu no kanja." Text: Shinhyaku.

Shin'ichi 真真都, *Noritsune* 教経 (2). *Bangai yōkyoku.* (Second category.) →Kakuichi-bon 11.10 "Noto dono saigo." Text: MYS 11.

Shirahata 白旗. *Bangai yōkyoku.* (Second category.) Yoshitsune cycle. →*Gikeiki*, Book 8. Text: MYS 16.

Shōgun no tsuka 将軍の塚. See *Amida no mine.*

**Shōzon 正尊. All five schools. Fourth category. Authorship attributed

to Nagatoshi. Yoshitsune cycle.→Kakuichi-bon 12.9 "Tosabō kirare";
Genpei jōsuiki, Book 46; *Gikeiki*, Book 4. Text: NKBT 41.

**Shunkan 俊寛. All five schools. Fourth category. Called *Kikaigashima*
鬼界島 in the Kita school. Author unknown, possibly Zenchiku or
Motomasa. →Kakuichi-bon 3.2 "Ashizuri." Text: Taikan 3; NKBT 41;
MLBZ 34. SNKS (*chū*); SNKZ 59; SNKT 57. Translation: Waley 1921
(extract); NGS (III) 1960; Kato in Brazell 1998.

**Shunnei (Shun'ei) 春栄. All five schools. Fourth category. Authorship:
sometimes attributed to Zeami. Dramatizes incident occuring after
the battle of Uji Bridge but with none of the details of the Kakuichi
account of the battle in Book 4. Text: Taikan 2; NKBT 40; SNKS
(*chū*). Translation: Smethurst 1998.

**Shunzei Tadanori 俊成忠度. Kanze, Hōshō, Kongō, Kita schools.
Second category. Author: Naitō Zaemon 内藤左衛門. →Kakuichi-
bon 7.16 "Tadamori no miyako ochi" and 9.14 "Tadanori saigo."
Text: KYS 2; Taikan 2. Translated in this volume.

Sotoba nagashi 卒塔婆流. *Bangai yōkyoku*. Also known as *Sobu* 蘇武
or *Yasuyori*康頼 (1). →Kakuichi-bon 2.16 "Sotoba nagashi"; 2.17
"Sobu." Text: MYS 2, 22 (variant).

Suma goto すま琴／須磨琴. *Bangai yōkyoku*. (Fifth category.) →Kakuichi-
bon 9.16 "Atsumori." Text: MYS 28.

Suma no fue 須磨之笛. *Bangai yōkyoku*. →Kakuichi-bon 9.16 "Atsumori."
Text: MYS 11.

Suzume no mori 雀森. *Bangai yōkyoku*. →Kakuichi-bon 9.16 "Atsumori."
Text: MYS 11.

Sumadera 須磨寺. *Bangai yōkyoku*. (Fourth category.) Yoshitsune cycle.
Benkei shows his skill in poetry. Text: MYS 5.

Suma no fue 須磨笛. *Bangai yōkyoku*. (Fourth category.) Atsumori's
spirit appears to a traveling monk. →Kakuichi-bon 9.16 "Atsumori."
Text: MYS 11.

*Suzuki 鈴木. *Bangai yōkyoku*. →*Gikeiki*. Text: Kokumin.

*Tachibori 太刀堀. See *Kurikara otoshi*.

**Tadanobu 忠信. Kanze and Hōshō schools. Fourth category.

Yoshitsune cycle. →*Gikeiki*, Book 5. Text: Taikan 3; MYSZ 7.

*Tadanobu 忠信. *Bangai yōkyoku*. Fourth category. Yoshitsune cycle. →*Gikeiki*, Book 5. Text: KYS 2; Taikan 3.

**Tadanori 忠度. All five schools. Second category. Author: Zeami. →Kakuichi-bon 7.16 "Tadamori no miyako ochi" and 9.14 "Tadanori saigo." Text: NKBT 40; SNKS (*chū*); SNKZ 58.; SNKT 57. Translation: Sadler 1934; NGS (II) 1959; Hare 1986; Shimazaki 1987; Yasuda 1989; Tyler 1992.

**Taisanbukun 泰山府君. Kongō school. Fifth category. Authorship: revised by Zeami? →*Genpei jōsuiki*, Book 2, cf. Kakuichi-bon 1.5 "Wagami no eiga." Text: KYS 2; Taikan 3.

*Takadachi 高館. *Bangai yōkyoku*. (Second category.) Yoshitsune cycle. Text: Bangai; MYS 22.

Takadachi Benkei 高館弁慶. *Bangai yōkyoku*. (Second category.) Yoshitsune cycle. Text: MYS 17.

*Takamura 篁. *Bangai yōkyoku*. (Fourth category.) Cf. Kakuichi-bon 12.9 "Rokudai kirare." Text: MYS 2; MYS 11 (*Ono no Takamura* 小野篁).

Taki mōde 滝詣. *Bangai yōkyoku*. →*Heiji monogatari*. Text: MYS 28.

Taki Mongaku 滝文学. *Bangai yōkyoku*. (Fifth category.) →Kakuichi-bon 5.7 "Mongaku no aragyō." Text: MYS 2.

Takiguchi 滝口. See *Yokobue* 横笛 (1).

Takikomori Mongaku 滝籠文覚. *Bangai yōkyoku*. (Fifth category.) →Kakuichi-bon 5.7 "Mongaku no aragyō." Text: KYS 2; Shinhyaku (*Mongaku Takigomori*).

*Tametomo 為朝 (1). *Bangai yōkyoku*. (Fourth category.)→*Hōgen monogatari*, Book 3. Text: MYS 23.

*Tametomo 為朝 (2). *Bangai yōkyoku*. (Fifth category.)→*Hōgen monogatari*. Text: MYS 12. Tametomo is mentioned twice in *Heike monogatari*, most notably in Kakuichi-bon 11.5 "Yumi nagashi" where Yoshitsune recalls his uncle's powerful bow.

**Tamura 田村. All five schools. Second category. The military exploits of Sakanoue no Tamuramaro (758–811) are summarized in *Genpei*

jōsuiki, Book 27, "Daijōe en'in no koto." In the Kakuichi-bon, his name is mentioned only in passing (6.5 "Megurashibumi"). Text: NKBZ 33; SNKS (*chū*); SNKZ 58. Translation: Sadler 1934; NGS (I) 1955.

Tankai 湛海. *Bangai yōkyoku.* (Fourth category.) Yoshitsune cycle. →*Gikeiki*, Book 2. Text: KYS 2; MYSZ (two variants).

*****Tatara Shigehira** 鑪重衡. *Bangai yōkyoku.* (Fourth category.) →Kakuichi-bon 5.14 "Nara enshō"; 11.19 "Shigehira no kirare." Text: MYS 6.

Tatsuzaki 竜崎. *Bangai yōkyoku.* (First category.) Also known as *Azuma Yorimasa* 東頼政 →Kakuichi-bon 4.12 "Miya no gosaigo" (and earlier episodes). Text: MYS 6.

Tokiwa 常磐. *Bangai yōkyoku.* (Third category.) Yoshitsune cycle. Text: MYSZ 10.

Tokiwa mondō 常磐問答. *Bangai yōkyoku.* (Third category.) Yoshitsune cycle. Text: MYS 6.

****Tomoakira** 知章. Kanze, Komparu, Kongō, Kita schools. Second category. →Kakuichi-bon 9.17 "Tomoakira saigo." Text: KYS 2; Taikan 4. Translation: Shimazaki 1993.

****Tomoe** 巴. All five schools. →Kakuichi-bon 9.4 "Kiso no saigo"; *Genpei jōsuiki*, Book 35. Text: NKBT 41; SNBZ 58. Translations: Sadler 1934; NGS 1960; Shimazaki 1993.

****Tomonaga** 朝長. All five schools. Second category. Sometimes attributed to Kanze Motomasa. →*Heiji monogatari*, Book 2. Text: SNKS (*chū*); NKBZ SNBZ 58. Translation: Shimazaki 1987.

*****Tomotada** 知忠. *Bangai yōkyoku.* (Fourth category.) Attributed to Kanze Kojirō Nobumitsu. →Kakuichi-bon 12.9 "Rokudai kirare"; Nagato-bon, Book 20. Text: MYS 6.

*****Tōya** 遠矢 ("Distant Arrows"). *Bangai yōkyoku.* (Fourth category.) →Kakuichi-bon 11.8; *Genpei jōsuiki*, Book 43. Text: KYS 2.

Tsuginobu 次信・継信 (1). *Bangai yōkyoku.* See *Yashimadera.*

*****Tsuginobu** 次信 (2). *Bangai yōkyoku.* (Second category.)→Kakuichi-bon 11.3 "Tsuginobu no saigo." Text: Zokugai . For another treatment of Tsuginobu's death, see the entry for *Settai.*

Tsukijima 築島 ("The Artificial Island"). *Bangai yōkyoku*. (Fifth category.) In Kakuichi-bon 6.8 "Tsukishima" 築島, Kiyomori is opposed the idea of human sacrifice. The lengthy play is based instead on a *kōwakamai*, *Tsukishima*, which gives an extended account of Kuniharu and his search for his daughter Meigetsu. Text: MYS 18.

Tsukimi 月見. *Bangai yōkyoku*. (Third category.) →Kakuichi-bon 5.2. Text: KYS 2; Shinhyaku. Related plays: *Matsuyoi, Matsuyoi no Kojijū, Tsukimi ryūjin*.

Tsukimi ryūjin 月見竜神. *Bangai yōkyoku*. (Fifth category.) →Kakuichi-bon 5.2 "Tsukimi." Text: MYS 29.

Tsukushi no urakaze つくしの浦風. *Bangai yōkyoku*. (Fourth category.) →Kakuichi-bon, Book 11. Text: MYS 29.

**Tsunemasa* 経政. All five schools. *Tsunemasa* 経正 in the Kanze and Komparu schools. Second category. →Kakuichi-bon 7.17 "Tsunemasa no miyako ochi," 9:17 "Tomoakira saigo." Text: KYS 2; Taikan 3; NKBT 41. Translation: Fenollosa and Pound 1916; Waley 1921; Shimazaki 1987.

Tsunemori 経盛. *Bangai yōkyoku*. (Fourth category.) →*Genpei jōsuiki*, Book 38; cf. Kakuichi-bon 9.16 "Atsumori no saigo." Text: MYS 2; MYS 20 (variant); MYSZ 9 (variant).

Tsurugaoka 鶴が岡; *Tsurugaoka Shizuka* 鶴岡静. *Bangai yōkyoku*. (Third category.) Yoshitsune cycle. →*Gikeiki*, Book 6; [*kōwakamai*] *Shizuka*. Text: KYS 2; Kokumin 2: MYSZ 9. Translation: Watson 2005.

Tsuruwaka 鶴若. *Bangai yōkyoku*. (Fourth category.) Yoshitsune cycle. →*Gikeiki*. Text: KYS 2.

Waka no uranami 和哥の浦なみ, 和歌の浦波. *Bangai yōkyoku*. (Fourth category.) →Kakuichi-bon 2.16 "Sotoba nagashi." Text: MYS 31.

**Yashima* 八島. All five schools. Known as *Yashima* 屋島 in the Kanze school. Second-category play). →Kakuichi-bon 11.5 "Yumi nagashi." Text: NKBT 41; SNKS; SNKZ 58. Translation: Ueda 1962 ("The Battle at Yashima"); Tyler 1978a; Tyler 1992; Shimazaki 1993.

Yashimadera 屋嶋寺. *Bangai yōkyoku*. (Second category.) Also known as *Tsuginobu* 次信(継信) (1). →Kakuichi-bon 11.3 "Tsuginobu no saigo"; *kōwakamai Yashima*. Text: MYS 7.

Yasuyori 康頼. *Bangai yōkyoku.* (Fifth category.) →Kakuichi-bon 2.16 "Sotoba nagashi." Text: MYS 15.

Yatsurugi 八剣. *Bangai yōkyoku* (Fifth category.) →Kakuichi-bon 11.12 "Ken" and versions of the "Book of Swords" ("Tsurugi no maki"). Text: KYS 3; Taikan 4.

Yōka 楊賀. *Bangai yōkyoku.* (Fourth category.) →Kakuichi-bon 7.9 "Genbō"; *Genpei jōsuiki*, Book 31, "Seizan no biwa Ryūsen takubaku no koto"; cf. Kakuichi-bon 7.9 "Genbō." Text: MYS 3, 24 (variant *Yōka* 陽嘉).

Yokobue 横笛 (1). *Bangai yōkyoku.* (Third category.) Also known as *Takiguchi* 滝口. →*Genpei jōsuiki*, Book 39; Kakuichi-bon 10.8 "Yokobue." Text: MYS 3.

Yokobue 横笛 (2). *Bangai yōkyoku.* (Third category.) Also known as *Yūrei Yokobue* 幽霊横笛. →Kakuichi-bon 10.8. Text: MYS 17.

**Yorimasa* 頼政. All five schools. Second category. Author: Zeami. →Kakuichi-bon 4.12 "Miya no gosaigo." Text: NKBT 40; NKBZ 33; SNKS (*ge*); SNKZ 58; SNKT 57. Translation: Tyler 1978b, Shimazaki 1993

Yoshiakira 義明. *Bangai yōkyoku.* (Second category.) →Kakuichi-bon 9.4 "Kiso no saigo." Text: MYS 31.

**Yoshino Shizuka* 吉野静. Kanze, Hōshō, Komparu, (Kita) schools. Third-category. Yoshitsune cycle. →*Gikeiki*, Book 5. Text: NKBT 40. Translation: Terasaki in Brazell 1988.

Yoshitomo 義朝. *Bangai yōkyoku.* (Second category). →*Heiji monogatari*. Text: MYS 15.

Yuki Yoritomo 雪頼朝. *Bangai yōkyoku.* (Fourth category.) →*Heiji monogatari*. Text: MYS 3; MYS 15 (variant); MYS 19 (variant).

Yukiie 行家. *Bangai yōkyoku.* (Fourth category.) →Nagato-bon, Book 19. Text: KYS 3; MYS 20.

**Yuya* 熊野. All five schools. *Yuya* 湯谷 in the Kita school. Third-category play. Author: sometimes attributed to Komparu Zenchiku or Kanze Motomasa. →Kakuichi-bon 10.6 "Kaidō kudari." Text: NKBT 41; SNKS (*ge*); SNKZ 58; SNBT 57. Translation: O'Neill 1954; NGS (II) 1959; Tyler 1978b; Shimazaki 1987.

*__Zaimoku Yoshihira__ 材木義平. *Bangai yōkyoku*. (Second category).
→*Heiji monogatari*. Text: Shinhyaku.

*__Zaron__ 座論 (1). Also known as *Zashikiron* 座敷論 and *Kajiwara zaron* 梶原座論. See entry for latter.

*__Zaron__ 座論 (2). *Bangai yōkyoku*. (Fourth category.) →Kakuichi-bon 11.1 "Sakaro"; *Genpei jōsuiki*, Book 20 "Ishibashi gassen." Text: MYS 27.

Works Cited

Abbreviations

NKBT   Nihon Koten Bungaku Taikei 日本古典文学大
          (Iwanami shoten)
NKBZ   Nihon Koten Bungaku Zenshū 日本古典文学全集
          (Shōgakukan)
SNKS   Shin Nihon Koten Shūsei 新日本古典集成
          (Shinchōsha)
SNKT   Shin Nihon Koten Bungaku Taikei 新日本古典文学大系
          (Iwanami shoten)
SNKZ   Shinpen Nihon Koten Bungaku Zenshū 新編日本古典文学全集
          (Shōgakukan)

Abe Yasurō 阿部泰郎. "Suisankō" 推参考. Osaka daigaku kokugo kokubungakkai. *Gobun* 52, 1989, 12–27.

Adolphson, Mikael S. *The Gates of Power: Monks, Courtiers, and Warriors in Pre-modern Japan*. Honolulu: University of Hawai'i Press, 2000.

Aida Jirō 相田二郎. *Mōko shūrai no kenkyū: zōhoban* 蒙古襲来の研究-増補版. Yoshikawa kōbunkan, 1982.

Akone no ura kuden 阿古根の浦口伝. In Sasaki Nobutsuna 佐々木信綱, ed., *Nihon kagaku taikei* 日本歌学大系 vol. 4, 398. Kazama shobō, 1973.

Amano Fumio 天野文雄. "'Heike no monogatari no mama' to iu koto: *Sanemori wo megutte*" "平家の物語のまま" と言う事：〈実盛〉をめぐって. *Kokuritsu nōgakudō* 国立能楽堂 45 (May 1987), 28–29.

Amano Fumio 天野文雄. "*Haku Rakuten* to Ōei no gaikō: Kume Kunitake to Takano Tatsuyuki no shosetsu wo kenshō suru" 〈白楽天〉と応永の外冠：久米邦武と高野辰之の 所説を検証する. *Zeami: chūsei no geijutsu to bunka* 世阿弥中世の芸術と文化 vol. 1, no. 1 (February 2002), 128–146.

Amano Fumio 天野文雄. "*Takasago no shudai to seiritsu no haikei: Ōei nijūkyū nen no Aso Daigūji zasshō no jōraku to Yoshimochi no chisei wo megutte*" 〈高砂〉の主題と成立の背景 —応永二十九年の阿蘇大宮司雑掌の上洛と義持の治世をめぐって—. *Engekigaku ronsō* 演劇学論叢, vol. 7 (December 31, 2004), 14–51.

Anzai Tsuyoshi 安西剛, ed. *Heike monogatari* 平家物語. E de yomu koten sirīzu 絵で読む古典シリーズ. Gakken, 1998.

Araki Hisashi 荒木尚. *Imagawa Ryōshun no kenkyū* 今川了俊の研究. Kasama shoin, 1977.

Araki, James. *The Ballad-drama of Medieval Japan*. Berkeley and Los Angeles: University of California Press, 1964.

Arnn, Barbara L. "Medieval Fiction and History in the *Heike Monogatari* Story Tradition." Ph.D. dissertation, University of Indiana, 1984.

Asahara Yoshiko 麻原美子, Haruta Akira 春田宣, Matsuo Ashie 松尾葦江, eds., *Yashiro-bon Takano-bon taishō Heike monogatari* 屋代本・髙野本対照平家物語. Three vols. Shintensha, 1990–1993.

Asahara Yoshiko 麻原美子 and Kitahara Yasuo 北原保雄, eds., *Mai no hon* 舞の本. SNKT 59. Iwanami shoten, 1994.

Asahara Yoshiko 麻原美子and Nanami Hiroaki 名波弘彰, *Nagatobon Heike monogatari no sōgō kenkyū, kōchū-hen jō* 長門本平家物語の総合研究校注篇上, vol 1. Benseisha, 1998.

Asahara Yoshiko 麻原美子, ed. *Nagato-bon Heike monogatari no sōgō kenkyū, kōchū-hen ge* 長門本平家物語の総合研究　校注篇下, vol. 2. Benseisha, 1999.

Asami Shinkō 浅見真高, Hirose Shintarō 広瀬信太郎, and Kiyoda Hiroshi 清田弘. "*Haku Rakuten* wo megutte" 白楽天をめぐって. *Kanze* 観世 (February 1984), 41–46.

Asao Naohiro 朝尾直弘. *Osaka to Sakai* 大阪と堺. Iwanami shoten, 1984.

Atkins, Paul S. *Revealed Identity: The Noh Plays of Komparu Zenchiku.* Ann Arbor: Center for Japanese Studies, University of Michigan, 2006.

Atkins, Paul. "The Index." Japanese Performing Arts Resource Center, 1998–1999. http://www.glopac.org/Jparc/eni/eni.html. Accessed September 1, 2012.

Azuma Kagami 吾妻鏡. In Kuroita Katsumi 黒板勝美, ed. *Azuma Kagami*. 4 vols. Shintei zōho Kokushi taikei 新訂増補国史大系 （普及版) 22. Yoshikawa kōbunkan, 1932; reprinted 1991.

Be Mun-gyŏng 裴文卿. "Yōkyoku to 'Hyakuren shōkai,'" 謡曲と『百聯抄解』. In Kodai chūsei bungaku ronkō kankōkai 古代中世文学論考刊行会, ed. *Kodai chūsei bungaku ronkō* 古代中世文学論考, vol. 5, 248–68. Shintensha, 2001.

Bialock, David. *Eccentric Spaces, Hidden Histories: Narrative, Ritual, and Royal Authority from The Chronicles of Japan to The Tale of the Heike.* Stanford: Stanford University Press, 2007.

Bialock, David. "Nation and Epic: The Tale of the Heike as Modern Classic." In Haruo Shirane and Tomi Suzuki, eds., *Inventing the Classics: Modernity, National Identity, and Japanese Literature*, 151–78. Stanford: Stanford University Press, 2000.

Bialock, David. "The Tale of the Heike." In Steven Carter, ed. *Medieval Japanese Writers, Dictionary of Literary Biography*, 73–84. Detroit: Gale Group, 1999.

Bloom, Harold. *The Anxiety of Influence: A Theory of Poetry.* New York: Oxford University Press, 1973.

Brazell, Karen. "Subversive Transformations: Atsumori and Tadanori at Suma." In Amy Vladeck Heinrich, ed., *Currents in Japanese Culture*, 35–52. New York: Columbia University Press, 1997.

Brazell, Karen. *Traditional Japanese Theatre: An Anthology of Plays.* New York: Columbia University Press, 1997.

Brown, Steven T. "From Woman Warrior to Peripatetic Entertainer: The Multiple Histories of Tomoe." *Harvard Journal of Asiatic Studies*, 58:1 (1998), 183–99.

Brown, Steven T. *Theatricalities of Power: The Cultural Politics of Noh.* Stanford: Stanford University Press, 2001.

Burton, R. F., trans. *Du Mu: Plantains in the Rain: Selected Chinese Poems.* London: Wellsweep Press, 1990.

Chang, Chung-Yuan. *Original Teachings of Ch'an Buddhism: Selected from* The Transmission of the Lamp. New York: Pantheon Books, 1969.

Chikamoto nikki 親元日記. Vol. 11 of *Zōho zoku shiryō taisei* 増補続史料大成. Kyoto: Rinsen shoten, 1994.

Chikanaga kyōki 親長卿記. Vol. 42 of *Zōho shiryō taisei* 増補史料大成. Kyoto: Rinsen shoten, 1975.

Collcutt, Martin. "Religion in the Life of Minamoto Yoritomo." In P. F. Kornicki and I. J. McMullen, eds., *Religion in Japan: Arrows to Heaven and Earth,* 95–101. Cambridge: Cambridge University Press, 1996.

Collection of Digital Images at Ikomasan Hōzanji. Accessed January 11, 2011. http://mahoroba.lib.nara-wu.ac.jp/y01/htmls/N10/index_eng.html.

Conlan, Thomas Donald. *In Little Need of Divine Intervention: Takezaki Suenaga's Scrolls of the Mongol Invasions of Japan.* Ithaca: Cornell East Asia Series, 2001.

Conlan, Thomas Donald. *State of War: The Violent Order of Fourteenth-Century Japan.* Ann Arbor: University of Michigan, Center for Japanese Studies, 2003.

Cranston, Edwin A. *A Waka Anthology, Vol. 1, The Gem-Glistening Cup.* Stanford: Stanford University Press, 1993.

Daijōin jisha zōjiki 大乗院寺社雑事記. Vol. 33 of *Zōho zoku shiryō taisei* 増補続史料大成. Kyoto: Rinsen shoten, 1994.

de Poorter, Erika. *Zeami's Talks on Sarugaku: An Annotated Translation of Sarugaku dangi with an Introduction on Zeami Motokiyo.* Amsterdam: J. C. Geiben, 1986. Reprint edition; Leiden: Hotei Publishing, 2002.

Ebrey, Patricia, Anne Walthall and James Palais, eds. *Pre-Modern East Asia: To 1800.* Boston: Houghton Mifflin Company, 2006.

Engyōbon chūshaku no kai 延慶本注釈の会, ed. Engyōbon Heike monogatari zenchūshaku 延慶本平家物語全注釈, vol. 1. Kyūko shoin, 2005.

Ennō kiroku chōsa kenkyū gurūpu (1), daihyō, Omote Akira. 演能記録調査研究グループ(1)、代表、表章. "Edo shoki nō bangumi nanashu (sono san)" 江戸初期能番組七種（その三）. *Nōgaku kenkyū* 能楽研究, Nōgaku kenkyūjo kiyō 能楽研究所紀要, no. 24 (1999), 1–52 (314–66).

Foley, John Miles. "The Impossibility of Canon," in Foley, ed., *Teaching Oral Traditions,* 13–33. Options for Teaching. New York: The Modern Language Association, 1998.

Foley, John Miles. *Immanent Art: From Structure to Meaning in Traditional Oral Epic.* Bloomington: Indiana University Press, 1991.

Franks, Amy. "Another *Tale of the Heike*: An Examination of the Engyōbon *Heike monogatari*." Ph.D. dissertation, Yale University. 2009.

Fujita Takanori 藤田隆則. *Nō no korosu* 能の多人数合唱 （コロス）. Hitsuji shobō, 2000.

Furukawa Hisashi 古川久, ed. *Kyōgenshū* 狂言集. Three vols. Nihon koten zensho.

Asahi shinbunsha, 1951–1953.

Furukawa Hisashi 古川久, ed. *Kyōgen kohon nishu: Tenshō kyōgen bon, Torakiyo kyōgen bon* 狂言古本二種：天正狂言本・虎清狂言本. Wanya shoten, 1968.

Furukawa Hisashi 古川久 and Kobayashi Seki 小林責, eds. *Kyōgen jiten jikō hen* 狂言辞典事項編. Tōkyōdō shuppan, 1976.

Furuya Chishin 古谷知新, ed. *Yōkyoku zenshū* 謡曲全集. 2 vols. Kokumin bunko kankōkai, 1911.

Gaun nikkenroku batsuyū 臥雲日件録抜尤. *Dai nihon kokiroku* 大日本古記録 Vol. 13. Iwanami shoten, 1992.

Geinōshi kenkyūkai 芸能史研究会, ed., *Nō* 能. Nihon shomin shiryō shūsei 日本庶民史料集成 3. San'ichi Shobō, 1978.

Genette, Gérard. *Narrative Discourse: An Essay in Method*, tr. Jane E. Lewin, ed. Jonathan Culler. Ithaca, New York: Cornell University Press, 1980.

Getsuyōkai 月曜会, ed., with Omote Akira 表章, general ed. *Zeami jihitsu nōhonshū* 世阿弥自筆能本集. Getsuyōkai, 1997.

Goble, Andrew. *Kenmu: Go-Daigo's Revolution*. Cambridge, MA: Harvard University Press, 1996.

Goff, Janet. *Noh Drama and The Tale of Genji: The Art of Allusion in Fifteen Classical Plays*. Princeton University Press, 1991.

Gohōkōin ki 後法興院記. *Zōho zoku shiryō taisei* 増補続史料大成 vol. 6. Kyoto: Rinsen shoten, 1994.

Goodwin, Janet R. "Alms for Kasagi Temple." The Journal of Asian Studies 46:4 (November 1987), 827–41.

Goodwin, Janet R. "Building Bridges and Saving Souls: The Fruits of Evangelism in Medieval Japan." *Monumenta Nipponica* 44:2 (Summer 1989), 137–49.

Gorai Shigeru 五来重. *Zōho Kōya hijiri* 増補 高野聖. Kadokawa sensho 79. Kadokawa shoten, 1975.

Gotō Yasuhiro 後藤康宏. "Suma-dera fue no iki to Saeda no fue monogatari wo megutte"『須磨寺笛之遺記』と『小枝の笛物語』をめぐって. Denshō bungaku kenkyū 31 (May 1985), 45–69.

Gotō Akio 後藤昭雄, Ikegami Jun'ichi, 池上洵一校注, Yamane Taisuke 山根對助, eds., *Gōdanshō, Chūgaishō, Fukego* 談抄・中外抄・富家語. SNKT 32. Iwanami shoten, 1997.

Haga Yaichi 芳賀矢一 and Sasaki Nobutsuna 佐佐木信綱, eds. *Kōchū yōkyoku sōsho* 校注謡曲叢書. Three volumes. Hakubunkan, 1914–15. Reprint edition, Rinsen shoten, 1987.

Hare, Thomas B. *Zeami's Style: The Noh Plays of Zeami Motokiyo*. Stanford: Stanford University Press, 1986.

Hare, Tom. *Zeami, Performance Notes*. New York: Columbia University Press, 2008.

Haretomi Sukune ki 晴富宿禰記. Meiji shoin, 1971.

Hayami Tasuku 速水侑. *Kannon shinkō* 観音信仰. 4th ed. Hanawa Shobō, 1976.

Hayami Tasuku 速水侑. *Kannon shinkō jiten* 観音信仰辞典. Ebisu Kōshō Shuppan, 2000.

Hayashiya Tatsusaburō 林屋辰三郎. *Chūsei bunka no kichō* 中世文化の基調.

Tōkyō Daigaku shuppankai, 1982.

Hazard, Benjamin Harrison. "Japanese Marauding in Medieval Korea: The Wakō Impact on Late Koryŏ." Ph.D. Dissertation, University of California, Berkeley, 1967.

Heutsch, James Barrett. "Wayfaring: Imagawa Ryōshun and his *Michiyukiburi*." M.A. thesis, University of California, Berkeley, 2002.

Hirota Tetsumichi 廣田哲通. *Tendai danjo de Hokekyō wo yomu* 天台談所で法華経を読む. Kanrin shobō, 1997.

Hirota Tetsumichi 広田哲通, Tanaka Takako 田中貴子, Kobayashi Naoki 小林直樹, Chikamoto Kensuke 近本謙介, and Abe Yasurō 阿部泰郎, eds. *Nikkō tenkaizō Jikidan innenshū: honkoku to sakuin* 日光天海蔵 直談因縁集 翻刻と索引. Kenkyū sōsho, no. 225. Osaka: Izumi shoin, 1998.

Hisamatsu Sen'ichi 久松潜一 and Nishio Minoru 西尾實, eds. *Karonshū, Nōgakuronshū* 歌論集・能樂論集. NKBT 65. Iwanami shoten, 1961.

Hokekyō jikidanshō 法華経直談鈔. 3 vols. Kyoto: Rinsen shoten, 1979.

Hokekyō jurin shūyōshō 法華経鷲林拾葉鈔. 4 vols. Kyoto: Rinsen shoten, 1991.

Hokuriku sanken no yōkyoku koseki annai 北陸三県の謡曲古跡案内 www.tvk.ne.jp/~mugiya/gosei.htm. Accessed January 11, 2011.

Hosaka Miyako 保坂都. "Tsumori-ke no kajingun (1): Tsumori ichimon to kakei" 津守家の歌人群 (1) 津守一門と家系. *Gakuen*, no. 421 (1975), 24–55.

Hosaka Miyako 保坂都. "Tsumori ke no kanjin gun (2): Sumiyoshi myōjin no shimei" 津守家の歌人群 (2) 住吉明神の使命. *Gakuen*, no. 433 (1976), 43–80.

Hosaka Miyako 保坂都. *Tsumori-ke no kajingun* 津守家の歌人群. Musashino shoin, 1984.

Hotta Yoshie 堀田善衛. *Teika Meigetsuki shishō* 定家名月記私抄. Chikuma bunko, 1996.

Hurvitz, Leon. *Scripture of the Lotus Blossom of the Fine Dharma*. Buddhist Studies and Translations, no. 94. New York: Columbia University Press, 1976.

Hyōdō Hiromi 兵藤裕己. *Heike monogatari no rekishi to geinō* 平家物語の歴史と芸能. Yoshikawa kōbunkan, 2000.

Ichiko Teiji 市古貞次, ed. *Otogizōshi* 御伽草子. NKBT 38. Iwanami shoten,1958.

Ichiko Teiji 市古貞次, ed. *Heike monogatari jiten* 平家物語辞典. Meiji shoin, 1973.

Ichiko Teiji 市古貞次, ed. *Heike monogatari kenkyū jiten* 平家物語研究事典. Meiji shoin, 1978.

Ichiko Teiji 市古貞次, ed. *Heike monogatari* 平家物語, NKBZ 29–30. Shōgakukan, 1973.

Ichiko Teiji 市古貞次, ed. *Nihon koten bungaku daijiten* 日本古典文学大事典. 5 vols. Iwanami shoten, 1984.

Ichiko Teiji 市古貞次, ed. *Heike monogatari* 平家物語, SNBZ 45–46. Shōgakukan, 1994.

Ichishima Kenkichi 市島謙吉, ed. *Gyokuyō* 玉葉, vol. 2. Kokusho kankōkai, 1906.

Ihon Tadasugawara kanjin sarugakuki 異本紀河原勧進猿楽記. Vol. 19 of *Gunsho ruijū* 群書類従. Yoshikawa Kōbunkan, 1984.

Ikeda Hiroshi 池田廣司 and Kitahara Yasuo 北原保雄, eds. *Ōkura Toraakira-*

bon: Kyōgen shū no kenkyū 大蔵虎明本 狂言集の研究. 3 vols. Hyōgensha, 1973.

Ikeyama Issaien 池山一切圓. "Kaidai" 解題. In *Hokekyō jikidanshō* 法華経直談鈔, vol. 1. Kyoto: Rinsen shoten, 1979.

Ikomasan hōzanji shozō kichō shiryō denshi gazōshū 生駒山寶山寺所蔵貴重資料電子画像集. "Zeami jihitsu Morihisa 世阿弥自筆盛久." http://mahoroba.lib.nara-wu.ac.jp/y01/htmls/N10/. Accessed January 11, 2011.

Imagawa Ryōshun 今川了俊. "Michiyuki buri" 道行きぶり. In Nagasaki Ken 長崎健, et al., eds., *Chūsei nikki kikō shū* 中世日記紀行集. Shōgakukan, 1994.

Inagaki, Hisao, ed. *A Dictionary of Japanese Buddhist Terms: Based on References in Japanese Literature*. In collaboration with P. G. O'Neill. 4th edition. Kyoto: Nagata Bunshōdō, 1992.

Inryōken nichiroku 蔭涼軒日録. Vol. 22 of *Zōho zoku shiryō taisei* 増補続史料大成. Kyoto: Rinsen shoten, 1978.

Iriya Yoshitaka 入矢義高 et al., eds. *Hekigan roku* 碧巌録, vol. 2. Iwanami shoten, 1994.

Ishida Takuya 石田拓也, ed. *Itō-ke-zō Nagato-bon Heike monogatari* 伊藤家蔵長門本平家物語. Kyūko shoin, 1977.

Ishiguro Kichijirō 石黒吉次郎. "Nō 'Morihisa' to bukkyō" 能 「盛久」と仏教. In Matsumoto Yasushi 松本寧至, ed. *Chūsei bungaku no shomondai* 中世文学の諸問題, 202–17. Shinchōsha, 2000.

Ishii Masatoshi 石井正敏, ed. *Zenrin kokuhōki* 善隣国宝記. In Tanaka Takeo 田中健夫, ed., *Zenrin kokuhōki Shintei zoku zenrin kokuhōki* 善隣国宝記新訂続善隣国宝記. Shūeisha, 1995.

Itō Hiroyuki 伊藤博之 et al., ed. *Nihon no chūsei bungaku* 日本の中世文学. Shin Nihon shuppansha, 1983.

Itō Hiroyuki 伊藤博之, Imanari Genshō 今成元昭, and Yamada Shōzen 山田昭全, eds. *Bukkyō bungaku no genten* 仏教文学の原典. Bukkyō bungaku kōza, vol. 1. Benseisha, 1994.

Itō Masayoshi 伊藤正義. *Yōkyoku zakki* 謡曲雑記. Osaka: Izumi shoin, 1989.

Itō Masayoshi 伊藤正義, ed. *Yōkyokushū* 謡曲集. 3 vols. SNKS. Shinchōsha, 1984–1988.

Itō Masayoshi 伊藤正義. "Sakuhin kenkyū: 'Bashō'" 作品研究『芭蕉』. *Kanze* 観世 46:7 (July, 1979), 4–13.

Iwasaki Kae 岩崎佳枝, Amino Yoshihiko 網野善彦, Takahashi Kiichi 高橋喜一, and Shiomura Kō 塩村耕, eds. *Shichijūichiban shokunin utaawase, Shinsen kyōkashū, Kokon ikyokushū* 七十一番職人歌合・新撰狂歌集・古今夷曲集. SNKT 61. Iwanami shoten, 1993.

Kaizu Ichirō 海津一郎. *Kamikaze to akutō no seiki: Nanbokuchō jidai o yominaosu* 神風と悪党の世紀 : 南北朝時代を読み直す. Kōdansha gendai shinsho 講談社現代新書, no. 1243. Kōdansha, 1995.

Kajihara Masaaki 梶原正昭 and Yamashita Hiroaki 山下宏明, eds. *Heike monogatari* 平家物語. 2 vols. SNKT 44–45. Iwanami shoten, 1991–1993.

Kanmon gyoki 看聞御記 (*Kanmon nikki* 看聞日記). Hanawa Hokiichi 塙保己
一, ed., *Zoku gunsho ruijū* 群書類従 (*hoi* 補遺), vols. 4–5. Zoku gunsho
ruijū kanseikai, 1930. Reprinted in *Zoku gunsho ruijū(hoi)*, supplementary
vol. 2, part 1. Zoku gunsho ruijū kanseikai, 1985.

Kanze Kiyoyuki 観世清之 and Maruoka Katsura 丸岡桂. *Kanze-ryū kaitei utaibon* 観世流改訂謡本. 45 vols. Kanze-ryū kaitei kankōkai, 1924–1925.

Kanze Sakon 観世左近, ed. *Kanzeryū yōkyoku zoku hyakubanshū* 観世流謡曲続
百番集. Taiseiban edition. Hinoki shoten, 1973.

Katagiri Yōichi, ed. Chūsei Kokinshū chūshakusho kaidai 中世古今集注釈書解
題. Six vols. Kyoto: Akao Shōbundō, 1973.

Katagiri Yōichi 片桐洋一. "Wakakami toshite no Sumiyoshi no kami" 和歌神とし
ての住吉の神. *Suminoe*, no. 175 (1985), 18–25.

Katano Tatsurō 片野達郎 and Matsuno Yōichi 松野陽一, eds. *Senzai wakashu*
千載和歌集. SNKT 10. Iwanami shoten, 1993.

Kawaguchi Hisao 川口久雄 and Shida Nobuyoshi 志田延義, eds. *Wakan
rōeishū, Ryōjin hishō* 和漢朗詠集；梁塵秘抄. NKBT 73. Iwanami shoten,
1973.

Kawaguchi Hisao 川口久雄, ed. Wakan Rōeishū 和漢朗詠集. Kōdansha gakujutsu
bunko, 1982.

Kawazoe, Shōji. "Japan and East Asia." In Kozo Yamamura, ed., *Cambridge History
of Japan: Volume 3, Medieval Japan*, 423–38. Cambridge: Cambridge University
Press, 1990.

Keene, Donald. *Travelers of a Hundred Ages*. New York: Henry Holt, 1989.

Kimbrough, R. Keller. "*Little Atsumori* and *The Tale of the Heike*: Fiction as
Commentary, and the Significance of a Name." In Michael F. Marra, ed.,
*Hermeneutical Strategies: Methods of Interpretation in the Study of Japanese
Literature*, Proceedings of the Association for Japanese Literary Studies, vol.
5 (2004), 325–36.

Kimbrough, R. Keller. *Preachers, Poets, Women & the Way: Izumi Shikibu and
the Buddhist Literature of Medieval Japan*. Michigan monogaraph series in
Japanese studies, 62. Ann Arbor: University of Michigan Center for Japanese
Studies, 2008.

Kinoshita Junji. *Requiem on the Great Meridian and Selected Essays*, tr. by Brian
Powell and Jason Daniel. Nan'un-do Publishing, 2000.

Kirihata Ken. "Kyōgen Costmes: The Fascinating World of Dyed Textiles." In
Sharon Sadako Takeda and Monica Bethe, eds., *Miracles and Mischief: Noh
and Kyōgen Theater in Japan*, 160–76 (Los Angeles: Los Angeles County
Museum of Art, 2002).

Kita Rokuheita 喜多六平太, ed. *Rō-Giō* 籠祇王. Wanya shoten, 1923.

Kitagawa, Hiroshi, and Bruce Tsuchida, trans. *The Tale of the Heike*. 2 vols.
University of Tokyo Press, 1975.

Kitahara Yasuo 北原保雄 and Ogawa Eiichi 小川栄一, eds. *Engyō-bon Heike
monogatari: honbun-hen*, 延慶本平家物語 [本文編]. 2 vols. Benseisha, 1990.

Kiyomizudera-shi hensan iinkai 清水寺史編纂委員会, ed. *Kiyomizudera-shi*

清水寺史. 3 vols. Kyoto: Hōzōkan, 1995.

Klein, Susan Blakeley. *Allegories of Desire: Esoteric Literary Commentaries of Medieval Japan.* Harvard University Press, 2002.

Klein, Susan Blakeley. "*Seijiteki gui toshite no nō: Haku Rakuten wo megutte*" 政治的寓意としての能—「白楽天」をめぐって. *Osaka Daigaku Daigakuin Bungaku Kenkyūka kiyō*, vol. 50 (March 2009), 29–68.

Kokinwakashū jo kikigaki: sanryū shō 古今和歌集序聞書：三流抄. In Katagiri Yōichi 片桐洋一, ed., *Chūsei Kokinshū chūshakusho kaidai* 中世古今集註釈書解題, vol. 2, 223–90. Kyoto: Akao shōbundō, 1973.

Kokusho kankōkai 国書刊行会, ed. *Heike monogatari Nagato-bon* 平家物語長門本. Kokushi taikei 国史大系, vol. 13. Kokusho kankōkai, 1906.

Komatsu Shigemi 小松茂美. *Yūzū nenbutsu engi* 融通念仏縁起. Zoku Nihon no emaki 続日本の絵, vol. 11. Chūō kōronsha, 1983.

Komatsu Shigemi 小松茂美. *Taima mandara engi, Chigo kannon engi* 当麻寺曼荼羅縁起, 稚児観音縁起. Zoku Nihon no emaki 続日本の絵巻, vol. 20. Chūō kōronsha, 1992.

Komatsu Shigemi 小松茂美. *Kiyomizudera engi, Shinnyodō engi* 清水寺縁起, 真如堂縁起. Zoku zoku nihon emaki taisei 続々日本絵巻大成, vol. 5. Chuō kōronsha, 1994.

Kōsai Tsutomu 香西精. "Sakuhin kenkyū: Sanemori" 作品研『実盛』. *Kanze* 観世 (January 1970), 3–9.

Kōsai Tsutomu 香西精. *Nō utai shinkō: Zeami ni terasu* 能謡新考：世阿弥に照らす. Hinoki shoten, 1972.

Koyama Hiroshi 小山弘志, Satō Kikuo 佐藤喜久雄, and Satō Kenichirō 佐藤健一郎. eds. *Yōkyōkushū* 謡曲集. 2 vols. NKBZ 33–34. Shōgakukan, 1973–1975.

Koyama Hiroshi 小山弘志 and Satō Kenichirō 佐藤健一郎, eds. *Yōkyōkushū* 謡曲集. 2 vols. SNBZ 58–59. Shōgakukan, 1997–1998.

Kubota Jun 久保田淳 and Hirata Yoshinobu 平田喜信, eds. *Goshūi wakashū* 後拾遺和歌集. SNKT 8. Iwanami shoten, 1994.

Kubota Jun 久保田淳, ed. *Shinkonkin wakashū* 新古今和歌集. 2 vols. Shinchōsha, 1979.

Kume Kunitake 久米邦武. "*Yōkyoku Haku Rakuten wa kessaku nari—yūdai naru taigai shisō to Ōei no gaikō*" 謡曲白楽天は傑作なり一雄大なる体外思想と応永の外冦. *Nōgaku* 能楽, vol. 14 (January 1916), 18–30.

Kurano Kenji 倉野憲司 and Takeda Yūkichi 武田祐吉, eds. *Kojiki Norito* 古事記祝詞. NKBT 1. Iwanami shoten, 1958.

Kurata Hyakuzō. *Shunkan: A Play*, trans. by Kan'ichi Ando. Kenkyusha, 1925.

Kurokawa Mamichi 黒川眞道, Hotta Shōzō 堀田璋左右, and Furuichi Michiyo 古内三千代, eds. *Heike monogatari Nagato-bon* 平家物語長門本. Kokushi taikei 国史大系, vol. 13. Kokusho kankōkai, 1906.

Kyōgaku shiyōshō 経覚私要鈔. Vol. 2 of *Shiryō sanshū* 史料纂集. Zoku gunsho ruijū kanseikai, 1971.

Kyōgen geinōshi kenkyū kai 狂言芸能史研究会, ed. *Kyōgen: "okashi" no keifu*

狂言 :「をかし」の系譜. Nihon no koten geinō 日本の古典芸能, vol. 4. Heibonsha, 1970.

LaFleur, William R. "Saigyō and the Buddhist Value of Nature." In *Nature in Asian Traditions of Thought: Essays in Environmental Philosophy*, ed. J. Baird Callicott and Roger T. Ames. Albany: SUNY Press, 1989.

Law, Jane Marie. "Violence, Ritual Reenactment, and Ideology: The Hōjō-e (Rite for the Release of Sentient Beings) of the Usa Hachiman Shrine in Japan," *History of Religions*, vol. 33, no. 4 (May 1994), 325–57.

Lim Beng Choo. "Performing *Furyū Nō*: The Theatre of Konparu Zenpō." *Asian Theater Journal*, vol. 22, no. 1 (Spring 2005), 33–51.

Looser, Thomas. *Visioning Eternity: Aesthetics, Politics, and History in the Early Modern Noh Theater*. Ithaca: Cornell East Asia Series, 2008.

MacWilliams, Mark. "Living Icons: Reizō Myths of the Saikoku Kannon Pilgrimage." *Monumenta Nipponica* 59:1 (Spring 2004), 35–81.

Mansai jugō nikki 満済准后日記. 3 vols. Ed. Kyoto Teikoku Daigaku Bunka Daigaku 京都帝国大学文科大学. Kyoto: Rokujō kappan seizōjo, 1918.

Maruoka Katsura 丸岡桂. *Kokon Yōkyoku Kaidai* 古今謡曲解題. Revised and augmented by Nishino Haruo 西野春雄. Kokon yōkyoku kaidai kankōkai, 1984.

Matisoff, Susan. "Kintōsho: Zeami's Song of Exile." *Monumenta Nipponica* 32:4 (winter 1977), 441–58.

Matisoff, Susan. *The Legend of Semimaru, Blind Musician of Japan*. Columbia University Press, 1978. Reprint edition, Cheng and Tsui, 2006.

Matsumoto Ryūshin 松本隆信, ed. *Otogizōshi shū* 御伽草子集. SNKS. Shinchōsha, 1980.

Matsumoto Ryūshin 松本隆信. *Chūsei shōmin bungaku: monogatari sōshi no yukue* 中世庶民文学 物語草子のゆくへ. Kyūko shoin, 1989.

Matsuoka Shinpei 松岡心平. "'Shigehira' no fukkyoku" 『重平重衡』の復曲. *Geinō* vol. 33, no. 2 (February, 1991), 17–19.

Matsuoka Shinpei 松岡心平. "Nō 'Shigehira' wo yomu" 能「重衡」を読む. In Kubota Jun 久保田淳, ed., *Ronshū chūsei no bungaku: sanbun-hen* 論集中世の文学 : 散文篇, 252–72 (Meiji shoin, 1994).

Matsuoka Shimpei. "Staging Noh." *Acta Asiatica* no. 73 (1997): 1–15.

Matsuoka Shinpei 松岡心平. *Nō: chūsei kara no hibiki* 能 : 中世からの響き. Kadokawa shoten, 1998.

McCullough, Helen Craig. *Yoshitsune: A Fifteenth-Century Chronicle*. Tokyo: University of Tokyo Press, 1966; Stanford University Press, 1966.

McCullough, Helen Craig. *Tales of Ise: Lyrical Episodes from Tenth-Century Japan*. Tokyo: University of Tokyo Press, 1968.

McCullough, Helen Craig. *Ōkagami: Fujiwara Michinaga (966–1027) and His Times*. Princeton: Princeton University Press, 1980.

McCullough, William H. and Helen C., trans. *A Tale of Flowering Fortunes: Annals of Japanese Aristocratic Life in the Heian Period*. 2 vols. Stanford: Stanford University Press, 1980.

McCullough, Helen Craig, trans. *Kokin Wakashū: The First Imperial Anthology of Japanese Poetry, with Tosa nikki and Shinsen waka.* Stanford: Stanford University Press, 1985.

McCullough, Helen Craig. *Brocade by Night: "Kokin Wakashū" and the Court Style in Japanese Classical Poetry.* Stanford: Stanford University Press, 1985.

McCullough, Helen Craig, trans. *The Tale of the Heike.* Stanford: Stanford University Press, 1988.

McCullough, Helen Craig, compiler and ed. *Classical Japanese Prose: An Anthology.* Stanford: Stanford University Press, 1990.

Meigetsuki kenkyūkai 明月記研究会, ed. "'Meigetsuki' (Jishō 4–5-nen) wo yomu)" 『明月記』（治承四五年）を読む. In *Meigetsuki kenkyū* 明月記研究 5 (November, 2000), 2–63.

Miller, Herschel, trans. "Stupa Komachi." In Haruo Shirane, ed., *Traditional Japanese Literature,* 936–52. Columbia University Press, 2007.

Miner, Earl, Hiroko Odagiri, and Robert E. Morrell. *The Princeton Companion to Classical Japanese Literature.* Princeton: Princeton University Press, 1985.

Minobe Shigekatsu 美濃部重克. *Chūsei denshō bungaku no shosō* 中世伝承文学の諸相. Osaka: Izumi shoin, 1988.

Miwa Masatane 三輪正胤. "*Chikuen shō* karon no seisei to hatten: kajin toshite no Sumiyoshi myōjin wo megutte." *Nagoya Daigaku kokugo kokubungaku* 名古屋大学国国文学13 (November 1963), 25–40.

Miyasaka Yūshō 宮坂宥勝, ed. *Kana hōgo shū* 假名法語集. NKBT 83. Iwanami shoten, 1964.

Mizuhara Hajime 水原一, ed. *Heike monogatari* 平家物語. 3 vols. SNKS. Shinchōsha, 1981.

Mizuhara Hajime 水原一, ed. *Shintei Genpei jōsuiki* 新訂源平盛衰記. Shin jinbutsu ōraisha, 1988–1991.

Mizuhara Hajime 水原一. *Engyō-bon Heike monogatari ronkō* 延慶本平家物語論. Katō chūdōkan, 1979.

Morris, V. Dixon. "Sakai: From Shōen to Port City." In John Hall and Toyoda Takeshi, eds. *Japan in the Muromachi Age,* 145–58. Berkeley and Los Angeles: University of California Press, 1977.

Mueller, Jacqueline. "The Two Shizukas: Zeami's Futari Shizuka," *Monumenta Nipponica,* 36:3 (Autumn 1981), 285–98.

Muroki Yatarō 室木弥太郎. *Zōtei katarimono (mai, sekkyō, kojōruri) no kenkyū* 語り物（舞・説経・古浄瑠璃）の研究. Fūkan shobō, 1981.

Nagaoki Sukune ki 長興宿禰記. Vol. 115 of *Shiryo sanshū* 史料纂集. Zoku gunsho ruijū kanseikai, 1998.

Nagazumi Yasuaki 永積安明 and Shimada Isao 島田勇雄. *Hōgen monogatari* 保元物語. NKBT 31. Iwanami shoten, 1961.

Nagazumi Yasuaki 永積安明 and Shimada Isao 島田勇雄. *Kokon chomonjū* 古今著門集. NKBT 84. Iwanami shoten, 1988.

Nakahara, Gladys E., trans. *A Translation of* Ryōjinhishō, *A Compendium of Japanese Folk Songs (Imayō) from the Heian Period (794–1185).* New York: Edwin Mellen Press, 2003.

Nakamura Eikō 中村栄孝. "Ōei no gaikō" 応永の外寇. In Kokushi Daijiten Henshū Iinka 国史大辞典編集委員会, ed., Kokushi daijiten 国史大辞典, vol. 2, 444–45. Yoshikawa kōbunkan, 1987.

Nakanodō Kazunobu 中ノ堂 一信. "Chūseiteki kanjin no tenkai" 中世的勧進 の展開. Geinōshi kenkyū 62 (July 1978), 12–35.

Nearman, Mark J., trans. "Kyakuraika: Zeami's Final Legacy for the Actor," Monumenta Nipponica 35:2 (Summer 1980), 161–97.

Nihon Kōtsū Kōsha. Japan: The New Official Guide. Japan Travel Bureau, 1975.

Nippon Gakujutsu Shinkōkai, ed. and trans. The Noh Drama: Ten Plays from the Japanese (Rutland, Vt., and Tokyo: Charles E. Tuttle, 1955).

Nippon Gakujutsu Shinkōkai, ed. Japanese Noh Drama. 3 vols. Nippon Gakujutsu Shinkōkai, 1955–1959.

Nishimoto Yutaka 西本泰. Sumiyoshi Taisha 住吉大社. Gakuseisha, 1977.

Nishino Haruo 西野春雄 and Hata Hisashi 羽田昶, ed., Nō kyōgen jiten 能・狂 言事典. Heibonsha, 1987; revised and expanded 1999.

Nishino Haruo 西野春雄, ed. Yōkyoku hyakuban 謡曲百番. SNKT 57. Iwanami shoten, 1998.

Nishiyama Masaru 西山克. Seichi no sōzōryoku: sankei mandara wo yomu 聖地 の想像力　参詣曼荼羅を読む. Kyoto: Hōzōkan, 1998.

Nobutane kyōki 宣胤卿記. Zōho shiryō taisei 増補史料大成　Vol. 44. Kyoto: Rinsen shoten, 1985.

Nōgaku zensho 能楽全書. Seven vols. Revised ed. Sōgensha, 1979–1981.

Nogami Toyoichirō 野上豊一郎, ed. Kaichū yōkyoku zenshū 解註謡曲全集. 6 vols. Chūō kōronsha, 1935–1936.

Nogami Toyoichirō 野上豊一郎. Nō nihyaku-yonjū-ban: shudai to kōsei 能二 百四十番：主題と構成. Nōgaku shorin, 1976.

Nogami Toyoichirō野上豊一郎and Tanaka Makoto田中允, eds. Yōkyoku shū 謡 曲集, 3 vols. Nihon koten zensho. Asahi Shinbusha, 1949–1957.

Nonomura Kaizō 野々村戒三 and Furukawa Hisashi 安藤常次郎, eds. Kyōgenshū 狂言集. Nōgaku shorin, 1970.

Nonomura Kaizō 野々村戒三 and Andō Tsunejirō 安藤常次郎, eds. Kyōgen shūsei 狂言集成. Nōgaku shorin, 1974.

Nonomura Kaizō 野々村戒三, ed. Yōkyoku nihyakugojū-banshū 謡曲二百五 十番集. Vol. 1 Honmon 本文, vol. 2 Sōsakuin 総索引. Revised by Ōtani Tokuzō 大谷篤蔵. Kyoto: Akao shōbundō, 1978.

Nonomura Kaizō 野々村戒三校, ed., Yōkyoku sanbyakugojū-banshū 謠曲三百 五十番集. Nihon meicho zenshū kankōkai, 1928. Revised by Ōtani Tokuzō 大谷篤蔵. Kyoto: Akao shōbundō, 1978. [This edition is being digitized. See: www.kanazawa-bidai.ac.jp/~hangyo/utahi/]

Nose Asaji 能勢朝次. Nōgaku genryūkō 能楽源流考. Iwanami shoten, 1938.

O'Neill, P. G. Early Nō Drama: Its Background, Character and Development 1300–1450. London: Lund Humphries, 1958. Reprint edition, Westport, CT: Greenwood Press, 1974.

Oda Tokunō 織田得能, ed., Hokekyō kōgi 法華経講義. 8 vols. Kōyūkazō, 1899.

Ōgushi Sumio 大串純夫. "Hitomaro zō no seiritsu to Tōji Sansui Byōbu" 人麿像 の成立と東寺山水屏風. *Bijutsu kenkyū* 美術研究, no. 164 (1952), 80–110.

Omote Akira 表章 and Itō Masayoshi 伊藤正義. *Konparu kodensho shūsei* 金春 古伝書集成. Wanya shoten, 1969.

Omote Akira 表章 and Katō Shūichi 加藤周一, eds. *Zeami, Zenchiku* 世阿 弥・禅竹. Nihon shisō taikei 24. Iwanami shoten, 1979. New Printing. *Gei no shisō, michi no shisō* I 芸の思想・道の思想 1. Nihon shisō taikei shinsōhan 日本思想体系　新装版. Iwanami shoten, 1995.

Ōsone Shōsuke 大曾根章介 and Horiuchi Hideaki 堀内秀晃, eds. *Wakan rōeishū* 和漢朗詠集. SNKS. Shinchōsha, 1983.

Ōsone Shōsuke 大曾根章介, Kinbara Tadashi 金原理, and Gotō Akio 後藤昭 雄, eds. *Honchō monzui* 本朝文粋. SNKT 27. Iwanami shoten, 1992.

Ōtani Tokuzō 大谷篤蔵, ed. *Yōkyoku nihyakubanshū sakui* 謡曲二百五十番集 索引 n. 2 vols.. Kaidai sakuin sōkan 6. Akaoshōbundō, 1988.

Ōwada Tateki 大和田建樹. *Yōkyoku tsūkai: zōho* 謡曲通解 増補. Hakubunkan, 1896.

Owen, Stephen, ed. and trans. *An Anthology of Chinese Literature, Beginnings to 1911.* New York and London: W.W. Norton, 1996.

Oyler, Elizabeth. "Giō: Women and Performance in *Heike monogatari.*" *Harvard Journal of Asiatic Studies,* vol. 64, no. 2 (Dec. 2004), 341–66.

Oyler, Elizabeth. *Swords, Oaths, and Prophetic Visions: Authoring Warrior Rule in Medieval Japan.* University of Hawai'i Press, 2006.

Oyudono no ue no nikki 御湯殿上日記. Vol. 3 of *Gunsho ruijū hoi* 群書類従補 遺. Zoku gunsho ruijū kanseikai, 1957.

Ozawa Masao 小沢正夫, ed. *Kokin wakashū* 古今和歌集. NKBZ 7. Shōgakukan, 1971.

Philippi, Donald trans. *Kojiki.* University of Tokyo Press, 1968. [Princeton: Princeton University Press, 1969.]

Pluschow, Herbert E. *Chaos and Cosmos: Ritual in Early and Medieval Japanese Literature.* Leiden: Brill, 1990.

Ponsonby-Fane, Richard. *Suminoe no Ohokami.* Kyoto: Nagai shuppan insatsu kabukishiki kaisha, 1935.

Quinn, Shelley Fenno. *Developing Zeami: The Noh Actor's Attunement in Practice.* Honolulu: Hawai'i University Press, 2005.

Rambelli, Fabio. *Vegetal Buddhas: Ideological Effects of Japanese Buddhist Doctrines on the Salvation of Inanimate Beings.* Kyoto: Scuola Italiana di Studi sull'Asia Orientale, 2001.

Rath, Eric. *The Ethos of Noh: Actors and Their Art.* Cambridge, MA: Harvard University Press, 2003.

Reizeike Shiguretei Bunko 冷泉家時雨亭文庫, ed. *Chūsei shikashū* 中世私家 集. vol. 2. Asahi Shinbunsha, 1994.

Rimer, J. Thomas, and Jonathan Chaves, tr. *Japanese and Chinese Poems to Sing: The 'Wakan Rōei Shū.'* New York: Columbia University Press, 1997.

Rimer, J. Thomas, and Masakazu Yamazaki. *On the Art of the Nō Drama: The*

Major Treatises of Zeami. Princeton University Press, 1984.

Robinson, Kenneth R. "From Raiders to Traders: Border Security and Border Control in Early Chosŏn, 1392–1450." *Korean Studies* 16 (1992), 94–115.

Robinson, Kenneth R. "The Tsushima Governor and Regulation of Japanese Access to Chosŏn in the Fifteenth and Sixteenth Centuries." *Korean Studies* 20 (1996), 21–50.

Rodd, Laurel Rasplica, with Mary Catherine Henkenius. *"Kokinshū": A Collection of Poems Ancient and Modern*. Princeton: Princeton University Press, 1984.

Roden, Donald. *Schooldays in Imperial Japan: A Study in the Culture of a Student Elite*. Berkeley: University of California Press, 1980.

Ruch, Barbara. "The Other Side of Culture in Medieval Japan." In Yamamura Kōzō, ed., *The Cambridge History of Japan*, vol. 3, 500–11. New York: Cambridge University Press, 1990.

Sakamoto Yukio 坂本幸男 and Iwamoto Yutaka 岩本裕, eds. *Hoke kyō* 法華経. 3 vols. Iwanami shoten, 1976.

Sakanishi Shio, *The Ink Smeared Lady and Other Kyōgen*. Boston: Marshall Jones, 1938; reprint, Rutland, Vt., and Tokyo: Charles E. Tuttle, 1960.

Sanari Kentarō 佐成謙太郎, ed. *Yōkyoku taikan* 謡曲大観. 7 vols. Meiji shoin, 1930–1931. [Reprint editions appeared in 1965, 1974, and 1982.]

Sanetaka kōki 実隆公記. Vol. 1. Ed. Takahashi Ryūzō 高橋隆三. Vol. 1. Zoku gunsho ruijū kanseikai, 1958.

Sansom, George. *A History of Japan: 1334–1615*. Stanford: Stanford University Press, 1961.

Sasaki Nobutsuna 佐々木信綱, ed. *Shin yōkyoku hyakuban* 新謡曲百番. Hakubunkan, 1912, reprint edition, Kyoto: Rinsen shoten, 1987.

Satoi Rokurō 里井陸郎. *Yōkyoku hyakusen, sono shi to dorama* 謡曲百選：その詩とドラマ. 2 vols. Kasama shoin, 1982.

Saya Makito 佐谷眞木人. "Otogizōshi *Ko Atsumori* no keisei wo megutte" 御伽草子『小敦盛』の形成をめぐって. *Mita kokubun* 18 (June 1993): 42-51.

Saya Makito 佐谷眞木人. *Heike monogatari kara jōruri e: Atsumori setsuwa no hen'yō* 平家物語から浄瑠璃へ 敦盛説話の変容. Keiō Gijuku Daigaku shuppankai, 2002.

Shimazaki, Chifumi. *The Noh, Volume III: Woman Noh Book 3*. Hinoki Shoten, 1981.

Shimazaki, Chifumi. *Battle Noh in Parallel Translations with an Introduction and Running Commentaries*. Hinoki Shoten, 1987.

Shimazaki, Chifumi. *Warrior Ghost Plays from the Japanese Noh Theater*. Ithaca: Cornell East Asia Series, 1993.

Shimosaka Mamoru 下坂守. *Sankei mandara* 参詣曼荼羅. *Nihon no bijutsu* 日本の美術, vol. 331. Shibundō, 1993.

Shinpen Kokka taikan 新編国歌大観, vol. 1: *Chokusenshūhen* 勅撰集編, *kashū* 歌集. Kadokawa shoten, 1983.

Shinshū Ōsaka-shi shi hensan iinkai 新修大阪市史編纂委員会, ed. *Shinshū Ōsaka-shi* 新修大阪市史, vol. 2. Osaka City, 1988.

Shirane, Haruo, ed. *Traditional Japanese Literature*. New York: Columbia

University Press, 2007.

Shively, Donald H. "Buddhahood for the Nonsentient: A Theme in Nō Plays," *Harvard Journal of Asiatic Studies* 20:1/2 (June 1957), 135-161

Smethurst, Mae. *The Artistry of Aeschylus and Zeami: A Comparative Study of Greek Tragedy and Nō.* Princeton: Princeton University Press, 1988.

Souyri, Pierre François. *The World Turned Upside Down: Medieval Japanese Society.* Translated by Käthe Roth. New York: Columbia University Press, 2001.

Stanford, James H. "The Nine Faces of Death: 'Su Tung-po's *Kuzōshi*.'" *Eastern Buddhist* 21:2 (1988), 54–77.

Tada Kōshō 多田孝正 and Tada Kōbun 多田孝文. *Hokkekyō ge: Kanfugenbosatsugyō hōkyō* 法華経 下 観普賢行法経. Taizō shuppan, 1997.

Taguchi Kazuo 田口和夫, ed. *Jōkyō nenkan Ōkura ryū aikyōgenhon nishu* 貞享年間大蔵流間狂言本二種. Nōgaku shiryō shūsei. Wanya shoten, 1988.

Takagi Ichinosuke 高木市之助 Ozawa Masao 小沢正夫, Atsumi Kaoru 渥美かをる, and Kindaichi Haruhiko 金田一春彦, eds. *Heike monogatari* 平家物語. NKBT 32–33. Iwanami shoten, 1959–1960.

Takahashi Sadaichi 高橋貞一. *Kundoku 'Gyokuyō,'* 訓読玉葉, vol. 4. Takashina shoten, 1989.

Takahashi Yoshio 高橋良雄. "'*Hotoke no hara' kō: 'Kaikoku zakki' no kōtei*," 「仏原」考: 「回国雑記」の行程. *Gakuen* 学苑, 481 (January 1980), 76–93.

Takakusu Junjirō 高楠順次郎 and Watanabe Kaigyoku 渡邊海旭, eds. *Taishō shinshū daizōkyō* 大正新修大蔵経. 85 vols. Taishō issaikyō kankōkai, 1924–32.

Takano Tatsuyuki 高野辰之. *Nihon engekishi* 日本演劇史 vol. 1. Tōkyōdō, 1945.

Takemoto Mikio 竹本幹夫. "*Heike monogatari* kanren enmoku ichiran 『平家物語』関連演目一覧," in Ōtsu Yūichi 大津雄一, Kusaka Tsukomu 日下力, Saeki Shin'ichi 佐伯真一, and Sakurai Yōko 櫻井陽子, eds., *Heike monogatari daijiten* 平家物語. Tōkyō shoseki, 2010, 617–609.

Takemoto Mikio 竹本幹夫. "Sakuhin kenkyū: *Haku Rakuten*" 作品研究：白楽天. *Kanze* 観世 (February 1984), 4–9.

Takemoto Mikio 竹本幹夫. *Kanami, Zeami jidai no nōgaku* 観阿弥、世阿弥時代の能楽. Meiji shoin, 1999.

Takemoto Mikio 竹本幹夫 and Hashimoto Asao 橋本朝生, eds. *Nō kyōgen hikkei* 能狂言必携. Gakutōsha, 1995,

Tamura Yoshirō 田村芳朗 and Fujii Kyōko 藤井教公. *Hokekyō* 法華経. 2 vols. Daizō shuppan, 1988.

Tanaka Makoto 田中允, ed. *Bangai yōkyoku (Kakuen-bon)* 番外謡曲 (角淵本). Koten bunko, vol. 33, Koten bunko, 1950.

Tanaka Makoto. *Bangai yōkyoku zoku (Kakuen-bon)* 番外謡曲続 (角淵本). Koten bunko, vol. 57, Koten bunko, 1952.

Tanaka Makoto 田中允, ed. *Mikan yōkyokushū* 未刊謡曲集. 33 vols. Koten bunko, 1963–1980.

Tanaka Makoto 田中允, ed. *Mikan yōkyokushū (zoku)* 未刊謡曲集 (続). 22 vols. Koten bunko, 1987–1998.

Tanaka Yoshinari 田中義成. *Ashikaga jidai shi* 足利時代史. Meiji shoin, 1923. Reprint edition, Kōdansha, 1979.

Tanaka, Takeo. "Japan's Relations with Overseas Countries." In John Whitney Hall and Toyoda Takeshi, eds. *Japan in the Muromachi Age*, 159–78. Berkeley and Los Angeles: University of California Press, 1977.

ten Grotenhuis, Elizabeth. *Japanese Mandalas: Representations of Sacred Geography*. Honolulu: University of Hawai'i Press, 1999.

Tokuda Kazuo 徳田和夫. "Etoki to monogatari kyōju" 絵解きと物語享受. *Bungaku* 文学 Vol. 54 (1986), 191–204.

Tokuda Kazuo 徳田和夫. "Otogizōshi *Ko Atsumori* no Kōshōji-bon wo megutte" お伽草子『小敦盛』の興生寺本をめぐって. *Gakushūin Joshi Daigaku kiyō* 4 (2002), 33–50.

Tokuda Kazuo 徳田和夫. *Egatari to monogatari* 絵語りと物語り. Heibonsha, 1990.

Tokue Gensei 徳江元正. *Muromachi geinōshi ronkō* 室町芸能史論攷. Miyai shoten, 1984.

Tomikura Tokujirō 富倉徳次郎. *Heike monogatari zenchūshaku* 平家物語全注釈. 4 vols. Kadokawa shoten, 1966–1968.

Tsuji Hikosaburō 辻彦三郎, ed. *Meigetsuki* 明月記, vol. 1. Zoku gunsho ruijū kanseikai, 1971.

Tsukamoto Tetsuzō 塚本哲三, ed. *Genpei jōsuiki* 源平盛衰記. 2 vols. Yūhōdō shoten, 1929.

Tyler, Royall. *Granny Mountains: A Second Cycle of Nō Plays*. Ithaca: Cornell East Asia Series, 1978.

Tyler, Royall. *Pining Wind. A Cycle of Nō Plays*. Ithaca: Cornell East Asia Series, 1978.

Tyler, Royall. *The Miracles of the Kasuga Deity*. New York: Columbia University Press, 1990.

Tyler, Royall. *Japanese Nō Dramas*. London, New York: Penguin Books, 1992.

Ubersfeld, Anne. *Reading Theatre*, tr. Frank Collins, ed. Paul Perron and Patrick Debbèche. Toronto: University of Toronto Press, 1999.

Utsumi Kōzō 内海弘蔵, ed. *Heike monogatari hyōshaku* 平家物語評釈. Meiji shoin, 1915; revised 1939.

Verschuer, Charlotte von. "Ashikaga Yoshimitsu's Foreign Policy 1398 to 1408 A.D.: A Translation from *Zenrin Kokuhōki*, the Cambridge Manuscript." *Monumenta Nipponica* 62:3 (Autumn 2007), 261–97.

Wakita Haruko 脇田晴子. *Josei geinō no genryū: kugutsu, kusemai, shirabyōshi* 女性芸能の源流―傀儡子・曲舞・白拍子. Kadokawa Sensho 角川選書 326. Kadokawa shoten, 2001.

Waley, Arthur. *The Nō Plays of Japan*. London: Allen and Unwin, 1921. Reprint edition, New York: Grove Press, 1957.

Watson, Burton, trans. *Records of The Grand Historian*. Translated from the Shih chi of Ssu-ma Chien. 2 vols. New York and London: Columbia University Press, 1961.

Watson, Burton, trans. *Records of the Grand Historian: Han Dynasty I*. Revised Edition. The Research Centre for Translation, The Chinese University of

Hong Kong and Columbia University Press, 1993.

Watson, Burton, trans. *The Lotus Sutra*. New York: Columbia University Press, 1993.

Watson, Burton, trans. *The Tales of the Heike*. Edited by Haruo Shirane. New York: Columbia University Press, 2006.

Watson, Michael. "A Narrative Study of the Kakuichi-bon *Heike monogatari*." D.Phil. thesis, University of Oxford, 2003.

Watson, Michael. "Spirits of the Drowned: Sea Journeys in *Bangai* Noh from the Genpei War," in Eiji Sekine, ed., *Travel in Japanese Representational Culture: Its Past, Present, and Future*, Proceedings of the Association for Japanese Literary Studies, vol. 8 (Summer 2007), 141–54.

Watson, Michael. "Noh Translations: noh plays in alphabetical order of the Japanese titles." Premodern Japanese Studies Website. http://www.meijigakuin.ac.jp/~pmjs/biblio/noh-trans.html. Accessed September 2, 2012.

Watson, Michael. "Genpei Tales and the Nō." Premodern Japanese Studies Website. http://www.meijigakuin.ac.jp/~pmjs/biblio/genpei-noh.html. Accessed September 2, 2012.

Wilson, William R., trans. *Hōgen monogatari: Tale of the Disorder in Hōgen*. Tokyo: Sophia University, 1971.

Yamada Yoshio 山田孝雄, ed. *Heike monogatari* 平家物語. Hōbunkan, 1933.

Yamanaka Reiko 山中玲子. "Ano yo kara furikaette miru ikusa monogatari あの世から振り返って見る戦物語," in *Gunki monogatari to sono gekika: Heike monogatari kara Taikōki made* 軍記物語とその劇化：『平家物語』から『太閤記』まで, ed. Kokubungaku kenkyū shiryōkan, Koten kōen shirīzu, vol.6. Rinsen shoin, 2000.

Yamashita Hiroaki 山下宏明, ed. *Genpei tōjōroku to kenkyū* 源平闘諍録と研究. Mikan kokubun shiryō series 2, vol. 14. Nagoya: Mikan kokubun shiryō kankōkai, 1963.

Yamashita Hiroaki 山下宏明. "Nō to Heike no ikusa monogatari: 'Shigehira' wo megutte 能と平家のいくさものがたり：『重平』をめぐって. *Bungaku* 1:6 (November, 2000), 112–24.

Yamashita Hiroaki 山下宏明. *Ikusa monogatari to Genji shōgun* いくさ物語と源氏将軍. Miyai shoten, 2003.

Yamashita Hiroaki 山下宏明. *Biwa hōshi no Heike monogatari to nō* 琵琶法師の『平家物語』と能. Kōshobō, 2006.

Yamazaki Masakazu 山崎正和. *Yabō to natsugusa* 野望と夏草. Kawada shobō, 1970.

Yamazaki Masakazu. *Mask and Sword: Two Plays for a Modern Japanese Theatre*. Translated by J. Thomas Rimer. New York: Columbia University Press, 1980.

Yasuda, Kenneth. "The Dramatic Structure of *Ataka*, a Noh Play," *Monumenta Nipponica* 27:4 (Winter 1972), 359–98.

Yasuda, Kenneth. *Masterworks of the Nō Theatre*. Bloomington and Indianapolis: Indiana University Press, 1989.

Yokomichi Mario 横道萬里雄 and Omote Akira 表章, eds. *Yōkyokushū* 謡曲集. 2 vols. SNKT 40–41. Iwanami shoten, 1960–1963.

Yokomichi Mario 横道萬里雄, Nishino Haruo 西野春雄, and Hata Hisashi 羽田昶. *Nō no sakusha to sakuhin* 能の作者と作品. Iwanami shoten, 1987.

Yokota-Murakami, Gerry. *The Formation of the Canon of Nō: The Literary Tradition of Divine Authority*. Osaka: Osaka University Press, 1997.

Yokoyama Shigeru 横山重 and Matsumoto Ryūshin 松本隆信, eds. *Muromachi jidai monogatari taisei* 室町時代物語大成, vol. 5. Kadokawa shoten, 1977.

Yōseki meguri 謡蹟めぐり
http://www.harusan1925.net/0321.html. Accessed January 11, 2011.

Yü, Chün-fang. Kuan-yin. New York: Columbia University Press, 2011.

Zeami 世阿弥. *Kintōsho* 金島書. In Omote Akira 表章 and Katō Shūichi 加藤周一, eds. *Zeami, Zenchiku* 世阿弥禅竹. Nihon shisō taikei 24. Iwanami shoten, 1974.

Zenrin kokuhōki 善隣国宝記. Ed. Ishii Masatoshi 石井正敏. In Tanaka Takeo 田中健夫, ed., *Zenrin kokuhōki Shintei zoku zenrin kokuhōki* 善隣国宝記新訂続善隣国宝記. Shūeisha, 1995.

Zenseki deetaa beesu: Zenseki no bu: goroku: Kidōroku 禅籍データーベース：禅籍の部：語録：虚堂録 (IRIZ) [Data base of Zen writings: Zen writings section: records of quotations; *Kidōroku*] http://iriz.hanazono.ac.jp/data/zenseki_208.html. Accessed January 11, 2011.

CONTRIBUTORS

Paul S. Atkins is Associate Professor of Japanese in the Department of Asian Languages and Literature at the University of Washington, Seattle. His publications include *Revealed Identity: The Noh Plays of Komparu Zenchiku* (University of Michigan Center for Japanese Studies, 2006). He was awarded the William F. Sibley Memorial Translation Prize in 2011.

David T. Bialock is Associate Professor of Japanese Literature at the University of Southern California, where he also serves as Chair of the Department of East Asian Languages and Cultures. He is the author of the monograph *Eccentric Spaces, Hidden Histories: Narrative, Ritual, and Royal Authority from* The Chronicles of Japan *to* The Tale of the Heike (Stanford University Press, 2007), and essays on classical Japanese poetry and other topics. His current research includes a book of essays on ecocriticism and Japanese literature; and work on a companion volume of *Heike* studies and translations.

Ivan Grail lives and works in western Massachusetts. He received his MA in East Asian Languages and Civilizations from Harvard University, where he studied poetry, literature, and historical documents.

Naoko Gunji is an independent scholar. Her publications include "Redesigning the Death Rite and Redesignating the Tomb: The Separation of Shinto and Buddhist Divinities at the Mortuary Site for Emperor Antoku" (*Japanese Journal of Religious Studies*, 2011), and "The Ritual Narration of Mortuary Art: The *Illustrated Story of Emperor Antoku* and Its *Etoki* at Amidaji" (*Japanese Journal of Religious Studies*, 2013). She is currently completing a book on the art, architecture, and rituals in Amidaji, a Buddhist mortuary temple for Emperor Antoku and the Taira.

Tom Hare is William Sauter LaPorte '28 Professor in Regional Studies, in Comparative Literature at Princeton University. His *Zeami, Performance Notes* (Columbia University Press, 2008) received the Hōsei University Noh Drama Prize in Memory of Kanze Hisao in 2009 and the 2010 Japan-U.S. Friendship Commission Prize for Translation of Japanese Literature. His current work engages problems of religious practice and artistic performance in medieval Japan. He is also the author of *ReMembering Osiris: Number, Gender and the Word in Ancient Egyptian Representational Systems* (Stanford University Press, 1999).

Keller Kimbrough is Associate Professor of Japanese in the Department of Asian Languages and Civilizations at the University of Colorado, Boulder. He has held teaching positions at the University of Michigan, the University of Virginia, Colby College, and the University of Colorado. His publications include *Preachers, Poets, Women, and the Way: Izumi Shikibu and the Buddhist Literature of Medieval Japan* (University of Michigan Center for Asian Studies, 2008), and *Wondrous Brutal Fictions: Eight Buddhist Tales from the Early Japanese Puppet Theater* (Columbia University Press, 2013).

Susan Blakeley Klein is Associate Professor of Japanese Literature and Culture, University of California, Irvine. She has published books on the Japanese postmodern dance form Butoh (*Ankoku Butō: The Premodern and Postmodern Influences on the Dance of Utter Darkness,* Cornell East Asia Series, 1989) and on the development of a group of secret medieval literary commentaries influenced by esoteric Shingon Buddhism (*Allegories of Desire: The Esoteric Literary Commentaries of Medieval Japan*).

Lim Beng Choo is Associate Professor in the Department of Japanese Studies, National University of Singapore. Her research interests include karamono nō, comedy film and translations. Her book *Another Stage: Kanze Nobumitsu and the Late Muromachi Noh Theater* (Cornell East Asia Series, 2012) is on the late Muromachi period nō practitioner Nobumitsu, "furyū noh," and modern nō discourse.

Susan Matisoff is Professor Emerita of Japanese in the Department of East Asian Languages and Cultures at University of California, Berkeley. Earlier in her career she taught for nearly three decades at Stanford University. She is the author of *The Legend of Semimaru, Blind Musician of Japan* (Columbia University Press, 1978) and numerous articles relating to Japanese medieval and early modern performing arts. Her most recent publication is a translation, with introduction, of the sekkyō-bushi *Oguri*. ("*Oguri*, an Early Edo Tale of Suffering, Resurrection, Revenge and Deification," *Monumenta Nipponica*, 66:1 (2011): 49–97.)

Stephen D. Miller and **Patrick Donnelly** are co-translators of the 141 Japanese poems in *The Wind from Vulture Peak: The Buddhification of Japanese Waka in the Heian Period* (Cornell East Asia Series, 2013). Their collaborative translations have appeared in numerous journals. Miller is Associate Professor of Japanese Language and Literature at the University of Massachusetts, Amherst, and author of *The Wind from Vulture Peak*. He is translator of *A Pilgrim's Guide to Forty-Six Temples* (Weatherhill Inc., 1990), and editor of *Partings at Dawn: An Anthology of Japanese Gay Literature* (Gay Sunshine Press, 1996). Donnelly is the author of *Nocturnes of the Brothel of Ruin* (Four Way Books, 2012), and *The Charge* (Ausable Press, 2003, since 2009 part of Copper Canyon Press); his poems have also appeared in many journals. He is an associate editor of *Poetry International*, director of the Advanced Seminar at The Frost Place, and has taught writing at Colby College, the Lesley University MFA Program, the Bread Loaf Writers' Conference, and elsewhere. He is a 2008 recipient of an Artist Fellowship from the Massachusetts Cultural Council. Both are contributing editors of *Trans-Portal* (www.transtudies.org).

Carolyn Morley, Professor of Japanese Literature and Theater at Wellesley College, specializes in premodern Japanese literature. Her publications include: *Transformations, Miracles, and Mischief: The Mountain Priest Plays of Kyōgen* (Cornell East Asia Series, 1993), "Mushrooms" (in *Traditional Japanese Theater*, ed. Karen Brazell, Columbia University Press, 1998), "A Woman's Journey Through Hell: Ominameshi Seen from the Perspective of the Kyōgen Interlude" (in *The Noh Ominameshi: A Flower Viewed from Many Directions*, ed. Mae Smethurst, Cornell East Asia Series, 2003), and "Bugaku" (in *Traditional Japanese Literature*, ed. Haruo Shirane, Columbia University, 2007).

Elizabeth Oyler is Associate Professor of Japanese at the University of Illinois, Urbana-Champaign. She is author of *Swords, Oaths, and Prophetic Visions: Authoring Warrior Rule in Medieval Japan* (University of Hawai'i Press, 2006) and articles on *Heike monogatari* and medieval performance traditions.

Shelley Fenno Quinn specializes in literature, culture, and performance traditions of medieval Japan. She is author of *Developing Zeami: The Noh Actor's Attunement in Practice* (2005). Currently she is at work on a monograph about reception of nō in modern contexts, with a focus on the life work of actor Kanze Hisao. She is Associate Professor in the Department of East Asian Languages and Literatures at Ohio State University.

J. Thomas Rimer is Professor Emeritus of Japanese Literature and Theatre at the University of Pittsburgh. Following his retirement, he taught for three years as the Terasaki Chair of U.S.-Japan Relations at the University of California, Losa Angeles. He is presently co-editing, with Cody Poulton and Mitsuya Mori, a volume of translations of modern Japanese plays for Columbia University Press.

Mae J. Smethurst is Professor of Classics and Adjunct Professor of East Asian Languages and Literatures at the University of Pittsburgh. She is also editor of *The Noh* Ominameshi: *A Flower Viewed from Many Directions*, co-editor, Christina Laffin (Cornell University East Asia Series, 2003) and author of *Dramatic Representations of Filial Piety: Five Noh in Translation* (Cornell University East Asia Series, 1998), which was granted a Japan-America Friendship Commission Award in 2002; *The Artistry of Aeschylus and Zeami: A Comparative Study of Greek Tragedy and Nō* (Princeton, 1989) granted an American Association of University Presses' Hiromi Arisawa Memorial Award, 1990, and translated into Japanese in 1994. Her *Dramatic Action in Greek Tragedy and Noh: Reading with and Beyond Aristotle* (2013) is from Lexington Books, Greek Studies: Interdisciplinary Approaches.

Roberta Strippoli is Assistant Professor at Binghamton University (SUNY), where she teaches premodern Japanese literature in the Department of Asian and Asian American Studies. She is the author of *La monaca tuttofare, la donna serpente, il demone beone. Racconti dal medioevo giapponese* [The Errand Nun, the Snake Woman, and the Drunken Demon: Tales from Medieval Japan] (Venice, Italy: Marsilio Editori, 2001).

Akiko Takeuchi is Professor of Comparative Literature at Hōsei University (Tokyo, Japan). She earned her Ph.D. in premodern Japanese literature at Columbia University. Her current work is on the oral narrative elements in Zeami's nō plays. Her other interests include: reception of nō in Western culture, rhetorics in nō plays, and intertextuality between nō and other literary/theatrical genres.

Michael Watson is Professor of Japanese Literature at Meiji Gakuin University, where he has taught since 1981. Recent publications have dealt with the earliest translations of *Heike monogatari* and the influence of the Chinese dynastic histories on Japanese medieval war tales and nō. His current research topics are the narrative style and reception of *Heike* variants and the development of nō after the Muromachi period.

CORNELL EAST ASIA SERIES

CORNELL
East Asia Series

eap.einaudi.cornell.edu/publications